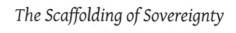

The Scaffolding of Sovereignty

COLUMBIA STUDIES IN POLITICAL THOUGHT / POLITICAL HISTORY

COLUMBIA STUDIES IN POLITICAL THOUGHT / POLITICAL HISTORY
Dick Howard, General Editor

Columbia Studies in Political Thought / Political History is a series dedicated to exploring the possibilities for democratic initiative and the revitalization of politics in the wake of the exhaustion of twentieth-century ideological "isms." By taking a historical approach to the politics of ideas about power, governance, and the just society, this series seeks to foster and illuminate new political spaces for human action and choice.

Pierre Rosanvallon, *Democracy Past and Future*, edited by Samuel Moyn (2006)

Claude Lefort, *Complications: Communism and the Dilemmas of Democracy*, translated by Julian Bourg (2007)

Benjamin R. Barber, *The Truth of Power: Intellectual Affairs in the Clinton White House* (2008)

Andrew Arato, *Constitution Making Under Occupation: The Politics of Imposed Revolution in Iraq* (2009)

Dick Howard, *The Primacy of the Political: A History of Political Thought from the Greeks to the French and American Revolution* (2010)

Paul W. Kahn, *Political Theology: Four New Chapters on the Concept of Sovereignty* (2011)

Stephen Eric Bronner, *Socialism Unbound: Principles, Practices, and Prospects* (2011)

David William Bates, *States of War: Enlightenment Origins of the Political* (2011)

Warren Breckman, *Adventures of the Symbolic: Post-Marxism and Radical Democracy* (2013)

Martin Breaugh, *The Plebeian Experience: A Discontinuous History of Political Freedom*, translated by Lazer Lederhendler (2013)

Dieter Grimm, *Sovereignty: The Origin and Future of a Political and Legal Concept*, translated by Belinda Cooper (2015)

Frank Palmeri, *State of Nature, Stages of Society: Enlightenment Conjectural History and Modern Social Discourse* (2016)

Elías José Palti, *An Archaeology of the Political: Regimes of Power from the Seventeenth Century to the Present* (2017)

THE SCAFFOLDING OF SOVEREIGNTY

Global and Aesthetic Perspectives
on the History of a Concept

Edited by
ZVI BEN-DOR BENITE, STEFANOS GEROULANOS,
AND NICOLE JERR

COLUMBIA UNIVERSITY PRESS
NEW YORK

Columbia University Press
Publishers Since 1893
New York   Chichester, West Sussex
cup.columbia.edu
Copyright © 2017 Columbia University Press
All rights reserved

Library of Congress Cataloging-in-Publication Data

Names: Ben-Dor Benite, Zvi, editor. | Geroulanos, Stefanos, 1979– editor. | Jerr, Nicole, editor.
Title: The scaffolding of sovereignty : global and aesthetic perspectives on the history of a concept / edited by Zvi Ben-Dor Benite, Stefanos Geroulanos, and Nicole Jerr.
Description: New York : Columbia University Press, 2017. | Series: Columbia studies in political thought/political history | Includes bibliographical references and index.
Identifiers: LCCN 2016045622 | ISBN 9780231171861 (cloth : alk. paper) | ISBN 9780231171878 (e-book)
Subjects: LCSH: Sovereignty—Philosophy. | Sovereignty—History.
Classification: LCC JC327 .S325 2017 | DDC 320.1/5—dc23
LC record available at https://lccn.loc.gov/2016045622

Columbia University Press books are printed on permanent and durable acid-free paper.
Printed in the United States of America

Cover design: Rebecca Lown

Cover image: Claes Janszoon Visscher, *Nova Totius Terrarum Orbis Geographica Ac Hydrographica Tabula* (1652) supported by grant

Figure Foundation

unexiled from idea we then be

For Zvi H. Schiffrin

For Andy Rabinbach and Sarah Carouso

To the memory of Yit Fung Jay

A King is as one set on a skaffold, whose smallest actions and gestures, all the people gazingly doe behold.

—KING JAMES I, *BASILIKON DORON*, 1599

A King is as one set on a stage, whose smallest actions and gestures, all the people gazingly doe behold.

—KING JAMES I, *BASILIKON DORON*, 1616

Contents

CONTENTS

CONTENTS

Foreword

DICK HOWARD

THE CONTRIBUTORS TO *The Scaffolding of Sovereignty* propose to rethink both the concept and the actual function of sovereignty. Their diverse work offers new angles of vision for the emerging academic discipline of "global intellectual history." While the project stands on its own, its scope and the reach of some of its rhetoric are clarified by its inclusion in the series Columbia Studies in Political Thought / Political History.

The principle that unites this collection was presented in the editor's foreword to Claude Lefort's *Complications* (2007): "no political thought without history; no history without political thought." Lefort's challenge to ideocratic interpretations of totalitarianism demonstrated that theories of the political cannot be easily separated from real political imperatives, of which they are one expression. Among the later volumes in the series, Paul Kahn's challenge to Carl Schmitt's notion of sovereignty, in his *Political Theology* (2011), and Warren Breckman's *Adventures of the Symbolic* (2013) probe the theoretical foundations of the concept of the political. In a different key, Martin Breaugh's *The Plebeian Experience* (2013) demonstrates that a political history of freedom must recognize that the experience of the political is "discontinuous." For its part, Dieter Grimm's history of *Sovereignty* (2015) is able to trace the historical transformation of the juridical vision of sovereignty, questioning its continued applicability in an increasingly global society, because Grimm recognizes an underlying conceptual continuity first articulated by Jean Bodin. A somewhat different version of this continuity is suggested by David Bates's *States of War* (2011), which underlines the "enlightenment origins of the political."

The Scaffolding of Sovereignty challenges a representation of sovereignty modeled on the Westphalian vision of the autonomous state facing other equally autonomous entities. As do the other works in the series, it rejects the reductive vision of sovereignty as power incarnate in a single centralized place. It goes a step further by opening a space for a wider and deeper account of the phenomenon of the political. The conceptual "scaffolding" erected and analyzed by the authors avoids the reductionism of "postcolonial studies" that stress the irreducible particularity of culture and denounce the imposition of universal norms. Digging beneath the historical framework of cultural modernity, and employing the insights of historical ethnography, the authors analyze the means by which, in diverse social contexts, the universality of the political, which represents the *symbolic* unity of diversity, gives meaning and legitimacy to the particularity of cultures.

The manner in which the expression (or the representation) of sovereignty depends on a "scaffolding" sets in motion a dialectic between what is represented (sovereignty) and the means by which it is represented (the scaffolding). Never at a loss for either erudition or creative readings of ethnohistory, the authors draw rich implications from this relation. They tease out aspects that are at once necessary (because sovereignty can only exist insofar as it is actually manifest in the world) and contingent (because this sovereignty can be represented by means of diverse social institutions, from quotidian everyday to formal courtly rituals, both of which may have religious referents). For this reason the aesthetic dimension—which is itself polysemic and never reducible to the simple sensible beauty of art—is seen to be fundamental to the understanding of the political. The aesthetic produces a type of "scaffolding" that supports the political edifice (or that is used for that purpose by those engaged in its construction). Understood in this way, "the aesthetic" can be defined as the sensible presentation of *concepts*, and thus as that elusive figure that unites the universality of the norm with the particularity of experience. The result is another potentially dialectical construction whose diverse historical and cultural appearances open to new themes developed in this volume. In a word, it becomes clear that it is not only Shakespeare or Schiller—or even the Greek tragedies—whose dramatic creations stand as the most sophisticated accounts of the tension that drives the dynamics of the political. With this, the limits of the Westphalian representation of sovereignty are clear even as the principles inherited from it are widened and deepened.

But the plot thickens. The editors point out that the scaffold is also the stage on which the execution of the monarch, and the demise of monarchy, takes place. This incarnation of the scaffold no longer expresses the being of the sovereign; it has lost its vivifying function. The gears of the dialectic are again engaged, this time in the conflict between sovereignty seen from above and that same sovereignty experienced from below. The institutions of the political, however defined, are not only the expression of an existing figure of sovereignty; they also determine what counts as belonging to (as well as what is excluded from) the sovereign. This active definitional function of the political can in turn become rigid; its reification then produces a deadening and destructive antipolitics that will wither and die unless it finds a new symbolic or aesthetic code that (re)vivifies the political. This sort of self-defeating dialectic appears in different cultures, diverse institutions, and at different historical moments. But readers must take care. The dialectic here is not Hegelian; the authors are perhaps searching for reason in history, but their questions do not try to define the Reason of History.

Political thought and political history come together in our present, which the authors put into perspective doubly: looking toward the origins of the political and fearing for its future. *The Scaffolding of Sovereignty* is neither purely philosophical nor simply historical; its use of ethnography is not backward looking, nor is its turn to non-Western examples marked by a longing for paradise lost. As with the other works in this series, the authors are offering new perspectives on the political history of sovereignty that open new frontiers for research even as they criticize the ideological simplifications that flood contemporary political life. From that point of view, the authors offer the seeds of a critical account of the emergence of a new type of scaffolding, an account that casts light on the tendency today to identify sovereignty with the political concept of *identity*. One sees this new figure of the political in forms of exclusionary populism that draw their energy from the fear of the Other. Rendered dynamic by the unrepresentable figure of the feared Other, the result is an identitarian vision of the political, which is doomed. It can only negate and deny; it is unable to affirm and create. As a result, it is a failure in all of the senses of the aesthetic as inter-preted here. Although it is no less real, or dangerous, its creative capacities are limited, and without the creation of new figures for political renewal, this identitarian vision of sovereignty is condemned to inaugurate a new barbarism.

The Scaffolding of Sovereignty

Editors' Introduction

ZVI BEN-DOR BENITE, STEFANOS GEROULANOS, AND NICOLE JERR

ANCIENT MESOPOTAMIAN SOVEREIGNS, beginning with the Assyrians, rulers of "the first intercontinental empire," were painfully conscious of the fragility of their rulership.[1] Their acute awareness of the tenuousness of sovereign power was arguably a condition intimately connected to the "normality of collapse" in Mesopotamian *mentalité*: since the common construction material in the region was mud brick, buildings and other structures made of it would eventually fall down, at times quickly and dramatically. Neglect, natural disasters, fires, and, of course, wars could easily bring down walls and buildings, and ancient Mesopotamian culture is full of records and stories around "successive falls and restorations" and about "restorer-kings" working hard to repair and maintain buildings and walls.[2] Royal palaces and temples were therefore probably often surrounded by scaffolding. The imagery of scaffolds surrounding a fragile structure can be applied to the realm of Assyrian politics as well: the shoring up of rulership involved immensely elaborate rhetoric, as Assyrian kings "bluntly proclaimed themselves masters of the entire globe, possessors of world 'from the great sea in the East to the great sea in the West.' "[3] They wielded power and control in varying degrees over vast territories—provinces, vassal states, buffer states, and enemies.[4] As they keep telling us in their stelae and inscriptions, the size and shape of their empire required Assyrian kings to contend with numerous and diverse situations in which their power was challenged in a concrete or

[1]

imagined way. Each Assyrian ruler "had to communicate meaningfully in two directions: with his own subjects and with the outside world."[5]

To handle their power and its vulnerability, the creators of the first great polity in the world—who made the eighth century BCE a contender for the first "great century" in world history—developed an elaborate repertoire designed to build, project, and maintain their rulership and define the territories to which it related.[6] Words denoting the boundary (*missru*) or territory/domain (*tahūmu*) of Assyria appear more than three hundred times in Assyrian sources.[7] The Assyrian king was "King of the Universe" (*šar kiššati*), but also "King of the four regions/quarters of the world" (*šar kibrāt arba'i/erbetti*), "Shepherd of the four quarters" (*rēû kibrāt erbetta*), in charge of the "protection of the [four] quarters" (*salūl kibrāti*),[8] even "King of *all* the four quarters" (*šar kullat kibrat araba'i*). Assyria, we are reminded repeatedly, occupied the whole world and was also ever-expanding.[9] The tandem use of "universe" and "four corners/regions/quarters" is replicated in the Assyrian deployment of two distinct terms that referred to their power: one (*kiššūtu*), authority, denoted direct hegemony; the other (*bēlūtu*), rule or lordship, was often associated with the claim to global rule.[10] Indeed, "lordship" or "rulership" was synonymous with "Assyria." The phrase *bēlūtu Aššur* meant both "the Lordship of Assyria" and "the lordship, viz. Assyria."[11] This was already then an old history. Assyrian sovereignty—relating to multiple forms of dominion and diverse territories and cultures—rested on the long tradition of Mesopotamian kingships it claimed to inherit, and was made of a powerful political and military machine, as well as of religious, artistic, literary, and architectural tools, all designed to erect and maintain rulership and to project a mighty image of sovereignty well beyond its actual domains.[12]

In some respects, Assyrian images and projections of sovereignty—its scaffolding—were stronger than real Assyrian power.[13] But in any event, they were inseparable from it. So strong was the projected image of Assyrian power that many of its elements still resonate with us today through the powerful biblical prophecies of Isaiah, who observed, and consumed, Assyrian propaganda avidly.[14] Isaiah's words reveal the "terrifying mask [that Assyria] deliberately turned towards the outside world and was undeniably effective."[15] When Isaiah had God declare, "O Assyrian, the rod of mine anger, and the staff in their hand is mine indignation," that Assyrian mask became part of Judeo-Christian theology as well.[16]

Not only do we find in the Assyrian conception of sovereignty a first claim to omnipotence that also masks the anguish associated with political negotiations, frailty, and even collapse; not only do we retrieve a model for sovereignty that would be based on physical structures and threats imposed by the natural world; but we also recover in this first great empire a set of priorities that shape our approach as we revisit, with historical, literary, and anthropological tools in hand, the scaffolding of sovereignty. By "the scaffolding of sovereignty" we mean that sovereignty is established and maintained as much by aesthetic, artistic, theatrical, and symbolic structures as by political claims over everyday life, war and peace, and life and death; sovereignty is mutable and fragile, requiring continual care and support; sovereignty is overpowering in the instant, yet never once and for all; sovereignty is defined by the rulers yet also by the ruled, the producers and the consumers of propaganda; sovereignty is a practice that not only colors but carves, defining the experience of space and time; sovereignty is at once inflected by theological problems and influential on religious belief; sovereignty is a subject of—and also a tool for—genealogical investigation; and insofar as sovereignty is a promise, it is, for the future of polities, a poisoned promise. Such, at any rate, is our claim in this volume.

The Dimensions of Sovereignty

Over the past two decades, sovereignty has emerged as a core concept across the humanities and social sciences. From history through anthropology, political science through comparative literature, scholars have pursued new perspectives on sovereignty, interweaving questions of authority, power, rights, law, and religious and popular foundations of leadership, not to mention self-sovereignty and human subjectivity. The theme has been no less significant in more popular discussions since 1989 on the rise of the new Central and Eastern European states, the expansion and crisis of the European Union, terrorism and the war on terror, the rise of China and India, the status of Daesh or Islamic State, the claims for an end to history, globalization (including the globalization of finance), human rights discourse, and the Internet.

Several trends are central to the recent academic return of sovereignty: the biopolitical approach to power, the concentration on empire and decolonization, the new history of international law and human rights, and the renewal of political theology. A general backdrop for such trends could be delineated in the pressures resulting at different times since the 1970s, from the weakening of the sovereign state initiated with the post-oil shock and continuing through the end of the Cold War, the ideological transformation resulting from it, and the transformation of the international order through globalization and the internationalization of finance. But too often in recent accounts sovereignty means little more than top-down secular political power, subjection, and scope of action: the modalities and styles of its exercise are reduced to vectors of the force with which it dominates, without much clear appreciation of the strange and complex theatricality involved, the rhetoric of its articulation as well as of claims or appeals to it, the dense interwovenness of its representations with other theological and aesthetic concepts, the frailty of its masks and the masks of its frailty. Much as current trends have rendered sovereignty a highly promising subject, they have rooted it in the narrower prospects of political science, often remaining blind to sovereignty's comparative, aesthetic, theatrical, and genealogical dimensions.[17]

The present volume proposes to recalibrate this discussion. Aiming at a comparative and theoretically rich understanding of sovereignty, we apply pressure on the concept by paying attention to those components of the scaffolding thanks to which sovereignty is both built into and sustained by social, aesthetic, and political practices. This introduction establishes the broader framework, as well as the stakes involved in understanding sovereignty in these terms, while the subsequent essays locate particular elements of this scaffolding in specific periods and areas, often foregrounding the tensions between its different constituents.

First, sovereignty needs to be understood as a *global* concept, a historical a priori that exceeds any single language, tradition, political regime, and inter-regime order. Not only does a sovereign force participate in the partitioning of a globe, tracing the framework for rule and the styles of subjection within a territory, but each particular form of sovereignty *constructs* a globe for its inhabitants, *maps* it, *makes it sensible*. Clashes between different regimes and powers are also clashes between different concepts, apparatuses, cartographies, and styles of sovereignty.

Second, for all its common characterization as a κυριαρχία that is ostensibly inflicted by a unilaterally operating and reigning power—a single indivisible hegemonic force that is subtended by one or other kind of law and rule—sovereignty has always been supported, complemented, and enforced by a complex aesthetic scaffold.[18] This structure includes the ways that sovereignty participates in the establishment of particular forms of representation, aesthetic and political; the political theology asserted by, or implicated in, its establishment and maintenance; the genealogies and citations, the legal, linguistic, and scholarly apparatuses through which it is legitimized; its complex interplays with forms of authority, legitimacy, and power; and the aesthetic and theatrical devices, the images, courts, styles, and media involved in its institution, persistence, transformation, and destruction. This complex scaffold includes even the devices used to mask it, to assert the supposedly unstaged univocity and force of sovereignty. Finally, the same term "scaffold" helps remind us of the destruction of sovereigns and sovereignties, each such sovereign anticipating and aiming to preclude (with varying degrees of success) his own undoing. Because of the similarities and differences of each architectonics that defines a particular sovereign regime, such regimes can be compared on the basis of these structures, in a manner not possible on the basis of "sovereignty's" direct application of power.

Third, and concomitantly, sovereignty needs to be examined on the basis of how it figures in literary and aesthetic works: to see sovereignty as an aesthetics is to attend to its operating and its grounding in aesthetic claims and practices from literature, theater, and art; if aesthetic practices of sovereignty are essential to its theater—its court element—such practices are also recounted, invented, experienced, or replicated in aesthetics and literature. "Aesthetics" here captures both senses of the word: aesthetics understood in terms of *sensation* and aesthetics as a pursuit of *the beautiful*. Sovereignty, we argue, is fundamentally involved in both; aesthetics, representation, and theatricality do not merely replay but contribute to staging, introjecting, reproducing, identifying with sovereignty and its experience. Aesthetics, literature, and especially the theater are no less sciences of sovereignty than law, economics, and the life and mind sciences.

Sovereignty as a Global Concept

This book is, in part, a response to the emerging need to offer a comparative theory of sovereignty in different places at different times. Sovereignty is not merely a Latin-derived, European, or Western imperial concept; it is a global one. Similar forms and styles of monarchic and hegemonic rule—not to mention of organized, legal, quasi-legal, and popular rule—can be charted across the globe. Even within Europe, as is often acknowledged, "there is no single agreed-upon concept of sovereignty for which one could offer a clear definition."[19] This demurral, however, is not sufficient; sovereignty is a different kind of concept, not one that *might* be reduced to a single definition but one that is attached to a mutable system of concepts, practices, and aesthetics. We understand sovereignty as a vector of power or force that is articulated, staged, negotiated, imagined, projected, refused, and even assaulted in and for its assertion as a unified, actually or figuratively embodied, *absolute* force that guarantees submission, carves space and time, organizes a society or community and its relations to other societies or communities, binds, commands, and demands. Sovereignty exceeds its particular cultural formations and *by definition* engages their interactions: it has done so across history without being itself ahistorical. That is, even if its particular forms and theories are untranslatable and non-globalizable— and precisely because it is not defined in the same terms in every culture— it has entwined populations and leaders in relationships that define the very concepts of society, power, and even sensation and beauty. Following this model (which is intended as a heuristic and adaptable one, not as a criterion), we think of sovereignty as integrating a spectrum of meanings and operations that ranges from the control of a geographic space or population to the representation and imposition of majesty or popular force; to the means and performance of political legitimacy; to the attempt to control natural, human, and material forces; to the citation of theologico-political and aesthetic themes.

One major aim of this project is to expand the geographical dimension and "de-Europeanize" the existing discussion of sovereignty by attending to problems and conceptions of sovereignty that integrate Islamic, Atlantic, Chinese, even nomadic and exilic approaches to the problem. To "de-Europeanize" is not meant in the harder sense of calling for a "provincializing" of Europe,[20] insofar as many crucial developments—especially modern developments concerning democracy, balance of power, law, and popular sovereignty—are (or derive from) fundamentally European practices. Rather, we use the phrase to argue that current discussions of sovereignty are usually based on schemata of a fundamentally European genealogy but nevertheless miss some of the importance and originality of even the European (and European imperial) case. In that Eurocentric schema, sovereignty properly understood dates to Roman law and arises in the early modern period together with the modern Western state; we ostensibly owe its "doctrine" to Bodin, Hobbes, Grotius, Pufendorf, and others. This post-Westphalian order is too often treated as the "source" of the notion because it assumes the existence of multiple sovereign states and a power balance between them. Its subsequent history is then described in terms of an attendant movement of secularization and liberalization, punctuated by the emergence of constitutions, the decline of royal and Catholic power, the later spread of popular sovereignty and revolutions, the nation-state, positive law, and the democratic division of powers.[21] Now, insofar as sovereignty is embedded in different ways in particular cases, times, and places, comparative attention can avoid the narrow temporal and spatial horizons that this doctrine generally assumes and offer a richer sense of both the status of power, subjectivity, and aesthetics within these cultures and the consequences of geopolitical and intercultural engagement.

Pursuing the "global" in "global concept" means showing and contrasting, implicitly or explicitly, the interstices—political, aesthetic, theologico-political, genealogical, legal—of sovereignty in, between, and across particular cultures. Comparisons have become imperative thanks to the advance of the historiography of empire, including major studies of sovereignty in the European Atlantic empires since the early modern period that have been influential in the rise of the Atlantic history field. In *A Search for Sovereignty*, Lauren Benton demonstrates that sovereignty in imperial contexts was a legally complex affair, a desideratum and not a given; she provides the ground for a serious international and comparative reconsideration of the theme and of its historical instability.[22] No less significantly, shifts in Asian historiography during the past decade signal forcefully that it is time for a much more informed and refined discussion about non-European sovereignties. The "New Qing History" has contributed greatly to a different polarization of the world that brings China front and center.[23] Looking at another set of problems, Aziz al-Azmeh, in *Muslim Kingship*, examined "parallels, analogues and continuities, conceived not as effects of abiding and continuing origins, but as ever-renewed redactions and forms of traditions which change signature and ostensible genealogy when transferred from one historical sense of continuity to another."[24] Seeking to show that Muslim kingship did not come out of thin air, al-Azmeh demonstrated his alternative by drawing on many locations in Asia and the Mediterranean, from the Pharaohs to

Pahlavi Iran, from Java to early modern Italy; such continuities, parallels, and analogues, he emphasized, were observed by people already in the distant past.[25] More recently, A. Azfar Moin's study of the "theater of sovereignty" in sixteenth- and seventeenth-century India—involving mystical attempts to "conquer time"—has opened the door to discussions about experiments in sovereignty in early modern Asian Islamic empires—Mughal, Safavid, and Ottoman.[26] From a different vantage point, scholars have exposed fascinating parallels between the Mongol Great Code of 1640 and the Treaty of Westphalia; Inner Asia, a lesser-known region in world history, now appears as a crucial link between empires and polities in Eurasia in general.[27] The boom in studies of the nineteenth- and twentieth-century advent of international law should engage the historical complexity of shifts in legality and authority, not only in the contexts of European imperial and international law but ultimately with a careful awareness of forms of globality and internationalism that long precede or geographically supersede the "rise of the West" scenario.[28] To reconsider Westphalia's ordering of sovereignty as one particular partition negotiated high up to organize rule over *one particular* globe is also to recognize that like other arrangements it divided up or parceled out sovereignty so that the order itself could "own" sovereignty across that globe and at the same time sanction it within the demarcated territories.

The "global" needs to be pursued in a second sense as well: "globality" is a concern because sovereignty—whether in the sense of the order imposed by the sovereign or in the sense of the order shared by sovereigns or states—has involved an ecumenism, an expansiveness to the corners of the known world. Within the very concept of sovereignty, there is a tendency to announce or promote every king as, in a sense, universal, in his understanding of his world or of his competition with other regimes. Often the king or sovereign order's power is described as extending not just to the borders of his terrain but (at least in potentiality) to much of, if not the *entire*, known world: the regalia of sovereignty require this possibility, which is essential to Christianity and Islam, European balance-of-power and colonial schemes, Soviet and Chinese communism, American democracy and empire since the Monroe Doctrine, and, more recently, international law. In this vein, Sheldon Pollock has argued that the spread of Sanskrit, like that of Latin, was shadowed by a "form of power for which this quasi-universal Sanskrit spoke," a diction for power that "was also meant to extend quasi-universally, 'to the ends of the horizons,' although such imperial polity existed more often as ideal than as actuality."[29] Such expansive claims to global control required complex theologico-political pursuits and sophisticated practices of rule: in China during Qing rulership, between 1644 and 1911, Manchu emperors pursued an alternative universality that made use of political, theological, and ritualistic ties and affinities in order to build, maintain, and represent their sovereignty to multiple ethnic and religious collectivities within the empire: Han Chinese, Manchus, Mongols, Tibetans, Buddhists, Daoists, and numerous other groups. The Qianlong emperor (r. 1736–1796) boasted this in the last years of his reign:

> In 1743 I first practiced Mongolian. In 1760, after I pacified the Muslims, I acquainted myself with Uighur (Huiyu). In 1776 after the two pacifications of the Jinquan [rebels] I became roughly conversant in Tibetan (Fanyu). In 1780, because the Panchen Lama was coming to visit I also studied Tangut (Tangulayu). Thus when the rota of Mongols, Muslims and Tibetans come every year to the capital for audience I use their own languages and do not rely on an interpreter . . . to express the idea of conquering by kindness.[30]

It would be hard to miss the parallel to a well-known contemporary passage by Napoleon: "My politics is to govern men as the greatest number among them wishes to be governed. Therein lies, I believe, the right way to recognize the sovereignty of the people. It is in fashioning myself a Catholic that I ended the war in the Vendée, in fashioning myself Muslim that I established myself in Egypt, in fashioning myself ultramontane that I won over minds in Italy. Were I to govern a Jewish people, I would reconstruct Solomon's temple."[31]

Comparing these passages forces a rethinking of categories (e.g., "Bonapartism") and, more importantly, a parallel recognition of both the globe as these emperors defined it and the scaffolds they built in their efforts to invade, inhabit, and refashion their worlds. What moreover should not be forgotten in these kinds of phrasing is that the Qianlong emperor's conquest ("pacification") means also the supersession of local competitors' sovereignty, a scaffold for their elimination and the elimination of their own scaffoldings. As first consul and then as emperor, Napoleon similarly proclaimed respect for "popular sovereignty" while precisely refiguring it as a *desire* for *his* dominion, and also indirectly to point out his disregard for the monarchies that battled this dominion—the Westphalian terms that had contributed to a semi-stable globe, which his postrevolutionary order committed to transforming through conquest and (civil) law.

Forms of globality instituted especially by colonialism involved as much a search for sovereignty on the planet as a weakening and destruction of competitors. These forms assume and encode forms of exceptionalism, universalism, and exclusion. The notion of Israel as God's chosen people effects not merely the exceptionalism that defines God's power over the people but also the complex theologico-political plane on which that exceptionalism operates; the Greek notion of barbarian pointed to the limits of the (Greek) world within which civilization was contained, limits more de facto and linguistic than political. Now, this kind of exceptionalist *and at the same time* ecumenicist expansion is usually not the property of lesser powers that are either quasi-sovereign or firmly constrained within an international order.[32] Still, it is worth recalling not only that Greeks and Hebrews constituted at most minor powers but that what was at stake in their claims too was the *order* of sovereignty over the known, experienced world, and a particular regime's manner for laying claim over it. This matter is of course not abandoned with the complexities introduced by modernity, democracy, nationalism, fantasies of the "end of history," dreams of world governance or democratic peace, and debates over human rights or what is often called the "responsibility to protect."[33] These too establish a broad span or purview for the sovereign regime, often all over the world, often in terms such as "humanity" and the presumed power of religion and the divine (a problem to which we shall return). Territories, borders, seas, even celestial bodies (physical or theological) are involved in this negotiation, articulation, and projection of power.[34] And sovereignty over nature itself is not merely a metaphor but a territorialization and politicization of space and life, a refusal of laws of the jungle, an institution of "law" in "natural law" and "right" in "natural right," a crucial sense of human mastery on a scale imagined, often even assumed, to extend everywhere.[35]

It is worth emphasizing the urgency of shifting scholarly understanding of sovereignty to the "global" sphere. Studying it as a culturally specific concept, figure, and dispensation allows access to its broad significance as well as to its forms, inflections, and receptions among different populations, and to tropes that range from political and aesthetic to the establishment of representation itself. Hent Kalmo and Quentin Skinner's edited collection *Sovereignty in Fragments* provides a useful foil here because in its broad claims it exemplifies the effort to at once establish and open up from the thoroughly traditional story of sovereignty as emerging with the rise of the modern, Western state and working its way across state power in the international system. The model that reduces sovereignty to state sovereignty and appoints Westphalia, Hobbes, and natural law as midwives of modern sovereignty, looking back to Roman law and forward to the post-1989 peace, appears even in the chapter titles: "The Westphalian Myth and the Idea of External Sovereignty"; "Double Binds: Sovereignty and the Just War Tradition"; "Prolegomena to the Post-Sovereign Rechtsstaat," and so on. Helpful as the volume may be in providing a history of the concept's attachment to the European state system, the forms of sovereignty that it proposes (e.g., "external sovereignty") need to be retheorized. To Kalmo and Skinner—and in this they are symptomatic rather than exceptional—sovereignty belongs squarely to the domain of *state theory* and *international interdependence*, to the negotiation of a power vested in state organizations. As a result they agonize over the extent to which "traditional" or "national" sovereignty has recently been "overcome," or "ended,"[36] and by extension over the conceptual confusion that ensues, which they then resolve by celebrating it as a "fragmentation" that is possible to study historically.[37] Other accounts often rely on too traditional conceptions of the rise of the West without engaging with or doing more than gesturing toward rival traditions.[38] When sovereignty *is* recognized as a global concept, this is largely in response to expectations within area studies or the recent globalization of history: sovereignty is then seen as part of the international political order and as linked to the inequities, hierarchies, and governance involved in globalization. These discussions, too, while breaking out of the European center, still await the appropriate conceptual framework for more capacious, far-reaching approaches.[39]

To proceed to a more properly global and systematic understanding of the concept, we rely instead on the recent rise of a subdiscipline of "global intellectual history" as a bridge between disciplines, periods, and areas.[40] The field allows us to consider the very different schemes on which sovereignty has been based or renewed, the stages and scaffolds on which sovereignty is erected or on which it perishes, the imaginations, myths, and notions on which its particular incarnations rely.[41] Likewise, global intellectual history as a rubric invites us to set three specific methodological priorities, namely (1) the need to conceive what *kind* of concept sovereignty is, and how it is embedded within broader conceptual webs; (2) the refusal, together with the

"European" model, of the model that starts and stops with the state; and (3) the study of sovereignty as involving the exploration, with anthropological density, of mutable, troubled, composite situations.

First, we regard sovereignty as a concept embedded within particular constellations of ideas, aesthetics, and practices. In our view, Kalmo and Skinner misjudge this embeddedness when they insist on a "need to disentangle . . . the complex links between concepts, institutions, practices, and doctrines—all of which have been seen as the true nature of sovereignty."[42] This is exactly what is not possible with sovereignty: rather than disentangle, the historian's purpose is to display at a minute level these entanglements and their consequences. Whereas sovereignty is conventionally discussed by reference to models in which it is characterized by the indivisibility and omnipotence of (sovereign) power,[43] to us this is a particular version of the image and stage essential for power to work at all, a self-definition that intentionally hides its own staging. Rather than abstract a foundational and universal definition, we propose that close comparisons with other forms of claims to horizonless power would not "disentangle" the concept but instead stage the particular frames and fictions involved in each formulation, retaining the embeddedness of each in its world.

Second, we decline to see the vesting of sovereignty in states as a given and therefore decline to reduce its study to that of state sovereignty, as political theory and international history too often have done. The concept of the state is itself too frequently taken for granted on the basis of an implicit or defined European model that does not easily satisfy the fact or form of power, control, or pressure elsewhere. As Clifford Geertz remarked,

"The state," particularly the postcolonial state—Kinshasa, Abuja, Rabat, New Delhi, Islamabad, Yangon, Jakarta, Manila (some of them seem, indeed, hardly to reach beyond their sprawling capitals, and their names have a habit of changing)—has . . . been the subject of a great deal of rather uncertain discussion as the enormous variety of its forms and expressions, the multiplicity of the regimes it houses, and the politics it supports have become apparent. There is talk of "failed states," "rogue states," "super-states," "quasi-states," "contest states," and "micro-states," of "tribes with flags," "imagined communities," and "regimes of unreality." China is a civilization trying to be a state, Saudi Arabia is a family business disguised as a state, Israel is a faith inscribed in a state—and who knows what Moldova is?[44]

Put differently, the Westphalian or statist model for sovereignty simply does not fit the state of the world today; we contend that it never did and that, nevertheless, the concept of sovereignty need not be abandoned together with this classic model in that the historical congealment of this model involves but one kind of setting of unitary power. Moreover, forms of interdependency, which involve transgressions of state boundaries so dear to the Westphalian model, bring up the question of how best they can be integrated into a thinking and representation of sovereignty (rather than being treated as frustrations or disruptions), given the history and international dimension of a system made up of nonequals, ever-permeable borders, invasions, internationalisms old and new, and—truth be told—mostly quasi-sovereigns. As Benton has argued, even within the major European empires, partial or divided sovereignty was far more often the case than the theory has let on, and this point could be further extended to an examination of the structures of composite monarchies, such as the Polish-Lithuanian Commonwealth, the English crown since James I, or the Habsburg dual monarchy.[45] Further inequalities and complications emerge with the way state officials in each case imagined other peoples, the place of court society in cultural as well as diplomatic confrontations,[46] and the interstate mirroring of sovereign figures, government, civilizing missions, or security, not to mention the warding off of both despotism and the index of backwardness.[47] Practices ranging from negotiation, diplomacy, and intelligence gathering to exchange, gift giving, and law, and still further to forms that permeate the necessary boundaries from trade to the Internet, expose the ambiguities and hierarchies involved in state building and quasi-sovereignty.[48] More recently, the globalization of finance and the transformation of the economic order have further embarrassed any claim that treating sovereignty at the state level alone is possible, and the problems associated with the economy that have emerged remain in this regard understudied.

The need for thicker descriptions of interstate systems is only part of the problem: domestically, sovereignty is just as much distended, unequally apportioned, negotiated, fought over, claimed, and pursued between different political forms. To quote James Sheehan, "The problem of sovereignty is the enduring tension between the order and unity promised by sovereign theory and the compromises and negotiations imposed by political practice."[49] Here too, sovereignty as *absolute* sovereignty is an image, never an uncontested, nonnegotiable reality beyond representation. To push the point further, under the illusory umbrella of continuity and stasis, sovereignty slides back and forth between states and leaders—a problem extending from traditional China and ancient Greece through the opening chapter of Machiavelli's *Prince* and Louis XIV's "L'État, c'est moi" to Hitler and Qaddafi,[50] and one engaged by Stanca Scholz-Cionca's and Yuri Pines's studies in this volume.[51] Sovereignty is similarly shared between states and political parties (Nazi Germany, the USSR and Eastern Europe in the 1945–1989 period, the People's Republic of China), regimes and the revolutions whose dynamism these incarnate, states and nations (especially with irredentist claims), not to mention nongovernmental and international units, including corporate and financial structures dating back to the East India companies.[52] Law, which since the early modern period, and especially since the rise of constitutionalism, has been so instrumental to the domestic and interstate establishment of figures of power and their limitations, has both settled on the sense of a constrained modern sovereignty and stretched the cat's cradle that ties together agents, parties, and movements, setting up claims to even limited authority. Here, too, the statist model offers little consolation or help.

Third, sovereignty should not be taken for a *well-established* concept—much less a *given* practice, a *particular* system for ordering populations or ethnic groups, or a *set* relationship between power and those who submit to it. It needs to be understood as far more mutable, context-specific, at times vibrant, at others precarious, almost always negotiated even for the maintenance of stability. That sovereignty is mostly—perhaps always—partial and elusive is no excuse for claiming that we might do away with the concept: the image of omnipotence and regulated order belies such a direction and demands attention to different forms of its construction. Especially when we look at nomadic cases, at contested or changing situations, or at sovereignty "from below," we find sovereignty first as practiced and only in consequence as theorized. This allows the historian to reconstruct conceptions out of dynamics of power that let us glean how different populations have constructed sovereignty itself. We have argued that the lack of a fully established concept of sovereignty can also be studied at the international or interstate level, where the signified of "sovereignty" is itself moldable, if not altogether amorphous. Domestically, too, as opposed to a univectoral force going from the head of the state to its subjects, we instead propose that even *this* univectoral force relies on the way it is perceived by *these* subjects and reflected back to *that* leader or political system, with the result that it is quietly reinstated or, at times, challenged with almost every act, event, or institutional change that affects major political matters. Sovereignty of the people similarly requires both the image of this "people" and an actual citizenry that exercises it, refracting it through the head of the state and back again to the population, such that this regime relies on contestation and self-transformation. Because of the embeddedness of sovereignty within the changing particularities (linguistic, legal, familial, religious) of given cultural landscapes, these mirroring effects contribute to the production of different and changing regimes and styles of power—even ostensible "transnational" or "transcultural" similarities quickly betray different devices and deployments.[53]

To those, then, who would warn (often correctly) that a history that aims globally tends to forget "the local," the current project uses these three methodological priorities to take up the challenge.[54] We obviously do not pretend to cover everything geographically and temporally; we hope that our approach can function as an initial template that others can work with. In the essays that follow, the "global," as a scale, points not to the particular formations of states but instead to the examination of local forms and assertions of sovereignty; to links, conflicts, and pressures that occur locally but hold broader political, theological, intellectual, and at times colonial resonance; and to engagements with particular conceptions of the globe, the world, the universe.[55] Li Chen's engagement with the affective basis of responses to the British Empire in nineteenth-century colonial China and A. Azfar Moin's discussion of the portrayal of the Mughal king as a mystical savior during the "Great Indian Mutiny" attend to the co-implication of real and phantasmal forms of power in colonial struggles. Nicola Di Cosmo's study of Nurhaci's rise from local Tungusic seminomadic chieftain to the founder of the Jurchen state allows us to engage with a rare moment when practices of power become negotiated as foundations of sovereignty—in this case in Qing China, one of the largest empires in history. Justin Stearns's discussion of Idrīs al-Bidlīsī's treatise on the plague, in the face of Qur'anic, scholarly, and political opposition, and Cathy Gere's examination of neurological studies of guillotined bodies during the Napoleonic wars show how the understanding of the body and power over it influenced early modern public health and the interstice of politics and neurology. Other contributors pursue comparisons and citations across considerable spatial and temporal periods:

Glenn Most, in his consideration of tragedy's ties to kingship, or Zvi Ben-Dor Benite, in his study of the ways that Muslims represented Manchu rulership over Islam by creatively rereading episodes from the biography of the Prophet Muhammad and writing them into their present time. Our aim throughout is to highlight the value of local work carried out with a more global conceptual, comparative, and theoretical horizon by offering thicker anthropological descriptions and close literary and philosophical readings, and by looking for their interdisciplinary utility in the establishment of political themes that are only in a weak manner divided by barriers of nation, region, language, and so on.

Aesthetics: Stage and Scaffold

The link between sovereignty and aesthetics has long been acknowledged, perhaps nowhere so nakedly as in the second edition of the *Basilikon Doron*, where King James I of England informs his son of the theater of power: "A King is as one set on a stage, whose smallest actions and gestures, all the people gazingly doe behold."[56] A king is an actor, one who plays a role; the king is watched, observed by an audience of subjects who will judge and acknowledge his performance. Even more shrewdly, in the first edition of the treatise, this line reads the same but for one word: "A King is as one set on a skaffold." Stage and scaffold are both terms of theater; scaffold contains the additional implications of being a structure erected to facilitate the maintenance and repair of a building, as well as of being a site of deposition and execution. In this way, the role of sovereign is both a performative and a precarious one, and the staging and scaffolding of sovereignty an ongoing project of attending to an edifice. What is this stage? How is it calibrated "from above" but also "from below" by all those people that "gazingly doe behold"? To what expected effects is it adjusted? How do different regimes rely on material and symbolic regalia, legal and cultural mechanisms, and citations of myth, theology, and their respective "classics"? And how does such reliance affect the use of power?

Our second broad claim in this book is that sovereignty—or, if one maintains the separation, its scaffold—should be studied in aesthetic terms. Particularly because it is a global and mutable concept with comparative value, "sovereignty" is the name not only for operations of unilateral or hegemonic power but also for the aesthetic conditioning of these operations. It needs to be theorized and researched across modes of theatricality and ritual, the lived experience of law and norms, art and aesthetic representations, economic foundations, and scholarship. To repeat: by "aesthetic" we do not only mean a matter of beauty—sovereign power is (also) beautiful or ugly depending on where one stands. We mean a broader anthropological domain that ranges from sensation and the experience of power to the legitimacy offered to political and international systems by ritual, symbolism, custom, religious negotiation and conviction, and exchange—all of which contribute to the scaffolding—to the ways that the exercise of sovereignty relies on a theatrical, representational, and artistic dimension and plays a normative role in the social and cultural establishment of the beautiful. In Western thought from Plato to Rancière, this much has been claimed as frequently as it has been disavowed: "politics is a question of aesthetics, a matter of appearances."[57] Whether one speaks of *the fiction of sovereignty*, the make-believe that some one or some force is indeed all-powerful; of *biopolitics*, for which sovereign power imposes itself on life itself; or even of *political representation*, questions of aesthetics, symbolism, and language arise.[58] Thus, to understand the operations and consequences of sovereignty, it is imperative to study its shape, the theater and garb that grant it legitimacy, appeal, believability, and normativity.[59] It is also necessary to speak of those who endorse, accept, tolerate, or suffer particular logics or effects of power thanks to this image and its legitimacy—even its varying characters as consuming, participative, or invincible—and to think about the local ways such a staged imagistic quality meets or folds into the experience of it. The semiotic, material, ceremonial, and spectacular dimensions structuring sovereignty myths (from coins to temples of worship) are part and parcel of this aesthetic scaffolding.

Court, Theater, Myth, Spectacle

That theatricality is intricately involved with kingship has long been a claim of democratic and revolutionary political thinkers who denounced in absolutism, in *régimes* they deemed *anciens*, a pomp and circumstance responsible for the perversion and insularization of power that was used to justify oppression. Since Max Weber, moreover, the administration of a territory or population has been regarded as largely distinct from the rituals of power, which for Weber served merely an ornamental purpose of legitimation. Yet as scholars have also established, theatricality—from dance, theater, and dress in court to the elaborate rituals for meetings of heads of state to legitimation concepts and aesthetic or narrative depictions—is almost never a mere accoutrement. It marks a court's and a king's separation from the rest of society; generates a religious, political, aesthetic, even psychological experience of unity; and provides a spectacle for domestic as well as international consumption. Geertz, in his account of the *negara*, goes so far as to identify the Balinese state with the spectacle of power and transpose each on the other:

> The whole of the *negara*—court life, the traditions that organized it, the extractions that supported it, the privileges that accompanied it—was essentially directed toward defining what power was; and what power was was what kings were. Particular kings came and went, 'poor passing facts' anonymized in titles, immobilized in ritual, and annihilated in bonfires. But what they represented, the model-and-copy conception of order, remained unaltered, at least over the period we know much about. The driving aim of higher politics was to construct a state by constructing a king. The more consummate the king, the more exemplary the center. The more exemplary the center, the more actual the realm.[60]

Such consummate identification was not essential to most states and courts, where the production of rituals—for example, to maintain and stylize the king's divine right in European courts—does not permit a directly causal relationship to the effects of sovereign power. Yet between Weber and Geertz there is a gamut of possibilities and effects, and it matters methodologically in what way these are theorized.[61] Styles and theaters of power condition the limits and forms for what can be claimed in particular regimes, not to mention how such claims are to be transmitted and interpreted. They also concede a theologico-political hierarchy tying a leader to the divine, to nature, and to the governed; they question what myths sustain political fictions, including ascent, glorified biography, the often quasi-autonomous status of internal power centers like aristocracies or religious elites, and the anxiety of succession; and they offer insight into how national systems—and mechanisms of exchange, including financial exchange—are legitimized and even naturalized. Sanjay Subrahmanyam has also recently situated the world of the courts at the center of interstate and long-distance cultural circulation and confrontation.[62] Nor are theater and scaffolding absent from the revolutionary chaos stamping out the dethroned sovereign's old theater: Jean Starobinski, for example, argued that the revolutionary speech or sermon in 1789 was "a punctual act, a brief event, inscribed in a passing minute, and the sermon engages a future and links energies that without it would disappear. The singular will of each is generalized in the instant where all pronounce the formula of the sermon.... The revolutionary sermon *creates* sovereignty, where the monarch received it from the heavens."[63]

Historians and sociologists—particularly in an earlier generation—have pursued accounts of political theater with an eye to its consequences. In *The Court Society*, Norbert Elias focused on the intricate rituals played out in French absolutist court and their effects on the French upper class: for him, etiquette, ceremony, and spectacle were essential to the recognition of the king as a *visible* presence and ruler whose distance from those he governed was established by a series of architectural and cultural separations.[64] In his analysis of czarist *Scenarios of Power*, Richard Wortman turned to "individual realizations of the myth [of governing, which] cast the new emperor as a mythical hero in a historically sensitive narrative that claimed to preserve the timeless verities underlying the myth."[65] Frances Yates, in her study of the *ballet comique* as a fête of the sixteenth-century French court, established that court entertainment relied on "an academic team of poets, musicians, artists, and humanist experts in mythology, and ... provided a field of action for the exercise of the dynamic power of poetry and music." Again, court entertainment was by no means embroidery: "The political aim of harmonizing the religious problems of the age through the use of court amusements is related to the philosophical aim of revealing the universal harmony through the power of 'ancient' poetry, music, and dancing."[66]

In these projects, as in research on China, India, and Japan (including the work by Zvi Ben-Dor Benite, A. Azfar Moin, and Stanca Scholz-Cionca here), the process of staging establishes a sovereign, marking him out, identifying him, even rendering him alien through signs like crown and scepter, physical carriage and comportment, kingly *manners*, court rituals bridging the spiritual and the everyday, and representations.[67] These signs expand outward from the court and its internal, even material, design,[68] binding together a whole world. "Pageantry" and "pomp" entail not so much a particular style of leadership but a form, in each case different, for the regime of power and of the potentials of its force. Even the democratic pretense to an absence of theater and the rejection of ornate regalia enforce new kinds of revolutionary theatricality, oftentimes at the most basic levels—theatricality in new claims on sovereignty, in competitions over it, in appeals to it, in dreams played out through it. For this reason, the language of civil religion does not quite suffice, and Walter Benjamin's famous phrase on the "aestheticization of politics" in fascism should not be taken to redeem other political regimes or their "civil religions" of major aesthetic considerations. Aesthetics may be "more" constitutive of the political in certain circumstances, but political claims cannot be divorced from their aesthetic underpinnings, implications, or coefficients: the political is political in part because it is aesthetic, symbolic, and mythical, because it is experienced and subjected to hermeneutic work at both the everyday and abstract levels, not "merely" as political but within aesthetic frameworks, traditions, and hopes. (Much the same could be said today of economic sovereignty, though a history of the aesthetics of sovereignty in capitalism remains to be developed.) Nor is it adequate to follow Carl Schmitt's defense of the absoluteness of sovereign decision and treat such "decision" as escaping aesthetic frameworks; Schmitt's formalization would overlook the extent to which a "pure" decision is mostly identified retroactively, once the stage has been cleaned up, re-presented as flat, and with only one decider standing on it. In the present volume, we thus pursue the question of theater as it extends beyond the traditional understanding of a "court": Dan Edelstein's examination of permanent revolution in 1789 and Marxist thought, Stefanos Geroulanos's discussion of the modern obsession with returning to an imagined origin to politically relaunch history itself, Alexei Yurchak's study of the still-continuing monumentalization and treatment of Lenin's corpse, and also his and Cathy Gere's studies of the co-identity between the body politic and the physiological body all argue that even if we start out in the court, we need to go far beyond it to find the traces and cascading effects of regalia in the persistent myths that weld together power, nature, and history, sometimes even time itself.

Representations

In a series of readings, beginning with his 1981 book *The Portrait of the King*, Louis Marin turned Hyacinthe Rigaud's 1701 portrait of Louis XIV into an image that did much more than simply depict the king; it defined the shape of power for Louis, his court, and his emissaries, becoming the image of what was proper to majesty. By exhibiting and substituting for him, it served as his first ambassador, as the "real presence" and body of the king (irrespective of the presence or absence of his physical body in the room), rendering the painting into the site of absolute, idealized, normative power.[69] Representation in Rigaud's painting weaves together the political and the aesthetic—the political became political because it was aesthetic, and vice versa.[70]

Despite the work of historians like Ernst Kantorowicz, Frances Yates, Peter Burke, David Howarth, Jonathan Spence, and Eric Michaud, contemporary scholars rarely treat the intertwining of *rulership* with the *image of rule* as a necessary component of the study of power.[71] This is often for reasons having to do with the supposedly nonimagistic basis of modern democracy, whereas less compunction is shown in scholarship of the non-Western world or in the study of "illiberal" regimes.[72] Nevertheless, questions of aesthetic representation are central to every conception of sovereignty, including popular sovereignty, and replayed in material or aesthetic artifacts, from coinage and seals to paperwork and weaponry.[73]

Figuration, narrative, and drama establish a whole other order for representations essential to the operations and majesties of power: witness the persistent figures of the king or leader in Western history from Odysseus to Obama—as grace giver or He Who Can Pardon;[74] as punisher;[75] as abdicator, as deposed, as the one who surrenders;[76] as lover (jealous, virginal, or manipulative);[77] as moral center; as usurper;[78] as judge of all and judged by none;[79] as healer,[80] or even as a patient who for the care of his body can only rely on foreigners—physicians alien to the body politic.[81] In these cases, each with its own history, the experience of sovereignty "from below" as well as "from above" pleats it in decisively aesthetic terms: what makes the king a king is not merely what the monarch decides or says *but how he appears* when so doing. Further concepts (aura, divine right, etc.), and images (e.g., the famous frontispiece of Hobbes's *Leviathan*, examined here by Jason Frank, Cathy Gere, and Bernadette Meyler) similarly influence our sense of the imposition and adjudication of force.[82] In each of these cases, as in Nicola Di

Cosmo's study of Nurhaci and Stanca Scholz-Cionca's examination of Toyo-tomi Hideyoshi, a hall of mirrors again enables the representational func-tion (and its masking) such that a leader may imbue a polity or community with particular characteristics and styles that in turn enable a particular image of him, an image that, reflected back to the polity, colors that polity anew. We might then speak of a different "mirror of princes" from that of the *specula principum* tradition: just as the praise and advice offered to princes (including instances of self-presentation such as Marcus Aurelius's *Medita-tions*) amounted to narratives of power and scenarios of sovereignty, other such narratives and scenarios became possible precisely because of the ways sovereignty (monarchic, legal, and/or popular) is represented and experi-enced by the population ruled. It is, to us, of paramount importance that once the matter of aesthetic representation has been broached, the issue of sovereignty is caught in a play of mirrors in such a manner that reigns, re-gimes (national, legal, democratic or not, etc.), and polities become entwined and self-represented in ways that construct the image of their agency and authority as one of sovereignty—monarchic, national, popular, or other. The resulting image of power has dynamic consequences for the political and aesthetic self-conception of a society and a regime.

Aesthetic representation matters, in other words, because it is essential for an understanding of the reach, requirements, and limits of power—for the ways that power and violence are legitimized and accepted by the pop-ulation that is governed, by those who carry out particular acts or orders, and by "the sovereign." Aesthetic representation matters just as much in administrative organization: cartography introduced a new aspect to the re-lationship between sovereignty and territory. After their conquest of China in the thirteenth century, Mongol rulers employed Muslim cartographers to map and teach them exactly what was and was not in their newly acquired domain.[83] Cartography in early modern Europe also projected power—at times once again in relation to Central Asian rulers: Christopher Marlowe's play *Tamburlaine the Great* (c. 1588), has Tamerlane crying on his deathbed: "Give me a map; then let me see how much / Is left for me to conquer all the world."[84] As Jordan Branch writes, a "novel shift has occurred toward using maps to picture territorial authority as a spatial expanse," and cartography subsequently would become a principal tool for the organization and depic-tion of nature and territory.[85]

Aesthetic representation is no less essential for the purposes of comparing forms of self-understanding, influence, domination (including colonial
domination), and violence. Bluntly put, any regime can kill, dominate, or ex-
clude; to ask how and why it chooses targets, how it appears legitimate in
doing so, is to engage the aesthetic question. How a naturalized aesthetics
complements power differentials in hierarchic and oppressive cultures; how
it enables subjection and maintains images of power and powerlessness; how
terms such as *resistance*, *liberation*, *continuity*, and *revolution* participate in an
aesthetic framework that would include their moral and theologico-political
experience—such questions animate several of the essays included here.
Cathy Gere examines how this ruler is also re-conceived on the basis of the
corpse of the condemned, once "sciences of life" stand next to the guillotine.
Jason Frank, A. Azfar Moin, and Stefanos Geroulanos each ask how an entire
aesthetics (and its transformation) is essential to the claims and entitlements
of power.

Even questions that at first sight seem irrelevant to aesthetics—such as ex-
ecutions and military equipment—are of no lesser concern here. The death
penalty, as a legally administered form of killing and punishment and also the
most basic of biopolitical acts, is generally recognized as shrouded in complex
symbolics and aesthetics. Insofar as "sovereignty and the death penalty have
been inextricably combined throughout history,"[86] the death penalty also has
rich cultural lives springing from "capital punishment's embeddedness in
discourses and symbolic practices," which range from the sentencing court
to the ruler to the act itself.[87] War has been attached to aesthetics ever
since the establishment of modern historiography, when Jacob Burckhardt
famously described Renaissance states as works of art forged by warfare and
tyrants' barbarism. Burckhardt's crediting of Frederick II with destroying
the feudal state and transforming "the people" into a "multitude destitute of
will and means of resistance" and his depiction of Petrarch as elaborating
"the modern fiction of the omnipotence of the state" both intertwine
warfare and the aesthetics of statehood.[88] The possession of an arsenal—
especially of a particular or powerful arsenal—has long been attached to
the establishment of sovereignty, such as Byzantine "Greek fire" or the
British *Dreadnought* in the early twentieth century. During the period leading up to World War II, "fear of loss of sovereignty" was one of the main
reasons why internationally coordinated disarmament efforts failed: this

was true particularly in the case of Western attempts to restrict the size of Japanese naval power, which Japan identified with its national and regional sovereignty.[89] Nuclear weapons—from the early refusal, by nuclear powers, of proposals to treat nuclear science as a matter of "world sovereignty" through to the Iranian insistence that any attempt to limit its nuclear program is a "breach of its national sovereignty"—have similarly served as not only tools guaranteeing survivability (of countries and regimes) but also particularly powerful rhetorical ornaments, ultimate signs of state sovereignty, thanks to the invulnerability and (self) extermination they symbolize.[90] As nuclear weapons are almost unusable, their function has become principally symbolic—aesthetic, rather than military; they have become the "'hidden juncture where the juridico-institutional model of sovereignty and the bio-political model of power' meet."[91]

Further reverberations of aesthetic representation become clearer when one attends to the multiplicity, coefficiency, and co-implication of sources of sovereignty—the aforementioned tendency for sovereignty to be ambiguously vested between persons, political units, and states, and especially the role played by conceptual or imaginary mediators for this sovereignty, such as nation, "the people," class, God, human rights, and so on. Carl Schmitt's famous dismissal of the *Rechtsstaat*'s claim to be the source of its own sovereignty involves precisely this question of the role of a mediation that would not be merely political. Harold Laski, identified with a different tradition of thinking about political and legal sovereignty in the early twentieth century, offered even harsher critiques of the idea that sovereignty is automatically vested, without negotiation or staging, in a personified or institutional vector, which it establishes its own realm that automatically underlies the sphere of law.[92] In the present volume, several essays engage the ways *aesthetic* representation sculpts both the self-image and mediating practices involved in this fashioning of sovereignty. Dan Edelstein engages with the figure of "permanent revolution" as one that not only recoded the Terror of 1793 but also allows Marx to conflate multiple categories (e.g., sans-culottes and an army of workers) and to transpose institutions onto one another in the instauration of "permanence" as a particular figure of popular sovereignty. Nicole Jerr inquires as to the meaning of a theater of revolution in relation to fears of crowd-based sovereignty in the twentieth century. Alexei Yurchak considers the odd survival, even past the end of the Soviet era, of Lenin's body as a living dead artifact with a history of both distortive and creative aesthetic and political effects on Soviet and now Russian sovereignty and history. Yuri Pines asks, with reference to traditional China: "Who is the supreme sovereign 'within the seas'? Is it a monarch personally, or is there a superior entity to whom the monarch's will should be subordinate?" For Amnon Raz-Krakotzkin, the clash between exilic Judaism and Zionism is central to the image of Jewish statehood and the recoding of the past. Stefanos Geroulanos examines how a rethinking of history as underwritten by ostensibly truer, deeper histories in the later nineteenth century anticipated the creation of "New Men" in twentieth-century Europe as new forms of aesthetico-political representation in theories of nation, power, and science.

Across these and other essays, the question of modernity and democracy also comes to the forefront: for all the shifts in sovereignty we usually associate with North Atlantic democracy, imperialism, and internationalism, the question of the role of aesthetics in structuring the force and image of sovereignty has to be raised anew. We propose that the effect of aesthetic representation in the establishment of the stage and scaffold of unitary or absolute rule—as well as in the contestations and reformulations of sovereignty—is a mirroring, a folding upon one another of different figures involved in casting the embodiments, organizations, and sources of sovereignty. Aesthetic mirroring and conflict nestle together reasons for historians to examine, even for the stakes of political history, the play of representation, from the understanding of kings and religious leaders in the European tradition as representatives of God on earth all the way to the democratic, nationalist, and even vanguardist revolutionary imaginaries. They are no less significant for the everyday experiences, contestations, or receptions of power, the images of sovereignty "from below." Aesthetic representation casts a plethora of images associated with the rule, with "the people," and with law in such a manner that these dynamically engage one another in order to generate the image of a structured source of power. Even in cases of "merely" political representation, a parliament, party, or dictatorial figure represents, say, "the people" (or "the will" of the people), speaks in "their" name, asserts "their" sovereignty.[93] Often, this institution or figure is itself not only invested with sovereign or quasi-sovereign power to represent "the people," so it can speak "in their name," but also casts back, as its own representative principle, as the figure counterrepresenting its own political work, this same and no less imaginary "people," constructing it as sovereign in turn.[94] Thus "people" elect the parliament, which speaks in their name, styles itself as speaking in their name, and establishes its own authority by inventing and styling this "people." To emphasize this mirror play of representation is not to stage a postmodern game of thrones; it is to ask *how* different regimes, claimants, appellants, and competitors articulate and depict forces and worldviews essential to the political schemes they play out; how these schemes clash with or reinforce one another; how sovereignties and sovereigns participate in the dynamic transformation of structures; how they present continuity, contingency, or rupture (and even continuous rupture, as Edelstein shows here); how they construct transcendentals and universes for their universalisms, often in the same gesture in which they designate those who speak for these universalisms; how they seek to displace existing schemes of power and representation for other ones, more efficient or more germane to their sense of rule.

Aesthetics and Political Theology

Canonical scholarly literature extends the problem of representation and aesthetics to engage political theology. In her influential study of the many mystical depictions of Elizabeth I as Astraea, Frances Yates examined both the figure of the Virgin Queen and the messianic implications inherent in the stylization of her rule.

> The symbol of the Virgin Queen—in whatever way understood, and all the more intensely because of the conflicts inherent in it—touched tremendous spiritual and historical issues. *The destiny of all mankind is at stake in the idea for which the virgin of the golden age stands*, and above both papacy and empire is Christ, praying in the words of St. John's gospel "that they may all be one; even as thou, Father, art in me, and I in thee." This is the sacred imperialism of the Prince of Peace, the Christian blend of Hebrew and Virgilian prophecy, uttered by the Messiah in the universal peace of the Roman Empire, that time of which Dante says that there will never be another like it for then "the Ship of the Human Family by a sweet pathway was hastening to its rightful haven." In the Elizabethan imperial theme, universal concepts are never far below the surface in the interpretation of history.[95]

Pursued in astonishing detail, Yates's claim concerns both the aesthetic representation of the sovereign discussed and the coextensiveness of that representation with religion and its experience. At least since Carl Schmitt's dismissal of representational democracy's claim to sovereignty in his 1922 book *Political Theology* and Ernst Kantorowicz's reconstruction of the late medieval shift from Christ-centered to law-centered kingship in *The King's Two Bodies*—and especially since the "rediscovery" of Schmitt in the 1980s—the problem of relations between religious, political, and state authority has motivated a scholarly pursuit of the very different functions involved in the concept of political theology. Kantorowicz established the theologico-political basis of late medieval and early modern kingship by detailing the juridical efforts to reconcile—with recourse to the christological divine incarnation—the representational problem posed by the king's duality: his mystical body (the body politic which is inviolable) and his natural body (which is susceptible to the usual physical vulnerabilities).[96] Crucially, he took this representational and theological problem as one that defined state formation. In a series of late essays, Kantorowicz also explored aspects of the aesthetic legitimation of royalty, from the motif of "mysteries" of state to the fashioning of emperors as rising suns.[97] Using material artifacts (coinage), jurisprudence, and literature, Kantorowicz reestablished sovereignty as a subject of theological study constructed in decidedly aesthetic and symbolic terms.

The rise of political theology in recent scholarship has taken several forms, from a renewed study of Paul of Tarsus to revisions of the secularization thesis.[98] These revisions have made clear that theopolitical problematization is hardly immune to questions of aesthetic representation and mirroring. As Jason Frank argues here, the effort to identify the "body of the people" so as to replace the religious and popular implications of the "body of the king" posed a crucial problem for the English and, later, French revolutionaries, who invested quite profoundly in the forms, rituals, and acts of power that could carry out this replacement. Amnon Raz-Krakotzkin similarly engages the complex picture—bypassing secularization—instituted by the concurrently theological and political figure of exile, especially when this is seen in contrast to the Zionist conception of the state. And in his study of Nurhaci, Nicola Di Cosmo asks about political theology's role in the transformation and legitimation of a nomadic empire into a contender for the Heavenly Throne of China against its Ming occupiers. In these discussions we return to the problem of territoriality and universality, as well as to the aesthetic and representational links that hold together the theologico-political chains in a meaningful experience of the everyday as this enfolds, dwells within, sutures with, or unleashes the divine. Quasi-secular aesthetic mythologization—including the quotidian representation of secular, religious, historical, and future-oriented political form—can be said to extend further, even to questions of the economy.[99] One way to pursue this concern is to follow Hent de Vries when he argues that not only have "pillars of sovereign power" been "theologico-political, if not mythico-religious," but that within that frame, "monetary flows," which have affinities with "mental dispositions," are no less historically and perhaps structurally theologico-political.[100] Accounts like this allow us to begin to extend the aesthetic and experiential assemblage involved in accounts of religion and power to capital itself.

Claude Lefort and Jacques Derrida have offered similar claims on the aesthetic, even theatrical, basis of political theology. In Lefort's account, "The Permanence of the Theologico-Political?," the obdurate, perhaps ineradicable, persistence of sovereignty in modern democratic society carries a mark of the tragic condition of modern democracy and the aesthetic establishment, through theology and politics, of an authority that still relies on the shadow cast over the "empty place of power" by religious and kingly power even after their fall. For his part, Jacques Derrida in his late book *Rogues* used theologico-political motifs in order to identify, as operating a single violent movement, the gestures that create the self and the sovereign. For Derrida, who was interested in proposing approaches to democratic authority, the self not only includes a propensity toward mastery but also creates myths that establish, on the scaffold of the executioner, this same self as both the foundation and the target of a theologico-politically derived sovereign power.[101]

Besides finding in Lefort and Derrida reason for studying ostensibly hard-political circumstances in terms of theater and myth, there is reason to ask about how political theology is not restricted to matters of regime construction and maintenance but involves occasions of theological conflict or negotiation as much as social policy. As Justin Stearns asks here, in addressing Islamic responses to the plague, "What theological, spiritual, legal, and medical concerns influenced rulers in responding to a challenge to the political and economic well-being of their realms?" Raz-Krakotzkin and Ben-Dor Benite pose similar questions relating to the theologico-political depictions and performances of territory and religious categories.

Linguistics, Law, and Scholarship

It is all but commonplace to note that claims to sovereignty, acts of sovereignty, and assertions made by different agents are aesthetic products of linguistic operations, that they are routinely founded on literary forms, religious as well as secular traditions of stylization, language games, and expressions aimed to convince rulers and ruled of a particular regime's (or claimant's) legitimacy, its capacity to institute and exceed norms, not to mention its ability to control and administer representative functions and formulas, their meaningfulness, and the overall narrative of power.[102] These arguments and claims are not covered by a framework that would simply designate them as performative acts, and the aesthetic problem is entirely concomitant, if not coextensive, with the plastic and formative processes they involve or invoke. Sovereign speech acts, institutional choices or establishments, legal orders, and claims matter well beyond their immediate consequences, marking the king, dictator, parliament, legal system, or people, and just as easily pleating or even *forming* hermeneutic practices: they are, we might say, wired with the images of rule as much as with the tokens and regalia involved in rule that we discussed earlier. Like the long-term influence of Confucianism in Chinese state institutions and practices, the tradition of *specula principum* in Europe—including Machiavelli and James I of England—contributed to the sense of a regulated form of ruling language, encompassing both aesthetics and morality. Discourse and literary tradition remained, in this regard, constitutive of how a prince must appear to act, partly through speech, while, conversely, a prince's actions affected the languages of rule. The same could be said in the modern arguments regarding national unification and language. As David Bell has argued, central to the nationalist efforts of the French Revolution was the standardization of French as a national language at the expense of vernaculars and dialects that had suddenly become politicized and deemed inaesthetic, insufficiently French.[103] Sheldon Pollock pursues a still broader argument in his chronicle of Sanskrit: for him, language in India was deeply implicated in the estab-lishment of power insofar as forms of power were rendered acceptable by the inflections of a narrow group of languages and rhetorical styles attached to specific classes. Sovereignty would thus be at times defined by linguistic opportunities and limits, at times by their violent transformation.

Deeply implicated with questions of language is the cultural and symbolic dimension of law in modern societies. A proper study of law, language, and sovereignty exceeds our space here, particularly given the growth of the field of critical legal studies. Suffice it to recall Paul W. Kahn's account of the value for legal scholarship of "cultural study (the practices and beliefs con-stitutive of law's rule)" and "the substantive form of the inquiry (genealogy and architecture)." His is a problematization that points toward an anthro-pologically richer discussion of law's linguistically based ordering and har-monizing of political and aesthetic representation, and through them, of everyday life in particular regimes.[104] Throughout the twentieth century, legal thinkers in Europe too, especially conservative ones—from Schmitt through Ernst-Wolfgang Böckenförde and his famous "dictum" on the limi-tations of the West German liberal state, and on to Pierre Legendre in France—have articulated the relationship of law to statehood and sover-eignty. Legendre, insisting on law's lineage, *textual* quality, psychic reach, and continuing dogmatic force ever since medieval canon law, has apostrophized the "anthropological function of the law" by emphasizing its extra-juridical origin and the way it codifies and reworks that origin:

> Fundamental juridical categories . . . do not conceal within themselves their own justification; they are juridical categories only because they are founded in, that is to say they refer to, the principle of division from which they spring. . . . In every society, the basic founding discourse is a celebration, a ritualization, because it is a matter of bringing alive, on a social scale, the rep-resentation of the foundations, the representation of what renders the func-tioning of the categories conceivable.[105]

Law as an oppressive and colonial form has also received considerable at-tention, and responses to this approach now formulate a broad, consequen-tial study of international and national practices of legal authority, not least in a symbolic framework.[106] On this subject, too, sovereignty resides not only in the possession and assignation of power but also in the drawing of juris-

dictional frontiers; the exercise of normative control; the language, metaphors, and images; the invocations of tradition and religion, innovation and
decision, rights and duties, contracts and cases; not to mention the aesthetic,
technological, and formal establishment of who may and who may not wield
legal power, under what conditions and with what rationale, following what
procedures, and permitting and underlying what further acts, norms, and
spheres of action. In the debates over particular legal formulations, language
becomes central as a form, formation, and regulation of life. Several essays
in this volume address the overlap and conflict of law with other realms. Bernadette Meyler examines the exception that is involved in a sovereign's act
of pardoning, from Kant and Schmitt back to early modern theater and up
to the present; Justin Stearns addresses conflicts of religious law and public
policy, and Miranda Spieler pursues French law and the absolutist practice
of prison banishment through *lettres de cachet* in an at once colonial and
urban context touching on slavery, regionalism, and legal identity.

One more point concerning the linguistic element of the scaffold should
be emphasized—namely, scholarship. We have already cited Yates on the
value of that scholarship for court entertainment in the French monarchy.
Scholarship in the legal and classics realms—perhaps especially in Britain—
was of course constitutive for domestic and colonial rule.[107] Unsurprisingly
perhaps, the dominant discussion of scholarship and aesthetics in recent
years has concerned the role of the sciences of life and mind, especially regarding biopolitical decisions over life and death. The role of these sciences—
in particular, racial, evolutionary, or eugenic biology, psychology, and
anthropology—in effecting or furthering social policies, biopolitical claims or
paradigms, particular concepts of the self, and specific regimes of power is
well documented and sometimes convincingly argued, especially when the
question of the normative and normalizing capacities of these sciences is at
stake.[108] Once again, though, "scholarship" need not be restricted to these
sciences, nor does it need to imply aesthetic disengagement: scholarship in
the classical and literary sciences has been of just as much service, and is
just as citable.[109] That political regimes are usually "regimes of citation"
binds scholarship and its culture once again to the political forms and their
symbolism.[110] Historiography on sovereignty needs to take the value of
citation and genealogy into account in its models of how sovereigns look to
the past and present. The significance of genealogy is evident, for example,
in the difference of the Skinnerian from the biopolitical approach—to pick

on two of the more influential recent approaches. Scholarship as critique has made similar claims. Agamben's biopolitics, from *Homo Sacer* until at least *State of Exception*, overlaps two genealogical efforts: one concerns the object of its study—a straight line from the *homo sacer* in Roman law to the extermination camps—the other establishes a tradition of precursors for the political claims of biopolitics (Schmitt, Benjamin, Foucault, Arendt). Each tradition is inscribed within the other in order to generate a sense that the overall project conducts an antiestablishment resistance on behalf of *homo sacer*. If this allows for political claims on behalf of the least of human beings, it also answers the question of sovereignty before it has been properly posed because it determines sovereign power as much through an identification with those at the limit of humanity as through a convenient genealogy of resistance. The complexity of modern legal and political norms is now treated as coefficient, contingent when compared to logics of "bios"; global and aesthetic problems also become lacunae clamoring for reengagement. It is worth emphasizing his schema's great difference from Kalmo and Skinner's emphasis on Westphalia, Hobbes, and liberalism. The language and genealogy generated in these scholarly claims remains structurally significant for their interpretations of linguistic and symbolic forms and effects. As scholarship is itself one of the sculptors of the aesthetics of sovereignty, the politics and aesthetics of scholarship on sovereignty instigate one of the central problems for several essays here, including Jason Frank's critique of political theory and Cathy Gere's link between depictions of sovereignty and neurological conceptions of the body during the English and French Revolutions.

Sovereignty and the Arts

Representations—whether a ceremonial appearance, a likeness reproduced on coins, symbolic reference in architecture and monuments, or characterization in poetry and narrative—work to tell a story of the sovereign and maintain the idea or fiction of his power. Crafting these stories and images are artists working across the visual, literary, and musical arts, and these arts, especially in the contexts of humanistic, Confucian, and Islamic traditions of learning, themselves came to profoundly shape the establishment, negotiation, and contestation of sovereignty.

Take, for example, a variety of portraits commissioned by the Qianlong emperor, depicting him as a Manchu warrior, a Confucian, a Mandarin, and a Daoist in an effort to identify him as ruler of each culture and all of them together. The paintings testify to far more than mere propaganda, not least because the artist responsible for them was the Italian Jesuit Giuseppe Castiglione, whose long tenure in the Chinese imperial court marks a significant art-historical moment of combined Eastern and Western techniques and conventions and demonstrates one significant way in which the relationship between sovereignty and the arts has held extensive influence.[111] The globality pursued by the Qianlong emperor comes to be entwined with a different, Catholic, globe and different implications of representation.

Another inscription of sovereignty into art emerges through the classic study *The Age of the Cathedrals,* in which Georges Duby notes that the birth of the very concept of a 'work of art' "depended particularly closely on royalty, its functions and resources."[112] Interwoven as it was with religious authority, royal authority in medieval Europe as elsewhere resulted in kings and emperors "comporting themselves as godly heroes," which prioritized making dedicatory gifts. "The sovereign was he-who-gives—who gives to God and who gives to men—and it was fitting that beautiful works should flow from his open hands."[113] The late medieval pinnacle of such works was the construction and maintenance of cathedrals, which were as much about sovereignty as about God: "The churches were in fact royal buildings par excellence, for God revealed himself to mankind as sovereign of the world, crowned and seated on a throne, there to judge the living and the dead. Moreover, every place of worship was supposed to enjoy the protection of the king himself, Christ's lieutenant on earth, and the king's offerings had helped to build it."[114]

Aesthetic representation thus generated a tradition in which kingship and its theological and aesthetic duties (from patronage to community building to establishing cultures of artistic power) became part of the setting of religious and aesthetic experience: they inscribed sovereignty into architecture, as elsewhere onto court culture and other arts. In Louis Marin's argument, aesthetic representation went a step further: it involved the direct inscription of sovereignty into aesthetics itself, into the unfolding of a visual semiotics that begins and ends with power. As Eva Giloi has argued, the rise of bourgeois material culture in nineteenth-century Germany had a similar effect in that it entailed intellectual clashes and a recalibration of logics of support for the Hohenzollern monarchy.[115] In this volume, Stanca Scholz-Cionca reviews the preeminent value of the theater in the court of the sixteenth-century Japanese warlord Toyotomi Hideyoshi, where Nô drama was supported on the level of institution, practiced on the level of personal obsession, and patronized on the level of a highly sophisticated sovereign scaffolding, telling even of future sovereign acts. Zvi Ben-Dor Benite similarly examines the Manchu Qing establishment of a mosque in Beijing, with its unexpected consequences, which led to an evocation of different Islamic laws and a meditation on Muslim perceptions of Chinese sovereignty.

At stake is not only the issue of sovereigns inscribing their sovereignty into art. Patronage aside, sovereigns have featured as figures hovering between divinity and humanity, not least in many of the foundational epics of world literature. The *Epic of Gilgamesh*, the *Iliad* and the *Odyssey*, the *Ramayana*, and the *Mwindo* epic—each follows the stories of hero-kings as they navigate these parameters—sometimes permitted to enter divine realms but then forced to confront their intractable mortality. What is more, these narratives provide key sites where the priorities and tensions of sovereignty have been worked out. Gilgamesh, for example, stops being an overbearing ruler when, after a long fight with Enkidu, his physical equal, a friendship ensues that changes his goals and values. Similarly, the tests that Rama endures when he is sent into a fourteen-year exile on the eve of his coronation ultimately show him to be a worthy king who knows to act in accordance with his dharma as well as that of others.

It is not our purpose to examine here the immense literature on sovereignty in the arts: these remarks are intended instead to indicate the often-osmotic solvency of blood and paint—sovereignty as a *phenomenon of power* and sovereignty in the *realm of aesthetics*. One might do well to consider art, theater, literature, and architecture as sciences of sovereignty. It is not just, for example, that Schiller's *Wallenstein* stages anxieties of power and tragedy during the Napoleonic reorganization of Europe. In guarding, often jealously, its own rules and manner of thinking, literature (like the other arts) seeks to control the latticework that joins the realms of the known and of tradition with those of the possible and the sublime. The scaffold of sovereignty—whether thought in terms of construction or of execution—is consolidated out of exactly this latticework.

In closing, it should come as no surprise that the specific art of drama has maintained a vested interest in the subject of sovereignty.[116] Since antiquity, the rise and fall of kings has provided drama with its principal tragic form. An implicit association of sovereigns with tragedy dates to the *Poetics*, where Aristotle specifies that a fine tragedy is about "one belonging to the class of those who enjoy great renown and prosperity, such as Oedipus, Thyestes, and eminent men from such lineages."[117] Glenn W. Most's essay "Sad Stories of the Deaths of Kings" considers the history of the relationship between sovereign figures and the genre of tragedy, suspended between political values of monarchy and those of democracy. Early modern drama unquestionably strengthened the relationship between sovereignty and theater as a result of the themes and structures it adopted. It is for no small reason that Shakespeare's plays feature regularly in political-theoretical discussions of sovereignty as demonstrated by the work of standard-bearers such as Kantorowicz, Schmitt, and Benjamin.[118] But Shakespeare is not alone in his dramatic relevance. The age of absolutism produced a vast body of drama with sovereignty at the center of its concerns, manifestly obvious in any survey of the major works of Spanish Golden Age drama, Japanese Nô, French neoclassicism, and the German baroque.[119] Nor is this an old-regime concern: as Lefort's reading of Jules Michelet indicates—where Lefort, in pursuing his interest on the empty place of power, inquires on the survival and afterlife of royalty—James I's concern with the scaffold/stage of sovereignty survives the destruction of absolutism. For Lefort's Michelet, theatricality plays a critical part in both supporting and dismantling the sovereign. Recent critical and philosophical explorations of sovereignty as it is related to these dramatic traditions abound, yet they are not given the seriousness they deserve in political theories of sovereignty, as if literary and aesthetic engagement simply occupied a discrete realm. Several essays in this volume explore the unique relationship between sovereignty and the theater. Indeed, so strong is the association between sovereign figures and tragedy that the very possibility of modern tragedy has been called into question as a result of its shift toward using common individuals as protagonists: in her essay, Nicole Jerr considers precisely this question—of the strange persistence of the relationship between sovereignty and drama even after political and aesthetic revolutions have ostensibly rendered "kings on stage" an obsolete trope. Bernadette Meyler follows threads within the writings of

Kant and Schmitt on the sovereign pardon that leads not only to theatrical metaphor but also to the consideration of theatrical text as a viable source of political theory.

Like this introduction, the current volume as a whole attempts to give a sense of the multiple sites for the examination of sovereignty and its scaffold. It does not pursue a wide-ranging comparison of concepts of sovereignty, nor does it sculpt a single model in deference to a false idol of coherence. The shift we advocate in the study of sovereignty by no means suggests a disciplinary priority, nor does it demand that all elements discussed here be addressed in each engagement with the subject. In putting forward the scaffolding of sovereignty, we are above all calling for strategies that do not decide in advance what sovereignty is but pursue, with varying degrees of interdisciplinary latitude, the interconnections of political theory, history, anthropology, and literature. In using conceptual and anthropologically attuned history to open the space where global intellectual history can handle at once comparative and aesthetic concerns involved in sovereignty's scaffolding, the essays we have brought together seek to give back to sovereignty both some of its elusiveness and some of its force. Our emphasis on the figure of the scaffold, with its inherent polysemy covering both scaffolding and site of execution, and our focus on the aesthetic dimensions of this scaffold do not aim to cross every meridian that traverses the problem, but they do mean to provide a capacious and amendable theoretical framework for further work.

We would like to thank the New York University Global Research Initiative and the Remarque Institute for supporting *Sovereignty: New Perspectives, New Frontiers*, a first conference on the subject that we organized in 2013, and then a Kandersteg Seminar in 2015. The participants at both of those events gave extremely helpful advice and suggestions. Further financial and organizational assistance was provided by the New York Area Consortium in Intellectual and Cultural History. We are also grateful for the valuable and often detailed comments we received from David A. Bell, Nicola Di Cosmo, Jason Frank, Cathy Gere, Udi Greenberg, Ethan Kleinberg, Mark Mazower, Jerrold Seigel, Natasha Wheatley, Larry Wolff, and two anonymous reviewers for Columbia University Press. Special thanks go also to Samuel Moyn for his support throughout. At the Press, we would like to express our appreciation to Wendy Lochner and Christine Dunbar for their enthusiasm and commitment and to Kathryn Jorge, who shepherded the book through production. Thanks also to Glenn Perkins for his superb copyediting.

Notes

1. Karl Moore and David Lewis, *Birth of the Multinational: 2000 Years of Ancient Business History from Ashur to Augustus* (Herndon, VA: Copenhagen Business School Press, 1999), 100–131; Philip J. King, "The Eighth, the Greatest of Centuries?," *Journal of Biblical Literature* 108, no. 1 (1989): 3–15.
2. Mario Liverani, "The Fall of the Assyrian Empire: Ancient and Modern Interpretations," in *Empires: Perspectives from Archaeology and History*, ed. Susan E. Alcock et al. (Cambridge: Cambridge University Press, 2001), 377–79.
3. Bustenay Oded, *War, Peace and Empire: Justifications for War in Assyrian Inscriptions* (Wiesbaden: Reichart, 1992), 163.
4. Bradley J. Parker, *Mechanics of Empire: The Northern Frontier of Assyria as a Case Study in Imperial Dynamics* (Helsinki: Neo-Assyrian Text Corpus Project, 2000), 127–28.
5. Oded, *War, Peace and Empire*, 163.
6. Bradley Parker, "Garrisoning the Empire: Aspects of the Construction and Maintenance of Forts on the Assyrian Frontier," *Iraq* 59 (1997): 77–87.
7. Simo Parpola, "National and Ethnic Identity in the Neo-Assyrian Empire and Assyrian Identity in Post-Empire Times," *Journal of Assyrian Academic Studies* 18, no. 2 (2004): 5–49.
8. Barbara Cifola, *Analysis of Variants of the Assyrian Royal Titulary from the Origins to Tiglath-Pileser III* (Naples: Istituto universitario orientale, 1995), 190.
9. Hayim Tadmor, *The Inscriptions of Tiglath-pileser III, King of Assyria: Critical Edition* (Jerusalem: Israel Academy of Sciences and Humanities, 1994), 97; see another list of universalistic titles in Cifola, *Analysis of Variants in the Assyrian Royal Titulary*, 157–58.
10. The term "four quarters of the earth" was also included in one of the titles of the Mesopotamian god Enlil (Jean-Jacques Glassner, *Mesopotamian Chronicles* [Leiden: Brill, 2005], 129).
11. A. H. Sayce, *Lectures Upon the Assyrian Language, and Syllabary* (London: Bagster, 1877), 56.
12. Leo Oppenheim, "Neo-Assyrian and Neo-Babylonian Empires," in *Propaganda and Communication in World History*, ed. Harold D. Lasswell, Daniel Lerner, and Hans Speier, vol. 1, *The Symbolic Instrument in Early Times* (Honolulu: University Press of Hawaii, 1979), 111–44.
13. For an uncritical classic perception of Assyria, see A. T. Olmstead, *History of Assyria* (New York: Scribner's, 1923). For a recent evaluation of Assyrian propaganda, see Mark W. Hamilton, "The Past as Destiny: Historical Visions in Sam'al and Judah Under Assyrian Hegemony," *Harvard Theological Review* 91, no. 3 (1998): 215–50.

14. On the representation of the Assyrian empire in Isaiah, see Peter Machinist, "Assyria and Its Image in the First Isaiah," *Journal of the American Oriental Society* 103, no. 4 (1983): 719–37.

15. Oppenheim, "Neo-Assyrian and Neo-Babylonian Empires," 133.

16. Isaiah 10:5. In 11:11–12, Isaiah speaks of the powers of God in assembling "the outcasts of Israel and gather[ing] together the dispersed of Judah from the four corners of the earth." Here is a clear case in which the ruled take an element from the ruler's scaffold of sovereignty and creatively use it in their own construction.

17. They have even renewed a measure of fatigue with the theme, which some characterize as both overbearing and reductive. See, e.g., Brian Goldstone, "Life After Sovereignty," *History of the Present* 4, no. 1 (2014): 97–118.

18. Compare, e.g., the discussion of the indivisibility of sovereignty in Jens Bartelson, "On the Indivisibility of Sovereignty," *Republics of Letters* 2, no. 2 (2011): 86. At pains both to confirm the priority of this indivisibility and to emphasize its troubled (because idealized) status, Bartelson calls sovereignty a symbolic form (in Ernst Cassirer's sense), "by means of which we have come to perceive the political world, but as such it does not stand in any determinate relationship to the world thus perceived." Bartelson later explains the eminence of the "indivisibility" approach as due to the "violent imposition of that [symbolic] form upon the world" (94). Useful as the notion of symbolic form is, this introduction takes issue with Bartelson's use of it in support of a conception of sovereignty that would supersede "facts on the ground."

19. Hent Kalmo and Quentin Skinner, eds., *Sovereignty in Fragments* (Cambridge: Cambridge University Press, 2010), 5. See also Jens Bartelson, *A Genealogy of Sovereignty* (Cambridge: Cambridge University Press, 1995), 13.

20. Dipesh Chakrabarty, *Provincializing Europe: Postcolonial Thought and Historical Difference* (Princeton: Princeton University Press, 2000). However, Chakrabarty critiques the claim that "modern politics is often justified as a story of human sovereignty" (15).

21. Kalmo and Skinner, "Concept in Fragments," in *Sovereignty in Fragments*; see also (with obvious differences) Hans J. Morgenthau, *Politics Among Nations* (New York: Knopf, 1967). Robert Jackson, *Sovereignty: The Evolution of an Idea* (Cambridge: Polity, 2007), interprets sovereignty as beginning with the sixteenth and seventeenth centuries and sees it as persisting through decline (159–60).

22. Lauren Benton, *A Search for Sovereignty: Law and Geography in European Empires, 1400-1900* (Cambridge: Cambridge University Press, 2009).

23. Pamela Crossley, *A Translucent Mirror: History and Identity in Qing Imperial Ideology* (Berkeley: University of California Press, 1999); Mark Elliott, *The Manchu Way: The Eight Banners and Ethnic Identity in Late Imperial China* (Stanford: Stanford University Press, 2001); Joanna Waley-Cohen, "The New Qing History," *Radical History Review* 88, no. 1 (2003): 193–206.

24. Aziz al-Azmeh, *Muslim Kingship: Power and the Sacred in Muslim, Christian and Pagan Polities* (London: I. B. Tauris, 1997), xi–xii.

25. Ibid., 140.

26. A. Azfar Moin, *The Millennial Sovereign: Sacred Kingship and Sainthood in Islam* (New York: Columbia University Press, 2012).

27. The Inner Asian Great Code recognized, and in effect established, the sovereignties of the greater and lesser principalities in the region. The Great Code played a similar role to that of the 1648 Treaty of Westphalia in the context of Europe and the Holy Roman Empire. Lkhamsuren Munkh-Erdene has discussed this issue in comparison to premodern Mongol conceptualizations of sovereignty in "The 1640 Great Code: An Inner Asian Parallel to the Treaty of Westphalia," *Central Asian Survey* 29, no. 3 (2010): 269–88.

28. Martti Koskenniemi, *The Gentle Civilizer of Nations: The Rise and Fall of International Law, 1870-1960* (Cambridge: Cambridge University Press, 2001), 7.

29. Sheldon Pollock, *The Language of the Gods in the World of Men* (Berkeley: University of California Press, 2009), 1.

30. Cited in Evelyn Rawski, *The Last Emperors: A Social History of Qing Imperial Institutions* (Berkeley: University of California Press, 1998), 6.

31. Napoleon Bonaparte to the Conseil d'État (August 16, 1800), in *Oeuvres du comte P. L. Roederer* (Paris: Didot, 1854), 3:334. In the years following this statement, Napoleon did pursue a specific policy toward Jews to include them as "full citizens" in the empire he was creating, and he tried to revive the Jewish Sanhedrin (assembly), dissolved by Roman imperial order in 358 CE (Simon Schwarzfuchs, *Napoleon, the Jews, and the Sanhedrin* [London: Routledge & Kegan Paul, 1979]; Franz Kobler, *Napoleon and the Jews* [New York: Schocken, 1976]).

32. See the proposal that sovereignty be conceived as socially constructed in Thomas Biersteker and Cynthia Weber, "The Social Construction of State Sovereignty," in *State Sovereignty as Social Construct*, ed. Biersteker and Weber (Cambridge: Cambridge University Press, 1996), 1–2, and Alexander Murphy, "The Sovereign State System as Political-Territorial Ideal," in ibid., chap. 4.

33. Mark Mazower, *Governing the World: The History of an Idea, 1815 to the Present* (New York: Norton, 2013); Glenda Sluga, *Internationalism in the Age of Nationalism* (Philadelphia: University of Pennsylvania Press, 2013).

34. For the history of the concept of territory in its Latin forms from the Romans to early modern Europe, see Stuart Elden, *The Birth of Territory* (Chicago: University of Chicago Press, 2013). See also Michel Foucault, *Security, Territory, Population* (New York: Picador, 2009). On contemporary affairs regarding territory, see Elden's *Terror and Territory* (Minneapolis: University of Minnesota Press, 2009); Wendy Brown, *Walled States, Waning Sovereignty* (New York: Zone, 2010); Saskia Sassen, *Losing Control? Sovereignty in an Age of Globalization* (New York: Columbia University Press, 1996); and Peter J. Taylor, "The State as Container: Territoriality in the Modern World-System," *Progress in Human Geography* 8, no. 2 (1994): 151–62. On piracy, besides Benton, *Search for Sovereignty*, see Daniel Heller-Roazen, *The Enemy of All: Piracy and the Law of Nations* (New York: Zone, 2009).

35. In the Western tradition, knowledge as sovereignty over nature can be traced most clearly to Bacon's "In Praise of Knowledge": "Therefore, no doubt the sovereignty of man lieth hid in knowledge; wherein many things are reserved, which kings with their treasure cannot buy, nor with their force command. . . . Now we govern nature in opinions, but we are thrall unto her in necessity; but

if we would be led by her in invention, we should command her in action" (*The Works of Francis Bacon*, ed. J. Spedding [Cambridge: Cambridge University Press, 2011], 8:125–26). As a concern in the philosophy of history, the problem of sovereignty over nature is of course a major subject of the Hegelian tradition; Theodor Adorno and Max Horkheimer cite Bacon in *Dialectic of Enlightenment* (Stanford: Stanford University Press, 2002), 1–2. The same problem is also a crucial consideration in the history of anthropology (with all its implications for European colonialism), not least insofar as questions of "animism," magic, and religion were concerned in the nineteenth and early twentieth century; see, e.g., James G. Frazer, *The Golden Bough: The Magic Art and the Evolution of Kings* (1896; London: Macmillan, 1920), 1:221: "if [the magician] claims a sovereignty over nature, it is a constitutional sovereignty rigorously limited in its scope and exercised in exact conformity with ancient usage." That this usage is clearly metaphorical should not blind us to the fact that it was also meant to identify the force of scientific and of magical work, and the designation of laws of nature (and obedience to them), as Frazer goes on to argue. The recent advent of environmental history has raised the stakes on the relation of the production of knowledge over nature.

36. Kalmo and Skinner, "Concept in Fragments," 23ff.

37. Ibid., 24–25.

38. Both Thomas Ertman's *Birth of the Leviathan* (Cambridge: Cambridge University Press, 1997) and Elden's conceptual history of territory, *The Birth of Territory*, fall within this category, even as they date the births mentioned in their titles to different periods.

39. Antje Flüchter and Susan Richter, eds., *Structures on the Move: Technologies of Governance in Transcultural Encounter* (Heidelberg: Springer, 2012); Douglas Howland and Luise S. White, eds., *The State of Sovereignty: Territories, Laws, Populations* (Bloomington: Indiana University Press, 2008). Flüchter and Richter's volume compares (and discusses encounters between) Germany and China, with useful chapters also on Mughal and colonial India. Howland and White's volume looks toward non-Western traditions, with essays that examine "extraterritoriality in East Asia" and "colonial sovereignty in Manchukuo," but the statist priority is in fact expanded, insofar as the system of colonial power and the emergence of international law as discussed in the book remain within the domain of states and international political effects alone.

40. Samuel Moyn and Andrew Sartori, eds., *Global Intellectual History* (New York: Columbia University Press, 2013).

41. David Armitage, *Foundations of Modern International Thought* (Cambridge: Cambridge University Press, 2013). Though thus far centered on the history of international law and political economy, we argue that this approach need not and perhaps cannot be sustained solely at those levels, and that a multifaceted anthropological and conceptual history, at once precise and suggestive, may offer a boon for further research. Because sovereignty engages at once the history of states, myths of legitimation, forms of power, and aesthetic practices, it offers a way to further this new paradigm in unexpected directions.

42. Kalmo and Skinner, "Concept in Fragments," 7. This claim is all the more mis-
    guided as a reading of the passage quoted from Wouter G. Werner and Jaap H.
    de Wilde, "The Endurance of Sovereignty," *European Journal for International
    Relations* 7, no. 3 (1986): 286. Werner and de Wilde had specifically foregrounded
    the conceptual embeddedness of sovereignty, not the possibility of "disentan-
    gling" it, when they asked: "To whom is a sovereignty claim addressed? What
    normative structures are used to determine the legitimacy of a claim to sov-
    ereignty?" Werner and de Wilde indicate that "disentangling" in the name
    of clarity and history may well undermine its own purpose. Biersteker and
    Weber also attempt to "disentangle" the components of "state sovereignty"
    ("Social Construction of State Sovereignty," 11).
43. In the Kalmo-Skinner model, this is simply self-evident. The ubiquitous refer-
    ences here are Hobbes's *Leviathan* and Schmitt's *Political Theology*. The classic
    critique of the unified sovereign state is Harold Laski, "The State and Sover-
    eignty," in *Studies on the Concept of Sovereignty* (New Haven: Yale University Press,
    1917), 1–26. In *Rogues* (Stanford: Stanford University Press, 2005), Jacques Derrida
    also criticized this sense of an indivisible and omnipotent agent, casting it
    instead as a pretense and counterproposing the model of a wheel that involves
    both the sovereign and the self (6–12, 16–17). See also the recent discussion of
    American popular sovereignty in Paul W. Kahn, *Political Theology: Four New Chap-
    ters on the Concept of Sovereignty* (New York: Columbia University Press, 2012).
44. Clifford Geertz, "What Is a State If It Is Not a Sovereign?," *Current Anthropology*
    45, no. 5 (2004): 578–79.
45. Benton, *Search for Sovereignty*, 28ff. Using a more strictly political sense of "sov-
    ereignty," and focusing on the British Empire and the case of Hyderabad, Eric
    Lewis Beverley engages a matter of partial sovereignty in *Hyderabad, British In-
    dia, and the World: Muslim Networks and Minor Sovereignty, 1850–1950* (Cambridge:
    Cambridge University Press, 2015).
46. Sanjay Subrahmanyam, *Courtly Encounters: Translating Courtliness and Violence in
    Early Modern Eurasia* (Cambridge, MA: Harvard University Press, 2012).
47. Classic examples of imagining others (and the consequences) include Larry
    Wolff, *Inventing Eastern Europe: The Map of Civilization on the Mind of the Enlighten-
    ment* (Stanford: Stanford University Press, 1994); Lucette Valensi, *The Birth of the
    Despot: Venice and the Sublime Porte* (Ithaca: Cornell University Press, 1993); Marc
    Crépon, *Les géographies de l'esprit* (Paris: Payot, 1996); and of course the entire
    discussion surrounding Edward Said's *Orientalism*.
48. Lucien Bély, *Espions et ambassadeurs* (Paris: Fayard, 1990); *L'art de la paix en
    Europe: Naissance de la diplomatie moderne, XVIe–XVIIIe siècle* (Paris: PUF, 2005); Priya
    Satia, *Spies in Arabia: The Great War and the Cultural Foundations of Britain's Covert
    Empire in the Middle East* (Oxford: Oxford University Press, 2008). The classic ref-
    erence on gift giving and sovereignty is Marcel Mauss, *The Gift: The Form and
    Reason for Exchange in Archaic Societies* (1954; reprint, New York: Norton, 2000).
    See also George Duby, *The Age of the Cathedrals: Art and Society, 980–1420* (Chicago:
    University of Chicago Press, 1981).
49. James J. Sheehan, "The Problem of Sovereignty in European History," *American
    Historical Review* 111, no. 1 (2006): 3.

50. Lucien Bély, *La société des princes* (Paris: Fayard, 1999). With regard to this particular issue, it is interesting to bring in the history of Arabic word *dawla*, which in modern Arabic means "state." *Dawla* was originally used during early Abbasid times (ninth–tenth centuries) to denote the "reign era" (of a specific ruler). Later on it came to denote the dynasty itself. During the late nineteenth century it emerged as the Arabic choice for the secular state modeled after Western examples. In the ancient Near East, kingdoms were often named after the dynasty. For instance, the ancient Kingdom of Israel is mentioned in contemporary steles as "House of Omri" (Beit Omri); Ancient Judah, as the "House of David" (Beit David). Premodern China identified as the names of the dynasty (e.g., Tang, Ming, Qing) and only during the twentieth century did the name of the state come to be separated from the name of the ruler or ruling dynasty.

51. Alexei Yurchak, "Bodies of Lenin: The Hidden Science of Communist Sovereignty," *Representations* 129 (2015): 116–57, claims: "The uniqueness of the Leninist polity lay in the novel way in which the sovereignty of that regime was organized. Sovereignty here was vested neither in the figure of the ruler (as in the premodern absolutist monarchy or Nazi state) nor in the abstract populace (as in the modern liberal democracy), but in the party. This model was not simply different from the other two but also functioned as their peculiar combination" (146).

52. On states and nations, see Sheehan, "The Problem of Sovereignty in European History," 10. On the British East India Company, see Philip J. Stern, *The Company-State: Corporate Sovereignty and the Early Modern Foundations of the British Empire in India* (Oxford: Oxford University Press, 2011).

53. In this, we agree with Geertz's objection to Michael Walzer's *Regicide and Revolution*:

Though both the structure and the expressions of social life change, the inner necessities that animate it do not. Thrones may be out of fashion, and pageantry too; but political authority still requires a cultural frame in which to define itself and advance its claims, and so does opposition to it. A world wholly demystified is a world wholly depoliticized; and though Weber promised us both of these—specialists without spirit in a bureaucratic iron cage—the course of events since, with its Sukarnos, Churchills, Nkrumahs, Hitlers, Maos, Roosevelts, Stalins, Nassers, and de Gaulles, suggests that what died in 1793 (to the degree that it did) was a certain view of the affinity between the sort of power that moves men and the sort that moves mountains, not the sense that there is one. (Geertz, *Local Knowledge* [New York: Basic Books, 1983], 143)

54. See the critique of global history in David A. Bell, "This Is What Happens When Historians Overuse the Idea of the Network," *New Republic*, October 25, 2013.

55. On the global as a scale, see Samuel Moyn and Andrew Sartori, "Approaches to Global Intellectual History," in Moyn and Sartori, *Global Intellectual History*, 5ff. On history as a mode of thinking across different globes, see Prasenjit Duara, Viren Murthy, and Andrew Sartori, eds., *A Companion to Global Historical Thought* (London: Wiley Blackwell, 2014).

56. *King James VI and I: Political Writings*, ed. J. P. Sommerville (Cambridge: Cambridge University Press, 1994), 49.

57. Jacques Rancière, "From Archipolitics to Metapolitics," in *Disagreement* (Minneapolis: University of Minnesota Press, 1998), 74.

58. The language of a "fiction" of sovereignty, frequently engaged in the work of Giorgio Agamben, is suggestive but insufficient when it promotes a dualism between the real and the fictitious. Without offering a detailed critique, we understand such fiction to be an integral part of the symbolic and aesthetic dimensions of sovereignty and of claims to it. See, e.g., Agamben, *State of Exception* (Chicago: University of Chicago Press, 2005), 59; Daniel McLoughlin, "The Fiction of Sovereignty and the Real State of Exception," *Law, Culture, and the Humanities*, May 14, 2013; and Colin Macquillan, "Agamben's Fictions," *Philosophy Compass* 7, no. 6 (2012): 376–87. See also Peter Gratton, *The State of Sovereignty* (Albany: State University of New York Press, 2012). On aesthetics, political representation, and history, and despite its difference in intent and theoretical aims from the current volume, see Frank Ankersmit, *Political Representation* (Stanford: Stanford University Press, 2002), 2–4, and *Historical Representation* (Stanford: Stanford University Press, 2002), 284; see also Paul Friedland's argument on the parallel transformation of theatrical and political representation in the later eighteenth century in *Political Actors: Representative Bodies and Theatricality in the French Revolution* (Ithaca: Cornell University Press, 2002).

59. As it is in so much legal thought, the argument on normativity is central to Schmitt's *Political Theology*. In a perhaps different register, for the co-implication of scientific knowledge and modern European norms, pursued with an evident if underacknowledged political purpose regarding knowledge and power, see also Georges Canguilhem, *The Normal and the Pathological* (New York: Zone, 1989).

60. Clifford Geertz, *Negara: The Theater State in Nineteenth-Century Bali* (Princeton: Princeton University Press, 1980), 124.

61. Contrast, e.g., the accounts of the Führerprinzip and rituals of Nazi power proposed by Ian Kershaw (in *The "Hitler Myth"* [New York: Oxford University Press, 1987], 8, 9), who relies on the Weberian model of the charismatic leader; by George L. Mosse (in *The Crisis of German Ideology: Intellectual Origins of the Third Reich* [New York: Grosset & Dunlap, 1964] and *The Nationalization of the Masses* [New York: H. Fertig, 1975]), who highlighted the irrational current in Nazi ideology; and by Eric Michaud, in *The Cult of Art in Nazi Germany* (Stanford: Stanford University Press, 2004), who interprets the aesthetic dimension of Nazism as constitutive of its worldview and focuses on Hitler as an artist-prince fundamentally sculpting norms for the reception of his persona and claims.

62. Subrahmanyam, *Courtly Encounters*, chap. 3.

63. Jean Starobinski, *1789: Les emblèmes de la raison* (Paris, Flammarion: 1973), 81, 89.

64. "Which development in a structure composed of interdependent people, which figuration of human beings, allows the formation of a central position with the particularly great freedom of decision that we call 'absolutism' or 'autocratic rule'?" Norbert Elias, *The Court Society* (New York: Pantheon, 1983), 24.

65. Richard Wortman, *Scenarios of Power: Myth and Ceremony in Russian Monarchy*, vol. 2, *From Alexander II to the Abdication of Nicholas II* (Princeton: Princeton University Press, 2000), 8.

66. Frances Yates, *The French Academies in the Sixteenth Century* (1947; reprint, London: Routledge, 1988), 270. In the Chinese case, the connections between the court, religious ceremonies, and theater and music are very strong throughout. In the ancient period, we learn from the *Zhouli*—composed before Confucius's time—about dances preformed at court in order to "promote harmony." Many ancient texts describe the ruler as personally intervening in drama and theater. From the Han dynasty on, imperial involvement in theater only increased, peaking during Yuan times (1267–1368) when China's Mongol rulers heavily supported Chinese drama. Of this long history we allow ourselves but one example: Emperor Zhuangzong (r. 923–26), known for his military capabilities, used to disguise himself and play on stage with his comedians. His love of theater cost him his life when one of his favorite actors stabbed him to death. See Chu Chia-Chien, James A. Graham, and Alexandre Iacovleff, *The Chinese Theatre* (London: John Lane, 1922), and Émile Guimet, *Le théâtre en Chine* (Paris: Musée Guimet, 1905).

67. Conversely, one might also ask the question of when the aesthetics of the court deteriorates to the point of amounting to mere aesthetics deprived of power, or to a theater where the sovereign plays at sovereignty. Alfred de Vigny's *Servitude et gloire militaires* (1835) stages the problem in an encounter between Napoleon and Pope Pius VII, in which the pope insults Napoleon as being merely a comic or tragic actor.

68. See Julia Reinhard Lupton, "Soft Res Publica: On the Assembly and Disassembly of Courtly Space," *Republics of Letters* 2, no. 2 (2011): 74.

69. Louis Marin, *The Portrait of the King* (Minneapolis: University of Minnesota Press, 1988). See also his *Politiques de la representation* (Paris: Kimé, 2005).

70. Marin, *Portrait of the King*, 5, 6, 7–8. "The king is only truly king, that is, monarch, in images. They are his *real presence*" (8, emphasis in original). See also Michel Foucault's contested argument about subjectivity, sovereignty, and representation in Velasquez's *Las Meninas* in *The Order of Things* (New York: Vintage, 1994), 16.

71. Peter Burke, *The Fabrication of Louis XIV* (New Haven: Yale University Press, 1994); David Howarth, *Images of Rule: Art and Politics in the English Renaissance* (Berkeley: University of California Press, 1997); Jonathan D. Spence, *Emperor of China: Self-Portrait of K'ang-Hsi* (New York: Vintage, 1988). See also Joan B. Landes, *Visualizing the Nation: Gender, Representation, and Revolution in Eighteenth-Century France* (Ithaca: Cornell University Press, 2003). For a detailed engagement with historians writing on the early modern image of rule, see Jason Frank's essay in this volume.

72. This is very evident particularly in the context of Cold War–era Western/anticommunist attempts to explain the nature of "illiberal" or "despotic" regimes in Asia. Karl Wittfogel's theory of "hydraulic empires" in *Oriental Despotism: A Comparative Study of Total Power* (New Haven: Yale University Press, 1957) famously argued that societies, mostly Asian, that had to rely heavily on large-

scale irrigation systems and therefore on massive coercive labor, gave rise to strong states which in turn became "despotic." We do not enter into a critique of this, now debunked, theory, but we do wish to point out that its heavy emphasis on the role of the state dwarfed and pushed aside issues of sovereignty and completely ignored questions related its trappings. Wittfogel saw the ruler simply as a despot produced by the state's bureaucracy, brushing aside his person and image as, at best, derivatives of the "strong state."

73. See William Monter, "Gendered Sovereignty: Numismatics and Female Monarchs in Europe, 1300–1800," *Journal of Interdisciplinary History* 41, no. 4 (2011): 533–64; Paul van Wie, *Image, History, and Politics: The Coinage of Modern Europe* (Lanham, MD: University Press of America, 1999); Jonathan Williams, "Imperial Style and the Coins of Cleopatra and Mark Antony," in *Cleopatra Reassessed*, ed. Susan Walker and Sally-Ann Ashton (London: British Museum, 2003), 87–94; Evgenia Shchukina, "Catherine II and Russian Metallic Art," in *Catherine the Great & Gustav III: Nationalmuseum, 9th October 1998-28th February 1999*, ed. Magnus Olausson (Stockholm: Nationalmuseum, 1999), 313–19; *Qianlong Imperial Seals: Legacies of Imperial Power from the Estate of Emile Guimet* (Hong Kong: Sotheby's, 2008); and Brigitte Bedos-Rezak, "The King's Sign," in *When Ego Was Imago* (Leiden: Brill, 2010), 75–94. On paperwork, see Ben Kafka, *The Demon of Writing: Powers and Failures of Paperwork* (New York: Zone, 2012).

74. See Natalie Zemon Davis's study of sovereignty instituted "from below" in *Fiction in the Archives* (Stanford: Stanford University Press, 1987), which examines letters appealing for pardon; see also the discussion of pardon by Bernadette Meyler in this volume.

75. Crucial to this form is of course Michel Foucault's work, though Foucault treated sovereignty as surpassed by the disciplinary state beginning around 1800. But see also Arlette Farge and Foucault's study of *lettres de cachet* in *Le désordre des familles: Lettres de cachet des Archives de la Bastille* (Paris: Gallimard, 1982), where, thanks to the form of the *lettres de cachet*, "political sovereignty comes to be inscribed at the most elementary level of social relations; from subject to subject, between the members of the same family, in relations of proximity, interest, vocation, in the relations of hate or love or rivalry we discern besides the traditional weapons of authority and obedience, the resources of 'absolute power.' . . . An entire political chain interlaces the weft of the everyday" (346–47).

76. Robin Wagner-Pacifici, *The Art of Surrender: Decomposing Sovereignty at Conflict's End* (Chicago: University of Chicago Press, 2005).

77. "Jealous": Rama and Sita in parts 6 and 7 of the *Ramayana*; "virginal": Elizabeth I of England; "manipulative": see Wendy Doniger, *The Bedtrick: Tales of Sex and Masquerade* (Chicago: University of Chicago Press, 2000), chap. 6. One could also point to other varieties of the reputation, especially but not solely among literary king lovers, such as stupid and pimpish (Caundales), cuckolded (Arthur), and lustful (David, Herod).

78. See Marin's discussion of the usurper in the "Finale" of *Portrait of the King*.

79. On the royal adoption of 1 Corinthians 2:15, see Ernst Kantorowicz, "The Sovereignty of the Artist," in *De Artibus Opuscula XL: Essays in Honor of Erwin*

Panofsky, ed. Millard Meiss (New York: New York University Press, 1961), esp. 278, and "Mysteries of State," *Harvard Theological Review* 48 (1953): 65–91, esp. 73–76.

80. See the classic work by Marc Bloch, *Les rois thaumaturges* (1924; reprint, Paris: Gallimard, 1983), translated as *The Royal Touch* (London: Routledge & Kegan Paul, 1973).

81. See Anne Marie Moulin's study of physicians practicing outside their native countries and kings relying on foreign doctors for their own health and, by extension, the stability of the state, *Le médecin du prince: Voyage à travers les cultures* (Paris: Odile Jacob, 2010).

82. For a reading of Hobbes and the stakes of terror and state violence today that is attuned to the spectacular dimension, see Carlo Ginzburg, "Fear Reverence Terror: Reading Hobbes Today" (European University Institute, Max Weber Lecture series, May 2008).

83. Tazaka Kodo, "An Aspect of Islam Culture Introduced into China," *Memoirs of the Research* 16 (1957): 75–160.

84. Christopher Marlowe, *Tamburlaine the Great*, act 5, scene 3, cited in Jordan Branch, *The Cartographic State: Maps, Territory and the Origins of Sovereignty* (New York: Cambridge University Press, 2014), 4.

85. Branch, *Cartographic State*, 4. See also Elden, "Coda," in *The Birth of Territory*; D. Graham Burnett, *Masters of All They Surveyed: Exploration, Geography, and a British El Dorado* (Chicago: University of Chicago Press, 2000); J. B. Harley, *The New Nature of Maps* (Baltimore: Johns Hopkins University Press, 2002); Matthew H. Edney, *Mapping an Empire: The Geographical Construction of British India, 1765-1843* (Chicago: University of Chicago Press, 1999); and Zvi Ben-Dor Benite, *The Ten Lost Tribes* (New York: Oxford University Press, 2009). Benton criticizes the overemphasis on maps in *Search for Sovereignty*, 1–3.

86. Judith Mendelsohn Rood, "The Palestinian Culture of Death: Shariah and Siyasah," in *The Cultural Lives of Capital Punishment*, ed. Austin Sarat and Christian Boulanger (Stanford: Stanford University Press, 2005), 233. The Palestinian example shows that the relationship between sovereignty and capital punishment is strong even in cases where the former barely exists: capital punishment in this case serves as one the markers of national sovereignty. See also Austin Sarat, *The Killing State: Capital Punishment in Law, Politics, and Culture* (New York: Oxford University Press, 1999), and Jennifer Culbert, *Dead Certainty: The Death Penalty and the Problem of Judgment* (Stanford: Stanford University Press, 2007).

87. Austin Sarat and Christian Boulanger, "Putting Culture Into the Picture: Toward a Comparative Analysis of State Killings," in Sarat and Boulanger, *Cultural Lives of Capital Punishment*, 1. See Michel Foucault, *Discipline and Punish: The Birth of the Prison*, trans. Alan Sheridan (New York: Vintage, 1995), chap. 1–2.

88. Jacob Burckhardt, *The Civilization of the Renaissance in Italy* (Mineola, NY: Dover, 2010), 3, 5.

89. Carolyn Kitching, *Britain and the Problem of International Disarmament, 1919-1934* (London: Routledge, 1999), 85–87.

90. See, among others, Mazower, *Governing the World*, 232, and, on the term "nuclear sovereignty," Seongho Sheen, "Nuclear Sovereignty Versus Nuclear Security: Renewing the ROK–U.S. Atomic Energy Agreement," *Korean Journal of Defense Analysis* 23, no. 2 (2011): 273–88.

91. Gregoire Mallard, "Who Shall Keep Humanity's 'Sacred Trust'? International Liberals, Cosmopolitans, and the Problem of Nuclear Proliferation," in *Global Science and National Sovereignty*, ed. Mallard, Catherine Paradeise, and Ashveen Peerbaye (New York: Routledge, 2009), 82–119. Mallard quotes from Giorgio Agamben, *Homo Sacer* (Stanford: Stanford University Press, 2001), 4.

92. Laski, *Studies in the Problem of Sovereignty*, 16. Laski's first reference is to John W. Salmond's *Jurisprudence* (London: Stevens & Haynes, 1913), 111.

93. David Runciman and Monica Brito Vieira, *Representation* (Cambridge: Polity, 2008), 5.

94. See J. G. A. Pocock, *The Ancient Constitution and the Feudal Law: A Study of English Historical Thought in the Seventeenth Century* (Cambridge: Cambridge University Press, 1987), on the struggle between the English Parliament and king and the respective efforts to craft their claims to sovereignty (e.g., 16–21, 51–55, 149–71). See also Jason Frank's conclusion, in this volume: "there is no people beyond their appearance and their act." In our argument, we follow Marin more closely than works from the Cambridge school of political thought, where often the different angles of representation are treated as distinct even as "throughout the long history of the concept they have come together in a range of different combinations and settings" (Runciman and Vieira, *Representation*, 6).

95. Frances Yates, "Queen Elizabeth as Astraea," *Journal of the Warburg and Courtauld Institutes* 10 (1947): 82. Republished in Yates, *Astraea: The Imperial Theme in the Sixteenth Century* (London: Routledge & Kegan Paul, 1975).

96. Ernst H. Kantorowicz, *The King's Two Bodies: A Study in Mediaeval Political Theology* (Princeton: Princeton University Press, 1957).

97. Ernst Kantorowicz, "Mysteries of State"; "The Sovereignty of the Artist"; "Oriens Augusti," *Dumbarton Oaks Papers* 17 (1963): 119–77.

98. See, e.g., Jacob Taubes, *The Political Theology of Paul* (Stanford: Stanford University Press, 2004); Daniel Boyarin, *A Radical Jew: Paul and the Politics of Identity* (Berkeley: University of California Press, 1997); Ward Blanton and Hent de Vries, *Paul and the Philosophers* (New York: Fordham University Press, 2013). On secularism, the list of recent discussions is endless, though frequently punctuated by Charles Taylor, *A Secular Age* (Cambridge, MA: Harvard University Press, 2007).

99. Giorgio Agamben has similarly elaborated a theologico-political premise of economics and administration in *The Kingdom and the Glory* (Stanford: Stanford University Press, 2011).

100. Hent de Vries and Lawrence Sullivan, preface to *Political Theologies* (New York: Fordham University Press, 2006), ix. De Vries's introduction can and should be read as a meditation on sovereignty as a concept suspended between religious thought and conviction, on one hand, and political phenomena, on the other.

101. Derrida, *Rogues*, 9–12, 17.

102. For a forceful and detailed analysis of the elaborate language games and hermeneutic efforts involved in appeals to the League of Nations, which doubles as a model of how to handle language in claims and appeals to sovereignty, see Natasha Wheatley, "Mandatory Interpretation: Legal Hermeneutics and the New International Order in Arab and Jewish Petitions to the League of Nations," *Past and Present* 227 (2015): 205–48.

103. David A. Bell, "National Language and the Revolutionary Crucible," in *The Cult of the Nation in France* (Cambridge, MA: Harvard University Press, 2001), 169–97.

104. Paul W. Kahn, *The Cultural Study of Law* (Chicago: University of Chicago Press, 1999).

105. Pierre Legendre, "The Lost Temporality of Law: An Interview with Pierre Legendre," *Law and Critique* 1, no. 1 (1990): 7–8. On the "anthropological function of the law," see Alain Supiot, *Homo Juridicus* (London: Verso, 2007), and on its politics, see Camille Robcis, *The Law of Kinship* (Ithaca: Cornell University Press, 2013), 1–2, 161, 215–16, 257.

106. Antony Anghie, *Imperialism, Sovereignty, and the Making of International Law* (Cambridge: Cambridge University Press, 2004).

107. See Max Müller's classic critique of the limits of classical education for colonial officials, *India: What Can It Teach Us?* (New York: Funk & Wagnalls, 1883).

108. The list here is endless; see the work of Nicolas Rose, esp. *Inventing Our Selves: Psychology, Power, and Personhood* (Cambridge: Cambridge University Press, 2010) and, with Joelle Abi-Rached, *Neuro* (Princeton: Princeton University Press, 2013), and Ian Hacking, "Making Up People," in *Historical Ontology* (Cambridge, MA: Harvard University Press, 2002). See also Vanessa Lemm and Miguel Vatter, *The Government of Life* (New York: Fordham University Press, 2014); Glenda Sluga, *The Nation, Psychology, and International Politics, 1870–1919* (New York: Palgrave Macmillan, 2006); Jan Goldstein, *Console and Classify* (Cambridge: Cambridge University Press, 1987); and Michel Foucault, *Abnormal* (New York: Picador, 2010) and *Psychiatric Power* (New York: Picador, 2008).

109. On rational choice theory, see Nicolas Guilhot, "Cyborg Pantocrator: International Relations Theory from Decisionism to Rational Choice," *Journal of the History of the Behavioral Sciences* 47, no. 3 (2011): 279–301. In *The Royal Remains* (Chicago: University of Chicago Press, 2011), Eric L. Santner proposes a theory of "the flesh" as the sublime substance that the various rituals, legal and theological doctrines, and literary and social fantasies surrounding the monarch's singular physiology . . . originally attempted to shape and manage" (ix–x). Jacques Derrida attended to aesthetic, fabular, and spectacular dimensions of sovereignty in some of his later writings and seminars, esp. *Rogues* and *The Beast and the Sovereign* (though in others, e.g., *The Death Penalty*, vol. 1, trans. Peggy Kamuf [Chicago: University of Chicago Press, 2014], 83, he worked directly from Schmitt's conception).

110. Eric Michaud, "Le nazisme, un régime de la citation," *Images re-vues* hors-serie 1 (2008), http://imagesrevues.revues.org/885 (accessed August 13, 2014).

111. In the Chinese case, portraiture of the ruler was an immensely important feature of the trappings of sovereignty and reached its moment of perfection during the Qing dynasty, particularly during the career of the Jesuit painter

Giuseppe Castiglione (1688–1766). See Cécile Beurdeley and Michel Beurdeley, *Giuseppe Castiglione, a Jesuit Painter at the Court of the Chinese Emperors* (Rutland, VT: Tuttle, 1971), and George Robert Loehr, *Giuseppe Castiglione: pittore di corte di Ch'ien-Lung, imperatore della Cina* (Rome: Istituto italiano per il Medio ed Estremo Oriente, 1940).

112. Duby, *Age of the Cathedrals*, 10.

113. Ibid., 12.

114. Ibid., 23.

115. Eva Giloi, *Monarchy, Myth, and Material Culture in Germany, 1750–1950* (Cambridge: Cambridge University Press, 2011).

116. For recent secondary works, see Edward Berenson and Eva Giloi, eds., *Constructing Charisma: Celebrity, Fame, and Power in Nineteenth-Century Europe* (New York: Berghahn, 2010); Bernadette Meyler, "Theater and Sovereignty," in *Oxford Handbook of Early Modern Law and Literature*, ed. Bradin Cormack and Lorna Hutson (London: Oxford University Press, forthcoming); and Philip Lorenz, *The Tears of Sovereignty: Perspectives of Power in Renaissance Drama* (New York: Fordham University Press, 2014).

117. Aristotle, *Poetics* 13.9–11.

118. Kantorowicz, *The King's Two Bodies*, chap. 2; Schmitt, *Hamlet or Hecuba* (Candor, NY: Telos, 2009); Walter Benjamin, *The Origin of German Tragic Drama* (London: Verso, 1998).

119. See, e.g., work by Alban K. Forcione, Christopher Pye, Stephen Orgel, Stephen Greenblatt, Franco Moretti, Paul Kottman, Julia Lupton, Anselm Haverkamp, and Philip Lorenz.

PART I

STAGES

IN *THE EMPEROR*, his account of the decline and fall of the regime of Haile Selassie, King of Kings, Elect of God, Lion of Judah, His Most Puissant Majesty and Distinguished Highness the Emperor of Ethiopia, Ryszard Kapuściński quotes an official of the court as follows:

> His Majesty spent the hour between 9 and 10 in the morning handing out assignments in the Audience Hall, and thus this time was called the Hour of Assignments. . . . His Majesty would take his place on the throne, and when he had seated himself I would slide a pillow under his feet. This had to be done like lightning so as not to leave Our Distinguished Monarch's legs hanging in the air for even a moment. We all know that His Highness was of small stature. At the same time, the dignity of the Imperial Office required that he be elevated above his subjects, even in a strictly physical sense. Thus the Imperial thrones had long legs and high seats, especially those left by Emperor Menelik, an exceptionally tall man. Therefore a contradiction arose, between the necessity of a high throne and the figure of His Venerable Majesty, a contradiction most sensitive and troublesome precisely in the region of the legs, since it is difficult to imagine that an appropriate dignity can be maintained by a person whose legs are dangling in the air like those of a small child. The pillow solved this delicate and all-important conundrum. I was His Most Virtuous Highness's pillow bearer for 26 years. I accompanied His Majesty on travels all around the world, and to tell the truth—I say it with pride—His

Majesty could not go anywhere without me, since his dignity required that he always take his place on a throne, and he could not sit on a throne without a pillow, and I was the pillow bearer. I had mastered the special protocol of this specialty and even possessed an extremely useful, expert knowledge: the height of various thrones. This allowed me quickly to choose a pillow of just the right size so that a shocking ill fit, allowing a gap to appear between the pillow and the Emperor shoes, would not occur.[1]

In one corner, we have a Polish—European and "Eastern" European— journalist, writing in the midst of communism's continued 1970s appeal and its spread in Africa. In the other corner, a minor courtier, as obsessive and brilliant at the tiny routine he had been used to carrying out as he remained pathetic to both his master and the Polish reporter, who writes of him with the sympathetic glance one would direct at a weak if exotic animal. In narrating this encounter, supposedly conveying his interlocutor's voice directly, Kapuściński speaks as much of power as of its regalia, its stuff, the pillows that prop it up, as much of styles and assignments as of courtliness and a theater of dignity, as much of a permanence of form as of the aesthetics of protocol. The Imperial Office—which one may ostensibly contradistinguish from the physically tiny but Most Virtuous emperor—requires thrones and courtiers for rulership to become reign.

Where is the sovereign? At first glance, he's settled in the gestures of the pillow bearer, his inventory, his memory—the techniques of the body that serve to symbolize Haile Selassie's power over his subjects, in this case the most intimate and established yet most silent ones. Sovereignty here is constructed as much by the emperor as by the pillow bearer and the narrator. But the sovereign is also doubled, multiplied, in Kapuściński's text itself, notably in the rhetoric of His Venerable Majesty and its permutations. Haile Selassie himself is already a memory surviving somewhere between absolutist comedy and admiring eulogy: he's been overcome by revolution just as his ancien régime accumulation of titles has been rendered irrelevant in the current international regime. At this point in the story, though deposed, he is not yet dead—though the book would first appear in Poland after his death. But is the sovereign even simply *here*? Polish readers, from 1976 to the eventual success of Solidarity and the collapse of the Communist regime, took Kapuściński's account to herald and describe not simply the fall of a distant outdated monarch in a military coup but the end of communism and the highly intricate regime that ruled Poland. More recent critics have pointed out that the forms of address Kapuściński gives for the deposed king (His Mellifluous Majesty, etc.) do not exist in Amharik and could not have been in use; their claim is thoroughly European and thus not only invented but "wrongly" redeployed as Ethiopian heraldry. The author and narrator appoint themselves heralds: just as the work itself turns out to involve more literary reinvention than reportage—just as it actively constructs a sovereignty of the (Polish, and not only Polish) narrator designed by Kapuściński over the accoutrements, style, even the form of Haile's power—the forms of pageantry belong to diplomatic norms governing protocol, the praise and order of power, and the stylization and ridicule of Old Regimes. Quotation, stage, and fiction weave together the "figure," "office," and power of the sovereign. Whether these belong to Haile Selassie, international norms, the pillow bearer, or the narrator, their compound and conflicting effect is clear: they describe power, even absolute power, but by negotiating it through its aesthetics (mediated by the narrator's aesthetics), its fiction (mediated by the narrator's fiction), its (retroactive) reach, its competing temporalities, its limits. Sovereignty, in turn, sets these values.

The essays in this first section of the book all focus on a relationship between staging and sovereign power: from conceptual to actively theatrical; our concern is with different varieties of staging—from the rhetorical establishment of Greek tragedy in its relation to kingship to the organization of formal relations between different contributors to the image of Chinese monarchy, the complexity of Mongol notions of sovereignty, and the figuration of a "body of the people" after the English and French revolutions.

Glenn W. Most's "Sad Stories of the Death of Kings" considers the relation between royal sovereignty and the literary genre of tragedy with particular attention to postclassical Greek texts. As he points out, nowadays, at least in Europe, a king or queen usually replaces another without any violence, but that is because true sovereignty resides not in the king but in the people's parliament. Richard II, in Shakespeare's play of that name, shows a different, older concept, in which the death of kings is the special province of tragedy in the theater. Aristotle, who ethicized tragedy, did not recognize this; but after him, the Peripatetic philosopher Theophrastus and late ancient grammarians like Donatus, Euanthius, and Diomedes formulated an essential generic link between tragedy and the fall of kings that went on to shape much of Western literature for well over a millennium.

Yuri Pines's essay "Contested Sovereignty" turns to ancient China, in particular to the monarchism that is considered the major feature of Chinese political culture. Traditional thinkers granted the monarch absolute authority on matters of substance: he was the supreme legislator and administrator, supreme judge and commander in chief, top educator and supreme pontific. Yet the monarch was not supposed to abuse his power; he was constantly reminded that he rules through the Mandate granted to his ancestors by Heaven, and the Mandate can be taken from him if he misbehaves. Heaven, however, was not a whimsical deity but acted on behalf of the people below: should they be maltreated, Heaven could sanction rebellion and replacement of the sovereign. The ruler was supposed to exercise sovereignty on behalf of Heaven above and the people below, but who would judge his performance? Here entered the intellectuals (scholar-officials), the empire's architects and its custodians. Having appropriated the right to interpret Heaven's omens and to air the people's grievances, scholar-officials hoped to counterbalance the monarch's absolute power and to preserve moral authority of their own stratum. The history of the Chinese empire appears here as the intellectuals' continuous efforts to restrain the absolute authority of the monarchs they themselves devised in the first place.

Nicola Di Cosmo's "Nurhaci's Gambit: The Concept and Praxis of Sovereignty in the Rise of Manchu Power" offers a unique perspective on the question of nomadic and state sovereignty. Di Cosmo offers a careful account of the rise of Nurhaci (1559–1626) and the early modern Jurchen state, which would become the Manchu Qing dynasty (1636–1911). Di Cosmo focuses on how Nurhaci's rise from local Tungusic seminomadic chieftain to founder of the Jurchen state involved subtle reworking of previous notions of sovereignty among the peoples of Inner Asia and Mongolia, as well as subtle negotiations with existing Ming concepts and Nurhaci's own innovations and political maneuvering. As opposed to other similar moments in world history (the rise of Chinggis Khan offering the clearest example), where accounts of rise to rulership were written long after the events, records from Nurhaci's own time allow a rare view of how sovereignty was "practiced" in "real time" before it was articulated by the later Qing emperors who sat on the throne in Beijing. At the same time, Di Cosmo exposes us to the dilemmas of the nomadic society in transition, coming to terms with a transformation into an entirely new political community and a state. This essay corresponds with, and complements, Yuri Pines's examination of Chinese sovereignty and rulership and Zvi Ben-Dor Benite's look at the question of Islamic "exilic" sovereignty under Qing rule.

Finally, Jason Frank's essay "The Living Image of the People" addresses an altogether different kind of stage: the figuration, as a body, of a people following democratic revolution. The transition from royal to popular sovereignty during the Age of Democratic Revolutions entailed not only the reorganization of institutions of governance and theories of political legitimacy but also a dramatic, though less-examined, transformation in the iconography of political power and rule. Monarchism, and especially the absolutist form it took in the seventeenth and eighteenth centuries, had a well-developed visual regime of power that centered on the body of the king and that helped enact and sustain an external sovereign authority over beholden subjects. The replacement of the personal and external rule of the king with the impersonal and immanent self-rule of the people posed representational difficulties both of institutionalization and law and of visualization and form. Monarchical divine right and popular sovereignty were embedded within two different cosmologies, and the revolutionary emergence of the people as the legitimate ground of public authority created the need for entirely new images of collectivity. How to envision and represent the people and their authorizing will is an aesthetic-political problem that haunts modern democratic theory, although it is usually overshadowed by democratic theory's preoccupation with the principles, norms, and procedures legitimizing democratic rule. Frank's essay examines some of the pressures of popular visualization that accompanied the victorious appearance of popular sovereignty at key moments of its emergence and how competing strategies of representing popular will were implicated in different conceptions of popular agency and power.

Note

1. Ryszard Kapuściński, *The Emperor* (New York: Vintage, 1989), 27–28.

Sad Stories of the Death of Kings

Sovereignty and Its Constraints in Greek Tragedy and Elsewhere

GLENN W. MOST

SOVEREIGNTY IS A WIDELY ATTESTED, if not geographically or historically universal, political claim, theological doctrine, and psychological aspiration, but it has been profoundly inflected by the varieties of circumstance and society. In this essay I track some of its transformations from our own times back to the Renaissance and ultimately to the fifth century BCE and from Western Europe to England to classical Athens.

On April 30, 2013, a remarkable event took place in Holland: Willem-Alexander Claus George Ferdinand became king of the Netherlands upon the abdication of his mother, Queen Beatrix. The passage of monarchy was staged in a highly theatrical performance at the symbolically charged central buildings of the city by legally qualified agents who followed a series of highly ritualized procedures defined to the tiniest details. The queen signed the Instrument of Abdication at the Royal Palace that morning; she and her son appeared together on the balcony of the palace to provide a visible demonstration of their harmony and of the continuity of their rule; King Willem-Alexander was officially inaugurated a few hours later at the Nieuwe Kerk in front of a joint session of the two houses of the States General, presided over by the president of the Senate, at a ceremony during which he was confirmed as monarch, swearing allegiance to the Constitution of the Netherlands and vowing that he would faithfully discharge all the duties of his office, while the members of the Houses swore first that they would uphold the doctrine (expressly codified in Article 42 of the constitution) that it is not the king but the ministers of the government who bear the responsibility for the government's acts and second that they would uphold the monarchy's rights. The credence table beside the king's throne bore various regalia—a crown, a scepter, and an orb—and also, conspicuously, the Constitution of the Netherlands.

This was a passage of power typical for the ordered constitutional monarchies of twenty-first-century Europe. Nations of this sort have a king or a queen, but real sovereignty is located not in their person or office but in the people of that nation and, through them, in the institution that they have created for that purpose and that purportedly represents their interests: the parliament. But if the people are sovereign and possess highly developed legislative, executive, and judicial mechanisms for exercising that sovereignty, why is there a king at all? Could they not do without one? Presumably the function of the monarchs in such countries is above all symbolic and psychological: unlike elected politicians, they embody the people not just for one or more terms of office but instead for their whole working lives (usually until death or incapacity, the Dutch tradition of abdication being a typically pragmatic exception), not just as one job among others that they perform during their careers but instead as their sole essential determination (whatever charities and other activities they may also be associated with), and not just as representatives of the interests of the members of whatever fraction of the electorate voted for them but instead as the expression of the totality of the populace, including those who cannot vote in its elections. The unity of the nation and the totality of its populace are manifested visibly in the oneness and integrity of the monarch's body, just as the temporal continuity of the nation and populace beyond any single generation is expressed in the hereditary character of the royal house—royal heirs are normally determined not on the basis of an evaluation, by the human members of an appointed committee, of the degree to which various candidates fulfill a set of agreed criteria, but by the genetic sweepstakes by which their royal parents have produced them. On the one hand, these monarchs, unlike politicians, who eventually are voted out of office, are not accountable (within certain limits) for their mistakes; on the other hand, their mistakes usually have little or no practical effect, for they themselves have no real power at all. Symbolically they provide a visible focus for their subjects' fantasies about the dignity and perpetuity of their country, but in reality it is the parliament and the government it expresses that possess all the power to make decisions that the monarch can at most only ratify. On that day in Amsterdam, what was made manifest at every moment of the ceremonies was the unquestioned and absolute prerogative of parliament: King Willem-Alexander, like his mother before him, became a sovereign devoid of sovereignty, and he inherited from his predecessor a sovereignty that she had never possessed and that she could pass on to him only by a kind of pacific fiction.

Now let us consider a different kind of passage of power, the one William Shakespeare staged in *The Life and Death of Richard the Second*. Richard II is a sovereign who becomes devoid of sovereignty because although he did indeed possess it once, he then came to lose it. The peripeteia around which the whole play is constructed occurs in act 3, scene 2, the central episode of its five-act structure. In the scene preceding this turning point, set at Bristol, Richard's rival Bolingbroke has had Richard's supporters Bushy and Green summarily executed; Richard knows nothing of their deaths at this point and so, unlike the spectators of the play, he is able to suppose that his sovereign power remains undiminished. In scene 2, set at Wales before Flint castle, where Richard is being besieged by Bolingbroke, Richard ends up yielding to Bolingbroke, leaves the castle, and joins him; Richard's actual abdication and Bolingbroke's investiture as King Henry IV will not take place until act 4, scene 1, but these formal procedures will only be the ceremonial confirmation of the transition of real power that we have witnessed being performed in the preceding scenes. Then the murder of Richard in act 5, scene 5 by Sir Piers Exton (who supposes that he is fulfilling Henry's wishes) is merely the inevitable consequence.

If in historical reality King Willem-Alexander attains a fictional sovereignty by his predecessor's peacefully abdicating, in Shakespeare's poetic drama King Richard II loses his genuine sovereignty by his successor's violently deposing him. The moment when Richard, at last coming to understand that he has lost the support of his allies and that Bushy and Green have been executed, finally reaches the same level of awareness of the facts as his interlocutors and the spectators have already achieved is the occasion for one of Shakespeare's most celebrated speeches:

No matter where—of comfort no man speak.
Let's talk of graves, of worms, and epitaphs,
Make dust our paper, and with rainy eyes

Write sorrow on the bosom of the earth.
Let's choose executors and talk of wills.
And yet not so—for what can we bequeath
Save our deposed bodies to the ground?
Our lands, our lives, and all, are Bolingbroke's,
And nothing can we call our own but death;
And that small model of the barren earth
Which serves as paste and cover to our bones.
For God's sake let us sit upon the ground
And tell sad stories of the death of kings:
How some have been depos'd, some slain in war,
Some haunted by the ghosts they have deposed;
Some poisoned by their wives, some sleeping kill'd,
All murthered—for within the hollow crown
That rounds the mortal temples of a king
Keeps Death his court, and there the antic sits,
Scoffing his state and grinning at his pomp,
Allowing him a breath, a little scene,
To monarchize, be fear'd and kill with looks;
Infusing him with self and vain conceit,
As if this flesh which walls about our life
Were brass impregnable; and, humour'd thus,
Comes at the last, and with a little pin
Bores through his castle wall, and farewell king![1]

Much has been said about this splendid speech. Richard, still alive, begins by composing an epitaph for himself as though he were already dead, and for that purpose he figures himself as a lowly scribbler who, stripped now of all the accoutrements of a professional author like Shakespeare himself, is reduced to employing as his instruments nothing but the poorest, most universal of natural phenomena, dust and rain and dirt; and in fact he is momentarily so alienated from any social dimension that he is driven to identify himself with these lowest natural common denominators, for he no longer possesses anything except his own body and his own death. But in the present context I wish above all to concentrate on the passage in which, with the impassioned exclamation, "For God's sake" (155), Richard moves to a higher register: he is now no longer even an impoverished poet writing a naturalized obituary for himself but instead merely some anonymous man, sitting in the company of other people and exchanging with them "sad stories" that tell of the deaths not just of one king but of many.

If these "stories" had to be assigned to a literary genre, what, we might wonder, would that be? To be sure, the mode of these stories is that of brief exemplary historical prose narratives gathered into collections—Richard's phrase suggests the exchange of more or (probably) less extended third-person narrations, one after the other, about less or (probably) more famous incidents from the past—and it is understandable that scholars who have commented on this line have thought above all of sets of tales recounting the fall of kings and other famous men such as the Tudor collection *The Mirror for Magistrates*.[2] And yet the catalogue of kinds of falls, for anyone familiar with the works of Shakespeare, has an immediate ring of familiarity: "How some have been depos'd," like Lear in effect and like Richard himself in this very play; "some slain in war," like Macbeth or Richard III; "Some haunted by the ghosts they have deposed," like Macbeth again; "Some poisoned by their wives," like King Hamlet in effect; "some sleeping kill'd," like King Hamlet and Duncan—what we have here is a catalogue of the plots of Shakespeare's own tragedies. And if we enlarge the corpus of tragic plots to contemporary Tudor dramas, the list could easily be extended even further. At this turning point of the plot of his own life, Richard suddenly discovers that he is no longer a real king but has become merely an actor in a tragedy about a king—his own tragedy, the one that is about him, the one that bears his name and whose identity is coextensive with his own.[3]

After all, although *King Richard II* is usually classified nowadays as one of Shakespeare's history plays (and was already categorized as such in the First Folio), in the Quarto it was entitled *The Tragedy of King Richard the Second*, and in any case the generic distinction between Shakespeare's histories and his tragedies is notoriously fluid. And in the following lines (160ff.), the theatrical hint of line 155 is expanded into a brilliant and complex metatheatrical conceit: the small round crown that surrounds the king's head increases in magnitude until it becomes the large round theater (we might call it "The Globe") in which an actor, using as best he can the "breath" and "little scene" (164) that his author has assigned him, "monarchizes" (165) or plays histrionically the role of being a king—while all the time the position of the real king is occupied by Death, dressed for the role of an "antic" (162) or buffoon, who "keeps . . . his court" (162) and knows full well, "scoffing his state and grinning at his pomp" (163), that what the fallen monarch cannot perceive otherwise than as a woeful tragedy is in reality nothing more than a risible comedy. Indeed, so thoroughgoing is the theatrical metaphor in this passage that it is tempting to read even the plea in its first line, "let us sit upon the ground" (155), not only as the mournful recognition of the sudden impoverishment of an ex-king who no longer has a throne to sit on and hence must sink down as far as a human being can go, to the very earth, but also as the self-protectively hopeful illusion that the man who used to be a king on the stage, and is no longer either the actor there or the royal or noble spectator in his box or on the stage, might have become a mere groundling, one vulgar commoner among others, sitting on the bare earth and telling of that king's (and of all kings') sufferings from below, protected from them at a safe distance.

For well over a millennium, from late antiquity until at least the Renaissance, "sad stories of the death of kings" was the paradigmatic definition of the genre of theatrical tragedy. Consider three influential poetological statements assigned by tradition to celebrated late Latin grammarians of the fourth century CE:

1. Donatus: Comedies received their name by ancient custom . . . "from the village" (kômê), that is, from the action of men's life, because they live in villages due to the mediocrity of their fortunes, not in royal palaces, like the characters of tragedy.[4]

2. Euanthius: Between tragedy and comedy there are many differences, above all that in comedy men's fortunes are mediocre, danger's assaults are slight, and the plots' outcomes are happy while in tragedy everything is the opposite: the characters are considered to be towering, the fears great, the outcomes fatal; and in the former the beginnings are turbulent, the endings serene, while in tragedy matters are arranged in the opposite order.[5]

3. Diomedes: Tragedy is a general treatment of a heroic fortune in adverse circumstances. . . . Comedy is a general treatment of the private fortune of an ordinary citizen without any danger to life. . . . In the latter are treated the fortunes of small villages, i.e., of humble homes, not, as in tragedy, of public and royal ones. . . . Comedy differs from tragedy in that in tragedy heroes, generals, and kings are brought onto the stage, in comedy humble and private people; in the former there is mourning, exile, mur-

der, in the latter love affairs and the ravishing of maidens; furthermore, that in the former there are often, and indeed almost always, sad outcomes for happy events and the recognition of children and of circumstances makes matters worse. So that they are distinguished by very different definitions.[6]

In many details, the definitions furnished by these texts differ markedly. Yet the basic conception underlying all three of them is identical. Tragedy and comedy are conceived as a binary opposition in terms of a set of contrary qualifications: tragedies have lofty personages, violent events, and plots that move from joy to grief; comedies have humble characters, trivial actions, and stories that move from turmoil to delight. Evidence for the persistence of this traditional definition at least into the Renaissance is provided for example by Scaliger's influential *Poetice*. In it he defined tragedy as "an imitation, by means of actions, of an illustrious fortune, with an unhappy outcome, in serious metrical discourse" and provided the following catalogue of its standard components:

> In tragedy: kings, princes, from the cities, castles, camps; the beginnings more serene, the outcomes terrible; the diction weighty, cultivated, avoiding the speech of the people, the whole appearance anxious: fears, threats, exiles, deaths. . . . Tragic matters are great, atrocious: the commands of kings, slaughter, desperations, hangings, exiles, bereavements, parricides, incests, burnings, battles, blindings, laments, screams, complaints, burials, epitaphs, dirges.[7]

Indeed, despite the lavish profusion of its catalogue of elements, Scaliger's view of tragedy seems, in comparison with his late ancient sources, to have become if anything even narrower in its doctrinaire limitation of the only genuinely tragic plots to sad stories of the death of kings.[8]

Scaliger, and before him the late ancient Roman grammarians, were looking back on two pertinent millennial traditions, one involving sustained theoretical reflections about the nature of literary tragedies and the other the practical composition of actual tragedies for performance and/or reading. What role, we might ask, do kings play in the texts that found both traditions, Aristotle's *Poetics* on the one hand and the ancient Greek tragedies on the other? It turns out that Aristotle never even mentions in his *Poetics* that kings ever appear in Greek tragedies—the standard Greek terms for king, *basileus* or *anax*, like the ones for tyrants, *turannos* or *despotês* or *monarchos*, do not occur even once in that treatise.[9] Yet there is not a single surviving ancient Greek tragedy in which there is not at least one ruling monarch, a king or a queen, who plays an important role. Aristotle's obdurate silence about the ubiquity of kings in Greek tragedy is remarkable—even astonishing—yet it can readily be understood if we recognize it as symptomatic of the basic orientation of his interpretation of Greek tragedy, which systematically suppresses political aspects of the plays in favor of ethical ones and in which the fundamental notion of catharsis as based on the emotions of pity and fear requires that the characters be of such a sort that they are not stationed at an elevation so far above us spectators that we are no longer capable of identifying with them and their sufferings.[10] But the tragedians' tenacious loquacity about kings deserves some further reflection.

As the appendix to this article demonstrates, almost all the surviving Greek tragedies include among their speaking characters at least one reigning monarch. Aeschylus's *Eumenides* might seem to be an exception, but at the end of that play Orestes leaves Athens to return to Argos and take over the kingship that awaits him there (furthermore, in a certain sense Athena is represented as a divine sovereign in charge of her city). The only true exception to this rule is the *Prometheus* traditionally ascribed to Aeschylus, in which the only speaking characters are Prometheus, the henchmen and subordinates of Zeus (Might, Hephaestus, Hermes), the sympathetic spectator Ocean, and Zeus's human lover and victim Io. Yet even in this case the exception is only apparent, for Zeus's threatening presence offstage is entirely real for the characters and the spectators during this play, and there can be no doubt that in the other two plays of the trilogy to which *Prometheus* belonged, Zeus's speaking role was central; hence it is the very absence from the stage of the young and tyrannical monarch Zeus that is one of the dominant theatrical effects of *Prometheus* and sets this play into significant contrast with the other two.

Thus there is no Greek myth without a king, and it is his story that almost every Greek tragedy is about. Often that story ends sadly for him, but not always: in Greek tragedies many kings do die or otherwise end badly, but others survive and even flourish. Almost always that king has a name, and sometimes his name is identical with the title of the tragedy.

So why is there a king in every Greek tragedy? To this simple question, an equally simple answer immediately suggests itself: all extant Greek tragedies (except for Aeschylus's *Persians*) represent events supposed to have taken place during the heroic age, and the Greeks believed that during that period all countries were kingdoms and hence that all the most important heroes, in particular those whose names and legends were still remembered, must have been kings.[11] This is of course quite true. But it is no less true that Greek tragedy is not an antiquarian exercise in historical research. Like Shakespeare's *Julius Caesar* with its notorious clock, the Greek tragedies are full of anachronisms that represent institutions and objects that did not exist, and could not possibly have existed, at the time of the events depicted—e.g., democracy, assemblies, rhetoricians, money, writing—but that succeeded without difficulty in conveying meaning to audiences who had a vague if distinct sense of a general difference between the lived present and the remote past but who were evidently not as troubled by certain kinds of historically inappropriate detail as some modern scholars have been.[12] This is not to say that an answer in terms of heroic kingship is simply false, but it is surely not enough by itself to explain this phenomenon—had the Athenians been convinced, wrongly, that their democracy was not a fairly recent innovation but instead an ancient institution, then the omnipresence of kings in their tragedies would have been very odd, but even presuming their belief that the heroic age was an age of kings this "historical" answer provides only an insufficient explanation.

It seems more fruitful to try to explain the ubiquity of tragic kings in terms of a structural opposition essential to the genre of tragedy. The name of the king is sometimes identical with the title of the tragedy in which he figures; however, as the appendix demonstrates, such a coincidence occurs only four times in thirty-three plays. More than twice as often (nine times), it is not from any speaking character but instead from the chorus that the play's title derives.

The chorus is as indispensable an element of tragedy as the king is; in fact, it is the systematic opposition and complementarity of these two elements that makes Greek tragedy what it is. There is no play without a king, but there is also no play without a chorus. The king is always an individual; the chorus is always a unified group (only rarely, and temporarily, does it divide into subgroups consisting of semi-choruses). The king declaims spoken verse as a single speaker (except in moments of high emotion when he can briefly sing); the chorus sings and dances and moves all together. The king almost always has a name; the members of the chorus are always, without exception, anonymous. The king has the highest status of any human being (above him are only the gods); the chorus is made up of people who always have a lower status than the king—indeed usually their status is not only lower (ordinary citizens) but also much lower (women, slaves, foreigners, or all of these together). The king interacts directly with the other characters (but if he prefers for whatever reason to interact indirectly by means of intermediaries, like the bodyguards that customarily accompany him, he can do so); the chorus usually interacts verbally with the speaking characters by the speaking mediation of an (always anonymous) chorus leader, to whom this intermediating role is delegated and who represents them for this purpose. The king acts, comments, plans, and suffers; the chorus reacts to the king's actions and sufferings but its members do not act themselves (sometimes they are tempted to become involved in the stage action; rarely, they almost do become involved, though only marginally, but there are strict implicit rules that govern and restrict the extent of their possible participation). Above all, there is one rule that is followed without a single exception by every Greek tragedy (and also, incidentally, by every Greek satyr play and comedy): at the end of the tragedy, whether or not the king is dead, the chorus is always alive. Under extreme circumstances, it can sometimes be threatened by a furious king (e.g., at the end of Aeschylus's *Agamemnon*), but never can those threats be fulfilled. At the end of the play, the chorus is no less alive than the spectators are.

The emphasis in theoretical discussions of tragedy, at least from the time of Plato and Aristotle, has tended to be placed on the heroic individuals whose actions and sufferings determine the tragic plot. The absence of the chorus from our own theatrical traditions makes its presence in the ancient texts so bothersome for many audiences and directors that it is easy to understand that the choral sections in modern productions of Greek tragedies are usually reduced, and indeed sometimes simply suppressed. But for the ancient texts, the complementary and interdependent relation between king and chorus seems to be essential and constitutive. How is this to be explained? My suggestion is political and moral in character: that the king represents the ethical values associated with monarchy and the chorus those associated with democracy, and that the genre of tragedy is intended, whatever else it does, to explore the interplay and conflict of these two sets of values.

An idea something along these lines was mentioned by Friedrich Nietzsche almost 150 years ago—only to be immediately and firmly rejected by him. In chapter 7 of his *Birth of Tragedy*, Nietzsche writes,

> This tradition tells us with total decisiveness *that tragedy arose out of the tragic chorus* and originally was only chorus and nothing but chorus—whence we derive the duty of looking into the heart of this tragic chorus as the genuine primal drama, without letting ourselves be at all satisfied with the ordinary phrases about art—that it is the ideal spectator or had to represent the people as opposed to the royal part of the scene. This last mentioned explanatory thought, which for many a politician sounds lofty (as though the immutable moral law were represented by the democratic Athenians in the people's chorus, which was always proved right against the kings' passionate violence, outrages, and excesses), as much as it may be suggested by a word of Aristotle's, has no influence on the original formation of tragedy, since from those purely religious origins the whole contrast between people and prince, indeed the entire politico-social sphere is excluded.[13]

Because Nietzsche is seeking the origin of tragedy and locates that in the chorus alone, he rejects the notion that it might be the contrast between chorus and actors that is central to the genre—his reference to the political contrast between democratic chorus and royal characters is his own idiosyncratic and creative distortion of a German tradition of interpretation of Greek tragedy that goes back to the Schlegel brothers and to Hegel.[14] But the ultimate origin of Greek tragedy is a mystery we are unlikely ever to unravel, and, more importantly, even if we did manage to do so, it would help us hardly if at all in understanding the real Greek tragedies that are transmitted to us. For by the time of the earliest surviving tragedy by Aeschylus (*The Persians*, produced 472 BCE), the political form of democracy (introduced by Cleisthenes in 508 BCE) and the dialogical form of tragedy had already been firmly established and tragedy had become a thoroughly politicized institution.

Instead of losing ourselves in the mists of speculation about primeval times, let us consider the tragedies we actually possess, in the light of the conflicts in values that they seem manifestly to presuppose, to elaborate, and to enact.[15] The king tends to embody competitive values that can turn, for himself and for others, either in a profoundly positive or in a profoundly negative direction. If he values others more than he does himself, then he is the unique instance capable of bringing salvation and other indispensable benefits to himself and his city: as a benefactor, he cares for his polity; he privileges his city over his family and himself; he safeguards justice for his citizens and piety toward the gods; he is successful in war. But if he values himself more than others, then his attitudes and actions have disastrous consequences for all: he yields to his passions, especially anger; he values his family and himself more than his city; he is unjust and impious, greedy and arrogant; his mistakes and his impetuosity lead to military defeat. By contrast, for Greek tragedy the values of democracy are, and can be, only positive in nature. The democrat's understanding of his life as being necessarily bound up with other people with whom he must collaborate if he is to survive and flourish leads him to embrace a set of cooperative values: moderation and self-control; reverence for tradition and respect for the rights of others; and the deepest of all values, the goal of survival. To be sure, the values of monarchy can be embodied not only in kings but also in other speaking characters (most often in the ambitious sons of kings who want to become kings themselves, like Polynices and Eteocles): conversely, speaking characters can sometimes embody democratic values (e.g., Ismene and Haemon in Sophocles's *Antigone* or Ion or Hippolytus in the eponymous plays of Euripides). Hence it is best to speak of monarchic values that are concentrated largely but not exclusively in kings and democratic values that are concentrated largely but not exclusively in the chorus.

It is not hard to find examples of bad kings and queens in Greek tragedy, ones who embody the negative aspects of monarchic values and inevitably come to grief. Xerxes in Aeschylus's *Persians*, Eteocles in his *Seven Against Thebes*, Clytemnestra and Agamemnon and Aegisthus in his *Agamemnon*, like Zeus in the *Prometheus* ascribed to the same playwright, all share the same moral characteristics—arrogance, disregard for the gods, preference of self and family over others and city, short-sightedness, infatuation with power and its trappings, inability to accept or even understand the good counsel provided by others—and all come to some form of grief, either in that very play or in a sequel. Aeschylus's *Persians* sets in sharp contrast to the bad king Xerxes a good king, Darius, who embodies all the virtues that are the contraries of Xerxes's vices and who is brought back from the grave in order to explain to the living why exactly his son was ruined. So too in Sophocles's *Oedipus at Colonus*, the bad Theban king Creon and the bad Theban aspirant to the throne Polynices are set, in their blind violence, ambition, and duplicity, in stark contrast with the good Athenian king Theseus.

By contrast, the choruses of Greek tragedy generally urge self-restraint, sociability, and piety, and they set their own survival as the highest of goals. A choral ode in *Prometheus* provides a characteristic example of this mixture of piety, fear, and the passionate desire to keep on living:

> May Zeus never, Zeus that controls
> the whole universe, oppose
> his power against my mind;
> may I never be lazy
> or slow to give my worship at
> the sacrificial feasts
> when the bulls are killed beside
> the quenchless stream of father Ocean;
> may I never sin in word;
> may these precepts still abide
> in my mind nor melt away.
> It is a sweet thing to draw out
> a long, long life in cheerful hopes,
> and feed the spirit in the bright
> benignity of happiness;
> but I shudder when I see you [i.e., Prometheus]
> wasted with ten thousand pains,
> all because you did not tremble
> at the name of Zeus: your mind
> was yours, not his, and at its bidding
> you regarded mortal beings
> too high, Prometheus.
> This I have learned while I looked on your fortunes,
> these deadly pains of yours, Prometheus.[16]

There are numerous scenes in which a chorus engages in animated discussion with a king: when he is just about to make some dreadful mistake, they urge him to adopt their own typical virtues—almost always in vain, as he is deaf to their wisdom and blind to their values.[17]

Kingship and democracy are of course political institutions, but it would be superficial to try to explain the ubiquity of the king and the chorus in Greek tragedy in purely political terms. After all, there had not been any hereditary kings in Athens since the legendary times even before and shortly after the Trojan War, and the last tyrant who had ruled the city, Hippias, had been overthrown in 510 BCE. Kings were, to be sure, a familiar feature of the contemporary world, but they were known to the Athenians as a political reality only from such alien examples as enemy Sparta and barbarian Persia. And, to be sure, individuals in fifth-century Athens who were thought to be aspiring to too much power in the city could sometimes be accused by their rivals of wanting to become tyrants, but the only times that tyrannical powers were actually introduced in Athens in the course of the fifth century BCE, they were assigned precisely not to single individuals but to relatively large groups of people, to four hundred men in 411 and to thirty in 404. So the kings of Greek tragedy most likely do not represent a purely political option in terms of contemporary local realities, one that Athenian audiences might hope or fear to see once again fulfilled as such in the real political institutions of their own city.

Instead, it surely makes more sense to see these characters as being moral or anthropological in essence rather than merely political. That is, the king figures not only actual or possible kings but all human beings, ancient and modern, viewed in the light of their aspiration for sovereignty: in this way he helps Greek tragedy speak both to the audiences of fifth-century Athens and to people in many places and at many times. The tragic king is a named individual who thinks he is free to pursue his desires, whatever they are, without having to submit to any constraint or limit—unlike ordinary people, who must live together with others and who must adapt to and negotiate with them if they wish to flourish, or even to survive. For the king, his freedom to pursue without let or hindrance, to the very end, exactly what he thinks to be good for him is not only important, it is his essential feature; it is what makes him what he is, and to him it seems (at least until, sometimes, almost at the play's end) to be far more important than mere survival. Unlike the king, who has no one above him but the gods who can tell him what he has to do and whose approval he needs to secure, the chorus members are bound up in all kinds of empirical circumstances that limit what they can wish for and what they can do. From the vantage point of their own safety (indeed, from that of their constitutive immunity), they watch everything that the king does and suffers, and if they are ever tempted to emulate him, their own commitment to the survival of their persons makes them able to resist any such temptation.

That is, the constitutive contrast between the individual character of the king and the group of the chorus allows Greek tragedy to pose the question of personal sovereignty not only for the king himself but for every human being. The spectators all come into the theater as individuals, but transformed into an audience they become part of a group: each still possesses his name, but as spectators they are all the anonymous, undistinguishable elements of a composite social mass. Aristotle, who thought that it is the speaking characters with whom the spectators identify, and Schlegel, who thought that it is the chorus, were both right—and hence they were both wrong, for every audience identifies both with the temptations of untrammeled individualism and with the consolations of solidarity and survival. Tragedy is a kind of laboratory experiment in social values, playing competitive values against cooperative ones in the form of a public spectacle, without any direct practical consequences, and permitting the members of the audience, who in their ordinary lives must constantly and problematically engage with the advantages and disadvantages of both kinds of values, to see what happens when extreme forms of both values are embodied in human agents and come into conflict with one another.

The narrator of epic had looked back onto the legendary events that he recounted from the vantage point of a time long after their conclusion; however lively and immediate his narrative could become, the past tense and his narratorial perspective inevitably created a distance between the audience and the events. In tragedy, by contrast, the action takes place in the full view of the spectators and occurs simultaneously with their own present time: even if the outcome of the events is always known beforehand, since it is determined by the familiar body of myth, the presence of actors unmediated by an external narrator and the present time of their actions and passions lend the tragic events not only a greater impression of vivacity but also even some degree of a semblance of open-endedness. This appearance of presentness is further intensified by the strong tendency of Greek tragedies, as Aristotle noted, to compress their whole action into the narrow limits of a single day and to indicate this limitation explicitly and conspicuously. And within this single day, Greek tragedy often focuses on the single moment during which a king will make a decision in order to resolve a crisis and to determine a future. On the one hand, the sovereign monarch in tragedy endeavors to make free decisions guided only by his intelligence and his desires, in terms of his own analysis of an immediately present set of circumstances and of the goals he wishes to pursue for the future. But, on the other hand, it turns out over and over again in Greek tragedy that as soon as he begins to make his decision about the present, it is discovered that some powerful, maleficent force from the distant past—an oracle, a curse, a crime—is reaching inescapably into that present to determine his choices and their outcomes in a way that makes a mockery of his human freedom. In Aeschylus's *Seven Against Thebes*, for example, King Eteocles strategically and rationally assigns to the first six gates of his city, one by one, the six champions who will successfully confront the first six enemy warriors of the attacking army. But when the messenger goes on to report that at the seventh gate there stands his own brother Polynices, Eteocles, despite the chorus's reasonable protests, can envision no possible course of action other than facing his brother himself in a mortal and morally polluted duel to the death, and he recognizes in this necessity the working through of their father's curse from which there is no possible escape for either brother. In Sophocles's *Oedipus the King*, Oedipus is a paradigm of rationality and decisiveness in his unrelenting investigation of the cause for the plague that is devastating his city—only to discover that he himself is its origin, thanks to an ancient curse on his family and the crime that he himself committed years before the action of the play began. Human decision, we might say, is revealed in tragedy to never be entirely autonomous: even for the king (let alone for the rest of us), there are always past events that condition the present and that limit any agent's ability to decide and to act according to what he perceives to be his own desires and goals. It is only because the tragic agent is so often a king, whose sovereignty over his decisions is assumed to be so absolute, that the past circumstance that reveals the falsity of any such pretention must take on as demonic and overpowering a form as it does in these tragedies.

At the end of the play, the king is often dead, but the chorus is always still alive to draw the moral of his story: every tragedy ends not with speech uttered by a character but with lines recited by the chorus, and even if these lines are often quite banal and indeed in some cases are identical from one play to another, they provide the final, unimpeachable comment on the passions and tribulations that the chorus and we have been witnessing for the past several hours. The chorus represents the continuous world of modest survival from generation to generation, in which the vicissitudes of a king are an immense but only temporary exception: it is the social values of democracy that provide the context and ultimate horizon for exploring the desires and the fate of the sovereign individual. In the end, of course, the tragic king is discovered, certainly by everyone else, and sometimes by himself as well, to be someone who not only no longer is a sovereign but in fact never was one. He turns out to be just like Richard II, who concludes his speech as follows:

> Cover your heads and mock not flesh and blood
> With solemn reverence: throw away respect,
> Tradition, form and ceremonious duty,
> For you have but mistook me all this while:
> I live with bread like you, feel want,
> Taste grief, need friends: subjected thus,
> How can you say to me, I am a king?[18]

Shakespeare, poet and lover, could not prevent himself from bestowing on the histrionic child of his imagination the ability to formulate this insight himself and to express it in language of such moving, because so uncharacteristic, simplicity. By contrast, it is usually not the kings of Greek tragedy who express this wisdom themselves (all too often they die before they get a chance to do so) but instead the chorus. So, for example, in Sophocles's *Oedipus the King*:

> O generations of men, how I
> count you as equal with those who live
> not at all!
> What man, what man on earth wins more
> of happiness than a seeming
> and after that falling away?
> Oedipus, you are my pattern of this,
> Oedipus, you and your fate!

Luckless Oedipus, as I look at you,
I count nothing in human affairs happy.

Inasmuch as you shot your bolt
beyond the others and won the prize
of happiness complete—
O Zeus—and killed and reduced to naught
the hooked taloned maid of the riddling speech,
standing a tower against death for my land;
hence you are called my king and hence
have been honored the highest of all
honors; and hence you ruled
in the great city of Thebes.

But now whose tale is more miserable?
Who is there lives with a savager fate?
Whose troubles so reverse his life as his?
O Oedipus, the famous prince
for whom the same great harbor
the same both for father and son
sufficed for bridal bed,
how, O how, have the furrows ploughed
by your father endured to bear you, poor wretch,
and remain silent so long?

Time who sees all has found you out
against your will; judges your marriage accursed,
begetter and begotten at one in it.
O child of Laius,
would I had never seen you.
I weep for you and cry
a dirge of lamentation.[19]

The oddity of the last lines of this passage has sometimes been overlooked. The chorus expresses the wish that they had never made Oedipus's acquaintance and become spectators of his triumph and his sufferings, yet all the same they mourn him and bewail his fall. Is there not some degree of tension between these two reactions? Does not the former suggest repudiation, the latter compassion? Certainly, we can understand that the chorus is somehow blaming Oedipus for the suffering his own suffering causes them, in their pity, to share. If only they had not known him, they would be saying, they would not be experiencing the grief that they now feel. The illogicality of their emotional turmoil is very human, and quite comprehensible. But perhaps there is also something deeper involved, something that may be hidden to the chorus but need not remain concealed to us: perhaps, too, in mourning the fall of Oedipus, the chorus is lamenting the inability of any human being to live the kind of life of superhuman triumph to which he, and not only he, had aspired. Seeing his poetically real, exemplary fall, they are reminded of the danger of other potential ones, figured in his case and applicable to their own and all others. Small wonder that they wish they had never witnessed it—and small wonder that Greek tragedy obliged them to do so, over and over again: for it is a lesson that cannot be repeated often enough.

Appendix: Kings in Greek Tragedy

This appendix lists all the ancient Greek tragedies that have survived whole, in approximate chronological order, and indicates for each one which speaking characters in it are ruling monarchs, either kings or queens. Parentheses indicate a king who is not physically present on stage but whose offstage action is essential to the play's meaning. Tragedies whose title is provided by the name of a king who is a character in them are indicated in boldface; those whose titles derive from their chorus have an asterisk. *Prometheus* is transmitted among the works of Aeschylus and *Rhesus* among those of Euripides, but many modern scholars doubt those attributions. *The Cyclops* is a satyr play. While it cannot be excluded that extending this catalogue to those tragedies extant only in fragments and/or testimonia might change the results obtained, it is unlikely that the difference would be significant.

AESCHYLUS

Persians*: Queen of Persia; ghost of Darius; Xerxes
The Seven Against Thebes: Eteocles
The Suppliant Maidens*: Pelasgus

Agamemnon: Clytemnestra; Agamemnon; Aegisthus
The Libation Bearers*: Clytemnestra; Aegisthus
Eumenides*: ghost of Clytemnestra; Orestes
Prometheus: (Zeus)

SOPHOCLES

Ajax: Menelaus; Agamemnon
The Women of Trachis*: Heracles
Oedipus the King: Oedipus
Antigone: Creon
Electra: Clytemnestra; Aegisthus
Philoctetes: Odysseus; Neoptolemus
Oedipus at Colonus: Theseus; Creon

EURIPIDES

Alcestis: Admetus
Medea: Creon; Jason; Aegeus
The Children of Heracles: Demophon; Eurystheus
Hippolytus: Theseus
Andromache: Menelaus
Hecuba: Agamemnon; Polymestor
The Suppliant Women*: Theseus; Adrastus
Electra: Clytemnestra; (Aegisthus)
Heracles: Lycus; Theseus
The Trojan Women*: Hecuba; Menelaus
Iphigenia Among the Taurians: Thoas
Ion: Xuthus; Ion
Helen: Menelaus; Theoclymenus
The Phoenician Women: Eteocles; Creon
Orestes: Menelaus; Tyndareus
The Bacchae*: Pentheus; Cadmus
Iphigenia in Aulis: Agamemnon; Menelaus
Rhesus: Rhesus
The Cyclops: Odysseus

Notes

1. *King Richard II*, ed. Peter Ure, 5th ed., Arden Edition of the Works of William Shakespeare (London: Methuen; Cambridge, MA: Harvard University Press, 1964), 101–3 (lines 144–70).
2. Ibid., 102 (line 156).
3. On "King Richard's Tragedy," see the detailed discussion in Ure's introduction, ibid., lxii–lxxxiii.
4. "Comoediae autem a more antiquo dictae . . . ἀπὸ τῆς κώμης, hoc est ab actu uitae hominum quia in uicis habitant ob mediocritatem fortunarum, non in aulis regiis, ut sunt personae tragicae." In Georg Kaibel, ed., *Comicorum Graecorum Fragmenta* (Berlin: Weidmann), 1:67.
5. "Inter tragoediam autem et comoediam cum multa tum imprimis hoc distat, quod in comoedia mediocres fortunae hominum, parui impetus periculorum laetique sunt exitus actionum, at in tragoedia omnia contra, ingentes personae, magni timores, exitus funesti habentur; et illic prima turbulenta, tranquilla ultima, in tragoedia contrario ordine res aguntur." In Paul Wessner, ed., *Aeli Donati quod fertur Commentum Terenti: Accedunt Eugraphi commentum et scholia Bembina* (Leipzig: Teubner, 1902), 1:21.
6. "Tragoedia est heroicae fortunae in adversis conprehensio . . . comoedia est privatae civilisque fortunae sine periculo vitae conprehensio . . . in ea viculorum, id est humilium domuum, fortunae conprehendantur, non ut in tragoedia publicarum regiarumque. . . . [C]omoedia a tragoedia differt, quod in tragoedia introducuntur heroes duces reges, in comoedia humiles atque privatae personae; in illa luctus exilia caedes, in hac amores, virginum raptus: deinde quod in illa frequenter et paene semper laetis rebus exitus tristes et liberorum fortunarumque in peius adgnitio. Quare varia definitione discretae sunt." In Heinrich Keil, ed., *Grammatici Latini* (Leipzig: Teubner, 1857), 1:487.
7. "Imitatio per actiones illustris fortunae, exitu infelici, oratione graui metrica. . . . In Tragoedia Reges, Principes, ex urbibus, arcibus, castris. Principia sedatiora: exitus horribiles. Oratio grauis, culta, vulgi dictione auersa, tota facies anxia: metus, minae, exilia, mortes. . . . Res Tragicae grandes, atroces, iussa Regum, caedes, desperationes suspendia, exilia, orbitates, parricidia, incestus, incendia, pugnae, occaecationes, fletus, ululatus, conquestiones, funera, epitaphia, epicedia." In Luc Deitz, ed., *Julius Caesar Scaliger, Poetices Libri Septem. Sieben Bücher über die Dichtkunst* (Stuttgart–Bad Canstatt: Frommann-Holzboog, 1994), bk. 1, chap. 6, 130–31, 132–33.
8. Bernard Weinberg, "Scaliger Versus Aristotle on Poetics," *Modern Philology* 39 (1942): 337–60, is helpful but limited to the comparison of Scaliger with Aristotle, and he neglects Scaliger's relations with his other sources.
9. In the *Problems* (19.48) transmitted in the Aristotelian corpus (but most likely not going back to him in its entirety) there is a single reference to the difference between the heroic characters and the popular chorus: "for the latter [i.e., the characters on the stage] imitate heroes, and among the ancients the

[sc., chorus] leaders alone were heroes, and the people, of whom the chorus consists, were mere men." In J. A. Smith and W. D. Ross, eds., *The Works of Aristotle Translated into English*, vol. 7, *Problemata*, ed. E. S. Forster (Oxford: Clarendon Press 1927), 922.

10. In chapter 2 of his *Poetics*, Aristotle says that the distinction between representing characters better than ourselves, worse than ourselves, or of the same sort as ourselves "separates tragedy from comedy: the latter tends to represent men worse than present humanity, the former better"; in chapter 13 he argues that pity and fear will only be produced in the spectators if they witness what happens to a man "who is not preeminent in virtue and justice, and one who falls into affliction not because of evil and wickedness, but because of a certain fallibility." Trans. Stephen Halliwell in *Aristotle's Poetics* (London: Duckworth, 1986), 32, 44.

11. In bk. 3, chap. 14 of his *Politics*, Aristotle distinguishes between five forms of kingship; the "fourth species of kingly monarchy—that of the heroic times ... was hereditary and legal, and was exercised over willing subjects." In Stephen Everson, ed., *Aristotle: The Politics and the Constitution of Athens* (Cambridge: Cambridge University Press, 1996), 84.

12. See esp. P. E. Easterling, "Anachronism in Greek Tragedy," *Journal of Hellenic Studies* 105 (1985): 1–10.

13. "Diese Ueberlieferung sagt uns mit voller Entschiedenheit, *dass die Tragödie aus dem tragischen Chore entstanden ist* und ursprünglich nur Chor und nichts als Chor war: woher wir die Verpflichtung nehmen, diesem tragischen Chore als dem eigentlichen Urdrama in's Herz zu sehen, ohne uns an den geläufigen Kunstredensarten—dass er der idealische Zuschauer sei oder das Volk gegenüber der fürstlichen Region der Scene zu vertreten habe—irgendwie genügen zu lassen. Jener zuletzt erwähnte, für manchen Politiker erhaben klingende Erläuterungsgedanke—als ob das unwandelbare Sittengesetz von den demokratischen Athenern in dem Volkschore dargestellt sei, der über die leidenschaftlichen Ausschreitungen und Ausschweifungen der Könige hinaus immer Recht behalte—mag noch so sehr durch ein Wort des Aristoteles nahegelegt sein: auf die ursprüngliche Formation der Tragödie ist er ohne Einfluss, da von jenen rein religiösen Ursprüngen der ganze Gegensatz von Volk und Fürst, überhaupt jegliche politisch-sociale Sphäre ausgeschlossen ist." From Giorgio Colli and Mazzino Montinari, eds., *Nietzsche Werke: Kritische Gesamtausgabe*, vol. 3.1, *Die Geburt der Tragödie: Unzeitgemäße Betrachungen I–III* (1872–1874) (Berlin: Walter de Gruyter, 1972), 48; the Aristotle reference is to the passage cited at n9.

14. See Barbara von Reibnitz, *Ein Kommentar zu Friedrich Nietzsche "Die Geburt der Tragödie aus dem Geiste der Musik" (Kapitel 1-12)* (Stuttgart-Weimar: J. B. Metzler, 1992), 186–87.

15. For the contrast between competitive and cooperative values that I presuppose here, see, e.g., Arthur W. H. Adkins, *Merit and Responsibility: A Study in Greek Values* (Oxford: Clarendon Press, 1960).

16. I quote the translation by David Grene in David Grene and Richmond Lattimore, ed., *The Complete Greek Tragedies*, 3rd ed., ed. Mark Griffith and Glenn W. Most,

Aeschylus I: The Persians, The Seven Against Thebes, The Suppliant Maidens, Prometheus Bound (Chicago: University of Chicago Press, 2013), 194–95.

17. One example among many is the interchange between Eteocles and the chorus in Aeschylus's *Seven Against Thebes*, ibid., 94–96.

18. *Richard II*, 3.2.171–77; Ure ed., 103.

19. I quote the translation by David Grene in Grene and Lattimore, *Complete Greek Tragedies*, 3rd ed., *Sophocles I: Antigone, Oedipus the King, Oedipus at Colonus* (Chicago: University of Chicago Press, 2013), 173–74.

TWO

Contested Sovereignty

Heaven, the Monarch, the People, and the Intellectuals in Traditional China

YURI PINES

OF THE MANIFOLD ASPECTS OF "SOVEREIGNTY," I want to focus on the issue most pertinent to early Chinese political thought, and indeed one related to the question of "political theology" in the West—namely, who is the source of supreme political authority? Is it a monarch personally, or is there a superior entity to which the monarch's will should be subordinate? This issue was debated—sometimes subtly, sometimes overtly—throughout the voluminous corpus of early Chinese political texts. Different conceptualizations of sovereignty coexisted before the imperial unification of 221 BCE and continued to influence the functioning of Chinese imperial polity (221 BCE–1912 CE). In what follows I argue that this coexistence of conflicting approaches reflected one of the basic tensions in Chinese political culture: the tension between, on the one hand, the unanimous conviction in the importance of a single omnipotent monarch as a stabilizer of the political system and, on the other hand, an awareness that an inept or malevolent monarch may harm rather than benefit this system. In my analysis, one may discern behind multiple concepts of sovereignty the desire of preimperial intellectuals and imperial literati—the architects and custodians of Chinese empire—to maintain their power at the ruler's side, and sometimes in the ruler's stead.

Monarch-Centered Thought

In the evolution of China's concepts of the ruler's authority, we can distinguish two important stages. The first, which may be considered a prologue to Chinese political thought in general, is the formation of the concept of Heaven's Mandate at the beginning of the Zhou dynasty (1046–256 BCE). Facing the need to justify the overthrow of their erstwhile masters, the Shang dynasty (ca. 1600–1046 BCE), the Zhou leaders claimed that they acted on behalf of the supreme deity, Heaven. According to their claim, Heaven originally mandated the Shang to rule, but once its monarchs misbehaved and discarded their responsibilities toward the people, "merciless Heaven" withdrew its Mandate from the Shang and granted it to the Zhou. This theory, which had a lasting impact on Chinese political culture, served both to justify Zhou rule and to caution future Zhou kings that unless they perform their tasks properly their dynasty may collapse as well. One of the early Zhou documents warns explicitly: "Heaven's Mandate is not constant."[1]

I return to the concept of Heaven's Mandate and its implications on the ruler's sovereignty below; here, suffice it to say that while the resort to divine legitimacy played an important role in ensuring initial stability for the Zhou regime, after a few centuries its effectiveness faded. Beginning in the eighth century BCE the Zhou world entered a period of prolonged crisis. First the Zhou "Sons of Heaven" were eclipsed by their nominal underlings, the regional lords; then those lords themselves lost power to leading ministerial lineages in their polities, and many of these lineages were in turn torn apart by fratricidal struggles. By the fifth century BCE, the would-be China was engulfed in a war of all against all, in which no victor could be expected and which gave the subsequent period its ominous name, the age of the Warring States (453–221 BCE).

The Warring States period was marked by ongoing military turmoil, but it was also an age rife with new departures in the sociopolitical and intellectual spheres. Politically, a series of profound reforms replaced the loose aristocratic polities of the past with centralized bureaucratic territorial states, which maintained a higher degree of control over the population than previously imaginable. Socially, the pedigree-based order was replaced by a new one in which individual merits played a more important role than birth rights in ensuring social status.[2] And intellectually, this era was marked by immense creativity, boldness, and diversity, which earned it the nickname of the age of the "Hundred Schools of Thought." Ideas, values, and perceptions developed during this period contributed decisively to the formation of the political, social, and ethical orientations that we identify today with traditional Chinese culture, creating an ideological framework within which the Chinese empire functioned from its inception in 221 BCE until its last decades. More specifically, concepts of rulership formed during this time continued to exercise immense influence on the functioning of Chinese emperors for millennia to come.[3]

The Warring States period was marked by remarkable intellectual pluralism. Ideas developed amid vibrant debate, uninhibited by political or ideological orthodoxies—a debate in which thinkers of different intellectual affiliations promoted highly distinctive approaches. Yet despite the variety of their ideas, thinkers of the Warring States period shared certain common perceptions. Two of these are of primary importance for the subsequent discussion: first, political unification of "All-Under-Heaven" is the only solution to perennial war; second, unification is attainable only under the aegis of a single omnipotent monarch. The monarchic principle of rule could be considered the effective bottom line of conflicting proposals.[4]

The thinkers' preoccupation with the idea of monarchism came against the backdrop of the crisis of monarchic rule in the preceding centuries. As mentioned above, the authority of the Zhou kings derived primarily from their exclusive religious power. In their capacity as "Sons of Heaven," the kings were the sole mediators between humans and the supreme deity; in addition, they had preferential access to the deified ancestors of the royal clan who acted as divine protectors of their progeny. This cultic power ensured to a certain extent the kings' ongoing mundane authority (and, mutatis mutandis, the authority of regional lords within their domains), but in the long term its effectiveness was limited. In the age marked by increasing skepticism toward the ability of divine forces to influence mundane affairs,[5] Zhou kings, as well as regional lords, were in the process of becoming ritual figureheads devoid of real authority. This uncertainty of the rulers' position was arguably the primary factor behind the political disintegration that plagued the Zhou world from the eighth century BCE, and it is to rectify this situation that thinkers of the subsequent Warring States period focused on the issue of the ruler's power. Their differences aside, the overwhelming majority of known thinkers came to an unanimous conclusion: ensuring supreme authority of the ruler—first within an individual polity and then in "All-Under-Heaven"—is the primary precondition for restoring universal peace and stability.[6]

Thinkers of the Warring States period provided manifold justifications for empowering the rulers and solidifying their authority; among these, two are particularly important for our discussion. First, the ruler was conceptualized as essential for ensuring proper sociopolitical order. The majority of thinkers agreed that to function properly, society should be stratified; this stratification would be impossible without the existence of a singular leader at the apex of social pyramid. Xunzi (ca. 310–230 BCE), arguably the most brilliant of preimperial thinkers, promulgated this understanding with the utmost clarity:

> In their lives the people cannot but create collectives; when they create collectives but there are no distinctions, there is contention; contention and then chaos; chaos and then separation; separation and then weakness; when [the people] are weak, they cannot overcome things; hence they cannot obtain palaces and houses to dwell in.... He who is able to employ his subjects is called the ruler. The ruler is the one who is good at [making people] flock together into a collective.[7]

Forming a social collective is the essential need of human beings. The collective, however, cannot be established without maintaining proper social distinctions, because otherwise, as Xunzi explains elsewhere, greediness of human beings and their desire to appropriate limited resources will lead to contention and turmoil. Maintaining distinctions, in turn, requires the unifying presence of the ruler. Xunzi emphasizes linguistic proximity between the terms "ruler" (君, jun) and "collective" (群, qun): the language itself reflects interconnectedness between the two. These ideas are further developed in "Relying on the Ruler," a chapter from a major preimperial compendium, the Lüshi chunqiu. The chapter, possibly penned by Xunzi's followers, explicates why a rulerless society is doomed:

> In high antiquity it happened that there was no ruler. The people lived together, dwelling like a herd. They knew their mothers but no fathers; had no distinctions between relatives, elder and younger brothers, husband and wife, male and female; had no way of superiors and inferiors, of old and young; had no rites of entrance, departure, and mutual greetings; had no advantages of

clothes, caps, boots, dwellings, and palaces; had no facilities such as utensils, instruments, boats, chariots, outer and inner walls, and defensive fortifications. This is the trouble of lacking a ruler.[8]

As in European modernity, many thinkers of the Warring States period looked at a primeval stateless society to find in its imagined past justifications for their recipes for the present.[9] The authors of the above passage learned from prehistory that a society without a ruler was a miserable one, one in which human beings could not attain minimal civilizational comfort. They sought to further prove this observation anthropologically, surveying a variety of uncivilized tribes at the fringes of Chinese civilization, and concluding:

These are the rulerless of the four directions. Their people live like elk and deer, birds and beasts: the young give orders to the old; the old fear the adults; the strong are considered the worthy; and the haughty and violent are revered. Day and night they abuse each other, leaving no time to rest, thereby exterminating their own kind. The sages profoundly investigate this trouble: hence when they consistently think of All-Under-Heaven, nothing is better than establishing a Son of Heaven; when they consistently think of a single state, nothing is better than establishing a ruler.[10]

The social necessity of establishing the ruler is clarified by both historical and anthropological examples: a society without a ruler is a society without rules; it is doomed to be enmeshed in nightmarish turmoil in which everybody loses. A ruler, therefore, is not a mere political function but rather a fundamental social desideratum. Yet merely establishing a ruler is not enough. If the authority is not fully concentrated in his hands, it will lead to inevitable turmoil, akin to that which destroyed the aristocratic polities of the preceding age. This is the second pillar of the ruler-centered discourse of the Warring States period, and the singularly important aspect of contemporaneous views of sovereignty. To function properly, the ruler should possess exclusive political authority. The *Lüshi chunqiu* explains:

The True Monarch upholds oneness and becomes the rectifier of the myriad things. The army needs the general: thereby it is unified. The state needs the ruler: thereby it is unified. All under Heaven needs the Son of Heaven: thereby it is unified. The Son of Heaven upholds oneness, thereby unifying it [the realm]. Oneness brings orderly rule; doubleness brings chaos.[11]

This short passage exemplifies the fundamental concern of the Warring States thinkers: any dispersal of the ruler's authority, any multiplicity of loci of power, will inevitably result in political crisis. The military simile is revealing: in the army, preservation of the chain of command and of the singular authority of every commander over his unit is essential for the proper functioning of the unit; so, the authors imply, it is in the political sphere. This simile was perhaps all too understandable for the dwellers of the Warring States world, who lived in a state that resembled a military machine.[12] The saying "Oneness brings orderly rule; doubleness brings chaos" recurs in a great variety of contemporaneous texts and may be considered a point of consensus for competing thinkers.[13] This consensus prevented creation of institutional means to check the ruler's power: any competing locus of authority was considered detrimental to the polity's functioning.

What does "oneness" mean in practical terms? First, the exclusivity of the ruler's position as the final decision maker: "he who is able to make decisions exclusively will therefore be the sovereign of All-Under-Heaven."[14] Second, the ruler's authority should be not just exclusive but absolute. Thinkers of the Warring States repeatedly invoked the line from the canonical *Book of Poems*: "Everywhere under Heaven is the King's land, each of those who live on the land is the King's servant."[15] This line was interpreted as referring to the comprehensive power of the monarch over property and social position of his subjects; or, in the words of a later text, "There are six things that the enlightened king maintains: to give life, to kill, to enrich, to impoverish, to ennoble, to debase."[16] Life, property, social position: all had to be determined by the sovereign. Indeed, in some of the Warring States, most notably the would-be unifier of Chinese world, the state of Qin, practical steps were taken to impose the ruler's control over his subjects' socioeconomic status by unifying political, economic, and social hierarchy.[17]

One can easily identify a despotic potential in the statements cited above, but we should not jump to conclusions. As I demonstrate below, thinkers of the Warring States period remained painstakingly aware both of the dangers of despotism and of the problem of unfitness of individual monarchs, and they sought multiple ways of mitigating the ruler's excesses. Advocacy of the ruler's exclusive decision making should not be confused with nullifying his aides. On the contrary, even the texts associated with authoritarian-minded thinkers repeatedly emphasize the collective nature of governance. For instance, the *Book of Lord Shang*, attributed to a staunch authoritarian, Shang Yang (d. 338 BCE), argues:

> The state is ordered through three [things]: the first is standards, the second is trustworthiness, the third is authority. Standards are what the ruler and ministers jointly uphold; trustworthiness is what the ruler and ministers jointly establish; authority is what the ruler exclusively regulates. When the sovereign loses what he should preserve, he is endangered; when the ruler and the ministers cast away standards and rely on their private [views], turmoil will surely ensue. Hence when standards are established, divisions are clarified and standards are not violated for private reasons, then there is orderly rule; when authority and regulations are determined exclusively by the ruler, [he inspires] awe; when the people trust his rewards, successes are accomplished; and when they trust his punishments, wickedness has no starting point.[18]

The emphasis on the singularity of the ruler's position at the top of the government apparatus is softened here by three clauses. First, the ruler is reminded that laws should be maintained jointly by the ruler and his ministers, not by the ruler alone. Second, the ruler is urged to preserve collaborative spirit ("trustworthiness") in relations with his aides. Third, and most importantly, just like the ministers, the ruler is strongly discouraged to cast away the law "for private reasons." The latter point is particularly important. Even those texts that adopt radical pro-ruler and antiministerial views, such as the *Book of Lord Shang*, remain adamant in their insistence that the ruler relinquishes his "private" (*si*) interests and whims. Institutionally omnipotent, the ruler is recognized still as a human being, and potentially an erring human being. How to prevent the monarch's personal weaknesses from damaging his institutional role without undermining his absolute authority became one of the trickiest problems in traditional Chinese political thought.

Heaven, the Ruler, and the People

In defending his commitment to the monarch's absolute power, Han Fei (d. 233 BCE), arguably the staunchest defender of the ruler's unlimited authority, conceded that at times villains could occupy the throne and that their rule would damage the very social and political fabric that rulers are supposed to protect. Yet he reminded his opponents that monsters on the throne—just as moral paragons—are exceptions: "Generations of rulers cannot be cut in the middle, and when I talk of power of the authority, I mean the average."[19] Overall, a ruler-centered system would remain effective enough and ensure smooth functioning of the government.

Han Fei's bold defense of a completely depersonalized monarchic system, sustainable under any but an exceptionally monstrous sovereign, was criticized by many thinkers, especially (but by no means exclusively) the followers of Confucius (551–479 BCE). While accepting in principle the idea that the ruler's institutional authority should be limitless, they were deeply concerned with the quality of individual rulers and, in particular, with potentially unfit sovereigns. This latter problem can be further subdivided into two: dealing with wicked despots, whose rule even Han Fei's system could not accommodate, and maintaining orderly rule under an inept (but not necessarily malevolent) ruler. In this section I focus on the dilemma of the despot, which was more directly challenging to the idea of monarchism shaped during the Warring States period.

The problem of malevolent monarchs was one of the earliest issues addressed by Chinese political thought. It was intrinsically connected to the replacement of the Shang dynasty by its Zhou subjects around 1046 BCE. As mentioned above, to justify their overthrow of the Shang, the Zhou leaders developed a theory of Heaven's Mandate, which could be withdrawn from a wicked sovereign. This theory, incorporated into canonical scriptures attributed to the Zhou founders, became a cornerstone of subsequent discussions of the issues of rulership. In a nutshell, it said that Heaven, the supreme and omniscient deity, supervises the political order below. Whenever a ruler behaves licentiously and oppressively, he is in danger of losing his forefather's Mandate, which would be transferred to the next, morally upright incumbent.

Using divine power both to support and to control the ruler's sovereignty may be considered a common feature of monarchies worldwide.[20] Yet Chinese Heaven was a peculiar deity. No prophet spoke on its behalf, no scriptures encapsulated its message; its omens were prone to multiple interpretations, and divination, once the major means of ascertaining divine will, was relegated in the Zhou era to the position of an auxiliary tool of "resolving doubts" but not a source of routine political guidance.[21] So removed was Heaven from everyday religious life that one of the leading scholars of early Chinese religion has suggested that its worship was less a religion and "more akin to a type of political philosophy."[22] The apparent weakness of the underlying religious belief in Heaven's Mandate explains why this notion remained of limited use in either bolstering or restricting the ruler's power throughout much of the Zhou era.

Being aware of the potential weakness of a pure appeal to Heaven, the architects of the early Zhou political culture introduced another important player to their nascent theology of sovereignty: the people. Many early Zhou documents explain that Heaven's interventions to punish or reward individual rulers are not whimsical; rather, Heaven acts on behalf of the people below and often speaks through their voices. One of these documents, "The Great Oath," allegedly created on the eve of the overthrow of the Shang, clarifies: "Heaven sees through the people's seeing, Heaven hears through the people's hearing." Elsewhere the text summarizes, "Heaven inevitably follows the people's desires."[23] It was on behalf of the people that Heaven punished the last rulers of the Shang and its putative predecessor, the Xia dynasty. Thus, pitying "the people of the four corners," Heaven replaced its "primary son," King Zhouxin of Shang (d. 1046 BCE), with the new incumbent, King Wen of Zhou (d. 1047 BCE). The latter was selected precisely because of his proven ability to care for the "small people." "Protecting the people" is further identified as one of the major tasks of Zhou government, insofar as the new leaders want to escape the miserable fate of the Xia and Shang.[24]

The interconnectedness of Heaven and the people created an effective mixture that can be considered an alternative source of sovereignty: a combination of divine and popular authority. Insofar as the people's well-being was the ultimate raison d'être of the polity, according to which the ruler's performance should be judged, and insofar as Heaven was acting on the people's behalf in selecting a new recipient of the Mandate, the combined authority of Heaven and the people was obviously superior to that of any individual monarch. Most consequentially, the fact that replacing a transgressing ruler was politically and religiously legitimate challenged the idea of a monarch as an absolute sovereign of the realm.

Being associated with early Zhou canonical texts, this acceptance of a supra-monarch locus of authority could not be easily dismissed even in the

Warring States period, when the primary source of the thinkers' concern was empowering monarchs rather than supervising and restricting them. Aside from a few dissenting voices, such as Han Fei's call to outlaw the very discourse of the Mandate's transferability as potentially subversive,[25] most thinkers had to look for ways of reconciling the Mandate's theory with the new understanding of the monarch's sovereignty. Individual solutions differed, but the dominant trend was to downplay the role of Heaven while stressing the importance of the people as ultimate kingmakers. This latter emphasis however was to serve as a check on the ruler's authority rather than squarely making the people an alternative source of sovereignty.

To be sure, the idea of Heaven as a sentient and interventionist deity was not abandoned altogether. It is particularly prominent in the writings of Mozi (ca. 460–390 BCE), who unequivocally assigned Heaven the role of the ultimate sovereign and the ruler's supervisor. Mozi argued that "the Son of Heaven cannot rectify himself; he is rectified by Heaven"[26] and that Heaven invariably inflicts rewards and punishments on the ruler. Mozi made Heaven a crucial actor in his political model. For instance, he advocated political centralization under a powerful ruler who would impose moral and intellectual uniformity on his subjects, yet this centralization presupposed Heaven as the supreme level of authority above the ruler: "If the hundred clans all conform upwards with the Son of Heaven but not with Heaven itself, then the disasters are still not eradicated. Now, frequent visitations of hurricanes and torrents are just punishments from Heaven upon the hundred clans for not conforming upward with Heaven."[27]

Heaven in the *Mozi* is an equivalent of absolute correctness; it is also the supreme rectifier, which actively monitors the human realm. This view was clearly a minority opinion, though; Mozi himself lamented that "today, officers and superior men of All-Under-Heaven all understand that the Son of Heaven rectifies All-Under-Heaven but do not understand that he is rectified by Heaven."[28] Many thinkers ignored Heaven's political role altogether; others interpreted it as an impersonal natural law that the ruler should understand and apply but that does not act consciously to punish him. Yet other thinkers, like Xunzi, explicitly stripped Heaven of its divine and sentient features. Throughout the Warring States the idea of Heaven's Mandate lost much of its erstwhile appeal, even though it was not completely cast away.[29]

In contrast to Heaven, not only did the people remain the focus of political discourse but their importance increased. Some of the pronouncements of contemporaneous thinkers sound almost like proclamations of the people's sovereignty. For instance, Mengzi (ca. 380-305 BCE), one of the leading followers of Confucius, claimed: "The people are the most esteemed; the altars of soil and grain [i.e., the state] follow them: the ruler is the lightest. Hence one who attains [the support of] the multitudes becomes Son of Heaven; one who attains [the support of] the Son of Heaven becomes a regional lord; one who attains [the support of] a regional lord becomes a noble."[30]

This statement is bolder than in other texts, but it is not exceptional. Time and again we are reminded that "All-Under-Heaven does not belong to the Son of Heaven but to All-Under-Heaven"; that "when the Great Way [of orderly rule] was implemented, All-Under-Heaven belonged to all"; and that "benefitting All-Under-Heaven" is the primary responsibility of the sovereign.[31] Xunzi quoted an unidentified "tradition: "The ruler is a boat; commoners are the water. The water can carry the boat; the water can capsize the boat."[32] The belief in the people's overwhelming political importance engulfed even the "people bashers" like Shang Yang, who notoriously claimed, "When the people are weak, the state is strong; hence the state that possesses the Way strives to weaken the people." Despite this and many similar statements, Shang Yang also called on the ruler to understand the people's "disposition" and to determine the laws accordingly, emphasizing that only he whose decisions are based on the people's opinion will succeed in his undertakings.[33]

It is tempting to read these plentiful pronouncements as related to the idea of popular sovereignty, but this would be grossly misleading. The thinkers recognized the importance of the people's well-being and their consent, and many made these the primary criterion of evaluating the ruler's performance, but none called the ruler to consult the commoners directly, or to allow their participation in decision making. The common belief was that the people would vote by their feet: if they were dissatisfied with the ruler, they may desert from the battlefield or leave their fields uncultivated and abscond to another state. It was for these reasons that the ruler had to constantly strive "to attain the people's heart"; but this recommendation by no means implied sharing power with the people or giving them a say on policy making.[34]

We may pause here and ask why, despite repeated proclamations about the centrality of the people and about their role as potential kingmakers, Chinese thinkers never moved toward the idea of popular sovereignty? I think the answer is related to the dilemma outlined by Jason Frank in this volume: the problem of the transfer of authority "from the personified body of the king to the independent but impersonal and anonymous will of the people." The "people" were simply too amorphous an entity to issue commands and to settle inevitable disputes among rival political actors. The idea "Oneness brings orderly rule; doubleness brings chaos" plainly precluded transfer of sovereignty from the hands of an individual monarch to the multitudes.

Going back to the perspective of the Warring States period, it may be noticed that invocation of the people as kingmakers and infrequent appeals to Heaven as the ultimate sovereign were of limited importance. Both of these could be used to curtail the ruler, but, as argued above, this was not the major concern of competing thinkers. Rather, they sought peace and stability, which, according to the thinkers' consensus, were attainable only under a powerful monarch; consequently, the goal was to strengthen the throne's power rather than reducing it. Yet the latent notion of the supra-ruler loci of authority had far-reaching consequences. It came to life shortly after the imperial unification, influencing political dynamics throughout the imperial era.

Between Mediocrities and Sage Rulers

Of the two problems of monarchism outlined in the previous section—despotism and the ruler's inadequacy—the former appears to be less pressing to the thinkers of the Warring States period. The ruler's potential for wickedness and oppressiveness was mitigated not so much by threats of the Mandate's revocation but by practical concerns. In the situation of intense competition between states, excessive oppressiveness would not be in a ruler's interest, as it could cause an exodus of gifted advisers to rival polities. The world of the Warring States resembled a huge market of talent; statesmen and thinkers could easily cross the boundaries in search of better patrons, a reality that granted ministers significant leverage vis-à-vis rulers. If historical records are reliable, most rulers of the Warring States appear to be more tolerant to their advisers' affronts than their imperial heirs were. To be sure, ministers and officials were at times persecuted, but these persecutions appear less frequent than in the subsequent imperial period.

Of more immediate concern to most thinkers was not the ruler's atrocities but his unfitness for office. Recall than in the meritocratic system of that age, ministers normally owed their position to their abilities, whereas a ruler was nominated due to his birthright alone. Inevitably, then, the throne was occupied at times by a mediocrity. Facing this problem, thinkers put forward a variety of methods to better the ruler: education, remonstrance, or even threats of insubordination. Yet, as everyone recognized, these methods had their limitations; some rulers simply could not be improved. Frustrated, a few thinkers suggested circumventing the system of hereditary succession in order to ensure the best possible monarch, but their efforts failed.[35] It was necessary to find a mode for maintaining proper order under an inept sovereign.

Thinkers' dissatisfaction with reigning monarchs of their age is visible throughout the entire corpus of political writings from the Warring States period: even Han Fei, the staunchest authoritarian, was frustrated with the problem of individual monarchs being the weakest link in the monarchical system.[36] In particular, thinkers unanimously considered themselves as intellectually (and morally) superior to the average rulers. This posed a harsh question: how to retain mediocre rulers' full political authority without jeopardizing political order due to their ineptitude?

The solution that ensued was a creative one: to preserve the image of the ruler's omnipotence while convincing him to refrain from active intervention in political routine. Should the ruler relegate power to meritorious aides and satisfy himself with the position of their ultimate supervisor, the political system would benefit from both the unifying presence of the supreme sovereign and from the skills of his underlings. Xunzi explains:

> Thus the enlightened sovereign is fond of the [guiding] principles, while the benighted ruler is fond of details. When the ruler is fond of the principles, one hundred affairs are [arranged] in their details; when the ruler is fond of details, one hundred affairs are disordered. The ruler selects one chancellor, arranges one law, clarifies one principle in order to cover everything, to illuminate everything, and to observe the completion [of affairs]. The chancel-

lor selects and orders heads of the hundred officials, attends to the guiding principles of the hundred affairs, and thereby refines the divisions between the hundred clerks at court, measures their achievements, discusses their rewards, and presents their achievements to the ruler at year's end. When they act correctly, they are approved; otherwise they are dismissed. Hence the ruler works hard in looking for [proper officials] and is at rest when employing them.[37]

Xunzi's proposal appears as an elegant solution to the delicate problem of a ruler's potential ineptitude. Since the ruler's aides are supposed to be the best men in the country, selected for their superb moral and intellectual qualities, entrusting them with administrative tasks will benefit the government and permit relaxation for the ruler. Moreover, relegating most tasks to his chancellor and other underlings will allow the ruler to overcome the limitations of his personal abilities, because a single person will never be able to comprehend the multitude of government affairs. The ruler will still preserve his supreme authority in selecting and supervising his chancellor and "clarifying the guiding principles," but everyday responsibilities will be in the hand of ministers (i.e., in the hands of Xunzi and his like).

Not all the thinkers shared Xunzi's optimism about cooperation between the ruler and his ministers; for instance, Xunzi's disciple, Han Fei, compared ministers to hungry tigers ready to devour the sovereign and seize his power.[38] Yet Han Fei also recommended that the ruler refrain from excessive activism: only thereby will the monarch avoid ministerial traps and preserve his good name; should a policy fail it will be the minister's fault.[39] Argumentation in favor of the ruler's quietude differed from one thinker to another, but the bottom line remained all the same: an ordinary sovereign should enjoy exclusive power of the final say but should relegate everyday tasks to his underlings.[40]

Ordinary sovereigns were the norm, but they were not the thinkers' ideal. The expectations focused rather on a truly impeccable ruler, named in various texts the Sage Monarch or True Monarch, a semidivine person,[41] the future unifier of All-Under-Heaven. Whereas current regional monarchs were repeatedly criticized for their inadequacy, the Sage Monarch was portrayed as superior to all in his intellect and morality. This superiority should enable him to unify All-under-Heaven, to engender universal compliance, and to bring about the long-expected peace and tranquility. Xunzi depicted his blessed impact: "When the sage monarch is above, he apportions dutiful actions below. Then, low and high nobles do not behave wantonly; the hundred officials are not insolent in their affairs; the multitudes and the hundred clans are without odd and licentious habits; there are no crimes of theft and robbery; none dares to oppose his superiors."[42]

The sage monarch would regulate every social stratum, ensure universal order, and impose uniform norms of morality. Elsewhere Xunzi is ready even to assign this future ruler the task of unifying intellectual realm: "he who unites with him is correct, he who differs from him is wrong."[43] That is, even such an independent-minded thinker as Xunzi will be ready to give up his intellectual autonomy if the sage monarch finally comes to occupy the throne.

Panegyrics to the towering figure of the sage monarch permeate late Warring States period texts. Yet they should not be considered simplistic manifestations of the thinkers' unwavering monarchism. Rather, Xunzi and his like employed the image of the True Monarch, an exceptional personality who appears "once in five hundred years,"[44] as a foil to contemporary rulers. While promising full obedience to this future ideal monarch, the thinkers preserved the right to criticize and occasionally to defy contemporary, inadequate sovereigns whose mediocrity was self-evident in comparison with the idealized sage unifier. What Xunzi could not possibly have anticipated is that one of his younger contemporaries, King Zheng of Qin, would not just appropriate the discourse of the True Monarch but also utilize it for an unprecedented assault on the intellectual autonomy of the educated elite.

Chinese Emperors: Limits to the Limitless Authority

In 221 BCE, King Zheng of Qin succeeded in attaining the unbelievable: having defeated all of his enemies in a series of brilliant campaigns, he had unified the entire known realm. Proudly proclaiming that his success dwarfed that of the former paragons, the king duly declared himself emperor, a newly invented title with overt sacral connotations (*huangdi*, literally the August Thearch). As the unifier of the realm, the First Emperor (r. 221–210 BCE) identified himself as the long-awaited True Monarch and became the first ruler in Chinese history to proclaim himself a sage. His newly designed image of a universal, omnipotent ruler synthesized most of the threads of the monarch-centered discourse of preceding centuries. Notably, there were some important modifications of this discourse as well. In particular, the idea of Heaven's Mandate, or more generally references to Heaven as supreme deity, are conspicuously absent from the First Emperor's propaganda. A man who saved humankind from centuries of warfare and turmoil was second to no one in either the mundane or celestial world.[45]

The First Emperor's appropriation of the idea of the sage monarch had immediate consequences. First, it allowed him to discard the notion of a sovereign who reigns but does not rule: indeed, his short but eventful reign was marked by unprecedented activism on his part. Second, it allowed him to redefine his position in relation to members of the educated elite: from now on, the ruler was not a disciple but a teacher of the intellectuals. In contrast to the preimperial period, the emperor no longer had to exercise self-restraint vis-à-vis his advisers. An imperial monopoly replaced the erstwhile interstate market of talent, and soon enough, the First Emperor's relations with the educated elite deteriorated: in 213 BCE this resulted in suppression of "private learning" and the infamous burning of books in private collections. This collision, as well as the collapse of Qin soon thereafter due to a popular uprising of unprecedented scale and ferocity, shaped the negative image of the first imperial dynasty and its founder for generations to come.[46]

Bad press notwithstanding, the First Emperor's impact on consequent trajectory of Chinese imperial institution was huge. His major innovations, including the title of August Thearch and the identification of a reigning emperor as a sage, were henceforth inseparable attributes of Chinese emperorship. The combination of pro-monarchic ideas of preimperial thinkers with the posture of an infallible sage, second to no one, became the most powerful ideological construct. The newly designed institution of emperorship became the pivot around which Chinese polity would revolve for the next 2,132 years.[47]

Imperial unification marked a major shift in the balance of power between the emperor and his aides. The disappearance of the erstwhile market of talent limited the ministerial leverage vis-à-vis the sovereigns, while the identification of the emperors as sages stripped the ministers of their important ideological weapon. The power of the throne—both symbolic and practical—became enormous, and while the ministers retained the right, and even the duty, to remonstrate with the ruler and to criticize his faults, they had to be more cautious. It was all too easy for a remonstrator to cross from legitimate criticism of the monarch to the crime of "great irreverence," which would result in the offender's execution. Although, *pace* a common view, despots were relatively infrequent in China's long history, their recurrence, and the resultant bloodshed, was common enough to require creation of a new system of moderating the ruler's excesses.[48]

The solution to the problem of despotism was multilayered. Most immediately, bureaucrats sought ways to restrain the emperor without imposing legal or institutional constrictions on his power. To attain this, they developed a system of invisible yet reasonably effective checks and balances. Through a variety of means—ranking from moral suasion to education of an heir apparent to bureaucratic tricks of the kind employed by Sir Humphrey Appleby from *Yes, Minister*—ministers tried to limit an emperor's intervention into everyday politics and confine him to a position of an arbiter in court disputes but not an independent initiator of new policies. These means were relatively successful, and indeed most rulers were satisfied with their nominal superiority and relegated much of the burden on their underlings. But not every ruler accepted the position of an omnipotent rubber stamp. To restrain these activists, more effective means were required.

It is on this basis that we can understand why the discourse of Heaven's Mandate was resurrected soon after Qin's downfall. This resurrection derived in part from the immediate historical context: the unprecedented magnitude of the anti-Qin uprising, the subsequent civil war, and the eventual rise of the Han dynasty (206/202 BCE–220 CE)—established by a mere commoner—all seemed to validate the centuries-old theory of Heaven's intervention into politics. These events also demonstrated that the commoners' "capsizing" the ruler's boat was not an empty threat but a real danger for the transgressing sovereign. Conditions were ripe for resurrection of the idea of a combined authority of Heaven and the people as being supreme to that of a monarch.

The imperial literati were quick to seize this opportunity. They proposed a new conceptualization of Heaven's interaction with humans in general and with emperors. Dong Zhongshu (ca. 195–115 BCE) and his followers were particularly effective in utilizing this idea in order to restrain the monarch. Their theory integrated previous views of Heaven, incorporating its image both as a sentient deity and as natural order. Heaven closely supervises the ruler: it reacts to his deeds by sending multiple omens and portents, and if these are unheeded, it can intervene in full, replacing him with a new ruler.

The theory clearly placed Heaven's sovereignty above that of the monarch, but it did not endanger the ruler directly. After all, the emperor remained the single mediator between humans and Heaven, and no religious establishment could speak on Heaven's behalf. Yet insofar as Heaven's omens and portents remained open to interpretation—and this interpretation was primarily done by the imperial literati, like Dong Zhongshu himself—those literati were the immediate beneficiaries of the new view of Heaven. To be sure, not every emperor could be manipulated by the invocation of omens and portents, but many were. For the literati, invoking omens was an advantageous means of presenting their interpretation of Heaven's intent in order to moderate some of the ruler's excesses.[49]

Yet portents and omens would probably not influence the emperors much, should Heaven's potential intervention into human affairs be confirmed from time to time by the outburst of popular rebellions. The rebellions became the singularly significant factor behind the dynastic change. They were a sensitive topic to discuss directly, but it was widely understood that they represented the clearest sign of Heaven's dissatisfaction with the dynasty. I shall not address here the impact of this view on rebellions' legitimacy, on their peculiar trajectory, and on their role in rejuvenation of the imperial polity, as I have done this elsewhere.[50] What is important for the present discussion is that the emperors' and elites' awareness of the permanent threat of popular insurrection caused them to be attentive to the people. Not only was the people's well-being repeatedly declared to be the dynasty's primary concern, but their sentiments had to be taken into account as an important, if not primary, criterion in devising new policies.[51]

Yet how could the emperors learn about the people's opinions? There were no regular means of communication, unless we consider collection of popular songs through which the rulers were supposed to learn about the people's mood.[52] Under duress, the commoners could turn in complaints against officials, and local protests were another quasi-legitimate way of displaying dissatisfaction. But each of these was considered an extraordinary and unwelcome manifestation of the commoners' needs. Normally, speaking on behalf of the commoners remained the prerogative of the educated elite. Just as in the case of Heaven, the literati appropriated the voice of those who had the potential of challenging the emperor's authority, posing as spokesmen of the uneducated masses and resorting to the "public opinion" to influence the emperor's behavior. In the final account, both *vox populi* and *vox Dei* were the voice of the literati.

Epilogue: Sovereign Entrapped?

The power and prestige of Chinese emperorship derived primarily from the fact that it was designed long before it materialized. The idea that a single individual must preserve absolute sovereignty over his subjects was a response to the political turmoil of the centuries preceding the imperial unification, and its validity was reinforced in centuries to come. In retrospect it appears to be a reasonable solution, even if not an ideal one, to the maladies of political disintegration. This rationale explains why the idea of an omnipotent monarch was never seriously questioned until the end of the nineteenth century.

Yet, their unwavering support of individual rule aside, the architects of the future empire and their heirs, the imperial literati, were well aware of the system's pitfalls and weaknesses, and they sought multiple ways to mitigate these. The idea of Heaven's *cum* people's sovereignty as superior to that of the monarch was one of the important devices employed to moderate the excesses of individual emperors. More importantly, it granted its designers, the literati, much higher power than their nominal position as the ruler's servitors could have allowed. Appropriating what Tu Wei-ming aptly names "the most generalisable social relevance (the sentiments of the people) and the most universalisable ethico-religious sanction (the mandate of heaven),"[53] the literati remained singularly well positioned to bargain with the throne and to direct it in the desirable direction. In the final account, behind their unwavering commitment to the idea of absolute monarchic authority, we may discern the persistent desire of Chinese imperial intellectuals to maintain the empire on the emperor's behalf—and at times in his stead.

Notes

1. "Kang gao" in the canonic *Book of Documents*; see *Shangshu jinguwen zhushu* (Beijing: Zhonghua, 1998), 371.
2. For sociopolitical reforms of the Warring States period, see Mark E. Lewis, "Warring States: Political History," in *The Cambridge History of Ancient China*, ed. Michael Loewe and Edward L. Shaughnessy (Cambridge: Cambridge University Press, 1999), 587–650.
3. For the political thought of the Warring States period, see Yuri Pines, *Envisioning Eternal Empire: Chinese Political Thought of the Warring States Era* (Honolulu: University of Hawai'i Press, 2009).

4. See more in Liu Zehua's essays collected in *Contemporary Chinese Thought* 45, no. 2-3 (2013–2014).

5. For this skepticism, see Yuri Pines, *Foundations of Confucian Thought: Intellectual Life in the Chunqiu Period, 722-453 B.C.E.* (Honolulu: University of Hawai'i Press, 2002), 55–88.

6. Pines, *Envisioning*, 25–53.

7. *Xunzi jijie* (Beijing: Zhonghua 1992), 9:165.

8. *Lüshi chunqiu jiaoshi* (Shanghai: Xuelin, 1990), 20.1:1322.

9. See more in Yuri Pines and Gideon Shelach, "'Using the Past to Serve the Present': Comparative Perspectives on Chinese and Western Theories of the Origins of the State," in *Genesis and Regeneration: Essays on Conceptions of Origins*, ed. Shaul Shaked (Jerusalem: Israel Academy of Science and Humanities, 2005), 127–63.

10. *Lüshi chunqiu*, 20.1:1322.

11. Ibid., 17.8:1132.

12. Mark E. Lewis, *Sanctioned Violence in Early China* (Albany: State University of New York Press, 1990), 53–96.

13. See, e.g., *Guanzi jiaozhu* (Beijing: Zhonghua, 2004), 52:998–99; *Shenzi jijiao jizhu* (Beijing: Zhonghua, 2013), 48; *Xunzi*, 11:223–24; and *Han Feizi jijie* (Beijing: Zhonghua, 1998) 7:39–43.

14. Shen Buhai (d. 337 BCE), translated from an extract in Herrlee G. Creel, *Shen Puhai* (Chicago: University of Chicago Press, 1974), 380.

15. *Mao shi zhengyi*, repr. in *Shisanjing zhushu* (Beijing: Zhonghua 1992), 13:463.

16. *Guanzi jiaozhu* (Beijing: Zhonghua, 2004), 45:912–13.

17. For Qin social engineering, see Yuri Pines, Gideon Shelach-Lavi, Lothar von Falkenhausen, and Robin D. S. Yates, "General Introduction: Qin History Revisited," in *Birth of an Empire: The State of Qin Revisited* (Berkeley: University of California Press, 2014), 24–26.

18. *Shangjunshu zhuizhi* (Beijing: Zhonghua, 1996), 14:82.

19. *Han Feizi*, 40:392.

20. See, for instance, constant invocations of Ahuramazda in the Behistun inscription by Darius I (c. 550–486 BCE), http://www.livius.org/be-bm/behistun/be histun03.html.

21. Divinations were an essential means of ascertaining the divine will under the Shang dynasty, but already in the late Shang period the scope of the issues about which the kings divined had gradually decreased (David N. Keightley, "The Shang," in Loewe and Shaughnessy, *The Cambridge History of Ancient China*, 261–62). For divinations as mostly a means to "resolve doubts" under the Zhou, see *Chunqiu Zuozhuan zhu* (Beijing: Zhonghua, 1981), Huan 11:113.

22. Poo Mu-chou, *In Search of Personal Welfare: A View of Ancient Chinese Religion* (Albany: State University of New York Press, 1998), 30.

23. "The Great Oath" was lost around the time of the imperial unification of 221 BCE (the current version in the *Book of Documents* is a later forgery). The quotation here is from preimperial texts that cite this document (*Mengzi yizhu* [Beijing: Zhonghua 1992], 9.5:219; *Chunqiu Zuozhuan*, Xiang 31:1184).

24. See Pines, *Envisioning*, 189–90, for further references.

25. *Han Feizi*, 52:465–66.

26. *Mozi jiaozhu* (Beijing: Zhonghua, 1994), 28:319.
27. Ibid., 11:110. "A hundred clans" stands for "the people."
28. Ibid., 28:319.
29. For Heaven as an equivalent of natural law, see, e.g., Randall P. Peerenboom, *Law and Morality in Ancient China: The Silk Manuscripts of Huang-Lao* (Albany: State University of New York Press, 1993). For overt negation of Heaven's political importance, see *Xunzi*, 17:306–20. For the decline of debates about Heaven's Mandate in the Warring States period, see Michael Loewe, *Divination, Mythology, and Monarchy in Han China* (Cambridge: University of Cambridge Press, 1994), 85–111.
30. *Mengzi*, 14.14:328.
31. *Lüshi chunqiu* 1.4:44; *Liji jijie* (Beijing: Zhonghua 1995), 9:582; *Shenzi*, 16; *Shangjun-shu*, 14:84.
32. *Xunzi*, 9:152.
33. *Shangjunshu*, 20:121, 5:40.
34. See the discussion in Pines, *Envisioning*, 198–214.
35. Ibid., 54–81.
36. Romain Graziani, "Monarch and Minister: The Problematic Partnership in the Building of Absolute Monarchy in the *Han Feizi*," in *Ideology of Power and Power of Ideology in Early China*, ed. Yuri Pines, Paul R. Goldin, and Martin Kern (Leiden: Brill, 2015), 155–80.
37. *Xunzi*, 11:223–24.
38. *Han Feizi*, 8:49–50.
39. Ibid., 5:27.
40. See more examples in Pines, *Envisioning*, 106–7.
41. For the proximity between sages and deities in early Chinese thought, see Michael J. Puett, *To Become a God: Cosmology, Sacrifice, and Self-Divinization in Early China* (Cambridge, MA: Harvard University Press), 2002.
42. *Xunzi*, 24:450.
43. Ibid., 18:331.
44. See *Mengzi*, 4.13:109.
45. For the First Emperor's self-propaganda and his image, see Martin Kern, *The Stele Inscriptions of Ch'in Shih-huang: Text and Ritual in Early Chinese Imperial Representation* (New Haven: American Oriental Society, 2000), and Yuri Pines, "The Messianic Emperor," in Pines et al., *Birth of an Empire*, 258–79.
46. Pines, introduction to part III, in Pines et al., *Birth of an Empire*, 227–38.
47. See Yuri Pines, *The Everlasting Empire: Traditional Chinese Political Culture and Its Enduring Legacy* (Princeton: Princeton University Press, 2012), 44–75, for further references. For the importance of the emperors' posture as sages and for despotic potential of this posture, see Liu Zehua, "Political and Intellectual Authority: The Concept of the 'Sage Monarch' and Its Modern Fate," in Pines, Goldin, and Kern, *Ideology of Power*, 273–300.
48. The discussion here and in subsequent paragraph is largely based on Pines, *Everlasting Empire*, 44–75.
49. See, for instance, Rafe de Crespigny, *Portents of Protest in the Later Han Dynasty* (Canberra: Australian National University Press, 1976).
50. Pines, *Everlasting Empire*, 134–61.

51. See, e.g., William T. Rowe, *Saving the World: Chen Hongmou and Elite Consciousness in Eighteenth-Century China* (Stanford: Stanford University Press, 2001), 373–77.

52. For the establishment of the office of song collectors in the Han period and its ritual background, see Martin Kern, "The Poetry of Han Historiography," *Early Medieval China* 10–11, no. 1 (2004): 33–35.

53. Tu Wei-ming, *Way, Learning, and Politics* (Albany: State University of New York Press, 1993), 20.

THREE

Nurhaci's Gambit

Sovereignty as Concept and Praxis in the Rise of the Manchus

NICOLA DI COSMO

"SOVEREIGNTY IN THE ALTAIC WORLD" was the theme of a PIAC (Permanent International Altaistic Conference) meeting held in Berlin in 1991.[1] The degree of uncertainty about the use and meaning of this term is clearly reflected in the contributions to the conference volume. For all its ambiguity, the concept of sovereignty in the political culture of Inner Asian nomads has never been seriously questioned or probed but instead remains most often identified with the ruler's ability to rule. The ruler, in an Altaic context, is above all the khan (*qan*), or khaghan (*qaghan*), a title that, according to widespread opinion, could be acquired by conquest or descent.[2] Around the question of "khanic" (if we can replace by this term more common adjectives such as "monarchic," "kingly," or even "imperial") sovereignty we need to consider the special features of a political system that is not based on a sedentary population, does not require urban centers to operate, and is founded on a social basis that is fluid, fissile, and fragmentary.

In the context of the present volume, a discussion of "Manchu sovereignty" intersects with several themes. First, in the area of comparative study of political concepts, terms such as "political community," "body politic," "legitimate authority," and "divine mandate to rule" have a clear relevance to any global approach to the question of sovereignty. Similar concepts exist in the broader Asian and European traditions; thus, we can find important points of comparison between political systems and ideologies of power that span world cultures from ancient to modern times. In addition to its global dimension, Manchu sovereignty relates, if perhaps in a more tangential manner, to the aesthetic dimension of sovereignty. Namely, it addresses questions of norms, traditions, laws, and international conventions that subtended the interaction among centers of power in the Sinitic and Inner Asian spheres. At the same time, the Manchus participated in the system of tribute relations, in its aesthetic as well as political and economic dimensions. The tribute system, as the chief framework of international relations in East Asia in premodern times, was heavily informed by ritualistic and aesthetic norms. The performative space of the sovereign-tributary relationship was the arena in which the Manchu leader and the Ming emperor negotiated power relations, with its highly codified ensemble of norms regulating the offer of tribute and the granting of titles. As we shall see, such granting of titles would acquire an entirely separate meaning once it was removed from that relationship and transferred to a different situation. In a Manchu context such titles enabled political agency and transformed symbolic capital into political capital. Finally, the political-ideological sphere became the arena of further ideological wrangling when the Manchu leader Nurhaci turned the tables on the Ming, claiming that if sovereignty were universal and granted by Heaven, it could not be regarded as the property of a single empire. In the name of a meritocratic Heaven, the contest is open to all, and the best will be the victor. In the same spirit, a concept of "just war" inspired the rhetoric of sovereignty of the early Manchus. If Heaven is impartial, then it will punish the abuses of the greater power, and war is justified by the need to redress an injustice. It is rather extraordinary that in the late 1640s, as the Manchus were swarming into central and southern China, the Jesuit Martino Martini used the same Manchu propaganda to justify the Manchu conquest of China and war against the Ming, thus laying the foundations for a Catholic accommodation with the Qing dynasty. But what are the roots of the ideas that informed such a multifaceted and sophisticated approach (albeit not formally theorized) to sovereignty? Are these ideas, concepts, and practices inherited, shared, borrowed, or created ex-novo?

The "Altaic" experience of rulership represented by the Turco-Mongol and Tungusic peoples has been central to the history of Eurasia for more than two thousand years, but it has been recognized only in a reflected way, through the mirror of the political culture of the peoples they conquered or in the context of diplomatic relations between nomads and sedentary empires. In the history of China the question of sovereignty emerges frequently in the relations between Inner Asian regimes and Chinese dynasties, or in the context of the rise of "conquest dynasties"—that is, periods of foreign rule over part or the whole of China. By the time "sovereignty," understood at its most basic level as the power wielded by the khan, makes its appearance in the Inner Asian political order, it is already a finished product, the result of the achievements of a "supratribal" leader able to unify nomadic peoples into a cohesive and threatening war machine.[3] Therefore, and this is the central and key concept, "sovereignty" in this particular political culture is identified with the attributes of a supreme leader ruling over multiple polities, not just a local chief or warlord.

Among the native concepts associated with the quality of being an empire builder are charisma (which can also be identified as divine support, the Turkic term *qut*), people, and something like authority or power. Perhaps the best way to characterize this last concept—which in Mongol, for instance, is called *jasaq*—is as the authority to issue edicts that people were expected to obey. In this respect—that is, as the supreme legal authority—Altaic sovereignty is not so distant from other cultural areas and historical contexts. The basis of that authority is the consensus (by recognition of charisma) of the people. These concepts, no matter how philologically or textually precisely we may define them, do not reveal the process through which the finished product—the creation of a large unified state—was attained, the nitty-gritty of the construction of both charisma and consensus. The political endeavor of a "sovereign" *supratribal* leader is typically long, bloody, and intensely contested, not least because the Inner Asian political culture is naturally disposed against these unifying projects. Various social "antibodies," first of all the privileges and independent status of local aristocratic families and "tribal" powers, are activated in a struggle of resistance against the establishment of a superior "sovereign" power. Sometimes the project fails, but sometimes it succeeds. One peculiar, and under-researched aspect is that historically most of these successful large projects originated in Mongolia and Manchuria, where this imperial tradition seems to hold greater sway than among the nomads of Siberia, Central Asia, or western Asia. The reason why this is so is unclear and needs to be investigated case by case. Generally speaking, however, the more sophisticated political cultures could mobilize a variety of concepts and resources, among which the idea of sovereignty itself is one deeply embedded in a political tradition that has not been sufficiently recognized and yet appears to be capable of informing and propelling extremely successful political projects, from the creation of the Mongol empire to the Manchu conquest of China.

If we regard the construction of such a unifying Inner Asian power as a "praxis" of sovereignty, we need to identify the tool kit, political arsenal, and building blocks of statecraft mobilized in this enterprise, and for that purpose it is necessary to consider simultaneously elements of conceptual history (i.e., what a term meant within a given polity at a given time) and elements contingent to the historical process itself (i.e., the strategic or tactical deployment of these concepts). Typically, however, such an analytical effort is hampered by two frequently encountered, yet problematic, approaches. First, it is common to assume that the political cultures of sedentary peoples intervened heavily in shaping Inner Asian ideas of sovereignty and attendant processes of political centralization, thus calling into question, in its more radical applications, the existence itself of a native "imperial" political culture.[4] Second, and diametrically opposed to the first assumption, interpretations and explanations often focus on identifying essential characteristics of Inner Asian nomadic cultures, shared by all of them across time—a quest that denies in principle the political dynamism and capacity of adaptation that is, possibly, one of the main reasons for the success of those polities.

Moreover, if we try to define a native concept of sovereignty common to all Inner Asian and Altaic peoples, we run immediately against another unproven assumption—namely, that a coherent and continuous tradition (both "native" and common to the different peoples that participate in the politics of the steppes) actually existed. In other words, can we speak of sovereignty as a concept that belonged to a general culture of the Eurasian steppes, or should we rather speak of more limited expressions of it—that is, within the confines of single imperial phenomena, such as the Xiongnu, the early Türks, the Kitan Liao state, the Mongol empire, or the Manchus? Are expressions of rulership and sovereignty across the empires and regimes created by Inner Asian peoples fungible, belonging to the same general political culture, or are they better studied as notions that were constantly reinvented and readapted by new instantiations of imperial power?

The question whether the political culture of nomadic empires belongs to the same "phylogenesis" poses, unfortunately, some theoretical obstacles that simply cannot be overcome. The most critical obstacle regards the absence of native written traditions that allow us to trace the evolution and transmission of these concepts. Ever since the first general history of nomadic peoples was written, it has been accepted as a necessary heuristic device that these empires and regimes belonged to the same general stock and molded their experience on the basis of a common stratum of ideas, concepts, and practices so that the variations we see among discrete polities are not sufficient to deny the existence of a unified political tradition.[5]

At its lowest common denominator, this assumption is grounded in the realization that every nomadic empire had to contend with similar issues, which are specific to nomadic steppe peoples. It is also based on cognate linguistic and semantic elements, whereby political terms, titles, and ideology appear to be similar. Comparative analysis, therefore, is not only essential to understanding contrasting ideas, but it becomes the key methodological approach to tracing the configurations, contours, transformations, and variations that these concepts acquired historically.

Three areas of inquiry are central to the comparative study of sovereignty in the Altaic tradition. The first concerns the political theology of sovereignty, and in particular the divine origin of rulership, and therefore the nature of the ruling "mandate" that a sovereign claims.[6] The second regards what we might call the "political community" over which the ruler exerts his sovereignty. Whether this is expressed as a "people" or as a "state," it has to be larger than a polity bonded by some type of group identity, be it based on common ancestry and kinship, territorial claims, or the sharing of a common religion or set of customs and laws. It must, that is, include multiple groups whose self-definitions are diverse but are nonetheless subject to, and partake in, the rule of a higher power than that expressed within the groups themselves. The third area refers to the praxis of sovereignty—that is, the process of the creation of an authority that could access both claims: that of having a divine right and the legitimate authority to rule a community larger than the ones defined by the bonds mentioned above. The assumption that a bounded political community could be replaced by an unbounded one by a military process of territorial conquest and subjugation of one's enemies ignores the political element involved in the acquisition not just of power but of *legitimate* power. The praxis of sovereignty is not about military conquest but about the creation of legitimate rule over an expanding and ideally boundless community.

In this essay I investigate the notion of sovereignty in relation to the rise of Nurhaci, the "great ancestor" of the Manchu state and of the Qing dynasty. He rose, like other Inner Asian empire builders, from relatively humble beginnings to lay the foundations of one of the greatest empire in Chinese and world history. Investigating how Nurhaci established his rule over an ever-widening community of peoples, expanded his legitimacy, and eventually maneuvered into claiming the Heavenly Mandate against the Ming as the ultimate step toward universal sovereignty is therefore presented as a contribution to the comparative and "global" understanding of expressions of sovereignty. More generally, I see this study as an attempt to move beyond static or rigid definitions of sovereignty and toward its interpretation as a political artifact.

The Jurchen Political Community

It is difficult to establish whether, at the time Nurhaci began his rise to power in the late sixteenth century, a notion of sovereignty could be applied to the various Jurchen communities that the Ming *wei-suo* system had in part inherited and in part created.[7] All Jurchen peoples were incorporated within the Ming frontier defense administration as "garrisons" (*wei*) and "outposts" (*suo*).[8] These came into being not just as an independent process of creation of Jurchen polities but as an evolution of frontier communities. This evolution began with the political and territorial restructuring of the polities under the Yuan dynasty and was continued under the Ming. As an integral part of the Ming defense system, they retained a degree of internal coherence consistent with the overall structure of the Ming frontier organization and within the general framework of the tribute system. In practice, the various chiefs owed their power to a dual mechanism of political legitimation: an internal process of acquisition of authority based on aristocratic lineages, military power, and personal qualities and an external process of recognition by the Ming emperor as overlord and sovereign.

Acknowledgment as a tributary entity by the Ming throne, which was accepted by all tribute-bearing peoples as the sovereign power, provided both economic incentives, such as permission to trade at frontier markets, and political obligations, which in practice meant loyalty to the emperor and willingness to defend the realm if needed. Jurchen aristocratic leaders exercised political authority within their community, but their power was conditional to their remaining subject to the Ming and accepting titles, ranks, and privileges that could only be allocated by the emperor. Subordination to the Ming made their position within their community, thus, less than "sovereign."

The Ming *wei-suo* system, however, was also based on ethnic and political divisions whose origins and development are embedded in local history. Jurchen politics was structured on three levels: within a polity, between Jurchen polities, and in relation to the Ming and other foreign entities, such as Koreans and Mongols. The internal organization of Jurchen politics was geared to preserving a balance of power among the different polities, which was the avowed goal of the Ming frontier system. The financial incentives provided by the Ming were meant to preserve local authority split among a series of separate and discrete aristocratic lineages. Under the Ming system, the Jurchen, allegedly one ethnic entity, were divided into separate political communities. Ethnic and political boundaries not only did not coincide but were kept rigidly divided.

The Jurchen people, or *gurun*, over which Nurhaci eventually established his "sovereignty," had therefore to be defined first of all as a single political community; in other words, the ethnic and political boundaries had to be brought into harmony so that only one center of power was allowed to exist. The process of redefining the scattered and divided Jurchen polities (or "nations," in the same sense of a Native American "nation"—also referred to as "tribes") as a single political community is what, in essence, can be considered the first phase of Nurhaci's rise to power. This culminated in 1616 with the establishment of an independent and "sovereign" regime that was called *jušen gurun* (that is, the Jurchen state), which was meant to replace the smaller gurun into which the Jurchen political galaxy was organized—namely, Jianzhou, Hada, Hulun, Haixi, and others.

The coming into existence of the jušen gurun as a new political actor is therefore a critical milestone within a strategy meant to expand Nurhaci's power beyond the polity of which he had become (not without bloodshed) the leader. The first mention of the term *jušen gurun* in Manchu records seems to appear in 1613 with specific reference to Nurhaci's polity.[9] Tracing the evolution of the term used in Manchu to indicate Nurhaci's own state is not easy because later sources anachronistically speak of *manju gurun*. Still, it is significant that we can find the term *niozi manju gurun* or "Jurchen Manchu nation" in the *Jiu Manzhou Dang*, and contemporary Chinese sources refer to Nurhaci's specific polity as the Jianzhou Jurchen (Jianzhou *nüzhen*).[10] Therefore, while all the various "nations" that Nurhaci attacked and subjugated (such as the Hoifa, Hada, and Ula) were considered to be Jurchen, the only jušen gurun ("Jurchen" nation) that appears in the early Manchu sources was the one created by Nurhaci.

At this point it is necessary to open a parenthesis to explain several possible translations of the term "gurun." This is often rendered as "state" in the same way that the Chinese term *guo* is translated as "state." As a state, gurun simply indicates a polity under a single legitimate authority, but it obviously does not reflect any modern sense of the state—that is, as a "nation-state." Another meaning for gurun is "people," understood as an organic ethnic unit. In this respect, perhaps, it could be rendered as "nation". To the extent that a gurun has a territorial dimension, another possible translation is "country." Finally, gurun could also stand for the term "dynasty," as for instance in *ming gurun* to refer to the Ming dynasty. The semantic mercuriality of this term is evidence not of a reduced and insufficient vocabulary but rather of a political culture whose operating terminology is open ended, malleable, and thus greatly dependent on context and process.

The invention of a "Jurchen nation" was an extraordinary and utterly bold move because it allowed Nurhaci to conjure up a much wider political community over which he could claim sovereignty. Yet the notion of a coherent community that could be extended to all Jurchens could not be created out of whole cloth. As a political artifact, it could be justified on historical bases, by reference to the Jurchens who created, half a century earlier, the Jin dynasty. The forcible subjugation of Nurhaci's Jurchen rivals could be presented, then, not as an act of conquest but rather as a logical step toward the reconstitution of a "Jurchen state" as a coherent political, ethnic, and historical community. Needless to say, such original, ancestral community was conjured up as a convenient conceit onto which the projection of a sovereign claim could be grafted.

The Creation of the Jušen Gurun

One key aspect of the strategy that would allow Nurhaci to annex other Jurchen nations before a concept of the jušen gurun could be created was that such annexation had to be regarded as legitimate in order to lay a solid foundation for the polity that would follow.

In purely ideological terms, Nurhaci presented the annexation of the Jurchen tribes against whom he fought as rightful retribution for attacks he and his family had suffered—within the Jurchen political culture, revenge constituted a legal cause for war. Moreover, the victories obtained on the battlefield were portrayed as an expression of the will of Heaven, which allowed Nurhaci to credit himself as one anointed by Heaven (*abka*). This notion, which is central to the building of imperial charisma, is given additional support when we consider the later appropriation of the origin myth of the Manchu royal house, the Aisin Gioro clan. The myth of the presumed ancestor of Nurhaci, Bukūri Yongšon, belongs to one of the most widespread political notions in Inner Asian history—namely, that legitimate sovereignty is associated with the restoration of order from the chaos that had plunged the people into a condition of war and violence. This myth, which was appropriated by Hong Taiji after the submission of the Hūrha nation, shows the political potency underlying the concept of a ruler who unites and pacifies the people. Taking the community from chaos to order was probably the most powerful claim to legitimate rule in the Inner Asian (as well as Chinese) political tool kit. It is no surprise that so much effort was directed to recruiting and propagating a suitable myth that presented Nurhaci as the descendant of such a "savior" figure and, by association, as the person who would once again pull together a nation that had plunged into political chaos.[11]

In order to realize his political project, Nurhaci had to paint a picture of the state of the Jurchen people that was consistent with his strategy. Thus, the people were no longer discrete autonomous nations (gurun) within the logic of balance of powers that had long been predominant in the region; instead, they were a single nation (also gurun) in a state of chaos and in need of a "unifier." The frequent references to the Jin dynasty (*aisin gurun*) were meant to stress the point that the Jurchen ethnic nation was once (and should be again) a single political community.[12] According to this logic, the separateness of the Jurchen peoples is taken as evidence of disorder and thus as a pretext to transform a political system based on a balance among discrete and equivalent minor "sovereignties" into one that reconstitutes an original unity. For Nurhaci, the path to expansion was not just based on the military subjugation of rival Jurchen nations. Rather, his political design from the beginning was based on the restoration of an ideal body politic over which he was to hold sway. In this exercise of artfully manipulated prescience, he transformed his original gurun into a progressively more inclusive and open community. Each of the political names in the progression from Jianzhou Jurchen (his original constituency) to jušen gurun (the state of all Jurchen) and to aisin gurun (a multiethnic dynastic state) is a milestone on the road of expanding his political community without loss of legitimacy in the process.

Naturally, Nurhaci's aggressive behavior angered the other nations, which could not passively accept their fate and tried to thwart his designs by forming a military coalition against him. The protracted violence that engulfed the Jurchen peoples was a central element of Nurhaci's claim that they required pacification and unification under a single authority. As the other Jurchen nations rose in defense of their independence and protected themselves, Nurhaci's strategy, as risky as it was, yielded results. The greater the chaos, the more persuasive his rhetoric of pacification and unification became, and the more support he received from the Ming.

The Logic of Nurhaci's Strategy

Nurhaci's rise to the head of the Jianzhou polity (a *wei* in the Ming system) and the later annexation of other Jurchen nations have been looked at mostly from the viewpoint of military strategy and political maneuvering.[13] The question of how "sovereignty" was claimed, established, represented, and proclaimed has attracted less attention. In order to achieve his goals, Nurhaci had to continue to be victorious in war, to avoid as much as possible his enemies joined in military alliances against him and especially to retain Ming support, or at least neutrality, for as long as possible. Had the Ming decided that Nurhaci's rise constituted a threat, his ambitious plan would have been thwarted early on. The first challenge in the state-building process, therefore, was to establish himself as the legitimate ruler over a political community inclusive of all Jurchen people—a strategy inherently antagonistic to the Ming frontier policy of "divide and rule"—before the Ming could oppose it. To bring the various Jurchen polities under his rule, mostly by force, and still maintain the legitimacy to do so, he needed a credible claim, which could not be entirely confined to his own propaganda. Such a claim had to be supported by external endorsements. Only after Nurhaci had acquired a level of 'international' recognition and support that allowed him to cast his shadow beyond his original power base (the Jianzhou Jurchen) could he move on to annex other polities.

The endorsements that Nurhaci gained in the late sixteenth and early seventeenth centuries from the Ming dynasty and from the Mongol Khalkha leaders should be read in this light—that is, as a form of legitimacy by which Nurhaci sought to expand virtually the political community within the reach of his power. His first step was acquiring Ming support in order to bring all the Jianzhou Jurchen (including several hostile towns and clans) under his control by portraying himself as the Ming order keeper.

In 1589 the Ming gave Nurhaci the important title of assistant commissioner in chief (*dudu qianshi*), which allowed him to begin a strong-arm policy vis-à-vis other Jurchen peoples. In a diplomatic exchange with the Yehe, who in 1591 warned Nurhaci that occupation of their lands would not be tolerated, the Jianzhou chieftain stressed the excellent relationship he had with the Ming and the titles he had been given, hinting that Nurhaci's authority could well extend beyond his own Jianzhou territory.[14] Nurhaci's aggressive tactics against other Jurchen polities were surely fueled by the high status that the Ming had given him. Such protection did not prevent a coalition of Jurchen tribes from mounting a military expedition against Nurhaci; however, he defeated them at the battle of Mount Gure (1593). This military feat further strengthened Nurhaci's hand and elevated his standing with the Ming as a local leader. He carefully cultivated this image and intervened militarily in support of the Ming on several occasions, for instance by volunteering troops to assist the Ming expedition to Korea during the Imjin War against Japan (1592–98). In 1595 the Ming regaled him with the coveted title of "Tiger and Dragon General" allegedly for his assistance in the protection of the frontiers, thus establishing him as their strong man in the region.[15] The Ming saw in him a loyal subject who repeatedly traveled to the court to present tribute. Consolidating his relationship with the Ming was essential to carrying his campaigns against other Jurchen gurun. Further military action against the Hada nation, however, met with criticism and reprimand from the Ming but could not prevent its annexation in 1601.

A second external recognition of high political status came from the Mongol Khalkha delegation, which in 1606 conferred on Nurhaci the title of *kündülen qaghan* following the opening of trade relations and other diplomatic contacts aimed at establishing peace.[16] The title *qaghan* (or *qan*) in an Inner Asian context was a lofty term, equivalent to Manchu *han*; it indicated a ruler with an especially elevated standing, above that of noblemen and chieftains. Until then Nurhaci had not claimed such a title and was referred to only by the aristocratic term of *beile*, roughly corresponding to "lord." The other Jurchen leaders also carried similar titles. The Mongol championing of Nurhaci was therefore exceptional because, at least in theory, it raised his status above that of any other Jurchen aristocrat. The endorsements received from the Ming court and Mongol aristocracy strengthened not only Nurhaci's political position in the region but also his particular claim to sovereignty over the other Jurchen chiefs.

If external support allowed Nurhaci to appear not as a usurper engaging in a policy of naked aggression but as someone who was "ordering" the Jurchen realm, bringing peace to it and thereby protecting the interests of his neighbors, the confirmation of the rightfulness of his actions came from victory on the battlefield, which was always presented as a divine augury and the tangible manifestation of Heaven's favor. Naturally, victory in battle helped consolidate power, but trumpeting victories in a manner that provided legitimacy was an essential component of Nurhaci's strategy in the construction of an expanding sphere of virtual sovereignty. As a preliminary observation, therefore, we can say that the shifting gap between the actual political community over which Nurhaci acquired authority at any given time and the "imagined community" to which he aspired to become the sovereign was filled with the appearance of external endorsements and diplomatic support that the Chinese and Mongol titles conveyed.

Sovereign Rule in Nurhaci's Claim of Independence from the Ming

The Ming dynasty eventually refrained from fully endorsing Nurhaci's rise to power, and the Yehe nation remained under Ming protection until the Ming themselves were defeated at Mount Sarhū in 1619. With the Ming resolution to quell his further ambitions, a point had been reached when Nurhaci's affirmation of Jurchen sovereignty had become incompatible with political support from a greater power, a power to which Nurhaci was still theoretically obligated to pay homage as a tributary subject. If external recognition helped Nurhaci to extend to all Jurchens the political community of which he aspired to become the sovereign, and if the Ming had fed Nurhaci's ambitions up until his full political design had been revealed, the withdrawal of Ming support in defense of the hostile Yehe persuaded Nurhaci that the time was ripe to proclaim not only sovereignty over the entire Jurchen political community but also independence from the Ming.

The creation of a unified Jurchen regime in the northeast did not necessarily require breaking the tributary relationship, but stiff internal resistance and the Ming court's growing suspicions complicated the process. One could even see in Nurhaci's marital diplomacy an attempt to use "soft" means to achieve his goal of unification rather than proceeding down a purely military avenue.[17] Given the economic benefits afforded by the tributary status, it seems that a declaration of political independence should have been delayed for as long as possible. It only ceased to be sustainable when Ming support for the Yehe ran directly counter Nurhaci's political project.

In 1616, with the founding of the Later Jin state (*amaga aisin gurun*) a new pattern emerged.[18] The political vision encapsulated in the notion of an "*aisin*" state was overtly inspired by the Jin dynasty of the twelfth century (1115–1234), foreshadowing a type of sovereignty whose reach might go beyond Manchuria and include at least a portion of Ming territory.[19] The association with the Jin dynasty allowed Nurhaci to conjure up yet another configuration for the political community ideally to be brought under his rule. Given the extent of the territorial expansion of the Jin dynasty, which had conquered northern China and ruled it for over a century, Nurhaci's sovereignty could then extend beyond the Jurchen ethnic community, even to Chinese peoples.

The transition from jušen gurun to aisin gurun should therefore be read as a significant turn in the definition of Nurhaci's sovereignty. It was not until the battle at Mount Sarhū (1619),[20] when Nurhaci defeated a large Ming army sent to crush him and destroy his capital, that he claimed Heaven's Mandate (*abkai fulingga*) as his reign title, even though his new dynasty had been proclaimed three years before.[21] The gap between the creation of a new political entity and the acquisition of a title that projected further political ambitions is significant for understanding the nature of Nurhaci's political strategy. Until the Ming had been defeated militarily it would have been easy to cast the confrontation in terms of a conflict between a legitimate dynasty and a rebel frontier warlord. The victory against the Ming was a gigantic military achievement. But even more than that, it called into question the very legitimacy of the Ming as the supreme, overarching, universal power. Nurhaci did not miss the opportunity to welcome his victory as Heaven's sign that his legitimate rule could reach beyond Manchuria. The transition from an ethnic and territorial definition of sovereignty, identified first with the Jianzhou Jurchen and later with the Jurchen nation, to a dynastic name (Jin, *aisin*) with direct historical reference to a bona fide Chinese dynasty with Manchurian roots, once again transformed the ideal composition of the political community and thus the "quality" of Nurhaci's sovereignty.

The contention that the Ming could lose Heaven's Mandate had been embedded in a complex text, known as the "Seven Great Grievances," issued in 1618. This document is, at its most basic level, a manifesto to justify the war against the Ming.[22] It retroactively establishes Nurhaci's sovereignty over Manchuria as an independent ruler, thus rhetorically transforming his previous relationship with China from subordinate (and tributary) to one of equal status. Several "grievances" refer to treaties and agreements between the Jianzhou Jurchen state and the Ming state that had been supposedly violated by the Ming. In the first grievance Nurhaci blames the Ming for the death of his father and grandfather, due in his view to the Ming's overstepping their authority and interfering with Manchurian politics by military intervention. The second grievance also refers to an episode of frontier violation by the Ming, even though according to Nurhaci an agreement had been reached to mark the boundary between his and Ming territory. There is probably no greater expression of sovereignty than the defense of "national" frontiers and the exercise of absolute power within them. By protesting that the Ming involvement in Jurchen politics was illegitimate, Nurhaci claimed his own unfettered sovereignty over the whole of Manchuria as a "fact" that predated his own declaration of independence from the Ming. Of course, the Ming saw in their own intervention into Jurchen affairs an effort to keep order among their subjects and the punitive expedition against a rebellious subject as their unequivocal right.

What is especially remarkable is that while Nurhaci was upholding his right to independent sovereign status, he was also, in the very same document, making parallel claims meant to extend that sovereignty to an even wider community. The seventh grievance makes oblique references to a theory of the Mandate of Heaven according to which universal rulership could be claimed by anyone favored by Heaven, and that the Ming throne, therefore, does not hold an exclusive right over it:

Under Heaven all people fight, but those who have sinned against Heaven are defeated and perish and those who are favored by Heaven prevail and survive. Is there a law according to which the dead in battle come back or the prisoners are given back? Is the emperor of a great state the Lord of every state? Why should I, alone, be left out from such a Heavenly decree? . . . The Hulun people united to attack me and since by doing so they sinned in front of Heaven, Heaven favored me. How can the [Ming] emperor judge negatively something good, and positively something bad? By helping the Yehe people, who are disliked by Heaven, doesn't he himself oppose Heaven?[23]

According to Nurhaci the emperor is sinning and will be punished for it, allowing the favored one, himself, to replace him. This direct challenge to the Ming emperor as a universal ruler was utterly arrogant for a mere frontier warlord, and it was certain to trigger the Ming armed response. But only after the battle in which Nurhaci defeated the Ming did he choose the extraordinary designation of Heaven's Mandate (*abkai fulingga*) for his reign title.[24] What this shows, consistently with the general strategy described so far, is not necessarily the will to conquer the whole of China but the extension of Nurhaci's sovereignty beyond the Jurchen ethnic and political community. One cannot fail to notice that Nurhaci conquered the Chinese territory of Liaodong and moved his capital there immediately after having expanded once again the theoretical reach of his legitimate rule.

Let us review the issues we have explored so far. At each stage of the process of expanding his sovereignty, the political community Nurhaci claimed was larger in name than it was in reality. External endorsements were taken as confirmation of the legitimacy of his ambitions and followed or accompanied by an actual expansion (and in this Nurhaci's ability as a military leader was clearly paramount) presented as a rightful act to "unify" a virtual realm over which Nurhaci lay his claim as sovereign. External recognitions came from the Ming, the Mongols, and "Heaven." A propaganda centered in "rightful expansion" (or even "manifest destiny") was meant, naturally, to counter the inevitable accusation that Nurhaci had embarked on a war of naked aggression. Had Nurhaci simply engaged in brutal conquest he would have lost the moral right and increased the number of his enemies, and his leadership may have been challenged inside his own camp. Indeed, challenges from clan and family plagued the early phase of Nurhaci's "state-building" and are reflected in the fratricidal struggle that in all probability led to the death of his brother Šurhaci.[25] Instead, the strategy of defining asymmetrically the political community actually under Nurhaci's control and the virtual political community that "should have been" under his rule allowed him to expand his sovereignty without losing legitimacy. The "Seven Great Grievances" was the crowning document and ultimate expression of this strategy.

If the expansion of Nurhaci's state beyond the Jianzhou polity required the invention of a jušen gurun and the invasion of Liaodong could take place as a new edition of an aisin gurun, the Mongol world posed a much more irksome challenge. The entirely different strategy pursued in relation to the Mongols reveals the complexity of establishing Nurhaci's legitimate rule over a people divided into many "nations" (some of them just as strong as the Manchus) over which he could not produce any credible political claim. The Mongol polities could not be said to be part of a jušen or aisin gurun, and Nurhaci had no connection to the Činggisid blood line, which might have provided at least a veneer of legitimacy. The painstaking diplomatic activity he carried out by forging treaties and marriage alliances was constantly accompanied by a "propaganda" in which Nurhaci, and later his son and successor Hong Taiji (r. 1626–43), stressed historical precedents for the transmission of the *doro*—that is, the principle of legitimate sovereignty—to show its transferability (a sort of *translatio imperii*) across separate political communities. The references in early Manchu sources to the transfer of rulership (or rightful sovereignty) from the Jin (*aisin*) dynasty to the Mongols at the time of the Mongol conquest—the Jurchen Jin dynasty fell to the Mongols in 1234—should therefore be read as an argument for the transferability of the doro between the Mongol and Jurchen communities, and thus for the possibility that Nurhaci, in his persona as the new *aisin* ruler, could reclaim it. If a sovereign's right to rule could be taken away from the Jin and enjoyed by the Mongols, there was no special reason why the Manchus could not reclaim it for themselves. What made this possible was the same Heavenly support so often invoked by the Mongol emperors, who were "oceanic rulers of the Mongol people by the power of eternal Heaven" ("möngke tngriyin küčündür yeke Mongol ulus un dalai-yin qan"), as it appears for instance in Güyük Khan's seal affixed to his diplomatic letters to Western powers. The Manchus missed no chance to stress that their military victories were indeed evidence of Heaven's favor. The connection established by Nurhaci and Hong Taiji with the glorious Mongol past (such as the well-known episode of the recovery of the Yuan dynastic seal) was meant to show how the long currents of Mongolian and Manchu history were braided into a common destiny and that sovereign rule between both communities was transferable and fungible.[26]

In political terms, however, any claim to sovereignty over the Mongols had to be sustained by a *practice* of sovereignty that demonstrated a right to rule beyond its ideological aspects. It is therefore in the context of the remaking of the Mongol political order by the competing project of imperial unification carried out by the Čaqar leader Ligdan Khan (1588–1634) that we find the roots of Manchu legitimacy with respect to the Mongol community.[27] While Ligdan's violent and ruthless rise challenged and endangered Nurhaci's own ascendancy, it also offered him and Hong Taiji the opportunity to present themselves as protectors of the Mongol people against a bloodthirsty tyrant. In the war against the Čaqars, Nurhaci assumed the position of guardian and tutor of the separate Mongol communities (*ulus*) that were being forcefully subjugated by Ligdan, whose own claim to sovereignty was entirely different from Nurhaci's. Ligdan's legitimacy was supported by his Činggisid lineage, which was a prerequisite for Mongol rulership, and by the external political-theological endorsement by powerful Tibetan Buddhist hierarchies. However, such support was not sufficient to overcome the resistance of the Mongol aristocracy, which, like the Jurchen chieftains in the Manchu camp, was not keen to be subjugated and offered staunch resistance. In Ligdan's case, however, his violent tactics were not accompanied by a state-building process comparable to that undertaken by Nurhaci. Against the exploitative and merciless policy carried out by Ligdan, Nurhaci's strategy of binding the Mongol communities to his political project by offering them protection and high positions, later continued by Hong Taiji, would prove eventually successful, thus further expanding the political community under the Manchu sway.[28]

Community and Sovereignty Among
the Early Manchus

In conclusion, I would like to make a few additional remarks on the actual Manchu terms deployed to denote the two concepts that have been central to our discussion: "gurun" and "doro," which I translate respectively as "political community" and "sovereignty." We have already examined the various meanings of the term "gurun" and its political fungibility. What is relevant to a discussion on sovereignty in the Manchu context is that the Jurchen concept of "state" appears to result from the combination of two components that are placed in dialectical relationship with each other: the gurun and the doro—that is, political community and sovereign power, or, to use different expressions, the body politic and the legitimate authority of the ruler. In order to appreciate fully the mechanisms underlying state-building strategies, we need to identify how these two concepts play against each other. To begin a conceptual history of gurun and doro, we should first turn to an analogous discussion that has developed around the Mongol terms *ulus* and *törü*, which, to go back to my initial remarks about a common stratum of Inner Asian politics, appear on the surface to be semantically close to the Manchu gurun and doro. According to Johann Elverskog's extensive analysis, *ulus* and *törü* correspond respectively to "people" and "state."[29] Without entering into the specific details of Mongol political terminology, the Manchu meaning of "doro," as expressed in our sources, does not support the notion that it is equivalent to "state," as defined by Elverskog in reference to the Mongol case, and therefore it cannot be regarded as a cognate of *törü*. Doro appears to be, rather, a transcendental quality of rulership that applies to the creation of an especially large and "transformational" political project. The concept of doro is most often linked in Manchu texts to the rulership of the Mongol and Jurchen empires and therefore to an imperial tradition that transcended any single ethnic community. In this respect, it may refer to a quality of "sovereignty" that may be understood not just as political power but as a praxis of rulership that is legitimate and righteous. The semantic field of doro eventually came to include other meanings, such as "rule," "doctrine," "ceremony," or *dao* (the Chinese philosophical principle of "path" or "pattern"), and was also related to other abstract concepts involving morality, propriety, and rituals.

In political practice, Nurhaci claimed that the doro of the Jin dynasty was inherited by him, as in the following sentence: "abkai kesi de sure kundulen han amba gurun de isabufi, aisin doro be jafafi banjire de." This could be literally translated as "at the point when by heavenly favor the wise and honored emperor had collected a great nation and wielded the sovereign power (doro) of the Jin."[30] Here gurun and doro are joined to indicate that a large political community had been "gathered" and that rightful sovereignty, handed down from the *amba gurun* (great nation) of the Jurchen Jin dynasty, had been established. This document, dated to 1613, precedes the establishment of the Later Jin dynasty by Nurhaci in 1616, but, as mentioned above, it prefigures it by creating a gap between the actual community over which Nurhaci had power and that over which he aspired to rule.

The gurun is also not a "state" (whatever we might mean by this) but the political community that provides doro to the ruler—that is, the base supporting the sovereign power of the ruler. State formation, understood as the rapid creation of institutions of government, both civil and military, is expressed neither by gurun nor by doro. In Manchu the terms that pertain to this process are *dasan* (government), *fafun* (law), *kooli* (statute, custom), and other administrative and legal concepts. If seeking an equivalent to the concept of "state" in the early stage of the rise of the Manchus would be not only difficult but most likely wrongheaded, this does not mean that one cannot define the Manchu power created by Nurhaci as a state, provided that we do not confuse or even compare it with the European conceptual history of this term. The state created by Nurhaci combined the formation of a new political community with the establishment of new sovereign rule through the transformative power of new social, military, and bureaucratic institutions. In this process, sovereignty was tightly connected with the process of constantly redrawing the boundaries of the political community within an overall strategy of military expansion. The state was the product of this dynamic and dialectic relationship between gurun and doro, but it did not gel into a fixed entity until the political community could itself be fixed and circumscribed. At the same time, fissures were preserved among the various ethnic groups and polities once united under a single sovereign. They retained their own individual character, and their respective relationships to the sovereign were articulated through specific and incommensurable cultures and traditions.

It is perhaps possible to conclude, at least as a suggestion for future interpretations of Manchu, and more broadly Inner Asian, approaches to sovereignty, that the strategy pursued by Nurhaci and foundational to the establishment of the Qing dynasty gives a particular flavor to Manchu rule in China, a flavor not be found in other dynasties. The existence of multiple sovereignties as a hallmark of Qing rule, as well as the extension of Qing rule to Mongolia, Tibet, Taiwan, and Xinjiang, cannot be regarded as extraneous to a political culture in which, as we see in Nurhaci's strategy, the concept of sovereignty was deeply inflected by a political praxis in which the construction of a political community (gurun) and the justification of legitimate rule (doro) had to be pursued in harmony with one another.

Notes

1. *Altaica Berolinensia: The Concept of Sovereignty in the Altaic World*, ed. Barbara Kellner-Heinkele (Wiesbaden: Harrassowitz, 1993).
2. See, for instance, P. B. Golden, "The Khazar Sacral Kingship," in *Pre-modern Russia and Its World: Essays in Honor of Thomas S. Noonan*, ed. Kathryn L. Reyerson et al. (Wiesbaden: Harrassowitz, 2006), 89.
3. On the concept of supratribal leadership, see Joseph Fletcher, "The Mongols: Ecological and Social Perspectives," *Harvard Journal of Asiatic Studies* 46, no. 1 (1986): 11–50, and "Turco-Mongolian Monarchic Tradition in the Ottoman Empire," *Harvard Ukrainian Studies* 3–4 (1979): 236–51.
4. For an overview of these points, see Daniel J. Rogers, "Inner Asian States and Empires: Theories and Synthesis," *Journal of Archaeological Research* 20, no. 3 (2012): 205–56.
5. Historiographically, the beginning of a unified history of the steppe can be traced back to de Guignes: see Joseph de Guignes, *Histoire générale des Huns, des Turcs, des Mogols, et des autres Tartares occidentaux, &tc.*, 4 vols. (Paris: Desaint & Saillant, 1758).
6. For an astute discussion of Mongol political theology, see Christopher P. Atwood, "Validation by Holiness or Sovereignty: Religious Toleration as Political Theology in the Mongol World Empire of the Thirteenth Century," *International History Review* 26, no. 2 (2004): 237–56.
7. Classic political doctrine defines the "sovereign" (be it a person, political body, or "people") as the ultimate and supreme authority of a political community and the source of lawmaking power. Sovereignty is therefore the quality possessed by the person or body of people who exercise that power. While other definitions are possible, and it would also be appropriate to contextualize and historicize this concept, such a definition is quite sufficient for our purpose. The notion of multiple "rulerships" of the Qing has been discussed particularly in relation to the Qianlong emperor (see Pamela Crossley, "The Rulerships of China," *American Historical Review* 97, no. 5 [1992]: 1468–83). However, there is a difference between rulership and sovereignty, and the construction of the Qing emperors' images and attributes belongs historically and conceptually to the post-conquest Qing dynasty, albeit with some references to the preconquest period. What has not been sufficiently analyzed so far is the evolution of a notion of sovereignty in the different phases of the pre-conquest period, and specifically in relation to the construction of a Jurchen state (*jušen gurun*) and, in the 1620s and 1630s, to an expanded multiethnic state. Also, attention to sovereignty has privileged some aspects over others. While performative, representative,

symbolic, and ideological facets have been studied closely, the establishment of "sovereignty" as a legally legitimate and internationally recognized authority over a political community and the concepts deployed in this process have not received equal attention.

8. For the establishment of this system, see Henry Serruys, *Sino-Jürčed Relations During the Yung-Lo Period (1403-1424)* (Wiesbaden: Harrassowitz, 1955).

9. *Manbun Rōtō/Manwen Laodang (MBRT)* (Tokyo: Tōyō Bunko, 1955-1963), 1:36, 63; *Jiu Manzhou dang (JMZD)* (Taipei: Guoli gugong bowuyuan, 1969), 1:80. According to another study the term "jušen gurun" was adopted starting in 1607 (see Xue Hong and Liu Hongsheng, "'Jiu Manzhou dang' suoji Da Qing jianhao qian de guohao," *Shehui kexue jikan* [1990] 2:83-90). However I could not find any mention of jušen gurun for this year in the *MBRT* and *JMZD*.

10. *JMZD*, 1:81.

11. Jun Matsumura, "On the Founding Legend of the Ch'ing Dynasty," *Acta Asiatica* 53 (1988): 1-23. See also Stephen W. Durrant, "Repetition in the Manchu Origin Myth as a Feature of Oral Narrative," *Central Asiatic Journal* 22, no. 1/2 (1978): 32-43; Pamela Kyle Crossley, "An Introduction to the Qing Foundation Myth," *Late Imperial China* 6, no. 2 (1985): 13-24.

12. For early references to Jin dynastic history in the Manchu documents, see *MBRT*, 1: 9 (1607), 90 (1618), 142-43 (1619), and 233-35 (1620).

13. Wada Sei, "Some Problems Concerning the Rise of T'ai-tsu, the Founder of Dynasty [*sic*]," *Memoirs of the Toyo Bunko* 16 (1957): 35-73.

14. For the text, see Teng Shaozhen, *Nuerhachi pingzhuan* (Shenyang: Liaoning renmin chubanshe, 1985), 67.

15. Gertraude Roth Li, "State Building Before 1644," in *The Cambridge History of China*, vol. 9, part 1, ed. Willard J. Peterson (Cambridge: Cambridge University Press, 2002), 29-30.

16. Nicola Di Cosmo and Dalizhabu Bao, *Manchu-Mongol Relations on the Eve of the Qing Conquest* (Leiden: Brill, 2003), 8.

17. Nicola Di Cosmo, "Marital Politics on the Manchu-Mongol Frontier in the Early Seventeenth Century." In *The Chinese State at the Borders*, ed. Diana Lary (Vancouver: University of British Columbia Press, 2007), 57-73.

18. *MBRT*, 1:68

19. The Manchu word *aisin*, meaning "gold," was the dynastic name of the Jin dynasty (1115-1234) founded by the Jurchen in the twelfth century and later conquered by the Mongols. This term is the same as Nurhaci's clan name: Aisin Gioro. The term "gold" has important connotations in the Altaic world, for it indicates a royal lineage, as in the Mongol term *altan uruq* for the imperial clan.

20. Ray Huang, "The Liao-tung Campaign of 1619," *Oriens Extremus* 28, no. 1 (1981): 30-54.

21. Nicola Di Cosmo, "Nurhaci's Names," in *Representing Power in Ancient Inner Asia: Legitimacy, Transmission, and the Sacred*, ed. Isabelle Charleux et al. (Bellingham: Western Washington University, 2010), 271-79.

22. On the Nurhaci's "just war" and the role of the "Seven Great Grievances" as his key political manifesto, see Nicola Di Cosmo, "La 'guerra giusta' nella conquista mancese della Cina," *Nuova Rivista Storica* 93, no. 2 (2009): 449-76.

23. For the complete text of the "Seven Grievances," see *MBRT*, 1:86–89.

24. Friedrich A. Bischoff, "On the Chinese Version of Some Manchu Imperial Titles," *Acta Orientalia Academiae Scientiarum Hungaricae* 51, no. 1–2 (1998): 55–61, 59.

25. Giovanni Stary, "From 'Clan-Rule' to 'Khan-Rule': Some Considerations About the Relations Between Nurhaci and Šurhaci," *Central Asiatic Journal* 58, no. 1–2 (2015): 149–54.

26. Hidehiro Okada, "The Yüan Imperial Seal in the Manchu Hands: The Source of the Ch'ing Legitimacy," in *Altaic Religious Beliefs and Practices: Proceedings of the 33d Meeting of the Permanent International Altaistic Conference, Budapest June 24-29 1990*, ed. Géza Bethlenfalvy et al. (Budapest: Research Group for Altaic Studies, Hungarian Academy of Sciences, 1992), 267–70.

27. Nicola Di Cosmo, "Military Aspects of the Manchu Wars Against the Caqars," in *Inner Asian Warfare (500-1800)*, ed. Nicola Di Cosmo (Leiden: Brill, 2002), 337–67.

28. On this issue, see Nicola Di Cosmo, "From Alliance to Tutelage: A Historical Analysis of Manchu-Mongol Relations Before the Qing Conquest," *Frontiers of Chinese History* 7, no. 2 (2012): 175–97.

29. Johan Elverskog, *Our Great Qing: The Mongols, Buddhism, and the State in Late Imperial China* (Honolulu: University of Hawai'i Press, 2006), 17–27.

30. *MBRT*, 1:28; *JMZD*, 1:58

FOUR

The Living Image of the People

JASON FRANK

THE TRANSITION FROM ROYAL to popular sovereignty during the Age of Democratic Revolutions (1776–1848) entailed not only the reorganization of institutions of governance and theories of political legitimacy but also a dramatic transformation in the iconography of political power and rule.[1] Monarchism, especially the absolutist form it took in the seventeenth and eighteenth centuries, had a well-developed visual regime of power that centered on the body of the king and that helped enact and sustain an external sovereign authority over beholden subjects. This form drew on and extended the medieval symbolism canonically examined by Ernst Kantorowicz in *The King's Two Bodies*, wherein the sacred and eternal *corpus mysticum* endowed the living mortal body of the king with political-theological vitality and significance.[2] The replacement of the personal and external rule of the king with the impersonal and immanent self-rule of the people posed representational difficulties not only of institutionalization and law but of visualization and form. Monarchical divine right and popular sovereignty were embedded within two different cosmologies, and the revolutionary emergence of the people as the legitimate ground of public authority—what Eric Santner, echoing both Kantorowicz and Sheldon Wolin, has described as "the epochal shift from the King's Two Bodies to the People's Two Bodies"— created the need for entirely "new images and mythologies of the collectivity."[3] How to image and envision the people and their authorizing will is an aesthetic-political problem that haunts modern democratic theory, although it is usually overshadowed by democratic theory's preoccupation with the principles, norms, and procedures legitimizing democratic rule. It is a problem that recent studies of popular constituent power and the paradoxes of peoplehood have brought into view but not yet fully explored.[4]

Edmund Morgan states one of the problems of the people's image and form succinctly in his influential history of popular sovereignty in the Anglophone seventeenth and eighteenth centuries. "The sovereignty of the people," he writes,

> is a much more complicated, one might say more fictional[,] fiction than the divine right of kings. A king, however dubious his divinity might seem, did not have to be imagined. He was a visible presence, wearing his crown and carrying his scepter. The people, on the other hand, are never visible as such. Before we ascribe sovereignty to the people, we have to imagine that there is such a thing, something we personify as though it were a single body, capable of thinking, of acting, of making decisions and carrying them out, something quite apart from government, and able to alter or remove a government at will, a collective entity more powerful and less fallible than a king or than any individual within it or than any group of individuals it singles out to govern it.[5]

While we might question whether the people must be personified in the way Morgan suggests in order to act (a point I return to below), he does helpfully draw attention to how the emergence of popular sovereignty in the Age of Democratic Revolutions relied on, elicited, sustained, and contested images of sovereign peoplehood. This essay examines some of the pressures of popular visualization that accompanied the victorious appearance of popular sovereignty at key moments of its emergence. I also look at how competing strategies of imaging popular will were implicated in different conceptions of popular agency and power. Images of peoplehood mediate the people's relationship to their own political empowerment—how they understand themselves to be a part of and act *as* a people. These images facilitate what Santner has described as "the metabolization of democratic authority" within the body politic.[6] I am particularly interested in the emergence of what I call "the living image of the people"—that is, the novel idea that collective assemblies, crowds, and mass protests were no longer understood merely as factious riots or seditious rebellions but instead as living incarnations of the people's authority, sublime expressions of the vitality and significance of popular will. In pursuing this argument, I do not intend to uncritically return to the hoary revolutionary myth of the direct expression of a unified and sacred popular voice, or its contemporary echoes in neo-Jacobin theories of popular will.[7] It is a mistake to see crowds, assemblies, and mobs as direct expressions of such sovereignty—they remain an image and potent political representation . . . but a living one. Understanding the historically specific mechanisms of their claims of popular representation helps make sense of the poetic condensations of such events, how, for example, a numerical minority of individuals physically gathered in a public space—whether it is called Tahrir, Zucotti, or Taksim—can be understood to speak and act on behalf of a superior but forever disembodied entity called the people. "In representation," as Carl Schmitt provocatively writes of such moments, the "invisible" becomes publicly "visible," and a "higher type of being comes into concrete appearance."[8] Schmitt's Catholic symbolism called on such moments to secure the transcendental authority of the state; the people's living image exposes a gap in that authority: it does not express a unitary presence of popular will so much as a surplus of immanence.

Alongside most democratic theory, contemporary social science has typically neglected these questions as well, hoping to avoid what Jon Elster describes as the dangerous sins of organicism, holism, functionalism, and teleology.[9] Some social scientists and historians, however, such as Charles Tilly and William Sewell, have traced the dramatic transformation in the repertoires and understanding of crowd actions during the eighteenth and nineteenth centuries, wherein the charismatic and extralegal authority that had been located in the king's body is transmitted through the living image of the people to mass assemblies and collectivities and through them made visible to the people themselves.[10] Sewell, for example, argues that the French Revolution's "act of epoch-making cultural creativity occurred in a moment of ecstatic discovery: the taking of the Bastille, which had begun as an act of defense against the king's aggression, revealed itself in the days that followed as a concrete, unmediated, and sublime instance of the people expressing its sovereign will."[11] The idea that popular assemblies and gatherings were manifestations of the people's voice assumes a distinctly modern and democratic form in this period, as does the related idea that this living manifestation is necessary for the people to apprehend themselves as a people, as a collective agent, a new heroic actor on the stage of history. A. V.

Lunacharsky, the "People's Commissar for Education" in the wake of the Russian Revolution, once wrote, "in order for the masses to make themselves felt, they must outwardly manifest themselves, and this is possible only when, to use Robespierre's phrase, they are their own spectacle."[12] The people must see themselves assembled, in other words, in order to feel their power, and this declaration of the vitalizing power of popular self-regard resonated widely among radical republicans, democrats, and socialists in the Age of Democratic Revolutions. Despite the common association of the people's living image with the fascist political aesthetics of mass assembly and state-orchestrated spectacles of domination—an association that works as a powerful obstacle to democratic theory's investigation of these questions—Lunacharsky's declaration continues to resonate in contemporary politics and deserves to be taken more seriously.[13] It challenges the familiar stories democratic theorists often tell themselves about the modern rejection of political aesthetics as antithetical to democratic politics.

Here are the basic outlines of that familiar story. The revolutionary rejection of monarchy during the seventeenth and eighteenth centuries corresponded with a concomitant rejection of mystifying pomp and ritualized authority, which, as Catharine Macaulay wrote in her refutation of Edmund Burke's *Reflections on the Revolution in France*, "blinded the people with the splendor of dazzling images."[14] The ancien régime, these republicans argued, relied for its authority on "the imposing glare of external magnificence to dazzle and so to awe the subjects into submission."[15] This powerful association of royal sovereignty with an illegitimate theater of power has shaped the stories that democratic theorists—from Thomas Paine to Jürgen Habermas—often tell about the progressive movement from heteronomous royalism to autonomous democracy. According to Habermas's influential formalization of this historical transformation, under feudal monarchies publicity and public representation were performances of authority on the part of the monarch and nobility: it was representation not *for* but rather *before* the people. Feudal authority's multiple public performances—coronation ceremonies, military parades, public feasts and celebrations—depended on the reverential consumption of these performances by an essentially passive *publicum*.[16] The emerging democratic authority of public opinion in the eighteenth century, by contrast, privileged epistemic transparency and consensus over dazzling aesthetic display as the basis of legitimacy. "Spectacle," in short, was replaced by "discourse."[17] In a democracy, contemporary democratic theorists tell us, the people are a deliberative "public," not a plebiscitary "audience."[18] The democratic age was supposed to stop the nonsense, transform subjects bedazzled by the spectacles of power into free and equal ratio-critical citizens capable of deliberating over political power's proper exercise and extent. Democracy, we are told, "has been disposed to eschew aesthetic devices as instruments of its politics."[19]

These tales of democratic disenchantment obscure the persistence of political aesthetics during the Age of Democratic Revolutions while also condemning political aesthetics as necessarily antithetical to democratic norms.[20] Maurice Agulhon, one of the greatest historians of the images and symbols of popular sovereignty and revolution, urges readers to reconsider "a common assumption that, in effect, symbolic language and imagery is most strongly linked to the politics of traditional societies, and must necessarily be weaker when politics are self-consciously modern, rational, secular, and conducted by enlightened rulers and citizens."[21] "For many men of the last century," he continues, "part of the logic of liberalism, rationalism and secularism involved the elimination or reduction of figurative symbols, the 'rattles' of power, in favor of simple politics, with a language of reason and common sense—a relegation of the sacred and the mystical to private life, well hidden."[22] Political theory has long been preoccupied with what Leo Strauss called the "theologico-political predicament," but it has only rarely taken up the parallel problem of political iconography, liturgy, and form, considering such questions to be, in Richard Rorty's words, no longer "salient" to the practical problems of our shared political life.[23] This essay—a brief historiographical survey with theoretical intent—offers a challenge to that logic and is part of a broader project to reexamine and reevaluate the interrelated terms of democracy's historical and normative disavowal of political aesthetics and to restore an appreciation of political aesthetics— what the editors of this volume describe in the introduction as the scaffolding of popular sovereignty—to contemporary democratic theory.[24]

I

The frontispiece to *Leviathan* is early modern political theory's most iconic attempt to visualize the incorporation of the multitude's dispersed power into the unified representation of the sovereign state; it is a visual condensation of the central arguments of Thomas Hobbes's great work (figure 4.1). We know that Hobbes carefully directed Abraham Bosse's design of the frontispiece from exile in Paris and that Bosse drew on long-established visual repertoires of royal portraiture in its design, as well as on Giuseppe Arcimboldo's influential compositional innovations, which revealed bodies and forms to be assembled from other bodies and forms.[25] These aesthetic innovations were vital for depicting a key aspect of Hobbes's argument: namely, that as an actor and representative, the sovereign's body is composed of the body of all contracting subjects and, conversely, that these subjects only exist as a unified collectivity—a people, properly understood—insofar as they are represented and cohered—produced—through their recognition of the sovereign's authority over them. "A multitude of men," Hobbes writes, "are made One Person, when they are by one man, or one Person, Represented . . . for it is the Unity of the Representer, not the Unity of the Represented, that maketh the Person One. . . . Unity cannot otherwise be understood in Multitude."[26] The frontispiece dramatizes Hobbes's epic theoretical construction of a "mortal god," a "visible power to keep [contracting parties] in awe," and a unifying and productive representation through which the multitude is converted into a single authorizing people capable of acting *as* a people through the delegated acts of their sovereign representative.[27] "The sovereign," as Hobbes writes, "represents the entire body of the State, encloses in himself all strength and all virtue, and possesses a power like the head over each member of the body."[28] Before Hobbes's preface commands his audience to read themselves into subjection, his frontispiece performs sovereign power's reliance on its own visibility to command the direction of the subjects' gaze.[29] Indeed, it suggests that the direction of the gaze is importantly constitutive of *Leviathan's* entire theory of subjection. The dynamic interplay and circulation of gazes between sovereign, viewer, and enthralled subjects performs the *Leviathan's* visual magic of subjection—for there can be no "Peace without subjection"—wherein the sovereign power is produced by the very subjects who take shape through their shared visual orientation.[30]

However paradigmatically modern Hobbes's great text is taken to be, it remains deeply embedded within the iconography of power associated with royal sovereignty. The care that Hobbes bestowed on the frontispiece, not only of the *Leviathan* but also of earlier texts like *De Cive* and his translation of Thucydides's *History of the Peloponnesian War*, mirrors the care shown by Tudor and Stuart kings and queens in crafting their own public image and

FIGURE 4.1 Frontispiece to Thomas Hobbes's *Leviathan* (London, 1651). Rare Book Collection, Cornell University Library, Ithaca, NY

attending to the close relationship between popular visuality and political power. "Throughout the early modern period," Kevin Sharpe writes, "image was central to the exercise of authority."[31] We need only think of the preoccupation with the theatricality of power in Elizabethan drama—Prospero's spellbinding spectacles—or in early modern political theory—Machiavelli's glorious acts of public cruelty—to provisionally verify such a claim. One illuminating background context for understanding the political-aesthetic intervention of *Leviathan*'s frontispiece is what Sharpe calls the "image wars" of the English Civil War.[32] As republicans and parliamentarians struggled against the power of king and court during the 1640s, they also confronted a deeply ingrained iconography of rule that supported and sustained, mystified and sacralized, that power, an iconography that "centered on the royal body and the representation of the royal body as the site of sacred kingship."[33] The sacred authority of the king as expressed in political rituals and religious ceremony, legal and theological doctrines, and literature and drama was organized around the visual appearance of the king's body and personality. According to Sharpe, it was Henry VIII who more than any previous king had "made the person and personality of the monarch more important than ever and affective relations with subjects more important than administrative procedures in establishing royal authority."[34] Elizabeth I continued Henry's effort to rely on carefully crafted symbolism and personal image to represent the sanctity of majesty and to portray herself as representative of the entire nation. "We princes," Elizabeth declared in 1586, "are set on stages in the sight and view of all the world."[35] Elizabeth's body became a "synecdoche for the body of the entire commonwealth," David Howarth writes, and Elizabeth "knew as well as any Medici, Hapsburg, or Valois the truth of Vitruvius' adage that royal spectacles had to be cast in such a way as to please the eye of the people."[36]

In the years leading up to the English Civil War, Charles I more than his immediate predecessors continued Henry VIII's and Elizabeth's preoccupation with ritual and symbolism that worked to sanctify the royal body and cohere the nation (figure 4.2), but the veils of opulent majesty were also being stripped away in the political debates of these years, to the point that "the Civil War, still more the regicide, was made possible only by the long process of demystification which had rendered monarchy a human condition and the monarch a man."[37] This corrosive process of demystification was a prominent theme in Shakespeare's royal tragedies. In *Richard II*, for example, Richard proclaims,

> Not all the water in the rough rude sea
> Can wash the balm off from an anointed king;
> The breath of worldly men cannot depose
> The deputy elected by the Lord.

But he soon concludes:

> Cover your heads and mock not flesh and blood
> With solemn reverence: throw away respect,
> Tradition, form and ceremonious duty,
> For you have but mistook me all this while:
> I live with bread like you, feel want,
> Taste grief, need friends: subjected thus,
> How can you say to me, I am a king?[38]

What can be more desacralizing of royal sovereignty, what de-coronation ceremony more visually astounding, than cutting off the head of the king? Even in death, however, the cultural authority of Charles's visual presence continued to resonate as he was converted by death into a martyr and Christ figure in widely disseminated books, prints, medals, and coins, which began circulating the day of his execution in the *Eikon Basilike* (Icon of the King), the purported account of his life and final days (figure 4.3). "With one stroke of the axe," as Cathy Gere writes in her essay in this volume, "the tyrant in the dock assumed a crown of thorns." While republicans and parliamentarians had won the Civil War politically and militarily, and made great inroads ideologically, they struggled against the persistence of a visual political culture that focused authority on the body of the king even in his death. "The execution of Charles I," Sharpe writes, "and still more the abolition of monarchy, necessitated not only a new constitution and government, but a different style and image, an entirely new form of visual representation, and, beyond that, a new aesthetic. When royal words and verbal forms such as proclamations and declarations might be appropriated and recast as texts of the republic, the visual images of authority, focusing as they had on the dynastic portrait, offered no obvious model for the commonwealth." Ac-

FIGURE 4.2 *Charles I (1600–1649), in Three Positions*, by Sir Anthony Van Dyck. Oil on canvas, 1635. The Royal Collection, London

cording to Sharpe, "the failure of the English Commonwealth is related to this failure of its iconography of power."[39]

There are many explanations for the Commonwealth's failure to provide a resonant and authoritative counterimage of popular—or at least parliamentary— sovereignty, or to visualize a body politic no longer cohered by the physical and sacred body of the king. The first and perhaps most serious obstacle to the development of a republican iconography of popular rule in the wake of the English Civil War was the congenital Protestant iconoclasm that animated so much antiroyal sentiment in the 1640s, and that continued to characterize radical forms of republican politics in the following century. Milton's *Eikonoklast*, a posthumous justification for the execution of Charles I and a pro-parliamentary response to the *Eikon Basilike*, offers the

FIGURE 4.3 Allegorical frontispiece to *Eikon Basilike*, by William Marshall (London, 1649). Special Collections, Cambridge University Library, Cambridge

most elaborate articulation of the need to crush the monarchy by also destroying the fetishized images and icons that sustain it; it offers an important chapter in the tangled modern history of popular revolutions with iconoclastic discourse.[40] The utilitarian strain of English republicanism, and its war against the decadent and corrupt pomp and luxury of royalism, also played an important role in the ideological struggle of the Civil War. Parliament had revealingly passed legislation removing the royal arms from all public places, attempting to cleanse the public realm of the iconography of royal power, again setting precedents for popular revolutions to come. Republicans also worried, however, about the considerable difficulties of disenthralling an idolatrous people from the ingrained spectacles of royalty. In *The Case of Commonwealth*, the republican propagandist Marchamont Needham lamented that "our former education under monarchy" had "rendered the people admirers of the pomp of tyranny and thus enemies to that freedom which hath been so dearly purchased."[41] Republicans worried that an "inconstant, irrational, and Image-doting rabble's" craving for images and sensory enthrallment would undo the gains of freedom and weaken the authority of the Commonwealth. "Like a credulous and hapless herd," Milton wrote, republicans were worried for a people "begott'n to servility, and inchanted with these popular institutes of Tyranny, subscrib'd with a new device of the Kings Picture at his praiers, hold out both thir eares with such delight and ravishment to be stigmatiz'd and board through in witness of thir own voluntary and beloved baseness."[42]

In addition to the ideological oppositions and the iconoclasm of the republican revolutionaries was the basic compositional difficulty of developing an image of popular republicanism that would not fall back on the visual repertoires of royal majesty associated with the singularity of the king's glorious body. Sharpe's enormous study of the image wars of the 1640s identifies only two efforts to visually depict the newfound popular authority of the Commonwealth, one a heavenly depiction of shaking hands evoking the contractual authority said to underwrite and legitimate the Commonwealth, and the other a portrait of the sitting Parliament. He judges neither effort a success in visualizing a headless republic freed from the unifying corporeal representation of the king. The persistence of the centered and sanctified authority of the royal body is demonstrated not only by the popular and resonant royal iconography of the martyred king but also by how quickly this personalist iconography returned, albeit in a modified republican plain style, once the Commonwealth came to an end and Cromwell's Protectorate was established. The iconography of Cromwell's personal power demonstrated, in Sharpe's words, "the failure of the republic to free itself of the cult of a single person."[43] Dramaturgical and pictorial conventions were powerful obstacles to envisioning a collective historical agent, the anonymous or impersonal heroism of the people.

This returns us to Hobbes's frontispiece. Political theorists have sometimes speculated about whether the face of the sovereign is modeled on Charles, Cromwell, or even Hobbes himself. The argument of *Leviathan*, after all, works to legitimate the rule of *any* power capable of maintaining order and securing peace, and by 1651 Hobbes's declared royalism was a lost cause. It is significant that Hobbes described *Leviathan* not only as a book that "fights on behalf of all kings" but also "all those who under whatever name bear the rights of kings."[44] However, the "image wars" context of the 1640s directs us away from the head of the sovereign and toward the body. Bosse, under Hobbes's direction, can be seen to be navigating the very visual dilemmas faced by the Commonwealth after the king's execution in 1649, but with greater compositional skill and aesthetic success. *Leviathan*'s frontispiece can be understood as a transitional object in the iconographic movement from royal to popular sovereignty. The frontispiece coheres the body of the people in the body of the sovereign, but it does not break dramatically from the iconography that sacralizes the royal body in doing so. In giving the body form through the people it simultaneously coheres, in forming the body entirely of the unified mass of other bodies, it also breaks from the visual mechanisms of the traditional royal synecdoche. If the visual metaphor of the body politic had traditionally worked, as Bruno Latour writes, to "fasten poor assemblies of humans to the solid reality of nature," to simultaneously allow the political community to be seen as a unity and to naturalize that unity,[45] *Leviathan*'s frontispiece makes an artificial assemblage of this metaphor—indeed, it dramatizes its artificiality—but without abandoning the inherited iconic political authority Sharpe and other historians have traced in their treatments of the aesthetics of royal power. The frontispiece reunifies the sovereign body riven by the Civil War, wherein, as Kantorowicz writes, Parliament, "in the name and by the authority of Charles I, King body politic," summoned "the armies which were to fight the same Charles I, king body natural."[46] If Charles I and his royalist supporters insisted on the inseparable identity of the mystical and corporeal body of the King, and Parliament divided the body politic against the king's mortal body, and pitted King against king, *Leviathan*'s frontispiece visually demonstrated them to be necessarily interdependent, each a condition of the other's possibility, and it suggested that this unity could only be brought about through a theory of political representation that was also what Horst Brederkamp has called a "picture-theory of politics": "There has been no philosopher or theorist of state before or since," Bredekamp writes, "who so emphatically pursued visual strategies as core political theory."[47]

II

Visual strategies were central to monarchical authority, and Charles was not the only mid-seventeenth-century spokesman for the sanctity of the royal flesh. Across the Channel, where he and his court sat in exile, the Sun King was developing the most elaborate and visually opulent articulation of the absolutist ideal (figure 4.4).[48] "As we are to our people," Louis proclaimed, so "our people are to us. The nation does not make a body in France; it resides entirely in the person of the king."[49] Or more famously: "L'État c'est moi." Robespierre would reverse this formulation's trajectory of authorization at the end of the next century, even while maintaining Louis's insistence on sanctified political embodiment, when he proclaimed on the floor of the National Convention: "I am neither the courtier, nor the moderator, nor the defender of the people: I am the people myself!"[50] The political theology of sacred kingship was more deeply established in seventeenth-century France than in England, and also more central to its discourses of democratic revolution after 1789. As Burke knew well, the revolutionary struggle against the ancien régime targeted this dense and interconnected network of ecclesiastical and civil authority, just as the counterrevolution sought to sustain or restore its shattered integrity. In his study of the Revolution's reliance on the metaphorics of the body politic, Antoine de Baecque argues that even more than in the English context, the "defeat of the body of the king represents a major caesura or gap in the French system of political representation"[51] just as the regicide marked the end of declared republican unity. The political theology centered on the ordering sovereign body of the king was destroyed with the beheading of Louis XVI, and the consequences reverberated in French political culture through the following centuries. The revolutionary emergence of the people was a more traumatic psychic event in France partly because it was portrayed as a necessary sacrifice enabling the political emergence of the autonomous French nation. "Louis must die because the *patrie* must live," as Robespierre famously declared.[52] The sacrificial structure of revolutionary democracy in France has been analyzed by political theorists as diverse as Georges Bataille and Michael Walzer, René Girard and Hannah Arendt, with some theorists affirming its structural necessity in the transition to constitutional republicanism and others lamenting its mythic investments in a dangerous political theology.[53] It has been familiarly portrayed "as the ritualistic founding act of a new social order, attributing to Louis the unusual sacred status of a sacrificial victim who possesses the supernatural ability to purify and regenerate the nation through his own death," as Susan Dunn writes in her study of the symbolism of regicide in French political thought over two centuries. "Regicide was regarded as the essential founding act and founding myth of the new French nation."[54] The revolutionaries did not simply want to destroy the mortal body natural and preserve the immortal body politic—as the English Parliament had done it its claim on behalf of the King against the king—but to destroy both simultaneously and replace it with an entirely new body politic of the independent and sovereign French people.

In his analysis of the trial and execution of Louis XVI, Michael Walzer examines the operation of this sacrificial logic in the trial and the broader public debate it engendered, and he defends the king's execution as a necessary step in the political and symbolic transition from royal to popular sovereignty. "The monarchy is not a king," as Saint Just would proclaim, "but is itself a crime."[55] According to Walzer, the French people required the sublime spectacle of the king's public beheading in order for the authorizing symbolism and political theology supporting the monarchy to be effectively shattered. "The ceremonies make the decisiveness," he writes. "Without the public acting out of revolutionary principles, not merely in front of the nation, but in ways that involve and implicate the nation, those principles remain a party creed, the revolution no more than a seizure of power."[56] Walzer's argument is more than a contextualized reiteration of what Arendt once described as "the age-old yet still current notions of the dictating violence of all beginnings," or the ancient idea that "whatever brotherhood human beings may be capable of has grown out of fratricide, whatever political organization men may have achieved has its origin in crime."[57] It is not only founding violence or the breach in established law that Walzer emphasizes in his interpretation of the king's trial but rather that the subsequent terrible spectacle of the regicide performed "the symbolic disenchantment of the realm as well as the establishment of a secular republic."[58] The king was killed not only as a "justiciable individual," in Walzer's words, accused of a crime (treason) but also as a sanctified symbol of royal sovereignty. For Walzer's provocatively extralegal political analysis, the spectacular beheading of Louis, the symbolic center of sacred kinship, was necessary for the more secure establishment of secular law in a republican

FIGURE 4.4 *Equestrian Portrait of Louis XIV (1638–1715) Crowned by Victory*, by Pierre Mignard. Oil on canvas, c. 1692. Chateau de Versailles, France

constitutional regime. In order for the new scaffolding of popular sovereignty to be erected, the old scaffolding had to be spectacularly destroyed.

It is a compelling argument, but as the revolutionary language surrounding the king's execution makes clear, the public beheading of the king should not be understood as an instance of secular disenchantment, and to this extent the secularization thesis that frames Walzer's argument is misleading: the execution marked the transference of sacred sovereignty, not its overcoming, from the destroyed body of the king to the living body of the sovereign people.[59] The familiar narrative of democratic disenchantment obscures the emergence of another political theology with an alternative set of political institutions and laws, as well as an alternative scaffolding of competing liturgies and iconographies, now centered on the sublime authority of the people's sovereign will. As with the iconoclasm of the English Civil War, in order to clear the way for the emergence of this newly sanctified source of sovereign power, the revolutionaries set about destroying not only the body of the king but also the enchanted visual tokens of kingship. "The revolutionaries had to deface, disqualify, and dispel the effigy of the sovereign by all means," Dario Gamboni writes, "including the beheading of the actual king, in order to destroy the symbolic order of the ancient regime."[60] The revolutionaries did not only present the severed head of the king to the exuberant crowds at the Place de la Révolution (figure 4.5), they melted down the king's scepter and crown, pressed the metals, and disseminated them as republican coins. Nobody grasped the political importance of this radical revolutionary iconoclasm—this "conquering empire of light and reason" and its destruction of "pleasing illusions" and the "decent drapery of life"—more clearly than Burke in his *Reflections on the Revolution in France*, the book that more than any other set the stage for subsequent counterrevolutionary calls for political-theological restoration.[61]

As with the English Civil War, the iconoclasm of the French Revolution was generated by powerful ideological forces, although forces more indebted to republicanism and the *philosophes* of the French Enlightenment than to radical Protestantism. French republicans, like their English counterparts, as Joan Landes writes, "generally distrusted the seductive quality of the image which they linked to the spectacular ceremonial culture of the old regime."[62] In eighteenth-century France, the republican critique of royal pomp and splendor—what Barbara Stafford has called the "republican discourse

FIGURE 4.5 *Fin Tragique de Louis XVI, exécuté le 21 janvier 1793 sur la place Louis XV, dite place de la Révolution*. Signed in the plate, *lower left and right*: "Dessiné d'après nature par Fious / Gravé par Sarcifu." Waddesdon, The Rothschild Collection (The National Trust)

of graphic despotism"[63]—was philosophically enhanced by empiricism, materialism, and the eighteenth-century conceptions of public opinion and deliberative discourse that Habermas makes so central to his story in *The Structural Transformation of the Bourgeois Public Sphere*. Condorcet, for example, had associated images with a more primitive and noncognitive form of human communication and writing with "higher processes of intellection."[64] Images seduced the passions, texts enlightened the mind; images elicited enthusiastic mobs or idolatrous throngs, texts circulated among a deliberative ratio-critical public. Expressing this confident empirical realism, the republican moralist Jean-Baptiste Salaville demanded that "the people will have to free themselves of the old allegories, and be accustomed to seeing in a statue only stone, and in an image only canvas and colors."[65]

While such iconoclasm animated the thinking of many French republicans, and some argued, in Lynn Hunt's words, that "a people with access to print and public discussion needed no icons,"[66] there was arguably an even more pronounced effort to transform passive royal subjects into active republican citizens through an education of the senses that involved immersing citizens-to-be in a radically reformed visual culture, especially as the Revolution radicalized under the Convention from 1792 to 1794. Sophie Wahnich has written that "we might consider the entirety of revolutionary political work as aiming to consolidate the principles declared in 1789 and 1793, and to make them operate as unreflecting prejudices, in other words to take them out of the possible sphere of discussion."[67] The Revolution, the Convention declared, "must create in man, as far as moral issues are concerned, a rapid instinct that will lead him to do good and avoid ill without the support of reasoning."[68] While "ridiculous hieroglyphs of the blazon are no longer for us [revolutionaries] anything more than historical objects," the Abbé Grégoire proclaimed in 1794, "when rebuilding a government anew, everything must be republicanized. The legislator who fails to recognize the importance of the language of signs would be remiss; should he omit any opportunity to impress the senses, to awaken republican ideas. This way the soul is penetrated by ever reproduced objects; and this composition, this set of principles, facts and emblems that ceaselessly retraces before the eyes of the citizen his rights and duties, shapes the republican mold that gives him national character and the bearing of a free man."[69]

As many historians of revolutionary France have documented, the visual culture of Revolution was a crucial part of this enterprise, and revolutionary iconoclasm was always entangled, if not entirely superseded, by revolutionary iconophilia. The revolutionary "veneration of the image and the destruction of the image," as Klaus Herding writes, "were very closely connected."[70] "The Revolution," Marie-Hélène Huet similarly concludes, "had a paradoxical relationship to images."[71] Among the most important questions facing leaders of the Revolution's projects of aesthetic and political reform, most notably Jacques-Louis David, was how to replace the mysticism of royal iconography, with its emphasis on the sacred flesh of the king and the cohering power of his body, with that of the people themselves, who had been proclaimed in Article 3 of the Declaration of the Rights of Man and Citizen "the source of all sovereignty": "No body, no individual can exercise authority that does not explicitly proceed from it." The transfer of sacred authority from the personified body of the king to the independent but impersonal and anonymous will of the people created an aesthetic-political dilemma for David and others. A central controversy and source of conflict was not only how to represent or institutionally embody that will but whether any representation could adequately or legitimately contain it.[72] This mistrust of representation distinguishes French revolutionary experience from the English revolutions that came before it. "French Revolutionaries did not just seek another representation of authority, a replacement for the king," as Hunt writes, "but rather came to question the very act of representation itself." During the Revolution, and especially under the Convention, "representation in all of its forms came under scrutiny."[73] François Furet first emphasized the extent to which the identity of the people was at "the heart of so many of the political contests in the vacuum opened up by the collapse of the *ancien régime*." "Which group, which assembly, which meeting, which consensus is the depository of the people's word?" Furet asks. "It is around this deadly question that the modalities of action and the distribution of power organize themselves."[74] The revolutionary suspicion of representation, the radical Rousseauean preoccupation with the unrepresentability of popular will, is the central condition of what Huet calls the "discourse of the revolutionary sublime" and its contribution to revolutionary and sometimes quasi-mystical efforts to envision popular sovereignty.

Revolutionary struggles over the political and institutional representation of popular will and their aesthetic corollaries were more closely connected than most democratic theorists acknowledge, although this fact is widely recognized by historians of the Revolution. The Revolution, Furet writes, was a "political phenomenon that involved powerful new forms of political symbolization," and the struggles over these symbols—visual and otherwise—was a key currency of revolutionary politics. In a wide-ranging interview, Claude Lefort and Pierre Rosanvallon pursue this issue through a discussion of the connections between the political and aesthetic representation of popular will. In his democratic theory Lefort influentially argued that popular will is fundamentally unrepresentable in its totality, that modern democracy is defined by the disembodiment of power and the "empty space" opened up by the killing of the king. "The Legitimacy of power" in a democracy, he writes, "is based on the people; but the image of popular sovereignty is linked to the image of an empty place, impossible to occupy, such that those who exercise public authority can never claim to appropriate it. Democracy combines these two apparently contradictory principles: on the one hand, power emanates from the people; on the other, it is the power of nobody. And democracy thrives on this contradiction. Whenever the latter risks being resolved or is resolved, democracy is either close to destruction or already destroyed."[75] Rosanvallon notes that during the Revolution the question of the visual representation of the people was taken up with just this problem of "resolution." "The painters and the engravers were not quite able to represent the people," he argues, and "their artistic debates became entangled with debates among different political factions over who the people were and how their voice could be authoritatively represented."[76]

Under the Convention these disputes temporarily subsided—and were dangerously "resolved"—as a relatively stable visual depiction of popular will emerged in the figure of a giant Hercules wielding his club. The Hercules had long been a heroic figure of French royal sovereignty—the "Hercule Gaulois" – and became especially predominant during the absolutist reign of Louis XIV.[77] The Hercules, as the municipal authorities of Valenciennes proclaimed in 1680, was the perfect figure to "express the image of . . . MAJESTY. He is the strongest and most celebrated of all the fabled Heroes, who will represent without exaggeration and with the greatest truth the most valorous and triumphant of all the Monarchs of the world."[78] In this figure's radical democratic redeployment under the Convention, Hercules not only embodied the massive power and unity of the popular will—in this image he was defined against the hydra of federalism (figure 4.6) and against the proliferation of intermediate institutions celebrated by such figures as Montesquieu—but also depicted the immediacy of popular will and its close relationship to necessity and force as represented in his giant club. Hercules is obviously not a figure of persuasion or deliberation but of instinctive virtue, courage, and force. Hercules is the figure of a mobilized radical democracy against the established procedures of liberal constitutionalism. In her reading of this symbolism, Hunt writes that the figure of Hercules was a "representation that strained against its own representative status . . . [a] diminishing point of representation."[79]

David was a central figure in revolutionary debates over the visual depictions of popular will, and he was the leading proponent of the Convention's adoption of the new Hercules iconography.[80] In a speech delivered before the Convention in 1793, David quite explicitly addressed the revolutionary transfer of sacrality from king to people and the dilemmas of depicting this political-theological transference in art:

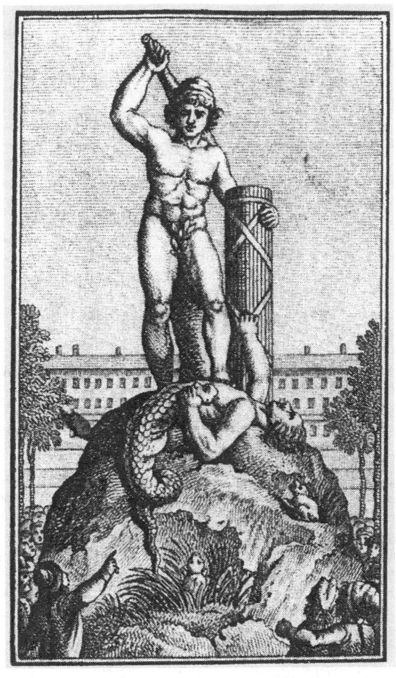

FIGURE 4.6 *The French People Overwhelming the Hydra of Federalism*, by Jacques-Louis David. Engraving, 1793. Musée Carnavalet, Paris. Photo by Lynn Hunt

Kings, not being able entirely to usurp the place of divinity in the temples, occupied the porticoes; they had their proud effigies placed there, no doubt so that the adoration of the people would linger with them before reaching the sanctuary. Accustomed to invading everything, they dared to dispute vows and incense with God Himself. You have turned upside down these insolent usurpers; they lie at this instant stretched out on the earth that they befouled with their crimes, objects of derision now to the populace finally cured of superstition. Citizens, let us perpetuate this triumph of reason over prejudice; let a monument be raised in the heart of the commune of Paris, not far from that of the very church they made their pantheon! Let us transmit to our descendants the first trophy raised by the sovereign people to mark its immortal victory over tyrants; may the truncated debris of their faces, confusedly heaped together, form a lasting monument to the glory of the people, and to the downfall of tyrants. . . . What I propose is to place this monument assembled from the piled-up rubble of those figures on the square of Pont Neuf and to mount above it the image of the giant people, the French people.[81]

David's proposal to erect a statue of Hercules as the symbol of the people's sovereignty on the rubble of the destroyed royal effigies taken from the porticos of Notre Dame expresses a common revolutionary fantasy that the shards of shattered royal sovereignty might be reassembled as the scaffolding of a new sovereignty, and it contributed to larger debates, especially among the Jacobins, over how the people could come to see their own power and natural virtue made manifest so they could live up to their own inner truth and capacity. "The radicals called on the people to look at themselves," Hunt writes, "to recognize themselves as central figures, to make their 'terrible cry resound in the halls of the Convention as well as the streets of Paris.' "[82] As Marx would later write in *The Poverty of Philosophy*, the people had to be made at once "authors and actors of their own drama,"[83] and these spectacles of democratic self-regard were important aspects of the emergence of this new collective actor on the stage of political history.

The fact that the Hercules was first erected during the Festival of Regeneration on August 10, 1793 raises other issues about the representation of popular will as inaugurated by the Revolution's radical political culture of festival and popular assembly, and in particular the expansive efforts to give aesthetic form to the radicals' most cherished self-understanding: the belief in their own Promethean powers, their constituent capacity to make the world anew, the central animating idea that, in Furet's words, "democratic politics had come to decide the fate of individuals and peoples," and that Rosanvallon calls "the radical project of a self-instituted society," a view of "politics as pure action, the unmediated expression of a directly perceptible will."[84] Rousseau's influence was everywhere in the debates over civic festivals and the great lawgiver's education of the popular will.[85] In his *Letter to D'Alembert*, Rousseau had contrasted the corrupt and alienated theatricality of the stage to the virtuous and authentic absorption of the peasant festival. In his *Government of Poland*, he had urged the Polish government to institute annual festivals commemorating the heroic sacrifice of the nation. And in the *Social Contract* the sovereign assemblies of the General Will are portrayed as sublime expressions of the people's inner virtue rather than spaces of political contention or common deliberation.[86] According to Mona Ozouf, in her study of the Revolution's festivals, "everyone dreamed of the revolutionary festival as a village festival without spectacle, enlarged to the dimensions of the entire nation."[87] The revolutionary festivals aimed for theatrical nontheatricality, an effort to make the people present to themselves, but purportedly without artifice and corrupting mediation, and through this revolutionary self-regard to instill into the senses and the heart of the people the civic myth and religion of their own popular constituent capacity. The people must see themselves assembled in order to feel their power, and Robespierre declared the "most magnificent of all spectacles is that of a great people assembled."[88] This spectacle of the people viewing themselves purportedly without mediation, without representation, was a powerful part of the resonant radical myth of the following century, the sublime myth of "revolutionary democracy."[89]

Michelet, the romantic worshiper of the sublime and rejuvenating vitality of popular will par excellence,[90] emphasized this heroically self-originating and constituent capacity in his *History of the French Revolution*, a book written during the revolutionary upheavals of 1848, when the discourse of the ineffable sublimity of the popular will reached its nineteenth-century apotheosis, partly due to the central political question of enfranchising the popular masses—which also raised the specter of "the social question"—but also due to the reappearance of a mobilized collective actor on the streets of Paris in February, May, and June. Looking back on the revolutionary festivals from the perspective of the upheavals of 1848, Michelet emphasized the radicals' effort to confront the intrinsic dangers of idolatry and reification in their representations of popular will. "It was objected," Michelet writes, "that a fixed simulacrum might remind the people of the Virgin and create another idolatry. . . . So a mobile, live and animated image was preferred. This image, changing with every festival could not become the object of superstitious adoration."[91] The Jacobins, in the words of Anaxagoras Chaumette, the elected president of the Commune and organizer of the Festival of Reason, aimed to replace "inanimate idols" of power with the "animated image" of the people through the sublime spectacle of orchestrated popular assemblies and festivals.[92]

The affirmation of the people's living image was reiterated by radical republicans against post-Thermidor efforts to make depictions of the people more allegorical, emblematic, and abstract—most obviously exemplified in the figure of Marianne—so that the people would become equated not with a living, acting, regenerative power but with the abstracted offices of the state and its authorized seals and legal symbolism. After Thermidor, as de Baecque writes, "the Revolution came to prefer the easily controllable, reassuring representation of a principle: the gentle figure of liberty."[93] This change in popular representation marked the transition from the people conceived as "actors of the narrative bound by their own adventure, to that of spectators of a body to be contemplated."[94] Marianne is the paradigmatic postrevolutionary example of what Jeffrey Schnapp describes as the "emblematic" mode of representing the sovereign people, symbolic allegories that emphasize defining principles or virtues over agency, and which he opposes to the "oceanic" mode of representing popular will, always "associated with moments of collective infusion within the framework of the political sublime."[95] In this transition we see alternative stagings for very different visions of democratic power.

The revolutionary fear of the people becoming a reification, a dead or inanimate idol, is reiterated in the "diffuse revolutionary populisms" of the nineteenth century and their commitment to the expressive and rejuvenating vitality of popular insurrection; Rosanvallon describes this discourse as the "poetry of the barricades."[96] Looking back on the revolutionary century from the Third Republic, Gustave Le Bon proclaimed it the "age of the crowd" and associated its politics with a politics of images: "crowds being only capable of thinking in images are only to be impressed by images. It is only images that terrify or attract them and become motives of action."[97]

Le Bon's reactionary view of the people's living image not only influenced the fascists, who mobilized it in their terrible seizures of power in the next century, but also the parliamentary democrats, who devised legal and procedural obstacles to what they conceived as the dangerous ascent of plebiscitary democracy.

Contemporary democratic theorists often seem to follow crowd theorists like Le Bon when they look back on the political catastrophes of the twentieth century and associate the politics of the people's living image with the new and dangerous styles of mass assembly and state-orchestrated spectacles of domination given fullest articulation in fascism. Such mass assemblies are understood as terrifying liturgies of a new "political religion," murderous efforts to reinvest the public realm with sublime significance.[98] In Lefort's words, the indeterminate "image of the people" associated with democracy's "empty space" is filled through the manifestation of this living image with the terrible visual fantasy of "the People-as-One."[99] In *On Revolution*, for example, Hannah Arendt portrays the French Revolution's crowds as the furthest thing from sublime instantiations of sovereign will; instead they are terrible manifestations of physical needs and compulsions that had hitherto remained hidden from the political space of appearances. "This multitude, appearing for the first time in broad daylight," Arendt writes, "was actually the multitude of the poor and the downtrodden, who every century before had hidden in darkness and in shame."[100] Arendt thought even less of the Revolution's festivals, which she described as "wretched and foredoomed substitutes for the constitution," substitutes that had moreover "failed utterly." The "ridiculousness of the enterprise," Arendt concludes, "was such that it must have been manifest to those who attended the initiating ceremonies as it was to later generations."[101]

Was the attempt to initiate and sustain a living image of the people so ridiculous—or worse, was it a grotesque anticipation of nationalist torchlight parades and state-orchestrated spectacles of domination? Many theorists of totalitarian democracy have thought so, but the revolutionary invocation of the people's living image should not be simply reduced to a dangerous effort to fill the empty space of power with the glorious body of the people or a wholesale rejection of political representation in the name of the direct expression of popular will. The living image of the people is not a unitary embodiment of the imminent "People-as-One" so much as the manifestation of the collective effort to burst the bounds of any formally authorized representation of sovereign voice. In these contexts, the assembled crowd inaugurates the people not as immanent presence but as surplus excrescence, revealing a surplus of democratic immanence and always less and more than the people in whose name they act.

In *Imagined Communities*, Benedict Anderson wrote that when we study the history of peoples we should not be primarily concerned with their "genuineness" or their "falsity" but rather with "the style in which they are imagined."[102] A particular style of imagining peoplehood is an unavoidable part of democratic theory, but one democratic theorists rarely explicitly engage. Confronting these questions helps us understand not only how a people is historically represented—who is included, their qualities and characteristics, their capacities for action—but also how individuals come to experience and feel themselves as a part of this mobilized and empowered collectivity in the first place. The people need such mediation to act as a people, even if their acts will also transcend the bounds of these mediating conditions. "Modern revolutions," Wolin writes, "involved the vast masses of human beings in action, not just fictionally as in the myth of popular sovereignty. More precisely, modern revolutions created the idea of collective action thereby contesting the monopoly on action previously enjoyed by kings, military leaders, aristocrats and prelates."[103] The living image of the people is an important part of the story of this transition in how we understand political action and collective political actors. Where the people's will is sovereign, such assemblies make available to the senses the agency, equality, and collective capacities of the people. At its heart is the question of how people come to experience themselves as a part of a sovereign power, how that authority is, again in Santner's terms, "metabolized." With democracy the people replaced the monarch, and "sovereignty was dispersed from the king's body to all bodies," Santner writes. "Suddenly every body bore political weight."[104]

As the crowds gathered in Tahrir Square in January and February 2011 they set up television monitors to watch themselves nightly on the evening news. It is not clear that this should be simply dismissed as ideological enthrallment to the spectacle, a revolution that must be televised. How we come to experience ourselves as free and equal parts of a collective entity capable of transformative action was a key question for theorists and actors of democracy at the time of its difficult emergence, and it is a problem left unresolved by appeals to formal democratic procedures, electoral representation, or public opinion polling. The living image of the people haunts the theory and practice of democracy in ways that we have yet to fully engage and understand. A closer examination of its history and its theory may help us see more clearly that there is no people beyond the people's appearance and act—and that the formation of a people is always both a political and an aesthetic problem. This is a useful reminder in a time when democratic theory proceeds largely without consideration of the demos and our most influential theories of collective action are premised on the impossibility of a collective actor.

Notes

I would like to thank Richard Bensel, Jodi Dean, Kevin Duong, Stefanos Geroulanos, Bonnie Honig, Alex Livingston, Davide Panagia, Camille Robcis, Kam Shapiro, and Sid Tarrow for their helpful and provocative comments on an earlier draft of this essay. I could not fully address all of their questions here, but the essay was improved by my attempt to do so.

1. R. R. Palmer, *The Age of Democratic Revolution* (Princeton: Princeton University Press, 1959).
2. Ernst H. Kantorowicz, *The King's Two Bodies: A Study in Medieval Political Theology* (Princeton: Princeton University Press, 1957).
3. Eric Santner, *The Royal Remains: The People's Two Bodies and the Endgame of Sovereignty* (Chicago: University of Chicago Press, 2011), xviii; Jeffrey T. Schnapp, "Mob Porn," in *Crowds*, ed. Jeffrey T. Schnapp and Mathew Tiews (Stanford: Stanford University Press, 2006), 1–45, 2. Clifford Geertz's classic work on the importance, and perhaps necessity, of "sacred centers" in cohering the symbolism of power, especially around the location of sovereignty, is directly relevant here. See his "Centers, Kings, and Charisma," in *Local Knowledge* (New York: Basic Books, 2000), 121–46. I am grateful to Richard Bensel for illuminating discussions of this issue.
4. See, e.g., Jason Frank, *Constituent Moments: Enacting the People in Postrevolutionary America* (Durham: Duke University Press, 2010); Bonnie Honig, "Between Decision and Deliberation: Political Paradox in Democratic Theory," *American Political Science Review* 101, no. 1 (2006): 1–17; and Sofia Nässtrom, "The Legitimacy of the People," *Political Theory* 35, no. 5 (2007): 624–58.
5. Edmund Morgan, *Inventing the People: The Rise of Popular Sovereignty in England and America* (New York: Norton, 1989), 153.
6. Santner, *Royal Remains*, 34.
7. See, e.g., Peter Hallward, "The Will of the People: Notes Towards a Dialectical Voluntarism," *Journal of Radical Philosophy* 155 (May/June 2009): 17–29.

8. Carl Schmitt, *Constitutional Theory*, trans. Jeffrey Seitzer (Durham: Duke University Press, 2008), 243.

9. Jon Elster, *Alexis de Tocqueville, The First Social Scientist* (Cambridge: Cambridge University Press, 2009), 4.

10. Charles Tilly, *Contentious Performances* (Cambridge: Cambridge University Press, 2008); William Sewell, "Historical Events as Transformation of Structures: Inventing Revolution at the Bastille," in *Logics of History: Social Theory and Social Transformation* (Chicago: University of Chicago Press, 2005), 225–70.

11. Sewell, "Historical Events," 236.

12. From "On Popular Festivals," originally published in the journal *Theatre Courier*, April 27–May 2, 1920, and reprinted in Vladimir Tolstoy, Irina Bibikova, and Catherine Cooke, eds., *Street Art of the Revolution: Festivals and Celebrations in Russia, 1918-33* (London: Thames & Hudson, 1990), 124.

13. On the fascist political aesthetics of mass assembly see George L. Mosse, *The Nationalization of the Masses* (New York: Fertig, 1975); and Simonetta Falasca-Zamponi, *Fascist Spectacle: The Aesthetics of Power in Mussolini's Italy* (Berkeley: University of California Press, 1997).

14. Catharine Macaulay, *Observations on the Reflections of the Right Hon. Edmund Burke, on the Revolution in France* (1790; Cambridge: Cambridge University Press, 2012), 39.

15. John Barrell, *Imagining the King's Death: Figurative Treason, Fantasies of Regicide 1793-1796* (Oxford: Oxford University Press, 2000), 15.

16. See Jürgen Habermas, *Structural Transformation of the Public Sphere: An Inquiry Into a Category of Bourgeois Society*, trans. Thomas Burger (Cambridge, MA: MIT Press, 1991), 8, 10.

17. Philip Rieff, "Aesthetic Functions in Modern Politics," *World Politics* 5, no. 4 (July 1953): 478–502, 480.

18. Nadia Urbinati, *Democracy Disfigured: Opinion, Truth, and the People* (Cambridge, MA: Harvard University Press, 2014), 171–227, 184.

19. Rieff, "Aesthetic Functions in Modern Politics," 480.

20. Claude Lefort once insightfully noted "the unavoidable—and no doubt ontological—difficulty democracy has in reading its own story," and democracy's failure to come to terms with the staging of its own sovereignty is a notable symptom of that difficulty. Lefort, *Democracy and Political Theory*, trans. David Macey (Minneapolis: University of Minnesota Press, 1988), 213–55, 255.

21. Maurice Agulhon, "Politics, Images, and Symbols in Post-Revolutionary France," in *Rites of Power: Symbolism, Ritual, and Politics Since the Middle Ages*, ed. Sean Wilentz (Philadelphia: University of Pennsylvania Press, 1985), 177–205, 187.

22. Ibid., 194.

23. Leo Strauss, *Spinoza's Critique of Religion*, trans. E. M. Sinclair (New York: Schocken, 1965), 1; Richard Rorty, *Contingency, Irony, and Solidarity* (Cambridge: Cambridge University Press, 1989). Rorty arguably returned to political theology in his later embrace of the civil religion of American exceptionalism in *Achieving Our Country: Leftist Thought in Twentieth-Century America* (Cambridge, MA: Harvard University Press, 1997).

24. There has been a growing call to reevaluate the role of political aesthetics in democratic theory. See esp. the essays collected in Nikolas Kompridis, ed., *The Aesthetic Turn in Political Thought* (London: Bloomsbury, 2014).

25. Horst Bredekamp, "Thomas Hobbes's Visual Strategies," in *The Cambridge Companion to Hobbes's Leviathan*, ed. Patricia Springborg (Cambridge: Cambridge University Press, 2007), 29–60; Dario Gomboni, "Composing the Body Politic: Composite Images and Political Representation, 1651–2004," in *Making Things Public: Atmospheres of Democracy*, ed. Bruno Latour and Peter Weibel (Cambridge, MA: MIT Press, 2005), 162–95; Noel Malcolm, "The Title Page of *Leviathan*, Seen in Curious Perspective," *Seventeenth Century* 13 (1998): 124–55; Christopher Pye, "The Sovereign, the Theater, and the Kingdome of Darknesse," *Representations* 8 (1984): 85–106.

26. Thomas Hobbes, *Leviathan* (1651; Cambridge: Cambridge University Press, 1991), 114.

27. Ibid., 88.

28. Ibid., 122.

29. See Pye, "The Sovereign, the Theater, and the Kingdome of Darknesse."

30. Hobbes, *Leviathan*, 119.

31. Kevin Sharpe, *Selling the Tudor Monarchy: Authority and Image in Sixteenth-Century England* (New Haven: Yale University Press, 2009), xxvi.

32. Kevin Sharpe, *Image Wars: Promoting Kings and Commonwealths in England, 1603–1660* (New Haven: Yale University Press, 2009).

33. Ibid., 230–66.

34. Ibid., 1.

35. Cited in Stephen Greenblatt, "Invisible Bullets: Renaissance Authority and Its Subversion," *Glyph* 8 (1981): 40–61.

36. David Howarth, *Images of Rule: Art and Politics in the English Renaissance, 1485–1649* (Berkeley: University of California Press, 1997), 3.

37. Sharpe, *Image Wars*, 436.

38. William Shakespeare, *Richard II* (1595; New York: Penguin, 1969), 110.

39. Sharpe, *Image Wars*, 426.

40. See Alain Besançon, *The Forbidden Image: An Intellectual History of Iconoclasm*, trans. Jane Marie Todd (Chicago: University of Chicago Press, 2009), and Norman Cohn, *The Pursuit of the Millennium* (New York: Oxford University Press, 1957).

41. Quoted in Sharpe, *Image Wars*, 445.

42. John Milton, *Eikonoklastes* [1649], in *The Complete Prose Works of John Milton*, ed. Don M. Wolfe et al. (New Haven: Yale University Press, 1953–82), 3:601.

43. Sharpe, *Image Wars*, 430.

44. Quoted in Quentin Skinner, *Visions of Politics*, vol. 3, *Hobbes and Civil Sciences* (Cambridge: Cambridge University Press, 2002), 16.

45. Latour, "From Realpolitik to Dingpolitik," in Latour and Weibel, *Making Things Public*, 14–41, 37.

46. Kantorowicz, *King's Two Bodies*, 21.

47. Bredekamp, "Thomas Hobbes's Visual Strategies," 30.

48. Jeffrey Merrick, "The Body Politics of French Absolutism," in *From the Royal to the Republican Body: Incorporating the Political in Seventeenth- and Eighteenth-Century France*, ed. Sara E. Melzer and Kathryn Norberg (Berkeley: University of California Press, 1998), 11–31.

49. Cited in Antoine de Baecque, *The Body Politic: Corporeal Metaphor in Revolutionary France, 1770–1800* (Stanford: Stanford University Press, 1997), 90.

50. Quoted in David P. Jordan, "The Robespierre Problem," in *Robespierre*, ed. Colin Hayden and William Doyle (Cambridge: Cambridge University Press, 2006), 17–34, 22.

51. Baecque, *Body Politic*, 29.

52. Maximilien Robespierre, speech of December 3, 1792, in *Regicide and Revolution: Speeches at the Trial of Louis XVI*, ed. Michael Walzer (New York: Columbia University Press, 1992), 138.

53. See Jesse Goldhammer, *The Headless Republic: Sacrificial Violence in Modern French Thought* (Ithaca: Cornell University Press, 2005).

54. Susan Dunn, *The Deaths of Louis XVI* (Princeton: Princeton University Press, 1994), 4.

55. Quoted in Walzer, *Regicide and Revolution*, 65.

56. Ibid., 88.

57. Hannah Arendt, *On Revolution* (New York: Penguin, 1965), 213, 20.

58. Walzer, *Regicide and Revolution*, 88.

59. On this point, see Dunn, *Deaths of Louis XVI*, 19.

60. Dario Gamboni, *The Destruction of Art: Iconoclasm and Vandalism Since the French Revolution* (London: Reaktion, 1997), 167.

61. Edmund Burke, *Reflections on the Revolution in France* (1791; Indianapolis, Ind.: Hackett, 1987), 67.

62. Joan B. Landes, *Visualizing the Nation: Gender, Representation, and Revolution in Eighteenth-Century France* (Ithaca: Cornell University Press, 2003), 27.

63. Barbara Stafford, *Artful Science: Enlightenment Entertainment and the Eclipse of Visual Education* (Cambridge, MA: MIT Press, 1994), 1.

64. Antoine-Nicholas de Condorcet, *Outlines of an Historical View of the Progress of the Human Mind* (1795; trans., Philadelphia, 1796), available at http://oll.libertyfund.org/titles/condorcet-outlines-of-an-historical-view-of-the-progress-of-the-human-mind.

65. Quoted in Landes, *Visualizing the Nation*, 28.

66. Lynn A. Hunt, *Politics, Culture, and Class in the French Revolution* (Berkeley: University of California Press, 1984), 91.

67. Sophie Wahnich, *In Defense of the Terror: Liberty or Death in the French Revolution* (New York: Verso, 2012), 76.

68. Quoted in ibid.

69. Quoted in Landes, *Visualizing the Nation*, 28.

70. Ibid., 56.

71. Marie Hélène Huet, *Mourning Glory: The Will of the French Revolution* (Philadelphia: University of Pennsylvania Press, 1997), 66.

72. Jon Cowans, *To Speak for the People: Public Opinion and the Problem of Legitimacy in the French Revolution* (New York: Routledge, 2001).

73. Hunt, *Politics, Culture, and Class*, 88.

74. François Furet, *Interpreting the French Revolution* (Cambridge: Cambridge University Press, 1981), 49.
75. Claude Lefort, *The Political Forms of Modern Society* (Cambridge, MA: MIT Press, 1986), 279.
76. Pierre Rosanvallon, "The Test of the Political: A Conversation with Claude Lefort," *Constellations* 19, no. 1 (2012): 4–15.
77. Rolf Reichardt, "The Heroic Deeds of the New Hercules: The Politicization of Popular Prints in the French Revolution," in *Symbols, Myths, and Images of the French Revolution*, ed. Ian Germani and Robin Swales (Winnipeg: Canadian Plains Research Center, 1998), 17–46, 38.
78. Ibid., 41.
79. Hunt, *Politics, Culture, and Class*, 99.
80. See esp. Warren Roberts, *Jacques Louis David, Revolutionary Artist* (Chapel Hill: University of North Carolina Press, 1989), 39–92.
81. Quoted in Baecque, *Body Politic*, 311.
82. Hunt *Politics, Culture, and Class*, 117.
83. Karl Marx, *The Poverty of Philosophy* (Beijing: Foreign Languages Press, 1966), 109.
84. Furet, *Interpreting the French Revolution*, 27; Pierre Rosanvallon, *Democratic Legitimacy*, trans. Arthur Goldhammer (Princeton: Princeton University Press, 2011), 125.
85. See Mona Ozouf, *Festivals and the French Revolution* (Cambridge, MA: Harvard University Press, 1991).
86. Jean-Jacques Rousseau, *Letter to M. D'Alembert on the Theatre*, trans. Allan Bloom (Ithaca: Cornell University Press, 1960), 125–26; Jean-Jacques Rousseau, *The Government of Poland*, trans. Willmoore Kendall (Indianapolis: Hackett, 1985), 19–26; Jean-Jacques Rousseau, *The Social Contract*, trans. Maurice Cranston (New York: Penguin, 1968), 73.
87. Ozouf, *Festivals and the French Revolution*, 42.
88. H. Morse Stephens, *The Principal Speeches of the Statesmen and Orators of the French Revolution, 1789-1795* (Oxford: Clarendon, 1892), 410.
89. Pierre Rosanvallon, "Revolutionary Democracy," in *Democracy Past and Future*, ed. Samuel Moyn (New York: Columbia University Press, 2006), 79–97.
90. Jules Michelet, *The People*, trans. John P. McKay (1846; Champagne-Urbana: University of Illinois Press, 1973), 18–19.
91. Quoted in Huet, *Mourning Glory*, 43.
92. Quoted in Landes, *Visualizing the Nation*, 29.
93. Baecque, *Body Politic*, 320.
94. Ibid.
95. Schnapp, "Mob Porn," 5.
96. Craig Calhoun, *The Roots of Radicalism* (Chicago: University of Chicago Press, 2012), 228–48; Rosanvallon, *Democratic Legitimacy*, 126.
97. Gustave Le Bon, *The Crowd* (1895; Atlanta: Cherokee Publishing, 1982), 54.
98. Emilio Gentile, *Politics as Religion* (Princeton: Princeton University Press, 2006).
99. Lefort, *Political Forms of Modern Society*, 304.
100. Arendt, *On Revolution*, 48.

101. Ibid., 100.
102. Benedict Anderson, *Imagined Communities* (London: Verso, 1983), 6.
103. Sheldon Wolin, "Transgression, Equality, Voice," in *Dēmokratia: A Conversation on Democracies, Ancient and Modern*, ed. Josiah Ober and Charles Hendrick (Princeton: Princeton University Press, 1996), 63–90, 68.
104. Santner, *Royal Remains*, 4.

PART II

COURTS

IN THE PEAK MOMENT OF PUCCINI'S *TURANDOT*, Princess Turandot orders that no one in Beijing shall sleep until she learns the name of the stranger who has answered the riddles she intended as guarantees of her celibacy and freedom. It is an expression of supreme sovereign power—but also, as we learn, of weakness. As everyone in the great capital stays awake, Calaf, the stranger whose royal identity is still concealed, sings to the Princess the following aria.

> No-one shall sleep!
> No-one shall sleep!
> You, too, oh Princess,
> In your cold room, watch the stars
> Trembling with love and hope!
> But my secret lies hidden within me,
> No-one shall discover my name!
>
> Oh no, I will only reveal it on your lips
> When daylight shines forth!

Everyone has been denied the bodily function of sleep because the ruler has simply ordered so, but Calaf reminds us that even the ruler shall not sleep. The words "in your cold room" should alert us that the entire scene is about bodies of royalty. Even the princess, late at night in her room in her palace, senses the drop in temperature (and Beijing can be very cold at night). All in all, she also has a human body that succumbs to nature. Calaf's own body is still the box where his true identity, itself identified with his royal blood, is kept, even when he is stripped of his kingdom and of the trappings of royalty.

In the original Persian tale by Nizami (1141–1209), the tension between the ruler's two bodies is established from the outset: in the wake of the loss of their kingdom, the khan Timurtash, his wife, and son lose all the trappings of royalty until nothing is left. They find themselves "almost naked in the midst of the mountains." It is at the desolate moment when, facing the nakedness of the khan, the young Prince Khalaf asks the key question: "How many rulers before us have been driven from their kingdoms, and after wandering about for years in foreign lands, sharing the lot of the most abject of mortals, have been in the end restored to their thrones! If God has the power to pluck off crowns, has He not also the power to restore them?"[1] For Nizami, a Sufi poet, the question is ultimately about fate. In Puccini's *Turandot*, the same question is about the body of kings. Calaf will reveal his identity only when the distance between his "abject" body and Turandot's royal body is canceled and he touches her lips.

The twelfth-century Persian tale and modern opera alike tighten the aperture on a series of touchy issues for sovereigns: the space between their "two bodies," the needs for courts and kingdoms in order to fuse their bodies, their relationship to laws and judgments. Are rulers comfortable with the space between the two bodies? Nizami asks whether the royal body remains noble, whether blood remains "royal," even once the kingdom is lost; Puccini reminds us that the king's "other" body is the physical one—even princesses feel the cold when they are alone in bed at night. Nizami asks the second question, on the place of a court, directly: does a king remain a king even after losing his kingdom and finding himself "almost naked in the mountains"? Puccini asks it when he inquires: Does Calaf remain a king even when he enters the Chinese capital with no kingdom to return to and with his identity concealed? Can the abject body invert into a royal body once again? And, as significantly, is Calaf nevertheless immune to judgment, beyond the law, as Puccini's opera argues? Does Turandot's injunction—the legal and veridical regime that she imposes—remain impossible to fulfill precisely and only because Calaf remains above the law?

The royal answer to these questions, as the endings of the tale and opera suggest, is a likely yes: the king remains a king and therefore there is no space between his two bodies. But the fact that questions such as these are raised inside, outside, and around courts—courts of a palatial or juridical variety—suggests that a great deal of unease about that space persists.

The essays in this section engage sovereignty from the perspective of the interplay of courts and bodies—as much courts intended to pass judgment as courts intended to celebrate and stage the king. At stake throughout are the often theatrical machinations that maintain and transform the fictions necessary for sovereignty over bodies, notably these two kinds of courts.

The subject of the first of four case studies on courts and bodies is the early sixteenth-century treatise addressed to the Ottoman sultan Selim by the Kurdish Muslim scholar Idrīs al-Bidlīsī (d. 1520), a brief explaining why he believed he was religiously justified in fleeing from an epidemic of the plague. Justin Stearns's essay on al-Bidlīsī considers his plague treatise in relation to the problem of sovereignty—in particular, the ways in which Muslim rulers and scholars related to each other and the degree to which both groups contested the field of what might be called public health in the premodern period. More specifically, the essay addresses how al-Bidlīsī constructed his own authority in the treatise in face of considerable scholarly opposition, and within the context of a long tradition of writings on epidemic disease by Muslim jurists and doctors. Beyond the theologico-political body of the diseased, the different courts that set health policy, the chapter addresses the nature of intellectual and political sovereignty in relation to the regulation and control of epidemic disease in the Muslim world in the sixteenth century.

Second, in "The Dancing Despot: Toyotomi Hideyoshi and the Performative Symbolism of Power," Stanca Scholz-Cionca presents a ruler acutely adept at harnessing the performative means available to him to establish his authority. Profoundly theatrical due to both personal temperament and political necessity, Toyotomi's reign was an ongoing staging of power and authority, whether hosting "the largest tea party ever recorded in Japanese history" or ordering the ritual suicide of the tea master with three thousand armed guards conspicuously surrounding his house. Hideyoshi both resembled Western monarchs—notably Louis XIV, famous for dancing ballet as Apollo through *Le ballet de la nuit*—and differed profoundly in his construction of expectations and customs to serve a sovereign, a construction, as

Scholz-Cionca emphasizes, made possible by a global network (including in particular Christian missionaries who were allowed at court) that facilitated firsthand knowledge of his persona and court. Of particular interest is the way Hideyoshi's relationship to theater goes beyond the ostentatious display and ritual of sovereignty on the public and court "stages" to a direct relationship with the art of Nô theater. Not only was Hideyoshi's support of Nô and its practitioners of instrumental and of lasting importance to the art, but he enthusiastically trained as an actor, sparking what would become an abiding passion and vested interest in Nô among the ruling elite.

In the third case, Bernadette Meyler focuses on the gesture of pardoning in relation to sovereignty. Theorists as diametrically opposed as Carl Schmitt and Immanuel Kant conceive of the pardon as an exception to the normal operation of law and associate that exception with the figure of the sovereign. This should not be surprising to those familiar with early modern political theory, which generally construed the pardon as one of the sovereign's most significant powers. Meyler argues that those setting up the foundations for liberal constitutionalism, like Kant, failed to generate a new account of pardoning that would render it an important component of either the rule of law or democracy rather than a relic of monarchical sovereignty. Hence the pardon seems to fit more naturally into the antiliberal Schmittian account of politics than into the contemporary U.S. constitutional order. As this essay contends, such a result was not inevitable; an alternative, nonsovereign conception of pardoning that appeared in early modern drama presented another possible basis for the act, one that was never implemented within politics. Kant associates pardoning with a particular kind of staging of the splendor of the king's majesty, one trumped only by the horror of the spectacle of revolutionary and counterrevolutionary violence. This theatrical version of the pardon scene as affirming the height of the sovereign above the people—a version that manifests itself in the spectacular finales of early modern plays such as Shakespeare's *Measure for Measure*—is countered by another kind of drama, in which forgiveness comes from a stranger or a friend and is passed among citizens to reconstitute the state. The article concludes by analyzing an example of one such play, *The Laws of Candy*, and the path offered by its nonsovereign staging of pardoning.

Miranda Spieler's essay, "The Vanishing Slaves of Paris," draws on newly unearthed dossiers in the Archives de la Bastille to rethink key features of the Old Regime state at the height of the French slave trade, during the explosive growth of Old Regime plantation societies, including Saint Domingue. These police documents chronicle the seizure and extrajudicial detention of slaves at the request of masters by Paris police from 1738 forward. When read in combination with other relevant archival sources from the period, (admiralty court records, notarial documents, decrees of the Royal Council), these materials (hitherto unknown to historians) draw attention to the remaking of domestic French law, legal institutions, and administrative practice under the influence of French Atlantic colonial wealth. Where historians have for decades argued that France observed a "free soil" principle in the later eighteenth century (by which slaves who set foot in domestic France were liberated by the Paris admiralty court), Spieler shows that the police in Paris intervened routinely at the request of slave masters to prevent the court's freedom decrees from taking effect. This chapter provides a revisionist portrait of the Old Regime state—hinging on the "colonization" of domestic France by the empire—and in the process examines the staging of sovereignty and the production of the "sovereign voice" in prerevolutionary France, as a transoceanic, imperial process.

Finally, Alexei Yurchak's "Re-touching the Sovereign: Biochemistry of Perpetual Leninism" discusses the project of the continuous maintenance and display of Lenin's body in Moscow for the past ninety years. The essay focuses on the scientific practice that emerged around this project, the ingenious medical innovations that accompanied it, and the unique political role this body performed in the structure of communist sovereignty. Following the (in some respects surprising) decision to preserve Lenin's body after his death in 1924, Yurchak reads the preservation in terms of "the material cultivation of the immortal, infallible, perpetually renewed body of the sovereign party" and attends to the Soviet commitment to Leninism in succeeding generations of leaders. Lenin's corpse, in its meticulous handling, turns out to provide both continuities with medieval and early modern forms (most notably the famous dual body of the King in Kantorowicz's study) and reasons to question the Communist Party's supposedly unmediated use of Soviet sovereignty. As a court, the mausoleum and laboratory has played a complex legitimating role: a site of rumors and a site for cultivating a representation of the population, of the revolution—whose "immortal body" was "Leninism, the foundational, unquestionable Truth located outside the system," as well as, now, the postcommunist future with a different, mysterious "embodied momentum."

Note

1. Julia Pardoe, *The Thousand and One Days; a Companion to the "Arabian Nights" (A Collection of Oriental Tales . . . Principally Derived from the Works of Different Oriental Scholars on the Continent)* (London: W. Lay, 1857), 62.

FIVE

Public Health, the State, and Religious Scholarship

Sovereignty in Idrīs al-Bidlīsī's Arguments for Fleeing the Plague

JUSTIN STEARNS

I

IN THIS ESSAY, I use sovereignty as a lens to examine a particular facet of the history of epidemic disease in the premodern Muslim Mediterranean. In placing the subjects of sovereignty and scholarly responses to epidemic disease into conversation with each other, I offer a few observations regarding the history of public health in the premodern Muslim world that, while speculative, are hopefully productive.[1] I should stress at the outset that unlike for the colonial and postcolonial periods in the Muslim Mediterranean, where recent scholarship has unpacked the ways in which sovereignty was contested at the intersection of politics and religious discourse, historians working on the premodern and precolonial Muslim Middle East have been much less successful in this regard.[2] In part, this is certainly a question of sources, as can be seen when we compare the recent and enlightening efforts of historians working on public health in late medieval Europe with the near complete absence of any comparable work done on the Muslim Mediterranean in the same period.[3]

By and large, we simply do not have the archival resources for the Islamicate societies in the southern and eastern Mediterranean that we possess for their northern, largely Christian neighbors.[4] The sources that we do have are for the most part normative and theoretical, including general works on medicine, treatises on specific diseases, legal responses (*fatāwā*) that have been shorn of much their historical and social context, and references in spiritual and religious commentaries and exegeses. I have previously discussed many of these sources as they related to the question of contagion and the transmission of disease, especially plague and leprosy.[5] Here, in a necessarily preliminary fashion, I examine the connection between sovereignty and debates on disease transmission and lay out a series of questions for which I do not think we have any definitive answers, but through which we may be able to productively reread sources previously examined in a different context: How did Muslim scholars and rulers in the premodern period construct sovereignty with regard to the public response to epidemic disease? What theological, spiritual, legal, and medical concerns influenced rulers in responding to a challenge to the political and economic well-being of their realms? How can we relate what we do know of the social response to epidemic disease with understandings of sovereignty in Muslim societies?[6] How best to consider the social and political life of a genre of medical and religious scholarship that previously has been discussed mainly within a comparatively narrow framework of intellectual history? This chapter offers no definitive answers to these questions but is more interested in what structures of sovereignty those attending to these issues are required to provide with scaffolding. Sovereignty is considered here, then, not as a political, religious, or legal concept so much as the terrain on which the ideas and policies that scholars and rulers can successfully represent and support are determined.

After some general reflections on recent discussions of sovereignty and Islamic thought, I take up the plague treatise of a prominent Kurdish scholar and politician, Idrīs al-Bidlīsī (d. 1520), a remarkable individual who wandered between the courts of three great Muslim powers at the beginning of the sixteenth century, the Safavids, the Ottomans, and the Mamluks. Al-Bidlīsī's plague treatise, which remains in manuscript, has principally attracted the attention of researchers interested in the claims of Muslim scholars regarding the significance of epidemic disease and how to regulate it.[7] In this framework, al-Bidlīsī was initially remarkable due to his strident defense of the contagious nature of the plague, a stance that previous scholarship had considered exceptional for a religious tradition that placed high value on the words of the Prophet Muhammad, who had denied contagion and had declared the plague to be martyrdom for believers.[8]

I am interested in placing al-Bidlīsī's plague treatise in the context of a question, which I believe is important for a more nuanced understanding of how religion, medicine, and political authority interacted in the regulation of epidemic disease in the premodern Islamicate world: how did the views of Muslims jurists, theologians, and mystics help determine the nature of the sovereignty claimed by various Muslim rulers when it came to regulating movement within and between their territories? It is a complex question, in part because these scholars, al-Bidlīsī among them, drew on discourses that transcended the legal question of who had what rights and responsibilities in the public and private spheres, which included the moral and ethical questions of what believers owed each other, what they should do (instead of what they had to do), and how they individually should orient themselves toward their Creator. Before going further, let me make a few general remarks about the relationship between temporal and religious authority and sovereignty in Islamic history.

II

For later generations of Muslims looking back, it was clear that during the Prophet Muhammad's lifetime he possessed absolute sovereignty over all temporal and religious matters.[9] He was, on the one hand, the vehicle through which God's word had been revealed to mankind, and his own words and acts gave the best indication of how this revelation was to be understood. On the other hand, he was also the political leader and arbitrator of the community that Muslims established in the oasis city of Yathrib—renamed prosaically the City of the Prophet, or City for short—in 622 after they had been persecuted in their hometown of Mecca during the preceding decade. Scholars have been rightly fascinated with the earliest Islamic political document we have, which must have been drawn up shortly after the Muslims arrived. The Constitution of Medina lays out a multireligious political alliance between Muslims and the Jewish tribes of Medina.[10] Importantly, the document recognizes Muhammad as final arbiter of community affairs. In the five years following the Muslim arrival, this alliance fell apart, but as the nascent Muslim community weathered its first challenges, experienced its first victories and losses on the battlefield, and returned victorious to

Mecca in 630, Muhammad's sovereignty was never portrayed as having been in doubt. His authority over temporal and religious matters was absolute.[11] This point is vital, for however much historians may rightly note the tendency of later jurists and political thinkers to project a fully developed state back onto the first years of Islamic history, Muhammad's lifetime was unique for political and religious authority being unquestionably united in one person. The critical term here is unquestionable. After the Prophet's death, in 632, there was some debate about whether his successors were in fact his *khalifa*, or representative, or God's. Almost thirty years ago Patricia Crone and Martin Hinds argued that the attempt to claim to be God's caliph was raised repeatedly by members of the Umayyad dynasty, which ruled from 661 to 750. That title clearly carried a greater claim to authority than being the representative of the Prophet for it permitted direct interpretation of God's revelation without the limitation of Prophetic precedent.[12] While Crone and Hinds's thesis continues to be influential, it has been challenged repeatedly, most recently by Ovamir Anjum, who argues that sovereignty in the early Muslim community did not rest with the caliph but with the Muslim community as a whole, and specifically with its scholars ('*ulama*).[13]

By the beginning of the Abbasid dynasty in 750, whereas the caliph's legitimacy as ruler was firmly linked to his being descended from the Prophet's family, the right to interpret and therefore also represent God's revelation was increasingly in the hands of a group of Muslims who specialized in just this (and who argued fiercely about how exactly to define and delimit this revelation). This group came to be known as the '*ulama*, the ones who have knowledge. Scholars have here, too, disagreed on how to interpret the relationship between the '*ulama* and the caliph, with an earlier thesis that religious and political spheres were effectively separated during the early Abbasid period facing the challenge of a more nuanced reading in which the Abbasid caliphs patronized those religious scholars whose views they shared, and the scholars in turn became increasingly politically quietist.[14]

While Abbasid caliphs may have continued rhetorically to assert their right to participate in debates over legal and theological issues, and may have been acknowledged by scholars to have the right to do so, it was the scholars themselves who increasingly embraced the task of doing so and who, with the establishment of law schools, enacted their own form of sovereignty over the Muslim community.[15] Political authorities continued, of course, to exert a huge amount of influence. Let us take the example of *fiqh*, or jurisprudence, after the four main Sunni law schools were fully articulated by the eleventh century. While the normative content both of legal theory and substantive law was determined by legal scholars who may or may not have had support from the state, and thus from the ruler, the judges who sat and gave the legally binding judgments on legal issues generally received a stipend from the state and were appointed by the ruler.[16] Yet even here the authority of the *'ulama* was limited, for in practice there were at least three courts, only one of which was directly within the purview of their interpretation of God's will, the *shari'a*. The other two were the *mazālim* courts, where representatives of the ruler could hand down discretionary punishments (*ta'zīr*) based on an understanding of law and politics that was inspired by revelation (*siyāsa shar'iyya*), and the court of the *muhtasib*, or market inspector, who enforced customary law in the public spaces of Muslim cities. These courts differed in part in rules of evidence, for a judge ruling according to the *shari'a* required all evidence to be brought to him and had no ability to independently investigate, whereas the *muhtasib* was, according to his job description, in a position to enforce justice in a proactive sense before a charge was filed against anyone. In a legal sense, then, we find no unified legal field; rather, there were overlapping jurisdictions and legal systems.[17] In a similar fashion, sovereignty itself was distributed throughout legal texts and practices, and more generally in the *'ulama*'s attempts to respond appropriately to the absolute sovereignty of God and His message to mankind. Here we must differentiate between the ideal of the revealed law (*shari'a*) and jurisprudence (*fiqh*) or man's imperfect attempt to ascertain this law. The sovereignty of the former was absolute and unquestionable, but the precise nature of the law was undefined; in mature Sunni legal theory, by contrast, the sovereignty of the latter was distributed between the four recognized Sunni law schools, all of which Sunni jurists recognized as having advanced equally valid claims to approximate divine law.[18] This admission by Muslim jurists that any given legal ruling by a trained jurist acting in good faith was at best a human approximation of God's revelation accentuated the need for jurists such as al-Bidlīsī, who were entering into contested legal and moral terrain, to make forceful and convincing arguments if they wanted to establish authority for their own interpretation of God's law.

III

So much for the nominal division between temporal and religious spheres. There was also within the revealed law of the 'ulama a principle, which in theory gave them license to question the power of the ruler directly, namely the injunction to "command the right and forbid the wrong" (al-amr bi-l-ma'rūf wa al-nahī 'an al-munkar).[19] Based initially on several Qur'anic references, this was potentially an absolute mandate for believers, placing them under the personal obligation to enforce Revelation and to take action if they witnessed God's will being perverted. Here, we might think, is a direct and permanent challenge to the sovereignty of the ruler, and in some branches of Islam, notably early Zaydi Shi'ism, this was indeed the case.[20] As Michael Cook has shown in great detail, by the eleventh century Sunni jurists, most notably al-Ghazālī (d. 1111), had interpreted this principle with great care to explain how it was to be implemented in a gradated fashion, with the ruler carrying it out with the hand, the scholar with the tongue, and the unlearned believer doing so in his heart.[21] Born out of a deep fear of civil war and social unrest, or fitna, Sunni scholars were clear that the ultimate authority in the public sphere lay with the ruler, whereas they could comfort themselves that they were responsible for the articulation of God's word and law, which had eternal significance. This relation between ruler and scholar was a symbiotic one, with rulers accruing legitimacy by supporting religious scholars and establishments, and many scholars, such as al-Bidlīsī himself, seeking out state sponsorship. It is not surprising then that al-Bidlīsī does not attempt in his plague treatise to claim political sovereignty but rather appeals to political authority to support his bid for religious authority and for the sovereignty of his own views on the proper way for Muslims and their rulers to respond to epidemic disease. This was not a sovereignty that was constitutive of orthodoxy so much as an argument for his views to be accepted as part of an orthodoxy that defined the boundaries of sovereignty.

IV

The overlapping spheres of legitimacy and authority that I have sketched out here were all housed within the caliphate and on the understanding that, at least in theoretical terms, there was only one political body that could rule over and represent the *umma*. By the tenth century however, there were three caliphates—the Abbasid, Umayyad, and Fatimid—functioning simultaneously, and Muslim legal theorists had to adjust their formulations accordingly, which was much needed, as by 1258, when the Mongols put an end to the Abbasid caliphate, it was nearly impossible to argue that the *umma* was still, even in theory, united by temporal or political rule.[22] Instead, and in a move that strengthened their own bargaining position, scholars developed the position that as long as the temporal ruler ensured and enforced the law as it was understood by the *'ulama*, his rule was legitimate.[23] It was religious and not political sovereignty that was thus reaffirmed as the only sovereign discourse that could aspire to be universal in the Muslim world. This, then, was the state of affairs during al-Bidlīsī's lifetime, when the Muslim world as he experienced it was under the rule of a rising and increasingly Sunni Ottoman dynasty in Anatolia, a nascent Shi'a Safavid dynasty in Iran, and a declining Sunni Mamluk dynasty that ruled over the Levant, Egypt, and the Hijaz.

V

Al-Bidlīsī was an extraordinary character whose life and works Ebru Sönmez has recently discussed in a detailed biography. He was born in the middle of the fifteenth century in Rayy, near Tabriz, at that time the capital of the Turkish Akkoyunlu state.[24] His father, Ḥusām al-Dīn al-Bidlīsī (d. 1495), was a well-known Sufi and held the position of secretary at the Akkoyunlu court. Al-Bidlīsī followed his father both in his interest in Sufism and in his service to the Akkoyunlu state, which he served as chancellor for a time, and he remained in Tabriz until 1500, shortly before its dissolution and absorption into the nascent Safavid Empire. Whereas many of the bureaucrats who had served under the Akkoyunlus chose to move to the Safavid court, al-Bidlīsī sought his fortune with the Ottomans. It is difficult to know why he made this decision, especially since he does not seem to have had any patron in Istanbul before his arrival there.[25] Sönmez has done an excellent job of portraying the tumultuous political scene in the eastern Mediterranean world at the beginning of the sixteenth century, a world where a wandering intellectual might try his luck at the Safavid, Ottoman, and Mamluk courts, provided that he could prove his value or ingratiate himself there.

Like many other refugees from the Akkoyunlu court, al-Bidlīsī found refuge in Istanbul, was appointed court secretary, and was granted a stipend. Some time later Sultan Bayazid II (r. 1481–1512) gave him the task of writing the history of the Ottoman dynasty. The resulting chronicle, *Hasht Bihisht*, has attracted most previous scholarship on al- Bidlīsī.[26] Al-Bidlīsī was integrally involved with the development of Ottoman policy along the frontier with the Safavids, but his chronicle found little favor in Istanbul, and he was frustrated and disheartened by the trajectory of his career.[27] In 1511 he set out to perform the pilgrimage and, after completing it, wrote to Bayazid from Mecca requesting redress for injustices he felt he had experienced at Ottoman hands. Receiving no answer, he remained in Mecca and perhaps contemplated seeking permanent service with the Mamluk sultan Qānṣū Ghawrī. In 1512 Bayazid's son Selim (d. 1520) forced him to abdicate and became sultan himself. Selim ordered al-Bidlīsī back to Istanbul. Apparently weary of being far from court, al-Bidlīsī happily complied. It was on his return from Mecca, as part of a caravan traveling from the Hijaz to the Levant (*shām*) that he heard of an epidemic having broken out in Cairo and decided to change his plans from returning via Cairo to heading directly to Ottoman territory.[28] Having heard of his decision—how is unclear—a group of scholars from Damascus and Aleppo, including a large number who acted like Sufis (*jamm ghafīr min al-mutashabbihīn bi-l-ṣūfiyya*) attacked him publicly for avoiding Cairo. Al-Bidlīsī described his initial reaction to this criticism as essentially nonplussed. He chose not to enter into argument with his opponents on the basis of what people had allegedly said (*bi-ṭarīq al-qawl wa-l-qīl*), and traveled on until he reached Kayseri (*Qayṣariyya*) in Anatolia.[29] There he took the time to consult all the relevant sources he could find and ascertained that, according to both revelation and reason, it was forbidden to approach a place where the plague had broken out: "Taking precautions and being wary in a country that is struck by epidemic and plague is a revealed ruling (*ḥukm sharʿī*) and a rational principle (*qānūn ʿaqlī*). It is in fact recommended (*mandūb*) and prescribed (*masnūn*)."[30]

Al-Bidlīsī recognized, however, that his opponents, made up of jurists and would-be Sufis, disagreed with him on this and argued that taking precautions and fleeing from the decree and judgment of God (*qaḍāʾ allāh wa qadarhu*) was forbidden since everything that happens, happens according to the will of God. Al-Bidlīsī was impatient with this line of argument and didn't hold back from expressing his frustration:

I said, addressing them, "Oh you poor souls, from whom the knowledge of the facts of the revealed laws and judgments have been kept—oh you pitiable ones, who have been deprived of insight into the foundations of the religion with regard to what is permitted and what is forbidden, do you not understand that your recommendation of the path of reliance on God, and to being satisfied with God's decree and submitting to the things that have been determined from time eternal (al-muqaddarāt al-azliyya), and entrusting the matter to the eternal Will is exactly the same as asserting that there is a choice to refrain from taking precautions and from being careful and a choice to entrust matters to the Chosen Actor?"[31]

It is clear to al-Bidlīsī that his opponents had erred in their reasoning, and that if they grant humans the ability to refrain from taking actions to protect themselves from the plague, they have implicitly acknowledged that they also have the choice to do so and that, by extension, both choices are in accordance with God's decree. Before looking further into al-Bidlīsī's plague treatise and the ways he chose to defend his choice not to approach a place where the plague had broken out, I should pause for a moment and address the genre of the plague treatise itself.

VI

Following his altercation with this group of obstinate scholars, al-Bidlīsī went on to have a largely though not entirely successful career at the court of Sultan Selim, playing an important role in the Ottoman consolidation of power over largely Kurdish-inhabited borderlands between it and the Safavid Empire.[32] His treatise on the plague, Risāla al-'ibā' 'an mawāqi' al-wabā' (Treatise of aversion to places where epidemics have broken out), has been mostly neglected by scholars, although it continued to be read in the Muslim world, as can be seen by its being cited by the Algerian scholar Ḥamdān Khoja (d. c. 1842) in the nineteenth century when he wrote a treatise of his own in favor of the quarantine.[33] In writing a treatise on the plague, al-Bidlīsī was advancing into well-traveled territory, although his own views on the contagion of the plague were somewhat exceptional for his time. In order to explain the significance of his perspective and to what extant it was novel in advocating a specific response to the challenge posed by epidemic disease, it is helpful to review briefly the history of this genre.

Islam emerged into the Middle East during what historians have traditionally referred to as the first pandemic of bubonic plague that lasted from the 540s to 750.[34] The Prophet himself did not experience the plague (ṭāʿūn) but had opinions and advice on a number of contagious diseases, such as mange in camels, leprosy in humans, and, in several famous hadith, on the plague itself.[35] This body of traditions appeared in some ways to be contradictory, for while denying the validity of a belief in contagion, along with other pre-Islamic superstitions, the Prophet warned of associating with lepers, even though he himself ate with them, and advised people not to approach an area where the plague had broken out yet simultaneously declared death from the plague to result in martyrdom for all believers. In the centuries after his death, those traditions attributed to the Prophet that Muslim scholars felt were trustworthy (and sometimes those that were not) were collected in compilations that went on to play a vital role in the articulation of the Sunni schools of law in the ninth and tenth centuries. Instead of rejecting some of the traditions on plague and contagion while affirming others, thereby preserving the apparent coherence of his legacy on the subject, some Sunni scholars as early as Ibn Qutayba (d. 889) in the ninth century chose to reconcile the apparently contradictory traditions by restricting their application and explaining that while diseases were transmissible, they did not transmit themselves by their own power.[36] In making this argument, they found support in a tradition in which the Prophet was challenged by a Bedouin who presented the case of a mangy camel that lay down with other camels, who then also became mangy. The Prophet, somewhat cryptically, retorted: who infected the first? The Prophet's point, it would seem, was that it was God who was first and foremost involved in the transmission of the disease. This line of thinking was particularly attractive to adherents of a school of theology called Ash'arism, which arose in the late ninth century and went on to become prevalent among Sunnis who followed the Maliki, and to a lesser extant the Shafi'i schools of jurisprudence.

Broadly conceived, the Ash'aris argued for a theory of occasionalism in which God created each and every thing and nothing but God had any ability to effect change.[37] The appearance that the world possessed something like a natural law that reflected an underlying web of secondary causes that possessed natures of their own—a position connected in Islamicate thought

with the position of the Aristotelian philosophers—was an illusion resulting from a false understanding of reality. For the Asha'ris, the appearance
of natural order was in reality the result of God's Habit (*'āda*) and His Wisdom (*ḥikma*) in arranging apparent causes and effects. The doctrine of occasionalism preserved the absolute unity of God by denying the existence
of other actors and played an important role in the Ash'ari understanding
of human action and human acquisition (*kasb*) of acts created by God.
Occasionalism, in other words, preserved the absolute sovereignty of God over
the natural world while God's Habit explained the apparent but illusory
existence of a natural order and man's ability to acquire acts created by God
ensured his moral responsibility for his actions. In this understanding,
plague and disease in general need to be accepted as part of nature, and thus
of God's Wisdom. While man may experience them as afflictions, scholars
could argue that he may not have understood their true purpose.[38]

Relevant for us here is that later Muslim scholars who were attracted to
occasionalism and who addressed the subject of contagion and of fleeing
from the plague did at times invoke it to justify not fleeing from the plague,
seeing that the Prophet had stressed that diseases didn't transmit themselves. If these same scholars were Sufis, and the majority of Sunni Muslim
scholars following the eleventh and twelfth centuries had had some experience of Sufism even though they differed widely on its nature and practice,
they would have found the concept of *tawakkul*, or reliance on God, relevant
in this context. *Tawakkul* played an important role in early Islamic asceti-
cism in the eighth–ninth centuries as well as in the later Sufi movements
of the ninth–tenth centuries, and while early examples of ascetics sitting
in the desert waiting for God to send them food remained attractive, especially in stories, prominent theorists of Sufism rejected such facile understandings of *tawakkul* as self-destructive. One influential justification for a
Muslim to take steps for self-preservation, including the use of medicine,
as part of a proper reliance on God was given by al-Ghazālī (d. 1111) in his
famous *Iḥyā' 'ulūm al-dīn* (Revival of the religious sciences), one of the few
sources that al-Bidlīsī explicitly cites in his treatise.[39]

A final line of thinking regarding epidemic disease that was absorbed and
debated by Muslim scholars during the same period that Islamic jurisprudence, theology, and mysticism were systematized was, of course, medicine.
Following the translation of Greek medical texts into Arabic in the ninth
century, Galenic humoral medicine was embraced by Muslim doctors and

was further developed and systematized in the works of scholars such as the physician Muḥammad b. Zakariyyā al-Rāzī (d. 923), in whose *al-Ḥāwī fī-l-ṭibb* a whole series of contagious diseases, including plague and leprosy, were described.[40]

Thus, when plague swept through the Muslim Mediterranean in the fourteenth century, Muslim scholars had a set of well-defined discourses to draw on when they set about describing the disease, the appropriate response to it, and the possible remedies for it. As described above with regard to Islamic law, however, no one of the scholars writing opinions on the plague was able to establish themselves as sovereign on the issue. Instead, the overall authority of the *'ulama* within Muslim societies was reaffirmed even as they differed on the subject, at times bitterly. This authority was defined by their being the recognized interpreters of God's sovereign revelation in all its legal, theological, and ethical complexity.

Until recently, the state of scholarship on the content of these plague treatises was largely framed by the seminal work of Michael Dols in *The Black Death in the Middle East*. Dols largely took the long plague treatise of Ibn Ḥajar al-Asqalānī (d. 1448), a prominent Egyptian Shāfiʿī jurist, as representative of the Sunni Muslim response to plague, although he acknowledged several fourteenth-century Andalusi treatises that claimed that the plague could be transmitted. Ibn Ḥajar's take on the plague can be briefly summarized as follows: (1) Revelation and empirical evidence prove that the plague is not contagious. (2) The plague is a martyrdom for believers who trust in God. (3) The immediate agent that causes the plague is jinn.[41] While there is no denying that Ibn Ḥajar's work was influential, I have argued that taken as a whole the plague treatises written during and after the Black Death show a broad spectrum of opinions regarding both contagion and whether it was permissible to flee the plague. By focusing on Ibn Ḥajar and by translating the treatises of Ibn al-Wardī (d. 1349) and al-Manbijī (d. 1383), who also largely denied contagion, Dols offered a generation of historians, especially European medievalists who had little else in the secondary literature to rely on, the impression that Muslims uniformly refused to flee the plague and held it to be a martyrdom.[42] It is here that al-Bidlīsī's treatise helps provide such a valuable corrective to Dols, for it shows that a scholar living in the Mashriq only two generations after Ibn Ḥajar was able to confidently assert the completely opposite view on plague—not just on the issue of contagion but also on the issue of martyrdom and the role of the jinn. Seen from one perspective, then, his treatise provides an Eastern parallel to the Maghribi treatises of Ibn al-Khaṭīb (d. 1374), Ibn Khātimah (d. 1369), and, to a lesser extant, al-Mawwāq (d. 1492).[43] Yet al-Bidlīsī exhibits such independence of thought in his treatise that it is far more than simply an Eastern replica of these earlier treatises. While it is beyond the scope of this chapter to give a full summary of his treatise, I will touch here on its main points and overall structure before returning to sovereignty and how reading al-Bidlīsī's treatise can help us in our understanding of the contested nature of public health in the premodern Islamicate world.[44]

VII

Following the introduction to his treatise, al-Bidlīsī notes that he intends it to be a gift to his Highness the Sultan. Since he will later make a brief, if striking, reference to the proper actions the ruler should take in a time of plague, it is notable that he intended his audience to be not only his scholarly critics but also his desired political patron.[45] As for the structure of the treatise, he has based it on three principles and structured it in three different chapters: (1) explaining the meaning of God's decree and judgment; (2) expounding on the meaning of compulsion and choice; and (3) explaining the world of barzakh, which is the place where calamities appear (maḥall ẓuhūr al-nawāzil wa-l-dawāhī). Al-Bidlīsī's discussion of these principles precedes the section in which he addresses the plague itself, and it is clear that he believes that addressing the relevant theological issues helps provide a theoretical framework that justifies and defends his later at times more prosaic discussion of the relevant legal traditions and medical remedies.

The first of these principles—the proper understanding of God's decree and judgment—may well have been the most important to al-Bidlīsī, for here he took on his opponents directly. The term qaḍā wa-l-qadar, or God's decree and judgment, is important in Islamic theology and was the subject of much discussion among the 'ulama. For al-Bidlīsī, a correct understanding of decree and judgment was essential to his treatise. The first term, God's decree, referred to God's eternal knowledge and determination of all that would ever happen. This was unquestionable. God's judgment, on the other hand, referred to the connection of that eternal knowledge with every existent thing, considering that substances are arranged in a chain of causes (*silsilāt al-ʿilal wa-l-asbāb*) and conditions. These created substances possess attributes necessary to existence that can change (*lawāzim ʿāriḍa la-hā fī-l-wujūd qābila li-l-taghayyur*) or be replaced, and these attributes include life, death, sickness, and well-being.[46] Seeing that this a complicated matter, al-Bidlīsī offers an extended metaphor as an explanation which is well worth summarizing here, as it explores what might be called the nature of God's sovereignty over His creation:

> Consider the case of a powerful, knowledgably and willing ruler, who makes a judgment and sends out a decree to his vizier that the latter should undertake with regard to the matter of twenty prisoners. The vizier should kill ten and spare ten for the good of the realm (*li-maṣlaḥat ṣalṭana*). The vizier follows the order, and after noting the faces that deserved to die and those that deserved to live, divides them into two groups of ten. When he presented to the ruler what he had chosen to do, the ruler was content with the vizier and with his decision, and he signed it. In this fashion, the ruler's final judgment was the result of a correspondence between his will and his power while also being in accordance with his decree, best understood as his all-encompassing knowledge.

Al-Bidlīsī explains that when we do not look at the specifics of what the vizier had done, we see that the particulars (i.e., choosing ten men to die) conform with the whole (the ruler's judgment that ten men would die and his knowledge of this). As for the correspondence between the ruler signing the vizier's decision and his initial order, al-Bidlīsī draws attention to two points: (1) Sparing ten prisoners and killing ten others according to the vizier's evaluation of them is not open to change, for the ruler had ordered it and the vizier had to carry it out. 2) What is variable is the inclusion of specific individuals among the ten for reasons and conditions determined by the vizier. If the vizier changed a specific selection, that would not conflict with the ruler's overall general command. In closing, al-Bidlīsī explains that, metaphorically speaking, the vizier is the judgment (*qadar*) he had previously defined as God's eternal knowledge.[47]

This is a striking metaphor and, in its equation of God with a king who has servants who carry out his will, has parallels with metaphors used by both al-Ghazālī and al-Sanūsī (d. 1490).[48] The recourse to royal sovereignty to explain divine sovereignty speaks perhaps first to the degree to which, in a world of competing caliphates, emirates, and sultanates, these authors were influenced by advice literature and the genre of "mirrors for princes," which was especially popular in Iran and which drew on the pre-Islamic identification of the King in the temporal world with God.[49] Like the two earlier scholars, who were also deeply influenced by Ash'arism, al-Bidlīsī is attempting to explain reality's apparent operation according to secondary causality; unlike them he is first and foremost interested in cutting the Gordian knot of predestination and freedom of will. Expanding on the second principle—the meaning of compulsion and choice—which is closely associated with the first, al-Bidlīsī goes on to explain his understanding of *kasb*, according to which God creates a power in the worshipper to choose between sequences of causes that God has created.[50] The upshot, al-Bidlīsī argues, is that whether you approach or flee an epidemic, you are doing this according to the decree and judgment of God.

The third principle that al-Bidlīsī examines deals with the *barzakh*, the world of images that exists between our physical world and the spiritual world and to which only the spiritually enlightened, including the prophets, the saints, and the most advanced of the scholars, have access.[51] This world mirrors what happens in our physical world, and those who have insight into it truly understand how and why things happen in our world, including falling ill and becoming healthy.[52] This section is important for al-Bidlīsī, for like Ibn Ḥajar he believes that the underlying causes of sickness are spiritual in nature, although unlike the Egyptian author he is able to reconcile humoral medicine seamlessly with the actions of angels, jinn, and spirits in the *barzakh*.[53]

On the one hand, al-Bidlīsī sees the origin of epidemic disease to be material, rooted in the corruption of the humoral balance of humans by polluted or poisoned air. On the other hand, these sublunar phenomena are caused directly by the states of the spheres, and both of these are mirrored in the imaginal world of the *barzakh*.[54] As should be clear from his exploration of human choice, al-Bidlīsī believes not only that it is permissible to flee from the plague or disease in general but that protecting oneself is mandatory, both according to revelation and reason, and he backs up this argument with the citation of numerous Prophetic traditions and episodes from early Islamic history.[55]

There are religious arguments that challenged al-Bidlīsī's position and, with a few noticeable exceptions, he addressed them all. The main one that is relevant here and related to public health is that opponents of flight, who also tended to deny the transmissibility of plague, often argued that Muslims should remain with the plague sick to tend to them and to bury the dead.[56] Al-Bidlīsī retorts that the damage done to the *umma* by the death of Muslims is so great that Muslims have a duty to protect their own lives above all else, seeing that the preservation of life is itself a foundational religious principle.[57] It is here that al-Bidlīsī states his one piece of direct advice to Muslim rulers: they should make rulings in accordance with the good of their followers, and regarding them the scholars have said that it is fine if they use some violence to preserve the greater good. Even if one does consider it legally permissible to stay in a country where the plague has broken out, a ruler is in accordance with what is desired by God if he encourages his people to flee, for to do anything else would lead to the suffering of his subjects and the weakening of his government. He should, instead, do what helps to strengthen Islam. This would be following Prophetic precedent.[58] It is thus the scholar's interpretation of God's revelation that defines the proper sovereign action of the ruler and the scholar's own authority.

In arguing that fleeing the plague is permissible, not only is al-Bidlīsī justifying his own behavior to his critics in Damascus and Aleppo, but he is going still further and making a bold assertion that Muslim political authorities should join him in seeing the plague and epidemic disease as a danger to the Muslim community. Al-Bidlīsī notably does not engage with the Prophetic tradition around which Ibn Ḥajar had based his entire treatise—namely, that the plague is a mercy for the Prophet's community and a martyrdom for the faithful. Instead he marshals a series of theological, legal, and mystical arguments for why epidemic disease is a danger that Muslims are obligated to avoid.[59]

VIII

How can the concept of sovereignty help us understand the complexities of al-Bidlīsī's argument for the right to flee the plague? Conversely, how do al-Bidlīsī's arguments and his use of jurisprudence, theology, mysticism, and medicine to articulate an appropriate response to epidemic disease complicate our understanding of the relationship between Muslim political leaders and religious scholars? Where did sovereignty lie in matters of public health and the public good? This chapter, with its rather broad overview, is only able to begin to answer these questions. Al-Bidlīsī, who had a tumultuous political career of his own and witnessed in his lifetime the collapse of both the Akkoyunlu and the Mamluk states, was not primarily interested in attaining political power himself, although he was intensely preoccupied with being recognized by Ottoman rulers and receiving state sponsorship. In his treatise on the plague he was principally concerned with scoring points against other scholars and demonstrating his authority as an intellectual figure. In one sense, then, the sovereignty in which he was interested was more intellectual than political; the power he wished to assert was linked to his personal scholarly stature and not to his own service to the Ottoman sultan. His few lines of advice to Muslim rulers on how to manage epidemic disease seem more a rhetorical device to support his own position than an honest attempt to dictate public policy. We know little of what Sultan Selim did, if anything, in response to al-Bidlīsī's treatise; although as Nükhet Varlik has shown, it was in the sixteenth century that the Ottoman state first developed an elaborate bureaucracy to count and regulate the bodies of its subjects and to take steps toward improving public urban health.[60] We can briefly consider other attempts to influence Muslim rulers in the Mediterranean to take action against epidemic disease.

There are few examples that I am aware of from the medieval period. The poetic advice a fifteenth-century jurist in Granada named 'Umar gave to that city's ruler that he should flee the city to protect himself following the outbreak of the plague of 1441 had no recorded effect, if the ruler even read it.[61] Contrast this suggestion with the legal debates from prior centuries among Muslim jurists regarding lepers, how safe it was to eat with them, buy goods from them, or have sex with them.[62] These debates were not solely theoretical, for we find, for example, in the twelfth-century manual of the muhtasib of Seville, Ibn 'Abdūn, that the general population should not interact with lepers.[63] While this is not a direct appeal to the ruler of the time, since the muhtasib was appointed by the ruler, it reflects his at least tacit approval of such a cautionary policy. We have no such references in a ḥisba manual to how plague victims should be dealt with.[64]

Within the Ottoman Empire, as noted above with reference to Nükhet Varlik's work, the Ottoman state made its first efforts to regulate urban sanitation in the sixteenth century, and notables fled urban areas in times of plague.[65] When we reach the nineteenth century, we are better informed of later disputes regarding the implementation of the quarantine.[66] The context of the debate had changed, and the European economic and colonial presence posed a serious challenge to the attempts of Muslim scholars and rulers to articulate their sovereignty over matters of public health. With regard to Tunisia in the eighteenth century, Nancy Gallagher has shown how while the debate over contagion continued to divide Muslim scholars, the desire of European merchants to preserve open ports and also markets was more influential.[67] Similarly, in the nineteenth century, due to an awareness of how plague was weakening the Ottoman Empire demographically, economically, and militarily, the Ottoman state repeatedly enforced quarantines and faced varying levels of opposition from its own population to its regulation of their movements.[68] In light of European colonial interests, and with them an increasing wealth of sources for the historian to ponder, it is easier to discuss political sovereignty explicitly, along with the ways in which Ottoman sovereignty over its territories and public health system was contested, when not violated outright, by outside powers. Here we find also the intriguing example of a figure like Ḥamdān Khoja (d. c. 1842), an Algerian religious scholar and nationalist who protested against the French invasion of Algeria while also advocating the use of the quarantine, despite its European provenance. In his plague treatise, he was able to carefully explain how Muslim sovereignty, scholarly and political, is not infringed upon through the adoption of the European policy of the quarantine. There were, after all, he argued, precedents in Islamic scholarship for arguing for the regulation of movement in times of epidemic disease, and one of these was the treatise of al-Bidlīsī.[69] Al-Bidlīsī's treatise was an awkward one to cite in support of quarantine—the temporary enforced holding of apparently healthy populations to make sure that they are not carrying disease before allowing them to reintegrate into healthy populations—when he was advocating the right, if not the necessity, to flee the plague, but Ḥamdān Khoja was more interested in al-Bidlīsī's claim that the ruler should intervene to protect his subjects than the form this intervention should take.

The example of Ḥamdān Khoja, and the fact that the Ottoman Empire did take steps to address the danger of the plague's contagion and at times justified these steps by citing supportive religious scholarship, makes us even more aware of how little we know of the response, if any, to the treatise of al-Bidlīsī and the related unanswered questions regarding sovereignty and public health.[70] It is tempting here to suggest that as the power of the state to centralize its operations and impose its will on its subject populations grew from the late Middle Ages into the early modern period that issues of sovereignty surrounding the regulation of disease became increasingly well defined. As Nükhet Varlik has demonstrated, this growing power of the Ottoman state went hand in hand with the facilitation of the spread of epidemic disease that resulted from an increasingly centralized political body.[71] Al-Bidlīsī, however, was living in an earlier period, when the relationship of sovereignty to public health was not as clear to Muslim scholars and rulers precisely because there was little scholarly consensus in Islamdom on what, if anything, could be done to remedy the spread of plague. This lack of clarity, however, made the debates over the proper response to epidemic disease all the more fierce. Reading al-Bidlīsī's contribution to these debates through the lens of sovereignty shows us not only how Muslim scholars sought to define the proper response of political authorities but also how this attempt was rooted in their establishing the proper understanding of God's sovereignty over both man and nature.

Notes

I am grateful to Nathalie Peutz for her careful reading of an initial draft of this chapter, to Nükhet Varlik for an engaging discussion on plague in the Ottoman Empire, and to Monica Green for her insightful comments on a later draft of this paper.

1. For a brief overview of public health in the pre-modern Muslim Middle East, see Peter E. Pormann and Emilie Savage-Smith, *Medieval Islamic Medicine* (Washington, DC: Georgetown University Press, 2007), 109–11.
2. Among the recent excellent studies for the colonial period, see, e.g., Ellen Amster, *Medicine and the Saints: Science, Islam, and the Colonial Encounter in Morocco, 1877–1956* (Austin: University of Texas Press, 2013).
3. See esp. Guy Geltner, "Public Health and the Pre-Modern City: A Research Agenda," *History Compass* 10 (2012): 231–45; "Healthscaping a Medieval City: Lucca's *Curia viarum* and the Future of Public Health History," *Urban History* 40 (2013): 395–415; and, with J. Coomans, "On the Street and in the Bathhouse: Medieval Galenism in Action?," *Anuario de estudios medievales* 43 (2013): 53–82.
4. Yet see the remarks in Tamer El-Leithy, "Living Documents, Dying Archives: Towards a Historical Anthropology of Medieval Arabic Archives," *Al-Qanṭara* 32 (2011): 389–93.
5. Justin Stearns, *Infectious Ideas: Contagion in Premodern Islamic and Christian Thought in the Western Mediterranean* (Baltimore: Johns Hopkins University Press, 2011).

My own work owes a particular debt to Michael Dols's seminal *The Black Death in the Middle East* (Princeton: Princeton University Press, 1977).

6. For an overview of what historical chronicles tell us about the social response to plague, see Dols, *Black Death in the Middle East*, 236–54. I have taken issue with Dols's comparison of Christian and Muslim responses to plague in *Infectious Ideas*, 160–67, and, with a slightly different framing, in "New Directions in the Study of Religious Responses to the Black Death," *History Compass* 7 (2009): 1–13.

7. I first encountered al-Bidlīsī's treatise when reading the work of a nineteenth-century Algerian jurist who supported the introduction of the quarantine. See Stearns, *Infectious Ideas*, 157.

8. Stearns, *Infectious Ideas*, chap. 1.

9. My remarks apply only to the Sunni tradition of Islamic religious thought, and even then they are general in the extreme and do injustice to what is rich tradition of political thinking.

10. See Uri Rubin, "The 'Constitution of Medina' Some Notes," *Studia Islamica* 62 (1985): 5–23, and the literature cited there.

11. Patricia Crone, *God's Rule: Government and Islam, Six Centuries of Medieval Islamic Political Thought* (Cambridge: Cambridge University Press, 2004), 10–14.

12. Patricia Crone and Martin Hinds, *God's Caliph: Religious Authority in the First Centuries of Islam* (Cambridge: Cambridge University Press, 1986).

13. Ovamir Anjum, *Politics, Law, and Community in Islamic Thought: The Taymiyyan Moment* (Cambridge: Cambridge University Press, 2012), 42–47. Anjum draws extensively on the work of other scholars, most prominently Uri Rubin.

14. The earlier interpretation was represented by Patricia Crone and Martin Hinds, among others. See Anjum, *Politics, Law, and Community*, 87–92. Anjum is drawing here on Muhammad Qasim Zaman's writings, in particular *Religion and Politics Under the Early 'Abbāsids: The Emergence of the Proto-Sunni Elite* (Leiden: Brill, 1997), esp. 6–10, 105–14, 204–13. Compare also with Ahmed El Shamsy, *The Canonization of Islamic Law* (Cambridge: Cambridge University Press, 2013), 86, where he argues that the shift that took place with al-Shāfi'ī (d. 820) in the early 'Abbasid period was one from a communal legal system administered by established authority figures to one that privileged the nominally disinterested reading of Prophetic tradition by jurists trained in textual hermeneutics.

15. On the 'Abbasid caliphs' support for what he calls "proto-Sunnism," Qasim Zaman writes perceptively: "Rather than dismiss such religious rhetoric for what it was—a prop of 'Abbāsid legitimism—it should be seen as a contribution, in some cases perhaps an inadvertent one, to religious discourse: if the caliph could not, or did not wish to, impose a proto-Sunnī ideology, he could at least symbolically proclaim the commitment of his state to the *sunna* and to those who, like himself, were engaged in reviving it. The state was not only representing itself as 'orthodox,' it was thereby also helping give a *concrete* expression to the notion of an 'orthodoxy.' Certain beliefs were being made visible, to adapt a phrase of Clifford Geertz, and so was the caliph's support for them" (Qasim Zaman, *Religion and Politics*, 206).

16. For a general overview of this complex relationship, see Knut S. Vikor, *Between God and the Sultan: A History of Islamic Law* (Oxford: Oxford University Press, 2005), 185–205.

17. Ibid.

18. On the admission of man's limited ability to access the meaning of divine revelation, and the consequences of doing so, see ibid., 104–6, and esp. Aron Zysow, *The Economy of Certainty: An Introduction to the Typology of Islamic Legal Theory* (Atlanta: Lockwood Press, 2013), 262–77.

19. Michael Cook, *Commanding Right and Forbidding Wrong in Islamic Thought* (Cambridge: Cambridge University Press, 2000).

20. Ibid., 227–47.

21. Ibid., 427–50.

22. For an overview of the issue of the debates on where to allocate sovereignty following the multiplication of the caliphate, see the third section of Crone, *God's Rule,* "Coping with a Fragmented World."

23. For Anjum's particular take on this phenomenon, see *Politics, Law, and Community,* 107. Much of Anjum's book is taken up with exploring what he sees as Ibn Taymiyya's (d. 1328) attempt to reassert the primacy of the community—mainly the 'ulama—in Islamic political thought.

24. Ebru Sönmez, *Idris-I Bidlisi: Ottoman Kurdistan and Islamic Legitimacy* (Istanbul: Libra Kitap, 2012), 30.

25. Ibid., 38–42. See also V. L. Ménage, s.v. "Bidlīsī," in *Encyclopaedia of Islam,* 2nd ed. (Brill Online, 2013), http://referenceworks.brillonline.com/entries/encyclopaedia-of-islam-2/bidlisi-SIM_1399 (accessed April 29, 2013).

26. Ibid., 18. See also Nukhet Varlik, *Plague and Empire in the Early Modern Mediterranean World: The Ottoman Experience* (Cambridge: Cambridge University Press, 2015), 234, 243.

27. Sönmez, *Idris-I Bidlisi,* 46–50.

28. Idrīs B. Ḥusām al-Dīn al-Bidlīsī, *Risāla al-ʾibāʾ ʿan mawāqiʿ al-wabāʾ,* Sulemaniye Esad Efendi 275, 102–61, 103b.

29. Ibid., 104a. I am not aware of the writings of al-Bidlīsī's critics being extant.

30. Ibid.

31. Ibid., 104b.

32. Sönmez, *Idris-I Bidlisi,* 53–60.

33. Stearns, *Infectious Ideas,* 102.

34. The usefulness of dividing the activity of bubonic plague into three pandemics has been increasingly disputed by historians, who have noted that the dates often given for these disparate outbreaks—roughly the 540s to 750, 1340s to 1722, 1896 to present—are fluid. On the plague treatise as a literary genre in Arabic, see Lawrence I. Conrad, "Arabic Plague Chronologies and Treatises: Social and Historical Factors in the Formation of a Literary Genre," *Studia Islamica* 54 (1981): 51–93.

35. The discussion in this paragraph is based on Stearns, *Infectious Ideas,* chap. 1.

36. Ibid., 30–31; Lawrence Conrad, "A Ninth-Century Muslim Scholar's Discussion of Contagion," in *Contagion: Perspectives from Pre-modern Societies,* ed. Lawrence Conrad and Dominik Wujastyk (Burlington, VT: Ashgate, 2000).

37. The literature on the subject is vast. For a discussion in relation to plague and its transmission, see Stearns, *Infectious Ideas*, chap. 5.

38. Accepting that there is a purpose does naturally not entail agreeing on the nature of that purpose, or on how to respond to the plague itself. Thus, Ibn Ḥajar could focus on the plague being a martyrdom for Muslims, and al-Ghazālī could ponder the ways in which disease causes believers to turn to God, while, without disputing either argument, al-Bidlīsī would advocate fleeing the plague.

39. See Stearns, *Infectious Ideas*, 144–45. Al-Ghazālī himself had prevaricated when it came to the precise issue of when and how to flee the plague, stressing the Muslim's duty to his Muslim community in a fashion that al-Bidlīsī rejected. See Al-Ghazali, *Faith in Divine Unity and Trust in Divine Providence*, trans. David Burrell (Louisville, KY: Fons Vitae, 2001), 132–35.

40. See Stearns, *Infectious Ideas*, 72. My gloss of medicine in the Muslim world as Galenic is imprecise, though more space would be required to give the subject its due. Nahyan Fancy, *Science and Religion in Mamluk Egypt: Ibn al-Nafīs, Pulmonary Transit and Bodily Resurrection* (New York: Routledge, 2013), has argued persuasively that much is lost when we refer to Islamicate medicine as a whole as Galenic for this obscures the substantial diversity of opinion that existed among doctors in the Muslim world over the years (71).

41. For Dols's discussion of Ibn Ḥajar's plague treatise, see *Black Death in the Middle East*, 110–21.

42. See Dols, "'Al-Manbijī's 'Report of the Plague': A Treatise on the Plague of 764–65/1362–64 in the Middle East," in *The Black Death: The Impact of the Fourteenth-Century Plague*, ed. D. Williman (Binghamton, NY: Center for Medieval and Early Renaissance Studies, 1982), 65–75, and "Ibn al-Wardī's *Risālah al-Naba' 'an al-Waba'*, a Translation of a Major Source for the History of the Black Death in the Middle East," in *Near Eastern Numismatics, Iconography, Epigraphy, and History: Studies in Honor of George C. Miles*, ed. D. Kouymjian (Beirut: American University of Beirut, 1974), 443–55.

43. See Stearns, *Infectious Ideas*, 79–85, 132–37.

44. Al-Bidlīsī was not the only sixteenth-century Ottoman scholar to write a plague treatise permitting flight from the plague. See Varlik, *Plague and Empire*, 243–44, where she briefly discusses the opinions of Kemalpaşazade, Taşköprizade, and Ebussuud.

45. See al-Bidlīsī, *Risāla al-'ibā'*, 105b; cf. 103a, where the Ottoman Sultan is listed as Salīm.

46. Ibid., 106b.

47. Ibid., 107b–8a. Al-Bidlīsī does make a point of clarifying that he is not adopting the stance of the philosophers according to which God does not know the particulars, for the potential changing natures that any particular could assume has been decreed (107a).

48. See Stearns, *Infectious Ideas*, 128–29, and the footnotes thereto.

49. See Crone, *God's Rule*, 153; also her discussion of al-Fārābī's treatment of the philosopher-king, ibid., 179–81.

50. Al-Bilīsī, *Risāla al-'ibā'*, 109b.

51. Ibid., 111b–13a; cf. 118a.
52. Ibid., 116a.
53. Ibid., 125a–28b.
54. Ibid., 119a, 121b, 122b.
55. Ibid., 131a–34b.
56. Ibid., 135b; also see the views of the Granadan jurist Ibn Lubb (d. 1381) summarized in Stearns, *Infectious Ideas*, 115–20.
57. Al-Bilīsī, *Risāla al-'ibā'*, 143b–44b.
58. Ibid., 147b.
59. There are many other aspects of al-Bidlīsī's plague treatise that are intriguing, including the author's description of the initial spread of syphilis and his own contraction and recovery from this disease through the use of mercury (ibid., 120a–b), but I cannot discuss these here.
60. Varlik, *Plague and Empire*, 249–53, and the following discussion, which, due to the limitations of the sources, relies largely on circumstantial evidence.
61. Stearns, *Infectious Ideas*, 130–31.
62. Ibid., 31–35, 112–13.
63. On the status of lepers in al-Andalus, see Christine Mazzoli-Guintard, "Notes sur une minorité urbaine d'al-Andalus: les lépreux," in *Homenaje al Profesor Carlos Posac Mon* (Ceuta: Instituto de estudios ceutíes, 1998), 1:319–25. For Ibn 'Abdūn's manual, see É. Lévi-Provençal, *Trois traites hispaniques de ḥisba* (Cairo: Institut français d'archeologie orientale, 1955), 50. The Christian doctor Qustā Ibn Lūqā (d. 910 or 920) made reference to the leper colonies of Jerusalem and Damascus in the ninth century (Stearns, *Infectious Ideas*, 71).
64. Yet see Kristin Stilt, *Islamic Law in Action: Authority, Discretion, and Everyday Experiences in Mamluk Egypt* (Oxford: Oxford University Press, 2011), 104–6, for a case in 1438 in which a *muhtasib* is given the explicit order to keep the women of Cairo indoors in the hope of improving public morality and thus lifting the plague by mollifying the wrath of God.
65. See also Varlik, *Plague and Empire*, 276–83.
66. For the account of a seventeenth-century Ottoman traveler who witnessed the use of the quarantine in Christian Europe, see *An Ottoman Traveller: Selections from the Book of Travels of Evliya Çelebi*, trans. Robert Dankoff and Sooyong Kim (London: Eland, 2010), 204. The Ottomans did not employ quarantines themselves, however, until the nineteenth century.
67. See Nancy Gallagher, *Medicine and Power in Tunisia* (Cambridge: Cambridge University Press, 1983), 31, 40–41. On the British regulation of the pilgrimage, see Michael Low, "Empire of the Hajj: Pilgrims, Plagues, and Pan-Islam Under British Surveillance, 1865–1908," *International Journal of Middle East Studies* 40 (2008): 269–90.
68. Andrew Robarts, "A Plague on Both Houses: Population Movements and the Spread of Disease Across the Ottoman-Russian Black Sea Frontier, 1768–1830s" (PhD diss., Georgetown University, 2010), 191–226.
69. Stearns, *Infectious Ideas*, 152–57.
70. Ibid., 152.
71. See, e.g., Varlik, *Plague and Empire*, 160.

The Dancing Despot

Toyotomi Hideyoshi and the Performative Symbolism of Power

STANCA SCHOLZ-CIONCA

I see their policie is great in doing thereof, and quite contrary to our
Comoedies in Christendome, ours being but dumbe shewes, and this
the truth it selfe, acted by the Kings themselves, to keep in perpetuall
remembrance their affaires.

—RICHARD COCKS, HIRADO, JAPAN, OCTOBER 13, 1613

"WE ROYALS ARE ALWAYS ON STAGE"—with this famous dictum that
conflates royalty with the lot of the actor, Queen Elizabeth I echoed a *basso
continuo* of her age. In fact, the theater metaphor applied to monarchic absolutism, frequent in discourses of the English Renaissance and Restoration,
reverberates in the dramatic works of Shakespeare and his contemporaries
across Europe. This perception is, of course, not confined to the Atlantic
space. At the same time, on the other side of the globe, in another island
country in the Pacific Ocean, a hegemon rose to power whose quick ascen-
sion and dramatic reign illustrates in spectacular ways what Christopher Pye
called in his seminal study "the irreducible relation between theatricality
and absolutism."[1] That hegemon, who pushed the theater metaphor to its
limits and also restored it to its basic meaning, was Toyotomi Hideyoshi
(1537?–1598), the second of three mighty warlords who unified Japan after a
century of devastating civil wars.[2]

In the history of Japan, this despot stands out not only as the most inventive and versatile performer of royal power, one whose acts unveil "sovereignty's true, and profoundly theatrical sources,"[3] but also as a devoted
amateur actor, who both impersonated on the Nô stage heroes of old and

confronted his own royal persona cast as a dramatic character, occasionally even representing himself in prodigious—and actually unique—acts of reduplication and reflection. Moreover, with his passion for the stage, this sovereign triggered a theatrical boom among Japan's leading elite, which impressed and baffled Europeans.[4]

Hideyoshi's role playing was not solely due to an innate histrionic temperament (which he undoubtedly possessed, as discussed below) but also induced by objective circumstances, which required extrovert performativity and self-fashioning on various stages of political action. In contrast to his English contemporary, Elizabeth I, who was born into her role as the daughter of a mighty king and legitimate heir to the throne and who relied on established state institutions to exercise and expand royal authority, Toyotomi Hideyoshi was an utter upstart of the lowest provenance who won his merits on the battlefield and fought his way to the top through prowess in arms and strategic genius as much as by intrigues, bargaining, and treason—to say nothing of some luck. Unlike his English counterpart, Hideyoshi was compelled to erect his scaffold of authority by reshaping the institutional structures of government and representation, an enterprise that implied a thorough refashioning of his own royal body. In order to legitimate his position, pacify the realm, stabilize his control of the nobility and the commoners, and impress the outside world, the hegemon had to adapt to existing frames and media and to find new forms for his symbolism of power.

In Japan, the set of media available for royal representation privileged performative acts over reified signs (such as statues of the king or effigies distributed on coins, more common in Europe)—that is, highlighting the royal body, his demeanor, and gestures as a central medium. Instinctively grasping this rhetorical potential, Hideyoshi used it in ostentatious acts of self-fashioning, achieved by diligent practice in disciplines and arts cultivated by the aristocracy and the warrior class. Besides his groundbreaking administrative reforms, the upstart sovereign is known as a renewer of ancient imperial ritual, an aficionado of theatricalized poetry contests, a generous patron and practitioner of the tea ceremony, a keen supervisor of stupendous architectural projects, and even as a landscape architect and designer of Zen gardens. However, his ultimate passion was—not surprisingly—theater, in which he displayed maniac addiction to the Nô.

These circumstances make Hideyoshi a unique case for the study of the royal body in premodern Japan, and the visibility of this hegemon is enhanced all the more by available handwritten private correspondence (which allows glimpses into his inner life) and by reflections in the Western gaze. His reign marks a hub of globalization in Japan's history, which, as we know, was followed by centuries of isolation from the outside world. During his reign, Christian missionaries admitted to the royal presence left an important corpus of documents on the extroverted sovereign—most based on encounters with the hegemon himself.[5] These accounts provide firsthand information on the royal body in performance—notably, postures, demeanor, and gestures—details hardly available from Japanese sources, which were subjected to strict conventions of historical discourse. In fact, the visibility of Hideyoshi is rather exceptional in premodern Japan, where secrecy (invisibility) was deemed to enhance the aura of sovereignty and therefore media representation was discouraged. The sculpture portrait, for example, though common in Europe, was reserved to Buddhist monks and nuns in Japan. So strong was the taboo of representing the royal body that on the Nô stage a sovereign could only be impersonated symbolically by a child.

The subject of this essay is the hegemon as a performer of political cum cultural acts. Both the configuration of real facts (the despot's foible for theatrical gestures) and the extant firsthand documents invite an investigation from the standpoint of the field of performance studies, highlighting theatrical elements in Hideyoshi's symbolic representation of royalty. I dwell on media and frames (royal pageants and punishing acts, courtly rituals and arts), on environment and setting (his *site-specific theater* avant la lettre), on the repertoire of roles, on rhetorical gesture, and on audiences and their responses. I also consider the hegemon's theater politics, which integrated Nô into court ceremonial—a far-reaching intervention that marks the institutional and aesthetic structures of the art down to the present day.

Names and Identities: Hideyoshi's Politics of Sight and Signs

For a commoner who became de facto leader of Japan overnight, performing sovereignty in a visible and distinctive way was a matter of vital importance, nothing short of a survival strategy in his insecure and contested position. However, acquiring the bodily signs of royalty—displaying prestige in a convincing way before his vassals and subjects, as well as before foreign ambassadors—implied learning the part from scratch, under continuous pressure of exposure and shame. During his reign, which extended less than one and a half decades (1585–1598), the upstart hegemon changed names,[6] roles, and functions, refashioning both his identity and appearance like an actor, in a continuous play of revealing and concealing, pretense and achievement.

His father's name remains unknown (his effort to conceal his origins is obvious), but he cherished and venerated his mother, adorning her with imperial titles, as he did for his half-brother, whose son he temporarily designated as his heir.[7] The circumstances and date of Hideyoshi's birth are hazy, veiled by mythmaking. He himself encouraged two versions. The first suggested a miracle, which implied a heavenly mandate, as he candidly reported in a diplomatic letter: "When I was about to enter my dear mother's womb, she had an auspicious dream. That night, the sunlight filled her room so that it was like noontime inside it. All were overwhelmed with astonishment. The attendants gathered, and the diviner proclaimed: 'This is a wondrous sign that when the child reaches his prime, his virtue will shine over the Four Seas, and he will radiate his glory to the ten thousand directions.'"[8] The second version, propagated in an official chronicle written by the hegemon's sycophant, Ômura Yûko, insinuates imperial descent. Both legends point to the despot's double strategy of combining "new and old principles of legitimacy."[9]

Elaborate shows are typical of Hideyoshi's reigning style. He used to baffle his subjects with rash and vigorous acts: rebuilding the capital at an incredible pace; erecting splendid palaces, residences, and monasteries; cutting new avenues through the city; or raising a huge moat around the capital. Equally striking are his acts of destruction, such as the overnight demolition of his former residence, donated to his nephew, Hidetsugi, when the latter fell into disgrace.[10] For more than a decade, Kyoto was a grand stage for Hideyoshi's demonstrations of power, a self-designed backdrop for flamboyant pageants and cruel acts of punishment, which lingered in popular memory as a lurid theater of despotic caprice. Such was the ritual suicide of the hegemon's intimate counselor, the tea master Sen no Rikyû, ordered by Hideyoshi in 1591 and staged as a spectacle that combined strategies of display and concealment, secrecy and crude visibility: while the seventy-year-old Rikyû was disemboweling himself in his residence, three thousand armed guards lined the streets surrounding it, abiding in uncanny silence. Another spectacle of horror was his nephew's ordered suicide, followed by the public execution of Hidetsugi's whole household—including the ladies-in-waiting and even their young children.[11]

Restoring Choreographies of Imperial Ritual

In Hideyoshi's political style, tradition was writ large and decorum of vital importance. His official chronicler, Ômura Yûko, noted that the hegemon "engaged in the study of several volumes of ancient histories and the genealogies of the various noble houses"[12] and ordered his sycophants to investigate and revive ceremonies of old that had fallen into oblivion during the long period of wars. However capricious the despot's acts, he staged his theater of power with a nod to the past, in a continuous search for famous precedents. His models were prominent members of the high nobility, known for their lavish style, but even more for their artistic taste. Restoring imperial structures and reviving (partly reinventing) court ceremonies was a reaction to his new surroundings. This allegedly illiterate upstart, with the coarse manners of a commoner, decided to live up to the elegant lifestyles of the court. An official portrait shows him with all the paraphernalia of a high courtier: sitting on a splendid multicolored dais, clad in the formal robes of a Heian courtier, wearing a black cap and holding in his right hand the minister's baton (*shaku*). The conventional setting sets off his physiognomy, painted with realistic accuracy: the emaciated face with dark circles around the eyes, a prominent mouth with thick lips, adorned with a tiny moustache and a thin beard—a rather unflattering portrait, calling to mind his nickname, Monkey, which hints at his lowly origins.

It is understandable that the upstart hegemon, exposed to the critical gaze of patricians of old descent, became a fervent defender of ancient traditions and was eager to bask in the sun of imperial splendor. By building a new palace for the emperor and by assuring a suitable income for the impoverished patricians, Hideyoshi not only signaled his own power and riches—displayed with even greater ostentation in his own residences—but also performed an act of *captatio benevolentiae*, a strategy to ensure loyalties. Imperial pomp and pageantry, revived in the old style of the Heian and Muromachi periods, offered an ideal stage for the glorification of the hegemon's persona: there he could pose as "the good patron and loyal minister of the court, the healer and ritualist, unquestionably the man of power and grace."[13] Hideyoshi deployed a remarkable gift for the mise-en-scène of huge ceremonies and entertainments, which symbolized social cohesion and order in a peaceful, prosperous reign. These included the pompous funeral ceremonies for his predecessor in 1582; a famous falconry hunting party in 1591, which resuscitated memories of Heian splendor; his huge flower-viewing parties and grand poetry contests; state processions and gorgeous tea ceremonies; and, last but not least, audiences for foreign ambassadors accompanied by extravagant exchanges of gifts.

Among his state pageants, the imperial procession of 1588—an official visit of Emperor Go-Yôzei to Hideyoshi's splendid Juraku palace—stands out for its long preparations: it allegedly took two years to reconstruct courtly requisites that had grown out of use. Hosts of artisans were commissioned with rebuilding the delicate palm-leaf ox-carriages as represented in Heian painted scrolls, but they were ordered to embellish them in the lavish style of his own reign: thus, for instance, the oxen's horns had to be gilded. The elaborate parades, banquets, and entertainments of all kinds that filled the five-day event displayed an ambiguous symbolism of power, for they stressed the hegemon's pacification of the realm, allegedly achieved under imperial protection. With a nod to Japan's glorious past (notably imperial visits to the residences of powerful shoguns in the fourteenth and early fifteenth century), the emperor's pageant actually framed a political act that was meant to reinforce Hideyoshi's leading role in the state: the despot exacted of the imperial dignitaries solemn oaths of loyalty—nominally to the emperor but actually to the chancellor, Hideyoshi himself.

His ambivalent body language in that event points to his politics of sight and signs: he performed humble submission when accompanying the imperial carriage on foot all the way to his own palace, bowing to hold the emperor's train in the procession. Still, he left no doubt as to his own role in the script: the courtiers called to perform the oath of submission to the throne were actually Hideyoshi's own vassals and acolytes, for whom he had obtained high functions within the courtly hierarchy, thus denouncing the refashioned imperial bureaucracy as a fake. Basking in imperial splendor, the chancellor's power appeared all the more evident. The grand mise-en-scène foregrounds royal authority split and reflected in two symbolic bodies: that of the emperor, offering a facade of legitimacy; and that of the real "king" and center of political power, the "Bountiful Minister" Hideyoshi. The latter's demonstration of loyalty to the emperor appears to be no more than a rhetorical device to clad his own claim to royalty, a claim candidly confessed elsewhere: "During the 104 reigns that have passed, there has never yet been a king who has ruled and governed the whole of Japan—and I have subdued all of it."[14]

A special record detailing the event, distributed to all the dignitaries present, was meant to preserve the memory of the royal pageant for coming generations but also, undoubtedly, to reinforce the oaths of submission that stood at the core of the performance, to strengthen the bonds of vassalage that sustained his reign. In an age of unstable loyalties and frequent acts of treason, that "stage script" would remind every potential renegade of his own proffered commitment to Hideyoshi. The despot's urge to ensure stable loyalties discloses anxieties concerning his position, which were to push him to rash acts during his last years.

Subverting the Protocol: The Royal Body Unchained

Although ceremonial was writ large in his symbolic representation of power, Hideyoshi also grasped by intuition the rhetoric of eccentric behavior, which could impress and awe his audience. In contrast to most of his predecessors and those following after him, he showed a histrionic propensity to disrupt the protocol by impulsive gestures and playful improvisation.

In the long practice of Japanese court ceremonial, the sovereign's body, if visible at all, was characterized by silence, immobility, and restraint. It inspired awe and stressed the unbridgeable distance between majesty and ordinary subjects—actually perceived as an ontological gap. Western visitors admitted to the court note the stiff immobility of the sovereigns. Thus, Luis Frois remarked, after a New Year's audience with the last Ashikaga shogun, Yoshiteru, in 1565: "During these visits he speaks to nobody, but he may make a gesture with the fan which he holds in his hand to some wealthy and important bonzes; but it is only a slight gesture and this is because of the dignity of the honorable position which he occupies. Persons of lower rank are not allowed to visit him, even though they may present him with a house of gold." At such visits, gifts or cups of tea passed through the hands of servants or ladies-in-waiting, but the potentate and his family members posed in rigid silence. The shogun's mother, Frois adds, "seemed to me like an abbess of a monastery and her household like a community of nuns, so great was the silence, modesty and good order of that house, and also because she was sitting in the doorway of a chapel of Amida."[15]

Unbridgeable distance is also reported at later audiences with Tokugawa shoguns, including Ieyasu (called "emperor"): one European visitor remembered: "There entered one of the greatest nobles of Japan . . . over a hundred paces from where His Highness was seated, this *tono* prostrated himself, bowing his head so low that it looked as if he wanted to kiss the ground. Nobody said a word to him nor did he raise his eyes towards the Emperor on entering and leaving. Finally he turned and withdrew with his large retinue, which, according to some of my servants, numbered more than 3,000 men."[16] The same impression is conveyed at an audience with Ieyasu's son, Hidetada, in 1611: "From inside the hall they gave a certain sign (albeit a very small one on the prince's part) giving the ambassador to understand that he should enter. Everything took place in such complete silence that it seemed like a dream, for it was as quiet as if nobody at all were present."[17]

In contrast, Hideyoshi's demeanor in similar situations often astounds due to his liveliness and impulsive gestures. His unforeseeable reactions and an unrestrained mobility suggest a histrionic character, doubled by the self-confidence of an absolute monarch. When receiving visitors seated on a chair, he would draw it near to the guests to converse with them; he would even borrow the belt of his Portuguese visitor to slap himself on the shoulders with it in a playful and casual way. Or he would candidly brag about his wondrous birth and his incomparable power before foreigners.

Rash and impulsive, this sovereign obviously enjoyed subverting the protocol, even using it as a foil for his own unconventional performance. While all the courtiers present remained immobile in prostrate position, the hegemon alone would move freely before his visitors, showing childlike curiosity for exotic people and objects, combined with a sharp power of observation. However, his impulsive, unrestrained gestures do not necessarily suggest an uncontrolled royal body. On the contrary, Hideyoshi appears in many instances to be aware of the effects produced by his unconventional acts, which he often used deliberately, alternating as he pleased distance and proximity, formal behavior and casual gestures that would baffle and awe his visitors.

The Royal Body Restrained: Hideyoshi and the Culture of Tea

Such lighthearted transgressions of courtly protocol were just one facet of Hideyoshi's bodily politics of power. His demonstrations of discipline and self-control were another. Actually, this hegemon of lowly extraction was obsessed with self-fashioning, and he spared no efforts to acquire noble bodily and spiritual accomplishments. His painstaking training in the art of poetry contests—a group practice, carefully orchestrated by etiquette and demanding competence in social intercourse—is well documented. Some of his *waka* (poetic form of thirty-two syllables) are preserved, but he also practiced *renga*, chain-poetry composed in coteries of poets, which were group performances in their own right. However, he showed even more interest in a codified practice that had become a fashionable pastime in warrior milieus: the tea ceremony.[18] In the subdued, minimalistic choreography of that Zen-suffused discipline, Hideyoshi found ample inspiration to expand and refine the rhetorics of the royal body.

In the latter half of the sixteenth century, the practice of tea had developed into a multimedia art, which implied a codified space and a compelling syntax of behavioral patterns. It trained composure of the mind, modesty and humility, and, not least, bodily control. It enhanced the sense of community; it cultivated camaraderie, simplicity, pureness, and fair-mindedness. A carefully designed space—a simple tea hut of two or three *tatami* mats with distinctive elements, including a ceremonial niche with a scroll painting, a shelf, and a crooked wooden pillar—put the mind at rest. The use of exquisite tools sharpened the senses, heightened the perception of nature and atmosphere, and refined the aesthetic taste of the participants. However, tea parties also promoted the cult of expensive—even fetishistic—objects, encouraging the collection and display of exclusive tools, such as costly teacups, fine teapots and kettles, and painted scrolls with exquisite calligraphy, exhibited in the niche of the tearoom.[19] Tea in Hideyoshi's time fostered contrasting and even polarized attitudes: restraint as much as gorgeous ostentation, the cult of poverty as much as the display of riches.

Hideyoshi's enthusiasm for the art of tea—according to his letters he practiced it regularly twice a day even during his military campaigns—was not only due to aesthetic inclinations. As he acknowledges in a letter, he became aware of tea as political capital when still in his predecessor's service: "For Nobunaga, tea was part of the Way of Politics. I shall never forget neither in this nor in my next life that Nobunaga allowed me to do tea."[20] Like his predecessor, who declared the practice a monopoly of the samurai elite and reclaimed for himself the right to bestow licenses to practice tea on his favorites, Hideyoshi used the ceremony's political and cultural capital, surrounding himself with the most famous tea masters of his time (among them Sen no Rikyû) and holding tea parties on strategic occasions: as a peace ritual after a battle; on the battlefield, to impress the enemy with his calm composure; as part of courtly protocol on important occasions (for instance, in 1585, in the festivities held after becoming chancellor); at receptions for foreign ambassadors, to impress the envoys with his splendid utensils; and, last but not least, in grand collective performances with mass participation to demonstrate benevolence and proximity to his subjects.

With the latter aim in mind, in 1587 he organized the largest tea party ever recorded in Japanese history—a telling example of the sovereign's political symbolism. Preceded by careful preparation, the tea party was intended to capture public attention and leave a lasting impression on the participants, to be transmitted to future generations. The setting was carefully chosen: the grove surrounding the Kitano shrine in the capital, dedicated to Sugawara Michizane, who was venerated as a deity of poetry and learning. The place was also inscribed in collective memory by grand poetry parties, *hana no moto renga* under blooming plum trees, held centuries before, during the heyday of the Ashikaga shogunate, on Michizane's memorial day in early spring (on the twenty-fifth day of the second lunar month). Such parties were occasions for the shogunate to display egalitarian and benevolent politics toward the masses, for they encouraged broad participation of amateur poets from all social strata, from the emperor to the beggar.

Hideyoshi was well aware of those lofty precedents when he invited a large audience to his tea party, planned to last for ten days. Announcements on wooden boards planted all over the capital advertised unlimited public participation, foreigners included (Chinese were expressly welcome!), though they stipulated strict rules: "[Persons] serious about the tea ceremony, whether they are [military] attendants, townsmen, or farmers, should bring along one kettle, one ladle, one drinking vessel, and either tea or barley."[21] The message contained an innuendo of compulsion and control, suggesting that failing to participate would be interpreted as an offense and even incur punishment.

The invitation was indeed accepted by huge crowds, and the hegemon kept his promise to personally serve his subjects a cup of tea. In the grove surrounding the Kitano shrine, where hundreds of improvised tearooms had been erected and the ground was spread with innumerable mats populated by tea amateurs from all layers of society, the hegemon sat in his famous tearoom plated with pure gold,[22] using tea utensils of inestimable value—and showing his exorbitant riches to awestruck guests. On what was planned as the first day of the performance, the despot is reported to have served with his own hands an impressive number of guests, chosen by lottery (in the sources, the number varies between 203 and 803). In any case, his physical performance surpassed by far all similar acts recorded and would have upstaged the dimensions of any tea party. The effort must have exhausted the monarch, who broke off the party at the end of the first day, sending everybody home. By putting an abrupt ending to his own *mise-en-scène*, the despot demonstrated once more his absolute power in a whimsical gesture. Typical for his technology of reigning, the party carried contradictory and ambiguous messages. On the one hand, it emphasized leniency and humility, promoting signs of consensus, community, and harmony between the sovereign and his subjects, displaying egalitarianism and democracy as inherent to Hideyoshi's peaceful and abundant reign. On the other hand, the party communicated absolute, tyrannical authority. The same ambivalence can be inferred from Hideyoshi's tea politics as a whole: although he introduced the tea ceremony to the imperial court, making it part of the state ceremonial and surrounding himself with the best tea masters, he not only defied the very spirit of tea by ostentatiously displaying his gold-plated tearoom but he would also order—for reasons still unknown—the suicide of his best tea master, Sen no Rikyû, four years later.

A Generous Patron of Nô

It comes as no surprise that a reign thus imbued with theatricality encouraged a broad range of performing arts. Indeed, in his fondness of spectacle and entertainment, Hideyoshi far surpassed his predecessors and successors. Even during military campaigns his entourage would include hosts of entertainers—musicians, singers, dancers, storytellers and rhapsodes, acrobats and wrestlers—who not only catered to the despot's own amusement but also heightened the spirits of his soldiers. Besides, the riotous atmosphere of Hideyoshi's camp would impress and scare his enemies. In his Kyûshû camp during the Korean campaign, he summoned from the capital more than eight hundred entertainers skilled in various genres—an impressive number by any standards.

Among those sundry arts, the medium that ultimately offered the most resounding space for Hideyoshi's display of royal power was Nô theater—an art form intimately connected to the warriors' culture and self-representation. From the surge of the art in the fourteenth century, the shoguns' patronage was decisive in the development of Nô. During the reign of the third Ashikaga shogun, Yoshimitsu (r. 1368–1394) and within the time span of two actors' generations—Kan'ami and his son Zeami—the genre shifted from a "beggar's occupation" practiced by pariahs on temple grounds to the status of a cultivated literary stage art suitable to be presented at court. Ever after, Nô performances—often elaborate programs lasting for several days on end— became a frequent part of courtly entertainment. The actors took advantage of their proximity to court life, blending courtly poetry into the dramas and polishing their stage practice, while samurai and patricians from the old aristocracy, for their part, started practicing Nô chant (*utai*) and dance (*shimai*) as an elegant pastime. In the new surroundings, Nô dance and stage movements were gradually influenced by courtly manners and etiquette, eventually becoming a model for princely demeanor.[23]

It was only natural for Hideyoshi to sponsor Nô troupes that would adorn his state banquets with their refined programs. Like Oda Nobunaga, Hideyoshi hastened to recall to the capital the best professional actors who had fled to the provinces in search of protection and employment in *daimyô* residences during the intestine wars. With peace restored and celebratory events mushrooming in the capital, the despot grasped all opportunities to summon famous actors to his residences. The frequent banquets and grand state ceremonies during Hideyoshi's reign contained daylong Nô programs performed by the more important families of actors—especially the Yamato troupes. The noble plays, featuring deities and demons, ghosts of famous warriors, or delicate love stories of old, provided an appropriate frame to the display of royal power.

Moreover, eager to monopolize Nô's cultural and symbolic capital, Hideyoshi took a decisive step to institutionalize the bonds between royalty and theater. He raised Nô to the position of state-sponsored art, integrated into the courtly ceremonial. Two official letters, issued in 1593 and signed in 1597 in his own hand and reinforced by his red seal, stipulated a special status to four family schools of Nô from Yamato, guaranteeing them a high yearly income to be paid by the leading warriors of the realm.[24] This was a measure of great portent, not only for the privileged actors who became practically state employees but also for the subsequent development of theater as a whole, since the Tokugawa shoguns following Hideyoshi reinforced the stipulations, thus confining Nô to the warriors' residences, where it gradually turned into a stiff ceremonial art shaped by its symbiosis with the warriors' etiquette. Even present Nô remains distinctly marked by that long cohabitation.

Hideyoshi on Stage

Creating new institutional frames was but one aspect of Hideyoshi's involvement with Nô; his own involvement in the practice of the art was another. His interest in Nô deepened during his campaign at Nagoya on Kyûshû, where he supervised the advancement and subsequent defeat of his troops on the Korean peninsula. Far from the actual battlefields and also cut off from the political stage in the capital, he found himself in an unusual position, one that favored leisurely activities. It is there he discovered Nô practice as a bodily and spiritual discipline that yielded an excellent tool of royal self-fashioning. In his endeavor to emulate aristocratic predecessors by acquiring mastery in the arms and arts (*bunbu*), Hideyoshi started to practice Nô as *via regia* to princely accomplishment, an ideal medium to attain that beauty and elegance of demeanor he thought most suitable for an accomplished sovereign. He advised his fellow warriors to follow him: "These days military men have ascended to high posts, but their appearance in court dress is utterly ignoble, so that they must all practice Nô."[25] Indeed, whereas the founder of Nô, the pariah Zeami, had striven to catch glimpses of the ways and manners of courtly life to imitate on stage, two centuries later it was the actors themselves who preserved the refined gesture repertoire of old and were in a position to teach it to the coarse warriors come to power.

Under the supervision of Nô master Kurematsu Shinkurô from the Konparu school and other leading actors, Hideyoshi applied himself to learning scores by heart and acquiring an actor's bodily skills. His private correspondence from the Kyushu camp discloses a growing enthusiasm for the practice. Thus he boasts in a letter written in 1593: "I have learned ten noh plays: *Matsukaze, Oimatsu, Miwa, Bahô, Kureha, Teika, Tôru, Kakitsubata, Tamura.* . . . To sum up, there are ten. I have become very skilled in these numbers and I will try to learn more."[26] A couple of months later, Nô dancing had apparently absorbed him altogether, reaching a state of mania. In a letter to his mother, the hegemon confesses in his sluggish diction:

> Although you have repeatedly sent me letters, I have sent no reply as I have had no free time because of noh. . . . My noh technique becomes more and more accomplished; whenever I present the *shimai* of various plays, the whole audience praises it very much. I have already done so for two plays, and after resting a little, I shall act again on the 9th day and show it to all the ladies in Kyoto. . . . I repeat: because I have been performing noh more and more, I am really tired and worried. . . . I shall perform noh at your residence to show (you and others). Look forward to it.[27]

Nô practice appealed to his fondness for masquerade, already exhibited on previous occasions: in his fancy for costumes *à la portuguaise* or for fierce makeup at public events (where he wore false eyebrows, a false moustache, and beard). Nô costumes, which in Hideyoshi's time had acquired the status of fetishistic goods, admired for their richness and splendor, became his most coveted presents.[28] In a letter, the despot thanked his wife, O-Ne: "You have very promptly given me a splendid *kosode* for noh with various patterns which you chose thinking they would suit me. Everyone I showed it to liked it very much. I am delighted that it was made just for me."[29] On another occasion, a set of costume items sent by a lady-in-waiting transported him into an exhilarated state: "You sent me some noh costumes which are beautiful; the pattern is especially original."[30]

Dancing Nô involved a heightened attention to his own body and appearance, which Hideyoshi watched with the self-critical gaze of an actor—that famous "distant gaze" (*riken no ken*) that Zeami advised the actors to train. The constant concern with his own persona also sharpened his sensitivity to the ravages of time on his own face. Private letters reveal an aging despot, embarrassed by his tired face, asking for his teeth-blackening cosmetic box to be sent from home, and confessing shame to show himself before his women after his long absence. However, in that critical phase in his life, the addiction to Nô may also have offered compensation for an unpleasant reality, an illusionary and temporary refuge from everyday worries. Hideyoshi was besieged by anxiety about the outcome of his campaign but also about the pending problem of succession. In spite of desperate efforts to impose his young son, born to a concubine during the campaign, as his legitimate heir, and notwithstanding the radical extermination of his nephew (his former favorite) together with all his household, Hideyoshi nevertheless anticipated the fragility of his scaffold of power. Indeed, the alliances enforced by oaths of loyalty were to prove volatile a couple of years after his death.

Many of Hideyoshi's utterances and acts during the last years of his life show an increasing discrepancy between his perception of reality and visionary states, a blurred distinction between facts and illusion. Not supported by his entourage, who only told him what he wished to hear (as one Jesuit put it), the increasingly lonely sovereign would mix up visions of his apotheosis as a glorious king with stage accomplishments. Thus, for instance, he deliberately misread the Ming emperor's harsh message—a demand for surrender—and preferred to concentrate instead on details of protocol, insisting on entertaining the Chinese ambassadors with his own Nô dances, as we learn from a letter addressed to his wife: "As imperial envoys have come from the Ming country to bring an apology, be assured that I shall agree with them about peace negotiations. . . . I shall be back in triumph around the 10th month. I shall try to put on noh (for the envoys)."[31]

The despot's Nô craze reached its peak after his return from the camp, when he repeatedly performed Nô together with professional actors before the emperor and other dignitaries. Enticing his vassals to emulate him, Hideyoshi also exposed high dignitaries in public by casting them in unfavorable roles.[32] During his last years, Hideyoshi's insatiable thirst for stage applause was only matched by his fits of self-aggrandizement. Few appreciations of his stage accomplishments have been preserved, but, alongside some ambiguous exclamations uttered by courtly spectators, one European witness offers critical remarks: Luis Frois (who was not impartial himself) noted after a Nô performance at Hideyoshi's Fushimi castle: "sometymes he also intruded himself, and danced amongst the rest, but with such an evil grace, as well argued an impotent, and dotinge old man."[33]

Panegyric Nô and the Hegemon's Rhetoric of Power

Hideyoshi may have been a poor actor; however, he undoubtedly proved a cunning dramaturge who made full use of theater's perlocutionary force in the symbolic representation of absolutist rule. Under his supervision, Nô became an excellent medium to impose on his subjects—by a skillful politics of sight and signs—the message of charismatic royalty. Thus, for the first time in history, Nô was unabashedly used as a bare political weapon to strategic ends. In 1594, the despot commissioned Ômura Yûko to write ten new plays in praise of "the piety, valour, grace and elegance, and wondrous deeds of the Prime Minister's [Hideyoshi's] reign." Such a bold innovation had to be defended: "There are many nô plays about heroes of old, but this time the venerable Yûko has been entrusted with recording the real events, excluding sham stories."[34]

Five of those taikô nô (plays dedicated to Hideyoshi) have been preserved: three "warrior plays" (shura-nô) and two celebratory plays of the deity type (kami-nô).[35] All are panegyric dramas attempting distinct dramaturgic strategies to represent, reflect, and reduplicate the sovereign's persona, a major challenge being the despot's insistence on performing himself all the main roles. After one attempt, Yûko abandoned direct dramatization of historical facts: among his plays, a single one, based on Hideyoshi's revenge on his predecessor's assassin, offered the sovereign-actor the chance to brandish his sword on the stage while impersonating himself in a "realistic" script, untypical of Nô.[36] The other two warrior plays tackle the sovereign's valor in an indirect way, using displacement and substitution: in them, Hideyoshi embodied ghosts of his enemies—two valiant knights who died while opposing the mighty general.

Conjuring the shadows of vanquished warriors killed in battles (or forced to commit suicide) was a time-tested pattern of the lyrical drama that evoked in elegiac mode the "nobility of failure," uttering prayers for the salvation of the unrestful souls.[37] Nô plays of the "warrior" type symbolically performed rituals of appeasement, especially because the revenge of those who had experienced violent death was deeply feared. Aware of this pattern, Yûko complied with the rules of classical warrior dramas. However, by casting the victor himself in the role of his dead victims, who proffered on the stage oaths of submission and praise of Hideyoshi, the author and his actor violated those very rules. In his mania of self-aggrandizement, the sovereign-actor inflicted postmortem humiliation on the dead, defying all considerations of piety.

Transgression is even more radical in the two deity plays dedicated to Hideyoshi, *Yoshino môde* (Royal Procession to Yoshino) and its pair, *Kôya sankei* (Pilgrimage to Mount Kôya). Embedded in state ceremonies, they reflect and reduplicate in their dramatic structure the display of the royal body in the framing events, relying on the expressive potential of site-specific performance. In contrast to the usual theater of memory in Nô, the deity plays dedicated to Hideyoshi are anticipatory dramas, which prescribed, described, and underpinned two royal pageants.

Yoshino môde prefigured the grand procession undertaken by Hideyoshi and his retinue in the second and third month of 1594 to an important religious site on Mount Yoshino. The pageant culminated in a blossom-viewing party (*hanami*) on the first day of the third lunar month in front of the Main Hall of the Yoshino temple complex, crowned by an elaborate Nô program comprising nine plays: three performed by Hideyoshi himself (among them *Yoshino môde*); two by his designated heir, Hidetsugi (who was ordered to commit suicide a couple of months later); and four by other high dignitaries.

Yoshino môde, which opened the program, casts the royal procession as *via sacra* crowned by divine epiphany—as usual in deity plays of the *incubatio* type. In contrast to the warrior dramas, the site is not connected to the hegemon's biography: it is not one of his battlefields but a place permeated by a *mysterium tremendum et fascinosum*, hosting a temple complex dedicated to Zaô Gongen, the fierce patron deity of the mountain ascetics' sect (*shugendô*). Moreover, the awe-inspiring site (*locus tremendus*), is also a well-known place of delight (*locus amoenus*), famous for its paradisiac landscape of cherry blossoms, which carries rich poetic associations reverberating in Nô rhetoric. This double connotation of the site provided a powerful setting for both the royal pageant and the Nô, echoing in the abundant felicitous words (*shûgen*) that embellish the libretto, pointing to the cosmic and religious dimensions of embodied political power.

The straightforward plot reduplicates the framing event: a high dignitary (*waki*) announces the hegemon's procession, praising the deeds of he "who rules the land at his heart's will [*kokoro no mama ni*], who conquered the three Korean lands and showed his benevolence to the Ming envoys, of he who put an end to the wars and built a splendid castle at Fushimi in Yamashiro."[38] A character Hideyoshi and his retinue—cast in side roles (*waki/wakizure*)—arrive at Yoshino where they encounter a mysterious old couple (*shite* and *tsure*) and engage in an elegant conversation about the holiness of the site. The old couple depart, to reappear in the second act in their real form as deities—the formidable Zaô Gongen himself, accompanied by a Heavenly maid—who extend their grace on the hegemon and promise to protect his reign.

The rather simple plot deployed its full effect in the performance in situ, which directed the spectators' gaze in an oscillating movement between the real act (the sovereign's procession) and the dramatic action on stage, relying on strategies of displacement, substitution, and reflection imposed by the sovereign's multiple roles. Hideyoshi was involved as main officiant of the state act (the procession and flower-viewing party); as dramaturge *and* spectator of the complex show (whose controlling gaze was feared, as he would punish the smallest lapse or deviation from the prescribed scenario); as a character in the play (the side character Hideyoshi, symbolically embodied by a child, as usual for imperial persons); and, last but not least, as the leading actor, who impersonated on stage the very deity of the place, Zaô Gongen. Iconographic similarities between the fierce deity (whose awe-inspiring wooden portrait is venerated in the main hall of the temple complex) and Hideyoshi's royal persona were not coincidental.

Symbolic gestures governed the drama: At the climax of the play—which was also a key moment in the "real" royal procession—the sovereign-actor, playing Zaô Gongen, offered the character Hideyoshi a blooming cherry twig, while solemnly promising divine protection for his reign. The stage gesture, which turned the audience's attention toward the real performance of charismatic royalty, insinuated divine sponsorship, uplifting the hegemon's human act in a divine space. By multiple reflections of the royal persona in the drama, in the staging and the "real" procession, the performance conflated sacred epiphany with the apotheosis of absolutist royalty, deliberately blurring the boundaries between poetry, theater, religion, and politics.

The sovereign had voiced his claim on the deity status before a foreign visitor as early as 1589, declaring *kami* (native deities) to be none other than the Lords of Japan, who were venerated by the people for their victories and exploits. The project was a pillar in Hideyoshi's scaffold of sovereignty, and Nô was instrumental in backing it. In fact, *Yoshino môde*, as performed in 1594 in situ, may be read as a symbolic act prefiguring his deification. This innuendo was reinforced on a gorgeous folding screen illustrating the procession to Yoshino (probably painted by Kanô Mitsunobu), which carries suggestions of the Buddhist paradise. It depicts Hideyoshi dressed in white, sitting like a bodhisattva among courtiers clad in bright colors in a pristine spring landscape of blooming cherry trees (an emblem of Yoshino but also a reflection of the hegemon's peaceful reign). In the lower left corner, a tiny Nô stage annexed to Yoshimizu-in indicates the performance held in front of the Zaô Hall, alluding to theater as a central tool of royal power.[39]

The claim to deification is reinforced in Yûko's second deity play, *Pilgrimage to Mount Kôya* (*Kôya sankei*), written for the despot's procession to his mother's mausoleum, erected in the precincts of the famous temple of esoteric Shingon Buddhism. In the play, the sovereign was cast in the role of his own mother, allegedly venerated posthumously as a bodhisattva. On the stage, the actor-sovereign was supposed to chant an elaborate praise of himself, voicing his mother's pride and gratitude to her royal son (actually impersonated by a child). Once more, the hegemon's body in multiple appearance—in human and divine form within the drama, as sovereign in the "real" pilgrimage—powerfully suggested sacred royalty. However, such overt conflation of royal with divine authority carried a seed of blasphemy, perceivable even to subjects living in a "charismatic social order" (Max Weber's term). Thus, when an earthquake accompanied by a violent storm interrupted the procession to Mount Kôya, it was understood as an ominous sign. According to an eyewitness, the hegemon's self-aggrandizement had infuriated the gods and an oracle announced that Kôbô Daishi himself, the venerated ancestor of the Shingon sect, had showed his discontent with the performance in his holy precincts. Thus, divine wrath precluded Hideyoshi's performance, and the sovereign hurried down from the mountain, leaving behind the Nô manuscript in the Kongôbuji (where it is preserved to the present day).

In both "pageant Nô," which belong to the category of "deity plays," the double *mise en abyme* of the hegemon's public parades was not simply an ornamental device but rather a tool for strong political messages, which blurred the boundaries between reality and show, religious veneration and royal charisma, and celebration and state parade. In a complex dramaturgy of sight and signs, Nô performances immersed in ceremonies of power display reinforced the hegemon's self-aggrandizement. For the sovereign-cum-actor, embodying deity roles within the frame of state acts foreshadowed his own deification, which was successfully promoted during the last years of his reign, although it proved short-lived after his death. In this respect, Hideyoshi is not an exception: all three major unifiers of Japan were deified, but only the third, Tokugawa Ieyasu—who was able to establish a long-lasting dynasty—is venerated as a deity to the present day in his Nikkô mausoleum. In contrast, Hideyoshi's vigorous performances of royalty on various stages of political representation and his aggressive self-fashioning, sometimes amounting to exhibitionism, proved in the end transitory—like theater itself, the leading medium of his reign.

Thus, the plebeian hegemon, who had to learn from scratch the grammar of power, skillfully used and expanded the performative spectrum available for royal representation. He embedded in the court ceremonials and state acts old and new performance patterns, to manipulate and control his subjects—like other absolute monarchs—by signs of authority and demonstrations of egalitarianism, gestures of magnanimity and spectacles of punishment. He was a master in alternating in fluid ways distance and proximity to his subjects, gestures of alliance and hegemonic pretense in foreign relations. Last, but not least, his manifold performances also reveal—in their ambivalence of reality and pretense, substance and appearance, fact and fiction—the deep anxieties and the dwindling sense of reality that lay at the core of royalty. How telling that the hegemon's favorite medium of self-representation was the theater stage.

Notes

1. Christopher Pye, *The Regal Phantasm: Shakespeare and the Politics of Spectacle* (London: Routledge, 1990), 1ff.
2. The other two were Oda Nobunaga (1534–1582) and Tokugawa Ieyasu (1543–1616). Following Japanese custom, surnames precede personal names in this chapter.

3. Pye, *Regal Phantasm*, 2.

4. Richard Cocks describes a performance given by "the Kings themselves, with the greatest Noblemen and Princes" in *The Voyage of John Saris to Japan, 1613*, ed. Ernest Mason Satow (London: Hakluyt Society, 1900), 70.

5. For a limited period—Japan's "Christian period" of roughly one century between 1543 and 1639—European missionaries won admission to the country and occasionally to the court.

6. In premodern Japan, it was usual to change names in the course of one's life. Most people had a childhood name, another after manhood initiation, names related to the profession and, as needed, honorary names, such as a posthumous Buddhist name. The right to use a family name was reserved to the elites.

7. The following biographical information on Toyotomi Hideyoshi is mainly indebted to Mary Elizabeth Berry, *Hideyoshi* (Cambridge, MA: Harvard University Press, 1982); Adriana Boscaro, *101 Letters of Hideyoshi: The Private Correspondence of Hideyoshi* (Tokyo: Sophia University, 1975); George Elison, "Hideyoshi, the Bountiful Minister," in *Warlords, Artists, and Commoners*, ed. George Elison and Bardwell Smith (Honolulu: University Press of Hawai'i, 1981), 223–44; *The Cambridge History of Japan*, ed. John Whitney Hall (Cambridge: Cambridge University Press, 1991), vol. 4; and Conrad Totman, *A History of Japan* (Oxford: Blackwell, 2000).

8. Contained in a letter demanding the submission of Formosa (1593) and sealed with Hideyoshi's golden seal. Cf. Elison, "Bountiful Minister," 223. A slightly different version is reported by St. Pedro Bautista Blanquez, in *They Came to Japan: An Anthology of European Reports on Japan, 1543-1640*, ed. Michael Cooper (Berkeley: University of California Press, 1965), 111.

9. Cf. Berry, *Hideyoshi*, 187.

10. Accused of treason, Hidetsugi was forced to commit suicide in 1594.

11. Beside the punishments in the capital, famously described in the reports of Jesuits is also the spectacular crucifixion of twenty-six Christians in Nagasaki, on February 5, 1597. See, e.g., Cooper, *They Came to Japan*, 385–95; also Michael Cooper, *Rodrigues the Interpreter: An Early Jesuit in Japan and China* (1974; New York: Weatherhill, 1994), 140–62.

12. *Kanpaku ninkanki*, quoted in Elison, "Bountiful Minister," 225.

13. Berry, *Hideyoshi*, 187.

14. Letter of St. Pedro Bautista Blanquez, O.F.M., in Cooper, *They Came to Japan*, 111.

15. Ibid., 109ff.

16. Rodrigo de Vivero y Velasco, 1609, quoted in ibid., 118.

17. Sebastian Vizcaino, in ibid., 119ff.

18. On the culture of tea in Hideyoshi's age, see e.g., H. Paul Varley and George Elison, "The Culture of Tea: From Its Origins to Sen no Rikyû," in Elison and Smith, *Warlords, Artists, and Commoners*, 187–222.

19. Contemporary descriptions of tea parties are offered by J. Rodriguez, in Cooper, *They Came to Japan*, 262ff.; see also Michael Cooper, *Joao Rodrigues's Account of Sixteenth Century Japan* (London: Hakluyt, 2001), 155–58, 272–81.

20. Letter of Hideyoshi, quoted in Herbert Plutschow, *Rediscovering Rikyu and the Beginnings of the Japanese Tea Ceremony* (Folkestone, UK: Global Oriental, 2003), 83.

21. Berry, *Hideyoshi*, 190.
22. The famous golden tearoom is described in the report of an audience with the hegemon in 1597: "They took us to a chamber completely lined with gold utensils—even the chopstick were of gold. And at the end of the repast they gave us a delicate drink which they call *cha*. Then the king came in & sat next to me" (St. Pedro Bautista Blanquez, in Cooper, *They Came to Japan*, 112).
23. For the convergence of the samurai bodily culture (martial arts, courtly etiquette) and Nô, see, e.g., Stanca Scholz-Cionca, "Halte den Fächer wie ein Schwert," in *Körper-Inszenierungen: Präsenz und kultureller Wandel*, ed. Erika Fischer-Lichte and Anne Fleig (Tübingen: Attempto, 2000), 131–47.
24. For details on Hideyoshi's Nô legislation, see Omote Akira and Amano Fumio, *Nôgaku no rekishi* (Tokyo: Iwanami Shoten, 1987–1992), 1:81–89; also Amano Fumio, *Nô ni tsukareta kenryokusha: Hideyoshi nôgaku aikôki* (Tokyo: Kodansha, 1997), 214–32.
25. Quoted in Elison, "Bountiful Minister," 243 n80.
26. Boscaro, *101 Letters*, 51 (letter 46, addressed to his wife and dated third month, fifth day, 1593).
27. Ibid., 67.
28. The symbolic value of masks, costumes and manuscripts within the Nô schools is discussed in Eric C. Rath, *The Ethos of Noh: Actors and Their Art* (Cambridge, MA: Harvard University Press, 2004).
29. Boscaro, *101 Letters*, 54.
30. Ibid., 64 (letter 96, to his concubine Tora).
31. Ibid., 57 (letter 51).
32. In the Kyôgen *Mimihiki* (Ear-Pulling) he probably pulled the ears of his partner "actor"—his former rival, Maeda Toshiie—before an audience sensitive to courtly decorum.
33. Quoted in Elison, "Bountiful Minister," 244.
34. Amano, *Nô ni tsukareta kenryokusha*, 88.
35. A play, preserved in the Komparu actors' family, possibly also belonged to the group: *Kono hana* (This [Marvellous] Bloom). For the following discussions of the plays, I used the texts in *Yôkyoku sanbyakugojûbanshû*, ed. Nonomura Kaizô (Tokyo: Kôbunsha, 1928); the comments of Hata in *Nô no sakusha to sakuhin*, ed. Yokomichi Mario, Nishino Haruo, and Hata Hisashi (Tokyo: Iwanami Shoten, 1992), vol. 3; Amano, *Nô ni tsukareta kenryokusha*; Nishino Haruo and Hata Hisashi, *Nô—Kyôgen jiten* (Tokyo: Heibonsha, 2011); and Kobayashi Seki, Nishi Setsuo, and Hata Hisashi, *Nôgaku daijiten* (Tokyo: Chikuma shobô, 2012).
36. Translated as *Conquest of Akechi* in Stephen T. Brown, *Theatricalities of Power: The Cultural Politics of Noh* (Stanford: Stanford University Press, 2001), 144–49.
37. Cf. Ivan Morris's popular book, *The Nobility of Failure: Tragic Heroes in the History of Japan* (New York: Holt, Rinehart & Winston, 1975).
38. Nonomura, *Yôkyoku sanbyakugojûbanshû*, 675.
39. *Yoshino hanami-zu byôbu*, http://bunka.nii.ac.jp/heritages/detail/43081 (accessed August 9, 2016).

SEVEN

Liberal Constitutionalism and the Sovereign Pardon

BERNADETTE MEYLER

WITHIN THE HISTORY OF POLITICAL THEORY, pardoning was characterized by Jean Bodin as one of the marks of sovereignty and by Immanuel Kant as the act that most enhances the majesty of the king. According to this tradition, pardoning itself constitutes a display of sovereignty and the location of the pardon power indicates the place of sovereignty within the state.[1] The pardon, however, sits ill with liberal political theory.[2] Rather than treating all citizens as equal under law, the pardon exempts an individual or group from punishment; an advantage for some could thus seem an injustice to others, especially those harmed by what has been pardoned. At the same time, pardoning revolutionary violence may serve the interests of the entire future citizenry, for whom the continuation or renewal of the state is enabled. As Alexander Hamilton claimed in *Federalist* 74, "in seasons of insurrection or rebellion, there are often critical moments, when a well-timed offer of pardon to the insurgents or rebels may restore the tranquility of the commonwealth; and which, if suffered to pass unimproved, it may never be possible afterwards to recall."[3] When it takes on the guise of amnesty, as in Hamilton's example, pardoning may itself constitute the political community for the sake of which it is given.

If the identity of those for whom and before whom the pardon is given has remained vexed, the connection between the one who pardons and the sovereign appeared much clearer from Bodin forward. Even within the American constitutional context, the pardon power that Article II accords the president has often seemed an undemocratic residue of the king's monarchical authority.[4] The structure of sovereignty analyzed by Carl Schmitt illuminates the nature of the relationship between pardoning and sovereignty. Although Schmitt himself devoted little attention to the pardon power, referring to it only in passing in *Constitutional Theory*, his account of the exception shares critical features with the dynamics of pardoning.

Nor is the isomorphism between pardoning and the exception simply an antiliberal Schmittian innovation. At the heart of the liberal tradition against which Schmitt launched his attacks, Immanuel Kant's writings themselves suggest both the necessity of pardoning in proto-revolutionary situations and the incompatibility of the pardon power with the liberal state grounded in the rule of law, or what we might call constitutionalism. Analysis of Kant's work on and around pardoning demonstrates the extent to which he remained captured both by the connection between sovereignty and pardoning and by the notion that pardoning might be required to preserve the polity from proto-revolutionary violence. Furthermore, following an earlier tradition, he continued at least nominally to link the power of pardoning with the king. It was, in part, precisely this association, however, that led Kant to resist the entailments of the pardon power, a power that served to aggrandize the king in the sight of his subjects and contravened the lawful character of the state—a principle on which Kant simultaneously insisted. The pardon hence proves an exception within the Kantian corpus as much as in the Schmittian critique.

The fundamental mistake shared by Kant and Schmitt may be the insistence on linking pardoning with sovereignty. To the extent that something like pardoning could be detached from sovereignty, it could be retained without compromising liberal constitutionalism. Although she refrained from fully elaborating the implications of the concept, what Hannah Arendt termed forgiveness—an ethical act between individuals that yet possesses political consequences—might furnish such a substitution for the sovereign pardon.[5] Several English plays of the seventeenth century likewise suggest ways of avoiding the association between sovereignty and pardoning, either by emphasizing forgiveness, like Arendt, or by insisting on a conception of clemency that resembles an equitable approach to law. These possible ways forward have never been taken up within the sphere of contemporary politics, which, recognizing the anomalous character of pardoning, has let it atrophy without adequate replacements.

The significance of this atrophy for criminal law has been widely discussed.[6] The consequences are, however, not confined to that realm. The absence of something like pardoning in contemporary politics possesses consequences for the nature of the political bond. In his writings on pardoning, Jacques Derrida emphasizes the significance of a "pure" pardon, which "would be a pardon without power: unconditional but without sovereignty."[7] For Derrida, the purity of the pardon is fundamentally compromised not only by a link with sovereignty but also by its instrumental deployment. Hence he contends:

> Each time that the pardon is in the service of an end, even if it were noble and spiritual (financial or spiritual redemption, reconciliation, salvation), each time that it tends to re-establish a normality (social, national, political, psychological) by a work of mourning, by some therapy or ecology of the memory, then the "pardon" is not pure, nor is its concept. The pardon is not, it should not be normal, normative, normalizing. It should remain exceptional and extraordinary, by proof of the impossible: as if it could interrupt the ordinary course of historic temporality.[8]

This linkage of pardoning "in the service of an end" with the "re-establish[ment of] normality" would render justifications for pardoning like Hamilton's impure. It would further seem to contravene any political use of pardoning. In connecting the pardon in service of an end and the goal of "re-establish[ing] normality," Derrida here paints with too broad a brush. A non-sovereign version of the pardon could serve the goal of founding or refounding a state without rendering the result "normal." Instead, it could help to generate new bases for the relations among political subjects or citizens and assist in the creation of a different form of political organization. Under this model, the pardon used for the ends of the state would itself generate a new basis for politics within that very state. It is this possibility to which the remainder of the essay will attempt to lend shape.

According to the now familiar mantra at the opening of *Political Theology*, "Sovereign is he who decides on the exception."[9] The exception, or emergency, as Schmitt defines it, "can at best be characterized as a case of extreme peril, a danger to the existence of the state, or the like."[10] The necessity of a decision on the exception controverts the possibility of a completely self-sufficient *Rechtsstaat*, or state characterized by the rule of law, and demonstrates the inevitably political—rather than exclusively legal—character of any constitution. As Schmitt explains in *Constitutional Theory*, the modern constitution must contain both *Rechtsstaat* and political elements: "for the Rechtsstaat understanding, the law is essentially a norm," whereas "'political' means a concept of law that, in contrast to the Rechtsstaat, results from the political form of existence of the state and out of the concrete manner of the formation of the organization of rule."[11] The error of liberal constitutional theory, in Schmitt's view, is to confuse the "constitution" with "constitutional law": "The distinction between constitution and constitutional law . . . [is] possible because the essence of the constitution is not contained in a statute or in a norm. Prior to the establishment of any norm, there is a fundamental *political decision by the bearer of the constitution-making power.* In a democracy, more specifically, this is a decision by the people; in a genuine monarchy, it is a decision by the monarch."[12] The political decision both precedes the establishment of the norm and intervenes at the moment of the emergency to re-ground the *Rechtsstaat.* The sovereignty of the constitution-making power reveals itself again when a decision is rendered on the exception.

Rather than recognizing the inevitably political component of the constitution, the bourgeois *Rechtsstaat* instead attempts to regulate the emergency from within constitutional law by "spell[ing] out in detail the case in which law suspends itself."[13] Many of the post-Weimar constitutions of Latin America and the post-Soviet ones of Eastern Europe attempted to avoid the abuse of emergency powers in precisely such a manner, depriving the executive of the capacity to decide, limiting the duration of the emergency, or protecting certain fundamental rights against abrogation during the period of exception.

The effort to constrain the exception through constitutional law coincides with the *Rechtsstaat*'s failure to disclose the source of sovereign power. As Schmitt contends, the *Rechtsstaat* "aspires, in fact, to not answer the question of sovereignty and to leave open the question of which political will makes the appropriate norm into a positively valid command. As noted, this must lead to concealments and fictions, with every instance of conflict posing anew the problem of sovereignty."[14] Despite these supposed fictions and subterfuges, "[i]nside every political unity, there can only be one bearer of the constitution-making power" and the constitution must rest "either on the monarchical or the democratic principle, on the constitution-making power of the prince or that of the people."[15] The fictions in question may result either from a compromise within the constitution—one that defers to the future the ultimate question of who will exercise sovereignty—or a refusal of the decision entirely.[16] In the absence of a decision embodied in constitutional laws, political precedent supplies the requisite determination of the identity of the sovereign.

While Schmitt devotes little attention to pardoning in *Constitutional Theory*—or in his other works—the position and specifications of the pardon power in the Weimar Constitution suggest a compromise akin to those he does discuss. The clauses pertaining to pardoning immediately followed the notorious article 48, the grant of emergency powers to the president of the Reich that later furnished Hitler with a legal excuse for suppressing individual rights. As they specified: "The President exercises the right of pardon [*das Begnadigungsrecht*] for the Reich. Reich amnesties [*Reichsamnestien*] require a Reich statute."[17] Harking back to the logic of monarchy, article 49 first endowed the president with the power of pardoning. This strategy is consistent with what Schmitt identifies as the grant of pseudo-monarchical capacities to the president within the bourgeois *Rechtsstaat* in order to generate a separation or balance of powers.[18] At the same time, however, the Weimar Constitution attempts to cabin even this allowance of authority rather than simply weighing other parliamentary powers against it. Distinguishing between "amnesty" and "pardon," the document limits the president's pardon by allocating amnesty to parliament. This strategy stands in contrast to Hamilton's comments in *Federalist* 74 about the scope of the pardon power as well as the Supreme Court's subsequent interpretation of the U.S. Constitution in *United States v. Klein* (1871), a decision insisting, "Pardon includes amnesty. It blots out the offense pardoned and removes all its penal consequences. . . . It is clear that the legislature cannot change the effect of such a pardon any more than the executive can change a law."[19]

Pardoning (or *Begnadigung*) and amnesty (or *amnestie*) do differ substantially; whereas pardoning in its legal acceptation denotes a "remission, either free or conditional, of the legal consequences of crime," amnesty consists in "forgetfulness, oblivion; an intentional overlooking" or "an act of oblivion, a general overlooking or pardoning of past offenses, by the ruling authority."[20] While pardoning usually occurs after conviction and simply removes punishment, amnesty or oblivion encourages forgetting the entire set of underlying events and suspending the question of culpability or innocence. The pardon generally touches an individual; an amnesty covers a collectivity.[21] And since at least the seventeenth century, efforts have been made in constitutional theory to restrict the pardon power of the king or chief executive by giving legislatures control over amnesty.

Nevertheless, the boundaries between pardoning and amnesty remain murky. In the early modern English context, general pardons were granted by the king and Parliament well before any efforts to divide amnesty from pardon or Parliament from monarch.[22] More recently, within the French setting, Vladimir Jankélévitch called attention to the possible proximity of forgiveness and forgetting in attacking statutes of limitations on genocide in L'imprescriptible. At the beginning of that polemic, Jankélévitch asks, "Est-il temps de pardoner, ou tout au moins d'oublier?," seeming to assimilate forgiveness with forgetting.[23] Statutes of limitations on crimes might themselves constitute a very broad form of amnesty.

Delineating the precise limits of the concepts of pardoning and amnesty itself requires a decision and may occasion conflict among the branches, as it did when Congress sparred with presidents Lincoln and Johnson about their authority to grant amnesty to members of the former Confederacy after the end of the Civil War.[24] Article 49's attempt to require a Reich statute for amnesty while allowing the president to exercise the pardon power hence leaves open the further determination of the boundary between pardoning and amnesty; in this way, it resembles the political compromises within constitutional law that Schmitt identifies and seems to await the gloss on its meaning provided by future practice.[25]

As with the state of exception, the Weimar Constitution tried to circumscribe pardoning by placing it within a separation-of-powers framework. In Schmitt's view, and in accord with his challenge elsewhere to the very possibility of separating powers, the efforts of article 48 to limit the president's decision on the exception remained of only nominal efficacy:

> According to article 48 of the German constitution of 1919, the exception is declared by the president of the Reich but is under the control of parliament, the Reichstag, which can at any time demand its suspension. This provision corresponds to the development and practice of the liberal constitutional state, which attempts to repress the question of sovereignty by a division and mutual control of competences. But only the arrangement of the precondition

that governs the invocation of exceptional powers corresponds to the liberal constitutional tendency, not the content of article 48. Article 48 grants unlimited power.[26]

The same might be said of article 49; to the extent that the president is, in the first instance, entitled to exercise the pardon on behalf of the state, the restriction of his power in the case of amnesty appears only belatedly and itself subject to circumscription. The discretionary decision on the pardon, like that on the emergency, determines what constitutes a pardon as well as when it should be employed.

The connections between the pardon and the exception extend further than the proximity of articles 48 and 49 of the Weimar Constitution. The decision on the exception and the determination to pardon resist circumscription by rule. Similarly, the specification of procedures for the declaration of emergency and the maintenance of restrictions on its scope have been notoriously insufficient in delineating the boundaries of states of exception. This is the case in part because what is perceived to be at stake is the very existence of the state itself; as Schmitt elaborates, "The state suspends the law in the exception on the basis of its right of self-preservation."[27] Such a Hobbesian account of the exception finds an analogy in the pardon power as well. Seeking peace was, for Hobbes, the primary dictate of natural law, and pardoning furnished the principal way of achieving peace within an already constituted—although perhaps revolutionarily overturned—polity.[28] Finally, both the exception and the pardon—like the other attributes of sovereignty—share theological roots. According to Schmitt, "The exception in jurisprudence is analogous to the miracle in theology."[29] The pardon itself, as an act of free gift, or grace, is likewise associated with the sovereignty of a Christian god, whose mercy displays a power even greater than that of judgment.

Even Schmitt appears to acknowledge this connection in a passage furnishing his most suggestive remarks about pardoning. Resisting the notion that the liberal state had managed to efface its own agency through law, Schmitt claimed:

Whoever takes the trouble of examining the public law literature of positive jurisprudence for its basic concepts and arguments will see that the state intervenes everywhere. At times it does so as a *deus ex machina*, to decide according to positive statute a controversy that the independent act of juristic perception failed to bring to a generally plausible solution; at other times it does so as the graceful and merciful lord who proves by pardons and amnesties his supremacy over his own laws. There always exists the same inexplicable identity; lawgiver, executive power, police, pardoner, welfare institution. Thus to an observer who takes the trouble to look at the total picture of contemporary jurisprudence, there appears a huge cloak-and-dagger drama, in which the state acts in many disguises but always as the same invisible person. The "omnipotence" of the modern lawgiver, of which one reads in every textbook on public law, is not only linguistically derived from theology.[30]

Here the state operates in dramatic terms, either serving as a deus ex machina or playing in a "cloak-and-dagger drama," its many personae substituting for a single surreptitious power. The deus ex machina form of the decision assumes a place analogous to that of the pardon. Despite the seemingly automated quality of the positivist state, it reaches out in various characters to affect what would otherwise seem a uniform rule of law.

Late in his career, after the dire consequences of his theories had become all too evident under the Third Reich, Schmitt would turn to an actual play— Shakespeare's *Hamlet*—to illuminate the relationship between aesthetics and history as well as between drama and sovereignty. A final intervention in the exchange between Schmitt and Walter Benjamin, and a response to Benjamin's use of Schmitt's thesis on sovereignty in his *Origin of German Tragic Drama* (1927), Schmitt's *Hamlet or Hecuba: The Intrusion of Time Into the Play* sees in the character Hamlet the formation of a myth, one that Jennifer Rust and Julia Lupton have aptly glossed as, in part, "the myth of sovereignty as presence."[31] The identification of Hamlet with a Schmittian sovereign might, on first blush, appear strange; as Schmitt himself describes Hamlet, he is a "procrastinator and dreamer . . . who cannot take the decision to act," an incapacity that would seem to accord poorly with the decisionism of *Political Theology*.[32] It is not exactly Hamlet's stance with respect to the decision, however, that renders him mythic but rather what that postponement of the decision signals about his connection with the historical figure of King James I.

The failure of decision within *Hamlet*, or "the transformation of the figure of the avenger into a reflective, self-conscious melancholic," itself indicates the "intrusion" (*Einbruch*) of history. As Schmitt writes:

The philosophizing and theologizing King James embodied namely the entire conflict of his age, a century of divided belief and religious civil war. The distortion that differentiates the Hamlet of this drama from all other avenger figures and that is otherwise inexplicable . . . —in short, the Hamletization of the avenger—finds a suitable explanation only here, in James. It is here that the connection between present history and tragedy emerges.[33]

Just as James here manifests himself in Hamlet, the "conflict of his age" imposes on James. Hamlet may represent both James and this conflict, but the form of representation is "personalized" rather than "impersonated."[34] The immediacy of the connection between Hamlet and James, and between James and the "conflict of his age" transcends "play" and renders *Hamlet* tragedy rather than *Trauerspiel*. Referring to the "unplayability [*Unverspielbarkeit*] of the tragic," Schmitt therefore explains that, "in distinguishing *Trauerspiel* and tragedy, we can recognize that incontrovertible core of a singular historical reality that transcends every subjective invention and can then understand its elevation to myth."[35] It is not just sovereign indecision but rather the historical problem to which that sovereign indecision points that renders Hamlet a mythic figure for the future.

The nature of this historical problem, however, remains less than perspicuous. On one level, Schmitt insists on a rather blunt comparison between Queen Mary Stuart's supposed culpability for the death of her husband—the future King James's father—and Gertrude's potential guilt in the demise of Hamlet's father, both of which subjects are "taboo."[36] Likewise, he associates the treatment of the ghost in *Hamlet* with Catholic and Protestant debates about the demonic quality of such apparitions and, in particular, the adolescent James's intervention in these debates with his 1597 *Daemonologie*.[37] More broadly, however, the problem concerns not only the division between Catholics and Protestants—and among various types of Protestants—that plagued seventeenth-century England but also the hypothesis of the "divine right of kings," which, in Schmitt's view, furnished King James's "true life's task, his existential problem."[38]

When James was writing and ruling, the prelude to the English Revolution had, in Schmitt's view, already commenced.[39] Because James's concerns would lead neither to the "state" characteristic of the continental European countries of the eighteenth century nor to the maritime economic empire of England, which Schmitt analyzed in *The Nomos of the Earth*, he was destined "to disappear from the stage of world history" and to remain in the modern consciousness only to the extent that the myth of Hamlet contains his relic.[40] If the myth of Hamlet furnishes this remainder and reminder of James, another seventeenth-century myth—that of the Leviathan—carried forward greater consequences for European political development, somewhat to Schmitt's chagrin.

In analyzing Hobbes's image for the commonwealth in an earlier book, from 1938, Schmitt claimed that the figure of the Leviathan gestured in two directions: toward a personalist vision unifying all of the components of the state into a single figure and toward a mechanistic and machinic one.[41] Whereas the first interpretation connected back to James himself and the Stuarts more generally, the second pointed forward to the continental European theories of the state.[42] As Victoria Kahn has persuasively argued, Schmitt's disillusion with the Hobbesian image of the Leviathan, the doubleness of which prevented Hobbes's philosophy from being received as decisionist and instead paved the path for the future liberal state, sent Schmitt back to search the seventeenth century for another hero of decisionism, which he ultimately located in Hamlet.[43] The passage from *Political Theology* quoted above, however, explaining the deus ex machina mode of the state's intervention, indicates the potential return of the person—or at least the god—in even the machine of the liberal state. The drama therefore continues as the god is put back into the machine. The pardon and the deus ex machina subsist only as the residue of the personalist sovereign in Schmitt's account though; rather than being identified with the divine-right monarch, they are personae adopted by the otherwise mechanistic state. At the same time, however, their existence may hinder the closure of the liberal state.

Schmitt's fascination with Hamlet and the Leviathan, images emanating from seventeenth-century England, might suggest a further engagement with the political developments of that century and the relationship of dramatic spectacle to what transpired. Oddly though, by positing the historical anomalousness of James's theories and their lack of inheritors, as well as claiming that Hobbes influenced continental Europe more than England itself, Schmitt managed to gloss over the space between *Hamlet* and Hobbes and to ignore the contest over sovereignty contained there.

In addition, by concentrating on the respective roles of monarch and legislature or, in their English incarnations, king and Parliament, Schmitt neglected the crucial function of the judiciary in the struggle among powers within seventeenth-century England. In the early seventeenth century, the king's capacity to pardon was challenged by and itself challenged the regularity of common-law decision making. The pardon thereby became a site for staging conflicts among not simply two but three forms of authority in the state.[44] Indeed, the common law component of the contest among powers may, more than the parliamentary element, have set the stage for the constitutional elements of the tradition of liberal constitutionalism, elements that come to the fore in the writings of Immanuel Kant.

Although Kant's work is associated with the inauguration of enlightenment reason and politics, and it promulgates a vision of sovereignty that is largely legislative rather than judicial, a certain singularity of sovereignty remains in the *Metaphysics of Morals*, one associated with the king's act of pardoning. While seeming to prioritize law giving—both in the context of individual ethics and the polity in general—Kant allows space for the pardon, a pardon that presents the tragicomic resolution of the revolutionary situation. Thus at the origins of modern liberalism lies an exception to the general rule of law.

The pardon intervenes, in Kant's writings, at the intersection between two dramas, that of the revolution and that of the sovereign who, in staging the pardon, dramatizes his own majesty. In the *Metaphysics of Morals*, Kant describes the pardon both theatrically and with great ambivalence:

> Of all the rights of a sovereign, the *right to grant clemency* to a criminal (*ius aggratiandi*), either by lessening or entirely remitting punishment, is the slipperiest one for him to exercise for it must be exercised in such a way as to show the splendor [*Glanz*] of his majesty, although he is thereby doing injustice [*unrecht zu tun*] in the highest degree.—With regard to crimes of *subjects* against one another it is absolutely not for him to exercise it; for here failure to punish (*impunitas criminis*) is the greatest wrong against his subjects. He can make use of it, therefore, only in case of a wrong done *to himself* (*crimen laesae maiestatis*). But he cannot make use of it even then if his failure to punish could endanger the people's security [*dem Volke selbst in Ansehung seiner Sicherheit Gefahr erwachsen könnte*].—This right is the only one that deserves to be called the right of majesty.[45]

Through pardoning, the sovereign commits an "injustice in the highest degree" that proves invisible to the people and instead enhances "the splendor of his majesty." Kant theatricalizes this "injustice in the highest degree," which derives from a display staged for the benefit of public opinion—the *Ansehung* of the people. The sovereign thus "shines" (*glänzen*) in the eyes of his subjects through the graciousness of his pardon. Pardon emerges here, however, as a responsibility that the sovereign should assume only in relation to himself, an act of forgiving someone who would injure him as a singular entity—but always *qua* sovereign. Kant assigns for pardoning the narrow space between circumstances in which political subjects would be injured by the absence of punishment—pardon defined here as an omission rather than a positive act—and those that, since involving only the sovereign, permit him the right to pardon.

This sliver constricts further when considered in the context of Kant's statements elsewhere defining sovereignty and discussing the nature of revolution. These remarks reveal the near impossibility of injuring the sovereign without simultaneously challenging the people; they also demonstrate that the ultimate offense against the sovereign would constitute the most unpardonable deed. Indeed, the right to pardon is accurately described as "the slipperiest," not because it can ever be exercised rightly but because it always engenders injustice and constitutes the element of sovereignty lying outside the law.

In a footnote to a passage in "Part Two: Public Right," Kant discusses the ultimate violence against a sovereign, that of "formal execution" (*der förmlichen Hinrichtung*), which he vehemently distinguishes from "murder" (*der Mord*), and employs as one example the trial and decapitation of Charles I during the English Revolution. The difference between "formal execution" and "murder" that Kant stresses, however, is undermined when he concludes that Charles and Louis XIV could not actually have been subjected to the first crime but instead were victims of the second and less egregious one. This confusion is made possible by the fact that the king functions as both a physical individual and a symbolic placeholder, so any attack against his literal body could signal either formal execution or murder. In order to ensure that he was targeted as sovereign rather than simply as individual, one would need to discover a revolutionary procedure that operated on a symbolic rather than material level. Asserting in the main text the principle that "a people cannot offer any resistance to the legislative head of a state which would be consistent with right, since a rightful condition is possible only by submission to its general [*allgemein*] legislative will,"[46] Kant further articulates the paradox of rebellion against the sovereign by explaining that the people's will would then be supreme, thereby negating the analytic supremacy of the sovereign. He concludes with the following summation: "This is self-contradictory, and the contradiction is evident as soon as one asks who is to be the judge in this dispute between people and sovereign (for, considered in terms of rights, these are always two distinct moral persons). For it is then apparent that the people wants to be the judge in its own suit."[47] Crucially here, Kant determines that because no "objective" standpoint can be attained, resolving the issue proves impossible. The opposition between people and sovereign cannot be reconciled.

Since Kant claims that judgment has reached an insoluble quandary when the people are pitted against their sovereign, it should not be surprising that he refers in his footnote to the case of the British monarch Charles I. Having created the High Court of Justice in 1649, the House of Commons proceeded to execute Charles for committing treason during the Civil War. When introducing the spectacle of Charles's death, Kant adds imaginary onlookers, alleging:

> It is the formal *execution* of a monarch that strikes horror [*Schaudern*] in a soul filled with the idea of human beings' rights, a horror that one feels repeatedly as soon as and as often as one thinks of such scenes [*Auftritt*] as the fate of Charles I or Louis XVI. But how are we to explain this feeling [*Gefühl*], which is not aesthetic feeling (sympathy, an effect of the imagination by which we put ourselves in the place of the sufferer) but moral feeling resulting from the complete overturning of all concepts of rights? It is regarded as a crime that remains forever and can never be expiated (*crimen immortale, inexpiabile*), and it seems to be like what theologians call the sin that cannot be forgiven [*vergeben*] either in this world or the next.[48]

As Kant explains, this feeling occurs because the criminal, here identified with the people, rather than simply making himself an exception to his own—in principle, universalizable—maxim, instead sets his maxim against the dictates of reason; thus, the fact that it takes place "beyond human reason"—or, in other words, violates the humanity of man—occasions the horrific quality of this crime, and perhaps also the reference to a theological analogy in the attempt to explain it. Although the passage denies aesthetic sympathy, the audience's reaction to a tragedy, it retains a dramatic structure so that the spectators simply experience a different generic drama, one connected with the sublime.

We can now return to the issue of the space left over for pardoning between the sovereign's right and the endangerment of the people, examining the paradoxical nature of Kant's double demand through a final passage. In this section, Kant asserts that the sovereign should remit capital punishment if the greater part of his citizenry would be eliminated by the *lex talionis* system of justice that Kant usually advocates. Although Kant claims that pardoning constitutes the sovereign's only "right of majesty," he yet refers to this mitigating function also as "an act of the right of majesty which, as clemency [*Begnadigung*], can always be exercised only in individual cases,"[49] setting the two almost indiscernibly close together. Again in this passage, Kant employs dramatic terminology to describe the situation, maintaining:

> If . . . the number of accomplices (*correi*) to such a deed is so great that the state, in order to have no such criminals in it, could soon find itself without subjects; and if the state still does not want to dissolve, that is, to pass over into the state of nature, which is far worse because there is no external justice at all in it (and if especially it does not want to dull the people's feeling [*das Gefühl*] by the spectacle [*das Spektakel*] of a slaughterhouse), then the sovereign must also have it in his power, in this case of necessity (*casus necessitatis*), to assume the role of judge (to represent him [*vorzustellen*]) and pronounce a judgment that decrees for the criminals a sentence other than capital punishment . . . which still preserves the population.[50]

If the civil order were to devolve again into the state of nature, the remaining individuals would be adversely affected, so here the amelioration of punishment, like pardon, allows for the well-being of lawful subjects. While the aggregate of the people cannot kill the king, the king as the representative of sovereign generality likewise cannot annihilate all his subjects. However, the hypothetical example that Kant invokes, since it involves such a large number of people, could be seen as an allusion to revolutionary violence as well. This conception would put the event on the verge of the unpardonable, lacking only the assassination of the sovereign himself. In order to retain the concept of legality here, the crime against legality must be pardoned and the law of the unpardonable compromised. This passage describes what should occur on the other side of revolution, but only if the revolution failed in its ultimate goal, that of deposing the monarch; we receive no advice here on how to respond when the sovereign no longer exists, and thus lacks the capacity to pardon.

Within Kant's narrative, the king stages his pardon both to accentuate his majesty in the eyes of his subjects and to transform what might, for the world audience, have been the sublime spectacle of the revolutionary overturning of law into a tragicomedy restoring the constitutional state. In both respects, the pardon shifts the signification of the performance for those watching, yet it fails to allow the "groundlings" of the polity or international community a means of participating more actively in the performance. A sublime form of tragedy finds itself contravened by the pardon, and only the king's majesty remains on display. In scattered comments, Hannah Arendt indicates the potential for rescuing the spectator from his passivity by replacing the sovereign's pardon of proto-revolutionary violence with the individual's forgiveness of the revolutionary act. Rather than furnishing a sovereign manifestation of political will, this forgiveness would arrive as an ethical gesture that yet carried implications for the reconstitution of the state.[51]

Long before Arendt's theoretical intervention, however, theater furnished examples of possibilities similar to those toward which Arendt would gesture. Written not in the twentieth century but instead in the early 1620s—during the very period Schmitt omits from consideration in moving immediately from Hamlet to Hobbes—The Laws of Candy, like other tragicomedies of its period, stages an alternative to the sovereign pardon.[52]

In The Laws of Candy—a a play now usually attributed to John Ford—a Senate governs Candy (Crete) instead of a monarch. One royal figure, the princess "Erota," does appear, but her authority seems more romantic than political. At the same time, however, there is no suggestion that the laws at issue in the plot were established democratically; instead, they appear to date back to time immemorial, or at least to the moment of the "elder Cretans" (LC, 669). Within the confines of the play, however, the Senate is responsible for issuing judgment; rather than having the state itself initiate prosecutions, individuals are given the power to hail each other into the Senate for condemnation.

In the first act, we are informed of two laws for which Crete is renowned, that of gratitude and that of reward for the individual who, by popular acclaim, is recognized as the foremost warrior on the battlefield (LC, 668–69). These two laws of Candy come into conflict, of course, during the play.

At the beginning, battle has just ended between Crete and Venice, with Crete claiming the victory. An older general, Cassilanes, and his son, Antinous, both claim the reward of honor, and because each possesses supporters within the army, they require the Senate to arbitrate the disagreement. For various reasons, the Senate prefers Antinous to Cassilanes. The ultimate result is that Cassilanes disowns Antinous, claiming that he has affronted his honor. Devastated, Antinous explains his plan to do his utmost to restore himself in his father's eyes and, if that fails, to exile himself to Malta (*LC*, 705).

A second strand of the plot circulates around the princess Erota, who is represented as enforcing a tyrannical love, the only relief from which would be her exercise of her seemingly sovereign mercy; the primary figure of devotion, Philander, the Prince of Cyprus, implores Erota, "If I offend with too much loving you, / It is a fault that I must still commit, / To make your mercy shine the more on me" (*LC*, 684). Gonzalo, the sinister and "politick" individual from Venice, rapidly enters into competition for Erota's hand, urging his birth and, more importantly, his wealth as reasons why Erota herself should wish the alliance. Erota's desire is, however, instead sparked by the dejected Antinous.

At the center of the play, act 3 begins with a revelation: Gonzalo, seemingly the friend of Crete, and Cassilanes's creditor for untold sums, reveals to Fernando, his captured countryman, that he has, in fact, been plotting against Crete the entire time. Indeed, he had arranged to bankrupt Cassilanes. We further discern that Gonzalo's ultimate goal involves marrying Erota in order to become King of Crete as well as Duke of Venice. The suggestion is not, however, that Erota herself will independently become sovereign but rather that, in conjunction, they can usurp the government and transform it into a monarchy. Through the instruments of civil war and financial ruin, Gonzalo thus hopes to usurp the state and to transform its mode of governance.

Gonzalo's plot is, fortunately, made known to Erota and the Senate by the prisoner Fernando, whom Cassilanes had agreed to keep for the Senate at his own home. Freeing Crete of Gonzalo's influence is not quite as simple as revealing his plot, however. Cassilanes is indebted to Gonzalo, a personal debt that parallels the financial obligation Crete itself supposedly bears to Venice. In exchange for agreeing to subject himself to her romantic wishes, Antinous extracts a promise from Erota to pay off Cassilanes's debt to Gonzalo without revealing that Antinous himself is behind the scheme. Even this well-intentioned plot miscarries, however, when Erota violates her vow and asks Cassilanes to pardon his son out of gratitude to her; as Erota explains her action, "for requitall [of my investment], [I] only made my suite, / That he would please to new receive his son / Into his favour, for whose love I told him / I had been still so friendly" (*LC*, 725).

What results is nearly the demise of the state; in act 5, a series of individuals accuse one another before the Senate of ingratitude and seek the penalty of death, each new person accusing the prior accuser until the Senate itself finds itself accused by Annophel, Cassilanes's daughter. The chain commences with Cassilanes himself, who urges an action of ingratitude against his son; Erota then follows suit, asking that Cassilanes be condemned; Antinous returns the favor, accusing Erota; finally, Annophel brings a charge against the Senate, claiming that it has been "unthankfull" to her father, and "crav[ing] / The rigor of the Law against you all" (*LC*, 729). The scene appears to be one of revenge, where each successive individual "strikes home" against another, but by means of an accusation rather than a sword.

The Senate then becomes a judge in its own case, a position that had been anathema since at least Sir Edward Coke's report in *Bonham's Case* (1610), and, in doing so, it condemns itself.[53] According to the senators:

POSSENNE: Though our ignorance
Of *Cassilanes* engagements might asswage
Severity of justice, yet to shew
How no excuse should smooth a breach of Law,
I yield me to the trial of it.

PORPHYCIO: So must I.
(*LC*, 730)

Although this self-condemnation might seem a departure from the prior proceedings, it is, in fact, in keeping with the earlier accusations and convictions, which generally occur by confessions or guilty pleas that the Senate is bound to accept. Thus, after Antinous insists on pronouncing his own guilt, the senator Possenne states, "You have doom'd your self, / We cannot quit you now" (*LC*, 725). The Senate itself seems incapable of issuing pardons and is restricted largely to confirming judgments made between the parties.

One might think at this point that the tragic end had arrived, the state on the verge of dissolution and Gonzalo still at large. Instead, however, an alternative manifests itself in the idea that Philander, the Prince of Cyprus who had haplessly loved Erota, must, at the behest of the Senate, serve as the "Moderator in this difference" (*LC*, 730). Elaborating on the "Scene of miserie" that Cassilanes has generated, Philander reproaches him and rehearses the curses that posterity will heap upon his memory (*LC*, 730). Cassilanes ultimately relents, not only forgiving Antinous—which has the effect, under the law, of freeing him (" 'Tis the Law, / That if the party who complaines, remit / The offender, he is freed")—but also asking his own forgiveness in turn (*LC*, 731). The chain of vengeance is then repeated in a chain of forgiveness until Philander proclaims, "Then with consent / Be reconcil'd on all sides" (*LC*, 731–32). With this ending, Philander's name takes on a new significance; previously simply designating him as a besotted lover, it now indicates his status as a lover of mankind in its entirety. The state then is new begotten just as Antinous tells his father that he "new beget[s]" him with forgiveness (*LC*, 731). The basis for this renewed state is a consent *between* citizens rather than a hierarchical structure of obligation. The exchange of forgiveness, like an exchange of gifts, binds individuals to each other in a condition of equality. As a foreigner, Philander, the deus ex machina who engineers the reconciliation, remains an outsider to the state but simultaneously underwrites its reconstruction, just as the founding moment can never be itself comprehended within what is founded. Although Erota accepts Philander in the end, it is in a changed capacity, her overweening pride tamed, as she herself admits. For the enemy alien Gonzalo is thus substituted the friendly stranger Philander, a foreigner within the state who will support it rather than undermine its existence.

The reversal from tragedy to tragicomedy here occurs not through the auspices of a god's intervention but instead through the activity of a foreigner, an outsider to the power structure of the state. Rather than a sovereign pardon provided from above, the forgivenesses in the play are exchanged between individuals, through a mutual consent that may represent a nascent form of social contract. By the end, the language of tyranny, which is deployed to characterize both Erota and Cassilanes throughout the play, has been replaced with an emphasis on equality and on lateral relations among the characters. Faced with the generalization of revenge into the threat of civil war or revolutionary violence, the play presents as its solution a non-sovereign version of forgiveness.

Kant associated pardoning with a particular kind of staging of the splendor of the king's majesty, one trumped only by the horror of the spectacle of revolutionary and counterrevolutionary violence. This theatrical version of the pardon scene as affirming the height of the sovereign above the people manifests itself in the spectacular finales of early seventeenth-century plays like Shakespeare's *Measure for Measure*,[54] in which Duke Vincentio returns and remits both the punishments that have accrued in his absence and those he himself has just imposed. Such a staging is countered by another kind of drama, that of *The Laws of Candy*, in which forgiveness comes from a stranger or a friend and is passed among citizens to reconstitute the state.

Those setting up the foundations for liberal constitutionalism, like Kant, failed to generate a new account of pardoning that would render it an important component of either the rule of law or democracy, rather than a relic of monarchical sovereignty. Hence the pardon seems to fit more naturally into the antiliberal Schmittian account of politics than into the contemporary U.S. constitutional order. Such a result was not, however, inevitable; an alternative, non-sovereign conception of pardoning that appeared in early modern drama presented another possible basis for the act, one that was never implemented within politics.

Notes

1. Natalie Zemon Davis confirms the intimate association between pardoning and sovereignty even in this early period. As Davis describes the power of the narratives told on behalf of the condemned in the letters of remission she analyzes, they allowed for "a complicity between sovereign and subject" because they permitted the king to strengthen sovereignty by "pushing [his will] beyond the law" while simultaneously helping the one given grace. Natalie Zemon Davis, *Fiction in the Archives: Pardon Tales and Their Tellers in Sixteenth-Century France* (Stanford: Stanford University Press, 1987), 58.
2. I am intentionally invoking a wide range of sources in this essay in order to make some theoretical remarks about the role of the pardon in the modern liberal tradition and those arrayed against that tradition; the work of Immanuel

Kant, in particular, remains one of the paradigmatic philosophical bases for liberalism, against which figures like Carl Schmitt aim their critiques. The essay turns at the end to an alternative theatrical conception of the pardon offered before the solidification of liberalism, an alternative that, I argue, avoids the principal problem of both liberal and antiliberal visions. If, as the introduction to this volume contends, "Aesthetics, literature, and especially the theater are no less sciences of sovereignty than law, economics, and the life and mind sciences," theater may help to furnish us with alternatives to sovereignty as well.

3. Alexander Hamilton, "Federalist 74," in Hamilton, James Madison, and John Jay, *Federalist Papers*, ed. Clinton Rossiter (New York: Signet Classic, 2003), 447.

4. The long-standing nature of this reservation, which even the founding generation expressed, is discussed in Kathleen Dean Moore, *Pardons: Justice, Mercy, and the Public Interest* (Oxford: Oxford University Press, 1997), 25–26.

5. I have elaborated elsewhere on the political dimensions of Arendt's concept of forgiveness: Bernadette Meyler, "Does Forgiveness Have a Place? Hegel, Arendt, and Revolution," *Theory and Event* 6, no. 1 (2002), https://muse.jhu.edu/article/32667.

6. Margaret Colgate Love, among others, has written extensively about this phenomenon: "The Twilight of the Pardon Power," *Journal of Criminal Law and Criminology* 100 (Summer 2010): 1169.

7. Jacques Derrida, "The Century and the Pardon," in *Le monde des débats* 9 (December 1999), trans. Greg Macon (2001), accessed at http://fixion.sytes.net/pardonEng.htm. In French, the primary meaning of the word "pardon" is forgiveness, not the juridical usage as in English, which would generally be translated as "faire grâce à" or "droit à grâce." Nevertheless, the term is sometimes deployed in legal contexts, generating an ambiguity that Derrida and others have used to productive effect. Although I cite Derrida's shorter essays on pardoning that have appeared in French and English, the basis for my discussion of his contribution is the as-yet-unpublished seminar on "Le parjure et le pardon" (1997–1999).

8. Derrida, "The Century and the Pardon."

9. Carl Schmitt, *Political Theology: Four Chapters on the Concept of Sovereignty*, trans. George Schwab (Chicago: University of Chicago Press, 2005), 5.

10. Ibid., 6.

11. Carl Schmitt, *Constitutional Theory*, trans. and ed. Jeffrey Seitzer (Durham: Duke University Press, 2008), 187.

12. Ibid., 75, 77.

13. Schmitt, *Political Theology*, 14.

14. Schmitt, *Constitutional Theory*, 187.

15. Ibid., 105.

16. Ibid., 86–87.

17. Weimar Constitution, 1919, articles 48 and 49, available at www.zum.de/psm/weimar/weimar_vve.php.

18. Schmitt, *Constitutional Theory*, 315–17.

19. United States v. Klein, 80 U.S. 128 (1871), 147–48.

20. *Oxford English Dictionary*, s.v. "pardon" and "amnesty."
21. Peter Krapp treats some of these distinctions in "Amnesty: Between an Ethics of Forgiveness and the Politics of Forgetting," *German Law Journal* 6, no. 1 (2005): 185.
22. Krista Kesselring thoroughly analyzed the use of the general pardon within the sixteenth century in *Mercy and Authority in the Tudor State* (Cambridge: Cambridge University Press, 2007), 56–90.
23. Vladimir Jankélévitch, *L'imprescriptible* (Paris: Editions du Seuil, 1986), 17. Derrida treats this aspect of Jankélévitch's theory in "To Forgive: The Unforgivable and the Imprescriptible." Whereas Jankélévitch in at least this context assimilates forgiveness with forgetting, Derrida insists that "forgiving is not forgetting (another enormous problem)." Jacques Derrida, "To Forgive: The Unforgivable and the Imprescriptible," in *Questioning God*, ed. John Caputo et al. (Bloomington: Indiana University Press, 2001), 23, 25–26. Many have noted the seeming incompatibility between Jankélévitch's account of forgiveness in *L'imprescriptible* and his more purely philosophical account in the subsequent book *Le pardon*. There he maintains that one can forgive even an unforgettable and inexcusable crime. Vladimir Jankélévitch, *Le pardon* (Paris: Montaigne, 1967), 204. Kevin Hart furnishes a plausible explanation of the difference, focusing on the distinction between the unpardonable or unforgivable on the one hand and the imprescriptible on the other: "One might take the whole of 'Should We Pardon Them?' (1965) to be a long, anguished counter-example to the case developed in *Forgiveness* (1967), one given both before and after the fact and not explicitly considered in the book. That would be a mistake, for the essay on Germany's role in the Shoah is concerned with another matter entirely, the imprescriptible rather than the unpardonable." Kevin Hart, "Guilty Forgiveness," in *Vladimir Jankélévitch and the Question of Forgiveness*, ed. Alan Udoff (New York: Lexington, 2013), 52. Ethan Kleinberg has persuasively argued that both of Jankélévitch's works must be seen as responses to the juridical debates about the punishment of crimes against humanity in the aftermath of the Holocaust. As he writes, "Both *Forgiveness* and *Pardonner?* must be read in the context of the twenty-year statute of limitations on Vichy War Crimes, the public debate and formal vote as to whether France should 'pardon' Germany and the Germans for Nazi war crimes, and the French law of 1964 that determined that 'crimes against humanity,' unlike other crimes, are not subject to any statute of limitations." Ethan Kleinberg, "To Atone and To Forgive," in Udoff, *Jankélévitch and the Question of Forgiveness*, 147.
24. This conflict is described in detail in Jonathan Dorris, *Pardon and Amnesty Under Lincoln and Johnson* (Chapel Hill: University of North Carolina Press, 1953).
25. Adam Sitze has similarly argued that Schmitt's *The Nomos of the Earth* "throws into relief a subtle but exigent problem in the philosophy of law," that of "*the relation of indiscernibility* that pertains between *the sovereign power to pardon* and *the theory and practice of amnesty*." Adam Sitze, "Keeping the Peace," in *Forgiveness, Mercy, and Clemency*, ed. Austin Sarat and Nasser Hussain (Stanford: Stanford University Press, 2007), 157.
26. Schmitt, *Political Theology*, 11.

27. Ibid., 12.
28. Thomas Hobbes, *Leviathan*, ed. Richard Tuck (Cambridge: Cambridge University Press, 1996), 92.
29. Schmitt, *Political Theology*, 36.
30. Ibid., 38.
31. Julia Lupton and Jennifer Rust, "Schmitt and Shakespeare," in Carl Schmitt, *Hamlet or Hecuba*, trans. David Pan and Jennifer Rust (Candor, NY: Telos, 2009), xxviii, xxxvii.
32. Schmitt, *Hamlet or Hecuba*, 9.
33. Ibid., 26.
34. Lupton and Rust, "Schmitt and Shakespeare," xl.
35. Schmitt, *Hamlet or Hecuba*, 40, 52.
36. Ibid., 15–18.
37. Ibid., 28.
38. Ibid., 29.
39. Ibid., 62.
40. Ibid., 65.
41. Carl Schmitt, *The Leviathan in the State Theory of Thomas Hobbes*, trans. George Schwab and Erna Hilfstein (Chicago: University of Chicago Press, 2008), 34–35.
42. Ibid., 79–80, 86.
43. Victoria Kahn, "Hamlet or Hecuba," *Representations* 83, no. 1 (2003): 80.
44. For further elaboration of this point, see Bernadette Meyler, " 'Our Cities Institutions' and the Institution of the Common Law," *Yale Journal of Law and the Humanities* 22, no. 2 (2010): 441.
45. Immanuel Kant, *The Metaphysics of Morals*, trans. Mary Gregor (Cambridge: Cambridge University Press, 1996), 109–10.
46. Ibid., 96.
47. Ibid., 97.
48. Ibid.
49. Ibid., 108.
50. Ibid., 107.
51. For a detailed treatment of Arendt, see Meyler, "Does Forgiveness Have a Place?"
52. *The Laws of Candy. A Tragicomedy*, in *The Dramatic Works in the Beaumont and Fletcher Canon*, vol. 10, ed. Fredson Bowers (Cambridge: Cambridge University Press, 1996), 666. Hereafter cited in text as *LC*.
53. Steve Sheppard, ed., "Bonham's Case," in *The Selected Writings of Sir Edward Coke* (Indianapolis: Liberty Fund, 2003), 1:264.
54. For a discussion of the Duke's pardons in *Measure for Measure*, see Meyler, " 'Our Cities Institutions' and the Institution of the Common Law," 461–65.

EIGHT

The Vanishing Slaves of Paris

The Lettre de Cachet *and the Emergence of an Imperial Legal Order in Eighteenth-Century France*

MIRANDA SPIELER

OUR TASK, as contributors to this volume, is to set aside received ideas and narrative conventions relevant to the meaning and structure of power and state authority. In view of that assignment, this historian must put her cards on the table: this is an essay about the state, its topic is law, and its terrain is France—the country that gave us words like absolutism, sovereignty, bureaucracy, and police.

Most of the people whom I discuss in this essay—enslaved domestics in eighteenth-century Paris—lived near a monument in the Place des Victoires composed of bronze bodies linked by gold chains in a circle around a statue of the king. The slaves—embodiments of Louis XIV's conquests in Europe—were unshackled and hauled off during the French Revolution on becoming "a spectacle that free men cannot abide," in the words of the legislator Alexandre-Theodore-Victor, Comte de la Lameth.[1] The slaves vanished (later to resurface in the Louvre) as Paris prepared, in spring 1790, for a huge festival—the Festival of Federation—on the theme of contractual government.[2]

The removal of slaves from the Place des Victoires followed changes to French law that expunged what revolutionary legislators, and members of the public, took for abuses of sovereign power, especially *lettres de cachet*. In principle, a lettre de cachet—also called an *ordre du roi* (order of the king)— was a note signed and sealed by the monarch enabling a person's exile or his detention at special sites, called *prisons d'état* (prisons of state), which lay beyond reach of the normal legal system.[3] During the eighteenth century, lettres de cachet multiplied, became banal, and (in Paris) made possible the roundup of prostitutes, vulgar neighbors, and above all family members— déclassé children, drunks, violent or mad spouses—at the discretion of the city's lieutenant general of police. It was a sign of the times that Antoine-René de Voyer de Paulmy, Marquis d'Argenson (1694–1757), in his posthumous *Considérations sur l'ancien et présent gouvernement de la France*, should propose, by way of radical reform, that the king actually consent to each use of his signature and seal on these documents.[4] The lettre de cachet was, in principle, the supreme expression of discretionary royal power. In practice, the manufacture and use of these documents in the eighteenth century had little to do with the king for reasons distinct from (though not unrelated to) the use of handwriting dummies for the production of all those *Louis*.

In *Le désordre des familles* (1982), Arlette Farge and Michel Foucault describe the widespread use of lettres de cachet by family members as the "legalization of private repression; royal power accorded legal authority to lock people up."[5] The use of state prisons to settle domestic crises in eighteenth-century Paris is pertinent to the study of sovereignty in several respects. This practice suggests a need to rethink how sovereignty is produced in daily life; to reflect on where sovereignty comes from in a spatial sense (the home? the court?); and even to reconsider the nature of despotism.

Petitions for lettres de cachet draw attention to the ambiguous meaning of "private life" and "family disorder." In aristocratic homes, *la légalisation de la répression privée* (in the phrase of Farge and Foucault) might mean using royal power to arrest an insolent lackey. For master craftsmen, a household dispute was invariably a labor dispute. As we shall see, the question of what counted as private and family-related became ever more complex in the eighteenth century, when Paris became an imperial capital full of imperial households. The private sphere—the precinct called home—is an imprecisely drawn social idea that lacks clear legal meaning. When Farge and Foucault trace the rise of lettres de cachet in eighteenth-century France to reveal "the legalization of private repression," they imply that private repression lacked a legal arsenal until the popularization of this alarming practice. Yet the so-called private space of the imperial household was also the slave master's dominion of authority. In the French colonial empire, home was a place of repression and violence organized by statute, in the form of the slave code or Code Noir (1685).[6]

When used against slaves, lettres de cachet allowed crown officials to safeguard the colonial property of masters sojourning in the capital. This point becomes especially clear when the police responded to complaints about newly sold people.[7] To enable the 1765 arrest by lettre de cachet of the slave Joseph Aza, the man's new master, a Neapolitan grandee, presented the police with a notarized sale document. Inspector Muron reported, "I discovered [Aza] to be living at the home of Gilles, wigmaker, in the Rue des Moulins on the Butte Saint Roche. I had the honor of informing the Prince [of Colonna] of the success of my research" at which the prince exhibited his "act of purchase of this negro—formerly belonging to Sieur Bernard who acquired him from the Count d'Artigue, grand chamberlain to their apostolic majesties—before Sauvage and Sauvigny, notaries at Chatelet, on the 29th of last May."[8]

The Aza *affaire* was more than a police matter. The sale of Aza before Paris notaries speaks to the new prominence of slaves in eighteenth-century legal documents linked to the French capital. Wherever they happened to reside—in Africa, the colonies, or the metropole—slaves could not avoid being present as figures in Parisian legal documents during the rise of the French slave trade and of the Saint Domingue plantation complex. Parisian courts not only heard cases dividing colonial property but also defined the very meaning of colonial property. It was the Parisian civil court at Chatelet, not a colonial court, that defined slaves as movables rather than real estate in 1705.[9] It was a Parisian notary who recorded the 1699 contract between "the royal companies of Senegal and Saint Domingue for the furnishing of 400 negroes a year." By the end of the eighteenth century, when the number of Africans captives disembarking in Saint Domingue reached forty thousand per year, the assets of Parisians came increasingly to include property in both France and the West Indies.[10]

The roundup of Parisian slaves by royal writ raises the question of what counted as the law of the land in that city and in prerevolutionary France more generally. Most obviously, the abduction of slaves by lettres de cachet defied the so-called free soil principle. According to the historian Sue Peabody, the doctrine that "there are no slaves in France" began as a medieval or renaissance legal maxim forbidding serfdom and slavery in the realm.[11] In her classic work on the subject, Peabody describes the successful efforts by slaves in Paris to sue for their freedom before two courts in the capital: the Admiralty Court of Paris, the highest court of its type in the land, and the Paris Parlement, an appellate court for civil and criminal matters with a vast territorial jurisdiction.[12] In Peabody's reading, the free soil doctrine assumed the status of a founding constitutional principle in eighteenth-century France and then declined in legal purport after 1770 due to the contaminating influence of racial thought from the colonies.[13] Historians Dwain C. Pruitt and Erick Noël have revised Peabody's account by suggesting geographical disparities in the application of the free soil doctrine. An enslaved footman who ditched his livery in Nantes could expect a different reception by courts there than in Paris. In Pruitt's reading, which relies on the records of admiralty courts and parlements outside Paris, French courts were beholden to slave owners to different degrees depending on place.[14]

However commonsensical this regionally sensitive reading might seem, there is something unsatisfying about the idea of law that sustains it. Law was the ideological expression of the ruling class except if you happened to be in Paris? Why did judicial institutions in the capital remain aloof to material concerns that proved so influential elsewhere? Sue Peabody suggests that religious conviction, linked to a keenness for liberty, lay behind the refusal of judges in the Paris Parlement to register a 1716 edict concerning slaves in France and a related 1738 declaration concerning their administration.[15] It is worth noting, en passant, that in 1716 the Paris Parlement did not mind registering the *Déclaration du Roy concernant La Guinée*, which concerned the fees paid to French merchants who had received royal passports from the late sovereign, Louis XIV, to trade in African slaves including children.

Parlement's refusal to register the 1716 edict did not keep Parisian men of the law from pressing the crown to help with the family's own slaves. Lawyers and judges in Paris included slave owners back from the colonies and their clients, in-laws, and blood relations. The slender 1756 police file concerning "A Negro Slave" includes a note explaining that "Monsieur Coustard, honorary councilor in the Grand Chamber [of the Parlement] demands an order of the king to arrest a negro slave belonging to Sieur Coustard, planter from Saint Domingue."[16] It is expressive of the developing character of Paris's legal establishment that a young Martiniquan charlatan hustled shopkeepers there in 1766—to enable a shopping spree for his lover (an opera girl)—by posing as a new councilor in the Paris Parlement.[17] Moreover, all Parisian police commissioners—including those who arrested slaves by royal writ—were also lawyers licensed to practice at the Paris Parlement.[18] It was

"I, Pierre Chenon, advocate at Parlement, royal councilor, commissioner at Châtelet," who recorded the arrest, by officer Buhot, of the mulatress Marie-Thérèse, an enslaved dressmaker, in a fourth-floor room on the Rue de Mail (1762). It was "Hubert Mutel, advocate at Parlement, royal councilor and commissioner at Châtelet," who recorded the arrest of the slave Papillon at the home of Marie, *femme de débauche*, near the Quinze Vingt Market.[19]

Did the Parlement's refusal to register the 1716 edict and the 1738 declaration matter? The 1738 text went into immediate effect in Paris in a form that would have been plain—a fact of daily life—for judges and lawyers of that court, who worked in the Palace of Justice. Where the 1716 act merely required masters to secure permission from colonial governors and register their slaves with the admiralty upon entering the realm, the 1738 text further specified that "the said permissions will also be registered with the clerk of the Marble Table at the Palace [of Justice] in Paris for slaves taken into our town." The Marble Table was a name for the Admiralty Court of Paris, which convened in the Palace of Justice, as did the Paris Parlement. As stipulated by the 1738 royal act, the admiralty court opened new slave registers, beginning in 1739, which indicated not only the names of slaves and masters arriving in Paris but also the name of the person who appeared before the Paris admiralty clerk to announce their arrival. For instance, on November 27, 1741, Joseph de Saint Laurent, advocate in the Paris Parlement, living in Paris at Rue Neuve in the Saint Eustache parish, "renewed the earlier declaration of Dame Petit concerning two slaves, Pierrot (age 20) and Charlot (age 9)." This item, in common with every slave registration before the admiralty clerk, ends with the phrase, "as stipulated by the declarations of the king given in Paris in the month of October 1716 and in December 1738." It was not uncommon for lawyers in parlement to handle admiralty matters. It would have been a quick errand for men who had business in the same building.[20]

Parlement's nonregistration of the 1716 and 1738 royal acts did not diminish the importance of these texts to slaves and lawyers. In this respect, police documents relating to the well-known case of *Jean Boucaux v. Verdelin* (1738) suggest that the 1716 edict made it possible for Boucaux to attain freedom. During this affair, the jurist René Hérault, then acting as Paris's lieutenant general of police, declined to issue a lettre de cachet for Boucaux's arrest in spite of appeals by the slave's purported owner—the notorious Bernard de Verdelin, Seigneur de Cabanac, whom Jean-Jacques Rousseau

described (years later) as "old, ugly, deaf, brutal, jealous, scarred . . . scream-
ing, reproaching, ranting, and causing his wife [Marie-Madeline d'Ars] to
cry."[21] Hérault, a former royal advocate at Châtelet who sat in the Royal Council, did not recognize Verdelin as Boucaux's rightful owner on legal grounds
(and perhaps also on personal ones). Boucaux's nonregistration with the admiralty in France (contravening the 1716 edict), and recent marriage to a
Parisian girl (who became pregnant during the *affaire*), led Hérault to side
with the slave against the master. According to the 1716 edict, the marriage
of a slave in France with the presumed consent of his master served as au-
tomatic grounds for manumission. It is even likely that Boucaux's allies
among the clergy opted to speed his nuptials by waiving the marriage banns
to prevent Verdelin from blocking the union altogether.[22]

The same year that Boucaux won his freedom, the crown removed the
very provisions in the 1716 law that cut this slave a path to liberty. The 1738
declaration imposed an absolute ban on slave marriage in France. It also denied freedom to unregistered slaves in France who were thereafter to be
confiscated by the king.

What, then, was the law of the land when it came to slaves in eighteenth-
century France, and in Paris in particular? What role did the lettre de cachet
play in defining it? To answer these questions requires that we revisit the
unregistered 1716 edict and the unregistered 1738 declaration concerning
slaves sojourning in France. Past historians who have analyzed these
texts have all overlooked key passages in these texts that do not relate in a
straightforward way to slave life in the metropole.

The 1716 edict and the 1738 declaration did not merely fashion a new law
of slavery for domestic France. These texts also concerned the validity of
colonial law on metropolitan soil. According to the first article of the 1716
text, "The edict of the month of March 1685 and decrees pertaining to its
execution and interpretation will be executed in the colonies."[23] Every other
article of this edict concerned slaves sojourning in France. The 1716 edict's
enactment depended on its registration by courts in France exclusively (not
on overseas courts). Moreover, the first article of this text would seem oddly
superfluous. The Code Noir took effect in the overseas empire decades earlier without needing to be registered by a single metropolitan court. In spite
of the metropolitan subject matter of this edict and in spite of the location
of the courts that were supposed to register and apply it, the first article of
this text claimed to enact a slave code in the colonies thirty years after it

took effect there. In view of these curiosities, it seems reasonable to assume that the goal of the 1716 act was *not* to enact the Code Noir in the colonies. Instead the 1716 edict was drafted slyly to oblige metropolitan courts to recognize the colonial slave code as part of the general law of France. It was written so that courts, in stealth, would enact the Code Noir on metropolitan soil subject to exceptions and amendments set forth in later paragraphs. For instance, where the Code Noir required the prior assent of masters to the marriage of slaves, the 1716 edict specified that slaves who married in France with their masters' approval "shall become free by virtue of their consent." Whatever ambiguity remained about the status of the Code Noir in France soon vanished, thanks to far more explicit language in the 1738 *Declaration du roi concernant les esclaves nègres des colonies qui interprète l'Edit du mois d'Octobre 1716*. This later text explained the new status of colonial slave law in consequence of the earlier act. According to the preamble of the 1738 declaration, "the account of the colonies we received on ascending the throne having led us to recognize the wisdom and necessity of dispositions in the letters patent, in the form of the Edict of March 1685, we ordered its execution by the first article of our Edict of October 1716."[24] The movement of slaves from the colonies to France gave the monarchy a reason to compel high courts throughout the realm to enact colonial slave law so that movable property in Saint Domingue, Mauritius, or Martinique (in other words, a slave) would remain movable property in France. At the beginning of the eighteenth century, these royal acts concerned with slave travel were written to guarantee the transoceanic mobility of legal categories that sustained colonial property.

Did the refusal of the Paris Parlement to register the 1716 law and its companion piece, the 1738 declaration, make slavery illegal in Paris? In 1766, Ripart de Monclar, prosecutor-general to the Parlement of Provence, addressed this question when reporting to the navy on a freedom suit before his court. The question of slavery's legality, he remarked, was straightforward inside the jurisdiction of courts that registered the 1716 and 1738 acts. "Slavery is legitimate and recognized by the laws. This was the subject of the 1716 edict and of the 1738 declaration."[25] In the jurisdiction of courts that declined to register these acts, he wrote, "one has recourse to lettres de cachet." For this jurist, the use of lettres de cachet in and around Paris had the effect of giving force to laws that lay dormant as a consequence of non-registration. In a sense, these lettres de cachet enacted slave law at moments of crisis, when slaves contested their status by fleeing or by entering freedom suits before the Admiralty Court of Paris.

Prisoner files from the Archives de la Bastille reveal that Parisian police agents captured slaves at the request of masters who sought either to keep their slaves from pursuing freedom suits before the admiralty court or to recover slaves who had already been declared free by that court.[26] Orders from the ministry of the navy typically lay behind this pattern of obstruction, which often meant arresting slaves in the dead of night and spiriting them away to prisons in the ports until their masters could arrange for their transport overseas. Of the forty-six people of color for whom I have police files, twenty were slaves who entered freedom suits before the Admiralty Court of Paris. Of these, three entered prison with collusion by the prosecutor of the admiralty court. It becomes possible to identify the arrest and removal of another seven slaves who sought freedom from the admiralty court by cross-referencing digitized colonial records (the IREL database), archives of the Paris prefecture of police, published judicial chronicles, and Eric Noël's invaluable *Dictionnaire des gens de couleur dans la France moderne* (2011).

Take, for instance, the 1777 case of Juliette from Bengal, whom documents of the period variously describe as *a jeune indienne*, a *négresse*, and a *négresse indienne*. Sold thrice at age seven before reaching France by way of Mauritius, she appeared before the admiralty clerk on September 24, 1777, at age fourteen, to demand her freedom. Soon her owner, Jean Corbin-Duplessis, a former soldier with a minor post at court (one of several stewards of the royal fruitery), obtained a lettre de cachet instructing Inspector Muron "to arrest the negress Juliette and conduct her to the prisons of Le Havre." The same writ instructs the jailer at Le Havre to retain her "until the moment of her embarkation." Her trace reappears in the archives of Normandy (Seine-Maritime), whence we learn that Juliette was to be sold again, in another country. On November 16, 1777, "Juliette, negress from Bengal, age fourteen, was embarked at Le Havre by the captain Louis-Nicolas Parquet on the *Duchesse d'Anville* . . . headed to Cap Français." She was off to Saint Domingue. The misfortunes of Juliette unfold in scraps taken from three different archival depositories (the National Archives in Paris, the Prefecture of Police in Paris, and the Archives of Seine-Maritime). However, she has no police file in the Bastille archival series. Her example and a few equally scattered cases from the same years make it clear that document destruction (also noted by Foucault and Farge), not an end to the vanishing system, accounts for the lack of slave police files after 1770.[27]

The refusal of the Paris Parlement to register the 1716 and 1738 laws amounted to a refusal to enact colonial statutes relevant to slavery on domestic soil. In consequence, lettres de cachet became an indispensable arm of the slave owner. These documents gave force to royal acts that hung in a kind of limbo because of their lack of promulgation. Instead of forcing the Paris Parlement to register the laws of 1716 and 1738 by the practice known as a *lit de justice* (the king goes into the Parlement to compel acceptance of his writ), the crown relied, in the case of slaves, on individual royal writs.

In *Les lettres de cachet et les prisons d'état* (1782), the future revolutionary, Honoré-Gabriel Riqueti, Count of Mirabeau (1749–1791) denounced the use of administrative power to circumvent the courts. "None can be condemned legitimately except by laws, and by laws that are covered in equity and authenticity, which alone makes them obligatory." By permitting masters to seize freedom-seeking slaves and imprison them pending transfer to the colonies, lettres de cachet subverted the authority of the admiralty court. In this respect, royal writs against slaves in no way differed from other sorts of lettres de cachet in enabling "the administration [to extend] its authority over things that the law does not sanction."[28] Nonetheless, royal orders for the roundup of freedom-seeking slaves in France were distinct from other forms of these documents. When accorded to slave masters, these writs did more than circumvent the law. They also gave force to a law of uncertain legitimacy—the Code Noir, as modified for domestic France by the 1716 edict and its companion piece. When turned against slaves, lettres de cachet functioned simultaneously as devices by which to circumvent the law (in freedom suits before the admiralty court) and as devices by which to apply the law (slave law).

While exceptional in several respects, the Bastille file on Pauline (1764–1765), which begins at the home of a lawyer at the Paris Parlement, is of special interest for what it reveals about the applicability of the Code Noir to the capital. Pauline's case, read against other documents of the period, further makes it possible to recognize an emerging custom of the country with respect to slaves in imperial Paris.[29]

Pauline became the property of Jean-Baptiste-Charles Bouvet de Lozier (1705–1786), a South Sea explorer, the discoverer of Bouvet Island (average temperature 0.7°C), and two-time governor of the French Mascarene Islands (average temperature 27°C), which then included Mauritius and Réunion. Bouvet returned to France in late 1763, at the end of the Seven Years' War, when a great number of defrocked imperial administrators, soldiers, stranded colonials, and people of color washed up in the metropole as a consequence of maritime war and a succession of imperial defeats. Disembarking in the port of Lorient, Bouvet de Lozier installed himself, his sister, and his three slaves at the home of his brother on the Rue des Blancs Manteaux, located on Paris's right bank, in the Marais (one short block away from the Hôtel de Soubise, the current site of the National Archives). In December 1764, Bouvet sought, and duly obtained, a royal writ from the Paris lieutenant general of police for the arrest of his slave on the pretext of *libertinage*. In fact, the arrest followed imbrications by Pauline against the former governor and his sister in front of two other enslaved domestics. Pauline claimed that her dead mistress had promised her liberty and that Bouvet de Lozier had reneged on that promise out of spite. She also claimed (plausibly) that he had confiscated her life savings (12,000 livres), the earnings (she said) of a "small business" begun with funds from Bouvet's dead spouse, Madame Dupleix. The former governor dismissed the figure as outlandish while hinting at an unsavory medical condition and prostitution.

In December 1764, Bouvet (through Inspector Muron) appealed to the police for a lettre de cachet by gesturing to his inability to punish Pauline in Paris as befitted a colonial slave. He "did not wish to use his authority here to punish her as he would on the isle of Bourbon. Nonetheless, the example of this negress has dangerous consequences for his other negroes and negresses, who are also slaves." As commissioners' reports from the 1760s attest, Paris police agents intervened to prevent the violent abuse of domestics in response to public clamor. Bouvet invoked social and policing norms in the capital to justify his demand for Pauline's arrest. He also appealed to a principle that had justified the arrest of other slaves in Paris, whose masters looked to extrajudicial depots, or prisons of state (Bicêtre, the Abbaye Saint-Germain, Salpêtrière, and For L'Evêque), as a substitute for lashes or internment in a plantation oubliette. For instance, in April 1761, the chemist, engineer, and administrator Trudaine de Montigny (1733–1771)—councilor of state, intendant of finances, director of the École des Ponts et Chaussées—requested a royal writ to enable the detention of Télémaque, age fifteen. With a view to stemming "a derangement, with fearful consequences," he asked that the boy be arrested and conveyed to the Bicêtre prison in the hope that "a rigorous correction might recall him to his duty." Trudaine immediately received a lettre de cachet for his slave together with a personal note and an order for the slave's liberation with the date left blank so that he might extract the boy whenever he wished. The instructions regarding Télémaque also indicate that Montigny's father, Daniel-Charles Trudaine (1703-1769)—founder of the École des Ponts et Chaussées—had sought help from the police in disciplining another slave a few years before. "Several years ago Monsieur de Marville [lieutenant general of police, 1740–1747] accorded the same favor to Monsieur Trudaine for a child of the same age in whom he took an interest."[30] At the For-l'Évêque prison in 1769, the teenage Aladin, who belonged to the Duc de Chartres, told police that "he did not know of any fault except that of missing the large Fête Dieu procession and of attending the small Fête Dieu procession without being attired in his dress uniform."[31] With respect to Aladin and Télémaque, royal writs both enforced the Code Noir and announced that document's invalidity in the capital. By arresting these slaves on the request of slave owners and their agents, police recognized the legitimacy of masters' property claims. Nonetheless, the arrest of these domestics and their detention in prisons of state arose precisely because colonial statutes relevant to slave punishment did not apply in Paris. Neither fugitive slaves nor insolent ones could be punished there by the methods of the islands.

In fact, Bouvet hoped to use the lettre de cachet quite differently than the Trudaines or the Duc de Chartres. These men envisaged the prison of state as a way of disciplining (and terrorizing) their enslaved adolescent retainers. By contrast, ex-governor Bouvet intended to unleash the fullness of what the Code Noir permitted—even to surpass it—to avenge Pauline's attempt at acceding to freedom. For Bouvet, the only pertinent law, as far as Pauline was concerned, was the law of the Mascarenes. As his lawyer explained to the admiralty court in 1765, Bouvet "has always intended and still intends to embark her at his expense and send her the Isle of Bourbon to be employed there in the service of the colony notwithstanding whatever punishment he should seek against her following the 1685 Declaration of the King [Code Noir]."[32] The financial value of Pauline did not matter to Bouvet. He intended to make her a public slave—to deliver her into perpetual penal servitude—by donating her to the colony he had long served as governor. Here the lettre de cachet offered Bouvet a means, or a potential means, of removing Pauline from Paris to enable the rigorous enforcement of colonial statutes. In every case but this one, masters in Paris who sought to remove their slaves to the islands used the lettre de cachet to secure their property when confronted with freedom-seeking domestics. In this case, Bouvet had no interest in retaining ownership of Pauline. She was a political problem that he intended to settle by staging her spectacular humiliation.

Pauline is exceptional in other respects. In contrast to all but one other slave with a surviving police file, she triumphed over the writ of the king and the wishes of her putative owner. Exiting the women's prison called Salpêtrière in January 1765, she holed up inside the Hôtel de Toulouse (now the Banque de France), an exquisite residence the size of a city block that belonged to Louis-Jean-Marie de Bourbon, Duc de Penthièvre (1737-1793), Admiral of France. Her case demonstrates, alas, that the only sure way for a person of color of uncertain status to avoid abduction from eighteenth-century Paris was to move in with the titular head of every admiralty court in the kingdom.

Bouvet intended to apply the letter of colonial law to Pauline. He and his amanuensis, Inspector Muron, envisaged the lettre de cachet as a tool for enforcing slave law. Ultimately, however, Pauline obtained freedom in a manner that defied both the Code Noir and the so-called free soil principle. She bought her liberty. While hiding in the Hôtel de Toulouse, Pauline proposed to buy herself out of slavery in Paris with the funds that Bouvet held on her behalf. Bouvet refused on the grounds that French colonial slave law forbade self-purchase. Only the intercession of Charles-Victor-François de Salaberry, judge at the Chamber of Auditors, led Bouvet to concede the point and sell Pauline (to herself) while confiscating her savings as payment.

Traveling on the backs of slaves who sojourned there, colonial slave law became the law in Paris insofar as this concerned the status of colonial property. Read this way, the coda to the unregistered 1716 and 1738 laws and subsequent royal writs against slaves in Paris consists of the creation (circa 1776) of a new imperial legal archive.[33] The new depository at Versailles would collect duplicates of all imperial civil records (certificates of birth, marriage, and death), all notarial documents, and all "judicial and extrajudicial acts concerning persons and property" from the overseas empire. The documents would "furnish information about those of our subjects who pass into the colonies that now can only be obtained with difficulty" and assure "the repose and security" of families overseas and at home. By design, legal acts that dealt with the sale or gift of slaves held a central place in the new archive. Slaves were dowry. Slaves were inheritance. Planters transacted in slaves by way of contracts drawn up by notaries. The new depository at Versailles aimed to create a unified world of legal meaning.[34] In making possible the trans-oceanic oneness of French legal culture, the new archive assured that overseas definitions of property (as well as persons) would remain constant at home. In this respect, the new archive made utter nonsense of the free soil doctrine, which could only exist in a fractured version of imperial France that enclosed multiple and contradictory legal orders. After 1776, colonial definitions of persons and things took up residence in the metropole. Thereafter, enslaved domestics in France, in common with slaves elsewhere, figured as *biens meubles* (movable goods) in the Crown's own legal depository.

The file on Pauline, read against other police, notarial, and admiralty sources, enables us to glimpse the emergence of a homegrown, improvised, Parisian adaptation of slave law. In Paris, the property claims of colonial masters remained valid while colonial criminal statutes concerning slaves did not. Ultimately, the refusal of the Paris Parlement to register the 1716 and 1738 laws opened a space for the development of a new set of customary practices in a rising imperial capital. Viewed this way, the arrest of slaves by royal writ was not just a convenient way for slave masters to circumvent the law of the land. In the case of slaves, lettres de cachet were also techniques of legal enforcement. These writs applied the law that defined colonial property. Much like the post-1776 imperial archive, lettres de cachet against slaves assured the "repose and security" of imperial families by imposing a new transoceanic legal order.

Notes

1. *Archives parlémentaires de 1789 à 1860: Recueil des débats législatifs et politiques des chambres françaises* (Paris: P. Dupont, 1862–), 1st series, 16:374 (June 20, 1790). The Parisian chronicler Louis-Sébastien Mercier (1740–1814) alludes to the removal of the bronze slaves at the foot of the king in his futuristic novel about the political remaking of Paris. See *L'an deux mille quatre cent quarante: Rêve s'il ne fut jamais* (Londres [sic], 1771), chap. 8, "Le nouveau Paris," 37.
2. "Décret de l'Assemblée nationale concernant l'enlèvement des quatres figures enchaînés au pied de la Statue de Louis XIV" (June 20, 1790).
3. For general works, see Paul Fabre, *Les lettres de cachet* (Béziers: J.-B. Perdraut, 1878), and Claude Quétel, *Les lettres de cachet: Une légende noir* (Paris: Perrin, 2011).

On prisons of state, see Jean-Claude Vimont, *La prison politique en France: Génèse d'un mode d'incarcération spécifique* (Paris: Anthropos-Economica, 1993). On uses of lettres de cachet in eighteenth-century Paris, see Arlette Farge and Michel Foucault, *Le désordre des familles: Lettres de cachet des archives de la Bastille au XVIIIe siècle* (Paris: Gallimard, 1982). For eighteenth-century denunciations of these royal writs, see [Honoré-Gabriel Riqueti, Comte de Mirabeau], *Des lettres de cachet et des prisons d'état, ouvrage posthume, composé en 1778* (Hamburg, 1782); for an overview of this literature, see Hans-Jürgen Lusebrink et al., *The Bastille: A History of a Symbol of Despotism and Freedom* (Durham, NC: Duke University Press, 1997).

4. Antoine-René de Voyer d'Argenson, *Considérations sur le gouvernement ancien et présent de la France, comparé avec celui des autres états; suivies d'un nouveau plan d'administration*, 2nd ed. (Amsterdam, 1784), 235.

5. Farge and Foucault, *Le désordre des familles*, 16.

6. Jean-François Niort, "Homo seruilis: Essai sur l'anthropologie et le statut juridique de l'esclave dans le Code Noir de 1685," *Droits* 50, no. 1 (2009): 119–41, and *Le Code Noir: Idées reçues sur un texte symbolique* (Paris: Éditions Cavalier Bleu, 2014). On the origins of the code, see Vernon Valentine Palmer, "The Origins and Authors of the Code Noir," *Louisiana Law Review* 56, no. 2 (Winter 1995): 363–407, and Bernard Vonglis, "La double origine du Code noir," in *Les Abolitions dans les Amériques*, ed. Liliane Chauleau (Fort-de-France: Société des amis des archives et de la recherche sur le patrimoine culturel des Antilles, 2001), 101–7. For an applied eighteenth-century history of the Code Noir focused on Saint Domingue, see Malick Ghachem, *The Old Regime and the Haitian Revolution* (New York: Cambridge University Press, 2012).

7. See petition of April 9, 1759, Archives nationales, Paris (hereafter abbreviated AN), Z-1d-131.

8. Archives de la Bastille, Bibliothèque de l'Arsénal, Paris (hereafter abbreviated AB), MS 12,230 (Joseph Aza, 1765).

9. Chambon, *Le commerce de l'Amérique par Marseille, ou, Explication des lettres-patentes du roi, portant règlement pour le commerce qui se fait de Marseillle aux isles françoise de l'Amérique, données au mois de février 1719* (Avignon, 1764), 2:225.

10. "Traité entre les compagnies royales de Sénégal et de Saint-Domingue pour la fourniture de 400 nègres originaires de Gambie, Cacher, Binao, dont 2/3 de mâles par an, en l'île de Saint-Domingue" (February 27, 1699), AN MC/ET/ XCV/722.

11. Sue Peabody, *"There Are No Slaves in France": The Political Culture of Race and Slavery in the Ancien Regime* (New York: Oxford, 1996); see also *Free Soil in the Atlantic World*, ed. Sue Peabody and Keila Grinberg (New York: Routledge, 2015). On free soil in the nineteenth century, see Peabody, "La question raciale et le 'sol libre de France': l'affaire Furcy," *Annales, Histoire, Sciences Sociales* 64, no. 6 (2009): 1305–34.

12. On the admiralty jurisdiction, see Jacques de Chastenet d'Esterre, *Histoire de l'Amirauté en France* (Paris: A. Pedone, 1906). See articles by Joachim Darsel (1905–1974) on Norman admiralty courts in *Annales de la Normandie*, vols. 19–31 (1969–1981) and vol. 36 (1986); by the same author, see *L'Amirauté en Bretagne des*

origines à la fin du XVIIIe siècle: Présentation de la thèse de Joachim Darsel, ed. Gérard Le Bouédec (Rennes: Presses universitaires de Rennes, 2012). For an eighteenth-century perspective on the admiralty, see René-Josué Valin, *Nouveau commentaire sur l'Ordonnance de la Marine du moi d'août 1681* (La Rochelle: Jérome Legier, 1766). For a sample of the vast literature on the Parlement of Paris in the eighteenth century, see Jean Egret, *Louis XV et l'opposition parlementaire* (Paris: A. Colin, 1970); François Bluche, *Les magistrats du Parlement de Paris au XVIIIe siècle*, rev. ed. (Paris: Economica, 1986); Richard Mowery Andrews, *Law, Magistracy, and Crime in Old Regime Paris, 1735-1789* (Cambridge: Cambridge University Press, 1994); Julian Swann, *Politics and the Parlement of Paris Under Louis XV, 1745-1774* (Cambridge: Cambridge University Press, 1995); and Peter Robert Campbell, *Power and Politics in Old Regime France, 1720-1745* (London: Routledge, 1996).

13. On racial law, see Yvan Debbasch, *Couleur et liberté: Le jeu du critère ethnique dans un ordre juridique esclavagiste* (Paris: Dalloz, 1967); Michèle Duchet, *Anthropologie et histore au siècle des lumières* (Paris: Albin Michel, 1995); Pierre H. Boulle, *Race et esclavage dans la France de l'Ancien Régime* (Paris: Perrin, 2007), esp. 59–80; and Guillaume Aubert, " 'The Blood of France': Race and Purity of Blood in the French Atlantic World," *William and Mary Quarterly*, 3rd ser., 61, no. 3 (2004): 439–78. On eighteenth-century French racial discourse, see Doris Garraway, *The Libertine Colony: Creolization in the Early French Caribbean* (Durham: Duke University Press, 2005); see also Mélanie Lamotte, "Colour Prejudice in the Early Modern French Empire, 1635-1767" (PhD thesis, University of Cambridge, 2015) and "Colour Prejudice in the Early Modern French Atlantic World," in *The Atlantic World*, ed. D'Maris Coffman, Adrien Leonard, and William O'Reilly (London: Routledge, 2015), 151–71.

14. Dwain C. Pruitt, "The Opposition of the Law to the Law: Race, Slavery, and the Law in Nantes, 1715-1778," *French Historical Studies* 30, no. 2 (2007): 147–74; Erick Noël, *Être noir en France au XVIIIe siècle* (Paris: Tallandier, 2006). See also Marcel Koufinkana, *Les esclaves noirs en France sous l'ancien régime (XVI-XVIIIe siècles)* (Paris: L'Harmattan, 2008).

15. Peabody, *There Are No Slaves in France*, 19–22.

16. Antoine Rouillé, Comte de Jouy, Min. de la Marine, Versailles, 10 March 1752, to Nicolas-René Berryer, lieutenant general of police, AB MS 11,807 ("un nègre esclave").

17. See petition to lieutenant general of police by Didier Colas, "loueur de carosses," AB MS 12,283 (Haillet, 1766).

18. On the legal profession, see David A. Bell, *Lawyers and Citizens: The Making of a Political Elite in Old Regime France* (New York: Oxford University Press, 1994); see also Martine Acerra, "Les avocats du Parlement de Paris, 1661–1715," *Histoire, économie et société* 1, no. 2 (1982): 213–25.

19. See AB MS 11,793 (Marie-Thérèse, 1752) and MS 12,252 (Papillon, 1765). On the daily life and professional practice of Mutel and Chenon, see Justine Berlière, *Policer Paris au siècle des lumières: Les commissaires du quartier du Louvre dans la seconde moitié du XVIIIe siècle* (Paris: École des Chartes, 2012), esp. 98–117; see also Vincent Milliot, *Un policier des lumières suivi de Mémoires de J. C. P. Lenoir, ancien lieutenant général de police de Paris* (Paris: Champ Vallon, 2011).

20. See *registres pour la déclaration des nègres*, AN Z-1d-139.
21. Jean-Jacques Rousseau, *Les confessions* (1782–1789), bk. 10, cited in Paul Tisseau, "Une amie de Jean-Jacques Rousseau: La Marquise de Verdelin," *Annales de la Société Jean-Jacques Rousseau* (Geneva: A. Jullien, 1905), 26–27.
22. Of Boucaux's marriage, see "Copie de l'extrait de mariage, Extrait du registre des mariages faits en l'église paroissiale de Saint Eustache à Paris," March 6, 1738, AB MS 11,380.
23. "Edit du roy donné à Paris au mois d'octobre 1716, concernant les esclaves nègres des colonies," http://arks.princeton.edu/ark:/88435/hh63sx27b.
24. "Déclaration du roi concernant les esclaves nègres des colonies qui interprète l'Edit du mois d'Octobre 1716, donne a Versailles le 15 décembre 1738," http://staraco .univ-nantes.fr/fr/ressources/documents/d%C3%A9claration-du-roy-1738.
25. Ripart de Montclar, prosecutor-general in Aix to Min. Navy, May 9, 1766, AN Marine B3/571.
26. On the creation of this depository for prison and police documents, see Frantz-Funck-Brentano, *Les archives de la Bastille: La formation du dépôt* (Dôle: C. Blind, 1890). For published documents from this series, see François and Louis Rav-aisson-Mollien, *Les archives de la Bastille: Documents inédits*, 19 vols. (Paris: Durand et Pedone-Lauriel, 1866–1904).
27. For documents on Juliette, see AN Z-1d-139; *ordre du roi* of October 31, 1777, AA3 (lettres de cachet), Archives de la Préfecture de Police; and AD Seine Maritime, 6P 6/11–12, cited in Erick Noël, ed., *Dictionnaire des gens de couleur dans la France moderne: Paris et son basin* (Geneva: Droz, 2011), nos. 1722 and 2569. Pierre Boulle notes the use of several *ordres du roi* against slaves seeking freedom on the eve of the 1777 edict creating a Police des Noirs. See Boulle, *Race et esclavage dans la France de l'Ancien Régime*, 85–87. For later cases of disappearance, see Jean Baptiste, slave of Héligon, in AN Z-1d 132 and C8b/12, no. 103, digitized at http:// anom.archivesnationales.culture.gouv.fr/ark:/61561/zn401hjhdiq. See also Jean-Louis and Jean Forestier, in AN Z-1d-134; on Forestier's deportation, see Col/E/188, digitized at http://anom.archivesnationales.culture.gouv.fr /ark:/61561/up424rrrlnh.
28. Mirabeau, *Des lettres de cachet et des prisons d'état*, 108, 120.
29. For the file on Pauline, see AB MS 12,252.
30. AB MS 12,137 (Télémaque, April 23, 1761).
31. AB MS 12,355 (Aladin, June 6–17, 1769).
32. Admiralty Court Session of March 18, 1765, AN Z-1d-132.
33. "Édit portant établissement à Versailles d'un dépôt des papiers publics des colonies, donné au mois de juin 1776 à Versailles, registré en la Chambre des Comptes le 15 avril 1777," http://gallica.bnf.fr/ark:/12148/btv1b8615078b.
34. On the theme of imperial consolidation in the English context, see Christopher Alan Bayly, *Imperial Meridian: The British Empire and the World, 1780-1830* (London: Routledge, 1989); see also Lauren Benton and Lisa Ford, *Rage for Order: The British Empire and the Origins of International Law, 1800-1850* (Cambridge, MA: Harvard University Press, 2016).

NINE

Re-touching the Sovereign

Biochemistry of Perpetual Leninism

ALEXEI YURCHAK

Original And Fake

WHAT KIND OF A BODY is lying in Lenin's Mausoleum in Moscow (figure 9.1)? Is it the real body of Lenin, a wax figurine, or an impostor? Rumors about its fake nature have circulated for over ninety years. They started even before Lenin's death, in the early 1920s, when he fell seriously ill and disappeared from public view. One rumor claimed that Lenin had already died and an imposter played his role.[1] In the first days after Lenin's death in January 1924, his body lay in state in the House of the Unions in Moscow, where enormous crowds gathered to bid farewell to the leader. For some, the experience of an endless line slowly filing past Lenin's body evoked the crowds that had gathered at the Panopticon Museum in St. Petersburg a few years previously to see a wax effigy of the Egyptian queen Cleopatra in a glass sarcophagus. In a reenactment of Cleopatra's death, every few minutes a snake slithered out and bit her exposed breast. Poet Alexander Blok wrote about being one of the hankering gawkers who "has come to glimpse the great profile, to see the waxworks advertised."[2] In January 1924, paying respects to Lenin, poet Vera Inber imitated the rhythm and imagery of Blok's stanza in her poem "Five Nights and Days," writing that she "has come to glimpse the pale profile, the medal red upon his chest."[3] The dim hall, Lenin's lit-up corpse, thousands of eyes fixated on his profile—it all reminded her of Cleopatra's wax model.[4]

FIGURE 9.1 Vladimir Lenin's embalmed body in the Mausoleum, Moscow. Public domain

When Lenin's embalmed body was publicly displayed in the Mausoleum in late summer 1924, Moscow was again awash with rumors. They did not disappear even in the 1930s, when repeating them could get one arrested. In the atmosphere of widespread denunciations, a young woman reported to the secret police that her acquaintances, the sister and daughter of the once powerful Felix Dzerzhinsky,[5] claimed in a private conversation that "the body lying in the Mausoleum is . . . a wax dummy."[6] These speculations were regularly repeated in Western newspapers. To dispel them, in the 1930s the Communist Party invited a group of Western newsmen to visit the Mausoleum. An American journalist remembered that Boris Zbarsky, one of Lenin's two original embalmers, "opened the hermetically sealed glass case . . . , tweaked Lenin's nose and turned his head to the right and left," demonstrating that "it was not wax. It was Lenin."[7]

One reason for the persistence of these rumors is that they seem believable. For some, the smooth sallow skin of Lenin's body glowing in the light of miniature lamps brings to mind the wax celebrities that populate Madame Tussaud's and its many imitations. For others, such rumors are credible because they seem cynically rational: why bother with the complex science of maintaining Lenin's body if creating its perfect wax replica would do the trick? In fact, drawing a line between real bodies and artificial models is not always easy. Many preserved bodies that are widely assumed to be real contain artificial parts. Internal liquids in the cells of Eva Perón's body have been substituted with wax, prompting the embalmers to nickname her "a candle."[8] Despite a popular assumption, the body of Jeremy Bentham at University College London is more artificial than real.[9] Bentham's skeleton was padded out with straw, dressed in his clothes and seated on a chair. An attempt to preserve Bentham's head by suspending it over sulfuric acid and drawing off the fluids with a pump went horribly wrong when his face shriveled beyond recognition. Instead, a wax replica of Bentham's head was attached to his skeleton, while the disfigured real head was preserved in a separate box.[10]

In 1976, a few days after Mao's death, a group of Chinese medics were unexpectedly charged with the task of preserving the chairman's body.[11] Having no experience in the matter and unable to turn for advice to the more experienced Soviet scientists (Sino-Soviet relations were at their worst), the Chinese had to experiment. It was so uncertain what the results would be, remembers Mao's personal physician Li Zhisui, that a wax copy of Mao's body was also created as a backup. Beijing Institute of Arts and Crafts dispatched two specialists to Madame Tussaud's in London to learn the newest methods of wax modeling. With surprise and satisfaction they telegraphed back "that in this technique, at least, China was already far more advanced than England."[12] Mao's waxen figure was created in secrecy and looked remarkably lifelike. Only a handful of medics, artists, and party leaders were aware of its existence. In 1977, both Maos, embalmed and waxen, were transferred to his mausoleum on Tiananmen Square. Which one is on display at a given moment depends on whether Mao's body has to undergo re-embalming.[13]

In the 1990s, after the Soviet collapse, rumors about Lenin's body being a fake intensified. Ilya Zbarsky, son of the original embalmer and himself a long-time member of the embalming team, felt it necessary to write in his memoir: "I worked in the Mausoleum for eighteen years and I know for a fact that Lenin's body is in a very good condition. . . . All sorts of rumors and fabrications according to which this is not Lenin's body but an effigy . . . or that nothing but Lenin's face and hands have been successfully preserved, have no foundation in reality."[14] However, the media was more ready to embrace stories about fake Lenin, and Zbarsky's statement was forgotten. At the same time, what he said in a later interview was misinterpreted. Zbarsky referred to the bodies of "Lenin's doubles" (dvoiniki), a slang term the lab's scientists used for bodies that have been embalmed in the lab using the same technique as Lenin's body. These "doubles" do not look like Lenin and are not preserved to be displayed. Lab scientists use them for experimental work on improving preservation techniques. However, the allusion to "doubles" morphed into a media story about "multiple Lenins," with the implication that whoever is displayed in the Mausoleum, it is not the real thing. In 2000, in an attempt to stop the rumor, Professor Yuri Romakov, the lab's deputy director, went on a popular radio show to assure the public that Lenin's body is his own and requires no substitutes.[15]

In 2008, a Duma deputy, Vladimir Medinsky—now Russia's minister of culture—announced from the Duma podium that Lenin's body was not real for a different reason. "Do not fool yourselves with the illusion that what is lying in the Mausoleum is Lenin. What's left there is only 10 percent of his body," he said alluding to the fact that most of Lenin's internal organs and liquids were gone. The respected political weekly *Vlast'* responded with its own half-ironic calculation that challenged Medinsky's figure: what is lying in the Mausoleum, it reported, is 23 percent of Lenin's body, not 10 percent as the deputy suggested.[16] The most radical theory was reported by Russian newspapers and TV in 2012: a professional criminalist investigation allegedly established that the body in the Mausoleum is not Lenin's "simply because such a person had never existed."[17]

In fact, if we looked at the material composition of Lenin's body more closely we would see that some of these rumors are not altogether unfounded. The task of the Mausoleum lab's scientists has always been to preserve the *dynamic form* of Lenin's body—its shape, color, weight, suppleness, firmness, flexibility, and so forth. Even today the body's joints can still bend, its torso and neck can rotate, its back and thighs remain flexible, its skin is firm and elastic, the hair on its chest and head is attached to the skin, and all of its bodily textures are supple, firm, and moist. However, to achieve this remarkable feat the lab has been gradually replacing this body's constitutive *bio-matter*—its liquids, fats, fragments of skin, muscle tissue, bone structure, and so on.[18]

In the Soviet times, special commissions of party leaders and scientists regularly examined every inch of this body in the naked state, checking its appearance, suppleness, volume, color, and weight and comparing them with the previous examinations. To this political-scientific gaze the body appeared as flexible, changing, improving. But to regular visitors Lenin's body always appeared as stiff, fixed, preserved once and for all in a distant past. They saw it lying in the sarcophagus dressed in a dark suit, with only the head and hands exposed. They never heard of the condition of this body as a whole. The existence of these two distinct regimes of visibility—one for the gaze of the political regime, the other for its common citizens—suggests that the political role of Lenin's body has always exceeded that of a simple propaganda symbol designed to boost popular support for the Soviet state. This body also played a distinct and publicly invisible political role that was important for the organization and reproduction of the regime. To understand this role we must first return to the period just before Lenin's death.

Lenin and Leninism

In spring 1922, Lenin felt ill and exhausted and left Moscow for the country estate of Gorki. He rested under the supervision of doctors but continued to lead the party and make occasional appearances in Moscow. But in May 1922, he had a stroke and temporarily lost ability to speak, read and write.[19] In response the party leadership introduced stricter rules isolating Lenin from the political life. While new rules reflected a real concern for Lenin's health, they were also an attempt to neutralize a powerful political rival. In June 1922, a secretary of the Central Committee complained in a letter to a friend that Dzerzhinsky and Smidovich[20] had isolated Lenin and "guard him like two bulldogs [not letting] . . . anyone come close to him or even into the building where he is staying."[21]

In the next year and a half Lenin's condition worsened, then improved, then worsened again. His imposed isolation became stricter. He was not allowed to read newspapers, write essays, or interact with important political figures.[22] Lenin experienced his situation as imprisonment, saying to a friend: "I haven't died yet, but under Stalin's supervision they are already trying to bury me."[23] In spring 1923, he had a third stroke and almost completely lost the ability to communicate;[24] meanwhile, the political rivalry in the leadership intensified.[25]

Lenin had not disappeared from the public view, however; his presence in fact intensified, but in a new form. While the living and ailing Lenin was isolated in the Gorki estate, a newly constructed canonized image of Lenin started to dominate the political discourse. Most of the familiar mythologized images and institutions around Lenin's cult that became well known throughout the Soviet history were created in those final months of his life, and in spite of his active protestations.[26] In early 1923, the term "Leninism" was introduced into public circulation,[27] and every party member had to pledge allegiance to it.[28] On March 31, 1923, the Lenin Institute was established in Moscow,[29] and the newspaper *Pravda* appealed to its readers to send "every scrap of paper bearing an inscription or mark made by Lenin" to the institute.[30]

At the same time, much of what Lenin was saying and writing after the autumn of 1922 was actively banished from this canonized image.[31] Lenin was not allowed to change his earlier positions or protest against misinterpretations of his earlier statements. It was now the Politburo that controlled what Lenin was "really" saying, not Lenin himself.[32] Lenin the political figure was doubled—into one Lenin who was banished from the political world and another Lenin who was canonized within it. In these two simultaneous processes, in the early 1920s the figure of "Leninism" was produced, which until the end of Soviet history served as the central, foundational, and unquestionable truth of the Soviet polity. In practice, Leninism was not a static doctrine that was formulated once and for all and later simply repeated; it was continually changed, reinterpreted, and reinvented.

Every Soviet leader from Stalin to Gorbachev produced his own version of Leninism, suppressing, reinterpreting, or reintroducing different aspects of "Lenin's legacy."[33] In 1990, less than two years before the Soviet state collapsed, the Communist Party finally admitted that every single version of Leninism involved distortions of Lenin's works. In his speech on the occasion of Lenin's 120th anniversary, in April 1990, Gorbachev said something unprecedented. Starting with the usual "Lenin still remains with us as the greatest thinker of the twentieth century," Gorbachev quickly added: "We must rethink Lenin and his theoretical and political work, and we must rid ourselves of the distortions and canonizations of his conclusions. . . . It is time to end the thoughtless and absurd manipulation of Lenin's name and image that turns him into an 'icon.'" Moreover, said Gorbachev, time has come to abandon the concept of "Leninism" altogether because it reduces Lenin's complex thought to a collection of canonical statements.[34]

Writing in a central daily, a philosophy professor lamented: "Our tragedy is that we do not know Lenin. We never read his original texts in the past, and we still do not do this today. For decades we have perceived Lenin through mediators, interpreters, popularizers, and other distorters."[35] A historian wrote in a widely circulating daily that Khrushchev and Brezhnev "were obviously not Leninists"; for them Lenin was only "an icon" behind which they could hide.[36] Another historian complained that even the Institute of Marxism-Leninism, the country's leading authority on Lenin's theoretical legacy, "for seventy years since its foundation has been fulfilling an absurd function . . . legitimating for publication [Lenin's] texts that matched the canon of the day, however different from real Lenin's words they were, and altering or modifying [Lenin's] texts that did not fit that canon."[37] A former speechwriter to the party leadership made an astonishing revelation: Mikhail Suslov, the powerful chief of ideology in the Politburo, for years had been skillfully manipulating Lenin's ideas by drawing on a vast collection of isolated quotes plucked out of Lenin's voluminous writings.[38] Using these quotes out of context Suslov assigned them with random meanings necessary to legitimate different political campaigns or speeches of the Soviet government, including diametrically opposing ones.

Form and Content

When Lenin died, on January 21, 1924, no plans to preserve his body existed. Professor Abrikosov conducted an autopsy and performed short-term embalming that would allow Lenin's body to be displayed in an open coffin for the five days of the public farewell. The incisions that Abrikosov made in the body cut across its major arteries and blood vessels. Later he remarked that had the plans to preserve Lenin's body for posterity existed at the time of the autopsy, he would not have cut these arteries and blood vessels because in long-term preservation they are used to deliver embalming liquids to all corners of the body.[39]

From January 22, Lenin's body lay in state in the House of the Trade Unions in Moscow with huge crowds of people from all over the country waiting in an enormous line, in extremely cold temperatures, to bid farewell to the leader.[40] It was announced that Lenin would be buried on January 27 in a newly built mausoleum on the Red Square, near the existing tombs of fallen revolutionaries. However, the crowds coming to see the body had not grown any smaller. At the same time, the body showed no signs of deterioration due to the extremely cold temperatures that winter and problems with heating in a war-devastated country (even inside the House of the Unions temperature never rose much above the freezing point).[41] For these different reasons, the official burial of the body in a temporary wooden mausoleum, in fact, amounted to placing it in an open sarcophagus in order to extend the public farewell. The funeral that started on January 27 was not yet completed; the interregnum was extended into the indefinite future. The body was displayed for another two months, until late March, when warmer spring weather finally arrived and the first threatening signs of decomposition were discovered.[42]

The extended period during which the body remained in an open sarcophagus allowed the party leadership and scientists to discuss it at endless meetings again and again. It was then that the idea that the body should be preserved and displayed for posterity gradually won. At first many party leaders considered this idea counterrevolutionary. Trotsky, Bukharin, and Voroshilov argued that preserving Lenin's body would be akin to creating a religious relic—an act that violated Marxist-Leninist principles.[43] Bonch-Bruevich stressed that while it was important to create a public memorial for Lenin, his body should be buried in a closed tomb.[44] But for many others it seemed important to continue displaying Lenin's body for some time, potentially for an indefinite future, allowing more people from all over the world to pay their respects to the leader.

Concluding an important meeting of the leadership on March 5, 1924, Avel Enukidze, a member of the Central Executive Committee, said that the body should be preserved and displayed, but "without promising to anyone that this is done for posterity." If it did not hold up after a period of time, "we will have to enclose it."[45] In late March, it was decided to try an experimental embalming procedure proposed by professor of medicine Vladimir Vorob'ev and biochemist Boris Zbarsky. Neither was certain if the experiment would succeed.[46] Vorob'ev and Zbarsky worked for four months and in late July 1924 reported to the leadership that if Lenin's body was regularly treated and re-embalmed according to the method they developed, it could be preserved for quite a long time. They did not specify for how long.[47] Following their success on July 24, 1924, the "Commission for the Immortalization of Lenin's Memory" issued a public statement:

We did not want to turn the body of Vladimir Il'ich into some kind of "relic," by means of which we could popularize and preserve his memory. He had

already immortalized himself enough with his brilliant teaching and revolutionary activities. . . . We wanted to preserve the body of Vladimir Il'ich . . .
[because] it is of great importance to preserve the *fizicheskii oblik* [physical
look, shape, form] of this remarkable leader for the next generation and all
the future generations.[48]

The long debates about Lenin's body among the party leadership in spring
1924, as well as the retrospective statement about its preservation in July,
suggest that the party leadership increasingly saw this body in two distinct
ways. This duality is reminiscent of how they had treated Lenin in the final
months of his life, when the flesh-and-blood Lenin was banished from
political life while the newly constructed "Leninism" was canonized within it.
Now, Lenin's body was treated in this dual way—it was officially "buried" but
continued to be on display; it was preserved for an indefinite future, but
not, the party claimed, to immortalize any concrete individual; it was the
biological corpse of a person but also a physical form that transcended
individual biology.[49] The body, in other words, was both the corpse of "Lenin"
and the embodiment of something that was different from Lenin and bigger
than him.

This way of thinking about Lenin's body in 1924 is strikingly similar to
how the scientists at the Mausoleum lab have viewed the goals of their work
since. Academician Valerii Bykov, the director of VILAR Institute, under
whose auspices the lab operates today, describes this task as the preservation of Lenin's "anatomical image" (*anatomicheskii obraz*).[50] This suggests that
maintaining the body's *form* is of greater significance than preserving its
original *bio-matter*. Academician Yurii Lopukhin, for several decades a leading scientist at the lab, prefers to describe Lenin's body as "live sculpture"
(*zhivaia skul'ptura*).[51] Lopukhin's phrase is an attempt to capture ambiguities
that such terms as "corpse," "mummy," or "relic" do not reflect. After decades of being re-embalmed and re-sculpted, the body has changed so considerably from its original biological composition, Lopukhin argues, that in
some way it is closer to a *representation* of Lenin's body than that body itself.
At the same time, Lopukhin stresses, this is not an external representation
as in sculpture or painting, because this is undeniably the *actual* body itself.
"Live sculpture" tries to capture this ambiguity—referring to a body that
both *is* and *is not* a representation, as if to say that this is a *sculpture of the
body that is being constructed out of the body itself.* The term "sculpture," how-

ever, does not fully satisfy Lopukhin either, since it tends to suggest a stiff and hard body, while Lenin's body is maintained to be flexible and supple.

Art and Biology

To keep this body's material form and dynamic properties, explains Lopukhin, "one must not only know the basics of anatomy, physical chemistry, and how to maintain the water balance.... One must also possess an artistic sense.... This is why not everyone is capable of doing this work."[52] Professor Vladislav Kozel'tsev, another veteran scientist of the lab, makes a similar point: during major re-embalming and reconstructing procedures, "every new wrinkle, cavity or protrusion [in Lenin's body] must be fixed. We are talking about tiny dimensions. Some amount of artificial substitutes has to be introduced, which is quite difficult. One needs experience and artistic sense to perform this work."[53]

During the Soviet period party commissions regularly examined the body and issued detailed reports on its condition.[54] On January 19, 1939, a "Commission of the People's Commissariat of Health for the Examination of Lenin's Body" reported that Lenin's nose, which lost its original form when Lenin's corpse was exposed to extreme cold after death,[55] finally had been rebuilt and was "in a very good condition." The report also wrote approvingly that the "elasticity of the eyelids" had been preserved and the face "makes a complete impression of a sleeping person, rather than a corpse."[56] A central criterion for maintaining Lenin's body that is underscored in these reports was to avoid an appearance of a stiff corpse, which invokes again Lopukhin's phrase "live sculpture." But there were also some problems that needed attention. Professor Nikolai Burdenko found new spots "on the outer side of the left forearm" and "in the lower part of the body, especially in the pelvic area." Alexei Busalov, director of the medical administration of the Kremlin, remarked that "on the soles and toes there are some signs of mummification. In the pelvic area there are hints of wrinkling and thinning [of the skin]."[57] The lab scientists had to solve these problems.

One reason for the development of new wrinkles, cavities, and spots on the body is hydrolysis—the process in which internal solid fats in skin and other tissues liquefy and move away from their areas. An examination commission three years later found that the wrinkles, spots, and depressions described earlier had been eliminated successfully. An important break-through was the development of an artificial material that solved the problem of hydrolysis. The material had similar physical characteristics to subcutaneous fats (the same consistency, softness and firmness), but unlike them it was chemically neutral and could not liquefy in normal temperatures. In November 1943, Zbarsky explained to the party leadership:

> After many experiments we developed a mix of paraffin, glycerin, and caro-tene with the melting point of 57 degrees Celsius. This mix in liquefied form can be injected under the skin, where it quickly hardens into a solid mass that can be easily shaped. After experiments in the lab it became possible to sub-stitute hydrolyzed fats with this new mass. From the chemical point of view this mass is inert and can be preserved without change. . . . Two years of ex-periments in this area produced such good results that they could be applied to fixing defects in Lenin's body.[58]

The material was applied by microinjections to various parts of the body where "depression or change of volume" was found, substituting "for the fatty materials that underwent hydrolysis." Georgii Miterev, People's com-missar of health, asked Zbarsky, "So, you insert artificial mass. . . . Does this mean that after a period of time all fats [in the body] will be replaced with this new artificial mass?"[59] Zbarsky replied positively, and Miterev and other dignitaries seemed satisfied. The commission also stressed that the elastic-ity and pressures of the skin and all tissues, and the flexibility of all small and large joints, had been perfectly maintained and in some cases im-proved.[60] From the commission's point of view, substituting original bio-matter with artificial materials was not a problem, as long as it helped to maintain the dynamic form of the body—the shape, volume and elasticity of its tissues, the smoothness and firmness of its skin, and the flexibility of its joints.

Mortal and Immortal

Why was maintaining the authenticity of this flexible form more important than preserving the bio-matter? Why did the scientists labor to maintain the precise shape, flexibility, and suppleness in those parts of the body that, unlike the head and hands, were never meant for public display? What was the political role of such a project? Some aspects of this role may become clearer if we compare this body with the bodies of sovereign rulers in different cultural and historical contexts. Western European kings, famously analyzed by Ernst Kantorowicz,[61] are a useful point of departure. Kantorowicz focused on late medieval and early modern legal theories that linked monarchic sovereignty and the king's body. Any sovereign power is absolute not only *spatially*, within sovereign borders,[62] but also *temporally*: it is potentially able to reproduce itself perpetually, surviving the demise of a concrete agent of sovereignty. But in what material form is the temporal perpetuity of sovereignty manifested, considering that bodies are mortal? When this question became important for political and theological reasons in late medieval England and France, it led to the development of a legal doctrine of "the king's two bodies." With the shift toward a new secularized model of monarchy, the king's legitimacy could no longer be based solely on the approval and consecration by the church and instead became purely "dynastic," coming not from grace but from *nature*. "Royal qualities and potencies" were now seen as natural traits that dwelled directly in the king's blood, creating "a royal species of man."[63] According to this view, the physical body of the king, unlike that of regular mortals, was *doubled*, consisting of two bodies that coexisted within one flesh—the mortal body (body of nature) and the immortal body (body of grace). The king's death was the demise of his mortal body, while the immortal body survived and, after the period of interregnum, re-inhabited the flesh of the next king.

During the interregnum the doubling of the monarch's body acquired an explicitly material manifestation, which came to be reflected in the construction of the monarch's effigy. The effigy looked uncannily similar to the deceased monarch but was different from his or her external representation. While sculptures and images of the dead are common in many funeral ceremonies around the world, they usually function as a *representation* of the dead person—that is, as a *substitute* for the missing corpse. But the role played by the effigy was different: it appeared only during a short period of time, before and during the funeral, always coexisting with the displayed corpse of the monarch instead of substituting for it.[64]

The pair of the corpse and the effigy manifested the actual material doubling of the monarch's body. To leave no doubt that this was the same body, only doubled, effigies were made to look like an exact, healthy (surviving) version of the monarch—so exact, that sometimes even the courtiers mistook the effigy for the living king. Effigies were produced in secret, with great artistic efforts summoned for this task. They were made of wax, leather, and wood. Their faces were meticulously modeled on the death mask of the monarch and carefully painted to look as alive as possible.[65] Real hair was used; artificial eyelashes were inserted; limbs were created with moving joints. In sixteenth-century France and England, during preparations for the monarch's funeral the effigy was displayed as prominently as the corpse. But because it functioned as the *surviving* body of the sovereign, often more attention was paid to it than to the corpse. The effigy was dressed in the monarch's clothes and seated on the throne; medics pretended to take its pulse and listen to its breath; it was served food and wine and after meals its mouth and hands were wiped.[66] During the funeral procession, the monarch's corpse and effigy both were carried through the city. Courtiers often jostled with each other for the position nearest to the effigy, ignoring the corpse (paying more attention to the surviving, perpetual half of the sovereign).[67] With the coronation of the next monarch, the mortal and immortal bodies became once again reunited within one person's flesh. The corpse of the previous monarch was buried and his effigy could no longer be publicly seen and was hidden or destroyed.[68]

In his book Kantorowicz discusses the theory of the king's two bodies as an artifact of late medieval–early modern Christian Western Europe. However, as anthropologists and historians have shown, many comparable rituals of the perpetual regeneration of sovereign power have existed in diverse sociocultural and historical contexts. The third edition of Sir James Frazer's *The Golden Bough: A Study in Comparative Religion*, published in 1916, describes the rituals of royal succession in the Shilluk kingdom of southern Sudan, which echo those described by Kantorowicz in some detail, including the rituals of doubling the royal body and using a wooden effigy.[69] Comparable cosmologies and rituals developed in other parts of the world and periods— from East India[70] to premodern Japan,[71] from ancient imperial Rome[72] to the modern Vatican.[73] It appears that a temporal discontinuity between the *impermanence* of the sovereign's human body and the *permanence* of the sovereign office, coupled with an attempt to avoid a crisis of power as a result of this discontinuity, led to the emergence of comparable cosmologies and rituals of bodily doubling in many different contexts.

The case explored by Kantorowicz, therefore, appears to be a significant but culturally specific variety of a broader phenomenon. In the Leninist system a distinct political cosmology that linked a doubling of the foundational body with the sovereignty of the political regime had also emerged. The link of this political cosmology with the body that is preserved for posterity was not formulated at once but developed gradually. With time this political cosmology shaped the peculiar requirements and constraints of the scientific practice that was designed to achieve preservation. This is not an argument about direct causality. The structure of Leninist sovereignty did not develop as a direct transformation of sovereign principles that existed in the Russian monarchy or in the institutions and beliefs of the Orthodox church. As Michael Cherniavsky, a student of Kantorowicz, has argued, a doctrine comparable to that of the king's two bodies in France and England never developed in the Russian czarist state.[74] However, in the Leninist polity the perpetual dimension of sovereignty at some point also became manifested materially, in the form of a doubled sovereign body. The importance of this doubled body in the political regime of the Bolshevik state was enabled not by the previous institutional structures of the prerevolutionary Russian state. It developed, rather, through a combination of circumstances—the relatively long presence of the unburied body in the months after Lenin's death, the political dissociation of Lenin from the artificially constructed "Leninism," and the peculiar combination of the *modern* revolutionary ethos and *traditional* form of power that defined the Bolshevik state. To clarify these points, we must compare the Bolshevik form of power with that in modern democracies and absolutist monarchies.

The King, the People, and the Party

Claude Lefort argues that the political institution of sovereign perpetuity in modern liberal democracy became negatively related to that institution in the absolutist monarchies that it replaced. In the European absolutist monarchies the sovereign's legitimacy was guaranteed by the monarch's link to "another place"—a place that was *external* to the political world of the monarchy, where the eternity of that sovereign power was anchored. It was in that external, other place that the physical body of each monarch was "located," until that monarch died. In a constitutive paradox of absolutist sovereignty, each monarch occupied the position of immortality, but only temporarily. In contemporary liberal democracies, argues Lefort, the center of sovereign power is also anchored in the immortal "other place," but now that place is *empty*. Democratic rulers cannot occupy it, as the absolutist monarch did, but they must act in the name of that place and refer to it for legitimacy. It is in that place that the foundational Truth of liberal democracy (its source of legitimacy) is anchored.[75]

Eric Santner has also argued that in liberal democracy, with the disappearance of the king's body the locus of sovereignty migrated into a new location. But unlike Lefort, he defines that location as the extra-personal body of the People (population, nation).[76]

In fact, despite their seeming inconsistency, Lefort's and Santner's arguments taken together describe how the doubling of the sovereign's body manifests itself in modern liberal democracy. This body is split between Santner's extra-personal body of the population and Lefort's external "empty space." The former is the collection of human bodies that continuously succeed the previous ones in the perpetual life of the nation; this is the modern equivalent of the succession of the *mortal bodies* of kings in an absolutist dynasty. The latter is the external place where the foundational Truth of the political system is located; this is the modern equivalent of the king's *immortal body*. The foundational Truth is external and prior to the system; it cannot be questioned in the political terms of the system and provides the system with legitimacy. In different modern systems this prior Truth is articulated in different terms—in the words of the Founding Fathers (United States),[77] in the maxims of Marxism-Leninism (Soviet Union), and so forth.

Comparing the structure of sovereignty in the premodern absolutist monarchy and in modern liberal democracy is helpful for understanding the structure of sovereignty in the Leninist polity, where it looked like a peculiar combination of the two.[78] No acting Soviet leader after Lenin's death could occupy the center of sovereign power, like the absolutist monarch did, because the relation of every leader to that power was mediated by the figure of "Leninism." Every Soviet leader, even Stalin at the height of his powers, had to refer to Leninism for legitimacy and could not question it. Any political figure in Soviet history was granted legitimacy if it could be demonstrated that he or she was faithful to Leninism, and was delegitimized in an instant if it was shown that he or she violated Leninism. The emergence of Stalin's personality cult and the collapse of that cult after his death, which did not lead to the collapse of the party and the Soviet system, illustrate this point. At first, Stalin was celebrated as the most faithful Leninist, someone who had unique access to Truth.[79] But after his death, in 1953, Stalin was accused of precisely the opposite—of having distorted the Truth of Leninism.[80] Like other Soviet leaders,[81] Stalin did not and could not occupy the center of sovereign power. But where was that center located? And what was the position of Lenin's body in relation to it?

Ken Jowitt argues that power in the Leninist system was centered neither in the traditional charismatic leader (as in the absolutist monarchy or the Nazi state) nor in depersonalized modern bureaucracy (as in liberal democracy) but instead in an institution that was organized as a combination of the two—the Leninist party. Jowitt defines that institution as *neotraditional* because it emerged when two seemingly incompatible principles were absorbed into one organizational structure: the traditional principle of "individual heroism" and the modern principle of "organizational impersonalism." Comparing two kinds of "totalitarianism," Leninism and Nazism, Jowitt points out that they both emphasized a "heroic ethic"; however, what *agent* each system designated as heroic was different. In the Nazi state that agent was the individual charismatic Leader, the Führer. Nazism was based on the Führerprinzip—on the personal charisma of the Leader, who "claims authority because he incorporates the idea in his person." In the Leninist system that agent was not an individual but the party, whose "heroism [was] defined in organizational, not individual, terms," and therefore its principle of organization was "charismatic impersonalism."[82]

The Leninist party was founded on and held together by the "correct line," a version of the foundational Truth. Every leader in the Leninist system claimed authority on the basis of his knowledge of the "correct line," and no leader could question it. At the end of Lenin's life and after his death the correct line became articulated as the newly constructed doctrine of "Leninism." However, since that doctrine was impersonal (no one could personally author or openly question it, and everyone had to refer to it for legitimacy), it potentially allowed for different interpretations.[83] This was why, argues Jowitt, the Leninist Party always generated many more internal factions than the Nazi Party.[84] And this was also why the Leninist Party always had the legitimate potential to criticize any leader, including the general secretary, if a group in the party leadership made a successful claim that

that leader had violated Leninism.[85] This was what Khrushchev claimed when he attacked Stalin's cult of personality at the Twentieth Party Congress in 1956.[86] And it was also what happened to Khrushchev when he was deposed by the Politburo in 1964.[87]

Jowitt's argument, combined with Lefort's and Santner's, adds clarity to how sovereign power in the Leninist system was organized. The center of sovereignty here was located neither in the twinned body of the charismatic Leader (the absolutist monarch) nor in the duality of "empty place" and collective body of the population (liberal democracy) but rather in a mixture of the two—the Leninist party. The party as a heroic agent was *impersonal*, *collective*, and *doubled* into mortal and immortal bodies. Its mortal body was the collection of all party members whose ongoing succession (like *the population* in liberal democracy) made the continuous existence of the party throughout Soviet history possible. Its immortal body was the doctrine of Leninism—the foundational, unquestionable Truth located outside the system.

What was the role of Lenin's body in this structure of power? That body served the role of the *material manifestation* of the doubled body of the party (akin to the role played together by the corpse and the effigy in the absolutist monarchy). Continuously reproducing "Leninism" as the foundational truth of the Soviet system involved not only manipulating and reinterpreting Lenin's texts and facts of his life but also resculpting and reconstructing his physical body in the Mausoleum. Similarly, the ongoing reforms, purges, and reconstructions of the party were comparable to the continuous regeneration of the population in liberal democracy—that is, to the practices of biopolitics. Reproducing Lenin's body at the level of physical *form* while altering and substituting its biological matter amounted to doubling this body into a *body-corpse* (mortal biological remains) and *body-effigy* (immortal physical form).

To the common visitor to the Mausoleum, Lenin's body has always appeared as the body-corpse—intact, preserved once and for all, fixed in the moment of death. But to the gaze of the political regime (the party leadership and the lab's scientists) Lenin's body appeared as the body-effigy—dynamic, regularly re-sculpted, located in the point of sovereign immortality.

In a way, Lenin's immortal body-effigy was reminiscent of the effigies of medieval kings. However, there was an important difference. The king's effigy existed only temporarily, during a short interregnum when the twinned body of the monarch was materially doubled into corpse and effigy. Conversely, Lenin's body was doubled into corpse and effigy *within one and the same body* and as *a perpetually renewed condition*. The regular "big procedures" of re-embalming and reconstructing Lenin's body that the lab has performed every one and a half years have played a role that can be paralleled to that of the interregnum and renewal of kings in the monarchy. To be more precise, both functioned as mechanisms of sovereign perpetuity.

Dead Leader and Living Patients

The "big procedures" last about two months. During that time all embalming liquids are drained from Lenin's body and subjected to a variety of biochemical, anatomical, and physical tests to identify unwanted biological and chemical processes.[88] Samples of different tissues in the body are collected and tested. Hundreds of photographs of the body's surfaces are taken with precision cameras and compared with the photographs taken previously to identify changes.[89] Microinjections of artificial substances, infusions of embalming and other liquids, and applications of plastics and other materials are used to reconstitute the original volume of body parts, landscape of its surfaces, skin pressure, joint flexibility, color, and weight. All this concerns not only the small parts of the body visible to the public (head and hands) but the parts the public can never see. Then the body is submerged for substantial periods of time (days or weeks) in baths with different solutions.

These elaborate procedures focus predominantly on maintaining the dynamic form of the body, which requires that its biological composition should be slowly changing. The body as a material artifact has been progressively detached from its original biological identity of a concrete individual. This detachment of the body from individual biology and the goal of preserving depersonalized form have enabled a particular kind of experimental work to develop that other types of preservation would not make possible. In addition, a special status that the lab had during the Soviet period meant that it was far better supplied with equipment (often Western), chemicals, and biological materials than most other medical research facilities. The lab was also supervised directly by the party leadership and the KGB, which freed it from many bureaucratic networks of control to which regular Soviet institutions were subjected. All this further enabled the kind of experimental work that far exceeded the immediate project of preserving a concrete body of Lenin and as a result generated many unique inventions, some of which have entered regular medicine and even found their way into Western medical practice. Consider two examples.

In the 1960s, Yurii Lopukhin and a team of lab scientists worked on an improved method for maintaining the form and volume of different tissues and organs in Lenin's body. They worked on a version of perfusion—the flowing of liquids (it can be blood or preservation liquids) through the capillary system of an organ to maintain its structure and volume over time. Perfusion is also used in regular medicine to maintain organs of recently deceased persons in a viable condition outside the body, making them available for organ transplantation. An approach to this problem that Lopukhin developed in Lenin's lab he later adapted for his work on kidney transplantation in living patients. Although maintaining tissues in Lenin's dead body is not the same as maintaining the viability of an organ, some technical designs that needed to be invented to perform complex perfusion in both projects, were similar. Lopukhin's long-time colleague Professor Kozel'tsev explained to me the connection between these two projects:

> You see, during the procedure of re-embalming it is crucial that the anatomical image [volume and dynamic characteristics of tissues] is preserved absolutely intact. It is important to maintain precise volume. To put it simply, no tissue should swell or shrink when liquids are added or drained. When Lopukhin worked on this challenging task he arrived at a very interesting idea, which he later applied to his work on kidney transplantation. A kidney is an appropriate organ for this approach because it's relatively isolated inside the body, like a separate vessel with an input and an output of liquids. Using a complex set of instruments that enabled perfusion of different tissues, when solutions flow through them, Lopukhin later applied this to maintaining the life and volume of a kidney outside of the body. To prepare kidneys for transplantation. The first instrumental set [*pribornoe oformlenie*] he designed here, in the [Mausoleum] lab.[90]

Lopukhin described the instrumental set he invented as a collection of "syringes, funnels, and cannulas—thin, thick, long, short, straight, crooked, of different sizes, capable of delivering liquids to various hidden places in the body where signs of softening or decomposition of tissues has been detected." They are unique, and their modifications are still used today. "If you saw what instruments the Mausoleum group still has at its disposal, you would be amazed," Lopukhin added with pride.[91] In 1969, for his work on developing a method of kidney transplantation Lopukhin won the State Prize of the USSR.[92]

One requirement of the work on Lenin's body has been that tissues should be damaged as little as possible; new punctures should be avoided. For example, it was important to develop noninvasive methods of testing the internal composition of the epidermis, the outmost layers of skin, without cutting the skin. A test method Lopukhin developed in this work later informed research on noninvasive techniques for measuring cholesterol levels in the skin of living patients, which he designed with a group of colleagues at the Research Institute of Physico-Chemical Medicine.[93] The method, known as the "three-drop test," involves putting on the surface of the palm a drop of a reagent, which enters into a reaction with skin cholesterol, applying a second drop of another reagent to the first solution to tie it, and then applying a third drop of a different reagent to that spot to change the color of the resultant mix, which can be accurately measured with a spectrophotometer. That color correlates with the level of cholesterol in the skin, and the method can quite accurately predict the overall level of cholesterol in the body (since approximately 11 percent of the human body's cholesterol is contained in the skin).[94] While one research focused on a dead body and the other research focused on living patients, both dealt with a problem that required noninvasive diagnostics, which allowed Lenin's dead body to affect the work on living patients. In 1992, Lopukhin described the three-drop test in an English-language publication,[95] and in 2002 it received a U.S. patent.[96] It was developed into an FDA-approved point-of-care diagnostic test called the "*PreVu* test" by the Canadian company Miraculins. Today the company successfully markets it in Canada, Europe, and the United States as "the world's first and only non-invasive skin cholesterol test."[97] The promotional materials make no mention of its link to Lenin's body.

In her study of the Lenin cult, historian Nina Tumarkin suggested that the Bolshevik leadership could have preserved Lenin's body to create a "sacred relic" that would "continue to legitimate Soviet power and mobilize the population," which was deeply Orthodox, largely illiterate, and familiar with saints.[98] However, while the display of this body may seem reminiscent of religious relics, the problem with Tumarkin's argument is that the party leaders from the beginning of this project explicitly tried to distance it from any association with relics and miracles, and they always emphasized that the preservation of Lenin's body was a great achievement of the Soviet science.[99] It has been also suggested that the decision to preserve Lenin could have been influenced by Nikolai Fedorov's philosophy of "common cause," which "sought human salvation in the physical resurrection of the flesh."[100] This argument, however, is also problematic, since the method of preserving Lenin's body, as I have argued, includes continuous substitution of its flesh with new inorganic substances, producing a kind of quasi-artificial flesh that is quite incompatible with the "remains" that Fedorov sought to resurrect.

To understand what the political meaning of Lenin's body was in Soviet times and what role it continues to play today, it is insufficient to analyze it only at the level of symbolism, as a tool of this or that ideology. It is equally important to investigate the materiality of this body—the condition of its tissues, cells and joints, the procedures and tests to which it has been subjected, and the scientific knowledge that has developed around it. Lenin's body has played a critical role in the system of Leninist sovereignty. That sovereignty was vested neither in the figure of the ruler (as in the "premodern" absolutist monarchy) nor in the abstract population (as in the "modern" liberal democracy) but in the collective agent that combined properties of the two: the Leninist party. This agent transcended every one of its members—each party member, including the party leader, could be found to be wrong and illegitimate, but the collective party was always-already legitimate and right. The legitimacy of this agent was guaranteed by the foundational Truth of Leninism, to which the party had unique access. The impersonal, collective, twinned body of the party was manifested in one concrete, material form—Lenin's body. Reproducing and readjusting "Leninism" as the foundational truth of the Soviet system involved constant manipulation and reinterpretation of Lenin's texts and facts of his life and constant resculpting and reconstruction of his physical body as a combination of a body-corpse (visible to the public) and body-effigy (visible only to the Party leadership).

In the end, persistent rumors about Lenin's body being a wax puppet have been neither quite accurate nor altogether wrong. This body is real and yet constructed; its bio-material composition is changing, but its dynamic form remains the same. Indeed, focusing on preserving its original biological matter would be a problem for the political regime. It would reduce this body to that of a concrete biological individual, undermining its role as the immortal sovereign body that transcends individual mortal concreteness. This body must inhabit Leninism but be different from Lenin. It must *feel* like Lenin but exceed concrete personhood. This is what Lopukhin's term "live sculpture" intuitively strives to convey.

This project emerged and evolved as part of a complex political cosmology that most participants—politicians and scientists—did not necessarily see for its underlying cultural and political logic. The cultivation of Lenin's body in the Soviet period was always performed in strict secrecy, behind closed doors, visible only to the gaze of the political leadership. The reason for this secrecy was the same as the reason for making invisible constant manipulations of Lenin's words, thoughts, and facts of his life.[101] This approach allowed for "Leninism" to appear as the foundational, ahistorical, unchanging Truth—a kind of truth that was anchored outside of the Soviet political process and functioned as the legitimate *source* of the party's actions instead of being a product of its arbitrary manipulations.

With the demise of the party, the Communist project, and the Soviet polity in 1991, Lenin's body became severed from this complex political system and lost its role in the system of sovereignty. The new Russian state neither closed the Mausoleum nor paid much attention to it. In the past twenty-five years it has deferred any decision on the fate of Lenin's body. And although today Lenin's body remains on public display and the lab continues its work, the body continues to exist mostly by inertia—the inertia of state institutions, historical imagination, and scientific practice. In this context one thing has become clear: for many scientists of the lab this project has long constituted first and foremost a unique scientific experiment. Their science has created a body that has never been static and preserved in a fixed state but has been dynamic, changing, and emerging. The collapse of the Soviet polity did not automatically spell the end of this embodied momentum, did not turn this body into a corpse, and did not reduce it to an effigy.

Notes

1. Olga Velikanova, *The Public Perception of the Cult of Lenin Based on Archival Materials* (Lewiston, NY: Edwin Mellen Press, 2002), 77.
2. "Cleopatra" (1907). In the translation of this stanza I drew on Andrey Kneller's version but changed it to be closer to the original. Alexander Blok, *The Stranger: Selected Poetry*, trans. Andrey Kneller (n.p.: CreateSpace, 2011), 45.

3. Vera Inber, "Piat' nochei i dnei," in *Lenin: Sbornik dlia rabochikh* (Vladimir: Vladimirskoe knigoizdatel'stvo, 1924), n.p. (translation mine).

4. Omry Ronen, "Leksicheskie i ritmo-sintakticheskie povtoreniia i 'nekontroliruemyi podtekst,'" *Izvestiia RAN, seriia literatury i iazyka* 56, no. 3 (1997): 40–41.

5. Dzerzhinsky directed the ChK and then GPU (predecessors of the KGB).

6. "Denunciation written by E. Pavlova," quoted in Alexandr Khinshtein, *Tainy Lubianki* (Moscow: OLMA Media Grupp, 2010), 147.

7. Louis Fischer, *The Life of Lenin* (New York: Harper, 1964), 675.

8. Calvin Sims, "Eva Peron's Corpse Continues to Haunt Argentina," *New York Times*, July 30, 1995.

9. F. Rosen, "Bentham, Jeremy (1748–1832)," *Oxford Dictionary of National Biography* (Oxford: Oxford University Press, 2004), http://www.oxforddnb.com/view/article/2153.

10. Nicholas J. Booth, "A Conservation Inspection of Jeremy Bentham's Mummified Head," UCL Museums and Collections Blog, September 6, 2015, https://blogs.ucl.ac.uk/museums/2015/09/06/jeremy-benthams-mummified-head/.

11. Mao had publicly voiced his wish to have his body cremated, so the Politburo decision to preserve it came as a surprise.

12. Li Zhisui, *The Private Life of Chairman Mao* (New York: Random House, 1994), 23.

13. Monica Hesse, "Stiff Challenge: How Kim Jong Il and Other Leaders Join the Ranks of the Preserved," *Washington Post*, January 19, 2012.

14. Ilya Zbarsky, "Ot Rossii do Rossii (vospominaniia uchenogo)," in *Pod "kryshei" Mavzoleia*, ed. Viktor Soloukhin and Ilya Zbarsky (Tver': Polina, 1998), 306–8. Zbarsky worked at the Lenin Mausoleum from 1934 to 1952.

15. Yurii Romakov. "Dvoinikov Lenina v byvshei laboratorii pri Mavzolee net," interview for "Ekho Moskvy" radio station, December 17, 2000, http://www.echo.msk.ru/news/25147.html.

16. "Leninskii raschet," *Vlast'* 29 (July 28, 2008): 20.

17. Anna Nadezhdina, "V Mavzolee lezhit ne Il'ich?," *Ekspress gazeta* 17 (May 1, 2012).

18. The "wet" internal organs that are most susceptible to decomposition—bowels, kidneys, liver, lungs, heart, brain, etc.—were taken out of the body during the initial temporary embalming in January 1924.

19. Boris Ravdin, "Istoriia odnoi bolezni," *Znanie-sila* 4 (April 1990): 21.

20. On Dzerzhinsky, see note 5 above. Petr Smidovich was a member of the Central Executive Committee of the Bolshevik party.

21. Letter of the Central Committee secretary L. P. Serebriakov to People's Commissar on Social Welfare A. N. Vinokurov, July 10, 1922, quoted in Yurii Fel'tishinskii, "Taina smerti Lenina," *Rossiia i sovremennyi mir* 4, no. 21 (1998): 207–24.

22. Ravdin, "Istoriia odnoi bolezni"; A. I. Zevelev, "Po povodu stat'i Yu.G. Fel'shtinskogo 'Taina smerti Lenina,'" *Vorposy Istorii* 8 (1999).

23. Quoted in V. Lel'chuk and V. Startsev, "Uroki dvukh publikatsii," *Znanie-sila*, November 1990, 51.

24. Ravdin, "Istoriia odnoi bolezni," 21–22.

25. L. E. Gorelova, "Istoricheskoe rassledovanie," *Russkii meditsinskii zhurnal* 13, no. 7 (April 2005), http://www.rmj.ru/articles_3695.htm.

26. Benno Ennker, *Formirovanie kul'ta Lenina v Sovetskom Soiuze* (Moscow: ROSSPEN, 2011), 66.

27. Mikhail Gorbachev claimed that the term "Leninism" was first coined by the Mensheviks (Bolshevik rivals among socialists) to ridicule Lenin's ideas. M. S. Gorbachev, "Slovo o Lenine, prezidenta SSSR, general'nogo sekretaria tsentral'nogo komiteta KPSS, M. S. Gorbacheva," *Pravda*, April 21, 1990. But Nina Tumarkin argues for a different origin: the term was invented by the Bolsheviks themselves and first publicly used on January 3, 1923. Nina Tumarkin, *Lenin Lives! The Lenin Cult in Soviet Russia* (Cambridge, MA: Harvard University Press, 1997), 120.

28. Ennker, *Formirovanie kul'ta Lenina*, 75.

29. Later it became known as the "Institute of Marxism-Leninism." It was closed down in 1991, when the Soviet state collapsed.

30. Quoted in Tumarkin, *Lenin Lives!*, 123.

31. In April 1925, the Central Committee made a decision that not one document or statement produced by Lenin could be published in the country without being first approved by Lenin Institute. The party's monopoly on Leninist discourse became complete.

32. This process is illustrated by the fate of several documents, which Lenin dictated in December 1922–January 1923 and which are known as Lenin's "Letter to the Congress." The letter was addressed to the delegates of the Thirteenth Party Congress scheduled to meet in Spring 1924. Lenin warned the delegates of the authoritarian tendencies of several party leaders, including Trotsky and especially Stalin. In May 1924, four months after Lenin's death, the letter was read to the delegates of the Thirteenth Congress. However, it was soon suppressed on Stalin's orders and never appeared in the published transcript of the Congress. When Stalin became the party's singular leader, in the early 1930s, Lenin's letter was accused of being a forgery produced by the enemies to undermine the party unity. It was briefly discussed in 1956, when Khrushchev denounced Stalin's cult after Stalin's death, but it remained unknown to the wider Soviet public until 1990, when perestroika reforms exposed many Soviet secrets. N. K. Gul'binskii, "K 120-letiiu so dnia rozhdeniia Vladimira Il'icha Lenina," *Ogonek* 17 (1990): 3.

33. See Alexei Yurchak, "Esli by Lenin byl zhiv, on by znal chto delat': golaia zhizn'vozhdia," *New Literary Review* 83 (2007): 189–204, and "If Lenin Were Alive Today, He Would Know What to Do," in *1990: Russians Remember a Turning Point*, ed. Irina Prokhorova (London: MacLehose Press, 2013).

34. Gorbachev, "Slovo o Lenine," 1.

35. V. Mel'nichenko, "Vera, nadezhda, Lenin," *Rabochaia tribuna*, December 4, 1990.

36. R. Kosolapov, "Ostorozhno martyshizm," *Leningradskaia Pravda*, December 22, 1990.

37. Ravdin, "Istoriia odnoi bolezni," 20.

38. Remembered by Fyodor Burlatsky, a former adviser and speechwriter to Khrushchev and Andropov. See Burlatsky, *Vozhdi i sovetniki* (Moscow: Politizdat, 1990).

39. Comment by Vorob'ev, "Protokol zasedaniia meditsinskoi komissii po sokhrane-niiu tela V. I. Lenina on 12 marta 1924 g.," Rossiiskii gosudarstvennyi arkhiv sotsial'no-politicheskoi istorii (RGASPI) [Russian State Archive of Socio-political History, Moscow], f. 16, op. 2s, papka 5, ed. kr. 54. The lack of uncut arteries in Lenin's body constituted a substantial problem for the Mausoleum lab in the following years, forcing the scientists to develop alternative methods for delivering embalming liquids.

40. Tumarkin, *Lenin Lives!*, 140.

41. See, e.g., "Akt N. 7 of the external examination of V. I. Lenin /Ul'ianov/" (February 21, 1924), RGASPI, f. 16, op. 2c, ed. khr. 52.

42. "Protokol po osmotru tela V. I. Lenina" (March 26, 1924), RGASPI, f. 16, op. 2c, ed. khr. 52.

43. Tumarkin, *Lenin Lives!*, 174; Ennker, *Formirovanie kul'ta Lenina*, 191.

44. Ennker, *Formirovanie kul'ta Lenina*, 191.

45. "Zasedanie tsentral'noi Komissii Prezidiuma Tsentral'nogo Ispolnitel'nogo Komiteta" (March 5, 1924), RGASPI, f. 16, op. 2c, ed. khr. 52.

46. Statement of the "Commission for the Organization of Lenin's Funeral," March 25, 1924, quoted in Tumarkin, *Lenin Lives!*, 185.

47. "Zasedanie Komissii Tsentral'nogo Ispolnitel'nogo Komiteta" (July 26, 1924), appendix to protocol no. 18, RGASPI: ed. khr. 48, papka N. 3, str. 73.

48. "Istoriia bal'zamirovaniia tela V. I. Lenina" (July 24, 1924), RGASPI, f. 16, op. 1, plenka N 522.

49. The reference to a "relic," and the denial that this body was one, emphasized this point. In the case of Christian relics it is crucial that the authentic biological substance of the person (saint) is preserved, while for Lenin's body, as we will see, biological substance is of secondary importance. See Yurchak, "If Lenin Were Alive."

50. "Mavzolei Lenina snova otrkoetsia dlia poseshcheniia 9 ianvaria 2007 goda," *Newsru.com*, December 25, 2006, www.newsru.com/russia/25dec2006/lenin .html.

51. Yurii Lopukhin, interview with author, Moscow, August 2009. Lopukhin worked in the lab from the late 1940s to the late 1980s, and today, despite old age, remains one of the lab's regular consultants.

52. Lopukhin, interview, Moscow, October 2009.

53. Vladislav Kozel'tsev, interview with author, Moscow, July 2009.

54. The commissions included ten to twenty people, members of the party leadership and leading medics and biochemists.

55. Lenin's body was carried in an open coffin from the Gorki estate to a nearby railway station in a temperature close to -30°C.

56. "Protokol zasedaniia komissii Narkomzdrava Soiuza SSR po osmotru tela V. I. Lenina, sostoiavshegosia 19-go ianvaria 1939 goda v Mavzolee," RGASPI, f. 16, op. 2, d.N. 110, comments by Nikolai Burdenko and A. A. Deshin.

57. Ibid., comments by Burdenko and Alexei Busalov.

58. "Doklad zasluzhennogo deiatelia nauki professora B. I. Zbarskogo 29 noiabria 1943 goda," RGASPI, f. 16, op. 2s, papka 5, ed. kr. 54.

59. Ibid.

60. "Protokol zasedaniia Komissii, obrazovannoi soglasno rasporiazheniiu SNK SSSR, N 12115/s, 29.06.42, po osmotru tela Lenina, sostoiavshemusia 13 i 14 ii-ulia 1942 g. v gorode Tiumeni," RGASPI, f. 16, op. 2c, papka 5, ed. kr. 54.

61. Ernst Kantorowicz, *The King's Two Bodies* (Princeton: Princeton University Press, 1996).

62. The spatial dimension of sovereignty has been much discussed in recent years, unlike its temporal side. See Carl Schmitt, *Political Theology: Four Chapters on the Concept of Sovereignty*, trans. George Schwab (Chicago: University of Chicago Press, 2005), and Giorgio Agamben, *Homo Sacer* (Stanford: Stanford University Press, 1998).

63. Kantorowicz, *King's Two Bodies*, 330–31.

64. Ralph E. Giesey, *The Royal Funeral Ceremony in Renaissance France* (Geneva: Droz, 1960); Elias Bickermann, *Consecratio: Le culte des souverains dans l'empire romain* (Geneva: Entretiens Hardt, XIX, 1972); and Agamben, *Homo Sacer*, 95, all make this observation in the context of ancient Roman funerals.

65. The effigy for Henry VII (died in 1509) was modeled on his death mask with such degree of precision that even "the slightly drooping left side of the mouth faith-fully reproduce[d] the physical contortions of the king's fatal stroke." Julian Litten, "The Funeral Effigy: Its Function and Purpose," in *The Funeral Effigies of Westminster Abbey*, ed. Anthony Harvey and Richard Mortimer (Woodbridge: Boydell, 1994), 3–19, 7. When Queen Elizabeth died in 1603, the face of the ef-figy that was modeled on her death mask contained meticulously reproduced "wrinkles and other features of ageing." Jennifer Woodward, *The Theatre of Death* (Woodbridge: Boydell, 1997), 90.

66. Kantorowicz, *King's Two Bodies*, 426; Giesey, *Royal Funeral Ceremony*, 144; Ralph E. Giesey, "Funeral Effigies as Emblems of Sovereignty: Europe, 14 to 18 Centuries" (lecture delivered to the Collège de France, June 10, 1987), 9, 17, www.regiesey.com /Lectures/Funeral_Effigies_as_Emblems_of_Sovereignty_Lecture_[English] _College_de_France.pdf.

67. Giesey, *Royal Funeral Ceremony*, 123.

68. Richard Mortimer, "The History of the Collection," in Harvey and Mortimer, *Funeral Effigies of Westminster Abbey*, 21–28.

69. See the discussion of this parallelism in David Graeber, "The Divine Kingship of the Shilluk: On Violence, Utopia, and the Human Condition; or, Elements for an Archaeology of Sovereignty," *HAU: Journal of Ethnographic Theory* 1, no. 1 (2014): 1–62 and Burhard Schnepel, *Twinned Beings: Kings and Effigies in Southern Sudan, East India and Renaissance France* (Göteborg: IASSA, 1995).

70. Schnepel, *Twinned Beings*.

71. The body of the emperor in modern Japan was viewed as "a 'receptacle' (*ire-mono*) for the immutable 'imperial spirit' (*tennorei*) that attached itself to each new emperor and was the source of the emperor's extraordinary authority." Takashi Fujitani, *Splendid Monarchy: Power and Pageantry in Modern Japan* (Berkeley: University of California Press, 1996), 157.

72. A wax effigy of the Roman emperor Antonius (second century CE) during the funerary period looked like the emperor, wore his clothes, and lay in his bed (Bickermann quoted in Agamben, *Homo Sacer*, 95). See also Aleš Chalupa, "How

Did Roman Emperors Become Gods?," *Anodos: Studies of the Ancient World* 6–7 (2006–2007): 201–7, and Jaś Elsner, *Imperial Rome and Christian Triumph* (Oxford: Oxford University Press, 1998), 29–30.

73. The principle of papal sovereignty, unlike that of monarchy, is not dynastic, which is why the theory of the pope's two bodies never developed. What survives the demise of each pope is the "absent presence" of the eternal papacy, invested not in a pope's effigy but in perpetual objects and rituals performed during the novena (interregnum). Agostino Paravicini-Bagliani, *The Pope's Body* (Chicago: University of Chicago Press, 1994); Gilbert O. Nations, *Papal Sovereignty* (Cincinnati: Standard Publishing, 1917).

74. The reason for this was that the Russian monarchic state had not undergone the same secularization that happened in England and France. Michael Cherniavsky, *Tsar and People: Studies in Russian Myths* (New Haven: Yale University Press, 1961).

75. Claude Lefort, "The Question of Democracy," *Democracy and Political Theory* (Minneapolis: University of Minnesota Press, 1988), 9–20; Claude Lefort, "The Image of the Body and Totalitarianism," in *The Political Forms of Modern Society* (Cambridge, MA: MIT Press), 292–306; Bernard Flynn, *The Philosophy of Claude Lefort* (Chicago: Northwestern University Press, 2005), xiii–xxx.

76. Eric Santner, *The Royal Remains: The People's Two Bodies and the Endgames of Sovereignty* (Chicago: University of Chicago Press, 2011), 33–34.

77. The opening words of the U.S. Declaration of Independence, "we hold these truths to be self-evident," refer to the political system's foundational truths that are prior to this system and cannot be proven in its political language. To be seen as legitimate, every U.S. politician must treat these truths as a priori unquestionable.

78. Lefort argues that if the leader in a liberal democracy reoccupied the "empty place" of sovereign power, democracy would slide into "totalitarianism." This happened, according to him, in Germany under Hitler and in the Soviet Union under Stalin (Lefort, "Image of the Body"). However, while Lefort is right about Nazi Germany, where the Führer's body indeed coincided with the center of sovereign power (see Ken Jowitt, *New World Disorder: The Leninist Extinction* [Berkeley: University of California Press, 1992], 1–6), his assessment of the leader's position in the Soviet Union is inaccurate.

79. Stalin was claimed to be "the Great inheritor [*prodolzhatel'*] of Lenin's cause" rather than the originator of a different cause. Stalin depended on "Lenin" as the source of his own legitimacy and could not supersede "Lenin" as the locus of Truth, contrary to a widespread argument—see, e.g., Jan Plamper, *The Stalin Cult: A Study in the Alchemy of Power* (New Haven: Yale University Press, 2012), 85. For a discussion, see Alexei Yurchak, *Everything Was Forever Until It Was No More: The Last Soviet Generation* (Princeton: Princeton University Press, 2006), chap. 2, and *Eto bylo navsegda poka ne konchilos: poslednee sovetskoe pokolenie* (Moscow: Novoe literaturnoe obozrenie, 2014).

80. Yurchak, "Esli by Lenin byl zhiv" and "If Lenin Were Alive."

81. But unlike Hitler in Nazi Germany.

82. Jowitt, *New World Disorder*, 1–8, 10.

83. For a major shift in the interpretation of the doctrine after Stalin's death as the "performative shift" of ideological discourse, see Yurchak, *Everything Was Forever*, chap. 2, and *Eto bylo navsegda*. For the crisis of doctrine in late perestroika, see Yurchak, "If Lenin Were Alive."

84. Joseph Nyomarkey, "Factionalism in the National Socialist German Workers' Party, 1925–1926: The Myth and Reality of the 'Northern Faction,'" *Political Science Quarterly* 80, no. 1 (1965): 45.

85. In contrast, in the Nazi system there was no external figure of Truth that could be used to delegitimize Hitler for violating the spirit of "true Nazism." See Christopher Hitchens, *Unacknowledged Legislation: Writers in the Public Sphere* (London: Verso, 2000), 281, and Slavoj Žižek, "Barbarism with a Human Face," *London Review of Books* 36, no. 9 (2014): 36–37.

86. In his "Secret Speech" at the Twentieth Party Congress in 1956, Khrushchev said, "We sharply criticize today the cult of the individual which was so widespread during Stalin's life . . . which is so alien to the spirit of Marxism-Leninism." "Nikita S. Khrushchev: The Secret Speech—On the Cult of Personality," *Internet Modern History Sourcebook*, http://legacy.fordham.edu/halsall/mod/1956khrushchev-secret1.html.

87. The October 14, 1964, decision of the presidium of the Central Committee, laconically titled, "On Comrade Khrushchev N. S.," stated: "As a result of the mistakes and wrong actions of Comrade Khrushchev, that *violate the Leninist principle of collective leadership*, an utterly unhealthy situation has developed in the Presidium of the CC," Rossiiskii gosudarstvennyi arkhiv natsional'noi istorii (RGANI) [Russian State Archive of National History, Moscow], f. 2, op. 1, d. 749, l. 78 (emphasis added). The statement was as unsubstantiated as it was damning: Khrushchev had violated Leninism. After that point all other arguments were superfluous.

88. Some tests occur in the Center for Scientific Research on Krasin Street in Moscow. Others are conducted in various medical institutes around Moscow. A whole network of research institutes is regularly involved in this ongoing work. Lopukhin interview, 22 October 2009.

89. According to interviews with the lab scientists. See also interview with a photo technician in Pavel Lobkov's film *Mavzolei* (NTV television channel, 1999).

90. Kozel'tsev interview.

91. Lopukhin interview, July 2010, Moscow.

92. Some aspects of this work are described in Yurii M. Lopukhin and B. M. Cheknev, "Biochemical Assessment of the Viability of Cadaver Kidney. Preservation of Kidney with the Use of Hypothermia and Hyperbaric Oxygenation," *Journal of Urology and Nephrology* 32 (1967): 19–24.

93. The work also involved specialists from the department of therapy at Moscow's Sechenov Medical University.

94. Lopukhin interviews, October 2009 and July 2010.

95. Yu. M. Lopukhin, "The Skin and Atherosclerosis (a Three-Drop Test)," *Physiochemical Aspects of Medicine Reviews* (Soviet Medical Reviews, Section B) 3 (1992): 1–124.

96. See www.google.com/patents/US6365363.

97. For Miraculins's visual illustration of the PreVu test, see www.prevu.com/USA /prevu.html.

98. Tumarkin, *Lenin Lives!*, 179. For a similar argument, see Graeme Gill, "The Soviet Leader Cult: Reflections on the Structure of Leadership in the Soviet Union," *British Journal of Political Science* 10 (1980): 167–86.

99. See also Ennker, *Formirovanie kul'ta Lenina*, 371. On another major difference between relics and Lenin's body, see Alexei Yurchak, "Form Versus Matter: Miraculous Relics and Lenin's Scientific Body," in "Death, Dying, and Mortality," special issue of *Collegium: Studies Across Disciplines in the Humanities and Social Sciences* 19 (2015): 61–81.

100. See also Tumarkin, *Lenin Lives!*, 179; George Young, *The Russian Cosmists: The Esoteric Futurism of Nikolai Fedorov and His Followers* (Oxford: Oxford University Press, 2012); and V. A. Kozhevnikov, *Opyt izlozheniia ucheniia N. F. Fedorova po izdannym i neizdannym proizvedeniiam, perepiske i lichnym besedam* (Moscow: Mysl', 2012).

101. Yurchak, "If Lenin Were Alive."

PART III

ACTS

I went to the middle of the room and called out,
"I know you're here," then noticed him in a corner,
looking tiny in his jeweled crown and his cape
with ermine trim. "I have lost my desire to rule,"
he said. "My kingdom is empty except for you,
and all you do is ask for me." "But Your Majesty—"
"Don't 'Your Majesty' me," he said and tilted his head
to one side and closed his eyes. "There," he whispered,
"that's more like it," and he entered his dream
like a mouse vanishing into its hole.

—MARK STRAND, "THE KING"

AS THE CURTAIN RISES on Mark Strand's marvelous poem "The King," the narrator crosses a room of unstated proportions, furnishings, period, and location.[1] The action of the first two lines seems to follow the logic of a game of hide-and-seek: the narrator shouting "I know you're here"—a statement that might be inflected as an expression of either taunt or frustration—before catching sight of the "you." But there is no mention of hiding, or of the room being appointed in such a way to allow for it. "I know you're here" could in this way be a statement of desire, hope, or even faith, and the utterance brings the desire or belief into being. For the king simply appears, and he appears first of all *unkingly*, "looking tiny." Size notwithstanding, he is recognizably the king due to the royal accoutrements that envelope and dwarf him.

The king's declaration reveals a frank, if fed-up, sovereign. "I have lost my desire to rule," he indicates, betraying a sense that authority is an optional privilege rather than an obligation. He has only the narrator as his subject. "All you do is ask for me," he accuses, rejecting the mere presence that is demanded of him. He is not interested in being the figurehead of such a territory, such a regime, such a facade. The narrator protests, but his rebellion is instantly quashed in the poem's most exquisite line: "Don't 'Your Majesty' me." Simultaneously an announcement of his abdication and an assertion of sovereignty, the imperial imperative both structures and undermines the relinquishment of power.

For the king, the decision has been made, and he presumes himself free to retreat into his private world. But he continues to be observed, and although his head may be tilted, there is no mention of the crown sliding off.

As in the other short introductions to the book's four sections, here too we open up from characterizations of a particular kind of sovereign, a king. Strand's poem serves as an apt introduction for what follows, for it articulates the desire for a sovereign—who is in some way missing or hidden—to be revealed, the marks of sovereignty that prop up as well as dwarf the human figure, the demands placed on the sovereign, and the sovereign's ability to command even when relinquishing power—indeed, even in death. At stake is this act that, perhaps more than any other, belongs to a sovereign at the same time as it is denied to him. Abdication, self-effacement, and self-abnegation put the lie to the obsession with the sufficiency of decision and action, those forms or expressions of sovereignty that deny their status as forms, deny sovereignty's ornamental, sartorial, or linguistic adornments, and provide an image or illusion of pure force. This section stages different problems surrounding sovereign activity and decision; in contrast to the Schmittian assertion that "sovereign is he who decides on the exception,"[2] the essays that follow ask how decisions and acts are imagined, presented, forged as sovereign—in what ways sovereignty is recuperated into the fabric of political life and the temples that make them possible. Where Schmitt presents the sovereign as deciding on the exception insofar as he decides on—accepts, creates, reframes, controls, modifies, sets aside, dismantles—the norm, we ask *how*? what norm(s)? resulting in what effects on the very concept of sovereignty, and thanks to what side-effects? within what theaters? grasping and submitting to what feedback over what kind of knowledge and information involved in sovereignty? Contextualizing and refiguring the problem of sovereign acts, these essays cast an unexpected light on sovereignty in relation to knowledge, repression, religion, theater, and revolution.

Building on the "New Qing History" that, since the late 1990s, has exposed a radically different style of Manchu rulership than what was portrayed before, Zvi Ben-Dor Benite's essay *"Hijra* and Exile" examines the tale of a mosque built by the Qianlong emperor and of the kind of sovereignty he sought and was accorded by his Muslim subjects. Whereas many of the new studies on Manchu rulership present a view from above, this essay presents a dual approach, examining Manchu-Muslim relationships from two directions: the ways the Manchus engaged their Muslim subjects and the ways Muslims wrote and represented Manchu rulership over Islam from below. Crucially, the Muslim community in question is one that lives under *non-Islamic* rule, which allows Ben-Dor Benite to expose and engage problems of Islamic sovereignty that have been overlooked in Islamic and Asian historiographies. Islam, ideally, maintains that Muslims should always live under Islamic rule, leaving no space within the body of Islamic law and tradition for cases where a community of Muslims lives under non-Islamic rule. Chinese Muslims "solved" the problem through creative rereading of specific episodes in the biography of the Prophet Muhammad and writing them into the body of Manchu rulership. In so doing they offered a means to overcome the limitations of Manchu multiple sovereignty itself on the one hand, and to resolve the problem of Muslim life under non-Muslim rule on the other.

Cathy Gere's "The Neurology of Regicide" casts a new light on the interrelation of neurology and political power. Between the execution of Charles I of England in 1649 and the restoration of Louis XVIII of France in 1815, a series of foundational decapitation experiments defined the methods and assumptions of modern neurology. Examining two such episodes, Gere argues that the natural philosophers who conducted these investigations were seeking answers to urgent political questions about sovereignty and the postrevolutionary social order. In the wake of regicide, a new approach to psychophysiology revealed how the body politic might function in a state of headless anarchy. Decapitation experiments in the Age of Democratic Revolutions constituted a science of sovereignty, establishing the structure and function of the central executive not only for the individual human subject but also for the commonwealth.

A. Azfar Moin turns to a quite different stage, peopled by millenarian hopes, anticolonial struggle, and the reinvestment of defunct sovereignty. In the Great Mutiny of 1857, the Indian soldiers of the English East India Company rose up against their colonial masters. As the rebellion gathered strength, the soldiers rallied around the feeble Mughal king in Delhi, an eighty-two-year-old puppet the British had been planning to pension off. Why the soldiers chose the defunct king as their symbol is a question that has since puzzled historians. The answer lies in the frantic rebel communiques from the battlefield, written mostly by Hindus, which portrayed the Muslim sovereign as a mystical savior empowered by the saints of the land. In these letters, soldiers complained not that the British had usurped Indian territory and wealth but that they had insulted their king and polluted the body politic—and ignored all the astrological and mystical signs of warning. They noted that British rule had begun in 1757 and now it was 1857; a century had passed, a fraction of the millennium, a time when all injustice would be undone in a messianic uprising. The rebellion, for these soldiers, was the last great act performed by the king's thaumaturgical body.

In "Exit the King?," Nicole Jerr attends to modern theatrical depictions of sovereignty. Among the various ways in which the political, theological, and social revolutions that marked late modernity manifested themselves in the theater, perhaps the furthest reaching, and seemingly most enduring, is the shift from royal protagonists to the common individual. By training the spotlight on the common individual, twentieth-century drama achieved nothing short of a theatrical revolution. And yet this revolution has not been as thorough as it might initially appear, for despite the political trend away from monarchical rule, and despite modern theater's deliberate and celebrated replacement of noble characters by ordinary individuals, sovereignty has nevertheless been staged and thematized within the many avant-garde movements of modern drama, and by some of its most significant playwrights (Yeats, O'Neill, Ibsen, Strindberg, Pirandello, Beckett, and Ionesco, to name a few). For Jerr, drama, perhaps more so than any other artistic genre, has decided that the stage direction "Exit the King" is optional; her essay, focusing on Alfred Jarry's *Ubu roi* (1896) and Eugène Ionesco's *Macbett* (1972), charts some ways the modern theater has offered its perspective on the subject of sovereignty and revolution.

Notes

1. Mark Strand, *Man and Camel* (New York: Knopf, 2006), 3.
2. Carl Schmitt, *Political Theology: Four Chapters on the Concept of Sovereignty*, trans. George Schwab (Chicago: University of Chicago Press, 2005), xxx.

TEN

Hijra and Exile

Islam and Dual Sovereignty in Qing China

ZVI BEN-DOR BENITE

Qiblah and the Limits of Qing Sovereignty

IN 1764 THE QIANLONG EMPEROR of the Qing dynasty (r. 1736–1796), a Manchu, built a mosque in Beijing. He dedicated the mosque to his "fragrant concubine" Xiang Fei, who was a Turkic Muslim from Xinjiang, the "New Dominion" newly conquered by the empire. The mosque was located in the area of the Huiziying (the Turkic-Muslim camp community)—Muslims forcibly moved from Xinjiang to Beijing after the conquest.[1] The gesture that the mosque signaled was also directed at Beijing's Sinophone Muslim community and, in effect, at the entire Chinese Muslim population (the Huihui).[2] The mosque could likewise be seen as a symbolic act, signaling a desire on the part of the Manchu court to patronize Islam after the conquest of Xinjiang, a clearly defined Muslim territory.[3] But the Huiziying Qingzhensi, as the mosque was called in Chinese, which cost so much to build, was congenitally crippled. Facing the imperial throne, which was to its north, and not Mecca (to its west), the mosque was rendered dysfunctional since it did not conform to Islamic law. As is well known, Islamic law mandates that the qiblah (direction, in Arabic) of all prayers should be the Ka'aba in Mecca—the most sacred location on earth.

However, the direction the mosque faced was a matter not just of Islamic law but also of Qing sovereignty. In this regard, the mosque presents us with a unique opportunity to think about the question of sovereignty and Islam in the Chinese imperial context—in which Muslims live under a non-Muslim ruler. Situated in an undefined realm between Islamic law and the Chinese throne, the question of the mosque's direction also had a great deal of political significance. A multilingual stele placed next to the mosque provides a small, but clear, clue with regard to this political significance.[4] The stele, whose text was undoubtedly written under the careful eye of the emperor and claims him to be its author, opens with the central idea of what in recent years has come to be known by scholars as Manchu-Qing imperial ideology:

> It is sublime to be master of the world, so that even in the remotest regions people submit to our control, and wherever our laws and methods have access, our customs and practice are adopted. . . . However . . . [i]t is only by accommodating the different ideas of different people that a real uniformity can be attained, in order that our civilization may be so comprehensive as to leave nothing outside.[5]

The stele ends with a poem describing Islam and the Prophet. It is there that we find the following stanza: "Western direction, northern direction / heading toward the same goal, [showing] one respect."[6] Our political clue is hidden in the phrase "western direction, northern direction"—or "western qiblah, northern qiblah," if you will. This phrase is not just an ornament; it is deliberately and carefully crafted to read something like this: "Bowing west toward Mecca, or bowing north toward the throne, Muslims respect the Prophet and the emperor alike." This reading fits the opening of the stele's text, which speaks of bringing "even the remotest . . . people" under "our [Qing] control" but at the same time refers to "accommodating the different ideas of different people" so that Qing "civilization may be so comprehensive as to leave nothing outside." To my mind, the inclusion of the above phrase betrays the fact that the emperor was quite concerned with the limitations of his rule when it came to Islam. He was aware that Islam posed a certain limit on the all-inclusive Qing universalism, which implied that the Qing emperor was the sovereign of all subjects, collectivities, and religions in his diverse empire. This concern, even anxiety, translated itself into a phrase in which the emperor declares that bowing north (toward the throne) is equal to bowing toward Mecca. It seems that the Qianlong emperor is conveying the message that he is equal to the Prophet Muhammad and shares the respect of Muslims with him. It is important to note here that the emperor does not replace the Prophet altogether or remove him from the equation. Indeed, he recognizes that the direction of the mosque should be toward the west, toward Mecca, but he states that in China, a "northern direction" is just as good. In this regard, the poem implies a sort of a shared responsibility, or partnership in sovereignty, vis-à-vis China's Muslims. Marshall Broomhall, an earlier (1910) translator of the same poem, commented on this stanza: "The Emperor always sits facing south, consequently all Chinese officials bow north.[7] The Moslems in China bow to the west, towards Mecca. The Emperor classes both acts together, and thus makes himself equal to Mohammed."[8] Furthermore, for the emperor the *qiblah* is a political issue: facing Mecca has nothing to do with the Ka'aba's holiness but with showing respect to the Prophet. This is a gesture that, politically understood, he cannot allow.

In this regard, the phrase that speaks of respecting the emperor and the Prophet alike also corresponds with the idea of imperial simultaneity, another crucial principle of Manchu-Qing imperial ideology. The concept of simultaneous rulership, probably the cornerstone of Qing rulership, allowed the Manchu emperors to present themselves simultaneously as the rulers of many different constituencies.[9] The Qianlong emperor's "vision of himself as the penultimate and only unifier of the diverse people under his rule also advanced the concept of separate cultural identities within the conquest elite. The emperor himself had to be all things to all people, but the subjects—Mongols, Tibetans, and Turkic-speaking Muslims—were to remain distinctly different in their religions, languages, and traditions."[10]

Thus, the poem should be seen as a fine illustration of Qing rulers' understanding of their political and religious roles vis-à-vis different collectivities in their empire, a polity in which "cultural diversity was unlimited."[11] It is certainly in keeping with the all-encompassing statement quoted above about having Qing "customs and practice ... adopted" and at the same time "accommodating the different ideas of different people" in order to attain "uniformity." Angela Zito, in her study of Qing relationships with the Tibetan Buddhists, explains that "encompassment" meant that imperial hierarchy was theorized "as a whole containing many, unequally valued but equally necessary parts." In this whole, rituals surrounding the Qing emperor brought about a "mode of social engagement" designed "not to overcome others by force but to include them in its own projects of rulership."[12] The "parts" in our case are the emperor and the Prophet. The above-mentioned idea of the emperor's being equal to, but not simply replacing, the Prophet resonates here. However, unlike in the case of Qing participation in Tibetan-Buddhist rituals, in this case all we have is a poem, and the dysfunctionality of the mosque still reminds us that the Qing's supposedly all-encompassing ideology in fact had limits. In this case, it was limited by Islamic law. The emperor built a mosque, but it did not meet the most basic requirement of proper mosque design—the *qiblah* to Mecca.[13] Ironically, the structure's spatial orientation on the globe—facing northward toward the throne and not westward toward Mecca—exposed the limits of the Manchu sovereign's universal aspirations.

Islam and Muslims seem to be in sharp contrast with other ethnic or religious groups within the Manchu empire. This presentation of things, a reasonable perspective concerning Islam and the Manchu empire that is based on cases such as the story of the mosque, places Muslims outside the pale even under a very attentive and "inclusive" emperor. Unlike with Confucians, Buddhists, and Daoists, for instance, the emperor could not simply situate himself at the center of the Muslims' moral world. Pamela Crossley has articulated best the Islamic limitation to Qing universalism as opposed to other groups within the empire: "Islam presented an absolute obstacle to the necessity of the [Qing] emperors to occupy the single point of transcendence at which all moral systems converge. A portion of Mongols might accede to the Qing representation of themselves as Chinggis [Khan]. A portion of Chinese might accede to Qing representations of themselves as avatars of Confucian benevolence and civilization. No portion of Muslims, accede as they might to the reality of Qing power, could accede to Qing moral centrality."[14] That is, the Qing-Muslim relationship was fundamentally restricted, and this limitation had two dimensions: On the one hand, Qing rulers were well aware of their inability to occupy the moral center of their Muslim subjects' universe. On the other hand, no Muslim could accept Qing claims to moral centrality. Crossley demonstrates these limitations the case of the Qing-Uighur relationship in Xinjiang.

In this regard the case of the Muslims of China and that of the Qing-Muslim relationship were radically different from the cases of other ethnic or religious groups in the empire. We can imagine the Qing court entertaining members or representatives of various religious and ethnic groups and engaging them through ritual and direct communication.[15] But while these complicated exchanges were taking place inside the court, outside stood the dysfunctional mosque as a reminder of the serious limitations and challenge that Islam presented to the dialogue.[16] The Qianlong emperor could be "all things to all his many peoples." He could appear as a "warrior, Buddhist deity, Taoist monk, writer, father, son, recluse, hunter, banquet host, beardless youth, future ancestor."[17] But he could not "perform" a Muslim, however "Muslim" might be defined. That is, the emperor of China could never "be" the Prophet, the caliph, the Mahdi, a Sufi saint, or the highest legal authority in an Islamic state (the latter role was hard even for powerful Muslim rulers to play). Ultimately, Islam—or, better yet, Islamic law and practice—could not serve as the basis for China's Muslims to become a coherent and well-defined constituency under Qing sovereignty.

But the perspective sketched above leads us to a certain historical dead end, which prevents us from writing this history in a fuller way. To write a different history, we should turn in a different direction. Instead of looking at things either from the throne down or from the vantage point of strict Islamic law, let us turn our gaze from law to culture and replace top-down perspectives with a more flexible approach. In other words, instead of setting Islamic law and Qing ideology against each other, the historian's task here is to look at concrete Muslim engagements with the question of sovereignty in this context. Therefore, the remainder of this essay is an inquiry into the ways that Sinophone Huihui educated elites engaged the question of "emperor or Prophet" as Muslims. This does not mean that the Qing rulers disappear altogether from now on. They quite actively, but indirectly, played a significant role in the ways Chinese Muslim elites portrayed and understood this question. These elites understood themselves as diasporic Muslims, for China was their home. In other words, their main concern was how to resolve the conflict arising from the fact that they were not strangers but actually Muslims at home in a non-Muslim state.[18] They worked to interpret Qing Chinese sovereignty in such a way as to produce a solution to their key problem: how to live as Muslims in a non-Islamic state and how to belong in it. We have seen above one imperial attempt to engage Islam, carried out in writing by the emperor himself under his guidance. Below we shall see how Qing emperors came to occupy a central place in the moral universe—a term I borrow from Crossley—of their Muslim subjects through those subjects' textual production. That is, we shall analyze how Chinese sovereigns were written into Chinese Islamic literary works. Simply put, although the emperor could not perform a Muslim, he could still play a significant role in the moral universe of his Muslim subjects—one that they created. Furthermore, it is true that Chinese Muslims could not engage the emperor through or with Islamic law and ritual. But they could still portray him as playing an important cultural role in the life of their community using other techniques that were equally important in the Chinese context.

The argument is simple: the fact that Qing emperors could not position themselves at the center of their Muslim subjects' moral universe does not mean that the Muslims could not position their emperors in that place on their own terms and for their own sake and needs. This is particularly true concerning the community of Chinese Muslims in China proper—the Huihui—who are the focus of this study. For them, as opposed to the Uighurs of Xinjiang (who were conquered and only partially incorporated into the Qing empire), engaging the emperor culturally was necessary and crucial for the creation and the articulation of the Muslim constituency in China. The exercise proposed here is therefore twofold: Instead of looking at Islamic law and at the Qing-Uighur relationship as the main ways to examine the Qing-Islam relationship, this essay focuses on the Muslims in China proper who had been living in China for many centuries. Moreover, instead of looking at top-down Qing policies toward the Muslims of China, I focus on how Muslims related to the throne and the emperorship.[19]

Finally, especially in the Muslim case, Crossley's term "moral universe" is crucial. My use of it here is flexible and allows us to look beyond the confines of law, religion, and orthopraxy. As good literate Chinese elites, the people discussed here did just this by writing the emperor into a very specific location in their symbolic world.[20] Speaking of a symbolic world and a moral universe rather than religion is not just useful here, it is imperative. One must not approach the Muslims of China as a community defined only by its religion. Rather, I argue that we must see the Chinese Muslim community as a collectivity defined also by its specific self-understanding and peculiar history as a diasporic community living in China. As Muslims, the Chinese Muslims were defined by Islam (however one defines that). But as Huihui—the term that became the main signifier for Chinese Muslims during the Ming and Qing periods—they were defined by their history and memory as foreigners who had made China their home.[21] This distinction between the narrower Islamic-based perception and the broader Huihui one is crucial, for the latter does make space for writing in the emperor of China. In other words, whereas Chinese emperors could not occupy a central place in the religious world of their Muslim subjects, they could occupy a central place in the symbolic or moral universe of their Huihui subjects.

In the following section I examine the main dimensions of Qing sovereignty that are relevant for this case and present the ways in which Chinese Muslims engaged that sovereignty on their own terms and for their own purposes.

The "Body Islamique" of Chinese Rulers

Let us begin with the Ming dynasty (1368–1644), which preceded the Qing. Elsewhere I have shown and elaborated on how learned Muslim elites in China exercised a great deal of autonomy and creativity in writing the body Islamique of Ming Taizu (Zhu Yuanzhang, r. 1368–1398), founder of the Ming dynasty. Simply put, using a variety of literary tricks, literate Chinese Muslims invented an image of the emperor as a crypto-Muslim ruler. They did so to help Muslims make sense of the transition from a multiethnic and diverse Mongol empire (the Yuan dynasty, 1267–1368) to a state that projected itself as homogeneously Chinese. Unlike its Mongol predecessor, the Ming dynasty "embodied a conscious effort to recreate an ethnic community of Han people who would be true to core principles of the Chinese great tradition." To this end, Ming subjects were required to "give up Mongol styles and customs in favor of Chinese practices," and "an effort was made to assimilate remnants" of the foreigners who until recently had ruled or governed China.[22] Muslims were one of these groups of foreigners, and thus the image of the crypto-Muslim emperor reflected their own transformation from Muslims residents of China into Chinese Muslims.[23] In other words, to turn this new (Ming) China into home for its Muslims, its founding emperor had to become Muslim in a certain regard. Since no one could openly claim he was a Muslim, legends about his crypto-Islamic nature emerged. The making of the Ming founder into a crypto-Muslim ruler began during the early Ming period in the form of traditions and rumors circulated orally and internally among Muslim communities in China.[24] When Chinese Muslim literary tradition took shape during the late Ming and early Qing, the body Islamique of the Ming founder was written in Muslim histories. This was how the population of Chinese Muslims explained in its own terms the history of the Ming dynasty and its place in that history. Significant for our purposes here is the fact that much of this cultural effort was centered on the image of the ruler himself.[25] He defined the dynasty, and he defined China.[26]

This phase, centered on the Ming ruler, is crucial in another regard: Muslims' autonomy in writing the emperor into the center of their moral universe. One can readily grasp why it is so important for rulers—perhaps imperial rulers in particular—to situate themselves at the center of their subjects' moral universes. We have seen above how the Qianlong emperor articulated this principle. Conversely, it is also often very important for subjects, particularly members of weak collectivities in a larger imperial society, to make a central space for their ruler in their world. Just as rulers try to organize or order their subjects' world and place themselves at its center, it is necessary for their subjects to do the same. This allows subjects to make sense of the ruler's actions and understand themselves as his constituents on their own terms. The case of Ming Taizu is a fine example of this need. The "body Islamique" of the emperor—his image as the patron of Islam—came to be seen as an entirely Muslim exercise, carried out with no interference or encouragement—direct or indirect—from the throne or the court. Ming Taizu simply did not know that his Muslim subjects had turned him into a Muslim. In a way, the turning of the emperor into a crypto-Muslim mirrors his own demand that all his subjects become Chinese.

The Qing dynasty oversaw a different China and was a different rulership. The Ming founder, known for his autocratic style, liked to communicate unidirectionally with his people through an unprecedented number of decrees and an extraordinary method he developed known as the Grand Pronouncements (Da Gao). Written by the emperor himself, the Grand Pronouncements "were directed at the broad spectrum of the population from high officialdom to village leaders and heads of families." In these pronouncements the sovereign voiced his own thoughts concerning good and evil, right and wrong, and the proper conduct of government.[27] In such a setting, there was little room even for the impression of a dialogue. This absence of real dialogue may also explain the unidirectional way in which Muslims attached a Muslim identity to their ruler. Qing rulers, as might have become apparent above, were more interested in engaging in a dialogue with their diverse body of subjects, and this worked for both sides. Crossley suggests that Qing activity concerning the better-known constituencies in the empire was not only advantageous for the court, it was "also a convenience to cultural elites who in the environment of simultaneous authorities were protected from being cast as minor, unorthodox, or subordinate because of cultural identity." This convenience relates to the process by which constituencies found "themselves and their histories expressed, contemporaneously, in the rulership."[28] I take this "convenience" a step further and think of it as a need or necessity to be "expressed in the rulership" in the case of elites belonging to constituencies such as the Chinese Muslims, groups that were even more minor and unorthodox than Han Chinese Tibetans, Mongols, Uighurs, Buddhists, and Daoists.

The Prophet and the Emperor

We have seen above how the Qianlong emperor created a "whole" containing "unequally valued but equally necessary parts" to bring Uighur Muslims under his rulership without, as he saw it, erasing their moral world altogether. The game he plays here revolves around the theme of the Prophet and the emperor. The most formative text expressing Huihui subjectivity in Qing China does the same thing, albeit from a different angle. It also elaborates on the same theme of the "unequally valued but equally necessary" Prophet and emperor. Situated in the early Tang dynasty (the seventh century), the *Huihui yuanlai* (Origins of the Huihui) is the most popular Chinese Muslim tale that recounts the story of Huihui origins. In various versions, the basic kernel of the tale was probably already circulating orally in China during late Ming times (the early seventeenth century). Yet we can be sure that the main story—involving communications between the emperor of China and Muhammad—only took shape well into the Qing period (the early eighteenth century).[29] The *Huihui yuanlai* was intended from the outset to be a foundation myth and therefore, unlike all other Chinese Islamic texts of the time, it appeared without an identified author.[30] We shall return to the connections between this text and the Qing emperors, their image, and their policies below. Let us first discuss the basic political meaning of the tale at the ideal level, that of bringing together the Prophet and the Chinese emperor.

Interestingly enough, the tale also begins with a story about a structure that, like the dysfunctional mosque, needs repair:

One night, the emperor Li Shimin [the Taizong emperor; r. 626–649] of the Tang dynasty dreamt that a roof beam of his golden palace was collapsing. The roof beam nearly smashed his head, but it was intercepted and pushed back by a man standing to the right hand side of the bed. The man wore a green robe, and a white turban was wound around his head. He had a towel draped over his shoulder and a water kettle in his left hand. He had deep eye sockets, a high nose bridge, and a brown face.[31]

The next morning, according to the story, the alarmed emperor summons his advisers, who tell him that the strange man must be a Muslim "from the Western Regions." The dream means, therefore, that "the great Tang Empire needed the Hui people for its defense." The advisers explain that a great sage, Muhammad, has arisen in the West, and the emperor must write him and ask for help. The emperor and the Prophet correspond, and Muhammad sends "3,000" Muslim soldiers to save China. These men, all "noble" Muslims, are led by the Sahaba (companion of the Prophet) Sa'd ibn abi Waqqas.[32] Soon after their arrival, however, the Muslims grow homesick and wish to return to Arabia. But the emperor of China still needs them and asks the Prophet to keep them there. The Prophet orders them to stay in China to fulfill their mission and instructs them to keep their Islamic traditions. The emperor and the Prophet thus make a deal: the Muslims will stay in China as long as they are allowed to practice Islam freely. And so, the tale concludes, the Huihui came into the world.[33] I have discussed this story elsewhere and explained its importance as both reflecting and affecting the rise of Chinese Islamic identity during the Qing. The *Huihui yuanlai* is the Huihui's communal biography, and its purpose is to legitimate the Muslim presence in China, a non-Islamic space. I have also argued that the text establishes the status of the Huihui as a sort of ahistorical collectivity of permanent sojourners in China. Note that in effect the Huihui are supposed to stay in China not forever but for as long as they are needed.[34]

Here I wish to emphasize the role the Chinese emperor plays in this tale and its political implications. At the most basic level, the Chinese emperor is the generator of the whole story. He is the reason why Muslims come to China, and his request that they stay produces their permanent sojourn there. The emperor also corresponds directly with Muhammad. The dialogue between the two produces a subtle set of relationships that are asymmetrical and symmetrical at once, making the Prophet and the emperor "unequally valued but equally necessary" as the story develops. On the one hand, Muhammad is superior. Heaven points to him as the one who will save China. He is the one who receives, and approves, the emperor's request for help. The Prophet is the one who sends the Muslims to China and commands them to stay there. He is also the one who stipulates that the Muslims should be able to marry Chinese women and practice Islam freely. On the other hand, the emperor of China is the one who receives a communication from Heaven about the danger to the empire and the Prophet, which means that he also has (albeit through dreams) some prophetic powers. The emperor also corresponds with Muhammad as an equal ruler. At no point does Muhammad ask, much less command, that the Chinese emperor or the Chinese people convert to Islam and accept his moral or political superiority. This means that Muhammad respects the emperor's religious autonomy and political dominion over China. Muhammad also responds favorably and without any conditions to the emperor's initial request to send Muslims to China. Muhammad's commands are directed only to his followers, the Muslims. Finally, the emperor is the one who is entrusted with the responsibility for the Muslims, who now become his subjects. They stay in China at his request, and he is responsible for them as their protector. In this way, the Chinese emperor becomes the protector of Islam, and of Muslims, in his domain.

The outcome of these symmetrical and asymmetrical mutual relationships is a delicate set of shifting hierarchies through which Muhammad and the emperor of China come to encompass each other. In this regard, a perception of dual sovereignty emerges from the tale, a duality that makes it possible for the Huihui to relate to the emperors as their sovereigns at the same time that they relate to Muhammad as their Prophet-sovereign.[35] The image of dual sovereignty suggested here can be seen as a Muslim response from below to the Qing message of the aforementioned imperial simultaneity emanating from above. If imperial simultaneity expresses the idea that the emperor can be more than one thing for many constituencies at once, his Muslim subjects can also worship two sovereigns simultaneously. From the Huihui point of view, the Muslims live in China because Muhammad sent them there and commanded them to stay. But at the same time, they live in China because of the invitation of the emperor. Moreover, while Muhammad is the generator of Islam, the Chinese emperor is its protector in China. Finally, Muhammad is the sovereign whose commands transcend history— they never change. The emperor of China is the sovereign whose dominion is within history. Above all, the notion of dual sovereignty allows the Muslims of China to relate to the emperor of China as their sovereign inasmuch as he acts as protector of Islam.[36] In simple terms, the two—Prophet and emperor—are partners of sorts. To be sure, this is not a partnership between identical, similar, or equal partners. The Prophet is not, and will never be, equal to the emperor as the ruler of China. The emperor is not, and will never be, equal to the Prophet as the messenger of God and ultimate source of Islamic authority on earth. But the two are partners when it comes to protecting Islam and the Muslims of China.

From a strictly Islamic legal point of view, the arrangement between Muhammad and the Chinese emperor seems unacceptable at first blush. Muhammad's own career as ruler suggests the same. As is well known, in his own polity at Medina the Prophet was at once the spiritual, political, and military leader of the *umma* (nation or community) of Islam, and he never shared his sovereignty with anyone. Nonetheless, there is in Islamic tradition a single, very important instance similar to the situation sketched above in the Chinese Muslim tale. We do not find it in Islamic law but in early Islamic history and in the biography (*sirah*) of the Prophet, a text that enjoys an almost scriptural status. The *Sirat al-Nabi* tells us that in 613, only three years after the Muhammad began his career as Prophet, a time when the small community of Muslims was still being harassed by the Quraysh in Mecca, he directed some of his followers to migrate to the Axum empire (Ethiopia, then known as Abyssinia). Two small groups of early Muslims left Mecca in 614 and 615. The migration (*hijra*) to Abyssinia is one of the significant events in early Islamic history. Known as the first *hijra*, it is viewed as a precursor to the most important event of all: the *hijra* to Medina in 622.[37] As in the Chinese case, it is a tale about Islam and a friendly country:

> When the apostle saw the affliction of his companions and that he could not protect them, he said to them: "If you were to go to Abyssinia it would be better for you, for the king will not tolerate injustice and it is a friendly country, until such time as Allah shall relieve you from your distress." Thereupon his companions went to Abyssinia.... This was the first Hijra of Islam.[38]

The Ethiopian negus receives the Muslims warmly and offers them hospitality. When a delegation of the Quraysh arrives with bribes, in the form of gifts, and demands that the Muslims be extradited back to Mecca, the negus tests the Muslims about their faith and, after realizing that Islam is compatible with Christianity, refuses to surrender them. He speaks directly to the Muslims, declaring that "you are safe in my country, I shall never give you up to your enemies." As one of these Muslims recalled later, "we have lived in the happiest conditions until we [returned] to the Apostle of God in Mecca."[39] The story concludes this way: after the negus's death, Muhammad "prayed over him and begged that his sins might be forgiven" (so he could enter heaven).[40] This episode earns Ethiopia, a non-Islamic land, a unique status in Islam. It neither belongs to the House of Islam nor is designated a House of War. "Leave the Abyssinians in peace, so long as they do not take the offensive," Muhammad is said to have declared in a hadith recorded in the eighth century.[41]

The Abyssinian episode at first seems quite different from the Chinese Muslim tale. But a closer look exposes some strong similarities. In both cases the Muslims who leave Mecca are companions of Prophet, chosen from among the community of his earliest followers. In both cases they arrive in a non-Islamic land, following his directive. In both cases they are protected by a sympathetic ruler. The relationship between the negus and the Prophet could be characterized as a relationship of shifting encompassments. The negus is the sovereign of his country, and the biography of the Prophet is clear about this point throughout. The negus, a non-Islamic ruler, even tests the Muslims about their faith. And he is the one who ultimately has the power to decide if he wants to protect them or not. For instance, he refuses to surrender them to their enemies when they demand the Muslims' return. When one of the Muslims, Ubayd-Allah ibn Jahsh, converts to Christianity, the negus sends the man's Muslim wife, Ramlah bint Abi Sufyan (circa 594–666), like a father who sends his daughter, to be married to the Prophet. Meanwhile, the Prophet respects the negus throughout and, when the negus dies, prays for him (a crucial reminder to us of who has the spiritual higher ground). In short, the negus protects the Muslims and in this regard shares sovereignty over them with the Prophet. For their part, the Muslims live in a non-Muslim land "in the happiest conditions." Again, all this does not suggest that Muhammad and the negus are equal. But in terms of their relationship as sovereigns of the Muslims in Ethiopia, there is a careful and subtle sharing of dominion. Muhammad is the distant sovereign in the sense that he is originator of Islam and the messenger of Allah; the negus is a sovereign as the protector of Islam and Muslims in his domain. This is the most basic link between this episode and the Chinese tale above. In the Chinese context, this is translated into a depiction of Muhammad as the distant (in terms of time and space) sovereign who is the originator of Islam.[42] The emperor, again, is the ruler of China—the country that hosts the Muslims—and the protector of its Islam and its Muslims.

Furthermore, there is room to think that the Chinese tale is modeled after the story of the Ethiopian episode, which was undoubtedly known among Chinese Muslims.[43] To begin with, in the biographies of the Prophet, the negus is mentioned as the first ruler outside Arabia who hears about the greatness of Muhammad. In the Chinese Muslim tale, the emperor of China is credited with the same merit, and later Chinese Muslim texts also insist on that point.[44] Another link between the two tales is Sa'd ibn Abi Waqqas: in the Chinese case, we meet him as the leader of the delegation to China; and in the biography of the Prophet, he is one of the leaders of the Muslims who had gone to Ethiopia.[45] Furthermore, in both stories there is a discussion about the relationship between Islam and host religions. In the Chinese tale, the emperor also tests the Muslims about Islam and ascertains that Islam is compatible with Confucianism. In the Ethiopian episode, the negus discusses the status of Mary and Jesus in Islam with one of the Muslims' leaders (Ja'far). In the Chinese tale, the emperor and Sa'd discuss the natures of sage and sagehood. In the wake of this discussion, the emperor proclaims that Islam and Confucianism both use the same meaning of sagehood and political virtue.[46] Finally, there are two interesting reverse parallelisms between the Ethiopian and the Chinese stories. First, in the Ethiopian case, the Muslims escape Mecca to save themselves in Ethiopia, while in the Chinese case, they leave Mecca to save China. Second, the Ethiopian story ends with the return of the Muslims of Mecca, who say that "we have lived in the happiest conditions until we [returned] to the Apostle of God in Mecca." The Chinese tale ends with a poem invoking the possibility of return but states that the Muslims are not in fact returning: "Who would know that Muslims were to dwell in China forever? . . . Even today [the eighteenth century] we protect the state, not moving again."[47]

The above linkages, correlations, and correspondences between the Chinese tale and the *hijra* to Ethiopia are not incidental, I would argue. At their base is an even stronger political—or political-theological, if you will—affinity. The Ethiopian episode is the first instance in Islamic history in which a community of Muslims is formed outside the community of believers, in what we might call exilic conditions. It is created during the lifetime of the Prophet and at his initiative. Therefore it has a different status than other, later, and more "this worldly" instances. It also is a moment in which Muhammad shares his responsibility for his followers with another ruler. Evidently, it was no small event at the time. The authors of the *Sirah* not only included this episode in the biography of the Prophet but also classified it as a *hijra* ("this was the first Hijra of Islam"). This is important. It should be recalled that the *hijra* to Medina, when Muhammad himself migrated out of Mecca, is the most significant date in Islamic history. It officially created the *umma*, and it was the moment when the Prophet turned into a sovereign in the fullest meaning of the term: a political and religious leader, military commander, and judge. A *hijra* is therefore not just a movement in space. It is also a politically and theologically charged event. The first *hijra* to Ethiopia, accordingly, should be seen as another type of *hijra*—as the time when another form of Islamic communal existence is created. This form is an exilic community, where the Prophet is not fully present and some of his functions are carried out by another sovereign. This, I suggest, is how the Chinese Muslims understood their own existence in China. And it is ultimately why they attached their story to the tale of the Ethiopian episode.

The most compelling evidence supporting the idea that the two cases are attached is found in the *Tianfang zhisheng shilu* (The veritable records of Islam's most sagely)—the Chinese version of the biography of the Prophet, produced in the 1730s by Liu Zhi (c. 1660–1740), who was closely related to the authors of the *Huihui yuanlai*.[48] This text is a translation of a fourteenth-century version of the *Sirah*. I have discussed the significance of this text in great detail elsewhere and showed why it should not be merely viewed as a translation. Liu Zhi tinkered with the original text in several key areas. One of which is crucial for our purpose here: In the section pertaining to the "second year of the Call" (612), we read that the "emperor of China, having seen an omen in the sky, sent an envoy to Arabia." In response, "the Prophet sent a delegation headed by Sa'd ibn Abi Waqqas to China. Only Sa'd returned back to Arabia." The text implies that the rest of the delegation, ostensibly the future forefathers of the Huihui (though the text does not say that just yet), remains in China.[49] Interestingly enough, the Chinese translation of the biography of Muhammad also fails to mention that the migrants to Abyssinia returned to Mecca. This is strange and clearly a deliberate omission. But let us read on. Twenty years later, we learn, the Chinese emperor sends another envoy to Arabia, and in response the Prophet sends Sa'd ibn Abi Waqqas to China again. This time he has the following instructions: "Several officers who went before have stayed in the east and have not returned. They must be increasing in numbers, and [thus] it is fitting that you [go there to] teach the Scripture and instruct them in the rites and ceremonies."[50] These sections do not exist in any version of the *Sirah* except the Chinese. Needless to say, they are not part of the biography of the Prophet as it is known in the Islamic world. The Chinese translator must have inserted them there, and he clearly did so with the *Huihui yuanlai* in mind. The dates that Liu Zhi picked are significant, and I suspect he crafted them carefully. The "second year of the Call" is one year before the migration to Ethiopia, which makes the journey to China, not the one to Ethiopia, the first *hijra*. The second date, twenty years later," is 632, just before Prophet's death in 633. The command to stay in China was therefore one of his last commands, which he never got to change.

These interpolations in a canonical Islamic source such as the *Sirah* of the Prophet cannot be understood unless we read them next to the *Huihui yuanlai*. The two texts only seem separate; in fact, they complement each other. The *Huihui yuanlai* tells us how things took place on the Chinese side, focusing on the emperor. In the Chinese translation of the *Sirah*, Liu Zhi wants the reader to read the same story as seen from Mecca, focusing on the Prophet. In this regard, the *Tianfang zhisheng shilu* not only complements the *Huihui yuanlai* but also authenticates it. Ultimately, in the biography of the Prophet we find the final proof that the Prophet and the emperor of China did communicate and that the Prophet sent Muslims to China, just he did to Ethiopia. The story is now complete. More important, we have assurance that the arrangement between the Prophet and the emperor was agreed to by both sides. The Chinese Muslim reader of the two texts is able therefore to imagine the emperor and the Prophet standing shoulder to shoulder, facing him as his dual sovereigns.

Back to the Qing: Writing the Emperor

Let us now turn back to the Qing concepts of rulership with which we began. It should be recalled that even though the Chinese Muslim texts discussed above project themselves back into distant times (the Tang dynasty and the first Islamic century), they were in fact written at the time when Qing rulers' dialogues with various constituencies in their empire were in motion. This was a time when "Qing policies stimulated social, cultural, and economic changes in the peripheries that encouraged the growth of ethnic identities" among peripheral groups.[51] Extending this argument to a marginal group such as the Chinese Muslims therefore seems logical. Let us also recall, again, that these dialogues were intended to express Qing ideas about simultaneous rulership, about expressing different constituencies in rulership, and about placing the emperor at the center of his subjects' moral universe. The story about the 1764 mosque is but one relatively late instance of such a dialogue, and it occurs when a new group, the Uighurs, is being brought into the fold. Evidently, the Chinese Muslim texts presented and discussed above were written within, and in response to, this particular political culture. Again, the interesting aspect of this is the Chinese Muslims' autonomy and agility in using Qing ideology for their own purposes.

One final and powerful clue connecting the Chinese Muslim texts to Qing ideology is found in an afterword written for the *Huihui yuanlai* that purports to explain how and why the text itself arrived in China. This makes some sense if we recall that the Chinese Muslim foundation myth pretends to have been written outside history with no identified author or time of composition. An afterword explaining what it is therefore seems necessary. Unlike the generic Chinese emperor who appears in the *Huihui yuanlai*, the afterword involves a real Qing ruler, the Kangxi emperor (r. 1661–1722). In fact, a somewhat cryptic title to the afterword labels him as the "source" or provider of the story:

The Qing Kangxi emperor, on his return from a journey beyond the Great Wall, stopped at the yamen of General Ma to rest overnight. One night, the emperor and the general discussed the Principle and the Dao. The emperor asked, "You Muslim, do you know the origins of your name and the meaning of *your* Dao?" The general answered, "I do not know." The emperor asked again, "Do you know why Islam is called 'the Pure and True' [*Qingzhen*, a Chinese name for Islam]?" The general answered, "I do not know [this either]." The emperor asked again, "Do you know why you came from the west to China? At what time and for what reason?" The answer was "I still don't know." The emperor said, "I have a book here for you to read that will inform you of these matters."[52]

At this point the emperor hands the book, which is of course the *Huihui yu-anlai*, to General Ma, who replies: "I cannot read, but I am glad to receive the book, and I beg permission to seek help from some educated person such that I might understand it." The general had the book transcribed and distributed it among other Muslims.[53]

The story is apocryphal, but it resonates with a great deal of real history. Let us begin with the simple case of identity of General Ma Jinliang (d. c. 1717). The real Ma Jinliang was a Chinese Muslim from Xining (then Gansu) and a high-ranking officer in Kangxi's armies. He played a key role in the 1690–1697 campaigns against the Zunghar Mongols.[54] At some point during these campaigns, the Kangxi emperor specifically mentioned him as one the four generals "hand-picked" by him.[55] Thus, as the highest-ranking Chinese Muslim general who marched with Kangxi, Ma Jinliang is the best character to be handpicked to play the emperor's Muslim counterpart in the fictional dialogue. Ma's presence in the dialogue also helps us locate the scene and helps explain what the phrase "journey beyond the Great Wall" means. We can be quite sure that the setting of the dialogue is in the wake of one of expeditions against the Zunghars, all of which involved crossing the Great Wall.[56] The military setting is clearly vital for the authenticity of the story. It also reminds us that the *Huihui yuanlai*, like the Chinese Muslims themselves, originates in a place that is not China but is "beyond the Great Wall." (If we remember, however, that the author is a member of the Chinese Muslim scholarly elite, we can understand why he ends with the general confessing that he "cannot read" and transmitting the book to "some educated person.")

Moreover, General Ma's inability to read the book suggests that the original *Huihui yuanlai*, the one that the emperor holds in his hands, is written not in Chinese but in a Muslim language. This also resonates with historical reality. Manchu emperors placed a great deal of importance on the connection between language and identity. The emperor's expressed concern about his general's Chinese Muslim identity and his irritation when he realizes that Ma does not know much about it also reflect concrete history. Some decades after the Manchu conquest of China, from the 1680s on, the court became more and more concerned with the weakening boundaries between Manchu and Han Chinese identities. Knowledge of the Manchu language was therefore key.[57] The Kangxi emperor, using himself as an example, was personally involved in making sure that Manchus received a proper Manchu education. The court also tried to educate Manchus about their origins, a project that would peak under the Qianlong emperor.[58] The Qianlong emperor, Kangxi's grandson, once even boasted that he knew all the languages of his different subjects and did not rely on an interpreter when he met with them "to express the idea of conquering by kindness."[59] The Kangxi emperor had expressed the wish to "know" his various subjects' heritages and ways of life and even "represent" them.[60] Thus, General Ma's "I cannot read" is a phrase that the Kangxi emperor probably heard many times from his Manchu generals, and it is safe to assume that he expected his different subjects to speak languages other than Chinese and to know them. In the passage discussed just above, we see him educating the Chinese Muslims about their origins, much as he would have done with Manchus. Finally, note also that the emperor behaves like an informed ethnographer. He appears to know what kind of questions he needs to ask his Muslim general and then gives the general a book that would teach him all that he needs to learn.

Of course, the Kangxi emperor did not really do all that. His Chinese Muslim subjects cast him in this role in what they wrote for their own consumption. They used a rhetoric of encompassment in order to encompass their ruler and cast him as encompassing them. It is clear that what is expressed in the texts is not merely fiction but a carefully crafted literary image of dual sovereignty shared by the Prophet and the emperor. The Chinese Muslims produced this using Islamic tradition that they reinterpreted for their own needs, and at the same time they made sure that what they wrote conformed to and corresponded with the cultural policies of China's rulers. In this way, the Kangxi emperor—and, by extension, the emperor of China—comes to sit in the center of his Chinese Muslim subjects' moral universe. He does not occupy the same place as the Prophet of Islam, who is the source of Islamic law and authority. But he still sits at the center as the protector of his subjects and the custodian of their Chinese Muslim identity. He makes sure they know their heritage and guards against their forgetting it. In a sense, the emperor who gives the general a book about the origins of the Chinese Muslims is like the negus who returned a Muslim woman to the Prophet after her husband converted to Christianity, thereby making sure she would remain Muslim. The emperor of China sits next to Muhammad, not instead of him. The relationship between the two can be characterized as a delicate set of mutual, shifting hierarchies.

*   *   *

I have argued that Chinese Muslim elites created this image of dual sovereignty because they needed it. This is a model, a mode, of sovereignty imagined by the Muslim subjects living under a non-Muslim ruler in order to avoid the conflicts such a condition might produce. But did all of this really work for them? Perhaps the best indication that it did can be gleaned by returning to the moment when it did not—the building of the dysfunctional mosque that faced north. In his discussion of dual sovereignty between a village headman and a priest in a village in India, Frank Heidemann insists that this type of sovereignty works because both sides always work together, next to each other. The headman and the priest carefully avoid facing each other directly because such a situation would immediately expose the different hierarchies between secular and scared, political and religious. Avoidance allows them to work together, "shoulder-to-shoulder" vis-à-vis the village people.[61] In a way, this can explain what was wrong with the mosque that the Qianlong emperor built. Instead of facing Mecca, the mosque was facing his throne. When he made the mosque, the domain of the Prophet, face him directly, he disrupted the delicate set of shifting hierarchies and exposed them in a way that no Muslim could work with. And no one attended the mosque.

Notes

1. The community of the Turkic-Muslim camp is far less known than the fragrant concubine. On its history, see Takahiro Onuma, "250 Years' History of the Turkic-Muslim Camp in Beijing," *TIAS Central Eurasian Research Series* 2 (2009): 1–59. On the fragrant concubine, see James Millward, "A Uyghur Muslim in Qianlong's Court: The Meanings of the Fragrant Concubine," *Journal of Asian Studies* 53 (1994): 427–58.
2. There is some discussion about the terminology and what to call Chinese-speaking Muslims of China. Here I use "Huihui" and "Chinese Muslims" interchangeably. "Huihui" was the main and clearest way Chinese Muslims identified themselves during the period discussed in this essay.
3. For more on the mosque, see Tristan G. Brown, "Towards an Understanding of Qianlong's Conception of Islam: A Study of the Dedication Inscriptions of the Fragrant Concubine's Mosque in the Imperial Capital," *Journal of Chinese Studies* 53 (July 2011): 137–53. Brown uses the Qianlong's dedication to ponder the lim-

itations of a possible imperial patronage of Islam. I am using it here for different purposes.

4. We have only rubbings of the stele today. Wang Dongping recovered the full Chinese text in 2007. See Wang Dongping, "Qianlong yuzi 'Chijian Huiren libaisi beiji' de liang ge wenti" (Two questions on the stele inscription of Uighurian [sic] mosque written by Emperor Qianlong), *Xiyu yanjiu* (2007): 70–75.

5. I use here the translation found in Marshall Broomhall, *Islam in China: A Neglected Problem* (London: Morgan & Scott, 1910), 94.

6. The Chinese phrase here—"Xi xiang bei xiang, tonggui yi zun"—is unique. (Note also that *xiang* here, coming after "west" and "north," is not transitive but nominative). It is loaded with meanings: *tonggui* means to "head toward the same goal," and *yi zun*, which I translate as "showing one respect," could mean "one statue of the Buddha" (in certain situations, of course).

7. Such a scene is beautifully depicted in Bernardo Bertolucci's *The Last Emperor* (1987), in which thousands of officials in the Forbidden City bow before the toddler Chinese emperor.

8. Broomhall, *Islam in China*, 97.

9. On Qing imperial simultaneity, see Pamela Crossley, *A Translucent Mirror: History and Identity in Qing Imperial Ideology* (Berkeley: University of California Press, 1999), 10–12, 133–34, 262–85.

10. Evelyn Rawski, *The Last Emperors: A Social History of Qing Imperial Institutions* (Berkeley: University of California Press, 1998), 60–61.

11. Pamela Kyle Crossley, "Pluralité impériale et identités subjectives dans la Chine des Qing," *Histoire, Sciences Sociales* 63, no. 3 (2008): 597–621.

12. Angela Zito, *Of Body and Brush: Grand Sacrifice as Text/Performance in Eighteenth-Century China* (Chicago: University of Chicago Press, 1997), 29. Zito elaborates on encompassment in Qing ideology in her introduction to the book.

13. Historically only one mosque did not fully comply with this requirement: the Masjid al-Qiblatayn (Mosque of the Two Qiblahs), which the Prophet built in Medina, faced Jerusalem (location of the original *qiblah* in Islam) and Mecca. Recently it was renovated, and the *qiblah* to Jerusalem was removed.

14. Crossley, "Pluralité impériale," 610.

15. See Rawski, *Last Emperors*, 197–263. On Qing ideology, see also Crossley, *Translucent Mirror*.

16. One exception again, to my mind, accentuates Muslim absence from the court. Rawski does mention some Muslims participating in rituals performed to bring rain in 1796. But her language is telling: "even Muslim rituals seem to have been performed for rain" (*Last Emperors*, 225). We can find more support for Crossley's assertion above in Rawski's words about Islam: "The rulers also supported Islam, the religion of the Turkic-speaking Muslims of Central Asia, but were much less successful in winning over this group" (ibid., 10).

17. Zito, *Of Body and Brush*, 13.

18. Zvi Ben-Dor Benite, *The Dao of Muhammad: A Cultural History of Muslims in Late Imperial China* (Cambridge, MA: Harvard University Asia Center, 2005).

19. There is also the related question of Muslims in Qing law and legal codes, but that is beyond the scope of this essay. On this question, see Jonathan Lipman,

"A Fierce and Brutal People: On Islam and Muslims in Qing Law," in *Empire at the Margins Culture, Ethnicity, and Frontier in Early Modern China*, ed. Pamela Crossley, Helen Siu, and Donald Sutton (Berkeley: University of California Press, 2006), 83–110.

20. On early modern Chinese literati culture in general, see Benjamin Elman and Alexander Woodside, eds., *Education and Society in Late Imperial China, 1600–1900* (Berkeley: University of California Press, 1994), and Benjamin Elman, *A Cultural History of Civil Examinations in Late Imperial China* (Berkeley: University of California Press, 2000) and *Civil Examinations and Meritocracy in Late Imperial China* (Cambridge, MA: Harvard University Press, 2013). On Chinese Muslim literati, see Ben-Dor Benite, *Dao of Muhammad*, 21–114.

21. I develop and elaborate on this theme in *Dao of Muhammad*, 12–21.

22. Edward Farmer, *Zhu Yuanzhang and Early Ming Legislation: The Reordering of Chinese Society Following the Era of Mongol Rule* (Leiden: Brill, 1995), 82.

23. Zvi Ben-Dor Benite, "The Marrano Emperor: The Mysterious Bond Between Zhu Yuanzhang and the Chinese Muslims," in *Long Live the Emperor! Uses of the Ming Founder Across Six Centuries of East Asian History*, ed. Sarah Schneewind, Ming Studies Research Series no. 4 (Minneapolis: Society for Ming Studies, 2008), 275–308.

24. I was able to show this through looking at Muslim family genealogies.

25. Ben-Dor Benite, "Marrano Emperor," 290–98.

26. The role of the ruler in sometimes even giving his or her name to the polity is discussed elsewhere in this book.

27. Farmer, *Zhu Yuanzhang and Early Ming Legislation*, 53–55.

28. Pamela Crossley, "An Early Modern Complex for Eurasian Empires" (unpublished paper, n.d.), 8, www.eastwestcenter.org/fileadmin/resources/education/asdp _pdfs/Crossley_Eurasian_Empire_1_.pdf (accessed September 2, 2016).

29. We can be sure that the kernel of the story did not appear before late Ming times. And we can be sure that the story involving the emperor and Muhammad appeared only after 1680. First, Chinese-speaking Muslim communities arose in China in significant numbers only during the Ming. Second, Ibn Battuta, who traveled and lived among Muslims in China and recorded many such stories, as well as stories of conversion to Islam in the region (e.g., that of the Chagatai ruler Tarmashirin Khan [r. 1331–1334]), does not mention anything remotely close to the story. Third, the story does not appear in any way in a document written in 1680 in which the basic history of Islam in China is discussed. In this document, the author—Ma Zhu, a Yunnanese Muslim—simply mentions that the Tang emperor had seen heavenly signs about Muhammad. Ma does not mention anything about a communication with the Prophet, which is key to the story. On Ibn Battuta and the Muslims of China, see Zvi Ben-Dor, "'Even Unto China': Displacement and Chinese Muslim Myths of Origin," *Bulletin of the Royal Institute for Inter-Faith Studies* 2 (2002/2003): 93–114.

30. We can be quite certain, though, that the author was Liu Sanjie, a prominent scholar from Nanjing. The *Huihui yuanlai* (in two volumes, collectively containing fifty-one leaves) has been widely circulated since 1712. The version available to us was already in this form in 1712. I am using here a Qianlong edition

(1759), the earliest available. For details about the history of this text, see Ben-Dor Benite, *Dao of Muhammad*, 204–5.

31. I am using the scholarly edition prepared by Ma Kuangyuan, *Huizu wenhua lunji: Fu "Huihui yuanlai" zhengli ben* (Beijing: Zhongguo wenlian chuban gongsi, 1998), 55–77. I am also consulting the original text. The translation of the specific passage above is excerpted from the *Huihui yuanlai* translated by Li Shujiang and Karl Luckert, *Mythology and Folklore of the Hui, a Muslim Chinese People* (Albany: State University of New York Press, 1996), 237–38.

32. The historical Sa'd (d. 671), a maternal uncle of Muhammad and one of the first in Mecca to accept Islam, never went to China. He was one the most eminent companions of the Prophet and the commander of the Arab armies that defeated the Sassanid Empire in 636.

33. Li and Luckert, *Mythology and Folklore of the Hui*, 238.

34. Ben-Dor Benite, *Dao of Muhammad*, 205–9.

35. In thinking of Prophet-sovereign, let us remember that unlike Moses and Jesus, Muhammad was at once the spiritual, political, and military leader of his followers.

36. My use of the term "dual sovereignty" is partially inspired by Frank Heidemann's discussion of the mutual relationship between the village headman and the priest and the ways sovereignty is "shared" between the chief political figure and the head religious figure in the Nilgiri Hills in India. Heidemann analyzes what he calls the "Rhetoric of Encompassment"—the expressions of this type of relationship. He characterizes this relationship as one in which both "sides claim to represent the world and include the sphere of the other at the same time." See Frank Heidemann, "The Priest and the Village Headman: Dual Sovereignty in the Nilgiri Hills," in *The Anthropology of Values: Essays in Honour of Georg Pfeffer*, ed. Peter Berger, Roland Hardenberg, Ellen Kattner, and Michael Prager (Delhi: Pearson, 2010), 110.

37. The first migration is discussed at length in all biographies of the Prophet. For an English version, see Ibn 'Abd al-Malik Hishām, Muhammad Ibn Ishāq, and Alfred Guillaume, *The Life of Muhammad: A Translation of Ishāq's Sīrat Rasūl Allāh* (Oxford: Oxford University Press, 1955), 146–55.

38. Ibid., 146.

39. Ibid., 153.

40. Ibid., 155.

41. On Ethiopia and the hadith about it, see Majid Khadduri, *War and Peace in the Law of Islam* (Baltimore: Johns Hopkins Press, 1955), 253–57.

42. On Islam as a *dao* and as the *dao* of Muhammad, see Ben-Dor Benite, *Dao of Muhammad*, 163–212. I would characterize the relationship among Muhammad, his *dao*, and his followers according to the *Sunzi* 1.5: "The Dao causes the people to be in complete accord with their ruler."

43. The *Tianfang Zhisheng Shilu* (Veritable records of Islam's most sagely), an early eighteenth-century translation of a biography of the Prophet from Iran, tells the story in great detail. But there should be no doubt that the Muslims in China were familiar with the story much before that time. See Liu Zhi, *Tianfang zhisheng shilu nianpu* (Yinchuan: Ningxia shaoshu minzu guji zhengli chuban

guihua xiaozu bangongshi, 1987). For an English version of the *Tianfang zhiseng shilu*, see Liu Jielian and Isaac Mason, *The Arabian Prophet: A Life of Mohammed from Chinese and Arabic Sources—A Chinese-Moslem Work* (Shanghai: Commercial Press, 1921). On the *Tianfang zhisheng shilu*, see Ben-Dor Benite, *Dao of Muhammad*, 167–70.

44. See Ben-Dor Benite, *Dao of Muhammad*, 15, 159, 185, 189–91, 221–12, 232–33.

45. Ibn Hishām, *Life of Muhammad*, 147.

46. This section is titled "Praise to Confucius and a Comparison of the Sages" ("Zan kong bi sheng"). See *"Huihui yuanlai" zhengli ben*, 65–67.

47. *Huihui yuanlai* (1759), 25a. For the Chinese original and my full translation, see Ben-Dor Benite, *Dao of Muhammad*, 206.

48. I am using here a facsimile of a paginated reprint of a Tongzhi (1874) edition. See Liu Zhi, *Tianfang zhisheng shilu* (Veritable records of Islam's most sagely) (Beijing: Zhongguo Yisilan huiyin, 1984).

49. Liu, *Tianfang zhisheng shilu*, 120.

50. Ibid., 265–66.

51. Rawski, *Last Emperors*, 301.

52. *Huihui yuanlai* (1759), 25b–26a. In a Daoguang edition, which I have used elsewhere, the question appears slightly differently: "One night, the emperor and the general discussed principle and the Dao. The emperor asked, 'You Muslim, do you know the origins of your name and the meaning of your Dao?'"

53. *Huihui yuanlai* (1759), 26a–26b.

54. On these campaigns, see Peter Perdue, *China Marches West: The Qing Conquest of Central Eurasia* (Cambridge, MA: Belknap Press of Harvard University Press, 2005). General Ma is mentioned several times in the *Qinzheng pingding shuomo fanglüe* (Chronicle of the Kangxi emperor's expeditions to pacify the steppe) (Taibei: Chenwen chuban she, 1970), vol. 23.

55. Quoted in Dai Yingcong, *The Sichuan Frontier and Tibet: Imperial Strategy in the Early Qing* (Seattle: University of Washington Press, 2009), 55.

56. Perdue, *China Marches West*, 182.

57. Crossley, *Translucent Mirror*, 108.

58. Pamela Crossley, "Manchu Education," in Elman and Woodside, *Education and Society*, 340–78, and "'Manzhou Yuanliu Kao' and the Formalization of the Manchu Heritage," *Journal of Asian Studies* 46, no. 4 (1987): 761–90.

59. Quoted in Rawski, *Last Emperors*, 301.

60. We see this in the case of the Miao in southern China. See Laura Hostetler, *Qing Colonial Enterprise: Ethnography and Cartography in Early Modern China* (Chicago: University of Chicago Press, 2001).

61. Heidemann, "Priest and the Village Headman," 104–19.

ELEVEN

The Neurology of Regicide

Decapitation Experiments and the Science of Sovereignty

CATHY GERE

1649

UPON HIS ARREST on charges of "treasons, murders, ravages, burnings, spoils, desolations, damages and mischiefs to the nation," Charles I demanded to know by what authority he was being detained. "I mean lawful," he clarified, for "there are many unlawful Authorities in the world, Theeves and Robbers by the high ways. Remember that I am your King, your lawful King."[1] In court, he refused to answer the charges, and continued to repeat the refrain: "Remember that I am your King . . . therefore let me know by what lawful Authority I am seated here."[2] This stonewalling was periodically interrupted by furious disquisitions from the bench on the history of parliaments, the ethics of sovereignty, and the limits of monarchical and imperial power. Reminding the king that the Emperor Caligula had *"wisht that the People of Rome had had but one neck, that at one blow he might cut it off,"* the judge commented: "the body of the people of England hath been . . . represented but in Parliament, and could you have but confounded that, you had at one blow cut off the neck of England."[3]

A scant three days after being compared to Caligula, Charles dined at noon on a piece of bread and a glass of claret before being marched to a scaffold in Whitehall "hung round with black and the floor covered with black and the Ax and Block laid in the middle." Before a great multitude, he protested his innocence once again, asserting that the people's "Liberty and

Freedom, consists in having of Government. . . . A subject and a soveraign are clean different things." In refusing to answer the charges against him, he argued, he was sacrificing his life for the liberty of his subjects: "If I would have given way to an Arbitrary way, for to have all Laws changed according to the power of the Sword, I needed not to have come here; and therefore, I tell you, (and I pray God it be not laid to your charge) That I Am the Martyr of the People."

Plaintively remarking that the block "might have been a little higher," Charles showed the executioner the sign by which he would communicate his readiness to receive the blow of the axe, extending his arms in front of his body. After murmuring two or three words to the sky, his hands aloft and eyes raised heavenward, he stooped down and laid his neck on the block. Contemporary engravings of the moment differ: in some he is kneeling as if in prayer; in others he is prostrate, nose to the scaffold floor. After a few moments of silence, Charles issued his final command as sovereign and law-giver: "The King stretching forth his hands, The Executioner at one blow, severed his head from his Body."[4] As he held up the dripping head, a great groan of lamentation arose from the crowd. The judge at Charles's trial had accused him of wanting to "cut off the neck of England," personifying the collective will of Parliament. But in condemning him to a martyr's death, Parliament unwittingly allowed that the neck of England might still be the grizzled column supporting the head of Charles Stuart. With one stroke of the axe, the tyrant in the dock assumed a crown of thorns, and the temporal crown of England and Scotland settled on the spotless brow of the languid, charming, and sexually rapacious Prince of Wales, in exile in Paris.

Regicide inevitably raises with heightened urgency the question of rev-olution's aftermath: whose head shall serve as the central authority, the unified will, the executive function? This essay examines these issues in the context of the history of the neurosciences. Between the death of Charles I in England and the restoration of Louis XVIII in France, a series of foundational decapitation experiments posed the regicidal riddles of the head of state in psychophysiological terms. All scientific, forensic, and punitive decapita-tions of the period—of animal and human, living and dead bodies—can be mined for their explicit or implicit theories of sovereignty; for reasons of space, this essay explores just two examples. Both exemplify what I call "the neurology of regicide": scientific investigations of nervous anatomy and physiology that rehearse the political tensions attendant on the execution of a sovereign king. The first example is from Restoration Oxford, the second from French-occupied Mainz in 1803, Year Twelve of the Revolution. A brief coda examines an experiment that took place in London in the same year and using the same technology as the German example, but with very different implications for the science of sovereignty. Arguing that physiologists adjudicated urgent questions about the postrevolutionary social order, this essay explores experimental science as a performance space in which new forms of sovereign power were legitimated through the investigation and redefinition of the human nervous system.

Re-capitating the Leviathan

By the time of the English regicide, Thomas Hobbes, sixty-year-old erstwhile mathematical tutor to the Prince of Wales, had already published two tracts condemning the error that the people might constitute themselves into a sovereign body and put to death a tyrant king. His *De Cive* of 1647 explained the political assertion of rights and liberties as arising from impulses as natural and as universal as they were dangerous and uncivilized. After the execution of Charles I, his arguments against political insurrection went even deeper into the fundamentals of human psychology. The *Leviathan* suggested that repairing the damage to the body politic would require nothing less than a science of mankind based on mechanical first principles, commanding assent by virtue of its geometric irrefutability. As a foundation for absolute certainty and absolute sovereignty, Hobbes defined the basic geometry of human behavior as movement toward and movement away, prompted by the primordial experiences of pain and pleasure.[5] Pointing out that all war, but especially civil war, caused untold suffering, Hobbes argued that our animal shrinking from bodily trauma was what mandated our submission to any sovereign authority capable of keeping the peace.

Hobbes's Leviathan was made up of a human multitude, all obeying the same invariant laws of hedonist psychology and bound by those laws to total obedience to the head of state. His prescription for the re-capitation of the body politic thus linked civil therapeutics directly to the medical variety, and to the nascent sciences of life. During the 1630s, in Paris, he had written about optics, assisted with dissections, and worked his way through Vesalius's great illustrated textbook of human anatomy.[6] His Leviathan was equipped with a correspondingly up-to-date nervous system. In a chapter entitled "Of those things that weaken or tend to the dissolution of a commonwealth," Hobbes argued that if the power of the state was split between spiritual and civil offices, the body politic would suffer "a Disease which not unfitly may be compared to the Epilepsie, or Falling-sicknesse." He likened the Church to an "unnaturall spirit, or wind in the head that obstructeth the roots of the Nerves," while the "Civill Power" he likened to the "Soule." When the Church was allowed to exert political power, it deprived the limbs of "the motion which naturally they should have from the power of the Soule in the Brain and thereby causeth violent, and irregular motions (which men call Convulsions)."[7] The soul of the Leviathan was not the Church, but the Civil Power, whose authority must be allowed to govern without interference or interruption, by analogy with the executive function of an individual brain.

The *Leviathan* exhorted submission to any absolute sovereign, whether anointed Sun King or self-styled Puritan Moses. Accordingly, upon Hobbes's return to Cromwellian London in 1651, the year of the book's publication, he was "much caressed" by the new regime, to the disgust of his Royalist friends.[8] But Oliver Cromwell—a head atop a rump—never created a symbolic order to rival that of the monarchy, and in 1658 he died, leaving the Commonwealth in chaos. In May 1660, Charles II rode triumphantly into London. A mere four days later, the king publicly forgave his puckish old mathematics teacher for his temporary defection and established Hobbes at the Restoration court.

After the coronation of Charles II, the rhetorical traffic established by Hobbes between political philosophy and nervous physiology began to flow in the other direction. Emerging from the same political and intellectual turmoil as the *Leviathan*, the nascent discipline of neurology forged similar links between monarchical sovereignty, personal safety, and the anatomy of the body politic. The word "neurologie" was coined in 1664 by a Royalist physician called Thomas Willis, who, in the aftermath of the interregnum, "addicted" himself "to the opening of heads" and founded a new science deeply inflected by the conflict that destroyed his world.

Willis was born in 1621 to a conservative family in West England. At age sixteen he had gone to Christchurch College, Oxford. In the summer of 1642, he graduated Master of Arts in preparation for the Anglican ministry, but the Civil War intervened before he could embark on a clerical career. That winter, Charles I, finding himself unable to march into London, made Oxford into the headquarters of the Royalist army, turning college quadrangles into stables for his horses and libraries into warehouses for military supplies. An elaborate system of earthworks was erected all around the city, with dams to strategically flood points of access, and palisades and trenches to fill in the gaps.

Willis left the city and went back to his family farm, where he lost both his parents to an epidemic of typhus. He mitigated his sense of helplessness with a meticulous account of the symptoms and the spread of the disease, his first excursion into medical observation. In 1644, ever the loyal monarchist, he returned to Oxford to answer a royal proclamation calling for volunteers to defend the city. He spent the next two years stationed in Magdalen Meadows on the eastern perimeter, under fire from the parliamentary forces that ringed the hills.[9] The efforts of Willis and the other student soldiers were to no avail, however, and in June 1646, the king slipped out of Oxford in disguise, leaving the garrison to surrender.

After the fall of Oxford, Willis's old Royalist allies who still held university appointments awarded him a medical degree as a token of their gratitude for his service to the cause. In 1647, the Puritans purged the town, and half of the university was thrown out. Willis hung on. Too obscure to raise the suspicions of Cromwell and his men, he quietly withdrew from the official life of the university in order to avoid taking the oath of allegiance to Parliament. He worked as a "pisse prophet" in Abingdon market—making diagnoses on the basis of the taste, smell, and color of urine samples—and set up an alchemical laboratory in his lodgings.

In the meantime, Cromwell had appointed a moderate Puritan and devout cosmopolitan called John Wilkins to the wardenship of Wadham College. Wilkins had traveled around the Continent and seen firsthand the devastation wrought by the wars of religion. In an explicit response to the religious fanaticism on all sides of the Civil War, he lured natural philosophers to the university, without regard for their political affiliation, to form the Oxford Experimental Philosophy Club, which met every Thursday afternoon to watch experiments and debate their meaning. "Their first purpose was no more, than onely the satisfaction of breathing a freer air, and of conversing in quiet with one another, without being ingag'd in the passions and madness of that dismal Age."[10] The free air at Wadham could be breathed by devout Anglicans and staunch Puritans alike, and Willis, despite his proven

loyalty to king and church, was invited to join. "Till about the yeare 1649,*
'twas . . . held a sinne to make a scrutinie into the waies of nature," John Aubrey remarked in the preface to his *Natural History of Wiltshire*, explaining
this suggestively regicidal chronology with a footnote: "*Experimentall Philosophy was then first cultivated by a club at Oxon."[11]

Willis had none of the polish of a gentlemanly physician; short and stam-
mering, he was described by Aubrey as having hair "like a red pig" and by
another chronicler of seventeenth-century Oxford as "a plain man, a man
of no carriage, little discourse, complaisance or society."[12] He was possessed,
however, of an accurate memory, kindly manner, and painstaking observa-
tional acuity, all of which began to win him patients among the impoverished
Royalists in the area around Oxford. The surviving casebooks of his practice in the years 1650 to 1652 show him beginning to replace traditional
humoral concepts with a new iatrochemistry of fermentations, distillations,
explosions, and sublimations.[13] He was not yet focusing on the nervous
system, but his observations of patients afflicted with "aberrations of the
mind" placed the cause firmly at the door of physical debility.[14] In his *Treatise
on Fermentations and Feavers*, first published in 1659, Willis reflected on the
iatrochemical causes of the "cruel Head-Aches," as well as "Delirium, Phren-
sie, Convulsion, etc." arising from the agitations of the blood "stirring up
inordinate motions in the Brain."[15]

By the Restoration, Willis was thirty-nine years old and in possession of
an enviable reputation for medical acumen, allied to proven loyalty to the
king and church. His friends were now the most powerful men in the land,
and in August 1660 the bishop of London rewarded him with an Oxford pro-
fessorship of natural philosophy. Resolving to dedicate himself "wholly to
the study of Anatomy," he transformed his lodgings in Oxford, which had
also served as a clandestine Anglican chapel during the years of the Republic,
into an "Anatomical Court." This metamorphosis from chapel to laboratory exemplifies the exceptionally harmonious relationship between the
restored church and the new natural philosophy. In an epistle dedicatory to
the archbishop of Canterbury, Willis confessed that he had "slain so many
Victims, whole Hetacombs almost of all Animals, in the Anatomical Court,
I could not have thought them rightly offered, unless they had been brought
to the most holy Altar of your Grace."[16] In Cromwellian Oxford, the Experimental Philosophy Club could claim the mantle of novelty and revolution; now

remade into the Royal Society for the Promotion of Natural Knowledge, they offered up dissection and experiment as Anglican sacraments revealing the providential order of nature.

On January 30, 1661, the twelfth anniversary of Charles I's execution, Oliver Cromwell was disinterred and decapitated, his head shoved onto a twenty-foot spike above Westminster Hall. At around the same time, Willis turned his full attention to the study of the brain and nerves. "I addicted my self to the opening of Heads," he later recalled, in order that "some truth might at length be drawn forth concerning the exercise, defects and irregularities of the Animal Government."[17] In search of the pathologies and fragilities of man's sovereign reason, he became the first natural philosopher to take the brain out of the skull entire, to study it as a whole organ, as opposed to taking off the skull from the top and slicing through the hemispheres like a soft-boiled egg. Renaissance anatomists had focused their attention on the ventricles as the most striking feature revealed by their technique; Willis focused instead on the solid tissues, immersing the delicate jelly of the brain in spirits of wine in order to harden it and then tracing the nerve pathways and blood vessels with the knife, examining them under one of the new microscopes.

In 1664 Willis coined the word "neurologie" in his treatise *The Anatomy of the Brain and Nerves.*[18] The book was crowned with a chapter on "the chief seat of the rational soul of a man, the chief mover in the animal machine, the origin and fountain of all motions and conceptions." Willis's first concern in delineating human cerebral anatomy—understandable in a man who had tried to defend the walls of Oxford against Cromwell's army—was with *safety.* The brain's defense strategy began with the most basic division of the cerebrum into two hemispheres "that there might be a provision made against the defect of one side by the supplement of the other." The hemispheres, in turn, were

> subdivided into two lobes, to wit, the Anterior and the Posterior; between which a branch of the Carotidick Artery, being drawn like a bounding River to both, distinguishes them as it were into two Provinces. Certainly this second partition of the humane brain also seems to be designed for its greater safety; that if, perchance any evil should happen to one or both the foremost Lobes, yet the latter, for that they are separated, may avoid the contagion of

the neighbouring and further spreading evil: so the Brain, like a Castle, divided into many towers or places of Defence, is thereby made the stronger and harder to be taken.[19]

The functions thus to be defended were those of peaceful agriculture, manufacture, and commerce. The surface of the brain was "plowed, or laid as it were with furrows . . . like a plot of ground, planted everywhere with nooks and corners, and dauks and molehills." Manufacture in this cerebral economy was concerned with the production, storage, and distribution of "animal spirits." After the animal spirits were manufactured, they were "brought at last into the *Callous Body*, as into a spacious field; where, as in a free and open place, these spirits . . . do meet together and remain as in a publick Emporium or Mart."[20]

Unfortunately for the equilibrium of the cerebral economy, Willis's "animal spirits were inclined to battle with one another, pitting the rational soul against the animal soul. When the animal soul had the upper hand, Man lost his reason and descended into madness and delirium. In the muscles of the extremities, the spirits were especially inclined toward rebelliousness, and in order for reason to be restored the "Army of Veterans" had to be disbanded—precisely the problem that faced the Restoration authorities in dealing with Cromwell's soldiers.[21] Willis's brain, with its castles and rivers, plowed fields and open markets, evoked the vanished order of prewar England, a place of organic harmony, ringed by rebel militias posing an existential threat to the whole Animal Government.

Most modern neuroscientific textbooks supply a diagram of the brain's basic morphology with the different structures named for their discoverers. At the base of the brain lies the Circle of Willis, an arterial ring connecting the four main blood vessels running from heart to head. Willis first noticed the structure that still bears his name during an autopsy of one of his patients. The man had suffered from terrible headaches for a time but then recovered and lived for many more years. Eventually he died, in full possession of his faculties. At the postmortem Willis observed that one of the four carotid arteries was blocked with a yellow mass while another was greatly enlarged. Observing that all four were connected by an arterial ring, he surmised that the whole structure served to provide blood to the brain should one or more artery fail. As with everything else in his account of the nervous system, his analysis stressed the providential protective function of the cerebral economy: "Nature has substituted a sufficient remedy against that danger of an Apoplexy."[22] In this case, he happened to be right. Willis's obsession with safety and redundancy in cerebral structures had secured him his scientific immortality. The image illustrating this structure from Willis's text—drawn by Christopher Wren, later architect of St Paul's Cathedral—remained the canonical view of the base of the brain until anatomical engraving finally became obsolete in the twentieth century.

For Willis no less than for Hobbes, human suffering and political danger were the ground on which counterrevolutionary politics and the physiology of the nervous system formed a continuous whole. The 1649 regicide had struck a mortal blow to the cosmic order of microcosm and macrocosm that underwrote Renaissance sovereignty, but the Leviathan was resurrected in the name of medical science. The Circle of Willis was part of the political anatomy of the brain of Restoration England, a supply line that might, God willing, help His Majesty's head stay attached to his body and spare the nation the trauma of civil war. Stamped with the seal of counterrevolutionary reaction, Willis's "neurologie" exemplified the tradeoff between security and freedom, the commitment to orderly markets, and the nostalgia of invented tradition, which the office of Britannic Majesty has represented from his time to ours.

Year Twelve

In 1788, the philosopher-priest Abbé Sieyès argued that true sovereignty lay in the common will, the "volonté commune" of the Third Estate, igniting a fiery debate about the location and structure of the executive function of the French body politic.[23] At the 1792 trial of Louis XVI, Jean-Paul Marat prophesied that as long as the defendant lived and breathed, there would be "no liberty, no security, no peace, no rest, no happiness for the French, no hope for other peoples of breaking this yoke, unless the tyrant's head is cut off."[24] Two months later, when the executioner held Citizen Louis Capet's head up for the crowd to admire, instead of a groan of lamentation there came a great cheer of joy.

All the neurological questions raised by the execution of the English monarch took on a new urgency in the wake of the public beheading of the French king. To what extent and for how long could the system continue to function in a state of headless anarchy? How might the "animal economy" of the body politic survive and thrive under the distributed action of a common will? By the end of 1793, the Committee of Public Safety admitted: "We have decreed a Republic, and we are still organized as a monarchy. The head of the monster is defeated, but the trunk still survives with its defective forms." In response to this crisis, the committee resolved "to strengthen all its parts, spread revolutionary vitality through its veins, immerse it in energy and complete its strength by the lightning of action." The life of the revived Republic would reside in a dispersed, anarchic force that traveled instantaneously along the limbs of the body politic: "Laws, which are the soul of the national body are immediately transmitted, and travel through it, circulating swiftly through all its veins, reaching from the heart to the extremities in an instant."[25]

In describing revolutionary vitality spreading through the veins of the body politic with "la fulgurance de l'action" (the lightning of action),[26] the Committee of Public Safety demonstrated at least a passing acquaintance with the latest developments in neurology. In 1781, the Italian physician Luigi Galvani had discovered that a headless frog twitched when touched by a metal object charged with static electricity. He subsequently found that a wire pointed at a stormy sky would make the decapitated animal jerk, as if alive, with every flash of lightning. For Galvani, the "animal electricity" that moved the frog was identical with the vital spirit, and it was distinct in kind from the "artificial" electricity generated by friction machines or the "natural" electricity of the heavens. In keeping with his impassioned vitalism, Galvani was an ardent supporter of the old regime, and a devout Roman Catholic. When Napoleon invaded his part of Italy in 1797, Galvani refused to swear an oath to the republic. He was removed from his chair of anatomy at University of Bologna and died a year later in poverty. His compatriot Alessandro Volta insisted that animal, artificial, and natural electricity were manifestations of the same underlying phenomenon and that Galvani's decapitation experiments actually proved the mechanistic character of living organisms. As befitted this prophet of mechanism, Volta harbored no nostalgia for the old regime and was invited to Paris by Napoleon himself, where he was made chevalier of the Legion of Honor and count of the Kingdom of Italy and was given a lifetime pension.

Mastery of animal electricity was one new tool of revolutionary neurology; another was the guillotine, attitudes toward which divided along the same lines as the Galvani-Volta controversy. In October 1795 the German anatomist Samuel Thomas Soemmerring issued a challenge to the revolutionaries, arguing that the guillotine was inhumane because consciousness persisted for a brief but morally salient interval after decapitation.[27] Soemmerring gave the imprimatur of medical science to the many circulating stories of severed heads whose play of expression seemed to indicate the continued existence of conscious life. The fact that facial features often grimaced in the seconds after execution was not in dispute, but these movements could be interpreted in one of two ways. Were they nothing more than meaningless, mechanical twitches, or were they manifestations of the soul, still inhabiting the brain?[28] The most infamous example was that of Charlotte Corday, who was executed for the murder of Jean Marat in 1793. It was said that when the executioner held up her head and slapped her in retribution for the deed, she blushed with indignation.

A swift response to this challenge came from the revolutionary philosopher-physician Pierre Cabanis. In a withering rebuttal of Soemmerring's claims about the guillotine, he dismissed as a "chimera" the idea that the twitches and grimaces of severed heads revealed the prolongation of consciousness or that Charlotte Corday's post-decapitation blush was truly a "moral movement."[29] Cabanis could claim some authority in this regard: in the course of the article, he referred the reader to the experiments that he had personally conducted at the Bîcetre Asylum on behalf of the Revolutionary government, guillotining cadavers to establish that the new machine cut cleanly through the spine, guaranteeing an instantaneous death.[30]

As the 1790s wore bloodily on, however, even this pioneer of medical execution technique recoiled against the Revolution's epidemic of decapitations, and by 1799 Cabanis was more than ready to embrace the aspirations of Napoleon Bonaparte, "the longed-for leader-philosophe who would . . . inaugurate an era of stability for the sake of science and learning."[31] In a 1799 speech to the docile rump of the Council of Five Hundred that remained after Napoleon's coup of 18 Brumaire, he mused on the physiology of the body politic, stressing the importance of unity of action and thought in the head of state, and suggesting that a distributed executive was in danger of producing a form of government that was a useless machine rather than a living organism.[32]

Four years later, in 1803, a group of men of science in French-occupied Mainz conducted a decapitation experiment that slavishly enacted every element of Cabanis's psycho-politics. During the years of Napoleonic rule, a bandit known as Schinderhannes had garnered a degree of popular notoriety for his prison breaks, his dashing defiance of French law, and his deliberate targeting of Jews. In 1802 he was captured and imprisoned in a wooden tower in the walls of Mainz. After the authorities threatened his common-law wife, he betrayed nineteen other members of his band, who were rounded up and thrown in jail. The following year, on 29 Brumaire, Year Twelve, all twenty were guillotined in front of the gates of the city.

Engravings of the Schinderhannes execution adhere faithfully to revolutionary iconography. A large crowd throngs around the scaffold. The guillotine rears up into the sky. The executioner holds up Schinderhannes's severed head for the mob to admire. For the artists who rendered the scene, this muddy corner of the German-speaking lands might as well have been the Place de la Concorde, the site of public execution in Paris. Missing from these stereotypical images of revolutionary justice is the wooden hut, sitting in a depression in the ground 150 paces from the guillotine, constructed by a group of local physicians, chemists, and medical students for the purposes of conducting electrical experiments on the severed heads and decapitated bodies as they came off the scaffold. In 1804 the experimenters published a report of their investigations, saturated with all the political aspirations and anxieties of Year Twelve.[33]

The pamphlet opened with a hymn of praise to Napoleon, hailing him as a new Alexander the Great, building temples of the arts and sciences on conquered lands and earning the gratitude of vanquished populations. There were benefits to such political loyalty: this motley group of experimenters was in a position to dictate the legal conditions for its own investigations. Hitherto, they claimed, "the laws of every civilized State" had forbidden "all investigations involving the forcible separation of the organic parts" only because of "the unreliability of the symptoms of death." Now, with the benefit of Dr. Guillotin's invention, all that had changed: "Given the certainty of death by execution, an exception is made in these cases to the usual practice of the legal authorities." The guillotine itself, by delivering such physiological certainty, created the forensic conditions under which the law might be renegotiated.[34]

According to the report, the wooden hut built for the purpose was spacious, with two rooms, four windows, and a stove in which a fire was kept burning, the day being foggy and wet. Electrical experiments were still marked by the Galvani-Volta debate, and the hut was equipped with two separate chambers, one containing a voltaic pile, the other a friction machine and two Leyden jars. The experimenters' stated goal was to ascertain what "effects are generated by the application of electricity to a dead body—both on the whole mechanism [*in der ganzen Maschine*] and on its individual parts—and, furthermore, how the effects of galvanic agent on a dead body might differ from these."[35]

The first body was brought into the wooden hut only four minutes after the execution and was "young, rather fat, and in all its parts very warm. Its muscles twitched of their own accord, and the blood spurted from the still-beating artery of the throat in short streams." Using the voltaic pile, the experimenters "brought the zinc pole to the spinal cord . . . and touched the copper pole to the skin of various external parts of the body." The results were satisfactory: "Strong movements occurred in the voluntary muscles with both the opening and closing of the current." They then "touched both poles to different apertures and points of the severed head," producing an effect that "was all the more remarkable for the assembled observers, on account of the importance of this body part." It must have been a macabre sight: "The rapid contractions of the face muscles, together with the gnashing of the teeth that resulted from the movements of the lower jaw, immediately suggested various fleeting physiognomies of the face."[36]

While the physicians were engaged in their electrical experiments, two of the junior members of the team were assigned an important role, described at the end of the pamphlet in a section entitled "Experiment on sensation and consciousness after decapitation":

On the day of the execution of the twenty criminals, Herr Pitschaft and Herr Größer, candidates of medicine, placed themselves under the scaffold, to undertake the following experiments on two of the heads (those of the so-called Schinderhannes and Black Jonas). One of the two candidates took the head in both hands as soon as it fell from the scaffold, and after they had carefully ensured that not the least deformation manifested in the face or in the half-closed eyes, called him in one ear and then the other, during which the one who was holding the head paid close attention to the results. Not the least alteration was to be observed. For the second head the two men swapped tasks, and still they observed nothing. This experiment was repeated for five other heads. The words "Do you hear me?" were shouted in their ears. Not the slightest movement of the eyes or any other sign was observed in any head to which the called out words were expressed.[37]

The Medical Society of Mainz took the question of the persistence of consciousness seriously enough to subject it to experimental investigation but resoundingly concluded that there was no spiritual significance to the movements of the facial muscles. In one single set of investigations the group simultaneously reconstructed the laws governing the scientific investigation of the dead, probed *die ganze Maschine* of the human body with electrical apparatus, and interpreted the mechanical grimaces of the severed head in terms favorable to the Revolution.

In stressing the mechanical death of the severed head, however, the Mainz experimenters also tacitly admitted that the body politic could not run on the lightning of law alone. The guillotine, in doing its work so cleanly, deprived both the body and the head of life, with no possibility of resurrection. In 1807, three years into Napoleonic empire, even the arch materialist Cabanis posited the existence of an ineffable spiritual principle guiding the physiological organization of the body:

> Is the *moi* the simple product of the successive action of the organs and the impressions that are transmitted to the sensorium commune? Or could it be that the systematic combination of the organs, their progressive development, and their faculties and functions are determined by an active principle whose nature is unknown, but whose existence is necessary for a reasonable explanation of the facts?[38]

Cabanis's admission of the existence of an "active principle," anterior to the physical being and perhaps outlasting it, was a straw in a counterrevolutionary wind that blew ever stronger after Napoleon's defeat. As the historian of French psychology Jan Goldstein has shown, the "post-revolutionary self" was the "indivisible *moi*" of the sacred individual.[39] This conception of individual sovereignty found experimental confirmation in the work of Pierre Flourens, the physiologist entrusted by the French Academy of Sciences in 1822 to ascertain the truth or falsity of the doctrine of phrenology. Flourens cut away at the brains of pigeons and found that the more of the hemispheres he removed, the more stupid the creatures became overall, without appearing to suffer the loss of any single, specific function. From this, he concluded that intelligence was one unitary phenomenon located in the cerebral hemispheres. For Flourens, the unitary faculty of the will could best be known through introspection, and its essential attribute was its freedom: "If there be anything that belongs to the *consciousness* it is . . . the sense of our personal unity; or, what is more, the consciousness of our moral liberty."[40]

In the German-speaking lands, after Napoleon's defeat and the restoration of the borders of the German Confederation, the reaction against Jacobin psychophysiology was, if anything, even stronger. Drawing on the transcendental psychology of Immanuel Kant and his followers, the most scientifically rigorous exponent of this Romantic neurology was Johannes Müller, whose *Handbook of Human Physiology* was the standard work in the field until it was surpassed by the work of his own students. For Müller all living things were imbued with a vital principle and all animals with mind or soul. The existence of a "purposeful, active, vital principle" was shown by the spontaneous development of whole organisms, capable of consciousness, from seeds and germs. The same soul force was "still active in the absence of a brain, in brainless and headless monsters," but mind, "in the narrow sense of imagination and thought, etc.," required the organic development of the brain in order to manifest.[41] Romantic or liberal, reactionary or Catholic, Kantian or Cartesian, the human frame of post-Napoleonic Continental Europe was endowed with a unitary mind or soul, indivisible, sacred, and immortal.

The Leviathan of Utility

The same year as the Mainz Medical Society was undertaking its decapitation experiment, Luigi Galvani's nephew traveled to London to conduct a similar performance, in a very different political register, however. In his capacity as Galvani's most loyal disciple, Giovanni Aldini had spent the previous few years touring the learned academies of Europe performing demonstrations of the distinctive properties of animal electricity. In January 1803, he undertook the electrical stimulation of the corpse of a malefactor who had been hanged in Newgate Prison for the crime of drowning his wife and child. Aldini was as sensitive to the prejudices and aspirations of his British hosts as the Mainz experimenters were to their Napoleonic patrons.[42]

Addressed to the Royal College of Surgeons, where the experiment took place, his report of his London adventure stressed commercial utility, therapeutic benefit, and bodily intactness.

Aldini had performed electrical experiments on decapitated bodies in Napoleonic Italy, but in London he was offered a quite different opportunity to test the effects of animal electricity. His subject, George Forster, was twenty-six at the time of his death, and of a sound and vigorous constitution. An autopsy revealed that he had suffocated quickly, as a result of his hanging, giving Aldini the chance to "ascertain what opinion should be formed of Galvanism as a means of excitement in cases of asphyxia and suspended animation."[43]

Experimenting on an intact corpse, Aldini felt that he had come closer than ever before to a medically significant result. Various chemical stimulants were in use at the time for the purposes of reviving unconscious patients, and he tested some of them in conjunction with electrical stimulation, to see if their action might be mutually enhanced. On administering Galvanic stimulus and volatile alkali together, the convulsions "extended from the muscles of the head, face and neck as far as the deltoid. The effects in this case surpassed our most sanguine expectations, and vitality might, perhaps, have been restored, if many circumstances had not rendered it impossible."[44] Unlike the severed heads that rolled off the revolutionary scaffold, the bodies produced by the British judicial regime might actually be restored to life, as witnessed by the effects of the electrical current spreading from the face and neck down to the torso.

Aldini was suitably modest about the implications of his resurrective powers, but he did hint that Britain of all places could make good use of such a technology:

To enlarge on the utility of such researches, or to point out the advantages which may result from them, is not my object at present. I shall here only observe, that as the bodies of valuable members of society are often found in similar circumstances, and with the same symptoms as those observed on executed criminals; by subjecting the latter to proper experiments, some speedier and more efficacious means than any hitherto known, of giving relief in such cases, may, perhaps, be discovered. In a commercial and maritime country like Britain, where so many persons, in consequence of their occupations at sea, on canals, rivers and in mines, are exposed to drowning, suffocation, and other accidents, this object is of utmost importance in a public view.[45]

By 1803, the British body politic had managed to weather the Glorious Revolution, the madness of George III, the loss of the American colonies, and the Napoleonic Wars without losing its head. It was not, and never would be, Year Twelve in London. Aldini was able to conduct his experiments on a whole body, hanged rather than decapitated, killed by suffocation like those "persons of consequence" who died in canals, mines, and rivers. His optimistic projections about the potential "utility" of his researches exemplified the practicality of the Whig compact between the crown, the aristocracy, and the rising middle class who were securing the nation's "commercial and maritime" prosperity.

On the Continent, the sciences of sovereignty adjudicated, above all, between mechanism and vitalism, body and soul. If the human body and the body politic were mere machines, then they could be successfully disassembled and reconstructed with human tools. The spectacular failure of this approach to the state in the years of the Terror sent nervous physiologists—reasoning, at this political impasse, from macrocosm to microcosm—back to conceptions of a sacred, indivisible soul-force inhabiting the brain. During the first Bourbon restoration, organicist notions of royal sovereignty were underwritten by vitalist notions of the sovereign individual will.

In Britain, by contrast, the legacy of Hobbes and Willis manifested as an emphasis on security over liberty, on bodily intactness and avoidance of physical trauma. Since 1660, British monarchical rule had been accepted more as therapeutic necessity than as divine right, and the physiology of the body politic was aligned with conceptions of happiness, prosperity, and utility owing more to medicine than to theology. In 1789, the unworldly Tory radical Jeremy Bentham announced the government of his "two sovereign masters, *pain* and *pleasure*."[46] Like Hobbes, Bentham would go on to argue against revolution on the grounds of pain aversion. Here was the lesson of the neurology of regicide: by allowing the sanctity of kingship to be displaced by the absolute rule of delight and misery, the British sovereign was able to keep his head on his torso and his crown on his head.

Notes

1. Walter Scott, ed., *A Collection of Scarce and Valuable Tracts* (London: T. Cadell & W. Davis, 1812), 488.
2. Charles Stuart, *King Charls, His Tryal at the High Court of Justice* (London: Peter Cole, Francis Tyton & John Playford, 1650), 20.
3. Ibid., 58.
4. Ibid., 79–83.
5. Thomas Hobbes, *Leviathan* (Harmondsworth: Penguin, 1968), 118–30.
6. Edmond George Petty-Fitzmaurice Fitzmaurice, *The Life of Sir William Petty, 1623–1687 . . . Chiefly Derived from Private Documents Hitherto Unpublished* (London: J. Murray, 1895), 5–6.
7. Hobbes, *Leviathan*, 371.
8. Quentin Skinner, *Visions of Politics: Hobbes and Civil Science* (Cambridge: Cambridge University Press, 2002), 23.
9. Carl Zimmer, *The Soul Made Flesh: The Discovery of the Brain and How It Changed the World* (London: William Heinemann, 2004).
10. Thomas Sprat, *The History of the Royal-Society of London, for the Improving of Natural Knowledge* (London: Printed by T. R. for J. Martyn & J. Allestry, 1667), 53.
11. John Aubrey and John Britton, *The Natural History of Wiltshire* (London: J. B. Nichols & Son, 1847), 5.
12. Robert G. Frank, "Thomas Willis and His Circle: Brain and Mind in Seventeenth-Century Medicine," in G. S. Rousseau, *The Languages of Psyche: Mind and Body in Enlightenment Thought: Clark Library Lectures, 1985-1986* (Berkeley: University of California Press, 1990), 110.
13. Thomas Willis and Kenneth Dewhurst, *Willis's Oxford Casebook (1650-52)* (Oxford: Sandford, 1981), 49.
14. Ibid., 108.
15. Thomas Willis, *A Medical-Philosophical Discourse of Fermentation; or, Of the Intestine Motion of Particles in Every Body* (London: Printed for T. Dring, C. Harper, J. Leigh, & S. Martin, 1681), 86.
16. Thomas Willis, *Anatomy of the Brain and Nerves*, ed. William Feindel (Montreal: McGill University Press, 1965), 51–53.
17. Ibid., 53.
18. Ibid., 136, 147, 178, 182.
19. Ibid., 91.
20. Ibid., 93.
21. Ibid., 130. See Michael Hawkins, "A Great and Difficult Thing: Understanding and Explaining the Human Machine in Restoration England," in *Bodies/Machines*, ed. Iwan Rhys (Oxford: Berg, 2002), 15-38.
22. Willis, *Anatomy of the Brain and Nerves*, 83.
23. Emmanuel Sieyés, *Qu'est-ce que le Tiers Etat?* (Paris: Au siège de la société, 1888), 65.
24. Michael Walzer, *Regicide and Revolution: Speeches at the Trial of Louis XVI* (London: Cambridge University Press, 1974), 165.

25. Antoine de Baecque, *The Body Politic: Corporeal Metaphor in Revolutionary France, 1770–1800* (Stanford: Stanford University Press, 1997), 310.

26. Antoine de Baecque, *Le corps de l'histoire: Metaphores et politique (1770–1800)* (Paris: Calmann-Lévy, 1993), 376.

27. Ludmilla Jordanova, "Medical Mediations: Mind, Body and the Guillotine," *History Workshop Journal* 28, no. 1 (1989): 39–52.

28. Roland Borgards, " 'Kopf Ab': die Ziechen und die Zeit des Schmerzes in eine medizinischen Debatte um 1800 und Brentanos Kasper und Annerl," in *Romantische Wissenspoetik: Die Künste und die Wissenschaften um 1800*, ed. Gabriele Brandstetter and Gerhard Neumann (Würzburg: Koenigshausen & Neumann, 2004).

29. "Sur le supplice de la Guillotine," in P. J. G. Cabanis, *Oeuvres Complètes* (Paris: Bossanges, 1823), 2:165.

30. Ibid., 2:171.

31. Martin S. Staum, *Cabanis: Enlightenment and Medical Philosophy in the French Revolution* (Princeton: Princeton University Press, 1980), 287.

32. Claude Lehec and Jean Cazeneuve, eds., *Oeuvres philosophiques de Cabanis* (Paris: PUF, 1956), 2:465.

33. Medizinischen Privatgesellschaft zu Mainz, *Galvanische und elektrische Versuche an Menschen- und Tierkörpen* (Frankfurt am Main: Andreäischen Buchhandlung, [1804]); Gunter Mann, "Schinderhannes, Galvanismus und die experimentelle Medizin in Mainz um 1800," *Medizinhistorisches Journal* 12, no. 1 (1977): 21–80.

34. Medizinischen Privatgesellschaft zu Mainz, *Galvanische und elektrische Versuche*, ix.

35. Ibid., xiii.

36. Ibid., 4.

37. Ibid., 49. Scholars of etiquette may be interested to learn that a severed head is addressed using the informal "*du*."

38. Lehec and Cazeneuve, *Oeuvres philosophiques de Cabanis*, 2:286.

39. Jan Goldstein, *The Post-Revolutionary Self: Politics and Psyche in France, 1750–1850* (Cambridge, MA: Harvard University Press, 2005).

40. Pierre Flourens, *Phrenology Examined* (*Examen de la phrénologie*, 1824), trans. Charles D. Meigs (Philadelphia: Hogan & Thompson, 1846), 45.

41. Johannes Müller, *Handbuch der Physiologie des Menschen*, vol. 2 (Coblenz: J. Hölscher, 1840), 507.

42. Aldini composed the report in his own limpid English. See Andre Parent, "Giovanni Aldini, from Animal Electricity to Human Brain Stimulation," *Canadian Journal of Neurological Sciences* 31, no. 4 (2004): 576–84.

43. Giovanni Aldini, *An Account of the Late Improvements in Galvanism with a Series of Curious and Interesting Experiments Performed Before the Commission of the French National Institute and Repeated Lately in the Anatomical Theatres of London* (London: Cuthell & Martin, 1803), 189–90.

44. Ibid., 194.

45. Ibid., 190–91.

46. Jeremy Bentham, *An Introduction to the Principles of Morals and Legislation* (Oxford: Oxford University Press, 1996), 11.

TWELVE

The "Millennium" of 1857
The Last Performance of the Great Mughal

A. AZFAR MOIN

WHEN FRANÇOIS BERNIER, a French physician who spent the 1660s working and traveling across Mughal India, went to see the Taj Mahal for the last time, it was in the company of a recently arrived countryman. Bernier admitted that both of them were mesmerized by the monument but also confessed that he hesitated to express his admiration, "fearing that my taste might have become corrupted by my long residence in the Indies." We can imagine his relief when his compatriot, still very French in his tastes, exclaimed that "he had seen nothing in Europe so bold and majestic."[1] The majesty of the Taj Mahal is emblematic of the energy the Mughals poured into the art of imperial performance. Perhaps more than any other in the early modern era, their empire depended on an overwhelming enactment of sovereignty.

The aspect of "sovereignty" examined in this essay, which dwells not on the living institutions of the Mughal empire but on the enduring memory of Mughal kingship, stems from the "aesthetic conditioning" of the operations of political power, its reverberations through time in symbols and rituals, and the experience and imaginaries left in its wake. Put in the simplest terms, monarchs maintained their sovereignty by performing it. Parades, progress, festivals, feasts, hunts, games, cults, monuments—the generic list of royal rites and symbols is long. But it is variable. Some kings depended on ceremonial display more than others. Clifford Geertz may have given us the extreme case where sovereigns existed to perform themselves to their subjects—ritual *was* politics.[2] But monarchical dependence on performance was not always politics by other means—a way to compensate for the lack of political control and social reach. In the Mughal instance we have high ritual and triumphant symbolism coupled with unprecedented levels of military power, bureaucratic sophistication, and systematic extraction of wealth. To appreciate the particularity of the Mughal context, it would help to compare their empire to those of their contemporaries.

The Mughal emperors were commonly called "Mongol" by dint of their original ethnicity. They traced their sovereignty from two Inner Asian world conquerors, paternally from Tamerlane (or Timur, d. 1405) and maternally from Chinggis Khan (or Genghis Khan, d. 1221).[3] Although they were Muslim, and are usually mentioned in the same breath as other early modern Muslim empires—the neighboring Safavids of Iran and the Ottomans farther west—in their "steppe" heritage, their vast territory, their great wealth, and the number and diversity of their subjects, the Mughals merit a comparison with their Qing contemporaries in China, as Victor Lieberman has shown so assiduously in his landmark work on Eurasian history.[4]

Like the Mughals, the Qing dynasty was another ruling group of Inner Asian—in this case Manchu—origins that ruled over a realm of immense geographic and ethnic variety. Indeed, if one reads Jonathan D. Spence's imaginative self-portrait of the great Kangxi (r. 1661–1722), the Qing emperor as he circulated with his mobile court and army across China—warring, feasting, and struggling to bring order to an empire of bewildering complexity—one could easily mistake the words to be those of his Mughal contemporary, Aurangzeb the "World Seizer" (r. 1658–1707), in whose reign and employ Bernier saw much of India.[5]

But if the scale and complexity of their cultural geographies make the Mughal and the Qing cases comparable, the factors that set their imperial projects apart are equally telling. When the Qing conquered China, they inherited a functioning imperial system from their Ming predecessors. The new rulers slotted themselves into their empire by adopting Mandarin Chinese and Confucian ethics. This was both convenient and necessary, for the Qing possessed hundreds of thousands of Manchu horsemen but lacked a literate culture. By contrast, when the Mughals conquered sixteenth-century India, they had to fashion a coherent polity out of a multitude of kingdoms and inner frontiers. They did so by imposing a Perso-Islamic literate culture across sixteenth-century India and dealt with the confusion of tongues and scripts by using Persian as a uniform language of administration. In military terms, however, the initial strength of the Mughal cavalry was miniscule—ten thousand or so—compared to that of the Manchus. This is why the Mughals had to recruit at length from an array of Turkic, Persian, and Indic warrior groups with whom they bonded via marriage and other inventive institutions of religion and kinship. As a consequence, though, they ended up dissolving their Inner Asian ethnicity and military core and increased their dependency on local collaborators. The Qing made no such sacrifice. Even as they Sinicized themselves culturally, they maintained their distinction and raised high barriers against competitors by preserving their Manchu ethnicity, kinship lines, and military core.

Put simply, what the Qing took for granted, the Mughals had to invent, and what the former could retain, the latter had to give up. Unable to depend on ascriptive identities of kin and clan and an established imperial language and ethic, the Mughals had to devise prescriptive identities for themselves and their local allies and to impose an overarching language and code of conduct. Given the scale of their empire, this was a formidable obstacle—one that no previous empire in South Asian history had overcome. These unfavorable odds are why Victor Lieberman declares the Mughal realm as structurally unstable in comparison to Qing China. While this may be so, we can derive another insight from Lieberman's astute analysis. We can argue that the creative—and hence performative—burden of sovereignty on the Mughals was far greater than on the Qing. In other words, to make their cultural system function—to give their newly minted imperial identities and institutions the semblance of being eternal—the Mughals had to put into circulation a greater quantity of social energy.

Indeed, the deliberately constructed and newfangled style of Mughal sovereignty is what makes it appear so strange to modern eyes. But it felt unsettling even then to contemporary visitors from Europe. Western Christians were used to seeing their "absolute" monarch's authority circumscribed by the status and power of the church. When they arrived in India, they were astonished to find Muslim kings being treated as saintlike beings, above the distinctions of religion. This was the stunned reaction of the Jesuits who spent several decades at the Mughal court in close dialogue with Muslim savants. As the Jesuit reports were printed, translated, and widely circulated, their European audience could scarcely believe what they read about the sublime self-fashioning of the sons of "Tamburlaine."[6]

The Jesuits had been invited to the Mughal court in 1579 by the emperor Akbar (r. 1556–1605), who was at the height of his power. The wealthiest and most productive regions of the subcontinent were firmly under his authority. A new tax regime had begun to harvest the vast agricultural wealth of northern India and exchange it for New World silver.[7] Minor kings and frontier warlords could now acquire more wealth and status by fighting for the emperor, as salaried servants, than in attacks and raids on one another. Furthermore, these major shifts in society and politics were taking place at a moment of cosmic significance. It was the end of the Islamic millennium. Mughal astrologers and sages were scouring the cosmos for signs; they awaited the manifestation of a new sovereign, a being who would usher in a new cycle of time. At this juncture Akbar celebrated his imperial success with a grand enactment of sovereignty. He declared himself the saint of the age and his subjects his devotees.[8]

Among the court rituals unveiled at this time was the institution of devotion (*muridi*). On the face of it a voluntary organization, the imperial order of disciples inducted men from the court and the army who, as initiates, accepted the emperor as spiritually supreme, above their own life, honor, wealth, and religion. The rollout of the new institution caused controversy in Muslim court circles since it implied that Akbar was sacred above all religions, including Islam. Despite the criticism, imperial discipleship was instituted in Akbar's reign and continued by his son and successor, Jahangir. That this was meant to be an inclusive institution accessible to ambitious men of all ethnicities and religions from across the world can be seen in the initiation of Sir Thomas Roe, the English ambassador to the Mughal court during Jahangir's reign.[9] In his official account sent to England, Roe did not reveal that he had been inducted as an imperial disciple, but simply wrote that he had been honored by the emperor and given a coin-sized portrait of the sovereign. He did boast, however, that the Mughal emperor, in his fondness for the Englishman, had absolved him from the requirement to prostrate before the sovereign. What Roe had received was a talismanic image in which the sovereign was shown framed in a window (*jharoka*), to be venerated (*darshan*) ritually like a Hindu divinity.[10]

A generation after Jahangir, the institution of discipleship widened and transformed into one of ritual kinship. Officers—Hindu and Muslim—began to be incorporated as "sons of the imperial household." At the same time, the veneration of the emperor was enshrined in the numerous imperial palaces and their new halls of public audiences, which also contained a ritual window (*jharoka*) for the emperor's throne.[11]

The burden of Mughal art and architecture, produced on an immense scale in the first century of the empire, was to uphold these new rituals of imperial sovereignty in which the emperor was put on display as the most sacred being of the realm. Mughal artists took Catholic icons brought by the Jesuits as a model for encapsulating their sovereign's sacred nature. Mughal architecture incorporated white marble, traditionally reserved for sacred buildings and saint shrines. The ultimate result was the magnificent white edifice that we now call the Taj Mahal but then did not have a name. Perhaps this grandest of all buildings did not need a designation because, as the final word on all sacred monuments, imperial or saintly, it was meant to defy categories. As one art historian argues, Shah Jahan had built for himself the paradisiacal Throne of God.[12]

Today in South Asia the strongly enunciated and publicly articulated divinity of the Mughal emperors jars national and religious sensibilities of all types. Secular nationalists find the cultic nature of Mughal sovereigns distasteful. For Hindu nationalists, the emperors remain too Muslim even in their saintlike exaltedness. To Muslim nationalists and Islamists, the Mughals appear unfathomably deviant in their transgression of Islamic norms, not the least of which was marriage to unconverted Hindu princesses. It is far easier, thus, to neglect the performative achievements of the Mughal sovereigns and instead focus on their political deeds. But if one puts modern distastes aside and pays heed to the historical circumstances that shaped the distinctive style of Mughal sovereignty—circumstances that set the political culture of Mughal India on a markedly different trajectory than that of Christian Europe or Confucian China—it becomes clear how successfully the Mughals launched a "social drama"[13] of sovereignty that shaped the nature of politics long after their empire had crumbled under its own weight.

The regional polities that replaced the Mughal realm were built on Mughal customs, and a majority of them functioned for nearly a century as if the "real" sovereign was still the emperor. This was, again, an unprecedented situation in South Asian history. When previous empires had disintegrated their rulers disappeared with them. In the Mughal case, however, the monarchy survived imperial dissolution and continued to play a key role in the theater of sovereignty. Why?

Here it is worth turning to a theoretical distinction between "ceremony" and "ritual" made by the anthropologist Victor Turner in his work on social drama.[14] Ceremony, for Turner, consists of collective acts that follow a coherent script. Ceremony is indicative—it "says" what is—and, hence, it is predictable. Ritual, by contrast, is ambiguously scripted. It is subjunctive—it also "says" what might be—and, hence, holds the seeds of social change. Especially in complex and hierarchical societies, social drama—the public evocation and collective enactment of a ritual scheme—should not be dismissed as ceremonial display. Rather, it must be examined for its transformative potential. If enacted energetically enough, Turner argues, social drama has the ability to ritually dismember and re-member society—it can create a new social order and the memory to sustain it. This was precisely the effect of the powerful new rites, symbols, and monuments with which the Mughals set their empire in motion in the sixteenth and seventeenth centuries. Theirs was not a monotonous, unchanging ceremonial order but a dialogic, evolving ritual process, one that adapted with every instantiation even as it forced its participants to adapt.[15]

By the time Bernier arrived in India, the Mughal ritual process had delivered strong results. The empire had developed a self-sustaining cultural logic that carried along with it both sovereign and subject. When the last of the "great" Mughal emperors, the Islam-inclined Aurangzeb, tried to change the script of his sovereign theater, he was, for the most part, ignored—by his sons, his allies, and his enemies, who continued to pretend as if the previous order was still in play.[16] After Aurangzeb's death, the pretense became permanent as the empire broke up into successor states that continued to act as "governors" of the Mughal sovereign. When the British entered Indian politics in the eighteenth century, they found themselves entangled in this "deep play" of sovereignty. They too adorned the robe of Mughal governorship in Bengal.

It is difficult to appreciate today the incongruity of the East India Company's situation: the world's first joint-stock corporation—the budding essence of capitalist modernity—had embraced the most divine of monarchies. Yet it is a testament to the endurance of the Mughal ritual theater that the British played their part for nearly a century. And, at the very end, when they were ready to draw the curtains, the British discovered much to their horror that the Mughal emperor had one last act left in him. It is to view this performance that we now turn.

The Mutiny of 1857

In 1757 the English East India Company, with help from Indian merchant groups, defeated the last Mughal governor of Bengal and became its de facto ruler. Within a decade, on the basis of another military victory, it negotiated from the Mughal emperor a formal and highly lucrative authority to collect taxes in what was the richest province of the empire. In exchange it agreed to send an annual tribute. By assuming the role of Mughal vassal to seal its political status, the company acted like many of the other regional South Asian powers in the eighteenth century. Gradually but relentlessly, it outspent, outfought, and outmaneuvered its political competitors. In 1803, when the company gained control over Delhi, it also assumed the responsibility of maintaining and protecting the Mughal emperor. This arrangement lasted for more than five decades, during which the company managed to eliminate or defang all its major rivals. However, in 1857, with their political and military hold over the subcontinent complete, a massive rebellion erupted among the company's own Indian soldiers. This violent episode, which nearly brought British rule in India to an end, became known as the Great Indian Mutiny.

The uprising of 1857, which spread throughout north and central India and raged for more than a year, did not have one central cause or unified strategy behind it. The episode began with a mutiny among the Indian soldiers of the company's Bengal Army. Some regional powers, especially those who had recently lost their dominion to English conquest, like the Maratha leader Nana Sahib, or were soon to lose it to the company's policies, like the Rani of Jhansi, also joined in. That there were so many motives and grievances behind the uprising made it politically incoherent and ultimately led to its failure. What is surprising, and still not properly understood or examined, is that the key symbol around which the diverse rebel groups rallied was the octogenarian Mughal emperor, Bahadur Shah Zafar.[17]

That Bahadur Shah's sole interest and chief accomplishment was classical Urdu poetry did not stop the rebels from declaring him their leader when they captured Delhi. When the English finally managed to crush the rebellion after severe losses and considerable savagery, they too held him accountable. During his trial, they charged him with leading an Islamic conspiracy against the British—a conspiracy with tentacles reaching out to Iran, Mecca, and the Ottoman Empire.[18] This was an odd accusation, as even a few contemporary Englishmen observed, since most of the rebel soldiers were upper-caste Hindus. The English prosecutor insisted, however, that the gestures made by the rebels to the rulers of Iran to invade India were proof of an international plot, and the fact that a few years before the mutiny a group of soldiers had formally requested to become disciples (*murids*) of the emperor showed that he had harbored ambitions to become a champion of Islam.[19]

The old emperor initially protested. He presented a short written explanation of his innocence. It stated that he had been powerless in the face of events and that his seal and signature had been indiscriminately used by rebel soldiers to issue orders without his permission or advice. Having made his case, he reconciled himself to nod through the remainder of the proceedings, not in apparent agreement but in fitful slumber. It was just as well because at the end of the farcical trial, Bahadur Shah was found guilty of all charges and exiled to Burma along with a handful of male and female family members who had survived the war and English retribution.

The Question of Sovereignty

In 1922, F. W. Buckler, a learned but unconventional historian of India, offered a controversial assessment of the Mughal emperor's trial. He pointed out that "if in 1857 there was any mutineer, it was the East India Company."[20] His assertion was based on the observation that the company had been a Mughal vassal de jure. This was a legal fiction the company had maintained for over a century by submitting itself to customs of Mughal kingship. However, in the years before the rebellion the English had begun to neglect the ritual privileges due the emperor. Thus, Buckler argued, "the army turned to its sovereign's allegiance against its rebel officer"—that is, the company. In strictly legal terms, the emperor and his men were in the right, Buckler insisted; it was the English who were the transgressors.

It should come as no surprise that Buckler's argument was roundly criticized by his fellow English historians as naïvely idealistic and wholly ignorant of social and political reality.[21] This may be so. But it has to be said in the eccentric historian's defense that some of the alternative explanations offered by his critics were no less whimsical. One English historian in his reply to Buckler argued that the mutiny was not, as the latter had suggested, a Muslim attempt to reclaim the dignity of their sovereign but rather it "was really the outcome of that fundamental Hindu antagonism to Western civilization and Western materialism, which in more recent times has formed one of the mainsprings of anarchical conspiracies and non-co-operation movements."[22] In other words, Buckler's chief fault was that his historical fancies ran counter to the colonial fancies of his contemporaries.

In any event, the enduring value of Buckler's scholarship was not in his grand explanation of historical causes but in the fresh interpretations he offered of the traditions and customs of Mughal sovereignty.[23] He noted that the company had maintained its ritual subordination to the body of the emperor by presenting offerings (*nazr*) upon gaining a royal audience and accepting robes of honor (*khil'at*) at least until 1843, when it abandoned these practices. Around this time, the company had begun to shed the cumbersome pretense of being subordinate to a man who had become in English eyes little more than a tourist attraction. Even as an attraction, the company kept the Mughal ruler in too impoverished a state to be presentable. One unimpressed English visitor to the emperor in 1838 had noted in his diary that the Mughal ruler was nothing but a "dirty, miserable old dog."[24]

This English disregard for Mughal traditions of sovereignty did not, as Buckler had insisted, create a legal breach of contract sufficient by itself to inspire Indian soldiers to revolt. However, it was highly symptomatic of a growing English disconnect from and disregard for Indian society. The decades leading up to 1857 had seen widespread social and economic transformation in many segments of agrarian society, and the colonial government had paid too little attention to the implications of these shifts for Indians, elite and commoner alike. The English had lost their affective connection to local knowledge. As C. A. Bayly has argued, an increasingly distant and unsympathetic attitude had by the middle of the nineteenth century made the colonial government tone deaf to India's "information order."[25] In the language of sacred kingship, it was as if the rulers had lost their ability to see the symptoms of distress and signs of disorder spreading through the body politic. The English were not listening when holy men began to dream and astrologers began to predict that the rule of the "Franks" was to last no longer than a hundred years, that it had begun in 1757 and so would end in 1857.

A Mutiny of Knowledges

The colonial archives on the uprising of 1857 contain a number of rebel pamphlets and letters that were collected for intelligence purposes or used as trial evidence. These artifacts preserve a "messianic" worldview that is strikingly similar to the one that had informed the institution and practice of sacred kingship in the classical Mughal period. They are full of signs, omens, and prophecies against the English. In these documents, the company was accused not of illegally usurping territory and political authority but rather of perverting India's moral order and upsetting its cosmological balance. According to this view, the earthly effects of this disturbance were being felt and seen all around, and the war was nothing less than a cosmically ordained corrective action.

One document, for example, contains a long history-prophecy of the world that predicted the end of English rule after a hundred years, followed by the rise of the Messiah and the end of time.[26] While the original document was in Persian verse, it survived only in a partial English translation made a few years after 1857. The translated section of the prophecy begins with the rise of Timur and continues through the reigns of his descendants in India, the decline of Mughal power, the rise of the Sikh empire, the coming of the English. It then predicts the imminent rise of the "Western King" (Shah Ghurbee) who would come from the west, presumably Afghanistan or Iran, and defeat the English in battle. The prophecy had apparently been printed in Delhi a few months before 1857 and was attributed to Shah Ni'matullah, a fifteenth-century Persian saint widely acknowledged as the "Nostradamus of the East."[27] The English officer who translated this prophecy described its international significance and political danger to his superiors as follows:

> The House of Timour no doubt had a good deal to say to the printing and circulation of the Prophecy, and through the influence of the late Kings of Delhi, it must have found its way into Afghanistan, and Persia, and the Furruchabad Nawab (Taffussool Hosain Khan) no doubt carried a copy with him to Mecca. This Prophecy in the hands of able men (Mahommedans) well versed in intrigue, is likely to do an immense amount of mischief in British India.[28]

In an insightful analysis of such rebel communiqués, Bayly observed that these texts represented a "mutiny of subordinated knowledges."[29] He showed that this form of political communication and those who had wielded it had been rapidly marginalized in nineteenth-century British India. The uprising of 1857, from this perspective, was as much a rebellion against an oppressive epistemology as it was against economic and political exploitation. We must add, however, that this insurgency of knowledges was also the last great sigh of the Mughal world in which sacred sovereignty was conceived of as messianic and millennial.

This cultural logic can be seen clearly at work in a long pamphlet issued from the rebel camp, entitled "Advice of the Royal Army." This mutinous document also contained references to the prophecies of Shah Ni'matullah, and it too began its justification of war against the English in explicitly millenarian terms: "Now the astrologers have ascertained and the Englishmen are convinced of the fact that their rule is not to last longer than one hundred years."[30]

The Advice of the Royal Army

Although written under the exigencies of war, the "Advice of the Royal Army" was a document designed to engage the imagination and excite the passions of its audience, "brethren in the faith throughout India, Hindoos as well as Mussulmans [Muslims], whomsoever God has exalted" (489). Like its audience, the pamphlet's authorship also transcended communal boundaries. It was produced under the authority of a Hindu leader, Kishori Lal Lahori. But it was composed by a Muslim scribe, Shaykh Said, whose flair for storytelling was proudly proclaimed in his nom de plume, Colorful Pen (*rangin raqam*). Indeed, much of the pamphlet was written in the entertaining and didactic style of a popular narrator or street preacher.

The pamphleteers acknowledged the stressful conditions under which they had prepared this document: "in camp during the confusion of a march and without having the proper printing materials at hand" (733). The hurried and unrevised nature of the document is evident in its jumbled organization, repetitions, digressions and confused juxtapositions of pious anecdotes, rousing verses, passionate pleas, and exhortations to fight. In its rough-hewn state, however, it preserves the voices and feelings of the rebellious soldiers in their diversity—brave and fearful, determined and wavering, hopeful and desperate.

The pamphleteers began by giving their former masters credit where it was due. The English had ruled successfully, they noted, as long as they had kept their promises, performed public service, built roads, maintained security, and administered justice. However, after they were defeated in Kabul—a reference assumedly to the first Anglo-Afghan war (1839–1842)—they had decided to "efface the religion of Muhammad." This effacement occurred not only through proselytizing Christian missionaries, the pamphlet implied, but via techniques of bodily pollution and miscegenation designed to corrupt the Indian body politic. Missionary schools had served to corrupt Muslim and Hindu children (495). Hundreds of Englishmen had seduced "females of Indian households" and sired many half-caste children. Women were given undue liberty. Historical texts were printed to heap contempt on Muslims and Hindus (497). Medicines had been mixed with cow fat, wine, and other forbidden things. Such actions could not be ignored. Thus, when an English doctor gargled into a bottle and gave it to a soldier as medicine, the soldier complained to his colleagues. They killed the doctor and burned his bungalow (499).

In the same vein, the pamphlet emphasized how under the English, the entire socio-moral order of India was being turned upside down. Indians were being incited away from their religions and social norms and turned into Christians and made to behave like Europeans. It maintained that in Lahore the English wanted to convert every Sikh to a Christian (499). The entire company army was to be made Christian (499–501). Instead of respectable Hindu and Muslim scholars, the company had appointed "low caste" converts to Christianity to courts of justice (503).

As part of the same effort, the English had also encouraged indecency and fornication (505). Wives who were not satisfied could now leave their husbands. Veiled women were required to appear in court (507). When a brother attacked his sister's lover to avenge family honor, he was imprisoned for years while the sister was set free to do as she pleased (509). In a reference to the latest instance of English conquest, that of the Punjab, the pamphlet noted that the company not only took the kingdom away from the reigning queen (*rani*) but also took her son and converted him to Christianity (515). A similar scheme was at work, it implied, when the English gave their Indian soldiers rifle cartridges made with pig and cow fat—a widely recognized source of the rebellion. The governor general, the pamphlet insisted, had devised this cartridge to Christianize all of Hindustan (517).

After relating in great detail the extent of social disorder and moral corruption spreading across the land, the pamphlet turned to describing its consequences. Holy men began to see visions of what was to come. One man who had constantly offered prayers prescribed by Ali saw the following vision: a hawk pounced on a group of paddy birds in a field and slit their throats; another group of paddy birds appeared and the hawk did the same thing. The English are the paddy birds, the pamphlet explained, and the Indian soldiers fighting them are the hawk. Similarly, in another dream, a man who had memorized the entire Qur'an (*hafiz*) saw that the second caliph Umar was conducting prayers at congregation mosque (*jami' masjid*) in Delhi (555). These dreams featuring Ali and Umar, symbols of Shi'ism and Sunnism, it should be noted, were meant to address a broad range of Muslims. But the pamphlet constantly emphasized throughout its narrative that its message was meant to be even broader: "In India there are two tribes Hindoo and Mussulman and neither of them feel disposed to embrace Christianity. Each is determined to uphold his respected faith" (527).

The pamphleteers pleaded that "with tears in our eyes" they had used many devices to correct these wrongs, but not one was successful. At last, a holy man dreamed that all the saints of God were assembled in front of the Prophet and complained against the oppression of the English. The Prophet, in response, took his Indian (Hindi) sword from the waist of Christ and entrusted it to his companion Umar. In this way, the pamphlet implied, the Prophet of Islam took the sovereignty over India away from Christians and gave it back to his own followers. This vision strengthened the rebels' resolve to uphold their faith and embrace death rather than "obey this race of unclean barbarians whose food is pork and wine and whose habit is lust and fornication" (555).

The imagery and language used in the pamphlet was Islamic but also universally designed to appeal to Indians of all faiths. It related the omens and auguries from well-known Muslim and Persian sources—the Qur'an, the poetry of Hafiz (d. 1390), and the mystical verses of Shah Ni'matullah (d. 1431)—to prove that English rule was fated to come to an end after a hundred years (557-59, 495). But it also maintained that these signs and prophecies were meaningful to both Hindus and Muslims. It accused the English of proscribing the use of the Islamic formula *Bismillah* (By the Name of God) even in children's books, while noting that both Hindus and Muslims used it (499). Moreover, it observed the harmful consequences for the English when they stopped using this formula: it became easier for the soldiers to kill them (599).

The pamphlet also used well-known cultural differences among Hindus and Muslims to good effect. For example, in an attempt to dismiss the soldiers' fears that the English possessed powers of sorcery, it offered three observations: First, it suggested, what appeared to be magic was typically a technical malfunction such as the "hang firing" of an incorrectly loaded cannon; second, if the English possessed magical power, it replied, then Hindus wielded it too; and, third, although Muslims considered magic forbidden, it pointed out, they used powerful techniques to negate its powers (597–605). The pamphlet then listed a series of Qur'anic verses, prayers, and incantations that would annul the effect of sorcery. The implication was that with such complementary abilities, Hindus and Muslims could perform their own magic and render useless that of the English. In this vein, the pamphleteers also cautioned the soldiers that rather than attribute their defeats to English magic, they should blame them on their own sins of looting and disobedience.

It was with such an outlook in which magic, sin, and the will of holy men shaped the outcome of events that the pamphlet narrated how the last Mughal king was reinstated and empowered by the rebel soldiers. This event was preceded by the following miraculous occurrence (563–67). A poor water carrier (*bihishti*) in Delhi was on the steps of the congregational mosque (*jami' masjid*) when he was drawn to a mysterious green glow nearby. He discovered that it was coming from the shrine of the Sufi saint Sarmad, buried near the mosque. Sarmad, it should be noted, was a famous seventeenth-century Sufi of Persian-Armenian origin best known for his mockery of formal religious doctrines. He described himself as a "follower of the Furqan (i.e., a Sufi), a (Hindu) priest, a (Buddhist) monk, a Jewish rabbi, an infidel, and an apostate Muslim,"[31] and the Mughal emperor Aurangzeb had sentenced him to death for apostasy. It is no accident that in this moment of crises, a holy man such as Sarmad was needed to miraculously overcome communal divisions.

According to the pamphlet, a hand came out of the mound at Sarmad's shrine and gave the water carrier a set of gold coins. A voice told him that these coins would lead him to the king and gave him a message for the Mughal ruler: "I have now freely pardoned the shedding of my blood. Up to this day my wrath has been boiling and in spite of intercession of the saints it has never grown less till now. Now, I freely and of my own accord grant an absolute pardon." When the water carrier tried to use the gold coins, he was arrested by the authorities on suspicion of theft. He was eventually brought in front of the Mughal king and so managed to give him the saint's message. The story implied that the saint had absolved the Mughal ruler for his ancestor's crime of shedding the Sufi's blood. This absolution cleared the path for the Mughal to become a true sovereign again. Soon after this incident, the pamphlet recorded, the rebels entered Delhi and put the king on the throne.

Not only were the saints of yore aiding the rebels' efforts. Present-day ones were also actively involved in defeating the English. The pamphlet related the following ongoing miracle featuring a black-clad messianic figure (679–81). A prediction had been made that a mendicant (*faqir*) in a black blanket would take over the English Fort William in Calcutta. When the English found a man of such a description near the fort, they arrested and imprisoned him. However, he disappeared, and now every Friday the sound of Muslim call to prayers (*azan*) came from the chapel in the fort. When the time was right, the pamphlet announced, this man would appear and wrest control of the fort away from the English.

Not all of the rebels' views were mystical and miraculous, however. They listed many of their complaints with historical precision and political pragmatism. They noted that the English via their "regulations" wanted to eliminate them as Christians had eliminated Muslims in Spain (653). They posed the question of why it was that the English had no influence in Rum (the Ottoman Empire) but so much in India (683–85). They provided a tabulated count of the Europeans they had killed (691). They compiled a list of grievances against the English to be sent to the kings of Iran, China, and other territories (693–729). They noted how the company had unilaterally broken its decades-long agreement with the kingdom of Awadh, and how they were trying to get the shah of Awadh to affix his seal to a deed of satisfaction to hide their legal transgressions (703).

In reading the pamphlet, however, one gets the sense that despite their historical awareness and political astuteness, what deeply puzzled the rebels was the nature of the company's sovereignty. How was it that a commercial, bureaucratic entity could take the place of a king? The company, in their eyes, did not behave as an organization subordinate to a sovereign. They wondered about the state of affairs in England itself. The queen of England, the pamphleteers reported, had become a debauched and helpless creature (575–77). They said that Victoria was not allowed see her own husband because he was suspected of harboring French loyalties; she was, instead, serviced by an Ethiopian boy who wanted to whisk her away to Africa. Indeed, the pamphleteers remarked, the company was plotting to take her kingdom just as they had stolen the kingdoms of India. Kingship was dying not only in India but also in England. It truly was the end of the world!

Buckler was right in a sense when he pointed out that the company's growing insults to Mughal sovereignty had caused the Indian soldiers to come to their emperor's defense. The relationship between cause and effect, however, was not as legally determined or politically transparent as Buckler had imagined it to be. It was not a breach of law or a sense of loyalty to old Bahadur Shah that turned the Indian soldiers and their compatriots against the English. Rather, it was a deeply and collectively felt perversion—felt as bodily pollution, social disorder, and cosmic chaos—at the new sovereign order ushered in by the company. It felt like the anarchy of the millennium. Social life was no longer governed by sacred traditions. Sexual relations were cut loose from the necessities of kinship ties. Taboos of pollution were publicly and forcibly flouted. Most seriously of all, a series of "regulations" had replaced the body of the sovereign as the basis of social order. The Great Indian Mutiny was, among other things, a rebellion against an inexplicable and unbearable dispensation that constituted, to use Foucault's aphoristic phrase, "sex without the law and power without the king."[32]

Notes

1. François Bernier, *Travels in the Mogul Empire*, ed. Vincent A. Smith, trans. Archibald Constable, 2nd ed. (New Delhi: Low Price Publications, 1989), 295. This anecdote from Bernier is also quoted in Ebba Koch, *Mughal Architecture: An Outline of Its History and Develoment (1526-1858)* (Munich: Prestel, 1991), 7.
2. Clifford Geertz, "Centers, Kings, and Charisma," in *Local Knowledge* (New York: Basic Books, 1983), 129–34.
3. The Central and Inner Asian heritage of the Mughals is traced in detail in Lisa Balabanlilar, *Imperial Identity in Mughal India: Memory and Dynastic Politics in Early Modern South and Central Asia* (London: Tauris, 2011).
4. The comparison in this essay between the Mughals and the Qing depends on Victor B. Lieberman, *Strange Parallels: Southeast Asia in Global Context, c. 800-1830*, vol. 2 (New York: Cambridge University Press, 2009), 709–12, 38–46.

5. Jonathan D. Spence, *Emperor of China: Self Portrait of K'ang Hsi* (New York: Vintage, 1975).

6. The history of the early Jesuit experience at the Mughal court is found in Pierre Du Jarric, *Akbar and the Jesuits*, trans. Charles Herbert Payne (London: Routledge-Curzon, 2005).

7. John F. Richards, "Mughal State Finance and the Premodern World Economy," *Comparative Studies in Society and History* 23, no. 2 (1981): 285–308.

8. A. Azfar Moin, *The Millennial Sovereign: Sacred Kingship and Sainthood in Islam* (New York: Columbia University Press, 2012), 130–69.

9. John F. Richards, "The Formulation of Imperial Authority Under Akbar and Jahangir," in *Kingship and Authority in South Asia*, ed. John F. Richards (Delhi: Oxford University Press, 1998), 285–326.

10. The role of painting in Mughal rituals is discussed in Moin, *Millennial Sovereign*, 189–210.

11. Ibid., 215–24.

12. Wayne E. Begley, "The Myth of the Taj Mahal and a New Theory of Its Symbolic Meaning," *Art Bulletin* 61, no. 1 (1979): 7–37.

13. For the concept of social drama, see Victor W. Turner, *From Ritual to Theatre: The Human Seriousness of Play* (New York: Performing Arts Journal Publications, 1982), 61–88.

14. Ibid., 80–81.

15. The Mughal imperial culture of having princes compete for the throne put into play such transformative processes and kept the system flexible and adaptive. Munis Daniyal Faruqui, *Princes of the Mughal Empire, 1504-1719* (Cambridge: Cambridge University Press, 2012).

16. Moin, *Millennial Sovereign*, 233–39.

17. For a sense of the discourse in which the Mughal emperor was used as a unifying symbol that transcended religious difference and treated as the "real" sovereign, see Nupur Chaudhuri and Rajat Kanta Ray, " 'We' and 'They' in an Altered Ecumene: The Mutiny from the Mutineer's Mouths," in *Mutiny at the Margins: New Perspectives on the Indian Uprising of 1857*, vol. 5, *Muslim, Dalit and Subaltern Narratives*, ed. Crispin Bates (Los Angeles: Sage, 2014), 36–48, 39. For a comprehensive overview of the latest arguments on the rebellion of 1857, see all seven volumes of *Mutiny at the Margins*.

18. My account of the trial of the emperor follows the one in William Dalrymple, *The Last Mughal: The Fall of a Dynasty, Delhi, 1857* (London: Bloomsbury, 2006), 435–41.

19. Ibid., 441.

20. F. W. Buckler, "The Political Theory of the Indian Mutiny," in *Legitimacy and Symbols: The South Asian Writings of F. W. Buckler*, ed. M. N. Pearson (Ann Arbor: Center for South and Southeast Asian Studies, University of Michigan, 1985), 46. This essay was first published as F. W. Buckler, "The Political Theory of the Indian Mutiny," *Transactions of the Royal Historical Society (London)* 5 (1922): 71–100.

21. S. M. Edwardes, "A Few Reflections on Buckler's Political Theory of the Indian Mutiny," in Pearson, *Legitimacy and Symbols*, 75–84; Douglas Dewar and H. L.

Garrett, "A Reply to Mr. F. W. Buckler's *The Political Theory of the Indian Mutiny*," in ibid., 85–113.

22. Edwardes, "Buckler's Political Theory," 79.

23. See, e.g., Buckler's critical remarks on the theory of "Oriental despot" prevalent in his days and his insightful reworking of this theory based on rituals of embodiment and incorporation. F. W. Buckler, "The Oriental Despot," in Pearson, *Legitimacy and Symbols*, 176–87. His contribution was reviewed and acknowledged in Stewart Gordon, ed., *Robes of Honour: Khil'at in Pre-colonial and Colonial India* (New Delhi: Oxford University Press, 2003), 1–30. Also see Bernard S. Cohn, *Colonialism and Its Forms of Knowledge: The British in India* (Princeton: Princeton University Press, 1996), 114.

24. Dewar and Garrett, "Reply to Buckler's *Political Theory*," 156.

25. C. A. Bayly, *Empire and Information: Intelligence Gathering and Social Communication in India, 1780-1870* (Cambridge: Cambridge University Press, 1996), 315–37.

26. "Documents from the Collections of Sir George Forrest, C.I.E.: Miscellaneous documents (1746–1859): Seditious Proclamation Issued During the Mutiny, a Muhammadan Prophecy of the Expulsion of the English," British Library, London, IOR/H/814.

27. Hamid Algar and J. Burton-Page, "Ni'mat-allahiyya," in *The Encyclopaedia of Islam*, 2nd ed., ed. P. Bearman et al. (Leiden: Brill, 2011); Edward G. Browne, *A Literary History of Persia*, 4 vols. (Cambridge: University Press, 1929), 3:465.

28. "Documents from the Collections of Sir George Forrest," 469.

29. He borrows the phrase from Foucault. See Bayly, *Empire and Information*, 330.

30. "Sir John Kaye's Mutiny Papers (1857–1858): Translation of 'Advice of the Royal Army,' a Pamphlet in the Handwriting of Shaikh Said Rungin Rakam 15th Sept. 1857, a Justification of the Mutiny After the One Hundred Years Rule of the English," British Library, London, IOR/H/727, 491. Subsequent page references given in text. This document is also briefly analyzed in Bayly, *Empire and Information*, 330–31.

31. Nathan Katz, "The Identity of a Mystic: The Case of Sa'id Sarmad, a Jewish-Yogi-Sufi Courtier of the Mughals," *Numen* 47, no. 2 (2000): 142–60.

32. Michel Foucault, *The History of Sexuality* (New York: Vintage, 1990), 1:91.

THIRTEEN

Exit the King?

Modern Theater and the Revolution

NICOLE JERR

Revolution in the Theater

IN HIS PHILOSOPHICAL treatise *Rhapsody for the Theatre*, Alain Badiou goes so far as to say that "great theatre of the revolution is so rare . . . we must conclude that the theatre avoids the revolution."[1] Badiou's complaint is that theater has not explicitly taken up historical revolutionary events as its subject matter. Failing to find the French Revolution on stage, he continues to search: "Is there," he asks, "a truly convincing Russian theatre with 1917 as its subject matter? A Chinese theatre on the sequence 1923–49? There are books, poems, movies, nobody will doubt that. But has the theatre, grand theatre, gone this way?"[2] Setting aside both Badiou's dogmatic standard of historical representation—the absence of blatant historical referents in a staged work of art hardly seems damning—as well as his assertion that theater's unwillingness to stage these revolutionary events is a manifestation of its alignment with the state, the general charge still carries force: theater avoids the revolution. What rankles about this imputation is that modern theater is understood to be, precisely, a theater of revolution, a "theater of revolt" (as it has been classically dubbed by Robert Brustein in his book by that title).[3] The long list of assorted avant-garde movements that constitute modern theater—symbolism, futurism, expressionism, surrealism, epic theater, theater of cruelty, theater of the absurd—whatever their particular preoccupations, these movements hold in common a spirit of rebellion, an emphasis on breaking with conventions. Individually and collectively, these movements constitute an aesthetic revolution, with parallels in other modernist arts, and closely tied, of course, to the political, theological, and social revolutions that mark late modernity. How, then, could theater be troubled by the revolution?

In this essay I explore certain complex contours and limits of the relationship between theater and revolution. To be sure, provocative examples of revolution do show up on the modern stage, and I consider two such plays: Alfred Jarry's *Ubu roi* (1896) and, at much greater length, Eugène Ionesco's *Macbett* (1972). It turns out that both plays, by two of modern theater's most significant avant-garde playwrights, "avoid the revolution" even as they stage revolution, providing compelling clues toward a more nuanced understanding of the interrelations at work between theater and revolution and, by extension, between theater and sovereignty.

As Badiou's several historical examples of "the revolution" indicate, it is a *certain* revolution missing in the theater: the revolution from absolute sovereignty to popular sovereignty. And yet, arguably the most significant, furthest reaching, and seemingly incontrovertible aesthetic revolution in the modern theater is the shift from royal protagonists to the common individual. This transfer of attention is the rallying cry within Arthur Miller's *Death of a Salesman*, where Linda says of her husband: "I don't say he's a great man. Willie Loman never made a lot of money. His name was never in the paper. He's not the finest character that ever lived. But he's a human being, and a terrible thing is happening to him. So attention must be paid . . . Attention, attention must finally be paid to such a person."[4] No longer bound to an interpretation of Aristotle that seems to call for tragedies to focus on characters from a privileged class, modern drama overwhelmingly relates the stories of those who had been sidelined in ancient and renaissance drama: bourgeois housewives, salesmen, peasants, and the disenfranchised. Broadly speaking, domestic concerns receive more stage time than matters of state, and the fates of citizens and soldiers receive more attention than those of the rulers and leaders.

The indisputable fact of this revolution notwithstanding, the adjustment in attention was not spontaneously achieved, nor was it as unalloyed as theater history accounts tend to portray it. Consider, for example, that even in *Death of a Salesman*, Willy Loman's son, Biff, insists, "You've just seen a prince walk by. A fine, troubled prince. A hard-working, unappreciated prince."[5] The

loaded invocation reveals at the very least a desire to make associations between the royal and the common person on the elementary linguistic level.
But just what this desire signifies is far from self-evident, particularly in an
American play, where, politically, royalism is anathema. Making it all the
more intriguing, this gesture toward sovereign figuration is hardly a rare
instance on the modern stage.

Indeed, despite the political trend away from monarchical rule, and
despite modern theater's deliberate and celebrated replacement of noble
characters by ordinary individuals, kings and queens not only survive in
modern drama, they conspicuously thrive—as evidenced by sovereign figures in works by influential playwrights as various in their political and
artistic commitments as Ibsen, Jarry, Yeats, Shaw, Pirandello, Eliot, O'Neill,
Anouilh, Genet, Brecht, Beckett, and Ionesco. In this way, drama, perhaps
more so than any other artistic genre, seems to have decided that the stage
direction "Exit the King" is optional.[6] As my brief list indicates, while hardly
uniform in tone or image, sovereignty has been staged and thematized within
the many avant-garde movements of modern drama, and by some of its most
exceptional playwrights, opening an important set of questions. What purpose do sovereign figures serve in modern drama? Are they put on stage only
to be dismantled? Is there something about theater that cannot do without
a sovereign? And how is it that theater historians have missed this counterrevolutionary tension?

Conveniently marking the rough chronological parameters of modern
drama (1896, 1972), both Jarry's *Ubu roi* and Ionesco's *Macbett* take their plot
cues from Shakespeare's *Macbeth*, allowing for comparison of modern theater's handling of revolution at the opening and close of this period. The
plays are significant for their farcical interpretations of Shakespeare's tragedy, generically demonstrating theater's ability to complicate the discourse
on sovereignty by introducing an ambivalence toward the notion of sovereignty understood narrowly in terms of force and might. But neither play is
content with simply generating laughter about political power and mock-
ing its potential for abuse. On the contrary, Jarry's fin-de-siècle play, as I will
briefly outline, introduces a set of concerns relating to the shift to popular
sovereignty that Ionesco's *Macbett* develops both more robustly and more
subtly, revealing some of modern theater's complex stakes in sovereignty.
For both playwrights, *personal sovereignty* emerges as a crucial but seldom
probed dimension of the shift from absolute to popular sovereignty. Rather

than understanding the shift in strictly political terms, modern theater draws attention to the responsibilities and burdens of sovereignty the common individual inherits. Indeed, in prioritizing the individual, modern theater reminds its audience that personal sovereignty underwrites the political structure as an indispensable element of its scaffolding.

Revolutionary Beginnings: The Crowd and Jarry's *Ubu roi*

The December 1896 premiere of *Ubu roi* at the Théâtre de l'Oeuvre is typically heralded as *the* theatrical event that ushered in many of the various forms of avant-garde theater. Theater history has delighted in the story of the uproar and mayhem on the opening night of the play, a charged beginning to an unmistakably new era in theater. *Ubu roi*—with its crude, craven, and raunchy sovereign wielding a toilet brush for a scepter—gave birth to far more than the sum of its swaggering, soiled parts. To be sure, Jarry's primary contribution is to be found in his comprehensive aesthetic challenge to the theater rather than strictly in the narrative content of *Ubu roi* (and my attention will be directed accordingly), yet the plot is what discloses a king who gets away—not only with copious scatological references but also with tyrannical atrocities. A rather obvious way to understand Jarry's choice of rank for Ubu is the contrast provided between the elevated position and the base person holding it. The disparity unmistakably heightens the comedic effect, but a study of the role of Ubu's sovereignty makes it clear that Jarry's artistic goals cannot be limited in any simple way to parody and antagonism.

Père Ubu is, after all, a colossal affront to conventional sensibilities, and not simply because he is on stage representing a king. From his off-color language to his off-putting diet, both often finding their source in excrement, to say nothing of his boorish, self-serving policies, childishly vain cowardice, and heinously violent procedures such as the notorious disembraining machine, Ubu is calculated to harass and disgust at every turn. Indeed, Ubu patently undermines traditional models of human nobility, revealing—in his plot to assassinate King Venceslas and his subsequent strategies to maintain the throne and rule his people—not the medieval ideal of a rational, deliberative mind that chooses the good and acts out of love, or even, like Shakespeare's Macbeth, a troubled conscience that manically seeks to reassure itself, but rather the base, untempered, animalistic desires and appetites that drive him and presumably, by extension, drive humankind. Ubu's assault is generally understood as an attack on the materialism of the bourgeoisie, but surely Ubu has staked out a larger, more complex kingdom than that. Critics throughout the twentieth century have also read Ubu as a critique of tyrannical regimes, and although tempting, this interpretation is anachronistic. So we must look further for the concept of sovereignty at work in this play.

In his January 8, 1896, letter to Aurélien Lugné-Poë, the manager of the Théâtre de l'Oeuvre, Jarry proposes a production of *Ubu roi*. He casually suggests it will be "interesting, perhaps" to the director and mentions that it would be "curious" to stage it in a certain way.[7] The nonchalance gives way, however, to what amounts to a systematic rejection of naturalist and realist theatrical principles, along with highly specific ideas for presenting Ubu on stage, animated by a strong *guignol*, or puppet, aesthetic. One seemingly innocuous point in Jarry's letter bears further scrutiny: the fourth item, which allows a single soldier to suffice for a crowd. His solution is noteworthy not only in terms of its simultaneous antirealism and theatrical restraint but also because it hints at an attitude Jarry will make explicit elsewhere: disdain for the masses. As he explains, crowds pose a theatrical difficulty and "are an embarrassment to intelligence."[8] Peppered throughout his other texts, the desire to minimize the crowd is shown to be not only a visual advantage and dramaturgical strategy but also a survival tactic for the theater. According to Jarry, theater has been plagued by an uncomprehending audience since antiquity, when the crowd only "understood or pretended to understand" what they watched because the stories were familiar.[9] He rejects, for this reason, theater that conforms to the taste of the public, scornfully referring to "the infinite mediocrity of the crowd," "the multitude," "illiterate, by definition."[10] In fact, pointing out that the substance of plays by Molière and Racine are lost on the crowd, Jarry bemoans the fact that the theater has "not yet acquired the freedom to forcibly remove those who do not understand."[11]

Jarry's contempt for the masses runs parallel to sociopolitical tensions of the fin-de-siècle. Discussions of the crowd—*la foule*—were embedded in concerns regarding sovereignty dating back at least to the French Revolution.

The question of *what kind* of popular sovereignty had replaced the divine right of kings with the execution of Louis XVI, and the question of how to control and organize this kind of sovereignty had been central to French (and more broadly European) writers since the event itself. The ongoing anxieties and uncertainties over issues of authority and the role of the masses became a matter of as much concern to socialists (from Henri de Saint-Simon through Karl Marx and on to Jean Jaurès and Georges Sorel) as to conservative thinkers loath to accept new democratic regimes.

Yet the disdain Jarry exhibits for the crowd is particularly significant for its appearance as a major motif concerning legitimacy and authority in the almost exactly contemporary work *The Crowd: A Study of the Popular Mind* (*La psychologie des foules*, 1895), which the social psychologist Gustave Le Bon published to considerable acclaim just as Jarry was working to bring *Ubu roi* to the stage. For Le Bon, the crowd is the defining sovereign power of the era, "the last surviving force of modern times" for which he has no admiration: "the tyrannical and sovereign force of being above discussion."[12] Le Bon views the masses as a force destructive to every level of society, consisting only of bearers of hypnotic suggestion rather than individual subjects. Jarry's misgivings (perhaps even influenced by Le Bon) are fundamentally in the aesthetic domain yet with similar concerns regarding popular sovereignty's tendency to efface the individual, especially as a being capable of critical thought and creativity.

The initial crowd that failed to find anything witty in *Ubu roi* provoked bitter criticism from Jarry. He accused the audience of being not only incapable of comprehending anything profound but moreover of having missed what is plainly and repeatedly articulated throughout the play by Mère Ubu: "What a stupid man! . . . What a sorry imbecile!"[13] Jarry's position could easily be taken as one of mere snobbery and elitism, yet the dangers of an unthinking public are embodied in the figure of King Ubu, giving particular force to Jarry's grievances.

He is full of vitriol in an article published just a few weeks after staging *Ubu roi*: "When the curtain was raised, I wanted the scene to confront the public like a [magic] mirror in which the vicious see themselves with bull horns and a dragon's body, according to the exaggeration of their vices." Although the crowd was appalled by what they saw—"the sight of its own ignoble double"—Jarry had taken pains to set up this equation. In a brochure passed out at the performance, the playwright announces his protagonist in precisely the same terms. "M. Ubu is an ignoble being, which is why we resemble him at all."[14]

Jarry chooses the word "ignoble" to describe Ubu both times, which neutrally could express Ubu's low or common status but more likely is meant to register Ubu's vile, unprincipled character. The term "ignoble" highlights the distance from nobility, whether of class status or mores, which in turn calls attention to the travesty of Ubu's sovereign status. In wanting the crowd to face its dishonorable double in the mirror provided by the theater, and making that other self turn out to be a king who rules "by the power of the lower appetites," Jarry is not calling attention to the dangers of tyranny but rather pointing to the dangers of a lack of self-governance.[15] At core, he is issuing a challenge to each member of the audience to participate in artistic creation, to rise above the crowd instead of being passive puppets moved by base instincts: in other words, to be a sovereign individual. He understands his own artistic motivation along these lines: "if there are, in the whole universe, five hundred people who, relative to infinite mediocrity, have a bit of Shakespeare and Leonardo in them," it is only fair to write plays for them and to give them "the active pleasure of creating."[16] Jarry's optimism even conquers the disappointment he feels about the crowd's response to *Ubu roi*; in the end he declares the crowd harmless despite its large numbers since it is fighting against intelligence. Intelligence, for Jarry, is explicitly equated with nobility (though not equated with class) when he triumphantly announces, "Ubu has not disembrained all the nobles."[17] Ubu's revolution, in which Ubu figures as popular sovereignty against individual sovereignty, has not been achieved. But neither has Ubu been dispatched. The Ubus are last seen fleeing by ship, at-large in the world, happily beginning a new adventure.

Revolution and Repetition: Ionesco's *Macbett*

The thinking, intelligent being versus the stupid person is also a concern in Ionesco's *Macbett*.[18] Indeed, Ionesco builds this theme into the title—that is, into the name "Macbett." With the alteration of just one letter—the final *-th* becoming a pair of *ts*—Ionesco not only begins the doubling and twinning that will guide the characters and plot of the play, but he also phonically registers the French pronunciation of "Macbeth," where the aspirated -*th* does not exist. This, in turn, introduces a beast, for the French hear *bête*: a term that can mean beast, as well as a stupid person, an idiot, a fool.

While the nuances of the French pronunciation are occasionally noted in the scholarship on this play, the implications have gone unexplored, as though it is self-evident just what Ionesco means to be doing by introducing this ambiguous *bête* into his play on sovereignty.[19] Audiences of the play should have no trouble identifying instances of Macbett, the character, acting both as a brutal beast, assassinating his sovereign, and as an idiot, taken in by the most banal of sexual seductions—to name only the most basic examples. But more important, in what ways might *Macbett*, the play, be understood to be negotiating the stakes of sovereignty with terms such as "beast" and "idiot" haunting it?

At a glance, with a Macbett, a Lady Macbett, a Duncan, a Banco, witches, and a Macol as the ultimate inheritor of the throne, the cast of Ionesco's *Macbett* looks to have straightforward parallels to Shakespeare's tragedy. As an ostensibly minor variation, Ionesco gives stage time to Candor and Glamiss, the traitorous equivalents to Cawdor and Glamiss—who are merely named and described by Shakespeare. A further twist is found in the provenance of Lady Macbett, who is, to begin with, an unhappily married Lady Duncan and who, it turns out, is one of the witches in disguise. The smaller walk-on parts are in line with a court or war environment, with the exception of two who are generally chalked up to Ionesco's absurdist aesthetic: a lemonade seller at the battle scene (raising the specter of Brecht's Mother Courage) and a butterfly hunter who wanders on stage just after the play's greatest moment of tension and appears again at the end, when all the other characters have left the stage.

Interchangeability is a crucial feature of Ionesco's aesthetics in *Macbett*, and nowhere is it more highly pronounced than in the characters of Macbett and Banco. The two generals so closely resemble each other that, as Macbett puts it, "People often take me for my twin brother. Or for Banco's twin brother."[20] Macbett and Banco have nearly identical soliloquies mid-battle (discussed below), where they reflect on the bloodshed and death count at their hands, and each reassures himself of his loyalty to his sovereign's cause. Significantly, when their dutifulness has run its course, their frustration takes the form of a near verbatim repetition of Candor and Glamiss's initial decision to revolt, restarting the cycle of insurgency and linking them in no uncertain terms with the play's original rebels (and the play's other set of doubles). The effect of the déjà vu is to introduce a sense of inevitability as well as banality to the revolutionary attempt. History is repeating itself in a predictable way: a sovereign is in power and the subjects rouse themselves to revolt with the same catch phrases as though learned by rote in school for just such an occasion.

The emphasis on interchangeability—and, related, on repetition—provides a significant way to begin to understand not only Ionesco's comic aesthetic (the category to which it has been limited by critics and scholars) but also, more importantly, Ionesco's approach to sovereignty. In *Macbett*, interchangeability points to the structure of sovereignty and subjecthood. Ionesco diminishes the particularities of individuals by twinning them, thereby laying stress on the singularity of the sovereign—who is always only one—over and against the plurality of the subjects—who are always many, and undifferentiated. Furthermore, the interchangeability of the subjects also indicates the crowd.

The *equivalence* at work in Ionesco's *Macbett*—between the pairs of characters he twins and, in the case of the war and later the assassination, between the sovereign and those who would be sovereign—is not to be confused with the *equivocation* at work in Shakespeare's *Macbeth*. Ionesco's slant underscores a critical difference worth spelling out precisely because comparisons with Shakespeare run the risk of understanding Ionesco as being no more than farcically reductive of the complexity found in Shakespeare's tragedy. The divergence between the two playwrights on this point is fundamental to their respective aims. In Shakespeare, antithetical values and ideas are shown to be confused ("Fair is foul and foul is fair"), in keeping with a focus on the moral aberrance of Macbeth's ambition for power and on the monstrousness of his choices. In Ionesco, resemblances verging on the identical are highlighted, in keeping with a focus on Macbett's lack of originality and on the prosaic quality of his desires.

The endless repetition of revolution is a pet theme of Ionesco's throughout his writings, and the equivalence and interchangeability underscored in his aesthetics in *Macbett* work to this end. In "More Pages from My Diary," published as a part of *Notes and Counter Notes* in 1962, Ionesco expounds on the misguided optimism that revolution will bring about change. "The word revolution is badly chosen by the revolutionaries," he points out. "Unconsciously it helps us to see through revolutionary action, which is itself synonymous with reaction, for etymologically revolution means a return, and is opposed to evolution."[21] Hannah Arendt made a similar point, though to different ends, one year later in her book *On Revolution*. She draws attention to the distinctly modern notion of revolution as tied to freedom and the creation of a truly new order, whereas the use of the term in antiquity was literal, implying a return to the same place.[22] But while Arendt understands a meaningful shift to have taken place in the sense and concept of revolution, Ionesco maintains the original definition, perceiving it as haunting modern attempts at revolution, despite the modern expectation of real change. For Ionesco, the office of power generates its own depravity, regardless of the party in authority. Emphasizing the return to the same is one way Ionesco's theater "avoids" revolution in general terms, but *Macbett* also registers a radical reluctance to "*the* revolution" more specifically in its critique of the subtler temptations and dangers of popular sovereignty.

Ionesco's views on revolution were immensely unpopular in artistic circles in the context of the highly volatile decades following World War II, and especially in late-1960s France, when revolution was touted as salvific. Leftist hopes in communism and Maoism dominated the French intellectual scene, and Ionesco—for failing to join in the fervor and, indeed, for speaking out against it—was understood to be a right-wing conservative. More accurately, his stance was one of radical skepticism toward any political regime promising a cure-all for humanity's difficulties. This was not a blithely held position of indifference; quite the contrary, given Ionesco's firsthand experiences. Shaped by the nightmare of witnessing not only his father but also intellectual colleagues—most notable among them the historian of religions Mircea Eliade and philosopher E. M. Cioran—submitting to and endorsing the Iron Guard, Ionesco made it his cause to resist commitments to political parties, even, and perhaps especially, when the trend was in their favor.

Journals and memoirs make no secret of the fact that as a result of familial betrayals and what he perceived as extreme emotional cruelty, Ionesco held his father in severe contempt. His abhorrence was further exacerbated by his father's shifting political loyalties, and these in turn (Ionesco himself suggests) had the effect of sealing the playwright's determination to abide by his own commitments rather than allow those who managed to be in power to dictate his beliefs. More interesting than providing a psychological explanation for Ionesco's approach toward political opposition is the way his reflections reveal not mere judgment but an attempt to come to terms with his scorn.

> My father was not a conscious opportunist; he believed in the powers that be. He respected the State. He believed in the State, no matter what it represented. . . . As far as he was concerned, the minute a party took over it was right. This was how he came to be an Iron Guard, a Freemason democrat, and a Stalinist. . . . What I reproached him for was his being like everybody else. What I reproached him for was going in the same direction as history. But haven't Heidegger, Jung, Sartre, and so many others done exactly the same thing? He did so in a cruder, more simplistic, more candid way perhaps. Waves of pure madness swept over the world. In order to resist these currents, one must tell oneself that history is always wrong, whereas it is generally believed that history is always right.
>
> He was like everyone else. That is what I held against him. That is what I was wrong to hold against him.[23]

Several things stand out in Ionesco's analysis of his father's political expediencies. He is careful to note his sense that the world itself was not in its right mind and that his father was not aware of the pattern of his behavior. Similarly, Ionesco observes that his father was not taken in due to nefarious desires but because of his sense of duty and respect for authority. Having exploitable principles, however, does not change the moral verdict. The repeated accusation is that his father was "like everybody else"—a charge easily extended to Candor and Glamiss or Macbett and Banco. That being indistinguishable from others is presented as an *indictment* goes some distance in underscoring the serious intent of Ionesco's aesthetics of equivalence, far surpassing humorous effect.

Indeed, over and above conveying the logic of sovereignty that mandates a single sovereign over indistinct subjects, similarity to others demonstrates a moral danger. The identical mid-battle soliloquies delivered first by Macbett and moments later by Banco offer a critical illustration:

> The blade of my sword is all red with blood. I've killed dozens and dozens of them with my bare hands. Twelve dozen officers and men who never did me any harm. I've had hundreds and hundreds of others executed by firing squad. Thousands of others were roasted alive when I set fire to the forests where

they'd run for safety. Tens of thousands of men, women, and children suffocated to death in cellars, buried under the rubble of their houses which I'd blown up. Hundreds of thousands were drowned in the Channel in desperate attempts to escape. Millions died of fear or committed suicide. Ten million others died of anger, apoplexy, or a broken heart. There's not enough ground to bury them all.[24]

A passage such as this—with references that conjure scenes from the Holocaust, the Allied airstrikes against civilian-occupied cities of Germany, and the Vietnam War—indicates Ionesco's willingness to extend a political critique while avoiding outright parallels that would render the play merely topical. The scope and numbers involved point to exaggeration, bombast, and fantasy. Ionesco walks a fine line between horror and humor. Yet before this can be summarily categorized as absurdist or as a simplistic attempt to wag a finger at perpetrators of war atrocities, it will be productive to consider a further resemblance that adds complexity to Ionesco's choices. Both in what has already been cited and in how it proceeds, this speech resonates in striking and disturbing ways with Hannah Arendt's description of German Nazi leader Adolf Eichmann in her 1963 report on his trial, *Eichmann in Jerusalem*.

According to Arendt, "Bragging was the vice that was Eichmann's undoing. It was sheer rodomontade when he told his men during the last days of the war: 'I will jump into my grave laughing, because the fact that I have the death of five million Jews [or "enemies of the Reich," as he always claimed to have said] on my conscience gives me extraordinary satisfaction.'"[25] As Arendt points out, his claim to such numbers was "preposterous." Even so, and more important, "Despite all the efforts of the prosecution, everybody could see that this man was not a 'monster,' but it was difficult indeed not to suspect that he was a clown."[26] The puzzle for Arendt lies exactly here, for the desire to account for evil craves easily identifiable villains replete with isolatable motives for cruelty, and, not finding such a beast, the temptation is then to see only farcical characters accidentally involved. The difficulty, of course, is that evil is not obliged to be recognizable in these terms. Referring to the text of a taped police examination, Arendt describes it as "a veritable gold mine for a psychologist—provided he is wise enough to understand that the horrible can be not only ludicrous but outright funny."[27] One has only to read this statement—replacing "playwright" for "psychologist"—to perceive that Ionesco has precisely this perspicacity.

The likeness between the historical war criminal and Ionesco's fictional creations extends beyond the comingling of horror and humor and toward what I am calling the moral danger of similarity and interchangeability. After cataloguing the numbers of victims at their hands, Macbett and Banco take a moment to rationalize their actions: "They were all traitors, of course. Enemies of the people—and of our beloved sovereign, the Archduke Duncan, whom God preserve."[28] The detachment and positive spin on the situation continues as each in turn talks himself out of feeling any guilt, remorse, or, indeed, physical pain: "I thrashed about a bit too hard. My wrist aches. Luckily it's nothing serious. It's been quite a pleasant day, really. Feeling quite bucked. . . . No. No regrets. They were traitors after all. I obeyed my sovereign's orders. I did my duty."[29] A correspondence with Ionesco's father can be heard in these rationalizations. Evoking phraseology and justification from both Soviet Communism ("enemies of the people") *and* medieval monarchism ("our beloved sovereign"), Ionesco's generals will use any idiomatic expressions they find to hand, even if they are ideologically contradictory. In addition to Macbett and Banco saying the same thing, making them indistinguishable from each other—and, by extension, "like everyone else"— they also operate from a rudimentary, unquestioned sense of duty to the sovereign (whoever that happens to be) in the same way Ionesco's father "believed in the State, no matter what it represented."

Returning to Ionesco's remarks on his father, his striking statement at the end—that he was *wrong* to hold it against him for being like everyone else— registers an important, if perplexing, qualification. His self-reproach suggests that similarity may be an unfortunate side effect, but it is not where Ionesco ultimately locates the problem. Macbett and Banco's justifications are marked by recourse to stock phrases and slogans without regard to their appropriateness, implying, at best, a sloppiness of mind, at worst, a willful desire to deceive both self and others. Arendt's penetrating insight about Eichmann and his role in the Holocaust was to identify the "banality of evil," by which she does not mean that Eichmann was simply an ordinary person (or even an ordinary criminal) or that evil is simply a widespread commonplace and therefore of trivial import.[30] Rather, of the paths that could lead to evil, there is a path devoid of clear criminal intent that does not necessarily look evil at all. As Arendt understands it, during the war such a path functioned as a survival tactic, and not only for high-ranking Nazis. She points out that the "German society of eighty million people had been shielded against reality and factuality by exactly the same means, the same self-deception, lies, and stupidity that had now become ingrained in Eichmann's mentality."[31]

The "means" to which Arendt refers, and the form the "stupidity" takes, is a habit of mind that expresses itself in language: "Eichmann, despite his rather bad memory, repeated word for word the same stock phrases and self-invented clichés (when he did succeed in constructing a sentence of his own, he repeated it until it became a cliché)."[32] Regarding Macbett and Banco alongside Eichmann provides an important opportunity for allowing the *bête* of *Macbett*—the threat of both the beast whose actions are outside the law and the stupid person who is unable to think—to come more fully into focus.[33] By paying attention to the human capacity to judge and articulate as constitutive elements of both personal, individual sovereignty and political sovereignty, the play goes beyond a predictable condemnation of tyrannical leaders to a consideration of how they come about.

When Candor is captured and faces execution for treason, his gallows speech has a distinctly different tone from that of his contrite counterpart in Shakespeare.[34] "If only I had won," he wistfully remarks, before rattling off two platitudes in an effort to comfort himself: "The victor is always right. *Vae victis*."[35] Candor, like Cawdor, presents himself as a cautionary tale, although in a bold departure he does *not* counsel against usurpation of the throne. In Shakespeare's *Macbeth*, that is where Cawdor—and after him, Macbeth—presumably go wrong, by taking up arms against the divinely anointed sovereign. Significantly, Ionesco's Candor gives voice to another understanding of the logic of sovereignty. Both of the cited phrases Candor relies on can be summed up in the plain expression, "Might makes right." Candor, like Ionesco's father, believes this. "If I'd been stronger," Candor announces, "I'd have been your anointed king. Defeated, I'm a traitor and a coward." The result of the action, not its motivating principle, determines the value and character of the agent. "If only I'd won," he continues, repeating his plaintive—and patently unremorseful—refrain before providing his explanation: "But History was against me. History is right, objectively speaking. I'm just a historical dead end. . . . The logic of events is the only one that counts. Historical reason is the only reason. There are no transcendental values to set against it."[36] Ionesco considers this a treacherous line of thought. Recall the reproach he leveled at his father for "going in the same direction as history." His exhortation to resist suggests that Candor's "logic of events" has missed the mark precisely in the assessment that "there are no transcendental values to set against it." In other words, according to Ionesco, there is indeed something transcendental to set against the fatalist notion that history is always right. (Just what this might be is discussed shortly.) Crucially, what Ionesco is fighting is a notion of sovereignty as well, the belief that whoever manages to be in power is meant to be there until someone stronger comes along.

In the final scene, in something of a coup de théâtre, Ionesco returns to his strategy of repeated speech, but with amplified stakes. Here, as nowhere else in the play, Ionesco gives Macol the exact lines—several dozen in sum—said by Malcolm in act 4 of Macbeth. Macduff has solicited Malcolm, Duncan's heir, to lead a war against the tyrant Macbeth and reclaim the throne. Malcolm's response, however, contains little comfort: "My poor country," he forecasts, "Shall have more vices than it had before, / More suffer and more sundry ways than ever, / By him that do succeed." "Black Macbeth," he promises, "Will seem as pure as snow; and the poor State / Esteem him as a lamb, being compar'd / With my confineless harms." Indeed, Macbeth may be "bloody, / Luxurious, avaricious, false, deceitful, / Sudden, malicious, smacking of every sin / That has a name," but according to Malcolm, "there's no bottom, none, / In my voluptuousness."[37]

The only difference in Macol's language when he says Malcolm's lines is a change from the conditional tense—"Had I power, I should / Pour the sweet milk of concord into Hell"—to the present active tense—"*Now I have power, I shall* / Pour the sweet milk of concord into Hell." It is not a potential threat but an imminent action. In Shakespeare's tragedy, these horrifying announcements are met with disgust and consternation by Macduff, as it is hoped they will be, for Malcolm claims he has spoken such only as a test to see whether Macduff has a finer sense of legitimate sovereignty or will simply throw in his lot with the stronger. (Macduff passes the test.) By the time Macol finishes his address in the Ionesco play, however, all of his would-be subjects and supporters are rendered speechless and have left the stage, and he himself vanishes in mist. Macol has the last word, not only on this subject, but in this play; Ionesco offers no soothing rejoinder to counter the bleak pronouncement. Instead, he offers a final theatrical gesture that is typically read as a signature mark of the "absurd": the butterfly hunter crosses the stage.

Considering Macol's harrowing, unchecked sovereign proclamation, it is not without reason that critics take Ionesco to be putting forward a picture of sovereignty bluntly at odds with Shakespeare's conclusion, for Ionesco's vision appears to be without any redemption or hope of a good king resuming rule, whereas *Macbeth* appears to finish with just such an optimism. On the face of it, Ionesco's *Macbett* seems resigned to the play's logic of the stronger. And yet his play works to resist the limited idea of sovereignty that dictates that "might is right" and, by extension, that history is always right.

Put another way, Ionesco is not making a simple pessimistic declaration; rather, he is creating a space—a theatrical space—in which the cycle might be reflected on or potentially even be broken. In no way do I suggest that there is redemption lurking, yet there is resistance. The question is where? As I read it, Ionesco is not quarreling with Shakespeare by reframing Malcolm's speech in the way he does but rather allowing the force of the language to hit the audience.[38] Instead of a confrontation between Malcolm and Macduff, Ionesco provides a confrontation between Macol and the audience, the only ones present to hear his vitriolic agenda. Who will rebuff Macol? Who will respond to him, as Macduff responds to Malcolm: "Fit to govern? No, not to live"?[39] Where is the thinking being who will weigh legitimate sovereignty against brute force? Who will pass the test? Here, the potential for being stupid or being a fool—the other kind of *bête*—comes directly to the fore. If it is proper to the human being to think, to consider, then it is at the risk of being an idiot or fool that one refrains from doing so. The test, as it is developed in the play, has to do with differentiating oneself from others, avoiding the sameness that works to dull thoughts, ideas, and actions. Ionesco is emphatic on this score: "What is important in a work or in an individual is not his resemblance to others but rather his difference, his originality, his uniqueness, his irreducibility. What is important is everything that I do differently from the others." Rather than stating an uncomplicated objective, Ionesco recognizes the difficulty and situates the aspiration to singularity in the human condition. "It is a cliché to say that 'nobody resembles anybody else,'" he continues. "It is also a truth. It is also true to say that 'everybody resembles everybody else.' This is man's contradictory truth."[40]

Ending *Macbett* with the figure of the butterfly hunter highlights the absurdity of the situation, but it also quite plainly represents the ongoing search for that which is elusive. At least one critic has proposed that the butterfly represents power.[41] Yet in Ionesco's play, power is not elusive, it is all too graspable; one must simply be the stronger. As he makes clear in *Rhinocéros*, Ionesco's concern is less with those who seek power—there will always be those—and more with those who grant them power, those who recognize them as leaders.

With this latter concern in mind, I would like to put forward another interpretation of Ionesco's butterfly hunter. Hunting was evidently on his mind, for a few months after Ionesco staged *Macbett*, he published a small essay in *Le Figaro* entitled "La chasse à l'homme" (The hunt for man, or The manhunt). There, discussing the way Nazism had made the word "humanism" ridiculous, he writes, "There is a word which one cannot use any more today without being laughed at, it is the word soul."[42] Ionesco, it goes without saying, is not afraid of generating laughter. I interpret his butterfly hunter as a hunter of man, and more precisely of the soul of man. The ancient Greeks held the butterfly to be a symbol of the psyche (ψυχή)—understood as the soul or the mind. With the elusive butterfly interpreted this way, Ionesco is registering dismay that no one is willing to play Macduff's role (arguably the only role of integrity in Shakespeare's *Macbeth*), a role Ionesco eliminated from his play—or rather, left open. The search continues for those who will not stupidly—that is, unthinkingly, mindlessly—accept the notion of sovereignty based on force.

My reading runs counter to the usual way of understanding Ionesco's *Macbett* exclusively in terms of political sovereignty. Finding a "soul"—even an elusive one—may seem an arbitrary spiritual insertion onto an absurdist play about political ambition and the abuse of power. But it may be easier to see that Ionesco's butterfly hunter represents a crucial tension within the play by recalling Candor's scaffold speech, in which he declares, "Historical reason is the only reason. There are no transcendental values to set against it." Above, I suggested that Ionesco, who insists on the toxic quality of such thinking regarding history's presumed right or reason (*raison* translates as both right and reason), must in fact harbor the suspicion—or hope—that there is indeed something transcendent at hand to aid in resisting it. Understanding the chased-after butterfly as the psyche in the ancient Greek sense of soul or mind deftly gestures toward the transcendent without any heavy-handed religiosity or moralism.

Giving the butterfly hunter the final moment on stage allows Ionesco to theatrically draw attention to what has been missing along the treacherous path of revolving absolutist sovereigns *Macbett* charts. The implication is not that human beings are soulless, but quite the contrary. In much the same manner that Ionesco rejected the interpretation of his early play *The Bald Soprano* as stressing the failure and impossibility of human communication (whereas Ionesco understood his work as "a plea, pathetic perhaps, for mutual understanding"), I am suggesting that in *Macbett*, Ionesco is not presenting a nihilistically pessimistic picture of political sovereignty but signaling a human faculty or resource that has not been fully utilized.[43]

A brief look at the "transformation" scene in which the witches secure Macbett's willingness to murder Duncan will demonstrate Ionesco's subtle and sophisticated insistence on Macbett's failure to adequately exercise his mind. The witches tempt Macbett with the idea not only of being the political sovereign but also, more interestingly, with the idea of being a sovereign individual: "Be your own master," the witches taunt, "instead of taking someone else's orders."[44] Ironically, although Macbett is drawn toward and ostensibly agrees to both forms of empowerment, what quite blatantly takes place is seduction and submission. When the witches are fully revealed as the beautiful Lady Duncan and her lady-in-waiting, Macbett's actions and terms of address are all in a sovereign register, but the sovereignty is not his. Macbett maintains his role as subject; indeed, he lowers himself even further. "Oh your Majesty!," he exclaims, falling to his knees. "Let me be your slave," he pleads, and, in a moment of inspired confusion he sputters, "Madam, sire, or rather siren. . . ."[45] While this scene obviously trades on the hilarity of hyperbolized sexuality, there is more to it than the comic predictability of Macbett's reaction, and still more to it besides the implied bondage of his character precisely when he would be sovereign.

Ionesco has gone beyond parody in his exploration of sovereignty. The Latin phrases throughout this scene reveal Ionesco's careful attention to matters of far more serious import than the way sex and power are enmeshed and rulers are enslaved. "*Alter ego surge*," the witches intone, calling forth not only their "other selves" as noblewomen but the "other self" of Macbett, the self that aspires to be the sovereign rather than a subject. Their lists of Latin adverbs and prepositions, arranged alliteratively for the most part, and peppered here and there with a line taken from Genesis and Virgil, give the impression of random, silly hocus-pocus. Yet the first and only line that Macbett repeats back to the witches—"*Video meliora, deteriora sequor*"—and that is chanted seven times as the climactic finale of the spell, could hardly be arbitrary. The line translates, "I see the better [course], follow the worse." Ionesco has made a slight change to the original phrase, taken from Ovid's *Metamorphoses*, book 7, where the line is said by Medea and has one additional word: "*Video meliora proboque, deteriora sequor.*" The left-out term, *proboque*, holds a key to Ionesco's sense of what is crucially missing in the battle against the logic of sovereignty that takes might for right. *Proboque* means "approve" or "esteem"; it is a term that designates value and judgment. The original phrase, "I see *and approve* the better course, but follow the worse," registers the acknowledgment of consideration, appraisal, and discernment. Without it, as it stands in the witches' curse, "seeing the better" is done with blank, uncomprehending eyes—stupid, unthinking, *bête* eyes.

Macbett's vision is explicitly called into question in the banquet scene, where, just as in Shakespeare's version, he unravels in front of his guests. When Macbett mistakes his portrait for that of Duncan's, accusing his subjects of disloyalty, they wonder among themselves "if myopia is brought on by power?" and conclude "it happens quite frequently."[46] Myopia, here, goes beyond literal near-sightedness to reflect small-mindedness and a lack of those things that are "proper to the human being," sovereign or no: insight and imagination. Again, while Ionesco is manifestly criticizing those in power, he is also, and more interestingly in my assessment, criticizing those who unthinkingly enable and support those who have risen to power. The banquet scene celebrates Macbett's coronation as well as his demise. As soon as Macol kills Macbett and is seated on the throne, the same guests who had gathered to honor Macbett shout, "Long live Macol, our beloved sovereign!" and others arrive holding placards that read, "Macol is always right."[47] Not only the sovereign suffers from myopia but also those who blankly accept the sovereign as right.

Counterrevolution in the Theater

Shakespeare's *Macbeth* is a tale of ambition gone awry. Jarry and Ionesco sidestep the traditional tragic tone, but their formal moves to farce only scratch the surface of the significant departures each playwright makes from Shakespeare's drama. *Ubu roi* and *Macbett* follow the trajectory of revolution and usurpation outlined in the Renaissance drama, and although each play sim-

ilarly presents a single king replacing another, both Ubu and Macbett epito-
mize characteristics of the crowd, fundamentally changing Shakespeare's
story of revolution to a modern story of *the* revolution: the shift from absolute sovereignty to popular sovereignty.

In their responses to the revolution, both Jarry and Ionesco express
anxieties about the crowd, revealing an important way theater "avoids the
revolution." Within the logic of absolute sovereignty, the crowd watches, defers to, acknowledges, and therefore corroborates the sovereign's authority.
Within the logic of popular sovereignty, the crowd rules—insofar as it must
at all times be taken into account, asserting its authority by virtue of size and
number. Jarry seeks to minimize the crowd's mass on stage and extends a
critique of the base desires and appetites that fuel the crowd and nurse its
power. Ionesco hints at the crowd with doubling of characters and explores
the repercussions on political life of the individual's failure to think and
judge *as an individual.*

The transition to democratic popular sovereignty created the challenge
of how to visualize and represent the people and its will.[48] By and large,
the modern theater does not stage popular will as such, in part because the
crowd is no less difficult to effectively represent on stage than it is in a
single image.[49] Yet as Jarry and Ionesco demonstrate, physical practicalities
present only the most literal obstruction. The crowd, even for a realist playwright dedicated to the common person, like Ibsen in his prose dramas,
turns out to be a threat—and precisely to the common person he studies and
celebrates. In his 1882 play *Enemy of the People*, Ibsen explicitly presents "the
People" as a menacing entity guided by the base desire of profit, but throughout his oeuvre the individual and personal sovereignty are determining
concerns.

If theater "avoids the revolution" in the overt historical terms specified
by Badiou, and "avoids the revolution" as well by failing to celebrate the
crowd, it is not the case that theater ignores the revolution, as evidenced by
the subsequent use of common individuals as protagonists rather than those
from noble ranks. The belief in the equality of human beings that entitles
popular will to its sovereignty also provides the common person the same
access to the modern stage as that enjoyed by the sovereign figures of ancient and baroque drama. In this way we can begin to understand the turn
to sovereign figuration in the modern theater. Drama, perhaps owing to its

reciprocal relationship with sovereignty, demonstrates a clear investment in the individual human being. Put succinctly, theater focuses on the ordinary *person*, not one or another version of the people.

By way of closing, I would like to return to a question posed at the beginning of this essay. With the counterintuitive yet undeniable recourse to sovereign figures in work by a wide range of modern dramatists, how is it that theater historians have missed this counterrevolutionary tension? In his case study of the scholarship on *Ubu roi*, Thomas Postlewait chastens scholars for being overly eager to accept and promote the narrative of modernism as a "story of revolt and controversy."[50] The enthusiasm for recording scandal and rebellion ironically betrays crowdlike, complacent assumptions that fail to register the complex and sometimes subtler ways in which the avant-garde forged its path. According to Postlewait, "We are not much interested in the various accommodations that modern artists made to the heritage. We tend to ignore the ways the traditions were modified yet continued. Our focus on innovation and confrontation usually rules out a history of continuity."[51] I take the failure to adequately acknowledge the ways modern theater negotiates a continued relationship with the figure of sovereignty to be one of the losses incurred by a preferred narrative of rogue artists abandoning all things traditional. Unfortunately, such an account is not only blinkered in terms of the history of modern drama, but it also misses an important way in which the integration of the past is precisely the mark of its modernity.

Notes

1. Alain Badiou, "Rhapsody for the Theatre," trans. Bruno Bosteels, *Theatre Survey* 49, no. 2 (2008): 205.
2. Ibid.
3. Robert Brustein, *The Theatre of Revolt* (Boston: Little, Brown, 1964).
4. Arthur Miller, *Death of a Salesman*, ed. Gerald Clifford Weales (New York: Penguin, 1996), 56.
5. Ibid., 114.
6. One does not, for example, find a similar rehabilitation of protagonists taken from the nobility in the novel, or sovereign subjects as a trend in modern painting.
7. Alfred Jarry, *Oeuvres complètes*, vol. 1, ed. Michel Arrivé (Paris: Gallimard, 1972), 1043.

8. Ibid.

9. Ibid., 405.

10. Ibid., 412, 408, 415.

11. Ibid., 405.

12. Gustave Le Bon, *The Crowd: A Study of the Popular Mind* (New York: Macmillan, 1896), 2, 4.

13. Jarry, *Oeuvres complètes*, 416.

14. Ibid., 416, 402.

15. Ibid., 402.

16. Ibid., 406.

17. Ibid., 417.

18. Ionesco, a noted member of the Collège de Pataphysique, proudly considered himself an heir of Jarry. Although his Macbeth play does not rely on scatological humor, Ionesco's farce pays homage to *Ubu roi* with characterization, imagery, and language. See, e.g., Curtis Perry, "Vaulting Ambitions and Killing Machines: Shakespeare, Jarry, Ionesco, and the Senecan Absurd," *Shakespeare Without Class: Misappropriations of Cultural Capital*, ed. Donald Hedrick and Bryan Reynolds (New York: Palgrave, 2000), and Jacqueline Sessa, "Deux avatars derisoires de *Macbeth*: L'*Ubu roi* de Jarry et le *Macbett* de Ionesco," *Travaux comparatistes*, ed. Lucette Desvignes (Saint-Étienne: Centre d'études comparatistes, 1978). In choosing to concentrate on these two "modern Macbeths," my study of modern drama and its relationship to this particular theme of sovereignty runs the risk of appearing limited to a distinct strain of French theater. Though neither purports to take place in France, it is certainly the case that France, with the contentious concept of sovereignty at the core of its dramatic modern political history, has an investment in the relations between sovereignty and drama. See, e.g., Ruth Morse, "Monsieur Macbeth: From Jarry to Ionesco," *Shakespeare Survey* 57 (2004): 112–25. Although she is dismissive of both Jarry and Ionesco, her account of the reception of *Macbeth* in France is helpful.

19. See, e.g., Rosette C. Lamont, *Ionesco's Imperatives: The Politics of Culture* (Ann Arbor: University of Michigan Press, 1993); Nancy Lane, *Understanding Eugène Ionesco* (Columbia: University of South Carolina Press, 1994); and Deborah B. Gaensbauer, *Eugène Ionesco Revisited* (New York: Twayne, 1996).

20. Eugène Ionesco, *Macbett*, in *Exit the King, The Killer, and Macbett: Three Plays by Eugène Ionesco*, trans. Charles Marowitz and Donald Watson (New York: Grove, 1973), 26.

21. Eugène Ionesco, *Notes and Counter Notes*, trans. Donald Watson (New York: Grove, 1964), 239.

22. Hannah Arendt, *On Revolution* (New York: Viking, 1963).

23. Eugène Ionesco, *Present Past, Past Present*, trans. Helen R. Lane (New York: Da Capo, 1998), 19.

24. Ionesco, *Macbett*, 15–16, 17–18.

25. Hannah Arendt, *Eichmann in Jerusalem: A Report on the Banality of Evil* (New York: Penguin, 2006), 46.

26. Ibid., 54.

27. Ibid., 48.

28. Ionesco, *Macbett*, 15–16, 17–18.

29. Ibid., 15–16, 17–18.

30. Arendt, *Eichmann in Jerusalem*, 252.

31. Ibid., 52.

32. Ibid., 49.

33. Just when Ionesco was writing *Macbett*, Arendt gave a lecture, "Thinking and Moral Consideration," *Social Research* 38, no. 3 (1971): 417–44, addressing precisely the moral hazard resulting from "clichés, stock phrases, adherence to conventional, standardized codes of expression and conduct." In it, she wonders whether "the activity of thinking as such, the habit of examining and reflecting upon whatever happens to come to pass, regardless of specific content and quite independent of results, could this activity be of such a nature that it 'conditions' men against evil-doing?" (418). As far as I have been able to establish, Ionesco does not intentionally or explicitly engage with Arendt's ideas, but for someone as politically concerned with the question of evil and its source, it is by no means far-fetched to imagine that he was familiar with her publication on the Eichmann trial. It is less likely that he would have known her 1971 lecture, but the overlap of themes and concerns in *Macbett* is fascinating to note, considering the proximity of their publications.

34. Cawdor's speech (1.4.5–7), by contrast, contains confession of wrongdoing, petition for pardon from the king, and demonstration of a remorseful spirit. Not only are these elements stock features of a Jacobean "scaffold speech," but they also serve in the tragedy of *Macbeth* to establish the rightful and legitimate sovereignty of the divinely anointed king by the very person who, hubristically, had sought the crown. For more on this, see Rebecca Lemon, "Scaffolds of Treason in *Macbeth*," *Theatre Journal* 54 (2002): 25–43.

35. Ionesco, *Macbett*, 30. The latter phrase, "Vae victis," is Latin for "Woe to the conquered" and first appears in Livy's account in *Ab urbe condita*. The former, "La raison du vainqueur est toujours la meilleure," literally translates as "The reason of the victor is always best." It is a slight variation on Jean de La Fontaine's "The reason of the strongest is always the best" ("La raison du plus fort est toujours la meilleure") with which he famously begins his seventeenth-century tale, *The Wolf and the Lamb*. This fable and specifically this phrase, have been eloquently explored by two important French theorists of sovereignty (among other things): Louis Marin, in his 1986 book *Food for Thought and Other Theologico-Political Essays*, and Jacques Derrida, in *The Beast and the Sovereign*. In this way, Ionesco, in 1972, is showing himself to be within a distinguished line of French thinkers of sovereignty, although neither Marin nor Derrida seems to be aware of Ionesco's theatrical intervention.

36. Ionesco, *Macbett*, 32.

37. William Shakespeare, *Macbeth*, ed. A. R. Braunmuller (Cambridge: Cambridge University Press, 2008), 4.3.46–99.

38. Ionesco had strong notions about adaptation. "I don't like the idea of *rewriting* Shakespeare and Molière, of sticking arms on the Venus de Milo," he claimed in 1966. "You have the right to give several interpretations of an author, to show his work in a new light, but not to distort the sense of his work to provide grist

for your own ideological mill." Charles Bonnefoy, *Conversations with Eugène Ionesco*, trans. Jan Dawson (New York: Holt, Rinehart and Winston, 1970), 159.

39. Shakespeare, *Macbeth*, 4.3.102–4.

40. Ionesco, *Present Past, Past Present*, 142.

41. Ruby Cohn, *Modern Shakespeare Offshoots* (Princeton: Princeton University Press, 1976), 85. The butterfly also suggests a potential reference to Shakespeare's *Coriolanus*. There, more interesting than merely as a symbol of elusive power, it is also linked with obsession and (self-) destruction. Though, intriguing as an unintentional gloss on another Shakespearean "power" play, nothing in Ionesco's stage directions, where the butterfly hunter seems more ineffectual than violent, invites a direct comparison.

42. Eugène Ionesco, "Journal de mon désarroi," *Le Figaro littéraire*, May 6, 1972, as printed in *Antidotes* (1977), 41–42; translation mine.

43. Ionesco, *Notes and Counter Notes*, 90.

44. Ibid., 50.

45. Ibid., 56–58.

46. Ibid., 89.

47. Ibid., 101 (in English in the original).

48. See Jason Frank, "The Living Image of the People," chap. 4 in this volume.

49. Groundbreaking and influential modern directors such as the Duke of Saxe-Meiningen, André Antoine, and Konstantin Stanislavsky—all with realist commitments—took up the challenge of staging the crowd, but their successes are noteworthy as much for their rarity as for their realist achievement.

50. Thomas Postlewait, *The Cambridge Introduction to Theatre Historiography* (Cambridge: Cambridge University Press, 2009), 65.

51. Ibid., 279.

PART IV

SHIFTS

IN HIS FAMOUS ESSAY "The Permanence of the Theologico-Political?" Claude Lefort juxtaposes histories of the French Revolution by Alexis de Tocqueville and Jules Michelet. He identifies one thing that escapes Tocqueville in the reduction of "the history of the ancien régime to the breakup of aristocratic society"[1]—this is "the figure of power," the figuration of sovereignty, its symbolic register, its form of representation. Michelet, by contrast, "having judged inevitable and visible to all 'the defeat of the nobility and the clergy'" reaches a profound conclusion about this sociopolitical upheaval: "The only obscure question was that of royalty. This is not, as it has often been said, a question of pure form, but a fundamental question, a question more intimate and more perennial than any other question in France, a question not only of politics, but of love and of religion. No other people so loved their kings."[2] Political *power* may have changed hands, but Michelet's account helps to locate the "obscure," "fundamental," "intimate," and "perennial" issue of *royalty* that remained for the new society to confront—as it also remained for the new aesthetics, especially theatrical aesthetics. It is from here that Lefort would build his well-known theory of the "empty place" of power that for him modern democracy institutes. For Lefort, Michelet's point regarding royalty speaks to an investment in a sovereign not as a political ruler (whose leadership was now superseded) but as a majestic figure whose sovereignty was both modeled on and supported by Christian theology.

Placing Michelet's wish to fathom "the mystery of the monarchical incarnation"[3] avant la lettre, in the tradition of scholarship that has come to be identified with Ernst Kantorowicz, Lefort allows us to ask precisely what happens once the "empty place" appears assured. What is this modern democratic shift supposedly away from royalty and sovereignty that to so many observers appears to have sealed the fate of sovereignty, through popularization and toward erasure? Lefort notes Michelet's remarkable insights that it is the *natural body* of the king that "exercises the charm that delights the people" and, furthermore, "because royalty is embodied in a man, the royal phantasmagoria is revived when the man is turned into a spectacle."[4] The physical body of the king registers royalty not only because it is understood to be combined with the mystical body but also because—and not despite the fact that—it is replete with all that is quintessentially human: mortality, fallibility, desires, and needs. The same corporeality of the king produces royalty as an *aesthetic* effect, "the charm that delights" when it is present as "a spectacle." Within the context of the Revolution, this becomes particularly problematic. Lefort explains Michelet's aggrieved tone regarding the detention of Louis XVI:

> It was believed, he suggests, that the deposition of the individual would have the effect of desanctifying him. On the contrary: "The most serious and the cruelest blow that could have been struck against the Revolution was the ineptitude of those who constantly kept Louis XVI before the eyes of the population, and who allowed him to relate to the population both as a man and as a prisoner." Why? *Because the more he was revealed in his human singularity, and the more visible the living individual became, the more he remained a king. . . . All the signs that designate him to be a man restore his kingship.*[5]

Paradoxically, what the king has in common with all—his physical humanity and familial relations—contribute to securing his royalty. Yet Lefort is careful to point out that this was not strictly a sympathetic reaction to human suffering; rather, the situation goes beyond affection for the king to reveal "the attraction of the unique object of every gaze."[6]

For the "empty place of power," this physical and symbolic ambiguity is critical. These descriptions help not only to suss out the politico-theological persistence of sovereignty, which Lefort ultimately designates "the royalty of spirit" and associates with a variety of humanism, but also to apprehend the crucial intertwinement of sovereignty and theater.[7] The presumed revolutionary and postrevolutionary democratic shift does not—indeed cannot—simply do without a complex engagement with these aesthetic, material, and semiotic forms. The essays in this section are interested in shifts, transformations, and transpositions of sovereignty, primarily modern ones. New forms of sovereignty—popular sovereignty, the sovereign state—require new forms of representation; the scaffold on which the sovereign is presented and sustained has changed form. The contexts in which problematics of modern sovereignty have reemerged (often with a vengeance) are the focus here.

Dan Edelstein's study "Revolution in Permanence and the Fall of Popular Sovereignty" engages the problem of "permanent revolution" and the sovereignty relevant to revolution itself. In their early modern incarnation, revolutions followed a constitutional script: after a brief, possibly violent interregnum, the new regime grounded its legitimacy by an act of popular sovereignty. How was it, then, that most twentieth-century revolutions did not rely on free elections to authorize their governments? Edelstein recounts how Karl Marx, in his commentary on the revolutions of 1848–1850, abandoned the constitutional model of revolution, substituting in its place a new, "permanent" model, based on the French Revolutionary Terror, and he traces a number of consequences for this rethinking of revolutionary power and authority, particularly with regard to questions of the image of the people and the assertion of their sovereignty.

In his seminal 1993 essay, translated here for the first time, Amnon Raz-Krakotzkin retrieves in Zionist thought a negation of the diaspora and the theologico-political concept of exile that sustained Judaism since the destruction of the Second Temple. As Zionism presents it, he argues, the concept of exile has meant nothing more than the absence of Jewish sovereignty, and therefore the restoration of that sovereignty means the negation of exile. In modern Jewish political consciousness this has become an all-encompassing central idea that shapes and distorts Jewish self-perception, the understanding of the Jewish past, and collective memory. Turning to Walter Benjamin and recent kabbalist scholarship, Raz-Krakotzkin offers a critical cultural analysis of the concepts of "exile," the "negation of exile," and their relationships to redemption and sovereignty, in the process show-ing how the negation of exile affects not only the understanding of Jewish reality but also the treatment of privacy today, as well as the treatment of the Palestinians.

Li Chen's essay analyzes how the post-Enlightenment discourse of sym-pathy and civilized sensibility became a popular epistemology and imperial ideology that served to redefine the basis of sovereignty in mid-nineteenth-century Sino-Western relations. However, the sentimental and conflictual nature of this discourse also generated ambiguities and ambivalence when dominated people appealed to similar sentiments and when violence and oppression were common fixtures of colonial empire. Studying the produc-tion and contestation of the resulting "affective knowledge" in Sino-Western relations allows us to see the frequently overlooked emotive underside of international politics and its effect on sovereignty.

Finally, Stefanos Geroulanos looks at the early twentieth-century figure of the New Man—the promised sovereign of an anticipated new era disbur-dened of the social, economic, and political failures of the present. As the "New Man" emerged in the nineteenth century and was radicalized in the post–World War I era, it came to inhabit fantasies of cultural and aesthetic regeneration not only in new, radical authoritarian regimes but also in most political, scientific, and avant-garde movements. Geroulanos foregrounds the case of Richard Wagner in relation to the problem of conceiving and stag-ing *new* or *futural* forms of sovereignty and tying them to the experience of secular and symbolic history. He argues that Wagner's theorization of the total artwork, together with his staging of *Siegfried*'s first act, articulates a relationship between artist/creator and hero/leader that contributes to un-derstanding both the complementary figures of the New Man—particularly their placement on the cusp of both the beginning and the end of history—and their complication, during the later years of the nineteenth century, by thick or dense concepts of symbolic history and by scientific discourses as-sociated with different political perspectives. Turning then to Carl Jung and Alfred Rosenberg, the essay examines how a staging of "the people" and of a symbolic heritage, which can supposedly only be interpreted and rede-ployed by the "genuine" national artist and philosophical psychologist re-spectively, can result in fictions of political participation and power in which the people, race, or nation is involved in an at once heroic and aesthetic self-deployment.

Notes

1. Claude Lefort, "The Permanence of the Theologico-Political?," in *Political Theologies: Public Religions in a Post-Secular World*, ed. Hent de Vries and Lawrence E. Sullivan (New York: Fordham University Press, 2006), 175.
2. Jules Michelet, quoted in ibid.
3. Ibid.
4. Ibid., 177, 179.
5. Ibid., 179; emphasis added.
6. Ibid.
7. Ibid., 186.

FOURTEEN

Revolution in Permanence and the Fall of Popular Sovereignty

DAN EDELSTEIN

FROM ITS ORIGINS in the Protestant Reformation until its global explosion in the eighteenth century, revolutionary thought went hand in hand with constitutionalism.[1] The same arguments theorists employed to justify insurrection against a despotic ruler also served as the principles of the new government to follow. The relation between constitution and revolution was symbiotic: precisely *because* an oppressive regime violated universal standards of justice and liberty the new government had to observe and cherish them.[2] What's more, both revolution and constitution shared the same ultimate authority: popular consent. It was only "the People [who can] be Judge" of whether a ruler's actions rose to the level of despotism, Locke concluded, and only the people who could contract a new government.[3] Popular sovereignty was thus the form of political authority that could legitimate an otherwise illegal rebellion and then sanction the new order that followed (through a ratification process). Revolution, in this early modern model, was always a means to a constitutional end.

The validity of this model is still recognized today, as can be seen in the Arab uprising, where revolutions against autocratic leaders were succeeded by constituent assemblies and open elections (in Tunisia, and at least initially in Egypt and Libya). But for a significant stretch of history, this model was left by the wayside. Indeed, between 1917 (Russia) and 1975 (Cambodia), roughly speaking, most revolutions did not have a constitution as their ultimate goal. If these revolutions did in some cases produce constitutions, those constitutions were often delayed (by sixteen years, in the Cuban case), and the vast majority of them were never ratified by popular vote (Iran being one exception).[4] What's more, despite many of these revolutionary states assuming the name of a "People's Republic," they did not, in fact, grant the people the right to free elections. As the fall of the Eastern Bloc in 1989 demonstrated, these people's republics were for the most part very unpopular.[5]

The twentieth-century history of revolution thus raises a different kind of red flag for the historian: how did a political concept (and term) that was originally joined at the hip with popular sovereignty become divorced from it? In this essay, which forms part of a larger research project, I analyze the role that Karl Marx played in tearing revolution away from popular sovereignty, through his theory of "permanent revolution." Marx's role in this story is really that of an intermediary: he first developed his theory, I argue, while studying the history of the French Revolution. As I have shown elsewhere, it was indeed the Jacobins who first moved beyond the constitutional model of revolution, with the proclamation of "revolutionary government" in October 1793.[6] Curiously, Marx did not make much of this decision by the Jacobin-dominated National Convention to suspend the French constitution but focused instead on a different, more "populist," feature of this period: the "permanence" of the Parisian sections. Through his study of the French Revolution, and his attempts to apply its principles during the 1848–1852 revolutions, Marx consumed the rift between revolutionary and constitutional thought. It was a consummation with wide-ranging consequences: while today we associate the theory of permanent revolution mainly with Trotsky, it was widely known and discussed in Russian social-democratic circles well before he embraced it.[7] Marx's reflections on Jacobinism thus provided a key theoretical justification for the anticonstitutional and antidemocratic model of revolution, which would triumph in October 1917 and for decades thereafter.

1848 and Marx

February 1848 witnessed two important events in revolutionary history: the publication of *The Communist Manifesto* and the outbreak of revolution in Paris.[8] There was no connection between these events, and Marx would update the two-stage theory of revolution presented in the *Manifesto* in response to the way revolutionary events unfolded in France and Germany.[9] As we will see below, the seeds of this revision had in fact been planted much earlier, but the actual experience of revolution provided him with a unique opportunity to adjust and refine his theory.

This practice of fine-tuning, for Marx, took the form of writing detailed articles on the French revolution of 1848–1850, articles that appeared in the *Neue Rheinische Zeitung* and would be published posthumously (by Engels, in 1895) under the title *The Class Struggles in France, 1848 to 1850*.[10] For the most part, this work consists of a remarkably detailed analysis of the day-to-day conflicts and debates. But Marx also drew on this analysis to derive broader, theoretical conclusions about revolution, and particularly about the role of workers in a "proletarian revolution."

Initially, Marx seemed content to analyze the February revolution according to the two-stage model outlined in the *Manifesto*: "Only bourgeois rule tears up the material roots of feudal society and levels the ground on which alone a proletarian revolution is possible," he recognized.[11] The workers could not have expected to take power in the spring of 1848, as the proletariat was not yet a sufficiently mobilized or self-conscious class in France.[12]

The workers nonetheless obliged the Provisional Government to acquiesce to some of their demands. These included the declaration of a republic, the proclamation of universal male suffrage, and the establishment of the Luxembourg Commission, charged with examining labor conditions.[13] Marx did not think very highly of this commission, describing it as a "ministry of pious wishes." He also viewed the creation of national workshops (*ateliers nationaux*) as a ploy to enlist worker support for the bourgeois government. Compared with the regime to come, however, Marx still described the early months of the Provisional Government as a "Republic with social institutions."[14]

All this changed, of course, once the April elections brought a more outspokenly conservative government to power. Curiously, Marx interpreted the subsequent June crushing of the workers' uprising as a return of sorts to the natural order of historical class struggle: "the real birthplace of the bourgeois republic is not the *February victory*; it is the *June defeat*," he remarked.[15] The early influence wielded by the workers was a historical anomaly; in Hegelian terms, their day in the sun of History had not yet arrived. But it was precisely through their clash with the bourgeoisie that the proletarians discovered their own class identity: "Only after being dipped in the blood of the *June insurgents* did the tricolor become the flag of the European revolution—the *red flag!*"[16] History itself thus allowed Marx to update the revolutionary theory he and Engels had laid out previously in the *Communist Manifesto*. In defeat, the proletarians had come out of the shadows of the bourgeoisie and assumed their own identity as a revolutionary class.

Where the establishment of constitutional rule had traditionally been regarded as the telos of revolution (at least up until 1793), Marx rejected this goal: "With the *Legislative* National Assembly the phenomenon of the *constitutional republic* was completed, that is, the republican form of government in which the rule of the bourgeois class is constituted."[17] The constitution, he claimed, was nothing more than the instrument that the party in power uses to retain power: "the interpretation of the constitution did not belong to those who had made it, but only to those who had accepted it.... [I]ts wording must be construed in its viable meaning and ... the bourgeois meaning was its only viable meaning." Employing a religious-legal analogy, Marx argued that interpretation was merely a means to power: "Bonaparte and the royalist majority of the National Assembly were the authentic interpreters of the constitution, as the priest is the authentic interpreter of the Bible, and the judge the authentic interpreter of the laws."[18]

This hermeneutical claim, however, masked a more radical stance. By rejecting the constitution's legitimacy, Marx refused to grant that popular sovereignty should have the final word in settling political outcomes. He had seen firsthand what happened when French peasants and villagers voted: they elected a Bonaparte.[19] In many respects, Marx's resistance to popular elections was driven by a paradox of authoritarian power in nineteenth-century France: direct democracy, in the form of plebiscites, was a central pillar of support of Bonapartism.[20] Constitutionalism, in nineteenth-century France, was counterrevolutionary. Marx had to make philosophical lemonade out of historical lemons.

But Marx's impatience with popular sovereignty cannot just be chalked up to a conservative electorate. Viewing all politics through the lens of class struggle, he castigated the Second Republic as nothing other than a "bourgeois dictatorship" (*Bourgeoisdictatur*). With this expression, he meant two things: first, it designated a regime that did not hesitate to use force to impose its will and repress dissent (as he shows in his analysis of the June 13,

1849, uprising). But the other half of the expression is equally important: politics was simply a matter of looking out for one's own class interests.

And so the ruthless defense of bourgeois interests that defined the Second Republic in Marx's eyes became a lesson in class domination. As in the past, the bourgeoisie was showing the way to conduct a successful revolution. Now that the proletariat had been fully elevated to the consciousness of its revolutionary-historical role, it should accordingly mimic the bourgeoisie in its pursuit and preservation of power. Or rather, in a more Hegelian mode, Marx argued that this was already happening: "the *proletariat* rallies more and more around *revolutionary socialism*, around *communism*, for which the bourgeoisie has itself invented the name of *Blanqui*. This socialism is the *declaration of the permanence of the revolution* [die *Permanenzerklärung der Revolution*], the *class dictatorship* of the proletariat as the necessary transit point to the *abolition of class distinctions generally*."[21]

This oft-quoted passage of the *Class Struggles* marks an important turning point in the history of revolutionary thought. Where the legitimacy of postrevolutionary regimes had previously been thought to rest on popular sovereignty, here Marx proposes a different form of political authority, which derives from the *future* accomplishment of a revolutionary program. The proletariat is the only class that can legitimately rule over the others because it is the only class destined to accomplish the true historical purpose of the revolution. Class sovereignty, which would later morph into party sovereignty, became the new guarantor of power in this permanent model of revolution.

This passage is also noteworthy because it associates this type of revolutionary authority with a concept that would become central to Marxist thought: "the revolution in permanence" or "permanent revolution." Marx does not expound on this idea in *The Class Struggles in France* ("The scope of this exposition does not permit of developing the subject further"), though the reference to Blanqui has led some commentators to seek its origin there.[22] But one does not find here, or in any other of Marx's discussions of permanent revolution (to which I turn shortly), the Blanquist notion that revolutionary dictators are to be drawn from the conspiratorial group that launched the revolution in the first place.[23] Since revolutions, for Marx, are the necessary outcomes of socioeconomic contradictions, it would be illogical for him to adhere to Blanqui's model of planned insurrections. Finally, there is no indication that Marx had in mind here a dictatorship of the type

Blanqui imagined—that is, an all-powerful Committee of Public Safety. As we will see, the French revolutionary practice that Marx preferred was fundamentally different.

What Marx sketches out in the *Class Struggles in France* is nonetheless much closer to the accelerated model of proletarian revolution *during* a bourgeois revolution later championed by Lenin and (even more explicitly) Trotsky, than the two-stage model of bourgeois revolution subsequently followed by proletarian revolution announced in the *Manifesto*. And this sketch was not a one-off draft. Indeed, Marx "developed the subject further" in a short piece published around the same time: the famous March 1850 "Address of the Central Committee to the Communist League," co-written with Engels. Here the battle-cry of the *Manifesto*, "Working Men of All Countries, Unite!" (also the motto of the Communist League) was updated with a more menacing one: The German workers' "battle-cry must be: *The Revolution in Permanence [Die Revolution in Permanenz]*."[24] As in the *Class Struggles in France*, Marx and Engels denounced constitutionalism again as a class instrument of "the constitutional-democratic petty bourgeois." But they also added two twists to the theory of permanent revolution. The first was temporal: the revolution should be permanent, in the literal sense that its actions must be of indefinite duration. Conversely, those who seek to end the revolution swiftly should be viewed with suspicion:

> While the democratic petty bourgeois want to bring the revolution to an end as quickly as possible, achieving at most the aims already mentioned, it is our interest and our task to make the revolution permanent [*die Revolution permanent zu machen*], until all the more or less propertied classes have been driven from their ruling positions, until the proletariat has conquered state power and until the association of the proletarians has progressed sufficiently far.[25]

Permanent revolution is thus once again associated with class dictatorship, even if this expression is not used in the text. Indeed, instead of the comparison with bourgeois rule found in the *Class Struggles in France*, Marx and Engels introduced a different historical parallel: "As in France in 1793, it is the task of the genuinely revolutionary party in Germany to carry through the strictest centralization."[26] They left no doubts about what it was specifically this earlier model had to offer. It was the Terror:

Above all, during and immediately after the struggle the workers, as far as it is at all possible, must oppose bourgeois attempts at pacification and force the democrats to carry out their terroristic phrases [*terroristischen Phrasen*]. They must work to ensure that the immediate revolutionary excitement is not suddenly suppressed after the victory. . . . Far from opposing the so-called excesses—instances of popular vengeance against hated individuals or against public buildings with which hateful memories are associated—the workers' party must not only tolerate these actions but must even give them direction.[27]

This passage reads in part like a revenge fiction of what might have happened in spring 1848 had the Parisian workers only harassed the Provisional Government more vigorously. But it can also be read as a socialist account of *quatrevingt-treize*, with the workers in the role of the sans-culottes. Either way, Marx and Engels defined permanent revolution on the model of the "decisive, terroristic [*terroristisch*] action against the reaction" that characterized, in their view, the radical phase of the French Revolution. The battle cry for permanent revolution was a literal call to battle: "the workers must be armed and organized," they wrote, "The whole proletariat must be armed at once with muskets, rifles, cannon and ammunition."[28]

This fixation on French revolutionary Terror raises the question of how much Marx's ideas about revolution were determined by the events of 1848–1850 and how much he was thinking about 1793. Some historians have characterized Marx and Engels's aggressive posture in the March address as a departure from the milder and more cautious attitude they had adopted at the beginning of the revolution. Jonathan Sperber recently argued, for instance, that "The policies [Marx] denounced in the March Address . . . were all central features of his own activities during most of 1848–49."[29] In Sperber's view, Marx became disenchanted by the failure of policies he had advocated in the *Neue Rheinische Zeitung* and subsequently moved closer to the more radical wing of the Communist League, represented by Andreas Gottschalk (from whom Sperber suggests Marx borrowed the phrase "permanent revolution"). While Marx clearly used the 1848–1850 revolution as an opportunity to think through and work out his own revolutionary theory, there is plenty of evidence that he hatched his more radical theory of proletarian revolution earlier. Already in the fall of 1848, he was making a strong case for provisional dictatorship and against constitutionalism, claiming that "every provisional organization of the state requires a dictatorship and an energetic dictatorship at that. From the very beginning we have reproached Camphausen for not acting dictatorially, for not having immediately smashed up and eliminated the remnants of the old institutions. . . . Herr Camphausen was lulling himself with constitutional dreaming"[30] In fact, the origins of Marx's theory of permanent revolution are to be discovered well *before* the revolution even broke out in 1848.

Marx and the French Revolution

In their illuminating history of the phrase "permanent revolution," Richard B. Day and Daniel Gaido note that Marx had used the expression three times before 1850, and first in 1843.[31] Each time, they remark, it was in the context of reflections on the French Revolution, and more specifically on the Terror. The importance of this context is particularly striking in the case of Marx's first usage of the term, in "On the Jewish Question." Marx introduces this notion by rapidly surveying some of the highlights of 1793:

> in periods when the political state as such is born violently out of civil society, when political liberation is the form in which men strive to achieve their liberation, the state can and must go as far as the *abolition of religion*, the *destruction* of religion. But it can do so only in the same way that it proceeds to the abolition of private property, to the maximum, to confiscation, to progressive taxation, just as it goes as far as the abolition of life, the *guillotine*.[32]

While the particular references in this passage obviously point back to the Terror, Marx is also attempting here to generalize these events: they are not simply characteristics of Jacobinism, but are what happens in "*periods* when the political state as such is born violently out of civil society." It is in this context of violent political birth that Marx first invokes the idea of permanent revolution:

> At times of special self-confidence, political life seeks to suppress its prerequisite, civil society and the elements composing this society, and to constitute itself as the real species-life of man, devoid of contradictions. But, it can

achieve this only by coming into *violent* contradiction with its own conditions of life, only by declaring the revolution to be *permanent* [*die Revolution für* permanent *erklärt*], and, therefore, the political drama necessarily ends with the re-establishment of religion, private property, and all elements of civil society, just as war ends with peace.[33]

Telling, the reference here to "permanent revolution" is unfavorable: this revolutionary phase resulted only in the restoration of the old regime. But the phrase itself invites further scrutiny. The term "permanent" is italicized in the original German text; while Marx often used italics for emphasis (including elsewhere in this passage), he may plausibly have used them here to indicate the foreign—and more specifically French—origin of the word.[34] It was not a term Marx had used often before.[35] What might explain its sudden appearance in his lexicon was his reading of that time. Day and Gaido do not mention that when Marx wrote "On the Jewish Question," he was immersed in the study of the French Revolution. He was living in Paris during this period (October 1843–January 1845) and contemplated writing a history of the National Convention.[36] He accordingly consulted Philippe Buchez and Pierre-Célestin Roux's *Histoire parlementaire de la Révolution française* (1833–1838), a largely documentary history of the Revolution, told from a sympathetic, neo-Jacobin perspective.[37] He may also have read Étienne Cabet's *Histoire populaire de la Révolution française, de 1789 à 1830*. And it is precisely around this time that Marx began affixing the qualifier "permanent" to revolution, notably in *The Holy Family* (published in 1845 but written the year before), where Marx remarks that Napoleon "*perfected* the *Terror* by *substituting permanent war* for *permanent revolution* [Er vollzog den Terrorismus, indem er an die Stelle der *permanenten* Revolution den permanenten *Krieg* setzte]."[38]

Here as well, the value of "permanent revolution" remains questionable; there is nothing yet to indicate that Marx admired this revolutionary model. But again, we can see the strong connection in Marx's mind between "permanent revolution" and the Terror of 1793. What made that connection meaningful? What exactly did Marx take away from his readings? A first step toward answering this question would be to resolve the philological mystery surrounding this expression: where did the term "permanent revolution" come from? As we have seen, scholars have suggested many different origins, though they are mostly speculative.[39] But there is in fact a clear source for this expression, which historians have curiously overlooked, and that is in the documentary record of the French Revolution itself.[40]

I am not claiming that Marx found the precise expression *révolution permanente* readymade in the revolutionary archives, even though it can, in fact, be found. Interestingly, the two uses of this expression that come closest to Marx's phrasing both employ it negatively. In a spring 1793 treatise dealing with constitutional matters, Jean-Baptiste-Moïse Jollivet, a former member of the Legislative Assembly, used it to warn against the dangers of weakening central political authority: "Then society would truly have no social aspect; it would be in perpetual and permanent revolution."[41] Jollivet's negative assessment of "permanent revolution" was echoed in another short text of the period, the *Adresse du conseil général permanent du département de l'Orne, à ses concitoyens*. Read at the beginning of the July 8, 1793, session of the National Convention, it summoned Frenchmen to be "continuously on guard against ill-wishers; since, to maintain you in a permanent state of revolution, of license and of anarchy, they will use all sorts of tricks."[42]

Given that we have no evidence that Marx knew of either of these documents, it would be foolish to claim that they constitute "the first" uses of this expression, particularly as they are conceptually opposed to Marx's theory. But consider this other address, made by the *citoyens en réquisition de la Section de Marseille* and presented to the convention on September 21, 1793: "the revolutionary army and canons will be maintained in permanence [l'armée révolutionnaire et les canons vont être en permanence]," they declared.[43] Here we find a very approving use of the expression *en permanence*. Rather than signaling perpetual disorder, it stands for constant alertness and preparedness in the face of counterrevolutionary threats. What is more, this choice of words was not fortuitous.

Indeed, the expression *en permanence* has a rich history in French revolutionary discourse. It can be traced back to the summer of 1792, when the people of Paris, and the Legislative Assembly, feared for the worst. France had declared war against Austria in April, but the king had vetoed a measure deploying twenty thousand national guardsmen outside of Paris to protect the capital.[44] In July, the assembly declared "la patrie en danger" (the homeland [is] in danger). It was in this context that the deputy Jacques-Alexis Thuriot relayed a demand expressed by the Parisian sections:

Many departments have already requested that their sections meet in permanence [La permanence des sections a déjà été demandée par plusieurs départements]. In Paris, it is the permanence of the sections that made the Revolution; it is the permanence that must consolidate it. I demand that the Assembly decree that the situation is urgent and that the sections meet in permanence.

His measure was promptly approved: "The National Assembly, having decreed the situation to be urgent, decrees that the assemblies of the Parisian sections will be held in permanence [se tiendront et seront permanentes], until otherwise indicated."[45] Here we find a very different understanding of revolutionary "permanence," one that is much closer to Marx's later usage. To declare the *permanence des sections* meant that instead of meeting on a regular basis, the Parisian sections (forty-eight in total) should keep their meeting places manned and open at all times. Practically, this amounted to mobilizing the armed citizens of Paris. The importance of this measure would soon become clear: on August 8, the Parisian sections voted massively in favor of overthrowing the king and then carried out their decision, storming the Tuileries palace on the night of August 9–10, 1792.[46] When, a year later, the section de Marseilles declared its intentions to meet *en permanence*, it expressed its continued faith in this belief that the Revolution could be saved through popular, armed defense. We are very close here to Marx and Engels's argument, in the March 1850 address, that "the workers must be armed and organized."

Can we be sure that Marx knew the revolutionary history of this term? It was certainly widely used, as simple word searches reveal: the phrase *en permanence* occurs in the *Archives parlementaires* more than two hundred times in 1792, and more than three hundred in 1793.[47] For the most part, this phrase was employed in reference to the Parisian sections: combinations of the terms "section(s)" and "permanent/permanence" occur more than 150 times in 1792, and more than 200 in 1793.[48] But other revolutionary bodies could also meet *en permanence*: as the Parisian sections were storming the Tuileries palace, the Legislative Assembly declared itself to be "en séance permanente."[49]

These quantitative measures are taken from the *Archives parlementaires*, a collation of primary sources similar to the *Histoire parlementaire*, without the political editorializing. Marx, however, read the latter. Was the theme of *permanence* as prominent in these volumes? As they have also been digitized, we can again marshal some numbers: volume 27, for instance, which covers the month of May 1793, contains ten mentions of "permanence," either in reference to the Parisian (or Marseillais) sections, sessions of the National Convention, or even the guillotine ("la guillotine est en permanence à Lyon").[50] Indeed, the phrase *en permanence* could be applied to almost any revolutionary institution, thus indicating its potency: Georges Couthon, a member of the Committee of Public Safety, declared (rather redundantly) this committee itself to be meeting "en permanence continuelle."[51]

In addition to these examples from the revolutionary texts, it is also worth paying attention to some of Buchez and Roux's editorial commentary. They make a point of underscoring the curious fact that the permanent session declared by the Legislative Assembly on August 10 was never lifted.[52] At a historical level, this detail might seem like a mere technicality. But it once again underscores the revolutionary symbolism captured in this phrase—and practice—of "permanence." When the going gets tough, the tough get permanent.

Finally, it's worth noting that the revolutionary practice of declaring permanence did not die out with the first French Revolution. As Jill Harsin has noted (without referring to Marx), revolutionaries in the 1830s would similarly declare section meetings to take place *en permanence* in cases of political emergency. As she writes, "the calling of meetings *en permanence*" was one of "the symbols of the revolutionary period of half a century before" that the July Monarchy men self-consciously invoked, along with the *Marseillaise* and the various section names.[53] Permanence remained part of the revolutionary repertoire up until 1848: indeed, on February 24, the day Louis Philippe abdicated, the deputy Charles Lafitte proposed that the Chamber of Deputies meet *en permanence*. His motion was seconded by Étienne Armand Napoléon de Cambacérès, whose uncle, Jean-Jacques-Régis de Cambacérès, had been a deputy in the National Convention (before becoming consul alongside Napoleon Bonaparte). The chamber dismissed the motion, but clearly the echoes of 1792 had not yet died out, as subsequent uses of this phrase during the 1848 revolution indicate.[54] Not only the chamber met in permanence, but in April so did the Parisian clubs.[55] The resurgence of this revolutionary memory may explain why Marx, in 1848, began considering "permanence" in a positive light and also why other revolutionary theorists, such as Proudhon or Gottschalk, latched onto this phrase at the same time.

The history of permanence in the first French Revolution also helps explain Marx's own understanding of the term. First, it's telling that in his very first use of the expression (in "On the Jewish Question"), permanence was something that had to be *declared*: "die Revolution für *permanent* erklärt." This corresponds to the original declaration of the "permanence of the sections" by the Legislative Assembly. Permanence is above all a performative. Its declarative origins are still on display in the *Class Struggles in France*, where Marx describes "die *Permanenzerklärung der Revolution*." This may also explain why the anonymous deputy to the Frankfurt National Assembly, whom Marx quotes in the September 23, 1848, issue of the *Neue Rheinische Zeitung*, announced that the assembly, in response to Frederick William IV of Prussia's counterrevolutionary action, had issued "a *declaration of permanence* which will probably lead to a new and very bloody *revolution*."[56] Second, let us remember that Marx only rarely uses the precise phrase "permanent revolution" (a point that gets lost in some English translations).[57] The "battle cry" issued in the 1850 address is rather *Die Revolution in Permanenz*. This phrase closely mirrors the French construction *en permanence*.

But the real payoff of this philological exercise is that it can illuminate Marx's own fleeting use of the concept of permanent revolution, and in particular its connection with the Terror. Viewed through the lens of "permanence," the Terror was first and foremost a *popular* affair, with armed sans-culottes taking the lead. These sans-culottes could easily be substituted, in Marx's mind at least, with armed workers. The key point to note here is that in this reading of the Terror the major players of the time—the Jacobin Club, the National Convention, the revolutionary tribunal, and even the Committee of Public Safety—take a second seat to the Parisian sections. In other words, the model of "permanent revolution" that Marx discovered in the Terror had very little to do with the more notable revolutionary institutions and individuals of the time. This meant that Marx could still be critical of the Jacobin idolatry that continued to afflict, in his eyes, French revolutionaries in 1848, without rejecting the value of the Terror (redefined as a popular movement) for future revolutions.[58]

This is not to say that Marx assumed no central organization was needed. Permanent revolution, like the Terror, was still compatible with dictatorship and "the strictest centralization," as Marx and Engels announced in their

1850 address—a line that Engels would furiously walk back in a post-Commune (1885) footnote praising local governments.[59] Class dictatorship might still require some actual dictators. Buchez and Roux, for their part, gave a hearty endorsement of the "Jacobin dictators," saluting the "high morality of their political doctrine."[60] But the "class dictatorship" that Marx had in mind could still have been construed as a kind of class sovereignty, since it was the armed sans-culottes who ultimately held the balance of power. "Permanence," in its 1792–1793 incarnation, entailed a different center of political gravity than Blanqui's theory of revolutionary dictatorship.

But the French Revolution origins of "permanence" also call attention to the central place of armed insurrection and popular violence in Marx's theory (recall "la guillotine en permanence"). Buchez and Roux presented this violence as not only necessary but wholly justified: in a preface entitled "De la terreur et de la crainte comme méthodes sociales," they laid out the neo-Jacobin *thèse des circonstances* in all its splendor: "Terror is thus sometimes obligatory; it is a duty to inflict it, though it always remains an exceptional method." It was nothing to be ashamed of since everyone did it.[61] To this *raison d'état* logic, Marx could add his own Hegelian argument that only history unveils the true and necessary processes of revolution. Since the Jacobins had had to use Terror, clearly the workers would as well. By fishing the concept of permanence out from the ocean of French revolutionary discourse, Marx elevated the Terror to a law of revolutionary history.

A Found and Lost History

If historians have not dedicated much effort to probing the origins of Marx's theory of permanent revolution, its family resemblance with Blanqui's idea of revolutionary dictatorship may largely be to blame. This resemblance even led fellow social-democrats to denounce it: as Day and Gaido recount, Eduard Bernstein, in his revisionist critique of Marxism, rejected permanent revolution as "Blanquism."[62] His accusation was all the more potent in that, in 1850, Marx and Engels had indeed collaborated with Blanquists, notably to form a short-lived "Universal Society of Revolutionary Communists." What's more, Marx himself invited this comparison by invoking Blanqui in his definition of permanent revolution in the *Class Struggles in France* and by praising him elsewhere.[63]

But as Day and Gaido also show, this identification was challenged in Bernstein's own time. Franz Mehring, who would later publish a biography of Marx, responded point by point to Bernstein, calling attention to the ways in which permanent revolution differed from Blanqui's "putschism."[64] Social-democrats of this period also remained aware of the French revolutionary roots of this concept. Equally critical of Bernstein was Karl Kautsky, who wrote a history of the French Revolution in which he argued that "the *sans-culottes* had to adopt ever more extreme measures; they had to declare the revolution in permanence [*revolution in permanenz*] and intensify all the more the terrorism that the war conditions had rendered necessary."[65] Engels similarly drew attention to this history, if in a somewhat roundabout way: "When later I read Bougeart's book on Marat, I found that in more than one respect we had only unconsciously imitated the great model of the genuine 'Ami du Peuple.'"[66] Alfred Bougeart had indeed highlighted Marat's defense of "permanence," discussing for instance his statement in favor of the "permanence de la commune" after the fall of the monarchy on August 10, 1792: since "the Commune's goal had not been achieved, the permanence of danger legitimates the permanence of its dictatorship."[67] What Engels depicted as unconscious imitation, however, was more likely to have been conscious modeling, at least in the case of Marx.

By reconstructing the turn of the twentieth-century debates surrounding permanent revolution, Day and Gaido have done a particular service to historians by demonstrating that, far from being particularly associated with Trotsky, this theory was well known and accepted among most social-democratic leaders, both German and Russian.[68] They point somewhat tantalizingly to a connection between these debates and what would become the Bolshevik party line: "In Russia, Lenin adopted Trotsky's view when he resolved to seize power from the Provisional Government."[69] But Lenin did not wait until 1917 to adapt the theory of permanent revolution: Lenin had already advocated for the creation of a "revolutionary-democratic dictatorship of the proletariat and the peasantry," in *Two Tactics of Social-Democracy in the Democratic Revolution* (written in 1905).[70] Here he collapsed the standard two-stage model of revolution into an accelerated one:

We must not be afraid (as is [the Menshevik Alexandr] Martynov) of a complete victory for Social-Democracy in a democratic revolution, i.e., of a revolutionary-democratic dictatorship of the proletariat and the peasantry, for such a victory will enable us to rouse Europe, and the socialist proletariat of Europe, after throwing off the yoke of the bourgeoisie, will in its turn help us to accomplish the socialist revolution. (chap. 10)

Due to Menshevik accusations that he had abandoned orthodox Marxism, and perhaps also to distance himself from Trotsky, who, under the influence of Alexander Parvus, began to champion the one-stage model at this same time, Lenin ended up downplaying his plans for dictatorship.[71] But there can be little doubt that Lenin was drawing on Marx's theory of permanent revolution, and through Marx, on the French Revolution example.[72] In *Two Tactics of Social-Democracy*, for instance, he quotes an 1848 article from the *Neue Rheinische Zeitung* where Marx writes, "The whole French terrorism . . . was nothing but a plebian manner of settling accounts with the enemies of the bourgeoisie, with absolutism, feudalism, and philistinism."[73] To be successful, Lenin argued, the revolutionaries would have to "settle accounts with tsarism in the Jacobin, or, if you like, in the plebeian way," and not fall prey to the "constitutional illusions" of the bourgeois parties.[74]

Through the medium of Marx, the French rupture with the constitutional model of revolution would thus come to be consummated in the Bolshevik revolution. While the nominal objective of permanent revolution was the eventual dissolution ("withering away") of the state, and by extension of all political sovereignty, the endless postponement of this goal led instead to the concentration of power in the hands of a revolutionary dictatorship. With the Bolsheviks, the party would in theory be the sovereign, though in practice power would often fall into the hands of a single leader. Marx's theory of permanent revolution thus led full circle back to a model of sovereignty that constitutionalism had been designed to thwart: the figure towering over the masses had become a Red Leviathan.

Notes

My thanks to Jeffrey Freedman, Anthony Grafton, Melvin Richter, Jerrold Seigel, Richard Wolin, Isser Woloch, and the participants of the Consortium for Intellectual and Cultural History in New York for their comments on this paper.

1. M. J. C. Vile, *Constitutionalism and the Separation of Powers* (1967; Indianapolis: Liberty Fund, 1998); Quentin Skinner, *The Foundations of Modern Political Thought,*

2 vols. (Cambridge: Cambridge University Press, 1978); Keith Baker, *Inventing the French Revolution* (Cambridge: Cambridge University Press, 1990), 252; Mark Edling, *A Revolution in Favor of Government* (Oxford: Oxford University Press, 2003).

2. Accordingly, it was in conjunction with actual revolutionary movements that the most important developments in constitutional theory occurred, most notably in England after 1649 (the separation of powers) and in 1688 (the bill of rights), in Corsica after 1755 (assertion of popular sovereignty), and in the United States (the amendment process). See notably Vile, *Constitutionalism and the Separation of Powers.*

3. John Locke, *Second Treatise*, in *Two Treatises of Government*, ed. Peter Laslett (1960; Cambridge: Cambridge University Press, 1988), §240.

4. On Cuba, see Marifeli Pérez-Stable, *The Cuban Revolution: Origins, Course, and Legacy*, rev. ed. (New York: Oxford University Press, 1999); for Iran, Saïd Arjomand, *The Turban and the Crown: The Islamic Revolution in Iran* (Oxford: Oxford University Press, 1988).

5. See, e.g., Timur Kuran, "Now out of Never: The Element of Surprise in the East European Revolution of 1989," *World Politics* 44, no. 1 (1991): 7–48.

6. See Dan Edelstein, "Do We Want a Revolution Without a Revolution? Reflections on Political Authority," *French Historical Studies* 35, no. 2 (2012): 269–89.

7. See *Witnesses to Permanent Revolution: The Documentary Record*, ed. Richard B. Day and Daniel Gaido (Leiden: Brill, 2009).

8. On Marx's 1848 experiences, see Gareth Stedman Jones, "Scripting the German Revolution: Marx and 1848," in *Scripting Revolution*, ed. Keith Baker and Dan Edelstein (forthcoming), and Jonathan Sperber, *Karl Marx: A Nineteenth-Century Life* (New York: Norton, 2013). On 1848 in general, see Sperber, *The European Revolutions, 1848–1851* (Cambridge: Cambridge University Press, 2005).

9. I am referring here to the argument, found in the last chapter of the *Manifesto*, that Communists should ally themselves, when necessary, with bourgeois parties engaged in revolutionary struggles and only turn against the bourgeoisie once the latter is victorious. See Stanley Moore, "Marx and Lenin as Historical Materialists," *Philosophy and Public Affairs* 4, no. 2 (1975): 171–94.

10. On this work, and the role of historiography in the development of Marx's revolutionary theory, see Leonard Krieger, "Marx and Engels as Historians," *Journal of the History of Ideas* 14, no. 3 (1953): 381–403; Jerrold Seigel, *Marx's Fate* (Princeton: Princeton University Press, 1978); and Peter Hayes, "Marx's Analysis of the French Class Structure," *Theory and Society* 22, no. 1 (1993): 99–123.

11. English translation from the Marx-Engels Archive, www.marxists.org/archive /marx/works/1850/class-struggles-france/ch01.htm. For pagination purposes, I provide page references to the *MEGA* edition, as well as the original German citation when the wording matters: *Die Klassenkämpfe in Frankreich 1848 bis 1850*, in *Karl Marx, Friedrich Engels Gesamtausgabe* (Berlin: Dietz Verlag, 1977), part 1, vol. 10, chap. 1, 127.

12. The above quote is preceded by the following passage: "The French working class had not attained this level; *it was still incapable of accomplishing its own revolution*" (emphasis added).

13. See Priscilla Smith Robertson, *Revolutions of 1848* (Princeton: Princeton University Press, 1952), and Sperber, *European Revolutions*.
14. *Klassenkämpfe in Frankreich*, chap. 1, 136.
15. Ibid., and chap. 3, 190–91. See Seigel, *Marx's Fate*, 206–13.
16. *Klassenkämpfe in Frankreich*, chap. 1, 140.
17. Ibid., chap. 3, 168. On Marx and Engels's anticonstitutional perspective during the 1848–1850 revolutions, see also Engels's "The Campaign for the German Imperial Constitution," which comes down very strongly against the constitutional model (in Day and Gaido, *Witnesses*, 7–8). This rejection of purely "political" solutions to social inequality can be traced back to Marx's early arguments about emancipation; see Seigel, *Marx's Fate*, chap. 4.
18. *Klassenkämpfe in Frankreich*, chap. 3, 169.
19. Ibid., chap. 1, 135. Note, however, that Marx also criticizes the bourgeois "Party of order" for suspending universal suffrage (at the end of chap. 3).
20. On Napoleon I's plebiscites, which included the 1804 confirmation of Napoleon as emperor, and the 1815 vote on the *acte additionel* to the constitution, see Isser Woloch, *Napoleon and His Collaborators* (New York: Norton, 2002). His nephew Napoleon III continued this tradition, holding plebiscites in 1851 (to confirm his coup d'état) and in 1852 (to confirm his imperial position). As I have argued elsewhere, the Jacobins suspended the 1793 constitution in part for similar electoral concerns; see my *The Terror of Natural Right* (Chicago: University of Chicago, 2009), chap. 4.
21. *Klassenkämpfe in Frankreich*, chap. 3, 192.
22. See, for instance, James Billington: "In propounding this doctrine, [Marx] drew close to Blanqui, whose ideas would also provide fortification for Lenin at a later time" (*Fire in the Minds of Men: Origins of the Revolutionary Faith* [New York: Basic Books, 1980], 282). In his biography of Marx, David McLellan reads the reference to Blanqui literally, suggesting that Marx genuinely is describing "the revolutionary socialism of Blanqui" (*Karl Marx: His Life and Thought* [New York: Harper & Row, 1973], 239). On Blanqui, see notably Patrick H. Hutton, *The Cult of the Revolutionary Tradition: The Blanquists in French Politics* (Berkeley: University of California Press, 1981). I am grateful to Biliana Kassabova for conversations about Blanqui's unpublished manuscripts.
23. Billington stresses the role played by Philippe Buonarotti's *Conspiration pour l'Egalité* (Brussels: La Librairie romantique, 1828), his account of Gracchus Babeuf's 1795 failed insurrection, in the development of Blanqui's own conspiratorial model of revolutionary dictatorship; see *Fire in the Minds of Men*. On Marx's own familiarity and interest in Buonarotti, see Bruce Brown, "The French Revolution and the Rise of Social Theory," *Science and Society* 30, no. 4 (1966): 385–432, esp. 423–24.
24. English translation from Marx-Engels Archive, www.marxists.org/archive/marx/works/1847/communist-league/1850-ad1.htm. For the original, see *Ansprache der Zentralbehörde des Bundes der Kommunisten vom März 1850*, in *MEGA*, part 1, 10:254–63.
25. *Ansprache der Zentralbehörde*, 258.
26. Ibid., 262.

27. Ibid., 259.
28. Ibid., 260.
29. Sperber, *Karl Marx*, 252. This was also McLellan's assessment; see his *Karl Marx*, 233.
30. *Neue Rheinische Zeitung* 102 (September 14, 1848), www.marxists.org/archive /marx/works/1848/09/12.htm#102. Lenin cites this passage in the epilogue to *Two Tactics of Social-Democracy*, in *Lenin Anthology*, ed. Robert Tucker (New York: Norton, 1975), 142. The November 23, 1848, issue of the *Neue Rheinische Zeitung* alludes to the "Organ der in Permanenz erklärten Revolution"; see also the issue of January 13, 1849, which refers to "die Revolution in Permanenz."
31. Day and Gaido, *Witnesses*, 3. Robert Tucker's *Marx-Engels Reader* (New York: Norton, 1972) already contained a reference to the earliest use in its index. See also Daniel Guérin, *La lutte des classes sous la première république* (Paris: Gallimard, 1946), 1:5–9.
32. English translation from the Marx-Engels Archive, www.marxists.org/archive /marx/works/1844/jewish-question/; *Zur Judenfrage*, in *MEGA*, part 1, 2:150–51.
33. *Zur Judenfrage*, 151.
34. For instance, in the preceding pages of *Zur Judenfrage*, Marx italicizes the words *bourgeois*, *citoyen*, and *Guillotine* (this last example comes from the quotation above).
35. I was only able to locate one prior use, in a May 12, 1842, *Rheinische Zeitung* article. My thanks to Adrian Daub for his comments on the German usage of *permanent*.
36. See Sperber, *Karl Marx*, chap. 4. On Marx's interest in French revolutionary history, see Brown, "French Revolution," esp. 422ff.; François Furet, *Marx and the French Revolution*, trans. Deborah Kan Furet (Chicago: University of Chicago Press, 1988); Michael Löwy, "The Poetry of the Past," *New Left Review* 177 (September/October 1989): 111–24; and Harold Mah, "The French Revolution and the Problem of German Modernity: Hegel, Heine and Marx," *New German Critique* 50 (1990): 3–20.
37. Marx cites Buchez and Roux in "On the Jewish Question" (*Histoire parlementaire*, vol. 28) and in *The Holy Family* (vol. 31–32). On Marx's other readings, see Brown, "French Revolution," 422–24, and Furet, *Marx and the French Revolution*, 20.
38. English translation at Marx-Engels Archive, www.marxists.org/archive/marx /works/1845/holy-family/ch06_3_c.htm. Emphasis added.
39. Billington traces the term back to German Illuminists; see *Fire in the Minds of Men*. I. Bernard Cohen has suggested that Proudhon may have been at the origin of this phrase; see *Revolution in Science* (Cambridge, MA: Harvard University Press, 1985), 274.
40. After researching this article, I discovered that Michael Löwy had suggested a related genealogy for Marx's expression: "It may be . . . that the phrase comes directly from Jacobin usage. During moments of revolutionary crisis the Jacobin Club would declare itself assembled 'en permanence'—in permanent session." *The Politics of Combined and Uneven Development: The Theory of Permanent Revolution* (1981; 2nd ed., Chicago: Haymarket Books, 2010), 8n20. While Löwy was on the right track, this historical reference is not exact: the origins of this

expression are not to be found with the Jacobin Club but rather with the Parisian sections. I outline below why this distinction matters and how it can help us to better comprehend what Marx had in mind when referring to "revolution in permanence." Guérin's mostly forgotten volumes on *La lutte des classes*, to which Löwy's article directed my attention, also establish a connection between permanent revolution and the Terror, though the author is mainly concerned with demonstrating the emergence of a "proletariat" class during the French Revolution.

41. See Jollivet, *Principes fondamentaux du régime social comparés avec le plan de Constitution*, in *Archives parlementaires* (*AP*) 61:644–66, 665, annex to the April 12, 1793, session.

42. *AP*, 68:396.

43. *AP*, 74:593.

44. See Jones, *Great Nation*, 459.

45. July 25, 1792; *AP*, 47:143. This episode is also recounted in the *Histoire parlementaire*, 16:179.

46. See Marcel Reinhard, *La chute de la royauté: 10 août 1792* (Paris: Gallimard, 1969).

47. Results obtained by a string search for "en permanence" in the AP (The Project for American and French Research on the Treasury of the French Language, or ARTFL, edition) and reporting results by frequency per year. Exact numbers: 223 and 344. Some of the metadata on the volumes is erroneous, however, so exact numbers are only provided to give a general order of magnitude.

48. Results obtained through a proximity search at the sentence level for "section* permanen*" and reporting results by frequency per year (ARTFL edition). Exact numbers: 169 and 232, but see qualifiers in preceding note.

49. *Histoire parlementaire*, 17:23.

50. May 15, 1793, *Histoire parlementaire*, 27:18. This term also features frequently in Etienne Cabet's *Histoire populaire de la revolution francaise*; in vol. 3, which deals with years 1792–1794, there are fourteen mentions of "permanence."

51. *Histoire parlementaire*, 32:197. Marx cites from this volume in *The Holy Family*.

52. "Ce fut la dernière du corps législatif; et c'est ici qu'il faut remarquer que la séance fut toujours considérée comme permanente depuis le 10 août. La permanence prononcée dans la nuit du 9 au 10 ne fut point levée. Les journaux du temps, le *Moniteur*, portent constamment en tête de leurs comptes-rendus: *Suite de la séance permanente du 10 août*. C'est donc à tort que presque tous les historiens ont écrit que la permanence avait cessé dans le mois d'août" (*Histoire parlementaire*, 17:17–18).

53. See Jill Harsin, *Barricades: The War of the Streets in Revolutionary Paris, 1830–1848* (New York: Palgrave Macmillan, 2002), 16–17 and passim. My thanks to Biliana Kassabova for this reference.

54. This event is described in numerous histories of 1848: for a fairly detailed account, see Jules Lermina, Émile Faure, and Edouard-Accoyer Spoll, *Histoire anecdotique illustrée de la révolution de 1848* (Paris: Pache and Defaux, 1868), 236–37; for some other examples, see 188, 271, 328, and 337. The website of the French National Assembly has a biographical fiche on Cambacérès: www.assemblee -nationale.fr/sycomore/fiche.asp?num_dept=9420.

55. This detail is mentioned in Edward Stillingfleet Cayley, *The European Revolutions of 1848* (London: Smith, Elder, 1856), 1:97.
56. English translation at Marx-Engels Archive, www.marxists.org/archive/marx/works/1848/09/23.htm.
57. See, for instance, the translation of the March 1850 address in the Marx-Engels Archive, which concludes with "Their battle-cry must be: *The Permanent Revolution*."
58. Hence, I disagree with Michael Löwy, who assumes that when Marx refers to the Terror he has in mind "the Jacobin model of 1793." But *permanence* was not a Jacobin concept at all: it was in fact the Jacobin-dominated National Convention that abolished the permanence of the sections on September 5, 1793. See Löwy, "Poetry of the Past," 122; on the convention, see Edelstein, *Terror of Natural Right*, 139.
59. See Tucker, *Marx-Engels Reader*, 510n4: "It must be recalled today that this passage is based on a misunderstanding."
60. *Histoire parlementaire*, 31:313.
61. *Histoire parlementaire*, 20:vi–vii.
62. See *The Preconditions of Socialism and the Tasks of Social Democracy* (1899), discussed in Day and Gaido, *Witnesses to Permanent Revolution*, 16–18.
63. Day and Gaido, *Witnesses*, 11–12. On this organization, and Marx's dealings with Blanquists in 1850, see also Christine Lattek, *Revolutionary Refugees: German Socialism in Britain, 1840-1860* (New York: Routledge, 2006) 52–57.
64. See Mehring, "The Revolution in Permanence" (1889), in Day and Gaido, *Witnesses*, 457–63.
65. See Kautsky, "The Sans-Culottes of the French Revolution" (1889), in Day and Gaido, *Witnesses*, 541. This text constitutes a chapter in his longer history, *Die Klassengegensätze von 1789: Zum hundertjährigen Gedenktag der grossen Revolution* (Stuttgart: Dietz, 1889); a French translation was also published, *La lutte des classes en France en 1789*, trans. Edouard Berth (Paris: G. Jacques, 1901), quote on 85.
66. "Marx and the *Neue Rheinische Zeitung* (1848–49)," in Day and Gaido, *Witnesses*, 14.
67. Alfred Bougeart, *Marat, l'ami du peuple* (Paris: Libraire internationale, 1865), 97.
68. Note also that Socialist Revolutionaries were similarly debating this theory around the same time; see Maureen Perrie, "The Socialist Revolutionaries on 'Permanent Revolution,'" *Soviet Studies* 24, no. 3 (1973): 411–13.
69. Day and Gaido, *Witnesses*, 54.
70. See Robert Service, *Lenin* (London: Macmillan, 2000), 173–74.
71. For Trotsky, too, the relation between permanent revolution and the French Terror was still evident; see his praise of Jacobinism in *Results and Prospects* (1906), chap. 3; English translation available from the Marx-Engels Archive, www.marxists.org/archive/trotsky/1931/tpr/rp03.htm.
72. According to one source, Lenin "knew [the 1850 March circular address] by heart" and "used to delight in quoting" it. David Riazanov, *Karl Marx and Frederick Engels: An Introduction to Their Lives and Work* (written 1927, published 1937), chap. 5, www.marxists.org/archive/riazanov/works/1927-ma/ch05.htm.

Referenced in Guérin, *La lutte des classes*, 1:473n14. Day and Gaido similarly note that this address "was destined to play a central role in all the debates over the class character and political alliances of the Russian revolution in 1903–7" (*Witnesses*, 9).

73. See, more generally, H. Gordon Skilling, "Permanent or Uninterrupted Revolution," *Canadian Slavonic Papers* 5 (1961): 3–30.

74. *Lenin Anthology*, 132. Lenin quotes from *The Class Struggle in France* in the conclusion to *Two Tactics of Social-Democracy*. See also Lenin's article "On Constitutional Illusions," in *Toward the Seizure of Power, Part I* (n.p., 1932), 62–75.

FIFTEEN

Exile Within Sovereignty

Critique of "The Negation of Exile" in Israeli Culture

AMNON RAZ-KRAKOTZKIN

The Negation of the Diaspora

THE "NEGATION OF EXILE" embodies the essence of the leading stream of Zionist ideology from which derive the different aspects of the Israeli Jewish-Zionist cultural experience. A central axis of an all-embracing viewpoint that defines the self-consciousness of the Jews of Israel, it informs their conception of history and collective memory, as well as cultural practices that both fashion and reflect Zionist-Israeli identity. Framing historical reality in terms of the "negation of exile" has far-reaching implications, especially on the bounds of the political and cultural discourse as well as on defining the political consensus in Israel.

"Negation of exile" denotes a viewpoint that sees modern Jewish settlement in the Land of Israel, along with the establishment of Jewish territorial sovereignty, as the return of the Jewish people to a land defined as their own after two thousand years of exile. In Zionist historical consciousness, the negation of exile fuses a continuum between the ancient past—in which there existed an entity defined as a sovereign nation—and the present, which *perceives itself* as the renewal of that same entity. The negation of exile is understood by those who express and define Zionist consciousness as the "normalization" of Jewish existence in terms of the full realization of Jewish history or, at least, its "solution." This approach, which has received countless authoritative expressions, has the status of a paradigm that directs all the streams of Zionism that accept it as a given.[1] They perceive the period of exile as an intermediary period; even if in its context important cultural values were created, it was in and of itself meaningless, a condition of deficient existence, partial and abnormal—a time in which the "spirit of the nation" could not find expression due to the external bounds that prevented its realization. The Land itself did not know a meaningful history apart from the history of the Jewish minority that settled there. The Land was an empty land, and its Palestinian population and culture had barely any part in the crystallization of Zionist self-consciousness. According to this perception, every Jew was "proto-Zionist" in that he lived a state of perpetual transience, yearning "to return" to the Land of Israel—the *only* territory where the nation can fulfill its mission.[2]

Contained within this historical perspective is an explicit assumption that the act of negating the condition of being a diaspora, the "return" to the Land, will lead, almost of its own, to the full realization of Jewish culture or the creation of a new national culture.[3] Inspired by European romantic ideas, the notion was formed to claim that the return of the people to its land and its connection to the soil of the homeland would ensure the revival of cultural creativity. This culture is understood to be "authentic": only external circumstances have until now prevented its appearance and development. It was against this background that the different images of the "new Jew"—the representative of the authentic culture and the symbol of its ideas—were created and crystallized. Over the years changes took place in the image of this symbol, as indicated by terms such as "Hebrew," "Sabra," or "Israeli," differentiated by their content and the ways in which they function. Nonetheless, all of these images come from the same principal departure point regarding the present Jewish existence in the Land, and all are incarnations of the same foundational aspiration. All of these images, and all of the explanations given to them, emphasize the difference that exists between them and the previous, exilic consciousness, whose erasure is the condition for liberation. Each in its own way symbolizes the "emancipated" Jew.[4] In seminal Zionist writings, as in the praxis that follows from them, the negation of images connected to exile serves as a founding basis of consciousness as well as a means and origin of legitimacy for the axioms and political activity of the state.

In this way, elements defined as exilic were rejected, and this rejection served as the basis for the establishment of the new, anti-exilic Jew, ostensibly liberated from the shackles of tradition. Characteristics ascribed to "exilic-ness" ("weakness," "passivity," etc.) were rejected, as were entire cultural traditions that were perceived as "exilic" (including, significantly, those of Jews from Arab countries). The declared policy was to bring about a cultural unification based on the system of values and images of the hegemonic elite. Even if this tendency was not fully realized, Israeliness remained based on repression and rejection. Phenomena that did not fall in line with this guiding principle, or that even expressed oppositional viewpoints, retained limited cultural status.

With time, the meanings of this radical trend became clear. Scholarship on the subject explicitly links cultural assumptions to prominent instances of denial and discrimination.[5] Components of early images of the negation of exile dulled over the years: the myth of the "Hebrew" or the "Sabra" lost the normative role it had played in the past, and new voices appeared that had been completely repressed or pushed to the margins. This new awareness did not lead to a fundamental clarification regarding the defining of historical reality on the basis of the myth of the "negation of exile" and its conception of history. The general outlines of this consciousness were perceived as obvious to the point that it was never examined or questioned, especially in a secular-Jewish context.[6] In particular, the direct link between this definition of Israeliness and the treatment of Palestinians was not discussed. The questions of the new Jewish identity and the Palestinian question were, and continue to be, perceived as entirely separate matters; and this despite the fundamental difficulty that stems from defining Israel as a Jewish state and its problematic outcome regarding the status of the Palestinian citizens.

The analysis outlined here considers the possibilities embodied in the concept of exile. I argue that concealed within the very concept of exile resides the potential for a comprehensive viewpoint that allows for a different relation with the various forms of Jewish-Israeli collectivity. It is possible to dredge up "exile" from past interpretations through to its current development and develop its idea as a general ethical-cultural position that enables a Jewish self-definition turning toward those same denied foundations of the present, and which enables their open existence and recognizes their point of view. As a cultural position, it grants meaning and value to a heterogeneous reality by turning toward the foundations repressed by the concept of negation of exile; moreover, it also recognizes the existence and rights of the Palestinian collective and its viewpoint. In the concept of exile is thus embodied a consistent moral position, on which critique can be grounded.

This alternative option has at its focus a concept of exile that comes from within the existing reality and recognizes the possibilities embodied in it. It does not constitute a return to the past, and certainly not an idealization of any exilic historical reality. In no way am I suggesting that we relate to exile as a positive historical condition to which we should aspire. A critical discussion must emphasize the basic element of oppression contained within exile as a historical condition, as well as its catastrophic results in certain historical contexts. It must take into consideration the dangers that Jews face in certain conditions of exile (without limiting the concern to the fate of Jews alone) and also the historical context that led to the growth of a consciousness that negates the diaspora. Nevertheless, being wary of the idealization of the exilic condition cannot invalidate either the fundamental meaning that is contained in the concept or the ethical-critical position that follows from it in concrete Israeli reality.

My use of "exile" here derives from the recognition that a critical attempt to present a cultural alternative requires the employment of concepts that delineate the culture being discussed. This direction differs from the position that presents "Israeliness" as a cultural option and the aspiration to turn Israel into a "normal" nation-state. The latter position is generally motivated by honest intentions to achieve the democratization of the state, as well as by a recognition of how problematic it is to define the state as "the state of the Jewish people." However, its pretension to define the collective in a way that will include the Arab citizens of Israel, alongside the trend to create an Israeli nationalism seemingly detached from Judaism, stipulates the acceptance of Arabs into the collective on their agreement to accept the cultural values of "Israeliness" as these are determined by the Jewish majority.[7] Talk of an Israeli nation preserves the same assumptions underlying the hegemonic Zionist culture. The bi-nationalism of Israel is not part of the suggested self-definition, which forecloses the Palestinian perspective and collective identity. The cultivation of this kind of Israeliness also deepens the disregard for the basic theological element bound up in the conceptual system of the Hebrew language in general, and in the loaded meanings of the concepts "exile" (*galut*), "redemption" (*geula*), or the "Land of Israel" (*eretz-yisrael*) in particular, as if language were neutral.

The Concept of Exile: The Theological Context

The fundamental problematic aspect of a Jewish collective definition based on the "negation of exile" stems, foremost, from the central place given to the concept of exile as the basis for Jewish self-definition as a historical phenomenon. If it is at all possible to speak of some common foundation to all of the historical expressions of Judaism, that foundation should be pinned to the definition of existence as a reality of exile. The destruction of the Temple became a symbol signifying the fashioning of a new collective historical-religious awareness in the first centuries of the Common Era (in exactly the same way that Christianity developed during that period) that based itself on an explicit bond to the past and that saw itself as the "real Israel." The foundations of this viewpoint preceded the destruction of the Second Temple and are already found in biblical texts, but only later on did they crystallize into a basis for defining Judaism, which in the context of rabbinic Judaism is the historical Judaism.[8] In Talmudic literature a concept of exile was formed that later developed corresponding to the changing cultural context. Talmudic literature, in its character and essence, reflects the consciousness of exile and creates the framework of belonging to a collective in which is embedded the consciousness of exile. This is what set Judaism apart in its own eyes (in the West at least until the eighteenth century).

Exile as a theological concept signifies the conditions under which it is impossible to uphold the commandments anywhere—including the Land of Israel.[9] Moreover, exile conditions a psychological-political consciousness that is not detached and that achieves rich expression in Jewish legal (halakhic) discourse; to adopt contemporary parlance, the consciousness of exile guides the existence of the Jew as a member in a minority group that criticizes the basic assumptions of the dominant majority. This consciousness played (and plays) a formative role in Jewish literature as well as in the concrete social frameworks of existence of the daily and yearly agenda. From this consciousness are derived conceptions of history, time, and fundamental assumptions about human existence. This is not merely *one* of the foundations of Jewish existence—it is the central foundation of its definition. The discussion of exile is not always explicit, but it appears in many of the texts that we identify as Jewish, and not only in the (many) texts whose focus is an investigation of the concept of exile. The concept also had a central role in the polemical reinforcement of Judaism. Exile does not only (or necessarily) symbolize the absence of power: conditions of powerlessness that existed in exile are of course well known, but they are perceived as dependent on some concrete historical situation and not on the condition of exile itself. Contrarily, the discourse on exile signifies a certain position in relation to the existing order, a position that exists in the given world but maintains a critical distance.

The concept of exile has acquired an extensive and rich and wide spectrum of interpretations and various responses across different political and social contexts. The Zionist perception of exile as the lack of realization of the political aspirations of the Jews and nothing more empties the concept of all of its deep contents in that it accepts the world order in its present form, adopts the modern system of values, and hopes for their realization *also* regarding the Jews. By the same token there is no place to claim that exile is apolitical or that it indicates passivity. This is the point of view of someone who has already defined the current reality as "negation of exile" while flattening the theological meaning. We need a clear distinction between "exile" as a broad concept aimed at reality in its entirety and "exile" (in its modern sense) or "diaspora," which highlight the existence of Jews in other lands and ignore the theological meaning of this condition.

Presenting exile as a temporary condition that connotes an aspiration for "return" to the Land of Israel does not satisfy, and generally does not serve, as a central component in the definition of exile and in its representation. Without diminishing one iota the centrality of the Land of Israel in past rabbinic Jewish thought, it should be noted that contrary to formulations widespread in Zionist discourse, the yearning for the Land of Israel was not defined in rabbinic thought as the result of the "negation of exile," and it was certainly not formulated in terms of ownership and attachment to an ancient past. It was the same when the messianic utopia included distinct foundations of return and rehabilitation. The fundamental meaning of exile and its sufferings in the Jewish consciousness are the symptom that represents the condition of the world in its entirety, and this symptom uses the fact that the world is not yet redeemed as the basis to be applied to reality. Therefore, in every discussion of exile as a theological concept, the discussion of evil—the perception of evil or the absence of good—stands at its center. However, this focus on evil does not come to be on its own. It is the basis for the traditional-religious stance and behavior that aims at redemption and that simultaneously signifies the distinct obligation of the created world in its present form; this approach is also at the basis of discussions of the "ignominy of exile," a discourse focused on the fate of Jews in one historical context or other expressing the determined cry for the change of that fate. Finally, exile is also the expression of the condition of divinity itself—God is in exile when His people are in exile.

The meaning of the concept of exile is especially prominent regarding the Jewish existence that developed in the Christian historical-cultural context. It should be noted that within this framework, the Christian historical-cultural defines itself as decidedly non-exilic in the sense exile is understood in Judaism. Christian consciousness relies on the Pauline and particularly the Augustinian conceptions of history, which claim that since the appearance of Jesus the world has entered a new age, "the age of grace," immersed in redemptive benevolence even as this era too is temporary and will end with the second coming of Jesus. For this conception, the "era of the law" (the pre-Christian, Jewish existence, before the new covenant with humanity), reflects a lack of benevolence. In this context, exile is what distinguishes between Jew and Christian, as indeed the Jew who is loyal to his exile negates the claim that the world has entered into the age of Grace and salvation. This stance explains why we should not conclude that the perception of exile is simply a condition forced on the Jew but a conscious choice: choosing to be a Jew is the same as choosing exile, and it has no other meaning. This exile indeed focuses on the messianic idea that negates it, but the determining factor is that for the sake of the existence of a messianic idea it is necessary to relate to this world as though it were a reality of exile.

Negation of Exile: The National Context

The fact that what defines Judaism as a historical phenomenon is a deeply theological concept of exile means that the "negation of exile" is in fact the negation of "Judaism." The Zionism that pretends to have a monopoly on Jewish history is in fact its negation, or at least the negation of foundational approaches that it defines as irrelevant. In the sense given to it by historical Zionist ideology and culture, a negation of the diaspora did not necessarily express the view that Jews could not exist in Europe any longer, in light of the dangers that lie in modernity and the clashes of modern culture. Indeed, that was the intent that motivated several of the first Zionists—Pinsker, Herzl, and, in an entirely different way, Lilienblum—even if they did not make explicit use of the concept. From their perspective, the rationale for Zionism was the need for shelter in light of the impossibility of Jewish existence in Europe, as well as the awareness of the dangers that lie within modern reality. Their motive did not necessitate the entire meta-narrative of the negation of the diaspora. The demand for *shelter* in no way required embracing the full myth. Nevertheless, this perception was soon exchanged for the now-hegemonic one, which sometimes even stood against the objectives to find "shelter" and to rescue Jews (in Hungary or America, for example), and which completely negates the legitimacy of a Jewish existence outside the Land of Israel and beyond the bounds of Zionist ideology.

In fact, the "negation of exile," in the broad sense of the term, is not reduced only to Zionist discourse; it is one of the foundation stones of the self-definition of modern Western Jewry in its entirety, and one of the characteristic expressions of modernity. The streams that developed around Moses Mendelssohn's thought (which served as a kind of axis that defined the new paradigms of modern Jewish discourse) and the responses to it all sought—except for orthodox circles—to build a new worldview in which Jewish identity would not be based on a consciousness of exile but instead on belonging to society and accepting the values of the dominant culture. The meaning of this trend was to make the definition of Judaism suitable not only to the language of modern culture but to its basic principles—which were understood to be neutral, that is to say indifferent to religious identity.

In the nineteenth and twentieth centuries, the discussion of the question of Judaism as a "religion" or "nation" was conducted from within this conceptual system. Seemingly contrary positions shared a common denominator: the definition of Jewish existence based on a break from the exilic principle and on the full acceptance of the concept of modern nationalism—the guiding principle of the dominant culture. In this way, exile ceased to be a significant factor and was no longer defined as a fundamental condition, only as a concept describing a historical reality stemming from the previous political order or the future one that would replace it. For many Jews, Judaism remained only a "religion"; defining it as such perpetuated, in effect, the problematic of belonging to the dominant society, defined as Christian, by restricting to the critical stance toward it that characterized the Jews as a religious minority group. Those who seized the opposite pole and cultivated a Jewish nationalism to be realized outside of Europe conceded this too. In both cases, exile was understood as an era and a condition that were forced on the Jews against their will. Indeed, there is a grave difference between the meaning and the implications of *that* viewpoint of the "negation of exile" and the historical perception embodied in it as a basis for the consciousness of the sovereign majority in the Land of Israel that defines itself in explicitly nationalist terms. In this context the "negation of exile" became the foundation that actively guided an entire cultural system.

The centrality of the concept of exile illuminates the special difficulty involved in the attempt at Jewish self-definition in terms of modern nationalism: it is not possible to treat historical Judaism as if it were a complete cultural framework given to examination as an autonomous system beyond the cultural contexts in which it existed and participated. The concept of exile is the basis for the self-definition of Jews in relation to the culture in which they exist: they constituted part of the place, but they were in exile *within it*. In order to be in exile in a certain place (i.e., Jewish in a certain place), the Jew must first of all be perceived as part of the framework because only in this way would his self-definition in relation to the dominant culture become clear. This self-definition always relied on a literary corpus that was more or less defined and that received concrete historical expression based on fundamental limitations dictated by Jewish law, but the very definition and the manner of existence, halakha in fact, of different halakhot are a culturally dependent matter. Exile is the framework in which the self-definition is formed within the tension between self-image and the self-image in the eyes of the other—the gentile.

It follows from the necessary bond to the cultural frameworks in which exilic Judaism exists that "symbiotic" relationship between Jewish self-image and the image in the eyes of the other is the essence of Judaism as a historical phenomenon. This relationship is expressed in the thought of nineteenth-century forerunners of Jewish nationalism such as Nachman Krochmal (1755–1840). However, modern nationalist understandings of Judaism (i.e., Zionism), break away from this understanding of symbiotic relationship. The demand for a "total Jewish existence" in modern nationalism is a demand for the negation of the symbiotic element within Jewish existence, and it is therefore the *explicit* demand for cultural repression. The astonishing term "destruction of the exiles" reflected this trend in a powerful and scathing way. Israeliness, which supposedly "liberated itself" from ideological proclamations such as this, also remained bound by the definition formulated through negation: the negative definition of culture as "negation of the diaspora" was and still is the definite, clear, and singular aspect of collective identity; it continues to serve as a mechanism of repression of elements that do not correspond to its meta-narrative.

Consequently, in the Jewish context the use of modern nationalist language provokes unique problems that do not stem from the concept of nationalism in and of itself. The difficulty is not couched in the actual definition of Jewish collectivity but in its concrete characteristics. In fact, in its basic meaning exile distinctly defines collectivity, although this collectivity relies on a type of shared memory that is entirely different from that which defines the later national consciousness. Jewish collectivity, as expressed for example in the concept "the people of Israel," is formulated in religious terms as an expression of partnership in a way of life and in a basic faith. National collectivity is not a new expression of the concept "the Jewish people," nor is it the secularization of that concept, in the sense that it is based on the negation of what preceded it—exile.

This fundamental problem at the heart of the Zionist definition has received almost no attention, and particularly not in the secular context. Some critics (the most prominent being A. B. Yehoshua and Eliezer Schweid) have pointed out that exile and scattering were not forced on the Jews and that it is "a constructed phenomenon in Jewish history."[10] However, in this they have arrived at a radical negation of the exilic experiences (to rid themselves of this "constructed phenomenon"), even of the right of Jews to live in the diaspora. Similarly, this negation is the source for the negation of the legitimacy of any aspect of privacy in the Jewish-Israeli context, as well as for a radical demand for total self-obligation to the collective. Consequently, negation of exile becomes negation of privacy—the right to feel exile—a feeling that on its own is perceived as subversive and menacing.

Among observant religious Jews, the problem of exile has served as a focus of discussion in light of both the need to acknowledge the theological meaning of the concept (or its other side—redemption) and the explicit oaths that forbid Jewish-political settlement in Israel. Two main approaches developed within the sector defined as "religious-Zionist": the dominant approach, advanced by Rabbi Kook and his students, claims that the present settlement is a stage in the messianic process. The state is perceived as preparation for redemption, and as a result an element of holiness is designated to it and its actions. Another approach has tried to differentiate between the two domains, political and religious. In the political domain, which it interprets according to secular-Western ideas, exile has ended; this is realized by recognizing Jewish sovereignty and by identifying with the state and its symbols. In the religious domain, that same reality is perceived as fixed in a state of exile; in other words, existence, in the theological sense, has not changed. Different thinkers tried to bridge these two domains and to describe the historical present as being caught in a liminal state, neither exile nor redemption. Religious thinkers were anyway needed for dealing with anti-Zionist approaches that persist in the ultra-orthodox community.[11]

Ultimately, all approaches that base their definition of Jewish existence in Israel on the concept of "negation of exile" view the political reality only vis-à-vis redemption—even when this redemption is secularized or not overt. In its various expressions, the negation of exile is accompanied by the consciousness of a redemption that guides the Israeli-Jewish collective. Either the state is given religious value to the point of being sacred, and at best pushes full redemption beyond history, or the state is described in religious terms taken out of their context. Paradoxically, the process of secularization never addressed the concept of exile itself; the negation of the diaspora simply rejected it and saw it as lacking relevant meaning. "Exile" was only thought of as a description of the status of Jews in other countries. In fact, the concept of exile was removed from the discourse on the existing reality (in the Land of Israel). Therefore it is not surprising that despite the attempt of some secular Zionist thinkers to shake off comparisons to earlier messianic movements, Zionist ideology was, from its inception, characterized by an active messianic element that existed regardless of the demonstrated efforts to avoid defining reality as an expression of "the work of God's hands." Even if different Zionist streams earnestly oppose the moral and political implications of the messianic position, they do not confront it with a stance based on other principles. Even the sincere use of "universal" terms, more than constituting an alternative to existing power relations, leads to a blurring of the way that these relations are rooted in widespread cultural definitions, particularly in regard to the treatment of Palestinians. While various approaches to historical reality developed in religious discourse, the secular-Zionist consensus is entirely based on axioms identical to those cultivated by radical Zionism in the style of Merkaz haRav (an important center of Religious Zionism). The negation of exile necessarily led to viewing reality in terms borrowed from the lexicon of redemption, and this view-point directed and established the Zionist interpretation. This is one of the main causes that enable the political and cultural power of political circles that developed around the thought of Rabbi Kook; their position is couched entirely in basic Zionist thought, and they see themselves, quite justifiably, as its prominent, legitimate successors.

Exile Within Sovereignty / Benjamin's Theses on the Philosophy of History

Exile is understood as the symbol of what is not sovereignty, and as the lack of the full acceptance of political sovereignty. At first glance it appears that there exists a fundamental contradiction between the concepts "exile" and "sovereignty." Yet it is precisely this tension, which remains without a definite solution, that gives my position its full meaning.

A reading of Walter Benjamin's "Theses on the Philosophy of History" an-chors the present discussion and directs the study of exile toward the cre-ative aspect of Israeli culture.[12] Benjamin's adoption of terminology from Jewish discourse grants special meaning to viewing them as a critical stance vis-à-vis current reality and the Zionist position, given that the latter relies on terms of redemption that originate in that same context.

In their concrete, completely oppositional position, the "Theses on the Philosophy of History" offer a fundamental critique of the positivist concep-tion of history—of "historicism" in the broad sense of the term. That con-ception views history as a continuous process, relying on the concept of "progress" and on faith in the linear advancement of humanity toward some complete future whose principal characteristics already exist in, or can be predicted from, the present. According to Benjamin, this conception of the continuity of history is that of the victors, and it is designed to serve the interests of the oppressive ruling classes. The concept of "progress" reflects the consciousness of those in power while silencing the voices of the op-pressed of the past. The memory of the oppressed is viewed as irrelevant in face of the faith in the continuous advancement of humanity. On the other hand, for Benjamin the praxis of the present should originate in the mem-ory of the oppressed, whose history is discontinuous and cannot be formu-lated in terms of bourgeois "progress."

Written in occupied Europe in 1940, in a "moment of danger" (255), the "Theses on the Philosophy of History" give meaning to the historical relation with the past by preserving the memory of that moment. In that same moment, memory is freed from the interests that use it as a means for their own realization. Liberated memory can see at that moment that "there is no document of civilization which is not at the same time a document of barbarism" (256). This state of emergency, understood from the viewpoint of the oppressed, is not exceptional but rather ordinary, the rule.

In that moment of the total victory of fascism, Benjamin is searching for the door to emancipation, and he suggests an approach that rejects the concept of progress and the concept of utopia to be realized at some certain moment in the future. Continued uncritical acceptance of historicism constitutes the acceptance of the cultural foundations of fascism. The surprise from the appearance of fascism stems from the fact that those who struggle against it hold the same values: "The current amazement that the things we are experiencing are 'still' possible in the twentieth century is . . . not the beginning of knowledge—unless it is the knowledge that the view of history which gives rise to it is untenable" (257). From this moment—that is, from within memory as it is perceived in the moment of danger—Benjamin outlines a theologico-political ethics derived from an alternative conception of time. The conception of history comes to acquire moral weight and brings the moral and the theological into contact with one another. According to Benjamin, without the theological aspect the Marxist position loses its validity.

In 1940, on the run as a refugee, writing *for* the ruling class *from* the position of the oppressed, Benjamin points out the demand directed toward our present, after the historic destruction caused by fascism and its apparent disregard for the state of emergency. He insists that it does not suffice to oppose historical fascism; rather, we must oppose the conception of history that made it possible: "the tradition of the oppressed teaches us that the 'state of emergency' in which we live is not the exception but the rule" (257). However, Benjamin is not satisfied with a critique of the concept of "progress" in merely pointing to its link to the rise of fascism; this act of criticism has no value in and of itself, for the sake of knowledge, if it does not situate as its focus the aspiration for emancipation-redemption. Redemption is embodied in the concept "remembrance"—a concept that maintains a central place in Benjamin's writings and that signifies a dynamic process of identifying with the memory of the oppressed. Remembrance stands in opposition to the monumental memory that is enslaved to the needs of the ruling classes and that serves them. Benjamin's position here is essentially different from Marx's, for whom the voices of the oppressed of the past hold no value. Contrarily, Benjamin posits, "*even the dead* will not be safe from the enemy if he wins" (255). Redemption is based on a turn to the past, on remembrance of the oppressed of the past whose oppression continues to be a part of the consciousness guiding the present. The turn to the past, for oppressed voices trampled by the dominant historical discourse, is crucial to the process of emancipation, and this is because the denial of oppression is part of the present. The foundations toward which remembrance is directed are found in the moment in which remembrance is carried out, although in a state of denial.

The alternative conception of history that Benjamin presents, and in which he sees a model with emancipatory power, is based on an enlightening interpretation of the Jewish concept of "messianism." In its very nature, the Jewish messianic conception cannot view history as a continuous progress that marches toward an end at some point in the future. In principle the messiah can come at any moment; he can come at any moment in the future, just as *he could* come at any moment in the past (which continues to function in the present). "Like every generation that preceded us, we have been endowed with a *weak* messianic power, a power to which the past has a claim" (254). The "messiah" (who here does not necessarily signify an individual person) becomes the existing element found at any time, the possibility within each and every moment. The realization of weak messianic power does not mean the transition of potential from power to action but rather—and this perhaps is Benjamin's original commentary on Jewish tradition—a search for that power and the desire to connect to it, the meaning of which liberates tradition from the conformism to which the ruling ideology has led it. The result is that the redemption of the present, a dynamic process that is not the sign of some terminal condition, is also stipulated in the redemption of the past—the "redemption" of the oppressed voice from the past, a voice whose subjugation is not the last word, and the discussion of which grants it a great deal of relevance for the needs of the present. The critique of the historical conception that informs collective identity is connected here to the process of emancipation: thus remembrance suggests a cultural praxis that leads to a dialectical change of reality. The past toward which remembrance looks is the foundation existing within the reality of the present, albeit in a denied state; identifying with the oppressed of the present becomes a basis for changing the oppressive reality. Therefore, to be occupied with the past is not for the sake of representing it in a continuum, "the way it really was" (255), but as a praxis that exists in the present in order to create "a history of the present" in the full sense of the word, and in this way to change the questions defining the discourse that relies on the present conception of history. As per the final line of the "Theses": "For every second of time was the strait gate through which the Messiah might enter" (264).

Despite his vigorous opposition to the concept of "progress," including the classic Marxist advance of history toward its emancipatory solution, Benjamin does not unfetter himself from the need to put forth an image of redemption; he posits that "a redeemed mankind receives the fullness of its past—which is to say, only for a redeemed mankind has its past become citable in all its moments" (254). It is a redemption in which the gap between past and present is completely nullified. Whatever we take this perception to mean, it is clearly not one of a social utopia to which history necessary leads, not an indication of a future reality to be realized. Instead, this should be seen as an illumination of the direction and path to which we should turn.

The conclusion is that striving for redemption *is* redemption, and in this context it is *exile*. The theses direct and gain valences from the discussion with which I began. Benjamin does not make explicit use of the concept "exile," but his use of the concept of redemption allows us go back and reread the Jewish literature that deals with exile, actualizing it. Exile (*galut*) is what imbues full meaning to "revelation" (*hitgalut*), which is also a condition for redemption. Exile contains the desire to escape from it, thus making redemption the companion of exile, a part of exile that is devoid of meaning if detached from it. In other words, exile embodies the possibility of redemption. By its very essence, exile is a condition whose end can arrive at any moment, and therefore it apparently contains a threatening apocalyptic potential. However, given that it is an all-embracing worldview in most of the historical revelations of Judaism that gives value to the condition of exile and the negativity within it, this condition is also the basis for establishing reality, and in it the messianic idea exists.

To be sure, the concept of exile signifies a lacking or partial essence in principle, yet the lack does not present a definite negation of the deficient reality but, on the contrary, a legitimization of a meaningful existence within it. Exile signifies absence, the recognition of an unfulfilled present, the consciousness of a defective world. In emphasizing the defective present, exile as a concept puts forth a position entirely different from the modern-positivist approach—one of whose expressions is Zionist ideology—and thus clarifies the meaning of remembrance. The yearning for redemption is based on the consciousness of exile and as such requires a turn to the oppressed foundations within a culture via undermining the memory of the rulers. It is therefore an action carried out in reality and is based on bestowing value to the viewpoint of the oppressed, a viewpoint *necessary* for a moral position to be developed. Consequently, only defining reality as exile can lead to the moral values that should guide political action. This is the site in Benjamin's thought that links Marxism and Jewish theology, two elements that become integrated with each other. Benjamin's critique of the Marxist approach is based on a fundamental identification with its goals as well as an obligation to its struggle. And in the context of Jewish thought, Benjamin is relating to different conceptions that exist in Jewish tradition, and he grants them political meaning, anchors them in a critique of modern Western culture, and formulates them in the conceptual language of that culture. Jewish terminology comes to serve as the basis for a position that has universal validity. Even more interesting is the way in which he internalizes kabbalistic mystical traditions, for which "remembrance" (sometimes through the use of the concept itself) had a central place in terms of coming nearer to divine knowledge and the experience of the full devotion of the individual. The path Benjamin suggests invokes theological projects, and it does so by seeing them as the sole path to emancipatory politics.

In this form, the turn to theology is, unsurprisingly, also the secularization of the theological in the sense that theology becomes a component guiding political action. The theological element ceases to be detached from reality and is understood as a positive aspect to any political stance, and in particular what is based on a value system derived from socialism. The concept of exile embodies this feature in that it is an essentially *political* concept; it underscores the full integration of the political and the religious, according to the modern definitions of these ideas. Exile is the platform in which what would, in the language of modern Western culture, be separated into "religion" and "nationalism" is integrated; that separation is part of the same historical approach that Benjamin attacks. As stated, this separation is problematic on its own in light of the theological meanings—both the revealed and hidden—that are embedded in the perception of reality. Exile is also the basis for the consciousness of the collective and the singular foundation that permits defining—in a very complex way—a certain kind of collectivity that grants meaning to the concept "Judaism" without the need to define it as redemption, and the definition will not be required to contradict and negate the foundational concepts that direct the historical development of Judaism.

A Benjaminian Turn to the Jewish Past

A position that draws inspiration from Benjamin's theses opens a particular lens through which to read Jewish sources. This position uses the memory of oppression not as a source for legitimacy in the present but rather as a basis to critique the history of the victors that denies the injustice, the memory of the victim. A Jewish history such as this is not a national history of Jews but a history written from the viewpoint of Jews, and in this way becomes on its own a "universal history." The memory of the oppressed that this history preserves is not a memory of misery and lachrymosity but an empathy nourished by the firm aspiration for the abolishment of the oppression that characterizes the present. This history does not pretend to be objective, but it maintains methodological strictness; its turn to the past is more attentive in that the past is not meant to serve a defined present but to *establish* a present. In this context, a discussion of the discrimination or oppression of Jews, of the element defined as "feminine" or "effeminizing" does not come from an opposite pole but from attentiveness to a repressed voice, the return to which is essential for understanding and critiquing the present. This framework prevents the division between those elements defined as "masculine" and "feminine" because their combination is a condition for the creation of an alternative position vis-à-vis hegemony, which is masculine in essence. This is not an ideology of suffering; the point of view of the oppressed is part of a praxis intended to examine "self-identity" mediated through the understanding of the oppressed other as well.

The Jewish past makes possible an approach of this kind perhaps because it is not a matter of a historical phenomenon of "complete oppression," of a totally silenced voice (excluding the expressions of terrible violence in the modern period, the apex being Nazi crimes). On the contrary, "Jewish history" (i.e., the contexts in which a Jewish existence was in a complex relationship with other elements of society and culture) expresses a liminal state. We are talking here about a collective that, despite its being understood and implicitly defined as a tolerated minority group (in both Christian and Muslim milieus), did not generally belong to the lower and oppressed classes in the society in which it lived. The discussion of the discrimination and oppression of minorities in instances where there existed discrimination and oppression is relevant only in the measure to which it is conducted on the basis of comparison with the state of other discriminated groups. Moreover, the fact that Jews preserve a history that is not silent makes "Jewish history" into a highly significant asset for studying the paradigms of general history; it enables an alternative writing of history.

In recent decades there have been many expressions of this alternative history in work that has deviated considerably from the picture of the past shaped by the "founding generation" of Zionist historiography. This new research presents Jewish history as part of the environment in which Jews lived, developing in different directions and thus blurring the dichotomy between "general" (i.e., European) and "Jewish" history. Presenting Judaism as part of the various cultural contexts in which it had developed, without conceding its uniqueness or ignoring the element of oppression raises difficult questions about the national narrative. Current research on Kabbalah, for example the work of Moshe Idel, Yehuda Liebes, and several of their colleagues and students, is directly relevant here. Their work can be presented as a "Benjaminian turn" to the past. These writers are influenced directly by Gershom Scholem's work, whose great value they recognize while remaining critical of it. They uncover elements of the "past" that were marginalized in the Zionist paradigm and rejected by the exceptional historiographical paradigm of the founder of the study of Kabbalah. Idel stresses the place of "prophetic," meaning ecstatic, Kabbalah. He assigns great importance to kabbalistic praxis in particular and focuses on explaining the techniques whose goal is the experience of union with the Jewish god. Scholem sought to minimize the value of this element by claiming that an essential difference between Judaism and Christianity is the complete absence of the personal experience of redemption in Judaism until Hasidism.[13] Focusing on these texts changes the historical picture of Jewish mysticism, blurring Scholem's sharp distinctions between Jewish and non-Jewish mysticisms. This kabbalistic stream also reflects an approach to the past similar to that which Benjamin develops in the language of modern culture. This fact grants these phenomena and the scholarship on them broad cultural significance.

This renewed discussion of different aspects of Jewish messianism sketches an essentially different picture from the accepted one that reduces the significance of the concept to a political-historical concept. Idel, for example, stresses messianic-mystical conceptions whose goal is the spiritual redemption of the individual, a psychological or philosophical process that takes place in the mind of the messiah and that does not exist on the stage of history. His—and others'—analysis reveals the concept of *messianism* that instills the Land of Israel with spiritual meaning, distances the conception of redemption from the physical land, and opens up a central place for the individual experience that is negated in the ideological world of Zionism. The exilic position couched in this concept of messianism allows for a balance between the individual and the collective; rather than the individual being totally subjugated to the "political" (understood exclusively as the sovereignty of the state), the former directs the latter. Liebes shows that Sabbateanism, usually understood as a political movement, a type of proto-Zionism, was in fact a movement of religious reform. In Sabbatean writings there is almost no mention of political activity tied to the Land of Israel, nor was this the essence of the movement.[14] The same goes for anyone who emphasized the cosmic essence of redemption and strove to heal the world, including divinity itself. (Mystical Judaism always insisted even the divine is a state of exile during the period of exile.) It should be noted that the existing expressions of political messianism do not correspond to the implicit conception of redemption that characterizes Zionist discourse; for example, it is not possible to equate the "accepted belief in the coming of the messiah," which finds its expression in liturgy, to the "yearning of generations" that Zionist ideologues depicted.

The Empty Land

Zionism's adoption of the "history of the victors" model has particular significance regarding the question of the treatment of the Palestinian minority. This is the second side of the national representation of Jewish history, whose critique through the concept of exile has clear ethical-political implications.

Defining Zionist settlement as an expression of "the negation of exile" and as the "return of the people to their land" prevented any acknowledgment of the collective aspirations of the local Arab population and its point of view; and it undoubtedly prevented the possibility of turning the existence of this collectivity into a positive element in the process of establishing the new Jewish identity. The conception of history of negation of exile, and the emptying of the Jewish time that spans from the loss of sovereignty over the Land of Israel until the renewed settlement there, were directly fulfilled by imagining the Land—the space of the realization and resolution of the history—as an "empty land."

Since early Zionist thinkers, the subject has been perceived as a question that should "be solved" so that it would cease to trouble the vision of redemption through the "negation of exile." Even many of those who warned that the "Arab problem" should be dealt with did not turn it into a part of their new Jewish identity. They too accepted the superficial, institutionalized partition between the question of "Jewish identity" and "the Palestinian question," and they agreed to relegate the Palestinians beyond the bounds of discourse. At least from the viewpoint of the images of self-identity, the Land continued to function as an empty land, and as such the massive "dialogue" with "the Land" (accompanied by images drenched in desire) was based on the denial of the native of the Land, the "other."

From a historical perspective, the denial of the Palestinian presence as a departure point for cultural identity finds its distinct expression in the worldview and value system that was consolidated during the period of the Second Aliyah, the context in which the fundamental cultural myths of the Zionist "negation of exile" culture were formed. It was then that the boundaries of the relations with Palestinians were defined in Zionist discourse, which became the boundaries of "the consensus" in its entirety (i.e., that which contains both supporters of "compromise" as well as their opponents). This was not a theoretical conception but the cultural basis that enabled a policy of repression and expulsion of Palestinians, a policy that was the realization of the image of the empty land. In the framework of this discourse the Palestinian always had to prove to his oppressors that he was not a threat; if he didn't prove this, all constituents of the Israeli consensus saw his punishment as legitimate.

Within the image of the "New Jew," which grows out of the negation of exile and the shedding of the exilic Jewish image, one can already find elements of the (symbolic and physical) expulsion of the Palestinians. The New Jew aspired to be "native," to be built by an unmediated link to the land, based on the image attributed to the Jews of the ancient past, the "Hebrews." However, this image, in its essence, was parallel in most of its characteristics to the image of the Arab. Thus, not only did the existence of the Arabs disrupt the realization of the concept of the empty land, but it also constituted a competing element vis-à-vis the image of the New Jew. A typical expression of this can be found in the adopting of the image of the Arab guard by the founders of the semi-military organizations of the Second Aliyah. However, this very image of the ideal Arab (which was seen as part of the "return" to the "Hebrew") led to the repression of the actual Arab who remained unimportant in and of himself. At the most the interest in the *fellaheen* (peasants) was maintained because they were perceived as preserving the authentic foundations of ancient Hebrewness and could therefore serve as role models for the creation of the new identity.[15] In other words, as a result of the fact that the image of the "Hebrew" that sought a "native" identity was (and had to be) based on all that the Arab represented, there was no place for the concrete Arab, whose existence had no value beyond a marginal role in the fashioning of Jewish self-identity. This came to fruition clearly in the slogans of the Second Aliyah, such as "Conquest of Labor and Preservation" (i.e., closing Jewish farms to Arab workers in order to maintain an autonomous economic framework).

The History of the Land

These implications of the dominant ideology that negates the diaspora receive full expression in the conception of the history of the Land of Israel since the inception of Zionist settlement in accordance with how it has been depicted in institutional historiography, as well as how it has been stressed in secondary-school education. This conception of history is the completion, or second side, of the Jewish history presented above. Historical images serve the myth of the return to the empty land: Zionist settlement is taught detached from the history of Palestinian presence in the Land and with no regard for it (something also expressed in maps that present Jewish settlement and ignore the layout of the Palestinian population). In high school education the "conflict" is taught as a separate subject, detached from the history of Zionist settlement. The Palestinians appear in the continuous narrative of "the development of Jewish settlement" only at moments of crisis, "incidents" in which violent opposition was revealed to continued Jewish immigration and Britain's pro-Zionist policy of a "national home." This disregard gives rise to a distorted system of images that disallows any understanding of the actions and resistance of the Palestinians. In institutions of higher education, disciplines are divided between "the history of Jewish settlement" (part of the "History of the Jewish People") and "the history of Palestinian nationalism" (in the field of Oriental Studies).

Key questions about the history of the Land of Israel are barely examined in this framework. In Israeli historical consciousness there is no memory of the Palestinian viewpoint on events, and the consciousness of the justice of the victors remains undisturbed. Central historical questions—such as the expulsion of Arabs from their land, the Palestinian relation to the British Mandate and their opposition to the Balfour Declaration, and especially the creation of the refugee problem—are virtually not discussed, and when they are discussed they do not become part of the cultural conversation about the question of self-identity and the formation of the collective consciousness. A sophisticated cultural mechanism shoves aside attempts to actualize these discussions. The gravest implication of the conception of history that is derived from the "negation of exile" is the denial of the Palestinian tragedy that accompanied the creation of the State of Israel. This denial, which is essentially a complete disregard of Palestinian memory and of the character of the Land pre-1948, is one of the distinct characteristics of Israeli culture, and this is emphasized by the central place in Jewish consciousness of the myth of '48 alongside the empty space left by forgetting the Palestinian tragedy.

It is especially important that political patterns of culture enable the systematic denial and forgetting of events, the total disregard for the fate of the Palestinians, and the drastic change that took place in Israel following the establishment of the state and its accompanying war. The silencing of the subject is an active cultural project that defines the bounds of the consensus and prevents a discussion of the fate of the refugees—whether because of the inability to deal with guilt or because of the tendency to preserve the myth. This project was also carried out in the erasure of the names of Palestinian towns that were destroyed as part of the trend to erase them from the story of the Land of Israel's past. The Palestinians are expelled along with the names of their towns. The expulsion brought the (partial) emptying of the Land and the creation of a new demographic map that correlated with the image of the empty land and the realization of the historical consciousness of the victors that preceded the expulsion. In the memoirs dedicated to the war there are nearly no references to the refugees, and certainly not to the action of expulsion. The prose literature that dealt with the margins of the subject, such as S. Yizhar's (Yizhar Smilanaski) famous stories, did not deal directly with the root of the events but only constituted a project of purification based on feelings of guilt that were channeled into concrete, individual instances and thereby succeeded in blurring the event itself, its scope, and especially its ideological origins. Thus a society intensively occupied with searching below the earth to find the remnants of its ancient "past"—in order to create a conscious continuum between this past and the present—completely ignores the map of the Land and its settlement as it was fifty years prior, and this reveals a surprising disregard for the fate of those defeated, who were almost entirely erased from the history of the Land and the geographic maps that depict it.

Historians who do not ignore these facts often justify those generally repressed elements of Zionist activity (expulsion, banishment, etc.) by claiming that any other policy would have caused the failure of the creation of sovereign Jewish settlement in the Land; in other words it would have prevented the creation of the present from which we are speaking. These are important historical questions, but they are not relevant to the present discussion, which departs from a consciousness of the present. The turn to the past demanded here is not a "historical alternative" whose only goal is to denigrate Zionism or reveal its sins. Historical research does not function as a tribunal, and it does not require one-dimensional, operative conclusions. Instead, it enables us to return the discourse to the foundations that have been systematically expelled from it. The goal is to make a turn to the past, and in particular to those denied elements of the past, as a basis for a consciousness of another kind in the present. Hence, the question is not what possibilities were really hidden in the past but what possibilities can be suggested in the present based on a critical discussion of that same formative past. A critical act such as this reveals the boundaries of the consciousness that is bestowed via the authoritative representation of the past and opens possibilities of a new consciousness.

Exile and Bi-nationalism

Benjamin's "Theses on the Philosophy of History" receives special meaning in this context. With the concept of exile signifying the resistance to negating the existing consciousness, the negation of the negation of exile becomes a way to turn to the denied past *through* this consciousness and to recognize the existence of an additional collective in Israel, as well as the consciousness of exile that became a central component of the latter's experience and historical memory,[16] and without needing to forego the concept of "shelter," even on the basis of a renewed and deepened connection to it from an emphasized reliance on the Jewish concept of exile. Moreover, there is also no need to deny the historic fundamental desire for the land that exists in Jewish consciousness. The meaning that the concept of exile receives here enables a definition of Jewish identity based on recognition of the potential hidden in the bi-nationalism of Israel. As a result a political discourse can be created whose departure point is the recognition of the existence of the Palestinians as a collective with a historical consciousness. Remembrance is directed simultaneously toward the denied Jewish past and the denied Palestinian past.

Bi-nationalism is not the call for the wanted type of political solution; it does not intend a "bi-national state," as the term is understood in the political jargon of the conflict between the two peoples; and it does not describe a yearned-for utopia. Bi-nationalism is a *moral* position that directs the attitude toward reality. It signifies first the dialogic element in the historical reality in a way that grants concrete meaning to the abstract theological element. Moreover, the bi-national position is crucial for any resolution whose goal is equal participation, whether or not it is two separate states or some other framework. The "two-state solution" cannot be constructed before there is a change in the consciousness of Israeli Jews. A condition for this change is bound up in the concept of exile and in openness to the theological element contained within it, and this in a way that will break the existing molds of political discourse.

Most importantly, situating the concept of "exile" as a basis for Jewish definition in Israel would mean distancing "the Land" as a loaded concept from the land as a place. A connection is necessary here to the same foundations in tradition that related to the Land of Israel as a spiritual concept, rather than a concrete geographic reality, and enabled the detachment of the concrete land from the concept of redemption. Of course, the yearning for the Land of Israel plays a central role in Jewish sources; it was emphasized and examined in different contexts, but in no way should this yearning be equated with the approach to the Land of Israel that was shaped by Zionist culture, even regarding Jews who settled there. The traditional yearning for the Land of Israel does not determine a necessary construct of concrete relations between Jews and the Land, and it is not formulated in terms of ownership. On the contrary, in many cases the desire to settle in the Land of Israel raised grave fears among Jewish halakhic authorities. It should again be emphasized that presenting exile as a temporary situation whose end is the longed-for "return" to the Land of Israel does not exhaust the concept of exile and does not serve as an important component in the discourse on exile. Moreover, the concepts "Land of Israel" or "Zion" served more as a pole of spiritual meaning (for defining the present situation) than as an expression of concrete aspirations.[17]

Furthermore, even in the framework of thought that emphasized the uniqueness of the Land of Israel, for example as the singular geographic space in which prophecy or connection to divine powers is possible, this viewpoint was detached from the concept of exile itself. Those like Maimonides, who were perceived to distinctly express the "yearning" for the Land, do not shape this attitude in the context of the negation of exile. The spiritualization of the Land creates an opening for recognition of the other as part of the self and enables equal dialogue; it leaves behind the concept of the Land as an expression of yearning in a way that dismantles the existing messianic baggage and demands remembrance. Paradoxically, the wish for redemption focuses on remembrance that in this context means recognition of the Palestinians as subjects possessing a position, as full partners in the discourse.

Exile here is intended to mean "de-colonialization" of the Jewish-Israeli entity, a concept that in this context expresses not only the end of occupation but a change in the basic colonial consciousness embedded in the concept of negation of exile that enables this colonial condition. "Colonialism" in this context is a type of memory work directed at forgetting. De-colonialization in this context is a type of de-territorialization, whose meaning is, again, not the abandonment of place but the work of remembrance that creates a space for the memory of the defeated. Exile within the place (the negation of "negation of exile") returns the longing for the theological-cultural role to a foundation that stresses existing reality and guides behavior within it. Exile in the place itself is also the only way to grant validity to the memory of the Jewish victim, the memory of the refugees searching for refuge, under the definition of sons of the Land returning to their "homes."

Notes

Translated by Aviv Ben-Or and severely abridged, by the editors, from Amnon Raz-Krakotzkin, "Galut betoch Ribonut: Le-Bikoret 'Shlilat haGalut' ba- Tarbut ha-Israelit," *Teoria u-Bikoret* 4 (Fall 1993): 23–54 and 5 (Spring 1994): 113–32.

1. See the opening passage of the Israeli Declaration of Independence and Ben-Zion Dinur's writings. Ben-Zion Dinur, *Israel in Exile* (Tel-Aviv: Dvir, 1938), 11–16 [Hebrew]. This approach is reflected in many other texts, including public education programs, and it is referenced casually by public figures who accept its irrefutability.

2. See Nathan Rotenstreich, *Current Studies in Zionism* (Tel Aviv: Am Oved, 1966) [Hebrew]; Charles Liebman and Eli'ezer Don-Yehiya, *Civil Religion in Israel* (Berkeley: University of California Press, 1983); Yaacov Shavit, *From Hebrew to Canaanite* (Tel Aviv: Domino, 1984) [Hebrew], 18–20; Ehud Luz, *Parallels Meet: Religion and Nationalism in the Early Zionist Movement (1882-1904)* (Philadelphia: Jewish Publication Society, 1988); Moshe Lissak and Dan Horowitz, *Distress in Utopia* (Tel Aviv: Am Over, 1990) [Hebrew], 143–66; Shmuel Almog, "Normalization and 'Light unto the Nations' in Zionism," in *Chosen People, Elect Nation, and Universal Mission*, ed. S. Almog and Michael Heyd (Jerusalem: Merkaz Zalman Shazar, 1991) [Hebrew]; Yosef Gorni, "The Relation Between the 'Poalei-Tziyon' Movement in the Land of Israel to the Diaspora," *HaTziyonut* 2 (1970): 74–89 [Hebrew]; Eliezer Schweid, " 'Negation of the Diaspora'—Two Paths," in *The Yishuv in the Modern Period*, ed. Shmuel Stempler (Tel Aviv: Misrad haBitahon, 1983) [Hebrew]; and Eliezer Schweid, "Two Approaches to the Idea of the Negation of the Diaspora in Zionist Ideology," *Hatziyonut* 9 (1982): 21–44 [Hebrew]. On the romantic aspects of this idea, see Yosef Gorni, "The Romantic Foundations of Second Aliyah Ideology," *Asufot* 10 (1966): 55–74 [Hebrew].

3. The tension between the desire for a "new" culture and the intention *to renew* reflects a fundamental tension that characterizes the messianic idea in Judaism. See Gershom Scholem, "Understanding the Messianic Idea in Israel," in *Explications and Implications* (Tel Aviv: Am Oved, 1975) [Hebrew], 155–90. From this perspective, Zionism touches on the central messianic question. These two trends become integrated in Zionist culture.

4. On the image of the new Jew, see Shavit, *From Hebrew to Canaanite*; Liebman and Don-Yehiya, *Civil Religion*; Yafah Berlovtiz, "The Model of the 'New Jew' in First

Aliyah Literature—Toward Zionist Anthropology," *Alei-Siah* 17–18 (1982): 54–70 [Hebrew]; Haim Nagid, "The Hebrew Revolution," in *The Yishuv in the Modern Period*, ed. Shmuel Stempler (Tel Aviv: Misrad haBitahon, 1983) [Hebrew]; and Boas Evron, *Jewish State or Israeli Nation?* (Bloomington: Indiana University Press, 1995). On images of the new Hebrew culture, see Itamar Even Zohar, "The Growth and Crystallization of Local and Native Hebrew Culture in Israel: 1882–1948," *Katedra* 16 (1980): 206–61 [Hebrew]. For debates about these depictions, see Nurit Graetz, ed., *Vantage Point: Culture and Society in the Land of Israel* (Ramat Gan: Open University of Israel, 1988) [Hebrew].

5. Tom Segev put forth a general discussion of the different elements for which the creation of Israeliness led to instances of radical repression. Tom Segev, *1949: The First Israelis* (New York: Henry Holt, 1998); Baruch Kurzweil, *Modern Hebrew Literature* (Jerusalem: Schocken, 1959) [Hebrew], 11–146; Ernest Simon, *Are We Still Jews* (Tel Aviv: Sifriyat Po'alim, 1982) [Hebrew].

6. In Zionist discourse different debates developed over how to implement the "negation of the diaspora" in practice, as well as regarding the character of the new culture and its measure of continuity in relation to the existing culture. See Luz, *Parallels Meet*.

7. See, for example, Yossef Agassi, Yehudit Buber Agassi, and Moshe Brant, *Who Is an Israeli* (Rehovot: Kivunim, 1991) [Hebrew]. Agassi and his interlocutors' point of departure is the problem that stems from defining Israel as a state of the Jewish People, a definition that places the Palestinian minority beyond the bounds of the collective. The "Israeliness" that they suggest is not based on granting linguistic value but rather on a radical aspiration for homogeneity. The Arabs have the "right" to participate in the collective but only on the condition that they accept its (Western-liberal) values and give up their "nonauthentic" Palestinian identity, according to the firm stance of the authors.

8. A foundation for this can already be found in Isaiah 2, which grants value to suffering. Jacob Neusner locates the crystallization of this paradigm in the period between the destruction of the First Temple and the establishment of the Second Temple. Jacob Neusner, *Self-Fulfilling Prophecy: Exile and Return in the History of Judaism* (Atlanta: Scholars Press, 1988).

9. See, for example, Amos Funkenstein, *Perceptions of Jewish History* (Berkeley: University of California Press, 1993).

10. See Eliezer Schweid, "The Magic of the Diaspora and the Problem of Normalization," in *Between Judaism and Zionism* (Jerusalem: HaSifriya Hatziyonit, 1983) [Hebrew], 139ff.

11. Those approaches continue to be generally ignored by "secular" thinkers.

12. Walter Benjamin, "Theses on the Philosophy of History," in *Illuminations*, trans. Harry Zohn (New York: Schocken, 1968), 253–64. Subsequent citations to this work given in text.

13. Gershom Scholem, "Toward an Understanding of the Messianic Idea in Judaism," in *The Messianic Idea in Judaism* (New York: Schocken, 1971), 1–36.

14. Yehudah Liebes, "Sabbatean Messianism," *Peamim* 40 (1988): 4–20 [Hebrew]; "New Directions in Scholarship on Kabbalah," *Peamim* 50 (1992): 135–55 [Hebrew];

"Zohar and Eros" (lecture in memory of Gershom Scholem at the Israeli National Academy for Sciences, Jerusalem, 1993) [Hebrew].

15. Gil Eyal, *The Disenchantment of the Orient* (Stanford: Stanford University Press, 2006), 33–61.

16. Edward Said, *Orientalism* (New York: Vintage, 1979).

17. Moshe Idel, "On Eretz-Yisrael in Medieval Mystical Thought," in *The Land of Israel in Medieval Jewish Thought*, ed. Moshe Halamish and Aviezer Ravitzky (Jerusalem: Yad Yitzhak Ben-Zvi, 1991), 193–214.

SIXTEEN

Affective Sovereignty, International Law, and China's Legal Status in the Nineteenth Century

LI CHEN

PRIOR SCHOLARSHIP has often focused on sovereignty as a philosophical, juridical, or political discourse and institution. Its sentimental dimension and history have received relatively little attention, and even the most recent surge of publications on the doctrine of humanitarian intervention has treated sovereignty primarily as a rationalistic issue. This essay focuses on the affective or sentimental aspect of the modern discourses of national sovereignty and international law in the context of Sino-Western relations during the nineteenth century. I first outline the rise of a sentimental culture in the eighteenth and nineteenth centuries and its implications for redefining the sovereign subject of the modern nation and international community. Next, I trace how incipient elements of this sentimentality had been incorporated into some earlier foundational texts of the law of nations and how they survived the subsequent positivist turn in the jurisprudence of international law. Finally, I illustrate the operation of the sentimental discourse in shaping the rights and obligations of sovereign states by examining the British public and parliamentary debates over the Second Opium War with China in 1856–1860. This analysis highlights the underexamined roles of the sentimental discourse in the historical transformation of modern international law and politics. More specifically, I argue that the sentimental discourse, structured by the core concepts of *primary injury* and *secondary injury*, played an important role in shaping China's sovereign status in relation to Western powers during the nineteenth century. While foreign domination in military, technological, and material strength was certainly important in turning China into a "semi-colonial" country after the First Opium War in 1839–1842, the foreign powers rarely justified their China policies in the next century simply because they were dominant empires. On the contrary, their policies were most effectively rationalized as necessary for redressing or preventing *injury* to life, property, treaty rights, or national feeling. This sentimental narrative of native injury to the dominant power was by no means confined to the Sino-Western relationship. Its popularity and efficacy in modern politics lies precisely in its *liminal* position—just like sentiment itself—which enables it to appeal to affect and emotions without being fully bound by formal legal or moral norms, and to claim legal and moral authority without losing its emotive power.

The Sovereign Subject of Modern Sentiments, Politics, and Civilization

By the end of the eighteenth century, a culture of sentimentality had become widespread in Euroamerican societies, producing "a new set of attitudes and emotional conventions" that regarded sympathy or compassion for other creatures' suffering as a universal attribute of humanity.[1] As articulated by Adam Smith and other thinkers of the eighteenth century, sympathy toward those in mental or physical distress was inherent in human nature and was a marker of an enlightened individual and community. Inflicting or exhibiting excessive pain, including state-sanctioned punishment, was considered to be barbaric and to have a barbarizing effect on both the inflictors and the spectators.[2] This "man of feeling" became prominent on the social and political stage of history as capitalism and colonialism spread rapidly across the world. Indeed, these Enlightenment ideas of *sympathy* not only exemplified the rise of a new bourgeois sensibility and identity in European metropoles but also created a new "epistemology and psychology," as Uday Singh Mehta has noted, for "understanding experience and power, especially in the unfamiliar context of the empire."[3] Historians have shown that this sentimental culture played a crucial role in facilitating the abolition of slavery, judicial torture, and public execution in many Euroamerican countries during the late eighteenth and nineteenth centuries.[4]

The sentimental discourse became so powerful in the nineteenth century partly because thinkers of rational liberalism also promoted it as a defining feature of societal or civilizational progress. According to John Stuart Mill's influential 1836 essay "Civilization," one thing that distinguishes modern civilization from the earlier period "is that the spectacle, and even the very idea of pain, is kept more and more out of sight of those classes who enjoy in their fullness the benefits of civilization." In the past, people were habituated to the spectacle of violence or "the alternate suffering and infliction of pain," whereas now all the tasks that involved inflicting pain for purposes of public order and benefit are delegated to some specialized classes of people, such as "the judge, the soldier, the surgeon, the butcher, and the executioner."[5] However, long before the industrialized West could confidently claim such a firm temporal boundary between its own rude past and its civilized present, a spatial boundary had already been asserted between the presumably liberal and enlightened West and the Oriental other. For instance, in *The Spirit of the Laws* (1748), Baron de Montesquieu, a founding theorist of modern political liberty and rule of law, canonized the idea that countries like China, Turkey, Japan, and India were Oriental despotisms governed by fear and corruption, in contrast to the law-based Western republics and monarchies governed by honor and virtue. Scholars have seldom noted that Montesquieu also incorporated the natural theory of moral sentiment into his comparative scheme of societies. Speaking as a man of feeling, he wrote, "When in reading history, we observe the cruelty of the Sultans in the administration of justice, we shudder at the very thought of the miseries of human nature." For him, despotic governments in general were defined by severe punishment because their people, under the yoke of tyranny, were so "inured to the cruelty" of punishments as to necessitate increasingly brutal penalties. This vicious cycle eventually reduced them to savages.[6] Drawing on Montesquieu's ideas on law and government, Adam Smith also noted that the "civilized" nations were distinguishable from the "barbarians" in their more lenient punishments.[7] Although Smith was relatively more tolerant toward non-Western societies than Montesquieu was, his theory of "commercial society" as the highest stage of historical development, as elaborated in *The Wealth of Nations* (1776), was often interpreted by other influential writers, including James Mill and John Stuart Mill, to classify non-Western societies as backward ones.[8]

As I further explain below, the interlocking operation of these influential strands of *rational* liberalism and *sentimental* liberalism hence created a subject of the modern world that was defined simultaneously by the underlying universal theories of humanity and natural sentiment and by the Europe-specific historical experiences and sociocultural sensibilities. Whether a non-European nation would be recognized as civilized enough for the full benefits of sovereignty under (European) international law was now determined not merely by the sophistication of its culture and institutions but also by its emotional practices or imputed sentimental attributes. There has been little discussion of the latter aspect in prior scholarship on the history of international law and sovereignty.

A corollary to such intellectual developments was the assumption that, as the London-based *Quarterly Review* implied in 1812, the "humane" and "benevolent" governance by European powers would more than liberate the Asian peoples from "under the yoke of a cruel and unfeeling despotism." Through the influence of imperial culture and pedagogy, the civilizing mission of the colonial powers would gradually "infuse" into the native minds English or Western "feelings."[9] The moral advantages resulting from its "humanizing policy and enlightened laws" would presumably better qualify a Western power like Britain to acquire a vast colonial empire and turn it into a "beneficent dominion" to improve the lot of millions of natives.[10] An 1850 editorial in the *North China Herald*, which would soon become the leading foreign newspaper in nineteenth-century China, cited judicial torture and punishments in Shanghai to conclude: "Let European nations compel these real barbarians to fulfill their treaties and another order of things must gradually ensue."[11] The treaties referred to were those between China and Britain, France, and the United States, respectively, as a result of the First Opium War, which granted the latter countries extraterritoriality and other privileges in China. Thus, the universalizing discourses of humanity, sympathy, and liberty generated the moral authority, ideological appeal, and intellectual framework for creating what Ann Stoler has called "different degrees of sovereignty and gradation of rights."[12]

Given the significant implications of the sentimental discourse, it is not surprising that an enormous body of what may be called "affective knowledge" was produced to visualize and narrate the cruelty and pain caused by social and legal practices in China, along with Japan, India, Vietnam, and so on.[13] In the process, numerous watercolor paintings, photographs, newspaper reports, and books depicting Chinese punishments were constantly being created, circulated, and consumed worldwide in the nineteenth and early twentieth centuries. Most of these visual and textual narratives emphasized the pain and emotions of the foreign spectators in contrast to the supposedly cruel or unfeeling Chinese criminals, executioners, and spectators. The resultant global spectacle of Chinese cruelty and barbarity shaped the identity of both the foreign viewers and commentators and their Chinese counterparts symbolized by such a spectacle.[14]

According to the Enlightenment theory of sympathy, as Dipesh Chakrabarty has recently pointed out, "the person who is not an immediate sufferer but who has the capacity to become a secondary sufferer through sympathy [by imagination] for a generalized picture of suffering, and who documents this suffering in the interests of eventual social intervention—such a person occupies the position of the *modern subject*."[15] In claiming sympathy for the pain of others, the sentimental spectator became both the speaking and feeling subject and a vicarious sufferer. The adopted pain or injury thus endowed him or her with a moral authority and a new legal right to protect the actual sufferer or humanity in general. This logic is at the root of the modern doctrine of humanitarian intervention, although few have discussed it from the perspective of sentimentality to understand how an unrelated spectator acquires legal standing by observing another's pain or injury. To better understand this, we need to trace the "prehistory" of this sentimental discourse in the canons of international law.

The Discourse of Injury in the Law of Nations and International Law

It is well known that the doctrine of just war is a cornerstone of international law and its early modern European predecessor. But at the heart of this key concept is a conception of inviolable rights and their vulnerability and necessary defense. Hugo Grotius, a Dutch jurist and one of the founders of the law of nations, cited St. Augustine and other classic sources in declaring in the early 1600s that "there is no other reasonable cause of making war, but an injury received" or threatened. The three main grounds for waging a just war were to defend one's life and property against injury, to recover what was unjustly taken away, and to punish past injury.[16] In other words, although just war itself was couched as a legal right, its juridical and philosophical origins lay in the idea of protection of oneself from *injury*. Agreeing with Grotius in this regard, Emer de Vattel, a leading eighteenth-century Swiss jurist, further defined "injury or injustice [as] being a trespass against the perfect right of another."[17] The just causes of war here had the claimant as the primary sufferer. Whether a war was considered just would depend on what constituted a legally recognized injury. As we shall see, the social and cultural specificities in constructing injury would be crucial for making that determination in international conflicts. It is worth noting that a successful claim to injury was, and still is, more than just a moral or legal issue. Among other things, seeking protection from alleged vulnerability and damages, a key element of the injury discourse, almost had an inherently emotive or sentimental dimension, implicitly or explicitly portraying the claimant as the sufferer of unjustified actions and worthy of sympathy and remedy.

In comparison with this doctrine of just war based on direct injury, the concept of secondary injury remained more controversial in modern international law, but this does not make it less important in certain situations. In fact, it has become one of the most extensively studied topics in international law over the last few decades. The recent debate over unilateral humanitarian intervention has focused on whether it is a morally justifiable doctrine or an abuse-prone pretext for military aggression.[18] What is overlooked in the debate is the fact that the sentimental discourse of humanity and sympathy was a major source of both the moral authority for the doctrine of humanitarian intervention on the one hand and of its susceptibility to manipulation for unrelated purposes on the other. A brief survey of a few influential treatises on the law of nations or international law illustrates this.

First, it is worth stressing that the sentimental discourse was and is much broader than is implied by the modern doctrine of humanitarian intervention. The latter doctrine has often been traced back to Grotius. Before him, however, Francisco de Victoria, a Spanish theologian and another founding jurist of the law of nations, had argued in the 1530s that the Amerindian governments' "tyrannical and oppressive" laws and treatment of their "innocent" subjects (e.g., their reported cannibalism) constituted a cause of just war by a benevolent Christian state like Spain on behalf of the native victims. For Victoria, it was irrelevant whether or not the natives desired such intervention, because they had no such "legal independence [i.e., subjectivity] as to be able to consign themselves or their children to death."[19] The native government's domestic cruelty was here *implicitly* treated as an *injury* to both humanity and the presumably sympathetic foreigners. Grotius expanded Victoria's argument to contend that war could be justly undertaken against foreigners who were "inhuman to their parents," ate human flesh, or committed other offenses against nature. Their "depravity of mind" was deemed so great as to have cut them off from human society and made them enemies of the whole world. Citing Aristotle and other classical authorities, Grotius stated that "the justest war is that which is undertaken against wild rapacious beasts and next to it is that against men who are like beasts."[20] Thus, by invoking the moral sentiments associated with the sensational image of cruelty and inhumanity, Grotius expelled the beastlike members from the universalized human society or law of nations, retaining them only as the objects of punishment under the law of nature. This doctrine of just war against another state in order to relieve the latter's subjects from tyrannical or cruel oppression served to override the prevailing view of an independent government's full autonomy over domestic matters.

Some scholars might argue that the image of suffering humanity evoked in such texts was just a rhetorical device, or that Victoria and Grotius justified the possible war against the Amerindians or Oriental countries on the basis of morality alone, having nothing to do with sentiment. The former argument is oversimplistic and tends to reduce these texts of international law to little more than pretexts of power politics. The latter argument assumes an over-rationalistic view of morality while dichotomizing morality and sentiment. Scholars have shown that claims to moral authority, political power, and legal rights sound more credible or legitimate when they appeal to human sentiments.[21] Likewise, the persuasive power of humanitarian intervention based on the doctrine of secondary injury, both morally and legally speaking, hinged on the emotional power of the image of humanity in pain. In Grotius's words, "if the injustice be [so] visible" under the foreign tyrannies that "no good man living can approve of, the right of human society shall not be therefore excluded" from interference with those foreign nations. In other words, the sentimental reactions to the "injustice" seen or imagined by the unrelated spectators created a moral obligation and a legal right for the latter to intervene. It was not injury to the foreign spectators' rights or property but injury to their feelings or moral sensibilities that constituted the grounds of intervention. Conscious of many recorded instances in which these sentiments were used as pretexts for "ambition and avarice," Grotius nevertheless concluded that abuses by the wicked shall not invalidate what is just.[22] Grotius had already begun to see humanitarian intervention as a "much more honorable [act] to revenge *other peoples' injuries*" rather than one's own suffering.[23]

The tensions between the general principle of respect for territorial sovereignty and the lingering influence of universalist ideas of natural law and justice continued into the next two centuries. Vattel was unequivocal that "nations are absolutely free and independent" and he explicitly criticized Grotius for advocating the right to punish another state for violating the law of nature. According to him, the right of punishment of nations could be derived "solely from their right to provide for their own safety" and claimed only against those by whom they have been "injured."[24] Insisting that foreign states should have "no right to interfere in the government of another independent state," Vattel nonetheless did include an exception to this general rule: unless the "oppressed people" requested foreign assistance against their own government. Therefore, despite his strong objection to Grotius's doctrine of intervention, Vattel's position was softened by this imagined scenario of cruelty and humanitarian sentiment: monstrous foreign rulers "render themselves the scourges and horror of the human race; they are savage beasts, whom every brave man may justly exterminate from the face of the earth."[25]

Henry Wheaton, an American diplomat and one of the few most influential international lawyers in the nineteenth century, witnessed the further positivist turn of international law whose ultimate source of legitimation was said to be based on the consent of sovereign states. He also played a leading role in developing what Antony Anghie has called the "recognition doctrine," which made the legal status of independent non-Christian states a matter to be determined by the Christian powers.[26] What was Wheaton's attitude toward humanitarian intervention in disregard of state sovereignty? In his widely cited *Elements of International Law* (1836), Wheaton justified the Christian European powers' collective assistance of the Greek rebels against the Ottoman Empire in 1827–1830 on the grounds that the Greeks, "after enduring ages of cruel oppression, had shaken off the Ottoman yoke." For him, this example "affords a further illustration of the principles of international law authorizing such an interference . . . where the general interests of humanity are infringed by the excesses of a barbarous and despotic government."[27] This passage has frequently been cited by modern scholars as a most eloquent articulation of the modern concept of humanitarian intervention. The passage conjured up for the modern sympathetic reader a vivid image of the suffering of the Greeks—as brethren not just in Christianity but also in humanity—from "the cruel warfare" and "merciless oppression" under a "barbarous and despotic" Oriental empire. In the interests of humanity and by invoking Montesquieu's notion of Oriental despotism, Wheaton's sentimental representation performed a dual function. It created a state of exception to the supposedly universal rule of state sovereignty, and it also made the Ottoman Empire, which was otherwise excluded by Wheaton and others from the benefits of "the general international law of Christendom," liable to punishment under the Euroamericentric system of international law.[28] The same arguments would be adopted by many Britons in their debates over the two wars with China in the mid-nineteenth century. Wheaton later revised his treatise to argue that contact with Western Christian nations had led African and Asian countries, including China, to adopt the Western legal principles and renounce their own backward customs and usages.[29]

Sovereignty and Sentimentalism in the Debate
Over the Second Opium War, 1856–1860

In the examples we have discussed, the sentimental conceptualization of injury was essential to the deliberation over when a just war could be launched against an independent state as an exception to the general recognition of state sovereignty. The ideas of both direct injury and secondary injury were invoked to call for military intervention in the context of Sino-Western relations in the nineteenth century. Nevertheless, together with the European intellectual tradition that raised questions about the moral legitimacy and corrupting effects of excessive imperial expansion, the universalist notions of justice and sympathy underlying the same discourses of liberalism and sentimentality also generated some of the most scathing critiques of the imperial project. In fact, Vattel had already observed in 1758 that "humanity revolts against a sovereign, who, without necessity or without very powerful reasons, lavishes the blood" of his people and exposes them to the danger of war.[30] He also thought that Grotius's unusually broad theory, authorizing an unrelated state to use force to punish another state for violating the law of nature, was to invite "all the ravages of enthusiasm and fanaticism" and create "numberless pretexts" for political ambition.[31] Then, the challenge would be to determine *when* humanitarian sentiment about the suffering of others would constitute an injury that is genuine and serious enough to justify intervention by a third party or foreign community. These challenges are illustrated in the debates over the Second Opium War in 1856–1860 and have continued to trouble thinkers and jurists of our own time.

In a monumental study of this conflict, John Wong has shown the so-called *Arrow* incident was a "manufactured" casus belli. Harry Parkes, British consul at Canton, and Sir John Bowring, fourth Governor of Hong Kong, got Britain into this war by maintaining that the Chinese seizure of the *Arrow*—a boat owned and operated by Chinese smugglers except for the nominal British captain and its expired Hong Kong registration—insulted the British flag and national honor.[32] Lord Palmerston, the British prime minister, adopted their "invented" story in support of a military expedition to punish the Chinese imperial commissioner, Ye Mingchen, both for insulting the British and for his behavior as an "insolent barbarian." Although Wong considers economic interests (such as the opium trade and Chinese goods and market in this case) to be the most "pivotal" and the ultimate cause of this war, he also notes that "public passion of imperial Britain at the time" enabled Palmerston to influence public opinion and the decision-making process.[33] Such passion, or what I call sentiment, was amply demonstrated by the debates in the British press and Parliament.

The conspiracy of Parkes and Bowring to cover up the expiry of the *Arrow*'s registration and their subsequent unauthorized bombardment of the city of Canton made it a formidable task for Palmerston's government to defend them or the use of force against China.[34] Even the British attorney general suggested that Britain might well be at fault under international law in this case. James Bruce, eighth Earl of Elgin, who led the China expedition in 1857–1860 as British plenipotentiary, privately lamented that his campaign originated in a "scandal" and that the bombardment of Canton was the "massacre of the innocent" in the Christian chronicle.[35]

When Adam Smith articulated his natural theory of sentiment in the 1750s, he assumed that "the impartial spectator" would be able to overcome self-interest or national prejudice to sympathize with those foreigners thousands of miles away.[36] In an essay that coined the term "international law" for the law of nations in the 1780s, Jeremy Bentham, a British philosopher and radical reformer with enormous influence on liberal thinkers including John Stuart Mill, pointed to the serious limitations of sentiment in the practice of empire: "Distant mischiefs make little impression on those on whom the remedying of them depends. A single murder committed in London makes more impression than if thousands of murders and other cruelties were committed in the East Indies." As a result, the impeachment of the former governor general of India Warren Hastings in London in 1788–1795 "excited compassion in those who heard the detail of the cruelties committed by him [in India] with indifference."[37] In the trial of Hastings, Edmund Burke called this kind of refusal to extend the metropolitan legal and moral standards to non-Western people a practice of "geographical morality."[38] For Burke, the disparaging representation of the Indian people as alien and inferior was more responsible than the geographical distance for the British refusal to empathize with those sufferers of British colonial injustice. As those distant people had "no other remedy but the sympathies of mankind," Burke considered the British refusal to extend sympathy a robbery in itself.[39] By construing the withholding of sympathy to the colonized population as an injury to humanity, Burke revealed the flip side of the now widespread discourse of sentimental liberalism and humanitarianism.

The charge of geographical morality was also what empowered the critics of the Second Opium War in their attack on the Palmerston government. When the debate over the war with China came up in the House of Commons in March 1857, Sir William Gladstone argued that Britain could not justify its bombardment of Canton and the war in terms of "municipal, imperial, or colonial law," "international law," or "the higher ground of natural justice."[40] Palmerston and his supporters tried hard to mount a defense by interpreting international law to suit their own arguments, but in the House of Lords in February 1857 the Earl of Carnarvon urged his audiences to attend to "the injustice committed by this country in enforcing the principles of international law when those laws applied in our own favour, and refusing to recognize them when their application justified the conduct of the Chinese."[41] However, it was John Roebuck, a leading radical reformer, who most clearly echoed Burke's criticism of geographical morality when he stated in the House of Commons: "I wish [those who supported the war with

China] would suppose that these transactions took place in the city of Liver-pool and the Mersey, for I have found that European and western people generally have one rule of morality for the west and another for the east." That principle had indeed been put forward in Parliament, but it was his be-lief that "the rule of morality extends over the globe (cheers), and what is just and unjust in the Mersey is equally just or unjust in the river before Can-ton. (Renewed cheers)."[42]

To rouse his audience's sympathy toward the Indians afar, Burke described both Indian suffering and British cruelty in vivid detail because he knew that his task, as Jennifer Pitts has noted, required careful "theatrics."[43] Burke stated, "I am sensible that a cold style of describing actions . . . [is] contrary to the justice due to the people, and to all genuine human feelings about them."[44] Therefore, his strategy in the impeachment debate was to create "deliberately shocking imagery to overcome what he feared was the insu-perable indifference" of the British elites and public toward the suffering of a distant people often despised and ignored by the British.[45] Interestingly, both critics and defenders of the Second Opium War deployed similar strat-egies. Just as Burke tried to make the Indians less alien to his audience, John Roebuck also stressed in 1857 that "China is among civilized nations" and that the Chinese "are a civilized people," even though their civilization "is not ours" and "is of a particular kind" in the sense that "they have not applied their intelligence to the art of war" as aggressively as the British. It is true that "they have been called barbarous [by us], but it must not be forgot-ten that they [also] call us barbarians." To impress his audiences further, he redirected their attention to the sharp contrast between their self-image and the actual consequences of British expansion overseas: The "citizens of Canton have seen their dwelling cut up and destroyed; they have seen their relatives butchered by the wonderous civilization of England; their blood has flowed, and for what? All because it is said the flag of England has been tarnished by the police officers of Canton." What would happen if "London were so shelled by a people of superior civilization to ourselves"? He had no doubt that every Englishman would then be ready to sacrifice him-self to "destroy the barbarians as we might call them who had battered the city about our ears."[46] As the British were supposedly the only great people with a constitutional government and large Eastern dominions, according to Roebuck, British acts in the East would be seen as representative of the en-tire Western civilization and of Christianity. A number of other members of

Parliament expressed a similar concern about the great damage done by this incident to Britain's national character. As Lord Malmesbury noted, "I feel that the honour of the country is at stake in this instance equally with its morality . . . [and] I feel shame for my country."[47]

Whether these critics' representation has the intended or unintended effect of giving due recognition to the sovereign and civilized status of China, Palmerston and his allies deployed the sentimental discourse to deny or displace that status. The government sent Parliament a volume of more than two hundred pages of *Correspondence Regarding Insults in China* during the years 1842–1856, which was designed to pile all the "outrages" on the back of the *Arrow* incident to "make it big enough" to justify the war.[48] It turned out that these thirty-seven "insults" included not only Sino-American disputes but also British outrages against the Chinese.[49] The British government survived a vote of censure in the House of Lords but lost in the Commons on February 26, 1857, by 263 votes to 247. In response, Palmerston dissolved Parliament and made an appeal to the people by calling a general election.[50]

News of Chinese resistance to or attack on the British, including a reported attempt by a Chinese baker to sell poisoned bread to foreigners in Hong Kong in January 1857, after the British bombardment of Canton, made for sensational headlines in English newspapers that condemned the Chinese for "cold-blooded murders" or "diabolic" cruelty.[51] The *Morning Post*, the British newspaper with the largest circulation after the *Times*, attributed the attempted poisoning to Commissioner Ye and described him as "the most truculent miscreant who had butchered seventy thousand of his own countrymen and who subsequently stimulated 'by a large reward, the murder of our countrymen.'"[52] Critics of Palmerston's government observed that all such attention to Chinese character as "uncivilized and cruel" was irrelevant to the current debate because it could not be understood as justifying the waging of war against them.[53] However, the sentimental discourse of Chinese punishments seemed to have precisely that effect. Consul Harry Parkes himself had published in the journal of the Royal Asiatic Society a lengthy account of the execution of fifty-three members of the Taiping Rebellion in Canton as witnessed by his colleague in 1852, writing that "owing to their hands being so constantly steeped in human blood, they do not shrink from the committal of the most inhuman practices." Discussion of the "cruelty" of Chinese punishments thus proved that the Chinese had only "semi-civilization" and among them "sympathy or feeling for the sufferings of others" was replaced by apathy or even brutality.[54] Likewise, Bowring wrote to the *Times* about the attempted poisoning in the heat of the debate in 1857 to defend the war and later published an article about "crimes and criminals in China."[55] These narratives about Chinese cruelty were directly translated by commentators and politicians into a justification for the military expedition. The *Globe*, another British newspaper supportive of Palmerston and the war policy, fabricated an alleged testimony to hold the Chinese authorities responsible for the poisoning.[56] This charge led some of the mainstream media to suggest that the Chinese be placed "outside the pale of all laws" and be "dealt with as noxious animals—as wild beasts in human shape, without one single redeeming virtue." Regarding such a people, it was useless to talk about international law; rather, only one law was applicable, "a law of severe, summary, and inexorable justice."[57] Besides recent Sino-Western disputes, century-old missionary stories about Chinese uncleanness, sensuality, avarice, and prejudice against women were also cited to confirm that the Chinese should not be negotiated with exactly like "a civilized state."[58] In any event, the "cold-blooded, machine-like" Chinese should be punished for their injury or offense to humanity, if not directly to the British.[59]

Capitalizing on the emotional power of this discourse of Chinese cruelty and barbarity, Palmerston and his supporters appealed to both the jingoistic sentiments of their audiences to defend the nation and their moral conscience to defend humanity in general. On March 20, 1857, right before the so-called Chinese Election, Palmerston delivered a public address before the entire cabinet, members of both houses of Parliament, and the entire diplomatic corps in London. He accused critics of his policy of being motivated by party agendas and being "instruments of national dishonour and disgrace." In response to the idea that his administration was "addicted to war," he reformulated the whole debate as one over whether the British should have the right to vindicate the "insult, outrage, and atrocity" suffered by their "fellow countrymen in a distant part of the globe." In the process, he skillfully identified the opposition and critics with the "Chinese barbarians," who were then equated with cold-hearted murderers. He pointed to "the logical and inevitable consequences" if the opposition were to come to power:

> They were bound . . . to have apologized to the Chinese barbarians for the
> wrongs we had done—to have rebuilt the forts which we gallant sailors had

destroyed, . . . and at the same time, in order to complete the measure of redress, they must have paid the rewards which had been given for the heads
of our merchants, and the cost of the arsenic which had been used in poisoning our fellow-subjects at Hongkong. (Cheers.) Gentlemen, I cannot envy
the feelings of those men who could witness with calmness the heads of
respectable British merchants on the walls of Canton, or the murders and
assassinations and poisonings perpetrated on our fellow-countrymen abroad,
and who, instead of feeling their blood boil with indignation at such proceedings, would have had us make an abject submission to the barbarians by
whom these atrocities were committed. (Cheers.)

The whole nation was urged to "rally together to vindicate the honour of
the empire."[60] Three days later, Palmerston released another election address
that was circulated nationwide, with a memorable account of the origin
of the war with China: "An insolent barbarian, wielding authority at Canton,
had violated the British flag, broken the engagements of treaties, offered rewards for the heads of British subjects in that part of China, and planned
their destruction by murder, assassinations, and poisons.'"[61] While members
of the opposition found Palmerston's speeches "full of deception and false-
hood," his arguments carried the day in the general election. Indeed, people
from all walks of life, not just those interested in the China trade, rallied
around the government to attack opposition members, many of whom had
to express their penitence to their constituencies.[62] Palmerston returned to
power in April 1857 with a landslide victory that swept away many of his
critics in Parliament. The war with China continued even after the Tory
opposition took over in February 1858; Palmerston was back in office in
June 1859 and stayed through 1865.[63]

These invocations of popular sentiments were not just rhetorical devices
but were embedded in the larger discourse of what I call sentimental liberalism and intimately connected with the sentimental facet of international
law and politics under study in this essay. As I have also shown elsewhere,
this sentimental discourse enabled Western lawyers and politicians to
redefine China's sovereign status and rights under international law and
order.[64] By the same token, the treatises and concessions that resulted from
the Second Opium War further undermined China's sovereignty. When it
came to 1900, the representation of China's cruelty and injury to its own
people and to foreigners during the Boxer Rebellion served to naturalize

the earlier bifurcation of the world into a community of "civilized" states as full subjects of international law and another group of states, including China, as partial subjects only for fulfilling legal obligations under their treaties with the former nations.[65] This bifurcation and the resultant gradations of sovereignty can be traced back to the debates over the two Opium Wars and the legal treatises of Wheaton and his predecessors such as Grotius and Victoria.[66] If "the history of sovereignty doctrine in the nineteenth century," as Antony Anghie has aptly put it, "is a history of the process by which Europeans states, by developing a complex vocabulary of cultural and racial discrimination," claimed the power to determine "who is and who is not sovereign,"[67] then it is also a history of how the sentimental discourse became a key part of this vocabulary and a significant source of this power.

Notes

1. Karen Halttunen, "Humanitarianism and the Pornography of Pain in Anglo-American Culture," *American Historical Review* 100, no. 2 (1995): 303. For literature review, see Daniel Wickberg, "What Is the History of Sensibilities?," *American Historical Review* 112, no. 3 (2007): 661–84.
2. Adam Smith, *The Theory of Moral Sentiments* (London: Millar, 1759); David Hume, *A Treatise of Human Nature*, 3 vols. (London: John Noon, 1739–1740).
3. Uday Singh Mehta, *Liberalism and Empire: A Study in Nineteenth-Century British Liberal Thought* (Chicago: University of Chicago Press, 1999), 16–17. See Lynn Festa, *Sentimental Figures of Empire in Eighteenth-Century Britain and France* (Baltimore: Johns Hopkins University Press, 2006).
4. See, e.g., Pieter Spierenburg, *The Spectacle of Suffering: Execution and the Evolution of Repression* (Cambridge: Cambridge University Press, 1984); Elizabeth Barnes, "Communicable Violence and the Problem of Capital Punishment in New England, 1830–1890," *Modern Language Studies* 30, no. 1 (2000): 7–26.
5. John Stuart Mill, "Civilization: Signs of the Times," *London and Westminster Review* 3, no. 1 (1836): 1–2.
6. Montesquieu, *The Spirit of the Laws*, trans. Thomas Nugent, 4th ed. (London: J. Nourse & P. Vallant, 1766), 1:118–19, 124–25 (on Japan). Given its very different focus, this chapter has no need or space for a detailed review of the intellectual genealogy, diversity, or internal contradictions of European representations of China or Chinese law. For most recent studies and citations to the relevant existing scholarship, see Li Chen, *Chinese Law in the Imperial Eyes: Sovereignty, Justice, and Transcultural Politics, c. 1740s–1840s* (New York: Columbia University Press, 2016); Teemu Ruskola, *Legal Orientalism: China, the United States, and Modern Law* (Cambridge, MA: Harvard University Press, 2013); Timothy Brook, Jérôme

Bourgon, and Gregory Blue, *Death by a Thousand Cuts* (Cambridge, MA: Harvard University Press, 2008).

7. Smith, *Theory of Moral Sentiments*, 228, 383 (comparing Chinese foot-binding and European body-squeezing).

8. About Smith's pluralism and later thinkers, see Jennifer Pitts, *A Turn to Empire: The Rise of Imperial Liberalism in Britain and France* (Princeton: Princeton University Press, 2005), 21–50.

9. "Papers Respecting the Negotiation for a Renewal of the East India Company's Exclusive Privileges (1812)," *Quarterly Review* 8 (1812): 283, 285.

10. J. Sydney Taylor's speech (May 30, 1831), in *The Punishments of Death* (London: Harvey & Durton, 1831), 27, 27–35.

11. "Punishment of the Canton and Fuhkeen Vagabonds," *North China Herald* 1, no. 4 (1850).

12. Ann L. Stoler, "On Degrees of Imperial Sovereignty," *Public Culture* 18, no. 1 (2006): 128.

13. See, e.g., Daniel V. Botsman, *Punishment and Power in the Making of Modern Japan* (Princeton: Princeton University Press, 2005).

14. Li Chen, "Sentimental Imperialism and the Global Spectacle of Chinese Punishments," in Chen, *Chinese Law in the Imperial Eyes*, 156–200. For some typical accounts in this regard, see, e.g., Old-Shanghai, "Chinese Massacre," *Times*, October 6, 1870; "Chinese Culprit Before a Magistrate," *Free Enquirer*, March 29, 1835, "Chinese Cruelty," *Chicago Tribune*, July 30, 1877. Also see Brook, Bourgon, and Blue, *Death by a Thousand Cuts*.

15. Dipesh Chakrabarty, *Provincializing Europe: Postcolonial Thought and Historical Difference* (Princeton: Princeton University Press, 2000), 119, 126–27.

16. Hugo Grotius, *Commentary on the Law of Prize and Booty* (c. 1604), ed. Martine Julia van Ittersum, trans. Gwladys L. Williams (Indianapolis: Liberty Fund, 2005), 102–7; *The Rights of War and Peace* (1625), ed. Richard Tuck (Indianapolis: Liberty Fund, 2005), 393–96.

17. Emer de Vattel, *The Law of Nations; or, Principles of the Law of Nature* (1758), ed. Béla Kaposy and Richard Whatmore (Indianapolis: Liberty Fund, 2008), 266, 482–84 (echoing Grotius's just-war theory).

18. See Ryan Goodman, "Humanitarian Intervention and Pretexts for War," *American Journal of International Law* 100, no. 1 (2006): 107–10; Sean D. Murphy, *Humanitarian Intervention: The United Nations in an Evolving World Order* (Philadelphia: University of Pennsylvania Press, 1996).

19. Franciscus de Victoria, *De Indies et De Ivre Belli Relectiones, Being Parts of Relectiones Theologicae XII* (1557), ed. James B. Scott and Ernest Nye, trans. John Pawley Bate (Washington, DC: Carnegie Institution, 1917), 156–62. See also Antony Anghie, *Imperialism, Sovereignty, and the Making of International Law* (Cambridge: Cambridge University Press, 2004), 13–31.

20. Grotius, *Commentary*, 1022–24, 1024. While Victoria did not consider it just to interfere with a country for offense against nature, Grotius held differently (ibid., 1024).

21. For the role of sentiment in shaping international politics or judicial process, see, e.g., Festa, *Sentimental Figures of Empire*; Eugenia Lean, *Public Passions: The Trial*

of *Shi Jianqiao and the Rise of Popular Sympathy in Republican China* (Berkeley: University of California Press, 2007); and Chen, *Chinese Law in Imperial Eyes*, 156–200.

22. Grotius, *Commentary*, 1161–62, 1159.
23. Ibid., 1021. Emphasis added.
24. Vattel, *Law of Nations*, 265.
25. Ibid., 292, 290–91. It is clear that the sentimental discourse already influenced him as he borrowed Montesquieu's passages about the brutalizing effect of severe punishment (ibid., 192).
26. Anghie, *Imperialism*, 75–114, 52–65.
27. Henry Wheaton, *Elements of International Law* (Philadelphia: Carey, Lea & Blanchard, 1836), 91, 94.
28. Ibid., 93–94. Wheaton also followed Vattel in emphasizing that the Greeks requested foreign assistance.
29. Henry Wheaton, *Elements of International Law*, 8th ed. (Boston: Little, Brown, 1866), 22, 178.
30. Vattel, *Law of Nations*, 482.
31. Ibid., 265.
32. John Y. Wong, *Deadly Dreams: Opium, Imperialism, and the* Arrow *War (1856–60) in China* (Cambridge: Cambridge University Press, 1998), 69–127, 4–5, 26–27, 459–63. About the war itself, see James L. Hevia, *English Lessons: The Pedagogy of Imperialism in Nineteenth-Century China* (Durham: Duke University Press, 2003), 32–117.
33. Wong, *Deadly Dreams*, 464.
34. See "House of Commons [Debates on March 3, 1857]," *Times*, March 4, 1857, and Wong, *Deadly Dreams*, 174–215.
35. John Newsinger, "Elgin in China," *New Left Review* 15 (2002): 130, 120; "House of Lords [Debates on February 26, 1857]," *Times*, February 27, 1857.
36. See his hypothetic earthquake in China, in Adam Smith, *The Theory of Moral Sentiments*, 2nd ed. (London: A. Miller, 1761), 211–14.
37. His *Principles of International Law* was drafted in 1786–89. See Jeremy Bentham, *The Works of Jeremy Bentham* (Edinburgh: W. Tait, 1843), 2:547.
38. Edmund Burke, *The Works and Correspondence of the Right Honourable Edmund Burke* (London: Francis & John Rivington, 1852), 7:380, 287–88; Pitts, *Turn to Empire*, 77.
39. See Pitts, *Turn to Empire*, 72–80, quotations at 74, 75.
40. Speech by Gladstone in "House of Commons [Debates on March 3, 1857]."
41. "House of Lords [Debates on February 26, 1857]."
42. "House of Commons [Debates on March 3, 1857]"; *Hansard's Parliamentary Debates*, 3rd ser. (London: Cornelius Buck, 1857), 144:1783–85.
43. Pitts, *Turn to Empire*, 75.
44. *The Speeches of the Right Hon. Edmund Burke, with Memoir and Historical Introduction*, ed. James Burke (Dublin: James Duffy, 1853), 250. See Pitts, *Turn to Empire*, 75.
45. Pitts, *Turn to Empire*, 76.
46. "House of Commons [Debates on March 3, 1857]." Also *Hansard's Parliamentary Debates*, 144:1783–85.
47. "House of Lords [Debates on February 26, 1857]."

48. "Correspondence Respecting Insults in China," in *Parliamentary Papers* (London: House of Commons, 1857). Quotation is from Goderich, "House of Commons [February 27]," *Times*, February 28, 1857.

49. "House of Commons [February 27]."

50. "House of Commons [March 5, 1857]," *Times*, March 6, 1857. About the candidates' speeches, see "The Elections," *Times*, March 30, 1857. For more on the "Chinese Election," see Wong, *Deadly Dreams*, 216–58.

51. "The Chinese and Persian Wars," *Times*, March 2, 1857.

52. Wong, *Deadly Dreams*, 226; also see 156–58 and 169–70 (on Palmerston's relationship with this paper).

53. See Mr. Henley's criticism of Ralph Bernal Osborne in "House of Commons [Debates on March 3, 1857]." Also see *Hansard's Parliamentary Debates*, 144:1759.

54. Harry S. Parkes, "Description of Proceedings in the Criminal Court of Canton, with an Account of an Execution at Canton by Frank Parish," *Transactions of the China Branch of the Royal Asiatic Society*, part 3 (1853): 43, 53–54.

55. "Sir John Bowring on the Chinese Barbarities," *Times*, April 18, 1857; John Bowring, "Recollections of Crime and Criminals in China," *Cornhill Magazine* 12 (1865).

56. *Globe*, March 24, 1857, quoted in Wong, *Deadly Dreams*, 227–28; see also 170 (on the media).

57. Wong, *Deadly Dreams*, 226.

58. "China," *Times*, April 6, 1857; *Morning Post*, February 28, 1857.

59. "Chinese Humanity," *Times*, May 5, 1857; Parkes, "Description of Proceedings," 56.

60. "Ministerial Banquet at the Mansion-House," *Times*, March 21, 1857.

61. "Lord Palmerston's Address," *Morning Post*, March 25, 1857.

62. "Election Intelligence," *Times*, March 21, 1857.

63. About British party politics then, see "England Since 1830," *Times*, March 17, 1874.

64. See Chen, *Chinese Law in Imperial Eyes*, 156–242.

65. "An Eyewitness Tells of Recent Frightful Chinese Torture," *San Francisco Call*, July 22, 1900; George Thin, *The Tientsin Massacre, the Causes of the Late Disturbances in China and How to Secure Permanent Peace* (London: Blackwood, 1870), 25–26, 66–67, 94; "The Note to China," *New York Times*, December 24, 1900. For foreign imperial politics in post-1860 China, see Hevia, *English Lessons*, 124–314.

66. About the First Opium War, see Chen, *Chinese Law in the Imperial Eyes*, chap. 5.

67. Anghie, *Imperialism*, 100.

SEVENTEEN

The Sovereignty of the New Man After Wagner

Artist and Hero, Symbolic History, and the Staging of Origins

STEFANOS GEROULANOS

Hier gebar ein neues Geschlecht eine neue Auffassung der Welt, indem es
durch ein uraltes Erlebnis schritt.

—ERNST JÜNGER, *STURM*

IN *DER MYTHUS DES ZWANZIGSTEN JAHRHUNDERTS* (1930), Alfred Rosenberg famously offered racial hierarchy as a restorative myth whose ciphers were already present in society but which still awaited its proper articulation, an "awakening" that was threatened as much by the enemies of national socialism as by a persistent, intentional neglect that had long and successfully relegated it to sleep.[1] Rosenberg proposed the following logic for the messianic awakening of the Nazi New Man:

> And while . . . we have not yet been gifted the authentic Genius who will reveal to us the Myth, who will educate us to the Type, this knowledge still does not relieve anyone thinking deeply of the duty of carrying out the preliminary work—work which has always been necessary—as a new vital feeling struggles for expression, generating spiritual tensions. Until the time has come for the Great Man who will teach and live what millions thus far could only stammer.[2]

The Genius that would emerge—the Genius that *was* emerging into consciousness across this self-referential formulation—would at once recalibrate the entire terrain of feeling and life, generate the new ideal or "Type," and incarnate and exemplify this ideal. Rosenberg's feint was to present his prophecy as mere preliminary staging work to "reveal" the Genius or Great Man, and nevertheless as an urgent vital duty, without which the myth and the new man would be lost altogether.[3] Still the Genius remained a gift to passively receive, one that had not yet been granted: carrying out the imperative "preliminary work" involved negotiating spiritual tensions, speaking in stammer, prophesying, and shaping, so as to make possible the moment of fusion in which the labored uncovering of the myth would coincide with the gift of the Genius and the consciousness transformed by it.[4]

Rosenberg's description of the present as a time of spiritual tension, work, and stammer—a precipice between a supposed redemption and an oblivion of Germany—expresses well one trend in the Nazi understanding of sovereignty as involving a future-oriented "awakening," a staged rebirth in which the unity and ascent to hegemony of a primordial German *Volk* would be guaranteed in the same gesture as it guaranteed the awakening. The New Man was to be willed into being through mytho-religious and aesthetic work, heralding the awakening he represented. As the Hero of the new era, the New Man was also to be above all not merely a political but a national-aesthetic creation.

This essay examines the interweaving of two problems at the juncture of aesthetics and radical politics in modern European history. The first of these is a conviction, occasional after 1848 but prevalent after 1900, at least among antibourgeois intellectuals, that modern sovereignty paled by comparison to both divine-right kingship and terroristic revolution.[5] Opponents of liberalism and parliamentarism who did not pine for monarchy routinely posited that the regimes controlling the major continental European states and empires were conceptually and aesthetically shallow operations that did not reach down to the true stratum of political or symbolic activity, did not go beyond a management of power, did not represent sources of political truth that could compete with revolutionary regeneration or with a belonging to a racial, national, or human community.[6] Nationalist and racial thought postulated that the pure springs of society and sovereignty were to be discovered at the fount of a longer, truer, deeper history—one whose symbolic unity guaranteed national unity at a frequently evolutionary, unconscious social level.[7] Revolutionary and anarchist activity often concurred that authenticity and political aura lay beyond, or more precisely *beneath*, these regimes, in their symbolic as well as political overturning. A return to the natural, to one's own, like an advance toward a truly new regime, supposedly involved a turn to a hidden symbolic truth, often a return to the beginning of history that could supposedly restore this hidden truth and harmony to society, political power, and aesthetics.

The second problem is the emergence of figures of the New Man as alternative, ostensibly more profound, forms of sovereignty. After 1918, the new regimes of the Soviet Union, fascist Italy, and Nazi Germany famously pursued projects of social and human regeneration. Promises of a New Man were also ubiquitous across the spectrum of political and avant-garde movements. Each assiduously staged its New Man as the embodiment of such promises, as the hoped-for sovereign of an anticipated new era disburdened of the social, economic, and political failures of the bourgeois present. Figures that were posited for the New Man were often complex, compound, and contradictory even within individual movements.[8] Targeting the bourgeois man and the new woman, such figures included the political leader or hegemon (a tradition exemplified in and by Mussolini)[9]; bearers of "the will" now raised to superhuman status (e.g., Stakhanovites or the SS); and the new, scientifically designed, aesthetically and eugenically articulated norms for a new man, ranging from cyborgs (in dada or *Metropolis*) to sublime beings now re-create human reality itself.

This essay threads these problems together by arguing that Wagner's quasi-Romantic fiction of a coexistence between an artist/creator and the hero/leader—an entwining through which each acquired a specific kind of sovereignty—was redeployed after World War I, buttressed by a conceptually recast understanding of history's effects on human nature. For this vision of human history, events and political circumstances formed merely a top stratum, underwritten by a symbolically dense, "truer," and more meaningful substratum (or series of substrata) that occasionally emerged at the surface. Sovereignty had disappeared from the political landscape because merely political power failed to affect the depths where human nature was properly plastic. The New Man was exciting partly as a response to this failure: in the promise that he would effect a transformation of human nature, the New Man was to reach beneath society and history, recuperate the lost beginning (or beginnings), admit the failures of history and the contemporary. "He" would be at once *new* and *primal*, extra-historical at both ends, untainted: the future-oriented scheme for building a new life was both one of raising, into everyday life, the power and authenticity of the veiled, unknown, symbolic history *and* one of restoring a primal state unspoiled by history and its perversions.[10] Moreover, identifying this forthcoming transformation granted power to authors, artists, or politicians reading their "authentic" history and announcing, staging, and managing the New Man. Carrying out this "preliminary work," the artist of the New World and supposedly true interpreter of history would become one who *shares* and *co-constructs* sovereignty with the New Man.

After discussing *Siegfried*, I turn to consider the motif of a "second" or "secret" history in the human sciences, then to the persistence of this motif in philosophy, and finally to scientific endeavors toward such a transformation. Fundamentally locked into one another, in a manner that affected both the aesthetic figuration of the new man and the political logics of sovereignty, artist-creator-scientists molded history and its limits for the heroes and leaders who would embody its transformation.

The Prototype: Siegfried

When Siegfried enters, early in act 1 of Wagner's *Siegfried*, guiding his pet bear (and his relationship to nature), the questions of his kinship, destiny, and status as hero-in-the-making are foremost on his mind and, for different reasons, on that of the audience. He knows that Mime, who has raised him and who declares, "Ich bin dein Vater und Mutter zugleich," cannot be either. The two of them lack all physical resemblance as opposed to the animals Siegfried has observed in the forest during his journeys and which are, he snarls, "teurer als Du, Baum und Vogel, die Fische im Bach, lieber mach ich sie leiden als dich."[11] Mime's claim to parentage must be "unnatural." The Siegfried leitmotif is played for the first time in the opera as Siegfried recounts how, during one of these adventures, he first saw his own image in the river water.[12] Having been played at the end of *Die Walküre* in reference to who might cross the ring of fire and awaken Brünhilde, the motif immediately identifies Siegfried as this musically and formally defined hero,[13] the one who will break Wotan's spear, end the punishment of Brünhilde, and act with the *free will* that his father, Siegmund, lacked.

A lot depends on this scene. First, the staging of the narcissistic moment bridges musical identity (the Siegfried leitmotif) and narrative self-recognition. For the rest of this act, as for act 2, Siegfried remains identifiable by his name and ever-expanding leitmotif, but his genealogy is as unknown to him as he is unknown to himself.[14] Wagner not only casts him through the Romantic theme of a wolf-child (in fact, a wolf-child twice over, a *Wälsungsproß* rather than a *Wälsung*)[15] but also systematically deprives him of the links to others, the social instincts (notably fear), and the intellect ("ach bist du dumm!")[16] that would allow him to engage meaningfully with his own background. Siegfried shifts from creature of myth to formal construct of the *Gesamtkunstwerk*—the one capable of true love in act 3, the one who, in breaking Wotan's spear early in act 3, breaks the Law—all laws, all relationships, all contracts, all the treaties that preserve the order of the universe—the one who destroys, à la Feuerbach, the rule of the gods for that of men and forces an anarchy in which order is promised only by the law of his sword.

Second, Wagner indicates here that Siegfried is attuned to a different set of signs than Mime, in that he is symbolically, musically at one with the course of the Ring itself.[17] The truth that sponsors him is provided not by cultural attachments, language, intelligence, sociality, but by the music as a mirror of his presence and a bearer of symbolism: hidden, invisible to Mime, but for us and for Siegfried all the truer, the music signifies symbolically, bears "destiny," and is wielded by Siegfried as power. Mime persists in relying on language, which both characters have reduced to malicious chatter; Siegfried has become a creature of musical symbolism: the horn, the forest bird, the weaponlike quality of his speaking his name, the ever-expanding leitmotif.

Third, as is well known, Wagner establishes a relationship of culture to nature; it is this relationship that, together with Siegfried's self-recognition and identification with musical form, casts the originality of his character. Commentators have routinely noted the scene as a restoration of nature against (Jewish) culture, a claim that hinges on the failure of Mime's ("cultural") upbringing of Siegfried to substitute for proper paternity.[18] Yet act 1 asserts little more than that all kinship must be explicitly rejected for a new relationship to nature to be instilled: Siegfried shows but a moment of sadness over his parents and immediately overrides the question of kinship for the reforging of the broken sword Nothung, which he demands of Mime, the "greatest of technicians" (*der weiseste Schmied*). Upon Mime's failure, he welds it himself, "naturally" or "instinctively." It is hardly accidental that in forging the weapon that will win him the Ring, Siegfried emerges as someone self-created, in charge of his own will and destiny.[19] Rather than follow the path laid out for him by Mime, Siegfried takes up this same path of his own; only through Siegfried's *own* subjugation of technique, tradition, and art to instinct and will do kinship and destiny come to be refracted into heroism. What wins here is not "nature" but rather an intimate absorption of nature that begins as much from destiny as from scratch, and that parallels the formal musical construction of the hero.

As Peter Caldwell elucidates, using Feuerbach, "the new myth was to *do* something, such as point to a new world. The modern mythmaker was interested in creation, not stabilization."[20] But how was this creation, this aestheticized purity, to work? Discussing his decision to work on Siegfried rather than Friedrich II, Wagner explained the role of myth as follows:

> [Germany], in its actual reality, could nowise satisfy my longing; thus I felt that a deeper instinct lay behind my impulse. . . . As though to get down to its root, I sank myself into the primal element at home, that meets us in the legends of a past which attracts us the more warmly as the present repels us with its hostile chill. To all our wishes and warm impulses, which in truth transport us to the Future, we seek to give a physical token by means of pictures from the Past, and thus to win for them a form the modern Present never can provide. . . . My studies thus bore me, through the legends of the Middle Ages, right down to their foundation in the old Germanic *mythos*; one swathing after another, which the later legendary lore had bound around it, I was able to unloose, and thus at last to gaze upon it in its chastest beauty. What here I saw, was no longer the figure of conventional history, whose garment claims our interest more than does the actual shape inside; but the real naked man, in whom I might spy each throbbing of his pulses, each stir within his mighty muscles, in uncramped, freest motion: the type of the true human being.[21]

In treating "the origin" as the most primal past through which to delve, in order to then dislocate and undermine the present time and recover an unwrapped Siegfried, Wagner identifies both a "conventional history" that has defined the modern German present and a moment that exceeds, transcends this history.[22] This text follows two movements: the second is Wagner's undressing of history and legend to get to the naked myth at its start—which he identifies with the naked, true human being.[23] Myth carries symbolic truth better than mere history. Wagner's use of the

Germanic *Nibelungenlied* hinges on this supposedly newly recovered northern Germanic identity being grounded in prehistory—not so much a racial unit but an Indo-European purity suspended between nature and history, whose racial and cultural coherence and authenticity had fallen to oblivion.[24]

The first movement, however, brackets instead this gesture of returning to the origin by crafting Wagner's aim as future-oriented: to mediate the presently formless "wishes and warm impulses" so that these might rightly and unproblematically "transport us to the Future." Wagner would, in other words, use the Siegfried myth to both criticize mid-nineteenth-century culture and promise an original man instated now as a new man. "Although the splendid type of Siegfried had long attracted me, it first enthralled my every thought when I had come to see it in its purest human shape, set free from every later wrappage."[25] The structural transformation of an old, conventional myth into a new aesthetic compound would make it possible for the purity of this "true human being" to restructure the present, propelling "wishes and warm impulses" toward an improved, more coherent future. The pure moment of anthropogenesis figured in Siegfried's solitary self-recognition at river's edge, now allowed Wagner to pinpoint and reconstruct the background out of which the aesthetic and mythical sovereignty of the new could emerge—a supposedly prehistoric background that could be rendered present with as much ease as it could be telescoped back to a time formally and historically exterior to the history that has veiled it.

Wagner's aesthetic-political engagement during the Schopenhauer-fuelled years around German Unification when he completed *Siegfried* is closely tied to this metahistory. Amid the reconsiderations of legitimacy and sovereignty that 1848 and its aftermath only rendered more urgent, Wagner's abandonment of familial and political forms of authority helped construct a dual-sovereignty fiction grounded on the work of art.[26] The recuperation of the prehistorical moment and its projection into a new sovereign hero, alongside the recasting of the artist as "co-sovereign" with this hero, translated into Wagner's aesthetics a way of addressing the frustrations with parliamentary and constitutional projects. The impossibility of trusting a Rousseauian hope for a renewal of the social contract combined here with a suspicion of the Feuerbachian progress toward a materialist apotheosis of Man that he had espoused before "A Communication to My Friends." Instead of tolerating traditional monarchy, paternal authority, parliamentarism, or socialism, Wagner framed an expanded, obverse political domain. Taking advantage of the myth of Germania—the myth, dating at least to Gibbon, of a "new" race having been born to Rome's north and having led to its destruction—Wagner now identified the *Volk* with this Germanic "origin" while re-positing it as a domain that is aesthetic and symbolic first, and as a result more deeply, more naturally, political.[27]

Choosing Schopenhauer's Will over Feuerbach's Man, Wagner also imported motifs shared at the overlap between naturalism and nationalism, some of them notably expressed in Jules Michelet's *Le peuple* (1846), whose Romanticism and egalitarianism found the Ur-figure in the unsocialized peasant genius.[28] Michelet had relied on the Genius combining its natural/ instinctual and critical faculties to become the redeemer who would restore *le peuple*. Wagner, treating aesthetics as the foundational technology of re-generation, used musical identification and the quasi-natural compound that Siegfried had now become to metonymically identify him with the art-work itself and present him as its liberating hero.[29]

That he intended this aesthetic to be political—indeed revolutionary—was crucial. Decrying, in "Art and Revolution" (1849), "many an honest friend of Art and many an upright friend of men" who followed "socialistic doctri-naires," Wagner specifically allied Art with Revolution. To destroy through Revolution the aesthetico-political regime defined by unfreedom and com-merce was to re-create in the present the framework uniting community, nation, and art last found in Greek tragedy.[30] *Pace* Koselleck's account of revolution, it remained for Wagner a circular, traditional movement essential for this reconstruction: "Only the great Revolution of Mankind, whose beginnings shattered Greek tragedy, can win for us this Art-work."[31] Both in the "circular," recuperative sense and in the future-oriented destruction of established forms, Wagner insisted that "with us, true Art is revolutionary." To call this an aestheticization of politics is altogether insufficient, for what he demanded, especially in "The Art-Work of the Future" (1849) was the art-ist's participation in a revolutionary movement that was *aesthetic* first and that would result in his particular coextensiveness of the Artist, Artwork, and *Volk*.[32] It is through this coextensiveness that the figures of Artist and Hero emerge.

In his expansion or inversion of the political, Wagner proposed a dual sov-ereignty around the *Volk*'s rebirth in the artwork: the sovereignty of the Artist who *is*, who *embodies* the *Volk* and gives it the artwork that mirrors it, and that of the Hero who *is*, who *embodies* the *Volk* in that he bears its need through true political will and ethical purpose. Neither can exist without *Volk* and Artwork, neither can be true asymptotically from its truth. Only thanks to the Artwork can they perfectly express and restage the *Volk*, acquiring as a result a sort of divine right over it. Just like the *Volk* itself, the Artist and the Artwork emerge from a true *want* or *need* [Noth—recall the name of Siegfried's sword], by contrast with the "enemies of the *Volk*" who "feel no want" and with the "fashion" and commerce which Wagner associated with the false, "egotistic," contemporary artist. The feeling of collective want ("eine gemeinschaftliche Noth") turned the *Volk* into the ground of the Artist's existence and the force that is propelled by his Artwork.[33]

A crucial second move involves the theorization of the artist's own place. The artist acquires his status as conduit of the vitality of the *Volk* into the artwork first as one of the set of artists that constitute the *Volk*'s aesthetic core.[34] Once he creates with and for it, he acquires a second, perfected identity with the *Volk*:

> Who, then, will be the *Artist of the Future*? The poet? The performer? The musician? The plastician?—Let us say it in one word: the *Volk. That selfsame Volk to whom we owe the only genuine Art-work, still living even in our modern memory, however much distorted by our restorations; to whom alone we owe all Art itself.*[35]

The Artist not only *expresses* the *Volk*, compressing it into the Artwork, but is tasked specifically with reuniting the *Volk* with itself, ironing out its folds, healing the fissures within it, and ensuring the supremacy of its *need*. This is clearest at the end of *Opera and Drama* (1851): rejecting "the State" and "the Philistine" that dominate current life, Wagner refuses to give up:

> We shall not win hope and nerve until we bend our ear to the heartbeat of history, and catch the sound of that sempiternal vein of living waters which, however buried under the waste-heap of historic civilization, yet pulses on in all its pristine freshness. . . . Where the statesman despairs, the politician drops his hands, the socialist plagues himself with fruitless systems, and even the philosopher can only interpret, but not announce . . . there it is that the *Artist*, with his clear eye, can see shapes [Gestalten] that reveal themselves only to a longing that demands the only truth—*Man*. The Artist has the power of seeing beforehand a yet unshapen world.[36]

Again, it is not a matter of the Artist's Will alone but of his conducting the *Volk*, and even nature itself, into the future.[37]

Wagner's theory of representation hinges on this point: the Artwork mirrors the *Volk*, constituting its self-expression and by the same token its self-recognition; the Artist serves as a mere conduit, but insofar as he also makes this self-identification and self-revelation possible, he is also exercising his own Will, which the *Volk* otherwise lacks. This Artist's Will consists precisely in its (asymptotic) self-erasure in the conduction of *Volk* into Artwork; it is heroic insofar as it constitutes the spark that restores this long-destroyed set of relations or provides the seed that "fecundates" and is by the same token exhausted in the Artwork as this mirroring and guiding *Zustand* of the *Volk*.

Hence the dual sovereignty model: the Artist is sovereign over the *Volk* insofar as he prefigures "a yet unshapen world" and dictates the superior, truer life he models on the Hero he draws out of the *Volk*. (In this regard, a lot could be said about *Lohengrin* and *Parsifal*, which complicate the picture by reinserting Christianity, and also about *Die Meistersinger von Nürnberg*, which is far more dominated by the *Volk* than *Siegfried*.) Wagner is, writes Adorno, " 'neither king nor emperor,' but one of the mass of citizens; yet he enjoys unlimited symbolic power over them."[38] By his will he shapes the supposedly formless human being into what the *Volk* already is, rendering the *Volk* dynamic and futural. As for his hero, the same mirroring effect is essential: when Siegfried sees himself as pure and unburdened by kinship and society, Wagner presents the self-recognition that the artwork is supposed to constitute. This is the looking glass for the *Volk* to become, so to speak, what it *already is*, and for the Artwork to become a guide of the *Volk*. Thanks to the temporal gesture of jumping to the beginning of history and thereby restoring a natural purity and a future, the *Volk* can now become an authentic, nonhistorical, true community. Siegfried and his Germania stand beyond history, half-liberated from it, "before" its beginning, and now anew in the restored futural present. Wagner stages the need for Need—which Siegfried gradually articulates as his—each figure supposedly forging the future. The Artist, who can do more than statesmen, politicians, and philosophers, reconstructs past and future, standing in control over the *Volk* while belonging to this same *Volk* through the Hero he raises from it. In the artist and the hero, the sovereign rises in two bodies once again.

A "Secret" History

When Wagner wrote of peeling history layer by layer, he meant layers of myth transformed by culture over time, and he inserted himself into several genealogies of the relation between history and human nature. As the nineteenth century ground on, pursuits of a secret, deeper, "truer" history through a symbolic universe awaiting its awakening and promising a superior understanding of human nature became more and more frequent. The figure of purity that had to be unveiled standing at the precipice of history with one foot outside and one in became a crucial motif. Herder and Hegel—especially the latter, with his famous preference for "philosophic" rather than "original" or "reflective" history—had already offered the quasi-Romantic basis for a history of meaning underlying the history of actions and events and requiring not merely narration and explanation but mining and management.[39] The complication of the human sciences in the later nineteenth century would multiply, thicken, and superimpose these layers of history to the point of giving the impression that history now carried geological strata, each of which had their own dynamics, logics, and force. Racial science and the theory of degeneration are only the best-known and most politically obvious versions of an inquiry where true meaning was supposed to reside deep beneath the surface of events. In dividing between groups, racial science called for the unitary depths of each of them to be sought out. Degeneration postulated new golden ages easily identifiable with a distant past.[40] Developments in several disciplines bound laws of human development with the history of either the species as a whole or particular groups within it. The anthropology of "primitive" societies established, from Tylor and later Frazer in Britain, Virchow in Germany, and Broca and later Durkheim in France, a series of fundamental metahistorical claims concerning the sources of meaningfulness (kinship systems, shared myths, skull morphogeny, etc.) underlying the evolution of complex societies out of more primitive ones.[41] "Animism," typically used to describe belief systems deemed too elementary to be categorized among religions, also privileged them by identifying an intimacy with nature proper to those far behind in the sociohistorical development of civilization. Historical linguistics, intimately bound since Friedrich Schlegel with the myth of an Indo-European (and at times specifically Aryan) provenance of European culture itself, adopted this commitment to historical derivation at a "fundamental," invisible level, which for it was language and mythology.[42] Indo-European linguo-mythology became an organizational principle that could be said to specifically underlie European society and history. (This continued all the way to the 1930s and beyond, when Georges Dumézil dodged Nicolai Trubetzkoi's criticisms of his scholarly rigor in linguistics partly by instrumentalizing language to ground Indo-European provenance on a mostly mythological and literary rhizome; the permutations and combinations of Indo-European semantics and its depths beneath European history were as complex as they were minutely differentiated.) *Völkerpsychologie*, beginning in the 1850s with Lazarus and Steinthal, and later continued by Wilhelm Wundt, eschewed biology to establish the laws of human societies on the basis of language and shared psychological elements that it defined at a minute, gestural, even psychophysical level. In his later work Wundt attempted to reconstruct this gestural and psychological basis in *Völkerpsychologie* as a proto-history.[43] Phylogenetic thought from Ernst Haeckel to World War II also contributed to the sense of the human body as subject to historical mutation—that is, as having acquired or developed specific characteristics over certain periods of time, characteristics that could nevertheless be quickly overturned (figure 17.1).[44]

With such pursuits, the sciences of man became sciences ostensibly researching the slightest ciphers of "true" human and historical meaning, and thus claimed the mantle of being the historically and structurally most fundamental, most primal ones. Further strategies and fictions of key epistemological significance were born and played out of this development. The fiction of "organic memory"—the notion that memory, including social memory, is inherited—provided space for an evolutionary model that bridged culture and not merely biology.[45] The epistemological gesture Thomas Henry Huxley identified in 1880 as "retrospective prophesy" allowed the reconstruction of codes in the deep past to look useful for the present, or even to appear true.[46] The standing attitude that "the savage" lay hidden just beneath the veneer of civilization—often identified with Freud but already quite widely held around 1900 and even more so in World War I—contrasted the limits of culture and the presumed force of natural laws beneath.[47]

Along these parallel, intertwined lines of inquiry—anthropology, phylogenetic thought, psychology, and linguistic derivation—the same historicity appears: the past extends back to "the origin," which is also the origin of the human; later developments constitute either rearrangements that cover over the origin (usually productively, in that they grow civilization)

FIGURE 17.1 Photogravure frontispiece to Ernst Haeckel's *The Evolution of Man* (New York: G. P. Putnam's Sons, 1905), with an androgynous classical Greek as the ideal point of an imagined history of youth

or divergences from its ostensibly true purpose. Just as geological discoveries undermined the chronology of religious history, projecting "worlds before Adam," so a pure, basic humanity could be projected into the distant past.[48] Tiers that could now be known subtended the prosaic history of events, people(s), states, wars, or eminent persons. These tiers were not merely theologies or "philosophic history" but sites of anthropogenesis and temporal continuity across epistemic-symbolic knowledge and value. Across the different sciences, a shared image was regularly drawn: the grain of "true" history lay beneath the scope of everyday affairs, and they generated particular scientific aesthetics. Like the musical symbolism that only Siegfried and the initiated audience could hear, the density of history was simply inaudible to others. Primal processes ought to be studied, especially because modernity appeared to involve a flattening, a homogenization (in Carl Schmitt's phrase, a "neutralization") of complexity, passion, depth, and conflict.[49] In the process, philosophical and Romantic history became saturated with what the discourses on heredity, culture, and symbolism located at its birth. In matters of sovereignty, true novelty and transformation required a movement that could reach *beneath* the scope and density of normal human affairs and that allowed for a mining of the depths of human nature across this history, which also meant a reach beyond this history— to a moment quite like that of *Siegfried*'s Germania.

New, Twentieth-Century Sovereigns

In *The Birth of Tragedy*, Nietzsche cast Wagner as the returning hero of "archaic" (preclassical) tragedy and the hope for aesthetico-political regeneration, playing out the very structure Wagner had invented on a new terrain (later, he in turn invented the Overman partly to outdo and deform this structure). By 1900 different designers of this metahistory doubled as creators of the future: out of the deep strata of the past, authors from Theodor Herzl in his Zionist *Altneuland* to Jack London in *Before Adam* could dredge and meaningfully deploy sovereign heroes and forces that were at once atavistic and new.[50] Wagner's strategy had purified and recuperated the myth so it would commandeer a metahistorical narrative of Germany and impose the mirror-system of Artist-*Volk*-Hero. Now, the announcement of a hero or new sovereign could deploy an alternative, deeper, or thicker history, which in turn located and justified the novelty of the hero/sovereign at the very beginning, at once in and out of the historical realm.

This was indeed common currency among theories of sovereignty and authority that cited a deeper history. Gustave Le Bon, in his "psychological" theory of the crowd, identified this with the "last sovereign force"; he proposed that to be successful, the leader, who is hypnotized together with the crowd he guides, *must* orate for that crowd images from its ancient racial past.[51] Imaginary prehistory and futural leadership combined in political and sociological thought. By 1918, as Boris Groys and especially Eric Michaud have shown, artists from Kazimir Malevich to Hitler's "government of artists" asserted themselves, their opposition to prosaic history, and their heroic new world all at once.[52] The motif appears in the supposed primitiveness of Weber's "charisma" and his sociohistorical accounts,[53] but it is nothing short of a structure in Carl Schmitt's work, especially *Political Theology* (1922). By slashing the Gordian knot of sovereignty in its famous opening sentence—"Sovereign is he who decides on the exception"—Schmitt announced a new sovereign who, to exceed and contain the neutralizing drive of liberalism, to refashion norms, *must* rely on the hidden (and historically longer) undercurrents of (Catholic) political theology.[54] This announcement and alternative history served as an Archimedian standpoint for Schmitt to extricate both *himself* and *his sovereign* from liberal legal thought, to found his own legitimacy as interpreter of sovereignty while proposing sovereignty as needing recovery from beneath the layer of liberal neutralization designed to cover it. The same dual gesture opened Schmitt's critical endorsement of Sorel's theory of myth in *The Crisis of Parliamentary Democracy* and buttressed his later eminence as "crown jurist" and arbiter of National Socialism.[55] The Russian/French philosopher Alexandre Kojève similarly constructed his early theory of authority by way of a Hegelian history of modernity culminating in the "end of history" that serves as a stage for only two figures to maintain ontological superiority over the rest: the sovereign God-Man who ends the Master-Slave dialectic and history itself (i.e., Napoleon or Stalin) and the interpreting Sage (Hegel and Kojève) who writes and guides that sovereign.[56] The anthropogenetic moment of the struggle for recognition that founds man and history is mirrored in the end-historical sovereign's creation of a world of equal citizens. Finally, it is quite possible to read Martin Heidegger's *Being and Time* with Heidegger in Wagner's role and authentic *Dasein* in Siegfried's. An emphasis on Heidegger's claim of the authenticity of *being-toward-death* as a rise above the inauthenticity of social existence can suggest that being itself, thanks to the restoration to prominence Heidegger proposes for it, serves him as the "deeper" stratum for asserting both *his* and *the authentic Dasein's sovereignties over das Man.*[57] *Being and Time* further establishes the history of being by announcing its forgetting since Plato, a forgetting of both the question of being and the history of being that Heidegger proposes to overcome by aligning the awakening of the question with the liberation of properly ontological history. In the newly recovered transparency of the ontological question, in the announcement of a figure of being-toward-death that can exceed the profane and inauthentic life of the present, Heidegger identifies the kind of authority that he would deploy as a logical political end of his ontology in his 1933–1934 attempt to guide the German Spirit and the National Socialist revolution.[58] Nor was the left immune to this language of a rise from the symbolic darkness of everyday history. Ernst Bloch directed dialectics (already an approach to sources of meaning) toward a specifically musical version of this "rise" in *The Spirit of Utopia*, citing Wagner and post-Beethovenian Germany, while Walter Benjamin struggled with awakenings—of memory, or elsewhere, à la Proust, from the dream—versus still other awakenings he engaged in relation to the writings of Klages and Jung.[59]

Scientific Engagements

The substrata of history proved as essential to scientists committed to the diagnosis of physical as well as social ills, scientists who took to the very same engagement with sovereignty in their proposals for scientific as social renewal. If philosophers made less of the biological and psychological bases for such an alternative history, scientific figures from different parts of the political spectrum found these bases definitive. Elements of the discourse on an alternative, deeper history were common to scientific writings from ethnography through archaeology, biology, and experimental psychology. I will glance at each in that order. Pursuing enduring sources of meaning, anthropologists (including interdisciplinary ones, from W. H. R. Rivers to Émile Durkheim) made a mixed use of recapitulation, organic and social memory, and *Völkerpsychologie* to suggest continuities beneath mere empiricism.[60] "Primitive communism" was a matter of considerable public fascination, adopted even by Rivers during his campaign with the Labour Party for a seat in the British Parliament.[61] By 1940, as Peter Mandler has shown, one of the standard-bearers of the field, Margaret Mead (during the war an American cultural ambassador to Britain), was mobilizing a concept of "national character"—as much a broadly shared rationale for deeper sources of meaning as an ethnographic and Boasian sociocultural construct indebted to Wundt's ethnopsychology. Prioritizing psychology as the basis for a "soft" social engineering, Mead employed her authority as participant-observer to show that it was possible "to change human nature" because "deep-seated cultural traits" were not biological but cultural in origin.[62] Mead was far from alone: while denouncing racial biology as pseudoscience, biologist Julian Huxley and anthropologist Alfred C. Haddon sought in *We Europeans* to describe the descent and difference of ethnic groups in Europe, relying on an ethnolinguistic model of cultural derivation.[63] Their rhetoric, which at times approximates Mead's on character, may have avoided proposing a new man, but it presented the often-deep cultural, ethnic, and linguistic mosaic of Europe as one that underwrote its history and present, and it offered social policy proposals ranging from opposition to miscegenation to the development of independent cultural spheres as a way out of Europe's (and racism's) current situation.[64] Cathy Gere has similarly shown such a return to the cusp of history in her studies of archaeologists Heinrich Schliemann and Arthur Evans, with Schliemann identifying the material basis for Greek epic and myth and Evans using and "rebuilding" Knossos in a modernist confection of a pacifist matriarchal and sexual prelapsarian utopia.[65] Their Mycenae and Knossos would be mobilized, not least by archaeologists and anthropologists, as sites of purity that offered Europeans a harmonious alternative future. Indo-European mythology received a major boon in the work of Georges Dumézil, who has been famously accused of imposing a fascist aesthetic onto his tripartite thesis on the structure of proto-Indo-European society and then obversely treating the last five thousand years as permutations of that structure.[66] Even if Mead and Evans may appear banal by comparison, their self-institution as scientific heroes of modernism and motivated purveyors of the present served precisely the sense of social/aesthetic engineering and promised new, purer worlds.

Biologists explicitly invested in radical political projects often used even stronger forms of the substrata-of-history argument to glance at prehistory and formulate the future. Finalism and vitalism in biology offered one well-known way for Romantic motifs to weave themselves into an understanding of history and sovereign agency. But this was a broader concern: in a 1923 lecture, the British socialist biologist John B. S. Haldane (later a key contributor to the establishment of the modern synthesis) surveyed the state, dangers, and promise of modern science, and cast the worker and engineer in the mold of Daedalus.[67] The choice (over Prometheus)[68] was far from a mere adornment: Haldane presented his recapitulation of the ancient myth as a modern, scientific deicide redeemed by the Daedalian worker who would remold "traditional mythology" and "traditional morals" as well.[69] The worker as Daedalus would be "conscious of his ghastly mission, and proud of it," as though he could redeem science from wartime technological violence and move society on a "true," improved path, as prehistoric, amoral, and idealistic, but secular.[70] Socialism would require scientific biology as much as the model thanks to which the worker announced the refounding of technical and social engineering.

Eugenicists from Charles Davenport on pushed far too. The French-American surgeon Alexis Carrel, in his 1936 book *Man the Unknown*, claimed that "biological classes" were fundamentally tied to social classes, and eugenics must aid in a reengineering that would restore premodern sociobiological harmony.[71] This harmony had been almost severed with the "base materialist" and "poor" mechanistic construction of modern man, and the democratic/egalitarian theorization of society since the Renaissance.[72] These had resulted in a fabrication that "infringed upon" and "transgressed against" natural laws, facilitating man's capacity to thwart natural selection in a way that allowed the survival of individuals of lower potential and thus facilitated the present crisis, resulting in the moral and spiritual destruction of man.[73] To Carrel, an aristocracy of geniuses should provide for humanity's future by distinguishing itself from people of lower biological rank—a neoproletariat. If technical science and politics had brought about moral, social, and intellectual decay, aristocratic eugenics could undo the consequences and redemptively reconstruct newly identical biological and social classes.[74] Carrel's argument relied on three widely held forms of alternative history: the Catholic identification of the Renaissance as the moment when things went wrong, the biologistic rhetoric of racial purity, which was supposedly undermined after the Middle Ages, and a modern techno-science that could be voluntaristically and eugenically controlled if and only if racial purity were reinstated on new ground.

Psychologists of different schools were just as convinced that their analytical work facilitated and even constructed truly new men, overcoming
bourgeois society while placing them, too, on a pedestal from which they
could structure not only this society but the past and future as well. Nitzan
Lebovic has shown this in the case of *Lebensphilosoph*-psychologist Ludwig
Klages, who was celebrated for providing a psychology that could renew and
refocus human life against a modernity that was supposedly erasing it.[75] But
the search for a deeper substratum was again not only property of the right.
For Lev Vygotsky, who in keeping with Soviet expectations did not project
purity to a moment prior to the past, psychology was nevertheless capable of
both mining history and remaking it. His 1930 essay "The Crisis of Psychology" identified the crisis of the discipline with the crisis of the bourgeois
world and heralded the capacity of psychology to become, in the "new society," the "science of the new man" precisely because of its capacity to dig
beneath bourgeois life and recover the truth of society itself.

> Our science could not and cannot develop in the old society. We cannot mas-
> ter the truth about personality and personality itself so long as mankind has
> not mastered the truth about society and society itself. In contrast, in the
> new society our science will take a central place in life. . . . The new society
> will create the new man. When one mentions the remolding of man as an
> indisputable trait of the new mankind and the artificial creation of a new
> biological type, then this will be the only and first species in biology which
> will create itself. In the future society, psychology will indeed be the science
> of the new man. Without this the perspective of Marxism and the history of
> science would not be complete. But this science of the new man will still re-
> main psychology. Now we hold its thread in our hands.[76]

It is too easy to read this approach as standing at a distance from the
Romantic motif of a beginning of history and the first man that stood on it.
Vygotsky's claim to be establishing, joining, analyzing, fabricating the New
Man at the moment of its true, *finally natural* inception carries precisely the
same variety of Romanticism, and the lack of a reference to a first man is
belied precisely by the suggestion that the remolding of man can disdain
the same (prosaic) history out of which it has emerged. Vygotsky's language,
bridging a rhetoric of "remolding" with one of anticipated humanistic self-

invention, establishes on a new plane the Marxist dialectical play of restoring precapitalist nature while synthesizing a new, properly proletarian universality. (Such romanticism is no more alien to Trotsky's understanding of "proletarian science," to Lukacs's *History and Class Consciousness*, or to Bloch's interwar work.)

More than anyone it was Carl Gustav Jung who established the psychological logic of "deeper," archetypal history by proposing concepts of a "collective unconscious" and an "archetype" that were forcefully dependent on the idea of a symbolic, mythical substratum underwriting everyday life. This became essential for his analysis of individuality and collectivities. After years of multiplying the symbols and complexes that structure the unconscious (tendencies Freud policed through the Oedipus complex), Jung claimed in 1912 that "psychoanalytic research into the nature of subliminal processes will be enormously enriched and deepened by a study of mythology," by which he meant "Indo-European" myth.[77] Though explicitly a form of *Völkerpsychologie*, his study radicalized earlier varieties of that field. As opposed to Wundt's focus on the laws of ethnopsychological development, whose history left behind the age of heroes for a rational modernity,[78] Jung expanded ethnopsychology into a vast symbolic and mythological reservoir that encompassed archetypes and iterable symbols of a collective unconscious. This was "self-identical in all Western men and thus constitutes a psychic foundation, superpersonal in its nature, that is present in every one of us,"[79] and whose shared forms each individual in turn appropriates and molds. By comparison to a subjective unconscious, the collective one is "sheer objectivity," a participation in the cultural and social forms and myths, and specifically an *inheritance* of the conditions for the regeneration of such forms.[80] Family environments and traditional forms of symbolic orientation fall by the wayside; instead, archetypes "can only be explained by assuming them to be deposits of the constantly repeated experiences of humanity."[81] What is more, the collective unconscious conducts *individuation*: in their persistence, archetypes render wholeness possible on different terms in each other. Still, only thanks to a "transcendent function" can the individual master the forms of the collective unconscious as they appear in his, or perhaps her, dreams and other unconscious activity—only through this "function" can individuation become complete. Jung's Wagnerian site for this transcendent function is, in 1917 as in 1940, one of heroism: the patient struggles to consciously dominate unconscious energies, like the hero who struggles and eventually triumphs over a monster and is reborn at the moment of his triumph; then, "the unconscious, robbed of its energy, no longer occupies the dominant position."[82] The domination of this unconscious is a heroic attempt at self-transcendence and individuation.[83]

The collective unconscious concept, Jung continued, has acquired particular salience in the period since 1789, marked by the "end of religion" and the diffusion and complication of the symbolic unconscious. Insofar as we do *not* believe, the symbolic collective unconscious has become confused, if not impoverished: whereas in, for example, Catholicism, one inhabits a given set of available symbols, for "us" the synthesis of individual and collective unconscious is more complicated and the need to study and deploy these archetypes all the more pressing. Jung claimed, in 1916: "Only in the age of enlightenment did people discover that the gods did not really exist, but were simply projections. Thus the gods were disposed of. But the corresponding psychological functioning was by no means disposed of; it lapsed into the unconscious, and men were thereupon poisoned by the surplus of libido that had once been laid up in the cult of divine images."[84] Only the psychoanalyst can cure the pathology caused by the loss of organized symbolic systems.

Hence the synthesis of this argument on subjective wholeness with the purpose of the philosopher/psychoanalyst and the artist who expresses it. In the artist or creative man, the collective unconscious "comes alive . . . like an all-pervading, omnipresent, omniscient spirit. It knows man *as he always was, and not as he is at this moment*; it knows him as myth."[85] As with the Artist in Wagner's *Art-work of the Future*, Jung's analyst and artist are bound to the unconscious (which replaces the *Volk*) and are capable of raising it to self-consciousness, individual and collective. Jung's self-conception as transferential facilitator enables precisely his sense of his project as one of organizing Indo-European archetypes and *Völkerpsychologie* in a manner that aided man to escape a relapse into a dark, deformed, partially speaking, quasi-ethnoracial collective unconscious. It is these elements that would triumph in Jung's racial and pro-Nazi claims of the mid 1930s, and that promised even unconscious collective renewal.[86]

The New Man and Dual Sovereignty

Were the dual sovereignty motif and the dense-history motif really about sovereignty, rather than mere utopian expectation? After all, the case could be made that the Second Empire, Paris Commune, and Third Republic in France; the unification of Germany and rise and decline of the German empire; the unified Italian kingdom; and the Austro-Hungarian compromise, to say nothing of the newly sovereign states of Eastern Europe after World War I, had far more reality to them—and affected governing relations in far more local and determined fashion than the imagination of a new man. Yet the lack of actual political power among many of the intellectuals discussed here should not blind us to the fact that a new sovereignty was not merely a desideratum and a matter of the exercise of power by post–World War I regimes or intellectual radicals unsatisfied with the political options immediately available for the transformation of society. Moreover, as Marcel Mauss recognized already in 1920, and with specific reference to Wagner, the search for absolute origins became both *during* and just *after* the Great War a distinct foundation of national sources of, and claims to, sovereignty.[87] In that form, the hero-artist doublet clocked a new way of understanding history and human nature—a demand that science, cultural or "biological" particularity, and technology be put to use toward a better world. An aestheticized conception of this better world premised on the New Man's atavism guided its power over the present and future. No less crucially, these were positions shared across the political spectrum, *even among liberals* who subscribed to at least some of the strata of history, who were at least tolerant of motifs of heroism and genius for arguments on liberal autonomy they proposed, and who were happy either to imagine the new man as the successful outcome of a colonial enterprise or, as Mosse has indicated, to adopt a limited version of this argument for bourgeois self-regeneration. The new man offered a far more radical and immediate imagination and analysis of modernity, a myth of historical depth and regeneration beyond economic, political, and legal problems, than negotiations of territory or immediate power relations at the domestic or international levels did. In its reliance on the new sciences of psychology and biology, not to mention archaeology, anthropology, and linguistics, it offered a way of conceiving past, present, and future, and of perceiving the social transformation of modernity at its violent limits. A new man seemed essential for the overcoming of the moral and political morass of bourgeois society, and he needed as much a designer (aesthetic or scientific) as he did historical substrata. In the recapitulation and administration of the compound, symbolically dense deeper layer of history, what was now called to the surface was the project of the artist/ author who would also be quasi-sovereign by way of his puppeteer-like attachment to the leader or new man he heralded. Thus, the New Man would remain at once pure of supposedly contemptible reality and imbued with true symbolic power, so as to serve as a sort of absolute regulatory ideal that restructures all political and aesthetic action. He would be truly *new* if he were ostensibly capable of sifting through and using this symbolic heritage while remaining unbound by it.

I close where I began, with Rosenberg: despite his obsession with the Gobineau-originating "myth of the blood," the only one he deemed "truly alive" because it was at once "new yet ancient" (*alt-neue*),[88] Rosenberg, too, relied on multiple strata. "Blood" was complemented by Wagner—including the dual sovereignty model. Yet if for Wagner the artist and hero stand juxtaposed as two non-coinciding figures mirroring the *Volk*, Rosenberg replayed the Wagnerian schema with a significant transformation that perfected and dissolved Wagner's logic—the fusion of artist and hero. National Socialism could be as much its own artist as its hero, with the true "new Genius" being anticipated, or rather at once "already here but yet to come."[89] "Blood" and "Wagner" were further complemented as strata by Rosenberg's versions of the Aryan or Indo-European fantasy with its "warrior nobility," of Madame Blavatsky's theosophy, and of a Norse/Teutonic north-south organization of racial hierarchy attached to a motif of artistic creation akin to German Grecophilia. The Will of the new was to be created aesthetically as well as politically: in its dual sovereignty over its supposed *Volk*, as at once artist and hero of the future, Nazism embodied and announced its compound New Man, dredging him out of a supposedly pure past in order to freeze the present under his anticipated power.

Notes

For invaluable comments and criticisms, I am grateful to Rania Ajami, Daniel Hoffman-Schwartz, Glenn Most, Anson Rabinbach, Andrew Sartori, Jerrold Seigel, Maria Stavrinaki, Natasha Wheatley, and Larry Wolff.

1. Alfred Rosenberg, *Der Mythus des 20. Jahrhunderts* (1930; Munich: Hoheneichen Verlag, 1939), 678.
2. Ibid., 601.
3. The book itself is supposed to serve as a dawning of the consciousness of the myth (e.g., ibid., 521–22). As Philippe Lacoue-Labarthe and Jean-Luc Nancy emphasize, for Rosenberg the world of myth is itself dated, obsolete, dead; yet in its Sorelian sense, "Myth is the power to bring together the fundamental forces and directions of an individual or of a people, the power of a subterranean, invisible, nonempirical identity." Lacoue-Labarthe and Nancy, "The Nazi Myth," *Critical Inquiry* 16, no. 2 (1990): 305.
4. Eric Michaud, *The Cult of Art in Nazi Germany* (Stanford: Stanford University Press, 2004), 84–100.
5. Michel Foucault usefully discusses Napoleon's mixing of personal, imperial, juridical, and disciplinary power in *Discipline and Punish: The Birth of the Prison*, trans. Alan Sheridan (New York: Vintage, 1995), 217. Chateaubriand's treatment of the coronation of Charles X in his *Memoirs from Beyond the Grave* (book 28, chap. 5) is one of the early formulations of a stylized but powerless sovereignty.
6. Reasons of brevity prohibit me from tracing this motif closely; suffice it to recall the writings of Jules Michelet, Ernest Renan, Friedrich Nietzsche, Gustave Le Bon, Vladimir Lenin, Hermann Kayserling, Stefan George and his circle, Oswald Spengler, Carl Schmitt, and Walter Benjamin.
7. Le Bon's *The Crowd* is exemplary of this tendency.
8. This element is largely left aside in efforts to account for the New Man; cf. Peter Fritzsche and Jochen Hellbeck, "The New Man in Stalinist Russia and Nazi Germany," in *Beyond Totalitarianism*, ed. Sheila Fitzpatrick and Michael Geyer (Cambridge: Cambridge University Press, 2009), 304–42. George Mosse presented the New Man as a specifically bourgeois fantasy of self-overcoming, with the focus on "bourgeois" rather than "self-overcoming."
9. Pierre Milza, "Mussolini," in *L'Homme nouveau dans l'Europe fasciste*, ed. Marie-Anne Matard-Bonucci and Pierre Milza (Paris: Fayard, 2004), 75–86; Milza, *Mussolini* (Paris: Fayard, 1999).
10. Foucault discusses a quite similar earlier theme—the fantasized return of a buried or lost king, together with the advent of early modern racism—in his treatment of sovereignty in *Society Must Be Defended: Lectures at the Collège de France, 1975-76*, trans. David Macey (New York: Picador, 2003), 55. Wagner's *Siegfried* clearly gains from this genre, but the terms in which the *modern* version of this motif has to be understood are somewhat different.
11. *Siegfried* 1.197–201, in Richard Wagner, *Der Ring des Nibelungen. Textbuch mit Varianten der Partitur*, ed. Egon Voss (Stuttgart: Philipp Reclam, 2009), 213.
12. *Siegfried* 1.265–80; Wagner, *Der Ring des Nibelungen*, 216.
13. Maurice Olender, *The Languages of Paradise* (Cambridge: Harvard University Press, 1992), 141–42, offers a helpful analysis of the use of myth in the contrast between the visible hero and the invisible Jewish God, even if his analysis of *Siegfried* is rather fast and meets with difficulties.
14. "Viel weiss ich noch nicht, noch nicht auch, wer ich bin," he tells Fafner to the sound of his twice-played leitmotif.

15. On the wolf-child, see Nicolas Pethes, *Zöglinge der Natur* (Göttingen: Wallstein, 2007).
16. *Siegfried* 1.251; Wagner, *Der Ring des Nibelungen*, 215.
17. Theodor Adorno, *In Search of Wagner*, trans. Rodney Livingstone (London: Verso, 2005), 92.
18. David J. Levin, *Richard Wagner, Fritz Lang, and the Nibelungen* (Princeton: Princeton University Press, 1998).
19. The sword's connotation of broken paternity and its restoration by Siegfried are essential themes; otherwise Fricka's objections to Wotan's claim in *Die Walküre* that Siegmund possesses free will could be raised anew.
20. Peter Caldwell, *Love, Death, and Revolution in Central Europe* (New York: Palgrave, 2009), 110. Wagner can further be said to have staged Siegfried—including his foibles, failure, and death in *Götterdämmerung*—in a manner that specifically brought to its close the domain of old Germanic myth. Instead of that domain, at the end of *Götterdämmerung* we find the deployment of a new world, a new aesthetico-political myth played out with the repetition of the first bars of the *Rheingold*'s prelude. In this reading, spectators could feel the cathartic end of the cycle to impose the new form of the old myth in order to *replace* their own world as well as the old myth at the same time.
21. Richard Wagner, "A Communication to My Friends" (1851), in *Wagner on Music and Drama*, ed. Albert Goldman and Evert Sprinchorn (New York: Dutton, 1964), 264.
22. For Wagner's "studies" and the origins of the "inner history" motif, see Friedrich Heinrich von der Hagen, *Der Nibelungen Lied* (Breslau: Max, 1816), xi, and the sources in Levin, *Richard Wagner*, 151n2.
23. For all their proximity, especially on the will, Schopenhauer and Wagner differ essentially on the use of the past—on the value of this symbolic dredging aimed to restore the will. See Schopenhauer's treatment of the past in *The World as Will and Representation*, trans. E. F. J. Payne, vol. 1 (New York: Dover, 1969), §57, 311.
24. Olender, *Languages of Paradise*, 6–9, 19; Stefan Arvidsson, *Aryan Idols* (Chicago: University of Chicago Press, 2006), chap. 4.
25. Wagner, "Communication to my Friends," 265. Egon Voss correctly warns against reducing Siegfried to a mere expression of Wagner's theoretical and social works from the 1840s and 1850. Egon Voss, in Wagner, *Der Ring des Nibelungen*, 461.
26. Wagner, introduction to "Art and Revolution," in *The Art-Work of the Future and Other Works*, trans. William Ashton Ellis (Lincoln: University of Nebraska Press, 1993), 24.
27. Edward Gibbon, *History of the Decline and Fall of the Roman Empire* (New York: Penguin Classics, 1996), 1:230; Herder, *Another Philosophy of History and Other Political Writings* (London: Hackett, 2004), 33. The theme dates to Tacitus's *Germania*; see Christopher B. Krebs, *A Most Dangerous Book: Tacitus's "Germania" from the Roman Empire to the Third Reich* (New York: Penguin, 2012), and Eric Michaud, "Barbarian Invasions and the Racialization of Art History," *October* 139 (Winter 2012): 59–76. For Wagner's appeal to Germania, see Wagner, "Hero-dom and Christendom"

(1881), in *Religion and Art*, trans. William Ashton Ellis (Lincoln: University of Nebraska Press, 1994), 278. On the relative absence of a racial purity argument in the early nineteenth century, see Brian Vick, "The Origins of the German *Volk*," in *German Studies Review* 26, no. 2 (May 2003): 241–56.

28. Jules Michelet, *The People*, trans. John P. McKay (Chicago: University of Illinois Press, 1973). Compare to Wagner, "Art-Work of the Future," 75.

29. Other thinkers distant from liberalism, pursued a similar strategy for art, describing it without irony or paradox as formative of the positive, scientific future. See, e.g., Auguste Comte, *République occidentale, ordre et progrès* (Paris: Mathias, 1848).

30. Wagner, "Art and Revolution," 54–56, esp. 56.

31. Wagner, "Art and Revolution," 53. On the dual meaning of revolution and the late eighteenth-century shift toward a singular, future-oriented meaning, see Reinhart Koselleck, "Historical Criteria of the Modern Concept of Revolution," in *Futures Past* (Cambridge, MA: MIT Press, 1985), 39–54.

32. This goes thus a step beyond Philipp Ther's claim that national operas (Verdi's in addition to Wagner's) involved "not just one but of two utopias of unity"— that is, the artistic unity of the *Gesamtkunstwerk* and the social unity of the theater itself. Ther, *Center Stage: Operatic Culture and Nation Building* (West Lafayette, IN: Purdue University Press, 2014), 13.

33. Wagner, "Art-Work of the Future," 75, 77; see also 194n.

34. Ibid., 195–96.

35. Ibid., 204–5, emphasis in original.

36. Wagner, *Oper und Drama* (Leipzig: J. J. Weber, 1869), 348, modified from Wagner, *Opera and Drama*, trans. W. A. Ellis (Lincoln: University of Nebraska Press, 1995), 374–75.

37. Wagner, *Oper und Drama*, 349–50, translation modified from Wagner, *Opera and Drama*, 375–76.

38. Adorno, *In Search of Wagner*, 20.

39. Hegel, *Introduction to the Philosophy of History* (Indianapolis: Hackett, 1988), 3.

40. See the classic accounts by George Mosse, *Toward the Final Solution* (New York: Fertig, 1978), 76–108, and Paul Weindling, *Health, Race and German Politics, 1870–1945* (Cambridge: Cambridge University Press, 1989), chap. 2–3. On the division of Germanic from Latin races, see Käthe Panick, *La Race Latine: Politischer Romantismus im Frankreich des 19. Jahrhunderts* (Bonn: Ludwig Röhrscheid, 1978), and Pierre Michel, *Les barbares, 1789-1848* (Lyon: PUL, 1981)

41. E. B. Tylor, *Primitive Culture*, 2 vols. (London: John Murray, 1871).

42. Max Müller's work, including his course for future colonial bureaucrats, *India: What Can It Teach Us?* (New York: Funk & Wagnalls, 1882), exemplifies these concerns. More broadly, see Anna Morpurgo Davies, *History of Linguistics*, vol. 4, *Nineteenth-Century Linguistics* (London: Longman, 1998), chap. 3. For philology and linguistic origins, see Olender, *Languages of Paradise*, 15, 19ff., as well as Judith R. H. Kaplan, "Language Science and Orientalism in Imperial Germany" (PhD diss., University of Wisconsin–Madison, 2012). On religion, see Arvidsson, *Aryan Idols*, introduction and chap. 2, and Tomoko Masuzawa, *The Invention of World Religions* (Chicago: University of Chicago Press, 2005), chap. 5.

43. For an explicitly historical perspective on *Völkerpsychologie*, see Wilhelm Wundt, *Elements of Folk-Psychology* (London: Allen & Unwin, 1916); Egbert Klautke, *The Mind of the Nation* (New York: Berghahn, 2013); and Stefanos Geroulanos, "The Plastic Self and the Prescription of Psychology," *Republics of Letters* 3, no. 2 (2014).

44. George W. Crile, *A Mechanistic View of War and Peace* (New York: Macmillan, 1915), 69. On the reach of Haeckel's recapitulation theory, see Knox Peden, "Alkaline Recapitulation," *Republics of Letters* 4, no. 1 (2014).

45. Laura Otis, *Organic Memory* (Lincoln: University of Nebraska Press, 1994).

46. Thomas Henry Huxley, "On the Method of Zadig," in *Science and Culture* (London, 1881), 128–48. See also Carlo Ginzburg, "Clues," in *Clues, Myths, and the Historical Method* (Baltimore: Johns Hopkins University Press, 1989), 117.

47. James G. Frazer, *The Golden Bough*, vol. 1 (1896; London: Macmillan, 1920), 236. For a phylogenetic version of this account attached to World War I, see Crile, *Mechanistic View of War and Peace*, 47–52.

48. Martin Rudwick, *Worlds Before Adam* (Chicago: University of Chicago Press, 2008). See also, e.g., Cathy Gere, *Knossos and the Prophets of Modernism* (Chicago: University of Chicago Press, 2009), 4, 7.

49. On neutralization, see Carl Schmitt, *Concept of the Political*, trans. George Schwab (Chicago: University of Chicago Press, 1996), 35, 70, 78.

50. Theodor Herzl, *Altneuland* (Leipzig: Hermann Seemann, 1903); Jack London, *Before Adam* (London: Macmillan, 1907); see also Georges Sorel, *Reflections on Violence*, ed. Jeremy Jennings (Cambridge: Cambridge University Press, 1999); Carl Schmitt, *The Crisis of Parliamentary Democracy*, trans. Ellen Kennedy (Cambridge: MIT Press, 1988), chap. 4.

51. Gustave Le Bon, *The Crowd: A Study of the Popular Mind* (1895; Atlanta: Cherokee, 1982).

52. Michaud, *Cult of Art*, 186–91; Boris Groys, *The Total Art of Stalinism* (Princeton: Princeton University Press, 1992).

53. See Max Weber, *Economy and Society: An Outline of Interpretive Sociology*, ed. Guenther Roth and Claus Wittich (Berkeley: University of California Press, 1978), vol. 2, chap. 14.

54. Carl Schmitt, *Political Theology: Four Chapters on the Concept of Sovereignty*, trans. George Schwab (Chicago: University of Chicago Press, 2005).

55. Schmitt, *Crisis of Parliamentary Democracy*, 73, 76; see also Schmitt's engagement with Mussolini and critique of "polytheism" for endangering Sorelian theory, 76.

56. See my *An Atheism That Is Not Humanist Emerges in French Thought* (Stanford: Stanford University Press, 2010), 162–63, 166, and the permutations of authority in Kojève's *La Notion de l'autorité* (1942; Paris: Gallimard, 2004).

57. Martin Heidegger, *Being and Time* (New York: Harper-Collins, 1962), §53.

58. See Richard Wolin, ed., *The Heidegger Controversy* (Cambridge, MA: MIT Press, 1992).

59. Ernst Bloch, *The Spirit of Utopia* (Stanford: Stanford University Press, 2000), 192.

60. W. H. R. Rivers, *Psychology and Politics* (London: Paul, Trench, Trubner, 1923), 91.

61. W. H. R. Rivers, "An Address on Socialism and Human Nature," in *Psychology and Politics* (London: Kegan Paul, 1923), 107–39. Rivers was criticized by Marcel Mauss

in *Manual of Ethnography* (1967; New York: Durkheim Press, 2007), 102 and, indirectly, by Bronislaw Malinowski in *Argonauts of the Western Pacific* (1922; London: George Routledge, 1932), 97.

62. Peter Mandler, *Return from the Natives* (New Haven: Yale University Press, 2013), 97; see also 58, 115.

63. For similarities to Mead, see Julian Huxley and Alfred Cort Haddon, *We Europeans* (New York: Harper, 1936), 15, 70–71, 74. A similar refusal of race compounded by alternative concepts can be found in Paul Rivet, ed., *L'espèce humaine* (Paris: L'Encyclopédie française [VII], 1937).

64. Huxley and Haddon, *We Europeans*, 235.

65. Gere, *Knossos and the Prophets of Modernism*, 11, 17, 80; Cathy Gere, *The Tomb of Agamemnon* (Cambridge, MA: Harvard University Press, 2006).

66. Carlo Ginzburg, "Germanic Mythology and Nazism: Thoughts on an Old Book by Georges Dumézil," in *Clues*, 126–45.

67. J. B. S. Haldane, *Daedalus; or, Science and the Future* (New York: Dutton, 1924).

68. Ibid., 46.

69. Ibid., 90.

70. Ibid., 92–93.

71. Alexis Carrel, *Man the Unknown* (London: Harper, 1935), 298.

72. Ibid., 271–73, 278.

73. Ibid., 272–73, 321.

74. Ibid., 298–99.

75. Lebovic further argues that a similarity between Klages, Freud, and Edward Spranger can be found in this pursuit, as in their sources in Dilthey, Nietzsche, and *Völkerpsychologie*. Nitzan Lebovic, *The Philosophy of Life and Death* (New York: Palgrave, 2013), 111.

76. Lev Vygotsky, "The Historical Meaning of the Crisis in Psychology" (1927), in *Collected Works*, vol. 3 (New York: Plenum, 1997), 342–43.

77. Carl G. Jung, "Therapeutic Principles of Psychoanalysis," in *Jung Contra Freud* (Princeton: Princeton University Press, 2012), 121. On Jung's role in the multiplication of symbols in the rewriting of the *Interpretation of Dreams*, see Lydia Marinelli and Andreas Mayer, *Dreaming by the Book* (New York: Other Press, 2003).

78. Jung was clearly aware of Wundt, and cites his *Grundriss der Psychologie* in "The Psychology of the Unconscious" (1917), in *Collected Works*, vol. 7 (New York: Pantheon, 1953), 17; so was Freud (in *Totem and Taboo*).

79. Jung, "Archetypes of the Collective Unconscious" (1934), in *The Integration of the Personality* (New York: Farrar & Rinehart, 1939), 52–53. The revised 1954 edition of this essay starkly avoids the "Western" focus of this point.

80. Jung, "Archetypes of the Collective Unconscious" (1934), in *Archetypes and the Collective Unconscious* (London: Routledge, 1968), 22; Jung, "The Role of the Unconscious" (1918) in *Civilization in Transition* (New York: Pantheon, 1964), 10–11. Jung would later compare his collective unconscious to the work on mythology by Mauss, Hubert, and Lévy-Bruhl. See Jung, "The Concept of the Collective Unconscious" (1936), in *Archetypes and the Collective Unconscious*, 42–43.

81. Jung, "Psychology of the Unconscious," 69.

82. Ibid., 77.

83. Jung, "The Psychology of the Child Archetype" (1940), in *Archetypes and the Collective Unconscious*, 166, 167.
84. Jung, "Psychology of the Unconscious," 92; see also Jung, *Archetypes and the Collective Unconscious*, 23.
85. Jung, "Role of the Unconscious," 10.
86. Jung, "The State of Psychotherapy Today," in *Civilization in Transition*, 166–67.
87. Marcel Mauss, "La nation," in *Oeuvres complètes III* (Paris: Minuit, 1969), 601.
88. Rosenberg, *Der Mythus des 20. Jahrhunderts*, 699.
89. The expression is Michaud's.

Contributors

ZVI BEN-DOR BENITE is professor of history and of Middle Eastern and Islamic studies at New York University. He received his PhD in history from the University of California, Los Angeles in 2000. Focusing on the question of interaction between religions in world history, he is the author of *The Dao of Muhammad: A Cultural History of Muslims in Late Imperial China* (2005) and *The Ten Lost Tribes: A World History* (2009) and coeditor of *Modern Middle Eastern Jewish Thought: Writings on Identity, Culture, and Politics* (2013).

LI CHEN is assistant professor of history at the University of Toronto and founding president of the International Society for Chinese Law and History. His research focuses on critical analysis of the intersections of law, culture, and politics in the context of Chinese and international history since 1500. His publications include *Chinese Law in the Imperial Eyes: Sovereignty, Justice, and Transcultural Politics, c. 1740s–1840s* (2016) and a coedited volume, *Chinese Law: Knowledge, Practice and Transformation, 1530s–1950s* (2015). He is working on another book, "Invisible Power, Legal Specialists, and the Juridical Field in Late Imperial China, 1651–1911."

NICOLA DI COSMO is Luce Foundation Professor of East Asian History at the Institute for Advanced Study, Princeton University. He holds a PhD from Indiana University, and a BA from the University of Venice. His research focuses on the history of Chinese and Inner Asian frontiers and the ethnic, social, and cultural history of steppe nomads. His authored and edited books include *Ancient China and Its Enemies: The Rise of Nomadic Power in East Asian History* (2002); *Manchu-Mongol Relations on the Eve of the Qing Conquest* (2003); *The Diary of a Manchu Soldier in Seventeenth-Century China* (2006); *Military Culture in Imperial China* (2009); and *The Cambridge History of Inner Asia* (2009). He is currently affiliated with New York University and Princeton University and is researching the role of Inner Asian empires in world history and the history of Mongolia's environment and the impact of climate change on pastoral nomads.

DAN EDELSTEIN is a professor of French and, by courtesy, history at Stanford University, where his research focuses mostly on eighteenth-century French literature, history, and political thought. He is the author of *The Terror of Natural Right: Republicanism, the Cult of Nature, and the French Revolution* (2009) and *The Enlightenment: A Genealogy* (2010). He is a principal investigator for the *Mapping the Republic of Letters* digital humanities project, and faculty director of Humanities+Design, both at Stanford. He is currently working on two books, one a history of natural and human rights, the other a comparative study of revolutions.

JASON FRANK is associate professor of government at Cornell University. He is the author of *Constituent Moments: Enacting the People in Postrevolutionary America* (2010) and *Publius and Political Imagination* (2014) and the editor of *A Political Companion to Herman Melville* (2013). He has published widely on democratic theory, American political thought, and politics and literature. His current book project is on the political aesthetics of popular sovereignty and is titled "The Democratic Sublime: Political Theory and Aesthetics in the Age of Revolution."

CATHY GERE is associate professor of history of science at the University of California, San Diego. Her last book, *Knossos and the Prophets of Modernism* (2009), examined the entangled histories of archaeology, psychoanalysis, and experimental literature. She is currently finishing a manuscript about utilitarian political philosophy and the neuroscience of pain and pleasure.

STEFANOS GEROULANOS is an associate professor of history at New York University and director of the Center for International Research in the Humanities and Social Sciences (CNRS). He is the author of *An Atheism That Is Not Humanist Emerges in French Thought* (2010) and *Transparency in Postwar France: A Critical History of the Present* (forthcoming 2017), and co-author of *Experimente im Individuum* (2014).

NICOLE JERR is assistant professor of English at the United States Air Force Academy. Her work has appeared in *Philosophy and Literature*, and she has contributed reviews to *Critical Inquiry*, and *MLN*. Her current book project, "Pretenders to the Throne: Sovereignty and Modern Drama," considers the political and aesthetic anomaly presented by the persistence of sovereign figures on the modern stage.

BERNADETTE MEYLER is professor of law and Deane F. Johnson Faculty Scholar at Stanford Law School. Her work stands at the intersection of constitutional law and law and the humanities. She has published numerous articles in venues such as the *Stanford*, *UCLA*, and *Cornell Law Reviews*; *Diacritics*; and *Theory and Event*, as well as various edited collections. Currently, she is completing book projects on theaters of pardoning and common law originalism. Until 2013, she served as professor of law and English at Cornell University and was the inaugural recipient of the Mellon/LAPA Fellowship in Law and the Humanities at Princeton University.

A. AZFAR MOIN is assistant professor of religious studies at the University of Texas at Austin. He received a PhD in history from the University of Michigan–Ann Arbor and is the author of *The Millennial Sovereign: Sacred Kingship and Sainthood in Islam* (2012). He studies the premodern Islamic world from comparative perspectives, with a focus on concepts and practices of sovereignty.

GLENN W. MOST is professor of Greek philology at the Scuola Normale Superiore di Pisa, visiting professor on the Committee on Social Thought at the University of Chicago, and external scientific member of the Max Planck Institute for the History of Science in Berlin. He has published numerous books and articles on classics, on the history and methodology of classical studies, on the classical tradition and comparative literature, on modern philosophy and literature, on literary theory, and on the history of art.

YURI PINES is Michael W. Lipson Professor of Asian Studies at the Hebrew University of Jerusalem. His studies focus on early Chinese political thought, traditional Chinese political culture, origins of Chinese historiography, and sociopolitical history of preimperial China and of Qin Empire (221–207 BCE). His monographs include *The Everlasting Empire: Traditional Chinese Political Culture and Its Enduring Legacy* (2012), *Envisioning Eternal Empire: Chinese Political Thought of the Warring States Era* (2009), and *Foundations of Confucian Thought: Intellectual Life in the Chunqiu Period, 722–453 B.C.E.* (2002).

AMNON RAZ-KRAKOTZKIN is a professor in the Department of Jewish History at Ben-Gurion University of Negev. His publications include *The Censor, the Editor, and the Text: Catholic Censorship and the Shaping of the Jewish Canon in the Jewish Canon in Sixteenth Century* (2007) and *Exil at souveraineté: Judaïsme, sionisme, et pensée binationale* (2007).

STANCA SCHOLZ-CIONCA, professor of Japanese studies at the University of Trier until 2013, also has taught in Munich, Berlin, and Oslo. Her research focuses on Japanese literature, comparative literature, and theater, especially Nô, *kyôgen*, and contemporary avant-garde. Her publications include *Aspekte des mittelalterlichen Synkretismus im Bild des Tenman Tenjin im Nô* (1991) and *Entstehung und Morphologie des klassischen Kyôgen im 17. Jahrhundert: Vom mittelalterlichen Theater der Außenseiter zum Kammerspiel des Shogunats* (1997), and the coedited volumes *Japanese Theatre and the International Stage* (2001), *Performing Culture in East Asia: China, Korea, Japan* (2004), *Befremdendes Lachen: Komik auf der heutigen Bühne im japanisch-deutschen Vergleich* (2005), *Nô Theatre Transversal* (2008), and *Japanese Theatre Transcultural: German and Italian Intertwinings* (2011).

MIRANDA SPIELER is associate professor of history at the American University of Paris and the author of *Empire and Underworld: Captivity in French Guiana* (2012).

JUSTIN STEARNS's research interests focus on the intersection of law, science, and theology in the premodern Muslim Middle East. His first book was *Infectious Ideas: Contagion in Pre-Modern Islamic and Christian Thought in the Western Mediterranean* (2011). He is currently working on a book on the social status of the natural sciences in early modern Morocco entitled "Revealed Science: The Natural Sciences in Islam in the Age of al-Hasan al-Yusi," as well as an edition and translation of al-Yusi's *Muhadarat* for the Library of Arabic Literature.

ALEXEI YURCHAK is professor of anthropology at the University of California, Berkeley, and the author of *Everything Was Forever Until It Was No More: The Last Soviet Generation* (2006).

Index